Sepher Sapphires:

A Treatise on Gematria

'The Magical Language of the Mysteries

Volume 1

Forward by

Chic and Tabatha Cicero

Written by

Wade Coleman

Edited by

Darcy Küntz

Published by Fraternity of the Hidden Light

2008

First Edition, 2001.
Second Edition, 2002.
Third Edition, 2003.
Fourth Edition, 2004.
Fifth Edition, 2005.
Sixth Edition, 2006.
First Renaissance Astrology Press Edition, 2006
Fraternity of the Hidden Light Edition, 2008

ISBN:978-0-9818977-0-7

Acknowledgements

I would like to thank **Kenneth Grant** for his permission to quote liberal sections of his book *Nightside of Eden*. His work on the Tunnels of Set are one of a kind.

I would like to thank **Ordo Templi Orientis** for permission to quote from the *Sepher Sephiroth* by Aleister Crowley which was the seed that formed this book.

Material in *True and Invisible Rosicrucian Order* by Paul Foster Case is quoted by permission of Red Wheel / Weiser Publishing.

Table of Contents

Foreword

Gematria, the Qabalistic numerology of Hebrew letters, is the life-blood of the Western Mystery Tradition. It is a system for investigating Hebrew words and names and learning their "secret sense" by examining the numerical value of the letters of the Hebrew alphabet which Israel Regardie called "the Alphabet of the Angels." This system relies on the fact that Hebrew is an alphabet in which letters stand for numbers, for there are no separate symbols for numbers. Words which have the same numerical value are often thought to have a significant relationship.

The ancient Hebrews devised several methods of using these letter-values to encode layers of special meaning into their sacred texts and mystical teachings. Thus the "Literal Qabalah," which specialized in using these techniques to interpret Hebrew Scriptures, came into being. In addition to straightforward gematria, the Literal Qabalah includes the more complex techniques of notariqon (creating and unraveling acronyms) and temurah (transposing letters in a manner similar to cryptography) to ascribe and uncover the hidden import of words. Consequently the Literal Qabalah is the perfect complement to the so-called "Unwritten Qabalah," which deals with the study of the symbol known as the Tree of Life.

The elegance of this Qabalistic symbol-system has always been evident to Western occultists such as Eliphas Levi:

> "On penetrating into the sanctuary of the Kaballah, one is seized with admiration at the sight of a doctrine so simple and at the same time so absolute. The necessary union of ideas and signs, the consecration of the most fundamental realities by primitive characters, the trinity of words, letters and numbers; a philosophy simple as the alphabet, profound and infinite as the Logos; theorems more luminous and complete than those of Pythagoras; a theology which may be epitomized by counting on the fingers; an infinity which can be held in the hollow of an infant's hand; ten numerals and twenty-two letters, a triangle, a square, and a circle's such are the elements of the Kaballah, such are the primary principles of the written word, shadow of that spoken Logos which created the world!" (From *Transcendental Magic.*)

Hebrew is not the only alphabet to use the numeral value of letters to decipher the mystical meaning of words. Greek has also been used by the Western Mystery Tradition for this purpose. Isopsephos (literally "equal stones") or Greek gematria as it is often called relies on an even greater range of numerical letter values. However, its use in esoteric circles has never been as popular as that of Hebrew gematria. Aleister Crowley, whose *Sepher Sephiroth* is a staple in many magical libraries, planned to write a comprehensive text on Greek gematria, but never got around to finishing it. His notes on the subject were later compiled and published by the O.T.O. but they were neither complete nor, in some instances, accurate. In addition, Crowley did not find Greek gematria as satisfying as its Hebrew counterpart. Author David Godwin, whose seminal book *Godwin's Cabalistic Encyclopedia* should be considered required reading for Western Esotericists, also wrote a book entitled *Light in Extension: Greek Magic from Homer to Modern Times*, which gives a section listing a number of relevant Greek words and their numerical values.

Wade Coleman's work is a welcome addition to the modern corpus of Qabalistic knowledge. *Sepher Sapphires* will prove to be one of the most valuable resources that the modern Hermeticist has at his fingertips.

Chic and Tabatha Cicero
Metatron House

May 8, 2004

Introduction

Gematria is the study of the numerical relation between numbers and words. Prior to the development of the separate numbering system, each letter was assigned a numerical value. The Hebrew Aleph, and the Greek Alpha α are numerically equal to one. Therefore each word has a numerical value. The study of the correlation of words with the same numerical value is called gematria. Appendix 1 in this book has tables showing the numerical relationship to words to numbers in Hebrew, Latin and Greek.

Let us take for example the words that are numerically equal to forty:

40

Number of days and lights it rained during the Biblical Flood.
Number of weeks of the gestation of a human child.
Numbers of years the Israelites wandered in the desert.

מ Mem. One of the 3 mother letters. Mem is attributed to the element of Water. Water is the source of form, associated with the creative letter Heh, and that the multiplication of forms is the apparent subdivision of the ONE into various parts.

בהל bokhal. the ripening (of figs); puberty of women.

ולד vahlahd. child boy; infant, embryo; young of an animal.

חלב chawlawb. milk, With different pointing *cheyeleyb*, meaning: fatness; the best of it.

גזל gawzal. to cut off or flay, to take away, to strip off, as skin from the flesh; to rob or plunder

להה lahah. To languish, faint, to be exhausted, to faint; to be foolish or mad.

בהל bakhal. to loathe, feel nausea

חבל chawbal. As a verb it means: to twist, to wind together, to bind; to pledge; to pervert, to damage, to act corruptly, to sin, to wound..

catena (Latin). A chain; things linked by common interest or logical series.

יד יהוה Yod Tetragrammaton. the hand of Jehovah (formative power).

טלא tahlah. To patch; to cover with spots.
לאט lat. Secret; to wrap, cover; to speak gently.

sol (Latin). The sun; gold.

By examining these words we see a common theme. Alchemical Water (Mem) is the source of our sustenance (chawlawb, sol). It is the creator of all things (bokhal, vahlahd).

The nature of water suggest that it is the twisting (chawbal) and limitation of the primal fire (Yod Tetragrammaton, The letter Yod ` is tongue of Flame and means "hand."). Limitation implies sorrow and hardship (gawzal, lahah, bakhal). The One Self must limit itself for the sake of creation.

To further your study of gematria, I recommend obtaining a copy of *Godwin's Cabalistic Encyclopedia*, *The Spice of Torah* (gematria of the first 5 books of the Bible), 777 (*Sepher Sephiroth)*, and the *Hebrew Tongue Restored*.

Wade Coleman.

July 2004

References and Notes

The following books, *Godwin's Cabalistic Encyclopedia*, *Sepher Sephiroth*, *Spice of Torah* are referenced without page number since these books are also referenced by numerical sequence of words.

Lt. is an abbreviation for Latin.

Gr. Is an abbreviation of Greek

The Greek letter Σ is used in calculus as the summation symbol. Therefore $\Sigma 6 = 21$ is a symbolic way of describing the theosophic extension of 6 is equal to 21, that is:

$1 + 2 + 3 + 4 + 5 + 6 = 21.$

Introduction to Qabalah

The Qabalah is a traditional body of wisdom dealing with God's creation of the universe and the laws of nature. It concerns the evolution of man and man's relationship to God. Qabalah includes the understanding of the spiritual spheres of creation, and the ways by which God administers the existence of the universe.

The Word Qabalah is from the Hebrew root word (קבל) to receive. it was traditionally taught as an oral tradition, imparted from teacher to student. In the Medieval and Renaissance times, more and more of the tradition was written down.

In the sixth century C.E. the Sepher Yetzirah (Book of Formation) was written. It is one of the cornerstone books in Qabalistic writings. It is the first work that describes the creation of the universe in terms of the letters of the Hebrew alphabet. Additionally, this is the first written work to speak of the ten Sephiroth, however, they were not named.

Another important work in the *Zohar*, written in the thirteenth century. The *Zohar* states the soul of man has three elements, the Nephesh, Ruach and Neshamah. The Nephesh is the lower or animal part of man's soul and deals with instincts and bodily needs and desires. The Ruach is the middle part and the word means "spirit" or "wind." It is here the facility of discrimination between good and evil is found. The Neshamah is the Divine Soul. This is the part of the soul that allows us to have the awareness of the existence and indwelling presence of God. It is the immortal part of the soul.

Another thirteenth century word is the *Gates of Light*, by Rabbi Joseph Gikatilla. This book includes one of the first descriptions of the Sephiroth and their attributions. However, the geometric arrangement of the Sephiroth and how they formed the Tree of Life were not discussed. Several arrangements were developed through the centuries. The one most currently used was developed in the 1650's.

There are two forms of the Qabalah, traditional Jewish and "Hermetic Qabalah." Hermetic Qabalah began in the Renaissance. A central point for its development is the Medici Academy in Florence. Almost all modern occultism can be traced back to the developments of the scholars in that time and place.

The Medici were a family of immense wealth, ruling Florence from the fifteenth century until 1737. Cosimo de Medici was the founder of the Platonic Academy, dedicated to the study of Greek and neo-Platonic philosophy. It was here that many Qabalistic text were translated in Latin. In this school there was a development of "Christian Qabalah" which incorporated elemental of Christianity (Jesus) into the Qabalah. One of the first practical works of their school was produced by Henry Cornelius Agrippa, *Three Books of Occult Philosophy*.

Hermetic Qabalah became well known in esoteric circles with the development of Hermetic Order of the Golden dawn in the late 1800's, a ceremonial magic order. Within the Golden Dawn, Kabalistic principles such as the ten Sephiroth were fused with Greek and Egyptian deities. Attributes of Divine, archangelic and angelic names were assigned of each Sephiroth in each of the four worlds.

The book *Liber 777*, attributed to Aleister Crowley was one of the first to create a set of tables relating various parts of ceremonial magic to thirty-two numbers representing the ten spheres and twenty-two paths of the Kabalistic Tree of Life.

This work is one of the first books published on gematria. Gematria is the study of words and phrases with the same numerical value are related in some way. Crowley's tabulations were the most extensive published to date. However, his book was not the first. Agrippa in his work, *Three Books of Occult Philosophy*, listed few dozen words relating Divine Names relating to each of the Sephiroth.

David Godwin's book, Godwin's Cabalistic Encyclopedia takes the study of gematria and order of magnitude beyond *Liber 777*. My book, Sepher Sapphires, began out of my love of numbers and as an indispensable aid in the study and practice of magic.

The important of numbers and the use of gematria cannot be underestimated. It is one of the pillars of magic. Agrippa states in Book 2, Chapter 1:

"The Doctrines of Mathematics are so necessary to, and have such an affinity with Magic, that they that do profess it without them, are quite out of the way, and labor in vain, and shall in no wise obtain their desired effect. For whatsoever things are, and are done in these inferior natural virtues, are all done, and governed by number, weight, measure, harmony, motion, and light."

Agrippa states in Chapter 2:

"… all things which were first made by the nature of things in its first Age, seem to be formed by the proportion of numbers, for this was the principal pattern in the mind of the Creator. … hence the motion of the Stars, and the revolution of the heaven, and the state of all things subsist by the uniting together of numbers. Numbers therefore are endowed with great and sublime virtues. … all things that are, and are made, subsist by, and receive their virtue from numbers. For time consists of number, and all motion, and action, and all things which are subject to time, and motion [Astrology]."

Therefore, the study of number, proportion, astrology, sound and color are keys to magic.

Additionally, without gematria and numerical relations, it would not be possible to create magical talismans. Agrippa continues in Book 2, Chapter 2:

"… and the proportions arising from numbers, do by lines, and points make Characters, and figures. And these are proper to Magical operations, the middle which is between both being appropriated by declining to the extremes, as in the use of letters. *And lastly, all species of natural things, and of those things which are above nature, are joined together by certain numbers* [emphasis added]. … Number has always a being. Yet there is one in voice, another in the proportion of them, another in the soul, and reason, and another in divine things.

Gematria is one of the pillars of magical practice. I hope the practicing ceremonial magician finds this book useful.

wade coleman

March 2006

Section 0

Numbers 0 - 99

0

I. "All the Power that ever was or will be is here now." [Saying assigned to 0 of the Pattern on the Trestleboard]

II. Absolute unity. The zero is nothing, that is, no-thing and is therefore a symbol of the power of life and potencies of growth and development.. The number zero comes before any other number, and is a symbol of all beginnings. It is nothing we can measure, because it is limitless. Any number that is divided by zero is not definable. The 0 sign looks like an egg, please note the symbol on the upper left hand corner on Key 13, Death.

1   (prime)

I. The Monad

II. Names for the number 1: see 12, 21, 37, 397, 422 or 1552, 620, 721, 559, 736, 837.

III. The number one is the first definite quanity. Eliphas Levi says: Unity may be conceived as relative, manifested, possessing duality, the beginning of numerical sequence. The number one is the initial impulse, initial movement, the beginning of a phase of manifested power. Note by its shape the number one is a phallic symbol, and suggest the ideas of to thrust, insert, and lead in to its meanings.

IV. "I am a center of expression for the Primal Will-to-Good, which eternally creates and sustains the universe." [1st Saying of the Pattern on the Trestleboard]

א Aleph. bull or ox. Oxen are symbols of the taming of natural forces. Culture power and Super-consciousness. Thus the letter Aleph is a symbol of creative energy, and of the vital principles of living creatures. This vital principle comes to us in physical form as the radiant energy from the sun and is asociated with the Key 0, the Fool. Aleph is symbolic of the element Air and **breath**. The noun "fool," is derived from the Latin *follis*, meaning a "bag of wind". Aleph is the Path of the Fiery of Scintillating Intelligence, linking Kether and Chokmah on the Tree of Life. See 214,37,111.

Aleph means oxen. Untill the turn of the century oxen (and horses) provided the power of movement, especially in agriculture. *Agriculture is the basis of civilization.* Aleph is a symbol of man using the forces available to him to adapt them to his own purposes.

I. Rabbi Ginsburgh says: "The union of higher reality, the upper Yod, with the lower reality, the lower Yod, by means of the connecting Vav, of Torah, is the ultimate secret of the letter Aleph." [The Alef-Beit,]

II. "The first character of the alphabet in nearly all know idioms. As symbolic image it represents universal man, mankind, the ruling being of the earth. In its hieroglyphic acceptation, it characterizes unity, the central point, the abstract principle of a thing. As sign, it expresses power, stability, continuity. Some grammarians make it express a kind of superlative as in Arabic; but this is only a result of its power as sign. On some rare occasions it takes the place of the emphatic article ה either at the beginning or at the end of the words. The rabbis use it as a sort of article. It is often added at the head of words as redundant vowel, to make them more sonorous and to add to their expression." [d'Olivet, 1976, p. 287.]

III. "*Aleph* (1): And behold: In this immense Dwelling, within these innumerable dwellings, everywhere there is creative immanence, spontaneous, always fresh and new; imperishable pulsation of life; recurrent sparks; life-death, life-death, death and resurrection: elusive, timeless. Its manifestation can be perceived and thought of only in this manner.

The non-thinkable has for its symbol the Aleph (1). The Aleph is always itself and never itself. It is ever recurring, though never the same. Aleph creates, it is creation, it is not created, yet it exists. It has no existence because all existence is continuous. It has no memory, having no past. It has no purpose, having no future. If one retains it, it remains retained. If one buries it, it remains buried. If one sets aside its obstacles, it is action. It breaks down resistances, though resistances are never broken by it. Without these, Aleph does not become manifest. Without Aleph, there would be nothing at all. Such is the image of the Aleph. Aleph itself is beyond all consciousness, human or cosmic. The image of Aleph is only an image, for Aleph belongs neither to time nor to space. Aleph is beyond the realm of our thought, beyond the reach of our mind." [Suraes, 1992, pp. 65-66.]

He adds: Aleph, no. 1, is the unthinkable life-death, abstract principle of all that is and all that is not. [ibid. p.61]

IV. The Ain, or Eye of the Void, represents absolutely No Thing. It is non-manifestation pure and simple. From it alone can manifestation proceed. The first formulation of No Thing, its reflection or reverse image was Some Thing, and this was represented by the number One, Aleph. The symbol attached to this number is that of a calf, the youngling; it was the child of the mother whom it had cleaved open in breaking from the womb or opening of the Abyss (Ain). The calf is thus the symbol of the Calif as the first cleaver or maker of the cleft. it was the clef or key of the mysteries of Initiation; the calf or 'child' of all later mythologies. Aleph, the whirling cross, the thunderbolt which broke open the firmament is the glyph of Air or Space. [Grant, 1994, p. 14.]

A Alpha (Gr). "Signifies, like the Hebrew Aleph, the beginning or a cycle of activity. It was one of the primary figures of the Gnostic mystery of Alpha and Omega, and was represented by the Tetrahedron, which it resembled in its primitive form." [Bond & Lea, 1977, p. 83.] see 40, 200, 800, 811.

2   (prime)

I. The Duad or Dyad.

II. Names for number 2: see 15, 37, 73.

III. The number 2 is the reflection of the number one. The number 2 is second in a series beginning with 1. Two represents continuation, in the sense of carrying onward or extending the initial impulse symbolized by 1. Therefore 2 is a symbol of prolongation, or lengthening in time or space. That is why the point is represented by the number 1 and the line by two.

IV. Key 2 in the Tarot is The High Priestess, a symbol of the mysterious working power of the supreme spirit working through the subconsciousness. It is also called Prakriti, the Great Womb or principal thing. It is feminine in relation to Kether. Key 2 is attributed to the Moon, the reflection of the sun, just as 2 is the reflection of one. Please note that Key 2 is the path that leads from Kether to Tiphareth.

V. Two is the symbol of duality, the symbol of the separation of the sexes, of space-time, etc. Any number that reductes of 2 has a characteristic of duality. In numerology the 2 is considered malific, this is based on the quality of duality asssociated with the number two. But the number two also concerns Wisdom, because duality is necessary for manifestation and consequently allows for man's evolution. In the Zohar the number 2 was sleced by God to begin creation. see 15, 37, 73, 106, 412 well as numbers which reduce to 2: 29, 11, 38, 47, 56, 65, 74.

VI. "Through me its unfailing Wisdom [Chokmah] takes form, in thought and word. [2nd saying of the Pattern on the Trestleboard]

ב Beth. house. Refers to whatever form may be termed a dwelling-place for Spirit, and the form particular referred to is human personality. "The Father who dwells in me, he does the works." As a preposition Beth means: in, at; among, with, by means of, through, against. It suggest movement from a point without to a point within. Beth is the Path of the Transparent Intelligence, linking Kether and Binah on the Tree of Life.

I. Rabbi Kushner: "Beth is drawn with two little points--one pointing above, the other pointing behind and toward the right. In this way when someone asks the Beth 'Who made you?,' it points above, and if they ask, What is his name?," it points toward the Aleph, as if to say, 'One is his name.'" [The Book of Letters]

II. Rabbi Blech: "Why does the Torah begin with the letter Beth, which corresponds to the number two? Because our Sages teach that God created not one world, but two. There is עשלם הזה, this world, and עשלם הבא, the world to come. Our life must always be lived with the awareness that the grave is not our end, but merely the second beginning." [The Secrets of the Hebrew Words].

III. "This character, as consonant, belongs to the labial sound. As symbolic image it represents the mouth of man, his dwelling, his interior. As grammatical sign, it is the paternal and virile sign, that of interior and active action. In Hebrew, it is the integral and indicative article expressing in nouns or actions... almost the same movement as the extractive article מ, but with more force and without any extraction or division of parts." [d'Olivet, 1976, pp. 300-301.]

IV. Paul Case: The Hieroglyph for Beth has been lost, as the square letters employed today are of comparative recent invention. Perhaps the first idea that will be suggested to most people be all arrow-head is sharpness. Then since every Hebrew letter stands for a kind of consciousness, Beth must be a sign of mental acuteness, or penetration. It represents the sort of intelligence that manifest itself in quick perception, accurate observation, keen discernment, sagacity, and the like. An arrowhead is a point, denoting position. In logical 'position' means affirmation or assertion, As when we speak of 'the proof of a position,' implying order-is derived. Beth, then represents affirmative mental activity, limiting its operation to a definite locality, and exercising itself in establishing order. Hence Beth suggest initiative, direction, control, the concentration of energy in a particular field, and its specialization in definite forms. This idea of concentration is inseparable from the original form of the letter. The word 'concentrate' is derived from the Greek Kentron, an arrow point. The same Greek work also means the point around which a circle is inscribed, which shows that it implies the very notions of definite locality, order, that we have been considering. The implicates of the letter name are closely related to those connected with the hieroglyphic. Beth means "house" suggesting enclosure, limitation, to a special field, definite locality, and so on. As a House is the dwelling of its owner, so is the kind of mental action related to Beth the abode of spirit, because it centers the cosmic mind in a particular, local expression. [The Secret Doctrine of the Tarot, The Word, June 1916, pp. 79-80]

V. "*Bayt* (2): Everything that exists is the conditioning of life and the life of the conditioning. Everything that is exists both internally and externally. Each germ of life has an envelope, which derives its movement from the great cosmic force of resistance to the life which is surging up from within (If the shell does not offer the right measure of resistance, the chicken will not hatch.) This whole duality of existence-and of our own thought-is conveyed by no. 2." [Suraes, 1992, p. 65.]

He adds: "is the archetype of all 'dwellings', of all containers: the physical support without which nothing is." [ibid. p. 61]

VI. Beth, we therefore discern the glyph of the biune god who is both (Beth) male and female, yet, being so, was neither the one nor the other, but the androgyne or hermaphrodite. Beth was ascribed to the Magician or the juggler, the twofold One who, on attaining puberty, becomes replete with creative potential symbolized by the camel, the letter *gimel*, which is the number three. In One Person are thus resumed the trinity of powers from Aleph, the Fool or innocent babe, through Beth the androgynous bi-sexual deity, to the fully equipped sexual procreatort, Beth is the double-wanded One, the Magician (male and female). [Grant, 1994, pp. 14-15.]

אא   An abbreviation for אריך אנפין , Arik Anpin, the Vast Countenance (Kether). see 422, 620.

ב An abbreviation of בנ, Ben (52) or בר (202). meaning "son of." Extremely rare use.

3   (prime)

I. Σ2 = 3

II. Names for the number 3: see 67, 42, 52, 265.

III. The number 3, as it relates to Key 3, The Empress, suggest the response of the subconscious (Key 2, The High Priestess) mental activity to the self-conscious (Key 1, the Magician) impulses in the generation of mental images (Key 3, The Empress).

IV. "Filled with its Understanding [Binah, 67 the third Sephirah] of its perfect law, I am guided moment to moment on the path of Liberation." [3rd Saying of the Pattern on the Trestleboard]

V. The mystic number of Chokmah. It manifest itself in mental life as creative imagination. As 1+2 is the union of the ideas of individuality (1) and repetition (2). The repetition of the unit (1) through the agency of the duad (2) is reproduction. Three is the number of production, formation, organization, propagation, elaboration.

ג Gimel. Camel. The number of the third Hebrew letter, Key 2 the High Priestess. Represents universal Memory, through the subconscious substance aspect (Water). The Uniting Intelligence, linking the universal self in Kether and the Ego in Tiphareth, on the Tree of Life. It is the bond between all created beings and like the camel, is a symbol of travel, communication and change. The direction Below on the Cube of Space. A key to the alchemical mystery of the First Matter-the Virgin Substance "whose purity naught can defile" [Book of Tokens, Gimel]. see 237, 882, 13.

I. "גה ג. This character as consonant, belongs to the guttural sound. The one by which I translate it, is quite a modern invention and responds to it rather imperfectly. Plutarch tells us that a certain Carvilius who, having opened a school at Rome, first invented or introduced the letter G, to distinguish the double sound of the C. As symbolic image the Hebraic Gimel indicates the throat of man, any conduit, any canal, any deep hollow object. As grammatical sign, it expresses organic development and produces all ideas origination from the corporeal organs and from their action." [d'Olivet,1976, p. 310.]

II. Rabbi Ginsburgh: "The Gimel is composed of a Vav, representing an erect man, with a lower Yod, a foot in motion...Our sages teach that the Gimel symbolizes a rich man running after a poor man, the Daleth, to give him charity." [Ginsburg, 1995, pp. 52, 54]

III. Gimel and Daleth were not used for creation because Gimel signifies beneficence, and Daleth poverty, which maintained each other. (Zohar 1, page 12).

IV. Paul Case: The Earliest sign for the letter Gimel was probably a conventionalized picture of a bow. As a bow is used for shooting arrows, the first idea it suggests is propulsive force. Since the letter Beth was originally in the form of an arrowhead, it becomes evident that Gimel, the bow, as the propulsive force behind the arrow, stands for something that incites the objective mind, represented by Beth, to express itself in concentrated attention. Thus, in a sense,

the bow is derived from the arrow; and this makes it an emblem of secondary existence; evolution, and the like. The bow, like the crescent, cup, sistrum, wheatear, oval, is related to the hieroglyphic as well as to the letter-name. Relaxed and unstrung, the bow is an emblem of peace; tense and strung, it signifies war. [The Secret of the Doctrine of the Tarot in the Word, July 1916, page 161, 163].

V. Gimel is a modified form of Yod. Thus the two parts of the letter hint at a concealed numeral value of 16, since Vav is 6 and Yod is 10. Among Hebrew words having the value of 16 are: אזוב, Hyssop, signifying purgation or purification; גבוה elevated, exalted, High; היא, She; and זוב, like equal to. The Uniting Intelligence (Gimel) is the most important means of purification. It links personal consciousness to the Highest plane of being. It is the wisdom personified in Proverbs as a woman. Its full exercise enables us to realize the identity of the Self in man with universal being.

VI. "Ghimel is the organic movement of every Bayt animated by Aleph." [Suraes, 1992, p. 61.]

VII. "Gimel is the lunar reflection of the *Ain* across the Desert of Set." [Grant, 1994, p. 15.]

אב Ab. Father. A name for number 2 and Chokmah. By notariqon אב stands for the 2 words Aima-Ben אימא בן . Mother (Binah) and Son (Tiphareth). In the Father these potencies are latent and concealed. The essential reality, the cause of existence. Also the 11th Hebrew month, July-August, corresponding roughly to the period when the sun is in Leo. This month is not mentioned in scripture. see 23, 73.

"The potential sign united to that of interior activity produces a root whence come all ideas of productive cause, efficient will, determining movement, generative force. In may ancient idioms and particularly in the Persian this root is applied especially to the aqueous element as principle of universal fructification.

All ideas of *paternity*. Desire to *have*: a *father*: *fruit*. In reflecting upon these different significations, which appear at first incongruous, one will perceive that they come from one another and are produced mutually." [d'Olivet,1976, p. 287.]

א‍ב. becoming, future. From this correspondence between Ab and Baw, Ab, the Father, is the cause of existence, and therefore antecedent to what is now part of our present experience, the life force named Ab is also the essential reality which is to find manifestation in every event and condition which, to our limited time-sense, appears to be in the future. Actually, the Eternal is beyond the limitations of past, present and future, it is the eternal NOW.

4

I. (2²)

II. The Tetractys or Tetrad

III. Number of faces and vertices on a Tetrahedron (associate with the element Fire).

IV. Names for the number 4: see 48, 72, 1626 (Greek).

V. The number 4 is symbolic of the square, and is associated with the orgin of forms and the manifest. Eliphas Levi wrote of four "... This number produces the cross and square in geometry. All that exists, whether good or evil, light or darkness, exists and is revealed by the tetrad, (it is) the unity of construction, solidity and measure."

VI. Four is associated with space-time and therefore with the first day of creation and the framework of the evolution of man. The 4th Sephiroth is Chesed (Mercifulness). Every number whose numerical reduction is 4 concerns the solid aspect of things.

VII. Four relates to the classifying activity of *self-consciousness* (Key 1, The Magician), induced by the response of *subconscious* (Key 2, The Empress) to to creat *mental images* (Key 3, The Empress). These mental images are arranged by the classifying activity is *reason* (Key 4, The Emperor).

VIII. Dominance is attributed to Key 4, the classifying activity of self-consciousness (induced by conscious response to sub-conscious mental imagery). In its highest aspect this dominance is the cosmic order, that which orders and arranges the substance manifested in every form. Key words associated with Key 4 are reason, measurement, record-keeping, tabulation, and beneficence.

IX. The number 4 is occultly connected with the completion of the 'sanctum sancitorum' -The ocean of a higher consciousness. [R.C. Allegory, page 16].

X. 'The Pythagoreans called the number 4 Tetractys (1626) because it is the foundation and root of all other numbers. [H.C. Agrippa of Occult Philosophy page 183-185].

XI. "From the exhaustless riches of its Limitless substance, I draw all things needful, both spiritual and material." [4th saying of the Pattern on the Trestleboard]

ד Daleth. Door. Daleth is attributed to Venus, the desire nature and creative imagination. Daleth is the Luminous Intelligence, uniting Chokmah and Binah on the Tree of Life. On the Cube of Space Daleth is the East face, source of Light. see 40, 400, 434.

I. Daleth means door (see Appendix 14) and is the leaf (a hinged or movable section of a door or gate), not the opening. It is the power to admit or bar, to retain or to let out, and entrance or exit. It is a passageway from within to without. Daleth is associated with Key 4, The Empress and creative imagination. It is the entrance (door) to new life and to new worlds. Because the value of Daleth is four, it is often cited in Qabalah as the sign of the 4th Sephirah, Mercy or Beneficence.

II. The door is a feminine symbol representing birth, reproduction, and the entry of life into manifestation. Daleth is the Womb, the door of personal life. It opens to receive the seed and closes to retain the germ during gestation. It opens again to send the new life into the world. This is activity occurs also on planes above the physical.

III. Rabbi Kushner: "And why does the roof of the Daleth extend backwards a little to the right, in the direction of Gimel? To teach us that the poor man, Daleth, must make himself available to the Gimel, the one who would lend him money. Nevertheless, the face of the Daleth is turned away--teaching that charity must be given in secret." [The Book of Letters]

IV. "This character as consonant belongs to the dental sound. It appears that in its hieroglyphic acceptation, it was the emblem of the universal quaternary; that is to say, of the source of all physical existence. As symbolic image it represents the breast, and every nourishing and abundant object. As grammatical sign, it expresses in general, abundance born of division: it is the sign of divisible and divide nature." [d'Olivet, 1976, p. 318.]

V. "Dallet is physical existence, as response to life, of all that, in nature, is organically active with Ghimel. Where the structure is inorganic Dallet is its own resistance to destruction." [Suraes, 1992, p. 61.]

בב An excavation or well; hollow a vein. From a root meaning: every idea of interior void, of exterior swelling: pupil of the eye.

אבא Abba. Father. A name for the number 4 and Chesed. The multiplication of Chokmah by itself (2x2). This links the derivation of the powers of Chesed from Chokmah, since Chokmah is called *Ab*, Father. It is through the path of Vav (the Hierophant, and in Italian Il Papa, the Father) that the power of Chokmah descends into Chesed.

גא conceited, haughty, proud. This word is associated with power, authority and magnificence expressed by Gedulah, Majesty (48). A typical Jupiterian sin, the negative polarity of persons of importance.

Gay and *Abba*, stand for opposite manifestations of Qabalistic ideas which correspond to the fourth Sephirah. This is precisely the significance of *gay*, as used in Isaiah 16:6. "We have heard of the *pride* of Moab, an excessive pride; Even of his arrogance, pride and fury; His ideal boasts are false." [New American Standard]

5 (prime)

I. The Pentalpha

II. The number of sides on a pentagon and the number of faces on a Icosahedron. Names for the number 5: see 64, 92, 216, 1200.

III. Five is midway between 1 and 10, therefore it is the number of adaptation and adjustment through the vehicle of self-consciousness. Thus 5 is the number of Man, because Man can achieve the full flower of self-conscious. This great work cannot be accomplished by the sub-human and subconscious levels of being. T

IV. "I recognize the manifestation of the undeviating Justice [Geburah] in all circumstances in my life." [The 5th saying in the Pattern on the Trestleboard]

ה Heh. Fifth letter of the Hebrew alphabet. Connected with the idea of meditation, the pentagram, the function of Binah [67] in creation. Also with vision, reason, observation which lead to definitions.

I. Rabbi Munk says: "The Heh looks life a lobby with three walls, but with one side completely open. This indicates that God allows man free choice. He is free to obey or disobey God's will, but he chooses to leave the safety of the Torah's spiritual and moral boundaries, he loses his foothold and slips, as it were, through the open space of the Heh into the abyss...however, Heh symbolizes God's readiness to forgive...A small opening is left in the top left leg of the Heh symbolizing that a space always remains through which a repentant sinner can return. [The Wisdom of the Hebrew Alphabet]

II. "This character is the symbol of universal life. It represents the breath of man, air, spirit, Soul; that which is animating; vivifying [Note the 1st Heh in IHVH is attributed to Binah, the creative world, the 2nd to Assiah, the material world]. As grammatical sign, it expresses Life and the abstract idea of being. It is, in the Hebrew tongue of great use as article." [d'Olivet, 1976, pp. 326-327.]

III. "Heh determines [Determinative Article] the noun. It draws the objective which it designates from a mass of similar objects and gives it a local existence. [i.e. Aries the Constituting Intelligences]. Derived from the sign ה, which contains the ideas of universal life, it presents itself under several acceptations as article. By the first, it points out simply the noun that it modifies and rendered by the corresponding articles *the*, *this*, *that*, *there*, *those*: by the second, it expresses a relation of dependence or division, and is translated *of the*; *of this, of that, of these, of those*: by the third, it adds to the noun before which it is placed, only an emphatic meaning, a sort of exclamation accent. In this last acceptation, it is placed indifferently at the beginning or at the end of words and is joined with the greater part of the other articles without being harmful to their movement. Therefore call it *Empirical article* and when I translate it which I rarely do lacking means, I render it by *o! oh! ah!* or simply by the exclamation point (!)." [ibid., pp. 111-112.]

IV. Carlo Suares: "Hay, is the archetype of universal life. When it is conferred upon Dallet, it allows it to play the game of existence, in partnership with the intermittent life-death process." [Suraes, 1992, p. 61.]

V. "Heh is the number 5, which is the glyph of Woman typified by her negative phase; it is also the equivalent of one hand (five fingers), the hand itself being typical of fashioning, moulding, creating. Its ideograph was the Kaf-ape or cynocephalus, the special vehicle of the god Thoth (the moon), thus indicating the lunar nature of this fashioning. Woman produces the blood from which the flesh is fashioned." [Grant, 1994, pp. 49-50.]

בבא. Door, gate, division, section (of an argument, exposition, or literary composition). May also be read as *Be-Bag*: "In time to come, in the future." A verbal symbol of transition from one state to another. Also of orderly classification, symbolized by Heh as the definite article.

גב Back; upper surface of anything; mound, the rim of a wheel, the vault of an arch; a hill or hillock. Whatever supports or sustains as a table supports objects laid thereon. The idea of something hollowed out, closely allied to all Qabalistic notions of the work of creation and specialization.

"The organic sign united by contraction to the root אב, symbol of every fructification, develops, in general, the idea of a thing placed or coming under another thing. גב *a boss, an excrescence, a protuberance; a knoll, the back,* everything convex. גב or גוב, *a grasshopper.*" [d'Olivet, 1976, p. 318.].

הא This. A pronoun. Five is considered to be the number of man. Man is "this." From a root meaning natural abundance and division [See D'Olivet's comments under Daleth].

אד fog, vapor, mist, to cover, to envelope. Genesis 2:6, "But a mist went up from the earth, and watered the whole face of the ground." Formed from the first two letters of Adam. it relates to the occult truth that the physical organism is something precipitated from, or condensed from a primary substance. Masters of wisdom know how to dissolve their physical vehicles into a "Mist," as did Jesus at his "Ascension," at which time "A cloud received him out of their sight." Qabalists associate this mist with the Malkuth. see 14, 41, 45, 55, 104, 72, 86, 158.

"This root, composed of the signs of power and of physical divisibility, indicates every distinct, single object, taken from the many. The Arabic expresses a temporal point, a determined epoch: *when, whilst, whereas. Ade* that which *emanates* from a thing: *the power of division, relative unity, an emanation; a smoking fire brand.*" [d'Olivet, 1976, p. 289.]

אבב to blossom, to bear fruit; to shine. See Book of Tokens under Heh.

אונא fugitive, to flee. The natural man does seem to be a fugitive.

בג food. Persian origin.

6

I. Σ3 = 6

II. Number of edges (lines) in a Tetrahedron (Fire), faces on a Cube (Earth) and vertices on a Octahedron (Water).

III. Names for the number 6: see 45, 52, 80, 311, 1081, 548, 666.

IV. The 1st perfect number (see Appendix) , and 6 symbolizes universal forces, like light, heat and electromagnetism.

V. Tiphareth is the 6th Sephiroth, therefore this number concerns beauty, harmony and symbolizes the union of the 2 worlds thourgh its associated with the union of the Fire and Water triangles. It a number of balance and contains 2 trinities (two triangles with 3 sides each). It is through the number 6 that man can contact the higher trinity.

VI. "In all things, great and small, I see the Beauty [Tiphareth] of the divine expression." [6th saying of the Pattern on the Trestleboard]

ו Vav. and. Vav is the path of the Triumphant and Eternal Intelligence linking Chokmah to Chesed. In grammar "and" is used as a conjunction, that which links a series of nouns or dependent clauses in a sentance.

I. Vav means nail or hook (see Appendix 14) and is symbolic of our connecting link With Universal Being. Vav is the link which fastens personal consciousness to universal life. As the number 6 it is associated with the Sphere of Tiphareth and the seat of the Soul on the Tree of Life. Tiphareth links Kether, the Indivisible One to the automatic consciousness in Yesod (The Moon and sub-consciousness). Vav is associated with Intuition. Intuition is the super-consciousness transmitting information through self-consciousness through sub-consciousness (Yesod).

II. "The Vav is a vertical line representing a pillar or a man standing upright. The world stands on pillars. The pillars, a symbol of support, hold hold Creation together." [Ginsburg, 1995, p. 97]

III. Rabbi Kushner: "This is the word of Vav: to join us all into a myriad of constellations each remaining different, each bound to the other." [The Book of Letters]

IV. "This character has two very distinct vocal acceptations, and a third as consonant. Following the first of these vocal acceptations, it represents the eye of man, and becomes the symbol light; the second represents the ear, and becomes the symbol of sound, air, wind: as a consonant it is the emblem of water and represents taste and covetous desire. As a grammatical sign the image of the most profound and inconceivable mystery. The image of the knot which unites, or

the point which separates nothingness and being [italics added]. In its luminous vocal acceptation וֹ, it is the sign of intellectual sense, the verbal sign *par excellence*. In its ethereal verbal acceptation ו, it is the universal convertible sign, *which makes a thing pass from one nature to another* [italics added]; communicating on one side with sign of intellectual sense וֹ, which is only itself more elevated, and on the other, with that of material sense עַ, which is only itself more abased: It is finally, in its aqueous consonantal acceptation, *the link of all things*[italics added], the conjunctive sign. The character ו, except its proper name וו, does not begin any word of the Hebraic tongue, and consequently does not furnish any root." [d'Olivet, 1976, p. 334.]

V. "Vav, expresses the fertilizing agent, that which impregnates. It is the direct result of Hay upon Dallet." [Suraes, 1992, p. 61.]

VI. "Six is the name and number of sex and it is represented by the letter *Vau* which means a 'nail', the phallic symbol of virility." [Grant, 1994, p. 17.]

בד Isolation, separation, thing separated from; alone; empty talk, lies, vain boasting. All its variation apply to the negative aspect of Tiphareth. With different pointing: twig of a tree, shoot staff, white linen and soothsayer; Rod; pole, limb of the body; cell (in skin), war, chatter; separable part of something; olive press.

"The root אד, which characterizes every object distinct and alone, being contracted with the sign of interior activity, composes this root whence issue ideas of separation, isolation, solitude, individuality, particular existence. From the idea of *separation* comes that of *opening*: thence that of *opening the mouth* which is attached to this root in several idioms, and in consequence, that of *chattering, babbling, jesting, boasting, lying,* etc. The Arabic signifies literally *middle, between*. As a verb, this root characterized the action of *dispersing*." [d'Olivet, 1976, pp. 301-302.]

גג roof, flat top of a house; the upper part of an altar; width, volume (geometry). This word indicated by the initials G.G., designating the sixth person called by brother C.R. to aid in the founding of the Rosicrucian order in the *Fama*. In certain esoteric societies, Yesod is represented by the alter. The top of the alter is referred to as Tiphareth. see 80, 1081.

I. "Third in order of these second four Brethren is Brother G.G. His initials spell the Hebrew noun *gawg*, meaning "roof," so suggesting both shelter and secrecy. Thus, the doorkeeper of a Masonic lodge bears the significant name of "tiler," and to "tile" the lodge is to make sure that none are admitted save those having the right to enter. Hence, Brother G.G. represents the human virtue of prudence. He also represents the principle of secrecy, as necessary today as ever before, If genuine occultism is to be propagated successfully. ...To give them to the unprepared is to violate the old alchemical maxim that before one uses the Philosophers Stone to transmute metals, the metals must first be purified. ... Thus, the *Fama* says Brother C.R. bound the Brethren to be not only faithful and diligent but secret also, and it speaks of the Brethren taking their knowledge into the world in order that it might be examined in secret by the learned. Similarly, in the ministry of Jesus, "Brethren G.G." appears side by side with "Brother B." For although Jesus held the multitudes spellbound with his verbal moving pictures, He withheld from all but a tested few the subtler meanings of his brilliant, colorful discourses." [Case, 1985, pp. 94-95]

II. "Every idea of elasticity; that which stretches and expands without being disunited. גג or גוג *The roof* of a tent, that which extends to cover, to envelop." [d'Olivet, 1976, p. 311.]

הא Lo, to behold, to see (variant of הה), a window. As one of the letters of יהוה, when Tetragrammaton is thought of as operating in Yetzirah, the World of Formation. Yetzirah has a special relationship to Tiphareth and to six. see 315.

"Every evident, demonstrated and determined existence. Every demonstrative movement expressed in an abstract sense by the relations *here*, *there*; *this*, *that*." [d'Olivet, 1976, p. 327.]

גבא a reservoir, cistern; form a root meaning "to gatherer, to collect." Refers to the function of the Tiphareth as a reservoir into which flow streams of influence from the Sephiroth above. see 60, 600, & 42.

אגב Through, by means of. A proposition signifying an agency that applies to 6 and Tiphareth as the mediator between the higher aspects of the Life-power and those which are subordinate. Found in Rabbinical Books but not the Bible.

דב a bear, she bear, Name of a constellation.

אבבא The Greek transliteration of Hebrew *Ab*, Father. This spelling occurs often in later Hebrew. It refers to the essential unity of Tiphareth with Chokmah. Title of Chokmah. see 3, 4, 73.

αββα. Abba (Gr). Father. Greek for אבא.

7 (prime)

I. Names for the number 7: 148, 525, 710.

II. The number of vertebrae in the human neck. Numerical value for the symbol of Sulfur. A numerical symbol of the diameter of the Archetypal World.

III. A seven pointed star cannot be constructed accurretly with a compass and straight edge. It requires human thought and trial and error before on is constructed with a degree of skill. The the number 7 is associated with mastery, conquest, peace safety, security.

IV. In the Tarot Key 7 is Temperance. The Angel shown of the Key is the Holy Guardian Angel and is a symbol of the power which can establish harmony out of chaos. It is a power of adaptation and adjustment. Equilibrium is the result of equilibration; the concrete application of the laws of symmetry and reciprocation bring poise, rest, art, victory.

V. *Panteuchia* was the Pythagorean name for Cheth. It is shown with armor. The Disposing Intelligence (Zain) is closely related to the Uniting Intelligence (Gimel); and in Key 6 it shows that the women (who looks at the angel) is the means of union with the super-consciousness, or angel.

VI. "In the Egyptian hieroglyphics the sign of 7 is the sign of a god, symbolized by the axe, a weapon of Set, the opener of the Mother. In the language of the secret gnosis Set is identical with his mother, hence his name Sept or Set, means seven. The number seven indicated the time for resuming sexual relations with the woman, and, in the symbology of the later Mysteries, it was attributed to the goddess Venus [Netzach, the shere of Venus is the 7th Sephiroth]." [Grant, 1994, p. 102.]

VI. "Living from that will, supported by its unfailing wisdom and understanding, mine is the Victorious [Natzach] life." [7th saying of the Pattern on the Trestleboard]

ז Zain, Zayin. Weapon, sword. A sword is an instrument of division and cleavage. It is the active principle in overcoming inimical entities or forces. Zain is found on the Tarot Key 6, The Lovers associated with the principle of *discrimination* and the sign Gemini ruled by *Mercury.*

I. Rabbi Munk: ...it is no coincidence that the letter Zain is the symbolic representative of both sustenance and armament. The two concepts are related to each other. The letter Zain is shaped like a spear, indicating that man's sustenance is obtained by his struggle. [The Wisdom of the Hebrew Alphabet]

II. "This character as consonant, and is applied as onomatopoeic means, to all hissing noises, to all objects which cleave the air. As symbol, it is represented by the javelin, dart, arrow, that which tends to an end: As grammatical sign, it is the demonstrative sign, abstract image of the link which unites things." [d'Olivet, 1976, p. 339.]

III. "Zayn is the achievement of every vital impregnation: this number opens the field of every possible possibility." [Suraes, 1992, p. 61.]

IV. *Zain* is the number seven, the number of sexual love. This number originally signified the womb through the symbolism of the Goddess of the Seven Stars, Ursa Major, the constellation of the Thigh which typified the birthplace of Light in the Dark of the Abyss [i.e. the Abyss as the nightsky or gulf of space]. Seven later became the number of Venus, the planetary representative of the Goddess, when the concept was romanticized and applied to sexual love between humans as distinct from the primary and stellar symbolism that signified bestial congress.

Seven thus became synonymous with the mechanism of sexual polarity symbolized by Gemini (the letter attributed to which is Zain) under the influence of Mercury, the masculine aspect of Venus or, more correctly, the positive aspect of the hermaphroditic polarity typified by the sephiroth Hod and Netzach. *Zain* is mystically associated with the yoni, the secret or hidden eye (*ayin*) which, together with the letter 'z' - the letter of the serpent -becomes *Z-ayin* or *Zain*. Zain is of major importance as being the S(word) of the Serpent, which is Silence. Hence, in the most secret Mystery Cults the Aeon of Zain is said to be devoid of a Word. It is the silent transmission of sexual energy in polarity that vibrates the Word in Silence, and that Word is as a Sword that cleaves the Abyss and it is heard of No-One. It is said that in the Aeon of Zain 'humanity is booked for a turn round the back of the Tree', which explains why no word will be heard, for there will be No-One (Nun = the Abyss) to hear it. The subject-object relationship will have ceased to exist. The Serpent and the Sword are the dual glyph of this arcanum and such is the special emblem of Set. [Grant, 1994, p. 18.]

גד Good fortune, luck, a tribe of Israel [Genesis 30:11], Hebrew tribe associated with Aries. Attributed to the function of sight, with calcination, the first stage of the Great work. Coriander is the name of the Babylonian god of Good fortune, similar to Jupiter. The path joining Chesed to Netzach is that of the letter Kaph, attributed to Jupiter. In astrology Venus is the Lesser Fortune, as Jupiter is the Greater. The Life-power always expresses itself in ways that are good, in forms that are Beneficent. see 10, 44, 95, 30, 570, 501, 54, 331, 830, 395.

"The root גא, symbol of that which augments and extends, united to the sign of abundance born of division, produces the root *gad* whose use is to depict that which acts in masses, which flocks, agitates tumultuously, assails in troops. *Gad. an incursion, an irruption*, literally and figuratively. *An incision* in anything whatsoever, a furrow; metaphorically, in the restricted sense, *a kid*: the sign of Capricorn; etc." [d'Olivet, 1976, p. 311.]

אבד to scatter, to disperse, to lose oneself, to wander, to be lost, perish, ruined. A word used in the Old Testament to indicate the "lost sheep of the House of Israel." This corresponds to the negative meaning of Zayin, the sword, as a destructive weapon. What is lost, as a sheep from a flock, is separated from its proper companions and from its environment, and this agrees with the idea of division suggested by Zayin. In its meaning to scatter, to disperse, it suggest dissemination or sowing. It diffuses, spreads, distributes and apportions. The archetypical world is the great reservoir of seed-forms, these being the platonic ideas. Symbolized by Yod, the male, sperm-giving principle of the Universe.

דבא influx, to flow in, prosperity, riches. This influx into the seeds of a forms which is the *Mezela* (78), or influence, is the source of all riches. with different vowels: strength, affluence; rest, quiet, compare with the meaning given to the number 7.

דאב to melt away, become faint, pine away, sorrowful, languish. There is a craving within the No-thing which causes in itself the will to create something.

דג A fish. The root-meaning of *dahg* is "to multiply abundantly". This is the singular form of the plural noun דגים, *dagim*, fishes. It is the name of the Pisces where Venus is exalted. and Jupiter rules. This intimates that the powers represented by 4 (Chesed) and 7 (Netzach) are related. *Dagah* דגה , to grow, to multiply, to become numerous, to spawn like fish, is derived from דג. It is used in Genesis 48:16. It is an occult reference to the infinite potentiality of the archetypal world, the plane of original ideas. see 12, 22, 14, 21, 44, 57, 66, 70, 28, 88 175, 700.

או desire, will, appetite; choice. All are attributes of Sulfur, the 2nd Alchemical principle. It is also used as a conjunction signifying: or, either, but, if, perhaps (suggesting uncertainty). The motive power of the Life-power's self-manifestation is its desire to actualize its own possibilities. "Either" and "Or" implies choice, selection, decision, the shaping of a course, the singling out of particular modes of expression. Thus *ow* connotes desire combined with decision. see 693, 73, 290.

"The potential sign Aleph united to the universal convertible sign Vav, image of the mysterious link which joins nothingness to being, constitutes one of the most difficult roots to conceive which the Hebrew tongue can offer. In proportion as the sense is generalized, one sees appear all ideas of appeteble, concupiscible passion, vague desire: in proportion as it is restricted, one discerns only a sentiment of incertitude, of doubt, which becomes extinct in the prepostive relation *or*.." [d'Olivet, 1976, p. 290.]

ברא to form, to devise, produce, invent; fabricate. The archetypal phase of the creative process is imagination, inventing a new forms of self-expression. The archetypal world is the plane of original ideas. In the negative sense, to feign, to pretend, to counterfeit.

האא 26th name of Shem ha-Mephorash, short form. see 22 & Appendix 10.

אהא Notariqon of Adonai Ha-Eretz, the Divine name of Malkuth, meaning "Lord of the Earth." see 361.

אגג flame. The proper name Agag.

בה in her.

8

I. (2^3)

II. The Ogdoad

III. Number of vertices on a Cube (Earth) and faces on a Octahedron (Water). Names for the number 8: see 15, 370, 585, 720.

IV. Key 8 in the Tarot is Strength. The Lion in the Key, the various symbols of life and wavy and undulation motion as well as the number 8 itself are symbols of the great magical agent. The great magical agent is the serpent power. It is coiling, spiraled and vibratory in motion. Key 8 is attributed to the secret of all spiritual activities, which is, all activities are spiritual or emanate from the One Source.

V. Eight is a numeral symbol of rhythmic vibration, the curves are reciprocal and alternating. It is endless activity. The two curves represent the paths of involutions and evolution, the descending curve for involution, and ascending curve for evolution.

VI. Eight is called the Dominical Number, or number of Christ, because 888 is Ιησους. Iesous. Jesus. It is also a symbol for the Holy Spirit, sometimes described as a feminine potency. Note that in Key 1 and 8 the number 8 (infinity sign) placed horizontally or feminine, position. See 888.

VII. Eight symbolizes that all opposites are effects of a single cause, and that balanced, reciprocal action and reaction between opposites results in harmony. Pythagoras called 8 *Harmonia*. This is a doctrine that should be put into practical application.

VIII. The extension of 8 is 36 [$\Sigma 8 = 36$]. 36 is 6x6 the magic square (see Appendix 6) of Tiphareth and is a symbol of the perfected expression of the One Ego (Tiphareth, the 6th Sephirah). Note that the 8th Sephirah of the Tree of Life is Hod (Mercury). Its color is orange attributed to The Sun (Tiphareth). The color of Tiphareth is yellow attributed to Mercury (Hod).

IX. "I look forward with confidence, to the perfect realization of the eternal Splendor [Hod] of the limitless light." [8th saying of the Pattern on the Trestleboard]

ה Cheth. Fence, field; the eighth Hebrew letter assigned to Cancer, the intelligence of the House of influence, to The Chariot, Key 7 in the Tarot and to the direction east-below on the Cube of Space, as well as to alchemical separation (95, 1360). It is the sign or symbol for the faculty of speech.

I. The character for Cheth is similar to that for Heh, but the line on the left is joined to the cross bar. This character is a combination of Daleth and Vav, implying its concealed numerical value is 10. By this number Cheth refers to the letter Yod, and also Malkuth, the Kingdom, of 10th Sephirah. It is a sign of the combination of the 4th (Daleth) and 6th Sephiroth (Vav), Mercy and Beauty.

II. The letter Cheth means a field, fence or palisade (a line of steep lofty cliffs usually along a river). This implies inclosure. This field can be the manifested universe, but in man is the personality. The One Self sets aside a particular point in space and time to cultivate the personal ego.

III. Rabbi Ginsburgh: "Cheth is used in technical terms to refer to drawing forth knowledge hidden in the subconsciousness, to the elucidation of mysteries, to the bringing of concealed meanings to the surface. "The form of the letter Cheth resembles a gateway. Through a gateway one enters and exits. One enters into an inner realm or chamber, a deeper state of awareness, a truer level of experience. One exits to return to one's pervious, stable state of existence, infused with the light of one's new experience." [The Alef-Beit,]

IV. Paul Case: "Since the Phoenicians carried their alphabets to the great centers of civilization in the ancient world, most of the symbols have undergone many alterations. To this rule, however, Cheth the eighth letter, as a notable exception. In the oldest records it consists of two, upright, joined by either two or three cross-bars. The Phoenician pictograph probably represented field, surrounded by a rectangular fence. It therefore suggest the same notions of particular location, enclosure, and specialized effort which are associated with the letter Beth. We may expect, on this account, to learn that the Tarot trump to be considered in this chapter symbolizes the same root ideas that are brought to mind by the picture of the magician. All cabalistic interpretations of Cheth agree that the letter stands for something that necessitates labor. Fabre D'Olivet was not always certain of his philology, but he was a thorough kabbalist; so that, while we must nearly always reject his views as a alphabetical origins we can often accept his explanation of the esoteric significance of the Hebrew letters. He says of Cheth: "This letter is the sign of the elementary existence; it is the image of a kind of equilibrium, and attaches itself to ideas of effort, of labor, and of normal and legislative action. It is a symbol of that which requires the expenditure of strength of power; and it implies that the energy so used is directed to a definite end.

Behind all these notions is the idea that the field stands in opposition to the worker. At the beginning of his labors it presents difficulties, even dangers. In its original state it gives trouble. It offers problems and puzzles that must be solved and mastered. After it has been brought under control it co-operates, in a manner of speaking, with the worker; but first of all it must be overcome by 'normal and legislative action.'

The outcome of such action is the establishment of order. Putting things in order is, in fact, the great secret of human achievement. No matter what you do, before you can succeed you must get rid of disorder somewhere. The more recondite significance of Cheth is related to the doctrine that this letter is a sign of elementary existence. The word 'elementary' as used by Fabre D'Olivet, means rudimental. What he speaks of is what the alchemist called their first matter, or chaos. The latter word implies disorder, Webster defines it as 'the confused, unorganized state of primordial matter before the creation of distinct and orderly forms! [The Secret Doctrine of the Tarot, The Word, June 1917, pp. 144-144]

V. "This character can be considered under the double relation of vowel or consonant. As vocal sound it is the symbol of elementary existence and represents the principle of vital aspiration: as consonant it belongs to the guttural sound and represents the field of man, his labor, that which demands on his part any effort, care, fatigue. As grammatical sign it holds an intermediary rank between ה, life, absolute existence, and כ, life, relative and assimilated existence. It presents thus, the image of a sort of equilibrium and equality, and is attached it ideas of effort, labor, and of normal and legislative action." [d'Olivet, 1976, pp. 345-346.]

VI. "Hhayt, is the sphere of storage of all undifferentiated energy, or unstructured substance. It expresses the most unevolved state of energy, as opposed to its achieved freedom in Zayn." [Suraes, 1992, p. 63.]

VII. Cheth, means a 'fence', 'vallum' or 'wall'; it is the Veil enclosing the Graal, the curtain concealing the Holy of Holies. This is also the mystical Veil of Paroketh (Paro-cheth) which was rent asunder the moment that deity became active and uttered the Word in oracles of thunder. *Cheth*, spelt in full, is 418, the number of Abrahadabra which signifies the uniting of the positive and negative currents, the accomplishment of the Great Work. [Grant, 1994, p. 19.]

א into that place, there; at that time; therefore. A demonstrative particle which originally meant "in that place, there." From this basic meaning, transferred to time, it came to mean "at that time, then," and was used in reference to both past and

future. *Awz* is used in Hebrew as "then" is employed English to indicate a casual relationship, like "therefore," or "on that account." All meanings of the word imply relationship, and designate some tie or connection of thought or activity between this place and that, this time and that (whether considered as being the cause of this event, or an effect or consequence yet to come. Additional meanings: whether, also, if.

"This root designates a fixed point in space or duration; a measured distance. It is expressed in a restricted sense by the adverbial relations *there* or *then*. The Arabic characterizes a sort of locomotion, agitation, pulsation, bubbling movement. As a verb it has the sense of *giving a principle; of founding*. The Chaldaic אזא expresses a movement of ascension according to which a thing is placed above another in consequence or this specific gravity. [d'Olivet, 1976, p. 291.]

דבב to go softly, to creep along, to flow gently; as wine poured carefully from a wineskin. Derived from it is the negative meaning, "to slander to disparage," based on the idea of the sneaky, creeping progress of a tale bearer. There is here also some hint of the serpent symbolism associated with Hermes. see 15, 2080, 217, 412, 421, 567, 626, 131.

דד the breast (of women) as the seat of love. Self-consciousness is the aspect of mental activity which makes possible the higher aspects of love and affection. It makes man able to relate cause and effect. It is what makes him a time-binder, uniting past and present and future. With different pointing: nipple, teat, nipple of citrus fruit; tap.

"Every idea of abundance, and division; of propagation, effusion and influence; or sufficient reason, affinity and sympathy. That which is divided in order to be propagated; that which acts by sympathy, affinity, influence, literally *breast, mammal*.

דוד Action of *acting by sympathy* and *by affinity*; action of *attracting, pleasing, loving*; *sufficing mutually*. In a broader sense, *a chosen vessel*, a place, an object toward which one is attracted; every sympathetic and electrifying purpose. In a more restricted sense, *a friend, a* lover; *friendship*, *love*; every kind of flower and particularly the *mandragora* and *the violet*." [d'Olivet, 1976, p. 320.]

אוא   Given, without explanation in *Sepher Sephiroth*. This word is not found in scripture or the Hebrew Lexicon and may be a notariqon. [Crowley, 1977, p. 1]

אבה   to desire, want or need; to consent; be willing. With different pointing: *ebeh*. reed, papyrus.

אגד   to bind or collect; tie, knot, bundle. With different pointing: *ehged*. bunch, bundle, tie, knot; union.

אהב   to love; love relationship, to be fond of, beloved. With different pointing: *ehab*, lust or desire.

זא   Notariqon for Zauir Anpin (478). the Lesser Countenance, or Microprosopus, a designation for Tiphareth.

באה   entrance, threshold. Cheth (Cancer) is the Humanity into incarnation. see Ezekiel 8:5.

הבא   heba. bring.

דאג   to be anxious, the proper name Doeg.

ב-ו   Mercury (ב) in Taurus (ו).

9

I. (3²)

II. The Ennead

III. Nine is the number of the Foundation [Yesod, 80], that is the basis of the Invisible, of its conjunction with our physical world. Every number which can be numerically reduced to 9 is linked to the 3 ways of initiation: Nine is 3+3+3, way of rigor (Fire), way of balance (Air), and way of Mercifulness (Water).

IV. Perfection or finish in the sense of 9 months of gestation for a human. Representing the ongoing cycle as the last number of a the series and therefore completion.

V. "In thought and word and deed, I rest my life, from day to day upon the sure Foundation [Yesod] of eternal being." [9th Saying of the Pattern on the Trestleboard] see 775.

ט   Teth. Teth is the 9th Hebrew letter, associated with Leo, with the Intelligence of the Secret of All Spiritual Activities, with the direction North-Above on the Cube of Space, and with alchemical digestion (419).

I. Teth means snake or serpent (see Appendix 14) and is a symbol of immortality and eternity. The form of the Teth is a coiled serpent and is a symbol of the Great Magical Agent. The motion of the Great Magical Agent is serpentine. It is wavy, undulating, and like a spiral.

II. Rabbi Ginsburgh: The form of Teth is "inverted," thus symbolizing hidden, inverted good-as expressed in the Zohar, "its good is hidden within it." The form of the letter Teth symbolizes the union of the groom and the bride consummating with conception. The secret of the Teth (numerically equivalent to nine, the nine months of pregnancy) is the power of the mother to carry her inner, concealed good--the fetus--through the period of pregnancy. [The Alef-Beit]

III. "This character, as consonant, belongs to the dental sound. As symbolic image it represents the shelter of man; the roof that he raises to protect him; his shield. As grammatical sign it is that of resistance and protection. It serves as link between ד and ת, and partakes of their properties, but in an inferior degree." [d'Olivet, 1976, p. 356.]

IV. "Tayt, as archetype of the primeval female energy, draws its life from Hhayt and builds it gradually into structures." [Suraes, 1992, p. 63.]

V. *Teth*, meaning a 'serpent', is the number nine. In the later Osirian Cults the serpent was equated with solar-phallic energy in the form of the lion-serpent which generated the spermatozoon. In the Draconian Tradition, however, Teth is the serpent symbolic of the female who periodically sloughs her old body as does the snake its skin. Hence, nine is the number of rejuvenation and renewal. [Grant, 1994, p. 20.]

אוא   to kindle, to heat. see 8 (אא).

אֵשׁ fire-pot, hearth, chafing dish, fire place. Also brother, relative, one, someone. With different vowel pointing: 1. meadow, pasture; 2. an interjection, cry of woe, AH!, Alas! Woe!

"The potential sign united to that of elementary existence ה, image of the travail of nature, produce a root whence results all ideas of equilibrium, equally identity, fraternity. When the sign ה characterizes principally all efforts, the root אֵח takes the meaning of its analogues אג, אֵק, and represents a somewhat violent action. It furnishes then all ideas of excitation, and becomes the name of the place where the fire is lighted, *the hearth*. אֵח, *Brother, kinsman, associate, neighbors*: *the common hearth* where all assembled." [d'Olivet, 1976, p. 291.]

בבה cavity, something hollowed out, the apple of the eye, apple.

בגד to cover, a cloak, covering, dress, garment; treachery, deceit, betrayal, unfaithfulness. With different vowel points: to act or deal treacherously. Note that Daleth, Gimel, Beth are the first of the 7 double letters; and the other 4 are Kaph, Peh, Resh, Tav is 700, which is equal to the cover (Kapporath) of the ark of the covenant or mercy seat (Ezekiel 25:17).

גו middle; midst, inside, center.

"גה, גו and גי The organic sign united either to that of life, or to that of universal convertible force, or to that of manifestation, constitutes a root which becomes the symbol of every organization. This root which possesses the same faculties of extension and aggrandizement that we have observed in the root גא, contains ideas apparently opposed to envelopment and development, according to the point of view under which one considers the organization. The Arabic word indicates universal envelopment, *space, atmosphere*.

גהה That which *organizes*; that which gives life to the organs: health, and metaphorically, *medicine*.

גוה Every kind of *organ* dilated to give passage to the vital spirits, or closed to retain them: every

expansion, every *conclusion*: that which serves as *tegument*; *the body*, in general; *the middle* of things: that which *preserves* them as, *the sheath* of a sword; etc." [d'Olivet, 1976, pp. 311-312.]

הד a sounding again, an echoing shout, shout, noise; echo. Variant spelling of הוד Hod, meaning: majesty, elegance; beauty, splendor. see 15.

"הד, like the root אד, of which it is only a modification, it is attached to all ideas of spiritual emanation, the diffusion of a thing *absolute* in its nature as the effect of *sound, light, voice, echo*. The Hebraic root is found in the Arabic root which is applied to every kind of sound, murmur, noise; but by natural deviation the Arabic root having become onomatopoeic and idiomatic. The Aramaic verb signifies *to demolish, cast down, overthrow* by similitude of the noise made by the thing which are demolished." [d'Olivet, 1976, p. 328.]

ד-ה Daleth-Heh. Venus (Daleth) in Aries (Heh).

ובא future, coming.

בדג to multiply abundantly.

בוא to enter, alight, to come into, till one comes.

גאה to swell, grow, rise or increase, become powerful, exalted, glorious; to be lifted up. These are activities of Yesod, or Foundation, the Pure Intelligence. "So called because it purifies the essence of the Sephiroth, proves and preserves there images, and prevent them from loss by their union with itself." see 18, 27, 36, 45, 54, 63 72, 81, 90, 80, 369, 3321.

אוב Magic. ghost conjurer, sorcerer; to mumble, a ventriloquist. The forced used in the Magic of Darkness. With different pointing: skin bag, bottle.

I. i.e. a soothsayer, who evokes the manes of the dead by the power of incantations and magical songs, in order to give answers as to future or doubtful things... Specially, it denotes a *python*, or a soothsaying daemon, of which these men were believed to be possessed. How then could it be that the same Hebrew word, should express a

27

bottle, and a ventriloquist? Apparently from the magician, when possessed with the daemon, being as it were, a bottle or vessel, and sheath of this python. [Gesenius, 1992, p. 18]

אדר to endure, to last, continue, era, duration, space and time.

באו In desire.

בגד covering, garment, robe; concealment.

10

I. $\Sigma 4 = 10$

II. A Greek name for 10 was Pantelia, signifying "all complete," or, "fully accomplished." Westcott says: "Note that ten is used as a sign of fellowship, love, peace and union, in the Masonic third token, the union of two five points of fellowship." Ten is also the number of complete manifestation, and is an all-embracing number. Because any number beyond 10 returns to units through reduction.

III. "The Kingdom of Spirit is embodied in my flesh." [10th Saying on the Pattern on the Trestleboard].

IV. Value of the Greek letter I (iota), the 8th letter of the alphabet. In the Pistis Sopina it is said "Iota (I) because the universe hath gone forth..." Parts of the Greek Mystery phrase I-A-Omega. see 811.

י Yod. the hand [of man], creative hand (see Appendix 14), a tongue of flame. It suggests that the primary Reality of the universe is identical with the power expressed by the handiwork of human beings. Yod is the foundation of the letters and resembles a tongue of flame. It is a component part of every Hebrew (actually ancient Chaldean, the "Flame Alphabet") letter. It is said that all letters are an adaptation of the letter Yod. It symbolizes the flame of spiritual energy which is present in all forms of the Life-power's self-expression. Yod is the channel of God's will [Zohar I, page 11].

I. The upper point of Yod represents the Primal Will (Kether), while the rest of the letter corresponds to Chokmah (Wisdom). This implies that all mental activity is derived directly from the essential Will of the One Identity. This mental activity, or volition, takes form as the Wisdom which is the basis for the entire cosmic order.

II. Yod is associated with Key 9, The Hermit and Virgo in Astrology. The path of Yod connects Chesed (cosmic memory) and Tiphareth (imagination) on the Tree of Life. see 23, 90, 18.

III. Rabbi Munk: "The tenth letter of the Alef-Beit, Yod, is barely larger than a dot and it cannot be divided into component parts. It alludes to God, Who is One and Indivisible, for although his attributes seem to be numerous and even contradictory, they flow from a unified purpose and existence. [The Wisdom of the Hebrew Alphabet]

IV. "This character is the symbol of all manifested power. It represents the hand of man, the forefinger. As grammatical sign, it is that of potential manifestation, intellectual duration, eternity. This character, remarkable in its vocal nature, loses the greater part of its faculties in becoming consonant, where it signifies only a material duration, a refraction, a sort of link as ו, or of movement as ש. Plato gave particular attention to this vowel which he considered as assigned to the female sex and designated consequently all that which is tender and delicate.

The Hebraist grammarians who rank this character among the *heemanthes*, attribute to it the virtue of expressing at the beginning of words, duration and strength; but it is only a result of its power as sign." [d'Olivet, 1976, p. 361.]

V. "*Yod* (10): Existence which both betrays and satisfies life. Continuity in the duration of that which duration destroys. Y*od*, projection of *Aleph*, confers reality upon all that tends to bury *Aleph* (dead or alive). Temporal Y*od* (10) is the finite which never rejoins the infinite. *Yod* is the manifested existence in time of *Aleph*, the timeless, the immeasurable." [Suraes, 1992, p. 66.]

VI. Yod is the sum total or end of the matter since it symbolizes the return of Unity (1) to the original state of non-duality symbolized by the Ayin (0), the Eye of Nuit. This demonstrates the ultimate identity of the Eye and the Hand. The latter, being the instrument of the holder, container, or womb, is an ideogram of the number 5 and hence of the female. The primal source of creationis the female whose symbols, Hand (1) and Eye (0), denote the mother-blood, the uterus in which and from which the Word issues and assumes flesh. [Grant, 1994, p. 21.]

הה Letter name Heh. Woe, alas. The first Heh represents <u>insight,</u> or the Life-power's own knowledge of itself. The second Heh is a symbol of <u>foresight</u>, directed toward the outcome of necessary consequences following from what insight reveals (see 514). It is written that creation took place with the letter Heh (understand 'takes' where you read 'took' for there is no time but an eternal present, for the One). Now Heh is the letter of vision, and it is spelled by its own self-duplication, that is, הה. Of these the first is the sign of the waters of Binah, and the second is the sign of the earth of Malkuth. Each is by number the half of the paternal Yod, for Heh is 5 and Yod is 10, thus may you see in the first Heh the Sephiroth from Kether to Geburah, and the second, those from Tiphareth to Malkuth. The whole tree is thus expressed by the name of this one letter. The first Heh is insight, the second is the same vision, tuned outward into manifestation .

אט gently, softly, secretly, slow. Also an enchanter, soothsayer, mutterer, magician, sorcerer. see 220.

"This root is scarcely used in Hebrew except to describe a sound or a slow, silent movement. The Arabic expresses any kind of murmuring noise. אט a *magic murmur*; *witchcraft, enchantment*." [d'Olivet, 1976, p. 292.]

אחד unity; to be united. Also a personal name.

בדד to divide, separation, separateness, separately; to scatter; alone, isolated, in a lonely state. see 6.

בוא to cleave asunder, destroy; to divide, cut through, spoil.

גבה height, altitude; exaction, pride, haughtiness. [Psalm 101:5, Proverbs 16:5]. With different pointing: 1. *gawboah*: high, tall, lofty,

exacted, elevated; 2. collect payment, 3. eyebrow. see 144.

גז Fleece; the shorn wool; shearing; mowing, mowed grass; field for mowing. Referring to Aries, the Ram to which the letter Heh is attributed.

"The root אז, which indicated the movement of that which tends to take away, united to the organic sign, constitutes a root whose use is to characterize the action by which one suppresses, takes away, extracts every superfluity, every growth; thence גזז, the action of *clipping wool*, *shaving the hair*, *mowing the grass*; *taking away* the tops of things, *polishing* roughness." [d'Olivet, 1976, p. 313.]

זאב to be yellow, a wolf. [Jeremiah 5:6] "Therefore a lion out of the forest shall slay them, and a wold of the evening shall spoil them, a leopard shall watch over their cities: everyone that goes out thence shall be torn to pieces: Because their transgressions are many, and their backslidings are increased.

"A wolf, on account of the luminous darts which flash from its eyes in the darkness. [d'Olivet, 1976, p. 339.] see זא (8).

חב Hiding place, a cherisher, i.e. the bosom.

"The sign of elementary existence united to the root אב, symbol of all fructification, forms a root whose purpose is to describe that which is occult, hidden, mysterious, secret, enclosed, as a germ, as all elementary fructification: if the root אב is taken in its acceptation of desire to have, the root in question here, will develop the idea of an amorous relation, or fecundation. This is why the Arabic taken in a restricted sense, signifies *to love*; whereas in a broader sense this root develops all ideas of grain, germ, semence, etc.

חב or חבב *to hide mysteriously, to impregnate, to brood*, etc. In a restricted sense, the Arabic *signifies to become partial, to favor*. As onomatopoeic root suggest the noise of whetting a sabre." [d'Olivet, 1976, p. 346.]

מא. to sweep away [Godwin]. This word is not found in scripture or the Hebrew Lexicon.

"Every idea of resistance, repulsion, rejection, reflection; that which causes luminous refraction. The Arabic develops the idea of every kind of bending, inflection. Thence the verb *to blow down*." [d'Olivet, 1976, p. 356.]

בגה to cover, a cloak, treachery, deceit.

ב-ח Mercury (Beth) in Cancer (Cheth).
דאה to fly, to soar.

דו two; (the prefix) bi-.

זג skin of a grape; husk, shell.

I. How do we use gematria to understand the secret meaning between words? Take for example אהד, to be united, unity; אט, gently, softly, secretly, an enchanter; בד to divide, separateness, separation; בא, to cleave asunder; גבה, elevated, exalted, high; דאה, flew, soared; הה, window, the name of the fifth letter; בח, hidden place, bosom.

How does one become united with the one source? First we are divided from that source. The magical operation must be done with gently and with secrecy. It starts when the skin or shell which is the cloak of deceit is devoured by the wolf, which is the same as the serpent, the Great Magical Agent. The pure is separated from the impure by the operation of the secret fire (Yod). This operation takes place in a hidden place. A clue to its location is in the Virgo region of the body. No more clues can be given.

11 (prime)

I. The general number of magick, or energy tending to change. [Crowley, 1977, p. xxv.]

II. The years in the Sun spot cycle to the closest whole number (11.1 years actual).

דהב Gold (Aramaic). Conceals an alchemical secret. Daleth (Venus) Cheth (a sign ruled by the Moon) and Beth (Mercury). Venus, Luna, and Mercury are the alchemical copper, silver and quicksilver. The first two are the best conductors of electricity. One the Tree of Life these correspond to the Paths which balance those

corresponding letters of אוד. *Dahab* is one of the alchemical name for the perfect red stone which is האדם אבן and also אדם. The Red Stone is also termed גפרית (sulphur, 693). See 103, 53, 157.

חג circularity of form or motion; a feast, festival; sacrifice. The magic force moves in cycles, it comes back to its starting point -it WHEELS, so to speak. For this reason every magical ritual is performed within a circle. see 789

גדד to tear out, attack, to cut off, to cut; to pick dates.

דז Proud, haughty; insolent; presumptuous.

חבא to conceal; to hide oneself, to be hidden.

גוב a locust; to dig; husband man.

אדו The English equivalent of several Hebrew names among whom was a prophet or seer [2 Chronicles 9:29, 12:15, 13:22].

אוד the fire of the magic light, firebrand, the magic power. Aleph is the divine Life-breath (Ruach, 214), Vav is the link which joins into all beings, and Daleth is the door of life through which all things are manifested. see 207, 363, 89.

The name שדי אל חי is 363, which is 11 times 11 multiplied by 3 (11 x 11 x 3) . Eleven is אוד (od) and 3 is Gimel. *Od* is the magic power and Gimel is the beginning of *Guph* the body. Aleph is the Breath, Vav is the Link, Daleth is the Door of Life and is Nogah also, which gives the Victory (The 7th Sephiroth). In Gimel (3) is Recollection and Union, and thus the letters of *ode* speak loud. In Yesod is all this centered and they who know the secret of Yod, become the extenders of the paternal Life and Light. Yesod is called the Sphere of the Moon, and The Moon (Key 2) in the Tarot is associated with the letter Gimel, the letter of Union (The Uniting Intelligence). Blessed are they who hear and understand, and understanding, live as they know. Note well the warning implied. There are many who seek to be spiritual at the expense of the body. They repudiate all that pertains to Yesod because they misunderstand its real significance. The mystery of the 9th Sephirah is a secret of Yod. see 343, 80, 214, 18 & C.27.

I. Llli Gelse: *Ode*. Positive emanation of the astral fluids or currents. It is the double, the phantom electro-magnetic, but of an electricity and a magnetism vitalized very strongly and related to the ether of all living beings, even of the plants, the minerals and crystals, which appear in a colored vapor in the darkness. And is the manifestation of the intimate will of native, the magical force, the astral forms of the universe center, the one which becomes concrete in the innumerable types of the world, its forms its imprints, the simple vestments of אוד or the astral. *Ode* is the negative emanation and united these two make אוֹר, the universal light, or the liquid Gold of the Hermetists. [note, circa 1920]

II. "This root, composed of the signs of power and of physical divisibility, indicates every distinct, single object, taken from the many. That which *emanates* from a thing: *the power of division, relative unity, an emanation*; *a smoking fire brand*.

אוד That which is done because of or *on occasion* of another thing: *an affair, a thing, an occurrence*." [d'Olivet, 1976, p. 289.]

אי Where?, How? Look to the Life-breath (א) expressed as Will (י) for the magic power. Also dry land, coast, country (Job 22:30), where one acts, where one is.

"Power accompanied by manifestation, forms a root whose meaning, akin to that which we have found in the root אי, expresses the same idea of desire, but less vague and more determined. It is no longer sentiment, passion without object, which falls into incertitude: it is the very object of this sentiment, the center toward which the will tends, the place where it is fixed. A remarkable thing is, that if the root אי is represented in its most abstract acceptation by the prepostive relation *or*, the root אי is represented, in the same acceptation, by the adverbial relation *where*.

Every center of activity, every place distinct, separate from another place. *An isle, a country, a region*; *where* one is, *where* one acts." [d'Olivet, 1976, p. 292.]

ג/ח Gimel/Cheth. Moon (Gimel) in Cancer (Cheth).

האגב the means by.

האנא the reservoir.

הבד separated.

גדד to tear out, attack, to cut off.

ואד vapor, mist.

ואבב and to bear fruit, to blossom.

ובבא gate, door.

וגב upper surface.

יא Oh! From a root meaning: all movements of the soul which spring from admiration and astonishment (Hebrew Tongue Resorted, p. 362].

בבוא When? The power used this moment in the Magic of Light. Also *ve-boa*: the coming of.

וד. proud, haughty.

אדה. to behold.

חבא. to conceal.

הבד hebed. garment, covering.

γη Gea (Gr). Earth. "contraction from a primary word; soil; by extension a region, or the solid part of the whole of the terrne globe (including the ocupants in each application): country, earth, ground, land, world." [Strong, 1996, p. 597.] see 2, 29, 38, 47, 56, 65, 74, 83.

12

I. The Tetrahedron has 4 triangular (3) faces (4 x 3 = 12).

II. Number of edges (lines) in a Octahedron (Air) and a Cube (Earth). Number of faces on a Dodecahedron (Akasha) and vertices on a Icosahedron (Air).

III. The sidereal revolution of Jupiter in years about the sun to the nearest whole number (11.86 years actual).

וו Letter-name Vav. nail, hook, pin. Something to support something else which hangs from it. Corresponding to Key 5, The Hierophant. The 16th path of Vav "veils the name of Him, the fortunate one" (הוא). Thus the Hierophant may be considered to be a symbol for the cosmic self, Yekhidah acting as the inner teacher of mankind. Vav represents also the Heart, seat of interior hearing or the ego in Tiphareth, suggesting that the seed the 6th Sephira is preexistent in Kether, the First. see 53, 177, 158, 508, 32, 168, 331, 506, 415, 6.

אוה desire, longing. With different vowel points: to desire, wish, long for.

"Action of *longing ardently, desiring, inclining with passion*." [d'Olivet, 1976, p. 290.] see Book of Tokens, (p. 71)

אזד confirmed, concluded (Aramaic). In Daniel 2:5 and 2:8 the Aramaic אזדא is used: the Authorized Version translation, "is gone," the Jewish translation, "is certain." Also "He departed, he went forth." Chaldean perhaps adjective "settled, firm, or decided." [C.F. The Talmud אזדא לטעמיה "decided to his purpose" (Daniel 2). The root perhaps akin to שות ימד "to set", hence different from אזל, which most prefer since ד = ל, as רעד = רעל, and so they render אזדא מני מלתא "the word (i.e. decree) is gone forth (i.e. has been issued) from me."] From Protestant Hebrew Dictionary.

חבב to cover, protect, love. see 10, (חב).

אחאב Father's Brother. [Jeremiah 29:21]. A prophet, denounced by Jeremiah. The second king of the Omir dynasty and early Israel's most conspicuous and important ruler (875-52 B.C.) Standard Bible Dictionary.

הוא Hu or Hoa. He (3rd person singular), Lord. One of the Divine Names associated with Kether. Hu or Hvan was a Druids name of the Sun. Hu or Yu, a Babylonian God of the Sky, a very ancient God. Compare with Jah, Jao [IAO], Jupiter, Allah, Hu.

"In a broad sense, *the Being*; the one who *is*: in a particular sense, *a being*; the one of whom one speaks, represented by the pronominal relations *he, that one, this*." [d'Olivet, 1976, p. 328.]

חד sharp.

"The power of division, expressed by the root אד which, arrested by the effort which results from its contraction with the elementary sign ח, becomes the image of relative unity. It is literally, *a sharp thing, a point, a summit*. The Arabic presents in general, the ideas of *terminating, determining, circumscribing, limiting*. it is, in a more restricted sense, *to grind*; metaphorically, *to punish*.

The point of anything whatever. Everything which *pricks*, everything which is *extreme, initial*: metaphorically, *a drop* of wine; *gaiety, lively and piquant*." [d'Olivet, 1976, p. 347.]

זה This. "Every demonstrative, manifesting, radiant movement: every objective expressed in an abstract sense by the pronominal relations *this, that, these, those*." [d'Olivet, 1976, p. 340.]

דוב A bear.

Westcott: "Parzala [Iron-פרזלא, 318], whose lesser number is 12, is of the same account as the name of that blood animal *Dob* [דוב], a Bear, whose number is 12 also.

And this is that mystical thing, which is written Daniel 7:5, 'And behold another Beast, a second like unto a Bear, stood on its one side, and it had three ribs standing out in his mouth, between his teeth; and thus they said to it 'arise, eat much flesh.' The Meaning is, that in order to constitute the Metallic Kingdom, in the second place, iron is to be taken; in whose mouth or opening (which comes to pass in an Earthen Vessel) a threefold scoria is thrust out, from within its whitish Nature." [Westcott, 1997, p. 24] see 318, 229.

בי Please, pray! [Genesis 44:18] "Then Judah went up to him [Joseph] and said, 'please, my Lord, let your servant speak a word to my Lord.

Do not be angry with your servant, though you are equal to pharaoh himself.'"

"Root analogous to the roots אב, בה, בו, which characterize the movement of a thing which advances, appears evident, comes opens, etc. This applies chiefly to the desire that one has to see a thing appear, an event occur, and that one expresses *by would to God*!" [d'Olivet, 1976, p. 304.]

גוג Gog; A prince of Magog, and descendant of Reuben (259) In 1 Chronicles 5:4: "The descendants of Joel: Shemiah his son, Gog, his son, Shimel his son..."

"...גג means elasticity; that which stretch and expands without being disunited. That which extends to cover, to envelop... the roof of a tent. [d'Olivet, 1976, p. 311.] see 6.

הבה A city of Edom [Crowley, 1977, p. 2]. Translated "come" in Genesis 11:3.

גט little book, pamphlet, letter, tools [Crowley, 1977, p. 2]. "This root is not used in Hebrew. The Arabic denotes a thing which repulses the effort of the hand which pushes it." [d'Olivet, 1976, p. 313.]

דגה to grow, spawn, or multiply. (as noun) a fish (fem.). As a verb: to move rapidly, to spawn, to become numerous, to multiply. Note the combination of the idea of rapid movement with that of the production of seed, or spawn. To multiply (like fish), suggesting the rapid multiplication of ideas which results from contact with the inner teacher.

ח/ד Daleth-Cheth. Venus (Daleth) in Cancer (Cheth).

אחאב Proper name see Jeremiah 29:21.

γαζα. gaza (Gr). treasury, treasure, riches. Originally a Persian word. Refers to the first path as the source whence all the riches of manifestation are drawn. see 3, 20, 21.

13   (prime)

I. The scale of the highest feminine unity; easily transformed to secondary masculine ideas by any make component; or, the unity resulting from love. [Crowley, 1977, p. xxv]

II. In Deuteronomy 6:4: "Hear, O Israel, the Lord our God is one Lord." The alchemical first matter is ONE, and contains within itself all that is needed. see 273, 372, 384, 395, 400, 441, 600, 636, 740. see 12 for D'Olivet comments on the root הו & 9 for his notes on אה.

III. "It is the name of no. 1 and it expresses in a stupendous way the metaphysical disappearance from our sight of Aleph, as it actually is projected into 8 [ח]and 4[ד]." [Suraes, 1992, p. 93.]

אחד echad, achad. Unity, one; alone, solitary.

בהו emptiness, void, terror, chaos. The primary chaos is the stuff thoughts are made of. The alchemist first matter is also called a "void". Applied to the first state of the earth. [Genesis 1:2] "And the earth was without form, and void, and darkness was upon the face of the deep; and the spirit of God moved upon the face of the waters."

"*An abyss*, a thing whose depth cannot be fathomed, physically as well as morally (see הו). The Arabic, as onomatopoeic root characterizes astonishment, surprise." [d'Olivet, 1976, p. 302.] see 19, 76, 411, 1152.

הגה sound, muttering, thought or musing, to contemplate, meditate; rumbling moan, sigh; rudder (of ship); to utter sounds, speak, murmur, moan, growl, coo; to read; pronounce; to remain. The primary chaos is a mode of vibration closely related to sound. Also: to divide, to separate dross.

איב to violate; to asperse; a female enemy; hatred; to be hostile, be an enemy of. Hate, the opposite pole of Love. Both are the same basic emotion.

הו here, this; this one. With different pointing: blossom, splendor.

I. "Every demonstrative, manifesting, radiant movement: every objectivity expressed in an abstract sense by the pronominal relations *this*, *that*, *these those* [see זה]. The Arabic expresses the action of shedding light, of shining. זו Absolute idea of *objectivity*; everything from which light is reflected." [d'Olivet, 1976, p. 340.]

חגב to pluck off, eat; a locust, grasshopper.

דוג a fisher, fisherman.
חדד the beast. see 9.

גהה healing, health. Proverbs 17:22: "A merry heart does good like a medicine."

"That which *organizes*; that which gives life to the organs: *health*, and metaphorically, *medicine*." [d'Olivet, 1976, p. 312.]

אבי father.

אגדה Collective unity, band, bunch, bundle, company; a joining together, a vaulted arch, the sky. A unity composed of the combination of parts.

גי Valley. Chokmah 42 fold name in Yetzirah.

דאגה anxiety, care, grief.
אהבה love (esp. between sexes), beloved.

יבא He comes [Genesis 49:10]. From a root meaning: to desire, long. [Strong, 1996, p. 382.] Refers to the alchemical new man, a product of mental analysis and synthesis. Associated with Shiloh (345) which refers to the Messiah (358).

14

I. The number of vertices, lines and faces on a Tetrahedron.

II. Height of the great pyramid in proportion to the length of its base line. Osiris body was divide into 14 parts.

אדה to join, stitch, piece together. See את.

די sufficing; enough, sufficient.

ד/י Daleth/Yod. Venus (Daleth) in Virgo (Yod).

דוד uncle; friend, relative; in medieval times, philosopher. With different pointing: *dude*. pot, kettle, boiler. From a root meaning: to boil, to be agitated. Also pronounced: *David*. Meaning, beloved, lover, to love, to compose love songs, friendship, caressing. With different vowel points: to receive, to adopt, to comprehend, to contain; a basket. see 137 (Lt), 155, 805.

I. "Action of *acting by sympathy* and *by affinity*; action of *attracting*, *pleasing*, *loving*; *sufficing mutually*. In a broader sense, *a chosen vessel*, a place, an object toward which one is attracted; every sympathetic and electrifying purpose. In a more restricted sense, *a friend*, *a lover*; *friendship*, *love*; every kind of flower and particularly *the mandragora* and *the violet*." [d'Olivet, 1976, p. 320.]

II. "The root of this name is a Hebrew verb spelled with the same letters, meaning primarily "to boil, to cook." Figuratively, it signifies "to love," and is fundamentally a verb designating love between the sexes. thus, "David" means "Love" or "Beloved." ...often the alchemical books assure us that the Great Work, or operation of the Sun, is nothing other than "coction," that is, cooking or boiling. What the alchemist are hiding behind this veil of language is the simple truth that love is the fulfilling of the law, that the pure gold of the Absolute is found through the working of the gentle heat of love, that the sacrifice of sacrifices is a broken and contrite heart purified in the fires of love, that only through love can the true pattern of that perfect golden cube, the New Jerusalem, be rightly perceived and understood." [Case, 1985, p. 138.] see 107, 222, 155.

אטד a thorn, a spine, the piercer. The basic meaning is phallic. Tradition associates אטד with Christ's crown of thorns. This seems to have little basis in fact, but is good symbolism nevertheless. With different pointing: the fastening or the fastener. From a verb meaning: to pierce, to penetrate, to fasten in. Thorns are symbols of union, connection, joining, fastening, association, accumulation and aggeration.

These ideas are fundamental in relation to Briah, the Creative World of Water, where archetypal ideas are combined with each other. Note that the rose, a symbol of love, has thorns. see 115.

אבח A sacrifice, an offer, offering (Aramaic). Both verb and noun, refers to the sacrifice of animals. Symbolizes control of the animal nature, energized by the Mars force. Refers to the fact that the life-power offers itself in an act of creation.

הדה to stretch forth the hand; to show the way; to seize, lay hold of. Note the Daleth between the two Heh's. That self offering is also a self-extension or self-direction. see 4, 104, 250, 41, 72, 86, 158.

גוה Body, or back. Root of גויה substance, a body. see 24.

יד hand. power, strength, place, monument. variant spelling of letter name Yod.

"The sign of potential manifestation, united to the root אד, image of every emanation, of every divisional cause, forms a remarkable root, whose purpose is to produce ideas relative to the hand of man. In the literal and restricted sense, *the hand*; in the figurative and general sense, it is the *faculty, executive force, power of acting, dominion*: it is every kind of *aid, instrument, machine, work, term; administration, liberality, faith, protection*: it is the symbol of *relative unity*, and of the *power of division*; it is *the margin, boarder, edge*; the point by which one grasp things; it is the *place, the point* that one indicates, etc." [d'Olivet, 1976, p. 363.]

זהב gold. Solar energy, the alchemical "gold", first matter and medicine. The gold of enlightenment, the philosophical gold which represents perfect verified truth. Zahab signifies primarily "That which shines." As a verb it means "to glitter like gold." see 200, 440.

I. *Aesch Mezareph*, Qabalistic alchemical treatise, says that when *zahab* is written alone, without any qualifying adjectives "It is refereed to Geburah, because gold cometh from the North." [Westcott, 1997, p. 13] This is a reference to Job 37:22 where the original has *zahab* for the word translated "fair weather" in the English

Bible. North is assigned to Geburah, the sphere of Mars. Like the Latin *Aurun*, which meant originally "the burning thing,"

II. "*Gold*, on account of its innate brightness." [d'Olivet, 1976, p. 340.]

III. Basil Valentine: "He that knows exactly this golden seed or magnet, and searcheth thoroughly into its properties, he hath the true root of life, and may attain that which his heart longs for, wherefore entreat all true lovers of mineral science, and sons of art, diligently to inquire after this metallic seed or root, and be assured that it is not an idle chimera or dream, but a real and certain truth."

IV. The intellect shall be silver, thy memory golden" [Waite, 1974, p. 59]. Note the moon is intellectual apprehension. Sun is right recollection', that is, 'the collecting intelligence' of 30th Path of Resh. The end of the work at the red stage (sun) is really a memory of something always true, but temporarily forgotten.

גיא deep gorge with lofty sides; rising ground. The "Earth" of Geburah. One of the 7 earths in the diagram of the 4 seas, so used it means "rising ground." Also undulating ground. see 291, 50, 365, 105, 302, 432, 337.

"*Valley, gorge, depth*. The Arabic indicates a place where water remains stagnant and becomes corrupt through standing." [d'Olivet, 1976, p. 313.]

דד "The sign of natural abundance united to that of manifestation, constitutes the true root characteristic of this sign. This root develops all ideas of sufficiency and of sufficient reason; of abundant cause and of elementary divisibility. די and דד: that which is *fecund, fertile, abundant, sufficient*; that which *contents, satisfies, suffices*." [d'Olivet, 1976, p. 321.]

הבהב a gift; a sacrificial offering. Refers to the fact that the Life-power offers itself in an act of creation. see אבח

alba (Lt). white. The feminine form of the adjective. As a noun, the name of the mother city of Rome, and is some occult texts it is used as an allusion to Amia (52). By sacrifice and purification, or making white (Alba) the animal and love nature (Mars-Venus) becomes Vhz, Gold. This is an alchemical Key.

15

I. $\Sigma 5 = 15$

II. 1/168 of a "week of times" (2520 years).

III. 15 is the theosophical extension of 5 ($\Box 5 = 15$). Thus Hod as a number, denotes the full expression of the powers symbolized by 5.

IV. The Sun (Tiphareth, 6) and The Moon (Yesod, 9).

הוד Hod. Splendor, Glory, the 8th Sephirah. From a Hebrew root derived from a noun designating the female breast, thus expressing ideas of nourishment, satisfaction of hunger. Hod signifies prominence, eminence, importance. A consequence of expansion from within of the essence of the 2nd Sephirah Chokmah. (Observe that on the Tree of Life, Chokmah and Hod are diametrically opposite.) The Perfect intelligence, seat of the personal intellect, is a focal point in which the will-force from Geburah, the image-making power of Tiphareth and the desire-force of Netzach are mingled. Connected with the intellectual operations of human self-consciousness. The full expression of the powers of Geburah (5), of which Hod is the reflection. Theosophic extension of 5 and the powers of Heh, the emperor. הוד may be read "Heh and Daleth," a combination of reason (Emperor), imagination (Empress), and intuition (the Hierophant). The desire for something different which disintegrates old forms in its early stages (Peh, the path between Hod and Netzach). see 8, 48, 193, 370, 550, 585, 720, & 2080.

I. Give some thought to the Sephirah Hod, where this Path descends. Consider its name letter by letter, in relation to the Keys of Tarot. The Sephirah *Hod* has through Tarot a link with the Path through which the Mezla descends to it from Geburah. Consider the Gematria of *Hod* and its relation to הד. Heh (ה) is the letter of the Emperor and ד the letter of the Empress, with ו between them to represent both אב and בן, and to intimate a conjunction also. This should put you on the track of the deeper significance of the

31st Path. That is to say, insofar as the specific nature of the descending influence is concerned. See 8 & C.39.

זוב to flow (as water), to melt, to gush. As a noun it designates the menstrual flux of women. An overflowing, abounding. "Action of *swarming as insects*; *of boiling, seething*, as water." [d'Olivet, 1976, p. 339.]

אביב the month of Exodus and Passover and resurrection. Its literal meaning is "blossom," or, "ear (of grain)." As the month of coming forth from the symbolic darkness of Egypt. *Abib* corresponds to Chokmah, as the first projection from Kether (73). Corresponds to the sign of Leo where Sol has his abode. See Deuteronomy 16:1.

HY Jah. Wisdom. The divine name attributed to Chokmah. A verbal symbol of the dual potency which brings the whole Tree of Life into manifestation Yod stands for *Ab*, the Father. Heh stands for *Aima*, the Mother. The short form of יהוה used principally in Hebrew poetry.

I. "ה. Absolute life manifested, eternity, the eternally living being: God." [d'Olivet, 1976, p. 363.]

איד distress, calamity, misery, misfortune. "*A vapor, an exhalation, a contagion*, that which *is spread* without." [d'Olivet, 1976, p. 293.]

ההו 41st name of Shem ha-Mephorash, short from. see 46 & Appendix 10.

הי Lamentation. In Ezekiel 2:10: (9) "Then I looked, and I saw a hand stretched out to me in it was a scroll, (10) which he unrolled before me. On both sides of it were written words of lamentations and mourning and woe."

"הי. Root analogous to the vital root הה whose properties it manifests. The Arabic represents the pronounial relation *she, that, this*. As a verb, this root develops the action of *arranging*, or *preparing* things and giving them an agreeable form... הי onomatopoeic root expressing all painful and sorrowful affections." [d'Olivet, 1976, p. 330.]

חז He who impels; to force, to move, to impel. "Every difficult movement made with effort; that which is done laboriously; a presumptuous, tenacious spirit." [d'Olivet, 1976, p. 341.]

חבה to cover, conceal, hide.

גאוה elevation, majesty; also, arrogance, haughtiness, pride.

אבוהא Angel of the 3rd decanate of Sagittarius.

חגב a locust

גבהה high.

XV (Lt). The last 2 letter of the word LVX (65). Minus the L (to instruct). Suggests the absence of the equalibrating, directive power symbolized by Key 11. Key 15, the Devil, represents the One Force, as it operates apart from human knowledge (למד). and human direction. yet XV is composed of the numbers V (5) and X (10), the Wheel of Fortune, the world of objective appearances and V, the principle of consciousness.

16

I. (4x4) or 2^4

אזוב Hyssop. Purgation or purification. Symbolizes the cleansing which comes from regulation. see 4, 64, 34, 136

אחז to apprehend, to lay hold of, to grasp, to handle, to fasten, to gird. With different pointing: to seize, clutch; to dazzle, delude. Refers to the grasp of cosmic laws which is based upon measurement.

"All ideas of *adhesion, apprehension, agglomeration, union, possession, heritage.*" [d'Olivet, 1976, p. 291.]

גבוה exacted, elevated, high. Refers to the idea of domination and authority derived from grasp of cosmic laws.

היא The personal pronoun She. Existence manifest through Prakariti (Isis) or Nature. The Uniting Intelligence (Gimel) is the most important means of purification. it links personal consciousness to the highest place of being. It is the wisdom personified in proverbs as a woman. Its full exercise enables us to realize the identity of the self in man with universal being. see הוא (12).

זוג to enclose, or, like, equal to. Refers to the essential identity of all manifestations of the One Life. With different pointing: 1. to pair or match, pair of scissors; married couple; 2. bell, rattle.

אחוד conjunction, union. Also powerful, strong or "the one", "the incomparable." In Judges 3:15: "But when the Children of Israel cried to the Lord, the Lord raised them up a deliverer, Ehud the son of Gera, a Benjemite, a man left-handed: and by him the children of Israel sent a present to Eblon the King of Moad." see 13.

חח "Hook." brooch, ring, Plural form in Ezekiel 29:4: [You say, 'the Nile is mine; I made it for myself'] "But I will put hooks in your jaws and make the fish of your streams stick to your jaws. I will pull you out from among the streams, with all the fish sticking to your scales."

"Every ideas of effort applied to a thing, and of a thing making effort; *a hook, fish-hook, ring; a thorn-bush.* חוח that which is *pointed, hooked*; that which exercises any force whatever, as *pincers, hooks, forceps:* thence the Arabic verb meaning *to penetrate, to go deeply into.*" [d'Olivet, 1976, p. 349.]

הי Alas! woe. "Onomatopoeic root which expresses disdain, disgust." [d'Olivet, 1976, p. 326.]

איה vulture, kite, Possibly hawk or falcon.

אודה I will thank.
הוה to be, to exist, mischief, ruin.
איה where?

אבדו perdition; the 2nd hell, corresponding to Hod [Godwin].

חבו 68th name of Shem ha-Mephorash, short form. see 31 & Appendix 10.

17   (prime)

I. The masculine unity. (Trinity of Aleph, Vau, Yod). [Crowley, 1977, p. xxv]

גיד sinew, vein, dried veins or tendon; penis. The sinew that shrank, in the story of Jacob's wrestling with the angel. "A *nerve, a tendon*; everything that can be stretched for action." [d'Olivet, 1976, p. 311.] see 67, 360, 377.

זבח to slaughter, to kill, to sacrifice. This is an alchemical name for the white stage of the Great Work.

זוד to boil, to seethe; to be fervid; to seethe with anger; to be proud or insolent. To act arrogantly or rebelliously. "Action of boiling, literally; of being swollen, puffed up with pride, figuratively, to act haughtily." [d'Olivet, 1976, p. 340.]

חדה to be glad, to rejoice, to gladden someone. see חד.

אוי Oh! Alas!

הגדה tale, legend; saga; narrative recital, homiletical portions of the Talmud; Haggadah, the order of the home-service on Passover night. Homiletical is teaching the principles adapting the sermons to the spiritual benefit of the hearer; the are of preparing sermons and preaching. See K.D.L.C.K p. 267

טוב fairness, good, a good thing; benefit, welfare. "This thy body is truly the heavenly vision of the *Goodness* of the eternal". [Book of Tokens] The importance of recognizing the true value and meaning of man's physical body cannot be overemphasized. Note that God said the Light [אור], was Good in Genesis 1:4. see 89, 170.

"טב. The sign of resistance united to that of interior action, image of all generation, composed a root which is applied to al ideas of conservation and central integrity: it is the symbol of healthy fructification, and of a force capable of setting aside every corruption. טוב. That which keeps a just mean; that which is *well, healthy*; that which defends itself and resists corruption; that which is *good*." [d'Olivet, 1976, p. 356.]

גדי fortunate one, sign of Capricorn. Sometime used as a title of Kether. "The root, גד. An *incursion, an irruption*, literally and figuratively. An *incision* in anything whatsoever, *a furrow*; metaphorically, in the restricted sense, *a kid*: the sign of Capricorn." [d'Olivet, 1976, p. 311.] see 207.

הזה to dream; to rave. "The root of זה. "Movement of ascension and exaltation expressed by the root א, being spiritualized in this one, becomes a sort of mental delirium, *a dream, a sympathetic somnambulism*. The Arabic restricted to the material sense signifies *to shake, to move to and fro, to wag the head*; etc." [d'Olivet, 1976, pp. 329-330.]

חוג to enclose, encompass; to describe a circle. In Job 26:10: "He hath encompassed the water with bounds." The American translation: "He described a circle on the surface of the water." What is meant is the horizon. As Emerson says, "The eye is the first circle, the horizon which bounds it is the second." This is connected with עין, Ayin (130), the eye.

"חוג. action of *whirling, dancing in a ring, devoting one's self to pleasure, celebrating the games*. Metaphorically, *an orbit, a circumference, a sphere of activity, the terrestrial globe*." [d'Olivet, 1976, p. 347.]

יהב. to give, to provide; to place. "Action of being fruitful, manifesting fruits; *a litter, a burden*. Action of bearing, producing." [d'Olivet, 1976, p. 363.]

והו 1st Shem ha-Mephorash, short form. see 32 & Appendix 10.

ההו 49th name of Shem ha-Mephorash, short form. see 48 & Appendix 10.

ההוא The He or Him. A reference to Kether. see 12 [הוא].

זבוב fly.

38

אגוז Nut (of a fruit of a tree). Used in the Song of Solomon 6:11 " I went down to the grove of the nut trees to look at the new growth in the valley, to see if the vines had budded or the pomegranates were in bloom." [New International]. The Zohar says this passage refers to Yesod. The "seed-principle" is the clue to the inner occult meaning.

יהב Lot, burden, what is given; fate (what bounds or limits). see 358, 830, 780, 130.

Adam (Lt). Man/Humanity (as a generic proper name). see 44, 45.

18

I. 2 x 3²

II. 1/40 of a "week of times."

חי life, living. Part of the Devine Name of Yesod (80). see 23, 9, 27, 36, 45, 54, 63, 72, 81, 90.

הוח to purify. "Action of *forcing, necessitating, constraining*; action of *expulsion*, evacuation, etc." [d'Olivet, 1976, p. 321.]

יאיא Notariqon of *yehi aur*. [Crowley, 1977, p. 3.]

איבה hatred. "The root איב. Every idea of *antipathy, enmity, animadversion*. It is an effect of the movement of contraction upon the volitive center א by the sign of interior activity ב." [d'Olivet, 1976, p. 292.]

חטא a criminal, one accounted guilty: offender, sinful, sinner. [Strong, 1996, p. 11.]

חט". The sign of effort united to that of resistance, constitutes a root whence come all ideas of frustrated hope; of failure, sin, error. חט or חטט (intens.) That which *misses* the mark, which is *at fault*, which *sins* in any manner whatsoever.

חטם (comp.) The root טם, symbol of effort united to resistance, being considered from another viewpoint, furnishes the restricted idea of *spinning*, and in consequence, every kind of *thread*, and of *sewing*; so that from the sense of *sewing*, comes that of *mending*; metaphorically, that of *amendment, restoration*: whence it results that the word חטא, which signifies a *sin*, signifies also an *expiation*." [d'Olivet, 1976, p. 349.]

הוח to purify.
אהבי my favorite, my beloved.

Dei (Lt). of God. see 74, 126, 56.

P.D. (Lt). Initials of one of the founders of the Rosicrucian order, according to the *Fama Fraternitiatis*.

19 (prime)

I. The feminine glyph. [Crowley, 1977, p. xxv].

II. At 19 brother C.R.C. finished his initiatory practices at Damcar (264). Key 19 in the Tarot is The Sun, which shows a boy and girl. They symbolizes regenerated human personality, the new vehicle for the Christos or Christ consciousness. They are shown with there back to a stone wall and to the limitations of the cousiousness of the five senses.

חוה Chavah. Eve (Life), "Mother of all Living." Literally, "to live, to be", originally "to breath". Wife of Adam (Humanity). A symbol of mother nature, or subconsciousness, the manifesting power of the cosmos . With different pointing: to be, exist, live, to say, relate, make manifest, to bend, to curve; a round tent, a circle of tents, a village, one of the names of Quicksilver. to show or declare. In Genesis 3:20: "So Adam called his wife's name Eve because she was the mother of all living." see 1577, 207.

I. The bride is Malkuth, and Malkuth is 496, a perfect number (see Appendix 6). 496 reduces to 19, the number of חוה, Eve, the Mother who is also the Bride. *Chavah* contains the beginning (1) and end (9) and their sum is 10, the Kingdom and the completion. Ten is the letter Yod, and the Yod in IHVH stands for Chokmah, the Father. see 496, 89 and C.9.

II. Paul Case: ...throughout the literature of ageless wisdom we have endless repetitions of the thought that the worlds of form and brought froth by sound, and continued by it. This doctrine is even hidden in plain sight in the Hebrew scriptures, where Eve is said to be the "Mother of all living.' The verbal form of this name means, 'To manifest, to show forth.' But the first letter of Eve in Hebrew, is Cheth, and to this Qabalists attribute speech. The second letter is Vau, attributed to the throat, where speech is generated. The third letter is Heh, which indicates definition (being the definite article) and also vision. Thus the very name of Eve is, to a Qabalist, a formula of the creative process. [Classic of Ageless Wisdom, 1931, p. 28]

III. "Here is a name where the changing of the vowel into consonant has caused a strange metamorphosis. The name which, according to the allusion that Moses makes, ought to signify, and signify effectively, *elementary existence*, being derived from the absolute verb הוה *to be-being*, by the sole reinforcement of the initial vowel ה, into ח has come to designate no more than a formless heap of matter, its aggregation, its mass; and by the hardening of the convertible sign ו sanctioned by the Chaldaic punctuation, serves as verb only to indicate the inert and passive existence of things. The change brought about in the derivative verb הוה, has been even more terrible in the absolute verb, חוה; for this verb, destined to represent the Immutable Being, expresses only an endless calamity, as I have explained in speaking of the sacred name יהוה... As to the reasons for the alterations undergone by this proper noun I can only refer the reader to the name of the volitive faculty, אשה [306] which, as we have seen, had preceded that of elementary existence חוה." [d'Olivet, 1976, pp. 117-118.]

IV. "A symbol of the emotional-nature united to the mental-nature of the lower mind... And the mind recognizes the life-principle within the soul to be the emotion-nature, for it is the originator of former of all qualities that subsist, that is, of all qualities that have in them the germ of the higher life." [Gaskell, 1981, p. 254.]

ובהו and emptiness or chaotic condition. Translated in Genesis 1:2 as "and void." see תהו (21). There must be a reason for the use of 2 words which mean about the same thing. see Bohu (13).

אהוז Angel of Sagittarius. Lord of the triplicaty by Day (L.T.D.). see 30, 95, 155, 216, 95, 267, 351, 550, 657.

אויב avib. an enemy, foe.
אחי awkhi. my brother (Genesis 4:9).

דיה diah. to be black.

איוב Job. "The greatly afflicted one." From the root איב meaning to hate (as one opposed tribe or parth); hence, to be hostile, be an enemy. [Strong, 1996, p. 304.]

חזו 24th Shem ha-Mephorash, short form. see 34 & Appendix 10.

Car (Lt). *CR* or *KR* and *Roke* (*RC* or *RK*). Words meaning respectively "Lamb" and "tenderness". Designations of the *Christos* particularly associated with the central figure of the Rosicrucian allegory, named in the *Fama Fraternitiatis*. "Our Brother and Father C.R." see 220.

20

Number of faces on a Icosahedron (Water) and vertices of a Dodecahedron (Akasha).

In the Fama, Brother C.R.C's 20th year was spent in a journey from Damcar to Egypt, a short stay in that country, and other journey to the place where he completed his work. see 444, 142 (Lt).

כ Kaph. Closed fist, grasping hand, palm of the hand. The hand of a man closed in the act of grasping. To grasp is to take possession. To grasp with the mind is to comprehend it and what we really comprehend is ours to control and use. In Key 10, attributed to Kaph, is a law of finite manifestation and is in our mental grasp.

I. This is a law operative through unimaginable immensities as well as a law so finite we can comprehend it. It manifest as the principle of rotation and evoolution. It is at work through the entire series of cosmic manifestations is an intelligible principle. We can understand and apply it. It has been symbolized from time immemorial by a turning wheel. The 8-spoked wheel is a symbol of this law as well as the force behind it.

II. Close your fist and turn it with the thumb toward you and notice how you forefinger and thumb form a spiral. The activity of the One Force circular and spiral in form. Thus, is growth and evolution possible. This motion of a spiral both returns to its source after a cyclic of manifestation as well as beginning it next revolution at a higher level.

III. Rabbi Ginsburgh says: The Kaph is composed of three connected lines with rounded corners, forming the image of a crown lying on its side, as if resting on the head of the king while in a state of prostration or self-nullification...The literal meaning of Kaph is palm...placing palm on palm is an act and sign of subjugation, similar to the act of bowing before a king. Whereas in bowing one totally nullifies one's consciousness in the presence of the King, in placing palm on palm one enters into a state of supplication and prayer to the King to reveal new will from His Supernal Crown (Will) to His subjects. [The Alef-Beit]

IV. Paul Case: In the pictorial alphabet of the early Semites, the sign for Kaph represented the palm of the Hand. From this pictograph two sets of implicits may be derived. The first is a development of ideas connected with the fact that the palm is the active working part of the hand, and all the implicits of this group have their origin in the verb 'to grasp'. The second chain of association begins with the universal belief that the palm is a map of life, which affords a skilled reader an accurate record of the past, and enables him to make a reliable forecast of future probabilities. [The Secret Doctrine of the Tarot, The Word in September 1917, p. 367]

V. "This character as consonant, belongs to the guttural sound. As symbolic image it represents every hollow object, in general; in particular, the hand of man half closed. As grammatical sign, it is the assimilative sign, that of reflective and transient life: it is a sort of mold which receives and communicates indifferently all forms. This character is derived from the aspiration ה, which comes from the vocal principle ה, image of absolute life; but here it joins the expression or organic character ג, of which it is a sort of reinforcement. In Hebrew, it is the assimilative

and concomitant article. Its movement in nouns and actions is similitude and analogy." [d'Olivet, 1976, p. 368.]

יוד Letter name Yod. Hand (as a formative power), creative hand. The qabalistic significance of יוד refers to it being a manual operation [C.F. "Immanuel", or "God with us"], performed by the aid of Mercury. *Yod* is the seed of all the letters, and is the secret of the covenant. This secret is the פה, (85), or יסוד, Ha-Yesod, the Foundation, and 85 is also מילה, the covenant which removes concealment form the paternal Yod. see 10, 61, 80, 85 & C.10.

דיו fluid darkness, ink. Darkness is an ancient symbol for all things pertaining to subconscious forces and activities. The secret of the 20th Path (י) is connected with the operation of the Mars force at subconscious levels. That is, the means whereby ideas are recorded in writing, the art said to be the invention of Hermes or Mercury, ruler of Virgo.

היה It was. to cause to become; to be; produce, make. The divine creativity of Yod is nothing new. 'of whatsoever is, thou mayest say with truth, it was.'" [Book of Tokens, p. 102]

חזה to have a vision of, to gaze at, to penetrate, pass through, to see, behold mentally, to comprehend, to see prophetically, to prophesy [Job 8:17]. All of these meanings correspond to the symbols of Key 9. The active participle of the verb is the noun *Khokeh*, prophet, seer. With different pointing: 1. chest, breast. 2. to select, to experience 3. contract, covenant in 2 Chronicles 19:29. The vision of the prophet is in truth a recollection of that which seems to belong to the past. see 107, 346, 701.

הה-הה Heh-heh. Letter name Heh (window) spelt in full. The Constituting Intelligence, attributed to Aries. see 10

דוי sickness, illness; melancholy. Putridity, loathsomeness, as 'putridity in my food', i.e. loathsome to me in Job 6:6. "Or can that which is unsavory [putrid] be eaten without salt? Or is there any taste in the white of an egg." This is a reference to the intestinal region correlated with

Yod (Virgo) is the seat of infection and of the intoxications which produce melancholy.

הטמאה Sinful things, sin. In Amos 9:8: "Surely the eyes of the sovereign Lord are on the sinful Kingdom. I will destroy it from the face of the Earth-yet I will not totally destroy the House of Jacob." variant spelling, see 418.

והו 62nd Name of Shem ha-Mephorash. see 51, & Appendix 10.

אחוה Brotherhood, fraternity; declaration, solution (of riddles). see Zechariah 11:14.

η γαζα ho gaza (Gr). The treasury. In Acts 8:20: But Peter said unto him (Simon), thy money perish with thee, because thou hast thought that the Gift [i.e. Treasury] of God may be purchased with money." The reference is to the laying on of hands or Baptism, a blessing so that the Holy Spirit may be received by the faithful. see 508.

21

I. Σ6 = 21

II. The diameter of the Formative World, Yetzirah.

III. Pernety: Twenty-one is a designation for the white stage of the work, call also: white copper, lamb, argent-vive, silver, white essence, Eve, white gum, foundation of art, hoe, hyle, virgin's milk, preparatory mean, root of art, unique root, rebis, Seth, companion, sister, sperm of the metals, field in which the Gold must be sown, glass, Zibach, ziva, veil, white veil, white rose, etc. [Great Art, p. 183]

IV. Twenty-one represents the combination of the Ego (1) with the non-ego (2), but it is a reversal of the order expressed by 12. In 12 the Ego is the vehicle and the non-ego the active principle; in 21 is the manifestation of the I through the me, the expression of the universal through the personal, the realization that the whole manifestation is the act of the Universal Ego.

V. Look at Key 21. It is a symbol of *union*, and is therefore the extension numerically of Key 6. What has become of the man in Key 6, when that Key's full expression is represented by Key 21,

and you will perhaps learn something to your advantage. Of course 21 is a representation of Binah, and the very number shows this because it reduces to Binah's number, 3; and in Key 21, if you look intently, you may see delineated in plain sight representation of the idea expressed in Hebrew as the word *Ain* (61), which is both *beten* (belly, womb, the inmost part) and *ammeka* (thy mother). This is a secret with many practical applications. see 61, 67, 400, 713 & C.32.

יהו A mystic name of 3 letters with which God sealed the six directions of space, creating the cube of space. *Yeho* is the name with which He sealed the height, and turned toward above, and sealed it with **יהו** [*Sepher Yetzirah*]. In the central point (Kether) are condensed or concentrated the potencies of all 6 directions. Connected also with the ancient Greek mystery name IAO (ee-ah-oh, see 811) and with Horus and Dionysus. (When a pentagram is traced, each line stands for Yeho or Eheieh. Forms the special name of Chokmah, **יה** (Yah). Yeho is compound in many Hebrew proper names. It may be considered, either as a short form of **יהוה**, or as being **יה**, Yah, ["high, elevated, swelling high"]. Since Yod, is assigned to Chokmah, Father; Heh is assigned to Binah, Mother, and Vav is assigned to Tiphareth, Ben, the son, perhaps the name may represent the holy family, father, mother and son, or Chokmah, Binah and Tiphareth [Gil Johnston]. see 17, 343 & *Sepher Yetzirah* 1:11.

הגיה deep meditation, musing [Psalms 5:1]. Also, murmuring, whispering. Carries out the idea of contemplation from the archetypal and creative worlds. All cosmic activities are aspect of the musing or meditation of the cosmic self Yekhidah. (I utter myself by seeing", Book of Tokens). The "substance" of light vibration radiated from suns. see 65.

זהו purity, referring to the unsullied state of the pattern-forms which exist in the plans of formation. see 7, 21, 14, 44, 66, 28, 88.

חזו vision, form, appearance. An Aramaic noun, used in Daniel 4:17, 7:7, & 7:20. In relation to Kether and Atziluth it intimates that what appears, however illusory the appearance may be and however men may misinterpret it, is actually a manifestation of the real presence of the Originating Principle seated in Kether. As a conjunction, *khesev* means "if," suggesting conditional existence. The Rabbinical writers employed khesev to convey the idea expressed by the English pronoun these, signifying the multiplicity of objects presented to the mind whenever it attends to the various phases of conditional existence.

Hawgeeg and *khesev* extend the meaning of the Logos doctrine by their indication that the process is exactly what is meant by a statement in The of Book of Tokens: "I utter myself by seeing."

אהיה Eheieh. "I am", Existence, Being, the Divine Name attributed to Kether which refers to the formative power of the Primal Will. The Name of Names. In Exodus 3:14, this word is translated "I AM." see 1032, 620, 37.

אך but, only, surely, indeed, yet, certainly, again, once more. A word having many meanings, but all representing some degree of restriction in the affirmative. It is the restriction of the specific, as opposed to the vague, of assurance as opposed to doubt. In Exodus 10:17: "Now forgive my sin once more and pray to the Lord your God to take this deadly plague away from me."

הוי Ah! Alas!

in (Lt). in. (movement) into; (presence) within. a preposition signifying active movement toward a center within. This refers to Kether as the initial concentration of Limitless Light into a small point. It is a movement toward a center within the boundless expanse of Pure Being. The whole field of cosmic manifestation is held to be within that expanse. Consequently, any point in space may be identified as that inner center. Hence the point within one's life to which he refers when he says "I" must be identical with the Central Reality of the universe, Yekhidah.

22

I. Circumference of a circle of the Archetypal World.

II. Brother C.R. left the city Fez. at age 22. Twenty-two represent the circumference of a circle (with a radius of 7), and the completion of a cycle of manifestation. In connection with Brother C.R.C. it indicates the full power of the Christ consciousness or God-Self are now ready to be manifested through the regenerated personality. Tenderness and empathy are the characteristics of an individual that has perfected their vehicle.

III. Note that the 22 letters of the Hebrew Alphabet are the connection paths for the holy influence, Mezla, as it flows down the Tree of Life. At the magical age of 22, one has become a master of all the paths. They are a living embodiment the the rose-cross.

חטה wheat. A seed-form, symbolically expressive of the archetypal world. see Key 3, the Empress.

טובה good. Refers to the goodness of primordial ideas. With different pointing: welfare, prosperity, happiness, bounty, favor, kindness, Good will. see 7, 14, 44, 21, 28, 66, 88.

זווג the state of puberty. With different pointing: marrying, marriage, pairing, coupling.

יאיא Notariqon of יהוה אלהים יהוה אחד, "Jehovah Elohim is One Jehovah" or "The Lord of Creation is One God."

יחד. Unity; to be united, joined. With different pointing: 1. to single out, set apart for special use, to cause to be alone, cause to meet privately; 2. to be done with, be set apart, be special; 3. points: union, unitedness. As an adverb, together, all together. see 65.

האאיה "Hearer in secret or Hidden God". 26th Shem ha-Mephorash. 126E - 130E Aphruimis. April 14, June 25, September 5, November 16, January 27. 8:20-8:40 A.M. Assocoated with Psalm 119:145: "I have called with my whole heart, answer me, O Lord (IHVH). "To win a lawsuit and render the judges favorable. Protects all who seek truth; it leads men to the contemplation of things divine. It rules politics, diplomats, ambassadors, treats of peace and commerce, and all conventions. Generally, it influences through couriers, dispatches, agents and secret expeditions.

Angel of the 2nd quinance [6-10°] of Sagittarius; angel by night of the 8 of Wands (Hod of Atziluth). This represents the subconscious influence of the sphere of mercury, in Atziluth, the archetypal world. see 22 & Appendix 10.

אבא 7th Shem ha-Mephorash, short form. see 37 & Appendix 10.

הדי 9th Shem ha-Mephorash, short form. see 53 & Appendix 10.

בך in thee, with thee. In Genesis 48:20: "And he [Jacob] blessed them that day and said, In your [in thee] name will Israel pronounce the blessing: May God make you like Ephraim and Manasseh. So he put Ephraim ahead of Manaseeh." Ephraim (331) corresponds to Taurus and alchemical fixation; Manasseh (395) corresponds to Aquarius and alchemical dissolution. see 182, 541.

בידו with (by) his hand. Related to Egyptian idea of creation. Also be-Yod [ב-יוד]. by Yod

חזוא (Aramaic) a magical vision. Designates the mental activity which is the embodiment of desire or longing.

Deo (Lt). God. As spelled in an inscription discovered in the vault of C.R. It is part of the phrase "From God we are Born."

C.R.C. Brother C.R.C.

23   (prime)

I. The glyph of life-nascent life. [Crowley, 1977, p. xxv].

II. The Sun (Tiphareth, 6) and Moon (Yesod, 9) with the aid of Mercury (Hod, 8).

חיה Chaiah. the Life-force, is that part of the constitution of man specially attributed to Chokmah. In organic life, it is a whirling force inherent in the order of the constellations. This is a conscious, vital, life-giving potency. It is the masculine dynamic energy and protective power that is the basis of physical procreation. In Atziluth it is the Fire, the irresistible urge in us of the Universal Will. All our drives to understand, all our yearning to comprehend the underlying forces of existence, are rooted in this drive to establish order out of chaos, rooted in the Chokmah, or Wisdom. And this fire is broadcast from Chokmah through Tiphareth, the Central Ego to every human being, incarnate or discarnate, via the path of Heh, the 15th path. The first letter of Chaiah, Cheth, means fence. The second and third letters IH, spell the diving name of Chokmah, Yah. It relates to he "protective" power of Chokmah and its being the primary filed of the Life-power's self-limitation by means of which all subsequent words of formation are made possible. He who knows the secret of this connecting relationship knows how to attract all things, whether spiritual or metaphysical. Magic is a mode of Life, a way of living, in which the Magician is a medium for conscious expression of the irresistible power of the heavenly order.

Life is Chaiah, seated in Chokmah, to which Yod particularly pertains. For Chaiah is אור, *Aur* and its number is 207, which is 9 times 23. Twenty-three is the number of חיה, Chaiah, and 9 is the number of Yesod. As stated before Chaiah is in Chokmah, and and Chokmah is the power of אב the Father. Thus Life and Light are one; that Light is always pure and always Holy, and the extension of Light is its multiplication through forms. Note that the mystery of the 9th Sephirah is a secret of Yod. Yod is the letter of *Ab*, and dilates upon Chaiah. The secret has to do with the radiance of the stars, that is with Light, which is one with Life. see 363, 11, 207, 430, 80, 10 and **27**.

אווי desire, hunger, appetite for. To bind is the essential idea. Desire is the binding cord. Life, wrongly interpreted, is the thing desired. When that false desires are removed, Babylon falls. Then all evil conditions are changed and the joy of the Lord is manifested. Briah is the world or plane associated with the power of desire in creating mental images.

אגידה tell. The Zohar [II:234B, pp.347 -348] comments: And I shall tell you." The word "tell" *Agidah*, contains an allusion to the esoteric wisdom. He sought to reveal to them their final destiny. It may be asked, seeing that he did not reveal what he sought to reveal, why are his words, which were afterwards believed, recorded in the scripture? The truth is that all that was needful to be revealed is completely stated and there is a hidden meaning within, and so nothing in the scripture is believed. In fact, everything is included in the scripture, and there is no word or letter short in it. Jacob said all that was needful for him to say, but not all openly, and not a letter was short of what was required."

חוט to string together, to join. As a noun: thread, line, a measuring tape. In Eastern Philosophy, sutratma, thread soul. The line or ray of the Life-power's outflowing influence which serves as a link of connection between successive lives of a particular soul. The Briatic watery substance holds the patterns which serve as a link throughout a whole series of incarnations related to a specific ray or individuality of the Life-power's self-expression.

יהגה He meditates. The connecting thread khoot, is mental in essence. God thinks the world into being, and the Life-Force is the activity of his unbroken meditation throughout a cosmic cycle.

יחח to be removed, be displaced, be agitated. see 262.

חדוה gladness, rejoicing, joy.

24

Octahedron has 8 triangular faces (8 x 3 = 24) and the Cube has 6 square faces (6 x 4 = 24). Since Air and Earth are represented by 24, or 2 x 12, we may regard them as corresponding to each other, and as being each a duplication, or twofold manifestation of Fire.

The mystical number for alchemical salt. Especially related to the Pythagorean triangle of Osiris-Isis-Horus, and to the 24 thrones of the elders in the Apocalypse, which refer to the positive and negative manifestations of the powers symbolized by the 12 signs, the 12 tribes, and the 12 apostles.

דך oppressed, humbled, miserable, cursed, down trodden. As a noun: pauper. Caused by ignorance and inertia-overbalance of Salt. see 504.

"The sign of natural abundance contracted with the root אך, symbol of concentric movement and of every restriction and exception, composes a root infinitely expressive whose object is to depict need, necessity, poverty and all ideas proceeding there from. The Arabic constitutes an onomatopoeic and idiomatic root which express the noise made in striking, beating, knocking; which consequently, develops all ideas which are attached to the action of *striking*, as those of *killing*, *breaking*, *splitting*, etc.... דך. that which is *needy, contrite, sad, poor, injurious, calamitous, vexation*, etc." [d'Olivet, 1976, p. 322.]

דוד . David, "beloved," the Biblical hero and King of Israel (variant spelling, see 14). "Love... is the substance of manifestation... it is abundance itself." [Case: The Flaming Cube].

I. "'David' means 'the beloved' or the man who realizes his true relation to the Infinite Spirit; and the description of Daniel as a man, greatly beloved and who realizes his true relation to the infinite spirit; and who had set his heart to understand Daniel 10:11, shows us that it is this set purpose of seeking to understand the nature of the Universal Spirit and the mode of our own relation to it, that raises the individual to the position of David or 'the Beloved.'" [Troward, 1942, p. 171.]

II. Paul Case: "Note that דוד = זהב, the alchemical Gold. The variant spelling, דויד = 24 = אהובי, 'He whom I love' = אהבי, 'He who love me' = בטחה 'confidence' [Isaiah 30:15] 'In quietness and in confidence shall be your strength.'" see 320 (ישי).

יחו 33rd name of Shem ha-Mephorash, short form. see 36, & Appendix 10.

כד a water pot, a large earthenware vessel, pitcher. It comprises the enclosure of all bodies and is the "earth vessel" of the alchemist. see 29.

"That which partakes of relative unity, isolation, division. In a restricted sense *a spark, a fragment*. The Chaldaic כד is represented in a restricted sense, by the adverbial relation *when*. The Arabic signifies in general, to act in one's own interest, to work for self; in particular, *to be industrious, to intrigue, to be fatigued, tormented.*" [d'Olivet, 1976, p. 370.]

גויה a body or substance. Alchemical salt is the substance of all bodies.

זיו abundance, plenty, superfluity.

All 3 of these words [האוהג, זחחז, ראב] are related to the meaning of alchemical Salt.

אובוגה "The shining one." Name of a planetary force. Fire is the extended manifestation of the underlying reality which gives body to all things. From a root [הבג]. see 14

אהובי He whom I Love.
אוהבי He who loves me.

Hoc (Lt). This. This beloved which is found in the salt of manifestation is "the shining one" centered in Tiphareth. Part of an inscription found written of the alter of the vault of Brother C.R. in the Rosicrucian Allegory. see 475, 122, 76, 106, 87

25

I. (5²)

II. The 25th Path is Samekh, between Tiphareth & Yesod.

כה thus, so; here, now. The brotherhood of light is destroyed here, on the physical plane by ignorance of the truth of unity.

"Root analogous to the root כב, but whose expression is spiritualize and reinforced by the presence of the sign ה. That which is conformable to a given model; that which coincides with a point of space or time, which can be conceived in an abstract sense, by the adverbial relations *yes, thus, like this; that; in that very place; at that very time*; etc." [d'Olivet, 1976, p. 370.]

יהי let there be [light]. Genesis 1:3. "*Yehy…* can only be translated "existence-life-existence". It expresses the coming into life (5) of a double existence (10 and 10) and thus describes the distinctive mark of organic life which is always a double process, inner and outer, of germ and shell or psyche and body." [Suraes, 1992, p. 84.]

אביהוא Worshipper of Hua. That is of Kether, the source of Light.

יהוד God of Geburah of Binah. Geburah is the sphere of the destructive Mars; Binah is the form-builder, the womb of manifestation.

חיוא An animal, beast. From the root חיא meaning to live, to keep alive. [Strong, 1996, p. 366.] A Cabalistic term for The Beast. The union of Samael, ("Poison of God", Angel of Death), and Isheth Zanunim (Demon of Prostitution), his wife. *Chioa* is the Archdemon of Tiphareth. These three constitute the Infernal Triad. Samael is the fifth of the archangels of the world of Briah, corresponding to the Sephirah Geburah. see 864, 1424.

היי 71st Shem ha-Mephorash, short form. see 56, & Appendix 10.

אכד A city and dynasty of ancient Babylonia. In Genesis 10:10: "The first centers of his [Nimrod's] kingdom were Babylon, Erech, Ankad and Calneh, in Shinar."

"ואכד *and Achad…* Two contracted roots compose this word: אך-כד. They depict energetically that sort of sentiment the result of which is, that each is excepted from the general law, flees from it, acts for his own part. The word אכד signifies properly, *a particle, a spark.*" [d'Olivet, 1976, p. 282.]

אכד destruction, collapse. In Psalm 90:3: "Then turns man to destruction, and says return you sons of Adam." The consequence of the apparent outgoing of personality into the field of conscious expression which involves the semblance of separateness. Acceptance of the illusion for reality leads to collapse (Key 16). Note that the number *dekah*, 25 is the square 5, the number of Mars. See 85, 124, 155, 1200, 1309.

Amo (Lt). Love. all manifestation is based on the attractive principle which unites one thing to another. see 671, 851.

Ex (Lt). From. From this attractive principle does the evolutionary growth and fruition of the soul take place. Part of an inscription found of the vault of Brother C.R. see 683 (Lt).

δακ (dak, Greek). Literally, the bit of dogs.

26

I. The number of vertices (or points, 8), lines (12) and faces (6) on a Octahedron and Cube, and therefore defines its limits. A cube is a symbol of the physical plane.

II. כ-ו The "length" of the Pillar of Mercy on the Tree of Life.

כבד weight, heavy, mighty; abundance, multitude. With different pointing: 1. vehemence, violence; 2. the liver, the innermost part (the heart); 3. glorious, magnificent; glory, wealth. The force of gravitation (electro-magnetism), the basis of all action.

Twenty-six is the number of IHVH. Therefore the Tree of Life is the practical mystery concerned with the direction of the serpent fire and relates to the utilization of the unknowable omnipresent power which makes matter attract. This is gravity, the force which holds planets in orbit and makes bodies fall to earth.

כוד to be heavy, to be burdensome; grievous; difficult; abundant, numerous.

כדב to lie, to tell falsehoods.

דבר to make heavy, harden; to honor, glorify; to sweep up, tidy (a room). With different pointing: *kabad*. to be honored.

יהוה Jehovah. the Unutterable Name. The Divine Name in Chokmah. Yah [יה] is the shorter form of יהוה. The divine creative name fundamental to the construction of the Tree of Life in the 4 worlds.

I. It is probable that the gentiles apprehended certain things concerning this name, and that from so doing they named their God Jupiter; thus the Latins were accustomed to use as their common and ordinary terms (for God) Jupiter or Jovis. For after all what difference is there between the Jovis of the Latins and the Jehovah of the Hebrews, as even more Jehovih, as it is written in certain versions of the Bible. [La Science Cablistique, Chapter 10]

This great mysterious name is the word of mystery, which has never been lost. This word is universal, and it produces all things, is short it is the word, by which God created the heavens, the earth, and al which is contained in space of his infinite circle." [IBID p. 151]

II.   "YHWH: 10.5.6.5, Existence-Life-Copulation-Life, expresses in existence the two lives (that of the container or shell or physical support, and that of the contained or germ or inner life) that fertilize each other. This double impregnation can only occur in Man and as long as it does not occur YHWH is immanent but unborn. We will often refer to this schema. For the time being, in Genesis 2, 5-6, Adam has not yet appeared. We will see him created in verse 7 before all the animals." [Suraes, 1992, p. 103.]

הגהי He meditates. God thinks the world into being and the Life-force of Chokmah in Briah is the activity of His unbroken meditation, which continues throughout the duration of a cosmic cycle.

חזה seeing, looking at. With different pointing: sight, vision. "I utter myself by seeing [Book of Tokens].

בידי into my hand. see Genesis 39:8.

27

I. (3^3)

II. Age of Brother C.R. after spending 5 years in his habitation, where he "ruminated his voyage and philosophy and reduced them together in a true memorial."

III. 27 is the 3rd cube (1 the 1st and 8 the 2nd) and suggest the symbolism of a geometric cube. The cube is a symbolism of the Holy of Holies and the Heavenly City mentioned in the 21st chapter of Revelations.

זך clean. pure. Though it is designated by another adjective, the idea of purity is associated with Yesod, meaning Basis or Foundation.

Twenty-seven is appropriate to designate the magical age at which brother CR becomes a Founder of the Fraternity. The Rosicrucian grade corresponding to Yesod is Theoricus, and in this grade the fundamental theory of the Great Work is explained. see 9, 80, 220, 570, 18, 36, 445, 63, 72, 81, 90.

חידה. Intricate speech, a riddle, an enigma; oracle, puzzle; a parable. A description of the magical language and writing.

בכה. to drop, distill, to flow down in drops; to weep, cry, wail. This describes the Hermetic work, and suggest also the measured outpouring of energy involved in such an undertaking.

Paul Case: *Bawkah* also means to weep, to cry. The Masters are moved by compassion for the errors of the unenlightened, by sympathy for suffers from the consequence of these errors of the unenlightened. They work without ceasing for the purification and regeneration of the Human race. "Here is a strong intimation that the cube of 3 units represent that which to the average man is a riddle indeed, and a cause for mourning; but also that which to the wise is a means for the establishment of purity, clarity and cleanliness of mind and body. [The Flaming Cube - Light of the Chaldees] see 132, *Chasidim*.

ידי. 40th Shem ha-Mephorash, short form. see 58 & Appendix 10.

28

I. Σ7 = 28. The mystical number of Netzach.

II. The diameter of Assiah in the material world. The second perfect number (see Appendix).

III. The number of days in a lunar month. By some accounts, the number of pieces the body of Osiris was divided.

יחוד. union or unity, indicates the fact that the material world, which we misinterpret as the sphere of manyness or multiplicity, is fundamentally the ONE expression of ONE reality, in which there is no separation whatever, each of the seemingly separate parts being combined with all the others.   This is a conception made understandable by modern rediscoveries concerning the electrical constitution of matter. With different pointing: 1. *yacheddaw, yechadu.* together, all together; alike. Union, unity; 2. privacy, private meeting; profession of unity of God (also separation) see 88, 7, 22, 14, 44, 21, 66, 440.

אבידוד Father or possessor of renown. One who has "strength."

החיה creature. In Genesis 1:21. "And God created great whales, and every living creature that moves, which the waters brought forth abundantly, after their kind..." From חיה Chaiah, living thing, animal; life; appetite; revival, renewal... Thus "the creatures."

חך to taste; to pass something through the plate; the throat; palate; mouth as organ of speech. The throat is connected with Venus and with desire. Job 34:3: (2) "hear my words, you wise men; listen to me, you men of learning. (3) for the ear test words as the palate (tongue) tastes food. Also in Job 6:30: "Is there any wickedness on my lips? Can my mouth not discern malice?" And in Proverbs 8:7: "My mouth speaks what is true, for my lips detest wickedness."

כח power, strength, might. Refers to the magic square of Venus. It represents by its total summation (2800 or 28 x 100) the formative power of desire. This work locates for us the place were we shall draw the power used in magic and other forms of practical occultism. The power we are to use is a physical power. The power is in plain sight. The alchemists tell us again and again when they intimate that the First Matter of the art is procurable everywhere, and without expense.

The reversal of the letter [כך] forms the word חך, *khake*, signifying the mouth as the former of words, or the power of verbal utterance. This power of verbal utterance is held in occult philosophy to be basic in the creation and formation of the universe. It is the power which supports all creation, and thus it is appropriate that of an area of a great lozenge [formed in the geometrical construction of the Tree of Life] corresponding to חך, *Khake*, by number should be shown as being what is outside and below the Tree of Life as its support [the number 28]. [Paul Case: Letter to J.W. Hamilton-Jones March 10, 1952 page 4].

יגיה will light. Psalm 18:28: "For thou will light my candle: the Lord my God will enlighten my darkness." [King James]. "You, O Lord, keep my lamp burning; my God turns my darkness into light." [New International]

טיט clay. A plastic medium easily impressed with the image of the artist. The substance out of which God formed Adam. Although different words for "clay" are used, the following quotes convey the thought: [Job 10:9] "Remember that you molded me like clay. Will you now turn me to dust again?" [Job 33:6] "I am just like you before God; I too have been taken from clay." Clay also refers to imperfect human beings, mired in the depths of materialism, and analogous to the "base metals" of the alchemist. They are transformed into the reality of "living stones" or "Gold". (Study this word letter by letter, and with the help of the corresponding Tarot keys, paths, etc.).

ידיד Beloved, lovely, pleasant. [Deuteronomy 33:12]. About Benjamin he said: let the beloved of the Lord rest secure in him, for he shields him all day long."

sal (Lt). salt. Corresponding to the 3rd alchemical principal, or Binah. The understanding of the Divine Mother is the bread which nourishes her creations on the physical or material plane. Salt crystallizes into cubes, relating to Saturn and Lead, as well as the cubic stone and cube of space. See 67, 78, 193.

Caeli (Lt) of heaven, or heavenly. Part of a phrase. see 75.

Commentary: From these words we see that the number 28 is associated with power [*kach, aebayhud*] that descends from higher levels [*Caeli, yechud*] and takes physical form [*sal, hachaiah, tiyt*].

28 is the sum of the numbers from 1 to 7. Note that Saturn in the 7th planet and is associated with time, or specifically the gateway between timelessness and time (see Binah, 67). Therefore 28 is the culmination of the process represented by 7 in time and space.

Netzach, the 7th Sephiroth on the Tree of Life and is the Sphere of Venus. Venus represents on a lower arc the receptacle of this descent of power initiated by Saturn. (Note that copper is attributed to Venus, a malleable metal [*tiyt*].) Humanitiy's ability to manipulative the physical form (time and space, *tiyt*) is through the power of speech (*chek*). In this connection note that Venus is attributed to the throat chakra and is associated with right desire, that is, desire in harmony with Divine Will. As a 5th Ray planet, it indicates the necessity of intelligent direction of this desire.

29   (prime)

I. The magick force itself, the masculine current. [Crowley, 1977, p. xxv].

II. When 7 = diameter of a circle and the circumference = 22 then 29 is a numerical representation of the symbol for alchemical salt.

הדב to break down, to overturn, cast down [Job 40:12]. The alchemical salt is the finitizing principle which breaks down the homogeneity of the infinite, the "complex illusion which deceives the ignorant."

כזב to fabricate, to spin, to bind together, to deceive. A complex illusion which deceives the ignorant. As a verb, *kawzab* means: to fabricate, to lie, to speak falsehood, to combine or devise, to bind together, to fail, to dry up (as a brook). As a noun: a lie, falsehood; deceit. see 22, 67.

דכה to be broken, be depressed. With different pointing: bruising, crushing (particularly of the testicles). Deuteronomy 23:1 "He that is wounded in the stones, or hath his primary member cut off, shall not enter into the congregation of the Lord."

magia (Lt). magic. The "web of illusion" (alchemical salt) is the true magic. Closely related to the Sanskrit *maya*, associated with Binah.

amen (Lt). amen. so be it. A title of Kether.

Via (Lt). Way; method or manner (of doing something.)

These words are related to the operation of alchemical Salt.

D.O.M.A. Initials for Deus Omnipotens Magister Artis. God Almighty Master of the Art.

30

I. The number of edges (lines) in a Dodecahedron (Akasha) and Icosahedron (Water).

II. The sidereal revolution of Saturn about the sun to the nears whole number (29.5 years).

ל Lamed. ox-goad. An ox-goad is used to guide oxen and to keep them on the road by the driver. Hence the idea of control, direction and incitement. The shape of the letter Lamed is that of a serpent. It represents the same force we discussed in Teth and Key 8. Teth is the coiled serpent, Lamed, is the same snake uncoiled and active. Thus the Book of Formation assigns action or work to Lamed. With slight change in pronunciation the letter is a verb, meaning, "to teach". Thus the ideas represented by our noun education. The character for Lamed is usually explained as being a conventionalized picture of a goad, or whip. But some authorities hold that it really represents an erect serpent.

I. "This character as consonant, belongs to the lingual sound. As symbolic image it represents the arm of a man, the wing of a bird, that which extends, raises and unfolds itself. As grammatical sign, it is expansive movement and is applied to all ideas of extension, elevation, occupation, possession. It is, in Hebrew the directive article...expressing in nouns or actions, a movement of union, dependence, possession or coincidence." [d'Olivet, 1976, p. 377.]

II. "As a Directive Article-It expresses, with nouns or actions whose movement it modifies, a direct relation of union, of possession, or of coincidence. I translate it by *to, at, for, according to, toward*, etc." [ibid., p. 112.]

III. Rabbi Yose liken the Lamed to a town watchman who stands on a high lookout and calls out his warning...Lamed. Oh so beautiful Lamed. Tall elegant like a palm branch (לולב) waved high...the Lamed is actually composed of two separate letters...it is the Vav (nail) perched on the roof of the Beth (house). [The Book of Letters, Rabbi Kushner] "A tower soaring in the air." [the Alef-Beit, Rabbi Ginsburgh]

IV. "*Lammed* is the organic movement that results from the overthrowing of obsolete structures. All organic structures have a necessary quality of resistance which deteriorates into rigidity and self-preservation. Evolution, according to Qabala, is a series of simultaneous destruction-construction of resistances, the biosphere being an interplay between structures and unstructured energies (analogically *Awr* [אור] and *Hhosheikh*) [חשך]." [Suraes, 1992, p. 89.]

יהודה Jehudah, Judah. praised, celebrated; the tribe of Israel assigned to Leo and the letter Teth. When masculine: *Judah*. Feminine: *Judea*. Related to alchemical digestion, the sense of taste and to the Intelligence of the Secret of all Spiritual Activities. The blessing of Jacob in Genesis 49:9: "A Lion's whelp is Judah; on prey you have grown up, my son. He crouches, he couches like a lion, like an old Lion; who dare disturb him?" see 419, 661, 216, 570 (Greek.)

אביטוב "Father of Goodness." Judah, as Leo is connected with the heart center and thus is Father of all that is good, i.e. love. see 17

כי that; when, while, as, for, because; but, only, indeed; in fact; lest; even if; although, though: mark burnt in, burning, burn. see 47 [כי טוב].

I. Isaiah 3:24: "Instead of fragrance, there will be a stench; instead of beauty, branding."

II. "Manifestation of any assimilating, compressing force. The Arabic signifies in a restricted sense, *a burn*. כי The force expressed by the root is represented in an abstract sense, by relations *that, because, for, then, when*, etc." [d'Olivet, 1976, p. 372.]

ייי Yeyeye. 22nd Shem ha-Mephorash , short form. see 61, & Appendix 10.

יהיה future tense of the verb "to be", "it will be."

חיב A party to an action at law; defendant, plaintiff. Note Lamed (30) is attributed to Justice.

δεκα deka (Gr). ten.

Arabia (Lt). Sterility. The place in the *Fama* where brother CRC became acquainted with the wise men of the temple in Damcar, and where he struck a bargain with the Arabians for a certain sum of money. This involves further experimental work, which was begun at Damascus.

"The vow of chastity implies by the place name Arabia. It refers to more than physical countenance, to more than merely refraining from the exercise of the sex-function. To receive initiation demands utter receptivity and that receptivity cannot be established or maintained unless, for this period there is abstinence from any kind of creative activity, mental or physical.

The temple of initiation is also of Arabia, and it is there brother CRC meets the wise men. Yet the bargain with the Arabians is for a 'certain sum of money'. Furthermore, Brother CRC sojourn at the temple is for a definitely limited time. The utter sterility which is necessary in order that one may pass safely through the trials of initiation is by no means imposed for life. It is an indispensable preliminary training in self-control, and this training is what Jesus meant by his cryptic statement that some persons make themselves Eunuchs "for the Kingdom of Heaven's sake..."

This temporary sterility establishes within the body a tremendous physical reserve of Life-force, and in the mind a like reserve of the subtler manifestation of the same force. After initiation, one heaves Arabia, that is to say, one returns to a more normal course of life." [Case, 1985. pp. 73-74.]

31 (prime)

I. The highest feminine trinity – zero through the glyph of the circle. [Crowley, 1977, p. xxv].

אל Al or El. strength, power, might, God the Mighty One. Divine Name corresponding to Chesed (4 of Wands). By its letters it is connected with the element Air and the Suit of Swords. Aleph: super-consciousness aspect of the airy power. Lamed: the ox-goad, denotes

direction and purpose. Perfectly free in Itself, the Life-power nevertheless guides Itself, during a cycle of manifestation, through self-appointed ways or channels of activity, corresponding to the formative power of Yetzirah. [Kether of Briah].

"This root springs from the united signs of power and extensive movement. The ideas which it develops are those of elevation, force, power, extent. The Hebrews and Arabs have drawn from it the name of God. Hieroglyphically, this is the symbol of nature or adverb relations *to, toward, for, by, against, upon, beneath*, etc.

The Arabic is employed as the universal designative relation, *the, of the, to the*, etc. As verb it expresses in the ancient idiom, the action of *moving quickly*, going with promptness from one place to another: in the modern idiom it signifies literally, to *be wearied* by too much movement.

אל and אלל (intens.) In this excess of extension, it is that which *passes away*, which is *empty, vain*; expressed by the adverbial relation *no, not, not so, nought, nothing*; etc." [d'Olivet, 1976, p. 294.]

לא not, or No-Thing. With other vowel-points, it, is a preposition meaning "to, toward, into, or against." Thus *El*, "God," is shown to be No-Thing, yet at the same time a strong power, which is the cause of motion toward, into, or even against. see 61, 48, 560, 538.

I. "This root is symbol of the line prolonged to infinity, of movement without term, or action whose duration is limitless: thence, the opposed ideas of *being* and *nothingness*, which it uses in developing the greater part of its compounds.

לא or לוא it is in general, an indefinite expansion, and absence without term expressed is an abstract sense by the relations, *no, not, not at all*, definite direction, that is to say, that which is restrained by means of the assimilative sign בּ, is opposed to it. see כה or בן." [d'Olivet, 1976, p. 377.]

חביה 68th Shem ha-Mephorash. Angel of 2nd quinance (6-10E) of Cancer; angel by night of the of 2 of Cups. This represents the subconscious influence of Chokmah, sphere of the zodiac, in Briah, the world of Creation. see Appendix 10.

הכאה A beating, striking, collision.

ייא King of Swords. see *The Key of Solomon*, figure 31. [Crowley, 1977, p. 4]

הוך A Chaldee verb meaning: "to go; to bring". The No-thing is the power which goes forth into every form of manifestation and brings about every phenomenon. see 511.

ויהי "And there was...." It is the manifesting force which came into operation when in response to the creative "let there be"... "And there was." [Genesis 1:3] This expression of for the compound word:
ויהי-אור "and there was light".

I. "ויהי. *and there (shall be)- became...* I must not neglect to say, that Moses, profiting by the hieroglyphic Genius of the Egyptian tongue, changing at will the future tense into past tense, depicts, on this occasion, the birth of light, symbol of intelligible *corporeality*, with an animation that no modern tongue can render except the Chinese. He writes first יהי-אור *there shall be light*; then repeating the same words with the single addition of the convertible sign ו, he turns suddenly, the future into the past, as if the effect had sustained before hand the outburst of the through ויהי-אור *and there-(shall-be) become light*.

This manner of speaking figuratively and hieroglyphically, always comes from the primitive meaning given to the בראשית [in the beginning, 913]: for the heavens and the Earth created in principle, and raising from power, into action, could unfold successive their virtual forces only as far as the Divine will announced in the future, is manifest in the past. The Being of beings knows no time. The Egyptian tongue is the only one in which this wonderful trope can take place even in the spoken tongue. It was a spoken effect which, from the hieroglyphic style passed into the figurative, and from the figurative into the literal." [d'Olivet, 1976, pp. 33-34.]

זהב טוב good gold in Genesis 2:12 and fine gold in 2nd Chronicles 3:5. Refers to Yesod. *Aesch Mezareph* 2:9: "*Zahav tob* is referred to Yesod, that is good Gold Genesis 2:12, for this kind is called good, after the manner of a good man." see also Lamentations 4:1.

איכ How? What? The no-thing is the reality which is the subject of inquiry in all questions beginning with How? or What? To attain this knowledge "Having emptied yourself, remain where you are." [Loa Tze]

ויהי. "And there was...." It is the manifesting force which came into operation when in response to the creative "let there be"... "And there was."

32

I. 2^5 or $(2 \times 2 \times 2 \times 2 \times 2)$

II. The 32 Paths of wisdom. The ten sephiroth plus the twenty-two connecting links (Hebrew letters and their associated Tarot Keys) between them.

כבוד weight, mass; Glory, brilliance. The symbol of the eternal presence of the divine glory, revealed by the inner voice. Refers to cosmic radiation materialized into electromagnetism and gravity. The substance of all that is. see 26 (*kabad*), 112. see 61, 63, 73, 78, 112, 508, 1081 (Greek), 832.

Thirty-two are the number of Paths and the number of כבוד, the Glory. Thus the paths and the Glory are one. The 32 Paths of Wisdom (Chokmah) are the paths of life. Chokmah is *Kachmah* and is the one and only power of life. The stars are physical condensations of the Glory of God, or the radiance known as electricity, magnetism and gravitation. These 3 are names for one power, and the words *Kachmah* and *Mezla* are other names for the same power. Man's body is a condensation on the physical plane of this power as is the physical body of a sun. With the exception of Hydrogen, all the elements in man's body comes from the stars. Whether as a human body, or as a solar form, however, the physical substance is the outer vesture of the Divine Glory. It runs from אין and flows back to אין, and through אין, into the unfathomable abyss of the radiant darkness. Everything, even man's physical body is from one substance inseparable from the Divine Glory. See **23**.

לב center, midst; heart (as the seat of knowledge, understanding and thinking). Note that לב is Libra and Mercury, the equilibration of action. In many esoteric schools, the heart is the point of initial preparation for admission. Man becomes ready for initiation only after the soul has made the necessary preparations in his heart. see 12, 406, 87.

"The expansive sign united by contraction to the root אב, image of every interior activity, every appetent, desires, generative force, constitutes a root whence emanate all ideas of vitality, passion, vigor, courage, audacity: literally, it is *the heart*, and figuratively, all things which pertain to that center of life; every quality, every faculty resulting from the unfolding of the vital principle.

The heart, the center of everything whatsoever from which life radiates; all dependent faculties: *courage, force, passion, affection, desire, will; sense.* [d'Olivet, 1976, p. 377-378.]

זיווג *copula maritalis*, sexual union, marriage coupling. Implies that divine union is likened to purified marital union.

חזיז zig-zag, forked lightning. The "lighting flash" of the Tree of Life proceeds from Kether to Malkuth. The kundalini flash proceeds from Malkuth (Saturn) to Kether (Mercury) in stirring the inner planetary centers. Lighting suggest illumination, however brief.

יחיד unity. 'an only one', alone, only, only one; lonely, solitary, indivisible; select, distinguished. Singular number (grammar) root of *Yekhidah* (37). Occurs 3 times in the Pentateuch and 9 times elsewhere in the Old Testament, 12 in all. Suggest that Divine illumination brings one in touch with the solitary Monad. See Key 9 - The Hermit) and K.D.L.C.K. (p. 432).

Thirty-two is the number of total manifestation; things as they are in their totality and finality, as represented by the whole Tree: the ten sephiroth and 22 paths. 32 is the number of *yawchid*, the

ego, self, or soul. The word *Ichid* derives from the Egyptian *Althet*, the spirit, the *manes*, the dead, which highlights the precise nature of the ego as an *upadhi* - an illusory entity masquerading as Being. [Grant, 1994, p. 46.]

אהיהוה Coalescence of אהיה and יהוה, Macroprosopus and Microprosopus, symbolized by the hexagram. Suppose that the 3 Hehs conceal the 3 mothers, א, מ, and ש, and we get 358. see 2, 26.

זכה to make clear, make pure; to pronounce guiltless, acquit; to obtain a privilege for, assign a possession to; to credit one's account with purification is essential for attainment of the heart's glory.

בל Bal. Lord. Aramaic word for heart.

והו . 1st Shem ha-Mephorash. "God raised and exalted above all things." One born under influence: A subtle spirit endowed with great wisdom, enthusiastic for science and the arts, capable of undertaking and accomplishing the most difficult things. Positive influence: Energy. Negative Influence: unquiet man. Anger. One born under influence:

Angle of the 1st quinance [0E-5E] of Aries and attributed to the 5 of Wands. see 32 & Appendix 10.

33

A mystical number in many parts of the world. The magical age of perfection. Represents the union of the 32 Paths with the concealed on of the 3 veils.

ג/ל Moon (Gimel) in Libra (Lamed).

גל ruin, a heap of stones; a spring, a fountain (because the water rolls out). Song of Solomon 4:12: Your are a garden locked up, my sister, my bride [Kallah, 55], you are a *spring* enclosed, a sealed fountain. Written גלל in Job 20:7 concerning the pride of the Godless man: "He will perish forever, like his own *dung*; those who have seen him will say, 'where is he.'" see Zechariah 4:2.

"This root can be conceived according to its two ways of composition: by the first, it is the root גּ, symbol of all organic extension, united to the sign of directive movement ל; by the second, it is the organic sign גּ, which is contracted with the root אל, symbol of elevation and expansive force. In the first case it is a thing which is displayed in space by unfolding itself; which is developed, produced, according to its nature, unveiled; in the second, it is a thing, on the contrary, which coils, rolls, complicates, accumulates, heaps up, envelops. Here, one can recognize the double meaning which is always attached to the sign גּ under the double relation of organic development and envelopment.

That which moves with a light and undulating movement; which manifest joy, grace, and ease in its movements. The revolution of celestial spheres. The orbit of the planets. *A wheel; a circumstance, an occasion.* That which is *revealed*, that which *appears*, is *uncovered*. That which *piles up* by rolling: the movement of the waves, *the swell; the volume* of anything whatsoever, *a heap, a pile; the circuit* or contour of an object or a place: *it confines.* [d'Olivet, 1976, p. 314.]

לג basin; a measure for liquids. see Leviticus 14:10.

"Every idea of liaison, if intimate, complicated thing; of *litigation.* The meaning of the Arabic is similar and signifies literally *to insist, to contest.* The Hebrew לג presents in the figurative, symbolic type, the measure of extent, *space.*" [d'Olivet, 1976, p. 378.]

באל Bael. Goetic demon by day of the 1st decanate of Aries. see Appendix 11.

Goetia: "The first principal spirit is a King ruling in the East, called *Bael.* He makes thee to go invisible. He rules over 66 Legions of Infernal spirits. He appears in divers shapes, sometimes like a Cat, sometimes like a Toad, and sometimes like a Man, and sometimes all these forms at once. He speaks hoarsely." [Mathers, 1995, p. 27].

ב-אל in (Beth) God (Al). In Hebrew Beth is the preposition "in."

בלא. to destroy, to decay. With different pointing: 1. *Bela,* a King of Edom; 2. *Blo,* the nothing.

ה-טיט the clay.

אבל to wither, to parch, droop, faint, sorrow, mourning, lament.

ו-וב Clean and pure.

אביך thy father.

ה-כח the power.

יחיה he lives. see Deuteronomy 8:3.

34

דל to move to and fro, to totter from weakness; weak, poor; a pauper, poor man; humble, lean, low; door, valve, wretched. In Psalm 141:3: "Set a guard over my mouth, O Lord; keep watch over the door (valve) of my lips."

"This root, conceived as the union of the sign of natural abundance or of divisibility, with the root אל symbol of elevation, produces the idea of every extraction, every removal, as for example, when one draws water from a well, when one takes away the life of a plant; from this idea, proceeds necessarily the accessory ideas of exhaustion and weakness. The Arabic root in particular, attaches more exclusively to the idea of distinguishing, designating conducting some one toward a distinct object. When it is weakened, it expresses a distinction of scorn; disdain, degradation. דל. That which *extracts; to draw* or *to attract above;* that *which takes away, drains;* that which *attenuates, consumes, enfeebles:* every kind of *division, distinction; emptiness* effected by *extraction;* any kind of *removal.* In a very restricted sense, *a seal;* a vessel for drawing water. [d'Olivet, 1976, pp. 322-323.] see 924.

לד Lydda, a town in Benjamin [Godwin].

"The expansive sign, joined to that of abundance born of division, or by contraction with the root אב, image of every emanation, composes a root whose purpose is to express every idea of propagation, of generation, of any extension whatsoever given to being. That which *is born, generated, propagated, bred, progeny, increase of family, race, lineage: confinement, childbirth,* etc." [d'Olivet, 1976, pp. 378-379.]

ידכ your hand. In Psalm 138:7: "Though I walk in the midst of trouble, you preserve my life; you stretch out your hand against the anger of my foes, with your right hand you save me."

Paul Case: The holy temple in the midst is the central point in our consciousness, where the throne is place, and this is the throne of the father, with the son at the right hand of the father. 'Thy right hand' is ימיני (130), equivalent to עין, the eye and הגאל מלאב, the angel of redemption. see 130, 10, 20.

בבל Babel. "*Babal* or *Bab-el* means the 'Gate of God', and, as such, is equated with the Northern gate of Eden (heaven) interpreted qabalistically as Daath. AL or EL is 31, the key number of the New Aeon." [Grant, 1994, p. 53.] see Genesis 10:10.

חהויה 24th Shem ha-Mephorash. "God good in himself." To obtain the grace and mercy of God. Governs: Exiles, fugitives, defaulters. Protects against harmful animals and preserves from thieves and assassins. Positive influence: Individual loves truth, the exact sciences, sincere in word and deed. Negative: governs harmful beings. Angle of the 3rd decanate (and 6th quinance) of Scorpio attributed to the 7 of Cups. see Appendix 10.

אל אב God the Father.

בלב ve-laib. (and) the heart.

חהויה Angel of 6th quinance of Scorpio.

35

I. Summation of every line of a magic square of Jupiter.

II. Sum of the 2nd (8) & 3rd (27) cubic numbers.

III. The measure of the perimeters of the heptagon forming the top and bottom of the vault of brother CR (7 sides times 5).

IV. Pythagoreans called 35 "harmony". This implies the perfect equilibrium of coordinated forces and agrees with other meaning of 7. Thirty-five is the sum of 8 and 27, the cubes of 2 and 9. Thus it represents the perfected expression of wisdom (2), combined with the fully manifested expression of understanding (3), because the cube, or threefold multiplication, of a number symbolizes the complete manifestation of the power of that number.

אל אב. God the Father. A divine name associated with Jupiter and Chesed. see 31.

גאל to ransom; to redeem, save, liberate, deliver. With different pointing *gawahl,* to profane, to pollute, contaminate, defile, desecrate. see 40.

גלא to reveal, to uncover, the Father cannot be seen face to face but is revealed in all his works. see 4, 16, 64, 136.

בבל confusion (cf. Tower of Babel, with its confusion of tongues).

ידד thy hand. [Psalm 138:7]: "Though I walk in the midst of trouble, thou wilt revive me: Thou shalt stretch forth thine hand against the wrath of mine enemies, and thy right hand shall save me."

גבל to draw a boundary, to set bounds, to border upon, adjoin. as a noun, edge, boundary, landmark. see 91, 231.

אגלא Notariqon for Ateh Gebur Le-Olahm Adonai. "Thine is the power through the endless ages, O Lord." see 858.

אלד 10th Shem ha-Mephorash, short form. see 50 & Appendix 10.

יהב he will go.

gaza (Lt). royal treasure, riches, wealth. The royal treasure is the indwelling presence of the One Power which is truly magical, because it is the power which sets the boundaries or defining limits of all forms. Through man it creates mental, emotional and physical riches which give dominion over the world of Assiah. To use our powers of desire correctly they must be set within exact bounds. Desire out of control is the cause of most of the sorrows and deprivations we experience in our incarnate existence. see 12 (Greek).

pax (Lt). peace. From a root akin to a Sanskrit word meaning "to bind." Literally, Pax is the "binding or fastening thing." It signifies dominion and empire. It implies silence as when we say "he held his peace." Note that this last meaning connects with those of Key 7 as representing control of speech. The dominion (pax) of spirit is the outcome of its ability to determine the exact limits of every one of its manifestations, form the least to the greatest. see 70 (הסה), 376, 31 (Lt).

per (Lt). through. it is through peace that we gain the royal treasure. Part of an inscription found in the vault of CR includes the phrase "through the Holy spirit we become alive again." see 214, 683 (Lt).

36

I. (6 x 6) or 2^2 x 3^2

II. $\Sigma 8 = 36$.

III. Value of the 7 constituent lines of a heptagram.

IV. The Pythagoreans call 36 "agreement" since it is the first number in which odd numbers being added together agree with even numbers. $1+3+5+7 = 16$; $2+4+6+8 = 20$. $16 +20 = 36 = 6 \times 6$. Attributed to Geburah, it means "The Confirmed". The Zohar [II:211A p. 298] says: "there being nine Hayoth [Living Creatures] on each of the four sides of the universe, the total number is 36."

בכחו by his (Her) power [Jeremiah 10:12]. Refers to the Life-power as dwelling within itself and as working throughout the field of manifestation from within. see 683, 46, 252, 315, 154, 224, 314, 29.

אהל tabernacle; tent [Rev. 21:3; Exodus 40:34]. Refers to the idea of the universe as the abode, or dwelling place, of the Life-power. The dwelling place of the *Shekhinah*.

אהל In the prologue of the Zohar [I:6]" MI, was the beginning of the edifice, existent and not-existent, deep-buried, unknowable by name. It was only called MI (who). It desired to become manifest and to be called by name. It therefore clothed itself in a refulgent and precious garment and created אלה (these), and אלה acquired a name. The letters of the two names intermingled, forming the complete name אלהים (Elohim-God)." see 86.

אלה God. A variant of אל. A metathesis of אהל, to hint that God is His own tabernacle. With different pointing: to be strong, strength, an oak. Goddess of Geburah.

הלא to removed, cast away; case far off. In Micah 4:7: "and I will make her that halted a remnant, and her that was cast off a strong nation: and the Lord shall reign over them in Mount Zion, from hence forth, even forever. see 165.

לו. perhaps, possibly; would that, O that! With different pointing: 'glory' in Deuteronomy 33:17: "His glory is like the firstling of his bullock..." see 806.

"לו or יל Every idea of liaison, cohesion, tendency of objects toward each other. The universal bond. The abstract line with *is conceived* going from one point to another and which is represented by the relations, *oh if! Oh that! would to God that!*

לוה. Action of being *adherent, coherent,* united by *mutual ties,* by *sympathetic movement: every adjunction, liaison, copulation, conjunction, addition,* etc." [d'Olivet, 1976, pp. 379-380.]

בדל be divided, separate, Root of הבדלה, *Habdalah,* a dividing, sundering, separating. Connected with Zain. see 46.

לאה weariness, exhaustion; the proper name Leah, daughter of Laban, and Jacob's first wife through the Father's ruse. In Genesis 29:23: "And it came to pass in the evening that he [Laban] took Leah his daughter, and brought her to him [Jacob]; and he went in unto her."

"This word is translated 'wearied' by Gesenius, and 'weary, or dull,' by Furst; both however are singularly inappropriate to an infant. Me may, more probably, consider that this word signifies 'she languishes,' and that is has reference to Astarte, or Ishtar. The idea of 'languishment' appears to have been associated in all hot countries with that of 'desire.' …the word may be a variant of לח, leah, which signifies 'vital force, freshness, and vigor;' the name being given with the same idea as was in the mind of Jacob, when he said, 'Reuben, thou are my might, the beginning of my strength' (Genesis 49:3), or variant of לוח, luh, 'he shines, glitters, or burns.'" [Inman, 1942, VII pp. 206-207.]

איכה How? where? How and where is the power of God to be found? In the glory of his silence. Hebrew title of the book of Lamentations.

וידוי confession.

כבדי my glory.

aqua (Lt). water. This water is the universal substance which fill the "deep". Here it should be remembered that Venus is fabled to have sprung from the sea.

Damcar (Lt). a "place" in "Arabia" where brother C.R. was initiated. As דם כר (264) Damcar means "the blood of the Lamb," which is the "water of life." This is a correspondence life that between *Argentum vivum*, the water of the sages, and דם ענב, Dam-enab, "The blood of the grape." Note the same colors, white and red. see 264, 166, 30 (Lt).

37   (prime)

I. The glyph of mercury. circle = 22, cross = 4, crescent = 11. ☿

II. Sattva, or alchemical Mercury, is the attribute of *Yekhidah*. The numeral value of *Yekhidah* (see below), is 37, which is number of degrees in the angle which determines the relation of the hypotenuse of a Pythagorean triangle to its base. Thus the number 37 signifies the principle which maintains the relation of the evolving forms of the Life-power to Isis, or Mother Nature. The Supreme SELF, *Yekhidah*, is this principle. It is the epithet of the soul of life of Israel. In Tarot it applies to Virgo [3+7 = 10; the numerical value of Yod, attributed to Virgo]. Thirty-seven is multiplied into many names and epithets of Jesus Christ. In the New Testament Jesus calls himself "Son of Man" 37 times (2380, Greek). The Zohar (123A) says from Isaac's birth to the time of his being bound were thus the real life of Sarah, as indicated in the expression "and the Life of Sarah was (ויהיו), the word ויהיו having the numerical value of 37". The *Garden of Pomegranates* gives 12 trials on the Tree of Life with a pendant Malkuth in Assiah. 3x12 + 1 = 37. [see Great Work Lesson 13]

III. Thirty-seven is the sum of the squares of 1 and 6, or 1 plus 36, so that its basic numeral properties are a combination of the powers of 1, or Kether, with those of 6, or Tiphareth.

IV. "The total numeration of the Sephiroth of the Middle Pillar, including Daath, is 37, which represents Unity itself in its balanced trinitarian manifestation [111 divided by 3]. 37 is also the word להב, meaning the 'flame', 'head', or 'point', which resumes the doctrine of the Head (in Daath) as the point of access to the universe of Pure Negation. Also, 37 is the number of לוא which means 'Non', 'Neque', 'Nondum', 'Absque', 'Nemo', 'Nihil'; not, neither, not yet, without, none, nothing." [Grant, 1994, p. 46.]

V. The unity itself in its balanced trinitarian manifestation. [Crowley, 1977, p. xxv].

הכבוד The weight. the glory. gravitation. The mass or potential working power concentrated at the center. The rolled-up scroll or see-idea of the High Priestess, concentrated in the Primal Will at the beginning of a cycle of the Life-power's self-expression. see 237.

יהידה Yekhidah. I AM, The Supreme Self, the Only One, the single, the indivisible. The cosmic SELF seated in Kether and associated with the Hermit, "He who stands alone." *Yekhidah* is the

Cosmic Logos, as the Solar Logos or Christos is the Logos of our system of planets revolving around the sun. *Yekhidah* is the Supreme Head of the universal system designated by the term *Rashith Ha-Galgalim*, "Head (or beginning) of the Whirlings".

Yekhidah (Hindu Ishvara) the Supreme Ruler, the One Identity, the Self is a point of expression for a dynamic energy, a point through which that energy passes continually. Yekhidah is the feminine form of יחד, meaning unity . The feminine form shows that although the I AM is one and alone, it is also the receptacle or vehicle for אין סוף אור, The Limitless Light. see 149 (Lt), 620, 111.

ולא and nothing. see Deuteronomy 5:22.

לאו 11ᵗʰ Shem ha-Mephorash, short form. see 52, & Appendix 10.

לאו 17ᵗʰ Shem ha-Mephorash, short form. see 52, & Appendix 10.

הבל "to breathe," or "a fleeting breath", vapor, hot air. The Talmud signifies "to evaporate." Denotes "transitoriness, emptiness," and is translated "vanity" (to be in vain), in the English version of Ecclesiastes. From it is derived the proper name Abel, given to the second son of Adam and Eve and killed by Cain (160). Refers to the volatility of the Mercury principle, and its close link with breath, or air, which the Hindus call Prana, the Greeks Pneuma, and the Hebrews Ruach. In Job 7:16: "I loathe it [my life]; I would not always live: let me alone, for my days are a fleeting breath." In Ecclesiastics 11:10: "So then, banish anxiety from your heart and cost off the troubles of your body, for youth and vigor (youth) are meaningless (vanity)." see 13, 345, 2368.

The root-word of all new testament appellations of Jesus (2368) which are multiples of 37. Thus it may be understood to be a type of the Messiah to whom the mystical name Shiloh is given. Since *abel* is from a root meaning "to breath, to wave" (the rhythmic motion of the Life-breath). It suggests that even the slightest and most fleeting expressions of the cosmic Life-breath are essentially identical with the eternal self.

ה can be read as the definite article "the." בל is "not" equivalent in meaning to לא, the metathesis of אל, El, strength. Refers to the truth that all things are transitory expressions of the strength (אל) which is not-anything. בל is the Aramaic word for "hearts", and originally meant "courage or strength." It is also a contraction of בול, Master or Lord. Thus הבל may be read as the (ה) No-thing, the Lord, whose strength is the heart or core of all things (בל). Also בל is 32 so that בלה may be read as "The 32," referring to the complete manifestation of the 32 paths of Wisdom.

אול might, physical power. from a root meaning "to twist." Sometimes used as a noun to designate the human body as being rolled together. In 2 Kings 24:15: "And he carried away Jehoichin to Babylon, and the King's mother, and the King's wives, and his officers, and the *mighty* of the land, those he carried into captivity from Jerusalem to Babylon." And in Psalm 73:4: "For there are no bands in their death, but their *strength* is firm."

אלאה Alah. a form of an Aramaic (Chaldee) name of God, compare with the Arabic Allah. see אלה.

אלו as a particle, "lo, behold" (Aramaic). As a conjunction, "if, but" (אלו)-suggests conditional existence. With different pointing: "these", as the multiplicity of "separate" objects presented to the mind as part of the various phases of conditional existence. see 21, *khesev*.

בלה to palpitate, to trouble, (a primitive Hebrew root) "The waters were troubled." From this basic idea are derived two opposite meanings: 1. to wear out, to decay; 2. to spend time; to be prolonged; to use; to enjoy.

הבל the heart (Aramaic). With different pointing: the lord, the husband, applied to the Christos, in a qabalistic sense.

גדל a primitive root like אול signifies primarily "to twist." It has a great variety of meanings as a verb, depending on the context; but, like these meanings always imply power, and also size and weight. It indicates the spiral, whirling motion associated with Key 10 and Jupiter, as well as with Kether. It has a secondary meaning of "to be strong, to be first, to be foremost or chief". This idea of magnitude is more definitely expressed by the feminine noun *Gedulah*, usually translated "magnificence."

הוזמי The 5 letter to which are attributed the 5 senses. ה: sight, ו: hearing, ז: smell, מ: taste, י: touch. A hint that the SELF is a focus for the subtle principles of sensation (tattvas).

זל giver, profuse, lavish. An intimation of the wealth of power centered in Kether. תת זל Tayth Zal (837) is one name for the Kether.

זו division of force.

כבודה glorious (Psalm 45:13). "The king's daughter is all-glorious within," Kebodah refers particularly to Malkuth, which is sometimes called "Bride," and "Daughter." Remember, "Kether is in Malkuth, and Malkuth is in Kether, but after another manner." This is akin to the Hermetic axiom: "That which is above is as that which is below, and that which is below is as that which is above." The root meaning of kabodah, is ponderability or weight, i.e., that which is manifest as gravitation. see 44 (להט)

דגל banner. The adytum of the One Self is the banner of deity.

להב flame. see 44.

אכאיה "God good and patient". 7th Shem ha-Mephorash. 31-35E. Genie. CLOÜS, Mercury. March 26, June 6, August 16, October 28, January 8. 2:00-2:20 AM. Attributed to Psalm 130:8. Rules patience, discovers the secrets of nature; influences the propagation of enlightenment and aids industry. Persons born: loves to instruct himself in useful things; glories in the execution of the most difficult works and discovers many useful processes in the arts. see Appendix 10.

Associated with the 1st quinance [1-5E] of Virgo; angel by day of the 8 of Pentacles (Hod of Assiah). This represents the operation of Hod,

sphere of Mercury, in Assiah, the material world. Davidson translates this name as "trouble", and says that in the Qabalah, he is one of 8 Seraphim [Davidson, 1971, p. 6.]

ואל Valu; Volac. Goetic demon #62 by night of the 2nd decanate of Sagittarius. see Appendix 11.

Goetia: "He is a president mighty and great, and appears like a child with angel's wings, riding on a two-headed dragon. His office is to give true answers of hidden treasures, and to tell where serpents may be seen. That which he will bring unto the Exorcist without any force or strength being by him employed. He governs 38 Legions of Spirits." [Mathers, 1995, p. 60]

וחזיר sanctuary, adytum

η θιβη He thebeh (Gr). Ark [Exodus 2:2 in the Greek Septuagint]. The ark in the bulrushes (Moses). The life-power is the ark which preserves us from every danger. Both it and Noah's ark suggest preservation of Life, and the transition from one cycle of the Life-power's manifestation to another. The point of "beginning," which is really a point of transition from relative quiescence to a period of relative activity, is symbolized as an ark.

linea (Lt). line, boundary, limit, goal. see 106 (*qav*).

non (Lt). Not, nothing. compare to אבל above.

Draco (Lt) Dragon. The Alchemical serpent power. see 358. In the book of Lambspring "A savage dragon lives in the forest [56 Latin], Most venomous he is, yet lacking nothing: When he sees the rays of the sun and its birth fire, He scatters abroad his poison, And flies upward so fiercely That no living creature can stand before him, Nor is even the basilisk equal to him." [Waite, 1974, vol. 1, p. 286]. Note that Draco (the dragon) and Panacea (universal medicine) are numerically equivalent. see 72 (Lt).

panacea (Lt). Universal medicine. Concerning the dragon, or serpent-power, it is said "He who hath skill, to slay him, wisely Hath escaped from all dangers. Yet all venom, and colors, are multiplied In the hour of his death. His venom becomes the great Medicine. He quickly consumes his venom, For he devours his poisonous tail. All this is performed on his own body, Form which flows forth glorious Balm, With all its miraculous virtues. Hereat all the sages do loudly rejoice." [Waite, 1974, Vo.1, p. 286]. see 72 (Lt).

tu (Lt). thou, you (singular form). "Thou art that."

vas (Lt). vase. An alchemical term describing the "vase of art." The vase is tu and tu is also יהודה. see 1630, 202.

mihi (Lt) to me. Part of a phrase, "Jesus is all things to me", and a second phrase found written on the altar in the vault of C.R. see 150, 475 (Lt).

cordo (Lt) hinge (of a door); the point round which anything turns, a pole; a chief circumstance, or consideration upon which many others depend, i.e. cardinal.

omega (Lt) Latin transliteration of Greek Omega, meaning the last, ending. Part of the a phrase. see 94, 717 (Lt).

38

Perimeter of a dodecahedron (Ether).

גלה to lay bare, to denude, to strip of concealment. to expose or reveal; to open (a book). Letter by letter גלה means: ג: Success in the Great Work depends on the discovery of the 1st matter. In order to expose it we must employ the power of recollection and association represented by the High Priestess (holding a rolled up scroll) who is a symbol of the 1st matter. ל: True faith which takes form in persevering action in the daily test and trial where no visible success is evident; ה: the discovery is to be made with the mind- in the light of reason and of the dominion over the conditions of physical existence. see 114.

לח vigor, natural force [Deuteronomy 34:7]. " And Moses was an hundred and twenty years old when he died: his eye was not dim, nor his natural force (vigor) abated." As an adjective *lakh*: moist, fresh, new, unused; liquid.

"Every movement directed toward elementary existence and making effort to produce itself, to make its appearance. Natural vigor; innate movement of vegetation; radical moisture: that which is verdant, young, moist, fresh; that which is glowing with youth, beauty, freshness; that which is smooth, soft to the touch; etc." [d'Olivet, 1976, pp. 380-381.]

איל moving one thning through another, spinning, "He departed." With different pointing: *awzal*, to go, to be gone, to be exhausted.

חל Wall, rampart. Root of חלט, *khalat*, to catch, to ascertain, to decide. With different pointing: *chol*, profane, unholy, to make a hole, hollow; to violate. see 6, 14, 10, 22, 47.

"חל Hel. This root, composed of the sign of elementary existence united to the root אל, symbol of extensive force and of every movement which bears upward, produces a mass of ideas which is very difficult to fix accurately. It is, in general, a superior effort which causes a distention, extension, realization; it is all unknown force which breaks the bonds of bodies by stretching them, breaking them, reducing them to shreds, or by dissolving them, relaxing them to excess.

Every idea of extension, effort, made up a thing to extend, develop, stretch or conduct it to a point or end, a twinge, a pain: a preserving movement; hope, expectation.

The Arabic, in a restricted sense it is the action of loosening, relaxing, releasing, resolving, absolving, etc. When the root receives the guttural reinforcement, it express in the state of privation, indigence; that which lacks, which is wanting, in any manner whatsoever. חל and לל (intensive) distention, distortion; contortion; endurance; solution of continuity; an opening, a wound: extreme relaxation, dissolution, profanation, pollution, weakness, infirmity, debility, vanity, effeminate dress, ornament; a flute; a dissolute dance, a frivolous amusement, etc." [d'Olivet, 1976, p. 350-351.]

גידי. "Valley of Vison". Servant to the prophet Elisha. see 2 Kings 8:4.

וכאי Innocent, guiltless, righteous, deserving, worth, entitle to.

חִיך to smile. also, the palate.

אואל Goetic demon #47 by night of the 2nd decanate of Cancer. see Appendix 11.

Goetia: "He is a duke, great, mighty, and strong; and appears in the from of a mighty dromedary at the first, but after a while at the command of the Exorcist he puts on human shape, and speaks the Egyptian tongue, but not perfectly. His office is to procure the love of women, and to tell things past, present, and to come. He also procures friendship between friends and foes. He was of the Order of Potentates or Powers. He governs 37 Legions of Spirits." [Mathers, 1995, p. 52]

Maria (Lt). Mary. Literally "seas". Relates to the great sea of Binah (67) as the mother of all manifested life. Mother of Jesus.

39

Diagonal of a rectangle 15 by 36.

זבל to enclose, reside; to exalt. As a masculine noun: *zabel*, dung, manure.

טל dew. Used in alchemical texts in relation to first matter. From a root: "to cover." see 343, 434.

יהוא אחד Tetragrammaton Echad. "The Lord is One." [Deuteronomy 6:4]. "Hear, O Israel: The Lord our God is One Lord." The great affirmation of unity which is the basis of Judaism. see 3, 12, 21, 30, 48, 7.

לט concealed, secret; enchantment. With different pointing: *lawt.* magic art.

אחיך your brother. Genesis 4:9, 10:11: "And the Lord said unto Cain, where is Abel thy Brother? And he said, I know not: am I my brother's keeper? And he said, what hast thou done? The voice of thy brother's blood crieth unto me from the ground. And now thou art cursed from the earth, which hath opened her mouth to receive thy brother's blood from thy hand." see 37, 160, 496, 519.

כוז metathesis of יהוה. see 26.

חובה misdeed, trespass, guilty, liability. "Three Mothers: Alef, Mem Shin. Their foundation is a pan of merit, a pan of liability and the tongue of decree deciding between them." [Kaplan, 1997, p. 139]

יהויה "God who knows all things." 33rd Shem ha-Mephorash. 161E-165E. 10:40 - 11:00 AM. "The Lord brings the counsel of the heathen to naught..." To know traitors, to destroy their projects and their machinations. Associated with the 3rd quinance quinance (11E-15E) of Capricorn; Angel by day of the 3 of Pentacles (Binah of Assiah). This represents the influence of Binah, sphere of Saturn in Assiah, the material world of action. see 24, 36, 965, & Appendix 10.

אבלו To mourn. see Joel 1:9.

אגלה I will lay bare. see Micah 1:6.

אובל I was carried. see Job 10:19.

אויבך Your enemy. see 1 Samuel 26:8.

אכל I will begin. see Deuteronomy 2:28.

בבלה To Babylon. see 2 Kings 20:17.

40

Number of days and lights it rained during the Biblical Flood. Number of weeks of the gestation of a human child. Numbers of years the Israelites wandered in the desert.

מ Mem. One of the 3 mother letters. Mem is attributed to the element of Water. Water is the source of form, associated with the creative letter Heh, and that the multiplication of forms is the apparent subdivision of the ONE into various parts. [So the verb ברא, *bawraw* (203), which is usually rendered "create", also means primarily "to cut out, to cut apart" -the diversifying power of Binah, the root of Water.

"Mem ...resembles a womb, which for the fetus is a "fountain of life." In Hebrew, the word אם, mother, also means "womb." Its essential consonant is the letter Mem. In most languages Mem is the basic sound of "mother." In general, the symbol of mother nature, Eve, "the mother of all life," is the womb of all (manifest) existence. This is after she ascends in aspiration--the secret of the letter Lamed--to receive from Adam the seed of life." [The Alef-Beit, Rabbi Ginsburgh]

"This character as consonant, belongs to the nasal sound. As symbolic image it represents woman, mother, companion of man; that which is productive, creative. As grammatical sign, it is the maternal and female sign of exterior and passive action; placed at the beginning of words it depicts that which is local and plastic; placed at the end, it becomes the collective sign, developing the being in infinitive space, as far as its nature permits, or unity by abstraction, in one single being all those of the same kind. In Hebrew it is the extractive or partitive article...expressing in nouns or actions that sort of movement by which a name or an action, it taken for means or instrument, is divided in its essence, or is drawn from the midst of several other similar nouns or actions." [d'Olivet, 1976, p. 385.]

Extractive or Partitive Article. The movement which this article expresses, with nouns or actions is taken for the means, for the instrument, by which they are divided in their essence, or drawn from the midst of several other nouns or similar actions. I render it ordinarily by *from, out of, by*; *with, by means of, among, between*, etc. [ibid., p.112]

בחל to loathe, feel nausea. The state of consciousness preceding the attainment of the consciousness symbolized by Key 12.

גזל to cut off or flay, to take away, to strip off, as skin from the flesh; to rob or plunder. Refers to the alchemical idea that the element water is the source of form, associated with the creative letter Heh and the multiplication of forms is the apparent subdivision of the ONE into various parts.

חבל As a verb it means: to twist, to wind together, to bind; to pledge; to pervert, to damage, to act corruptly, to sin, to wound. As a noun *cheybel*: a cord, a rope; pain, sorrow; a measuring line; a snare. Limitation and measurement are inseparable from creation--the

One Life sacrifices itself for manifestation, which is a source of pain and sorrow. This world is a delusion and a snare to those who misapprehend the meaning of its appearances. Also with different points: woe! Oh! Alas!; what a pity! This mixture is a breaking up of "the still calm of Pure Being..." A sense in which the original purity of the subsisting ONE is damaged or destroyed by the creative process.

חלב With different pointing *cheyeleyb*, meaning: fatness; the best of it. The "Virgin's Milk" or alchemical water. From the element of Water the Wise derive all their supplies of substance for manifestation.

יד יהוה Yod Tetragrammaton. the hand of Jehovah (formative power). Ezekiel 1:3 "The had of the Lord was upon him." Signifies the formation power of the One Reality. Alchemical Water is the agency or power whereby the One Reality projects its creative energy into specific forms. see 90.

ילד child boy; infant, embryo; young of an animal.

גואל redeemer, savior, messiah, liberator, a title of Yesod. With different pointing: kinsman, relative. Jeremiah 59:20: "and a redeemer will come to Zion."[It is important for the understanding of the passage cited, Job 19:25 (My redeemer, 44), to know that the fundamental meaning of גול, "Redeemer" is a <u>blood</u> relative, or one next of kin.] see 233, 4, 400, 233, 44.

לי to me, to mine. We shall come to the redeemer, when we hear the call. We are driven (Lamed) to the Father (Yod).

טלא To patch; to cover with spots [Genesis 30:20].

בחל the ripening (of figs); puberty of women.

להה To languish, faint, to be exhausted, to faint; to be foolish or mad. "Water" causes illusion, delusion and snare, as well as being the great healer.

לאט Secret; to wrap, cover; to speak gently.

בלדד The second of Job's three friends. He is called the "Shuhite," which implies both his family and his nation [Job 2:11]. Shuhite is a region on the western side of Chaldea, bordering on Arabia where the Tsukhi, a powerful people, are found. [William Smith-dictionary of the Bible] Shuah was a son of Abraham [Genesis 25:2, 6]. Bilad means "Bel loves". Bel was the Babylonian analog of Jupiter, connected with champion of the gods and savior.

catena (Lt). A chain; things linked by common interest or logical series. Used in Secret Symbols (plate 33) to illustrate the same basic idea as that which is symbolized by the Tree of Life, with its connecting paths.

sol (Lt). The sun; gold.

41   (prime)

I. $(2^4 + 5^2)$

II. The yoni as a vampire force, sterile. [Crowley, 1977, p. xxv].

איל strength, power. with different vowel points: *terebinth*, 1. oak. 2. ram, head, chief, mighty one; 3. pilaster, buttress. The meaning ram relates it to Aries (טלה, a young lamb). All these meanings are connected with the letter Heh through the sign Aries. see 44.

אם womb. origin, commencement; mother; basis. Refers of Binah (Aima) as when it is said חכמה אב בינה אם "Wisdom is the Father, Understanding the Mother." see 67, 155.

אם if, whether (conjunction); when, on, condition, in case.

גבול to set bounds; border, boundary, limit, territory, district, province (as a distinct from Jerusalem and the temple). Used in the Book of Formation to indicate the 12 directions of space corresponding to the edges of the cube. They are called "the Boundaries of the World." [Chapter 5, section 2] With different pointing: kneading.

אלי my God, my Hero. Also a proper name. Refers to the deity name of Chesed and has the same basic meaning of strength as its metathesis [איל]. [Psalm 18:3].

יה יהוה Yah Tetragrammaton. Lord God. [Psalm 118:5,6] "I called upon the Lord in distress: The Lord answered me, and set me in a large place. The Lord is on my side: I will not fear: What can man do unto me?" In this Psalm יה, Yah, ends the 5th verse, and יהוה begins the 6th; and the Qabalistic use of this combination is to represent the union of Chokmah, Father (יה) with Tiphareth, Son (יהוה). see 67, 4, 15, 105.

אחלב fatness, fertility. Name of the City of Asher [sublimation = Libra = 501] In Judges 1:31: "Neither did Asher drive out the inhabitants of Ahlab."

בטל To stop, cease, to cease to exist; to be idle, stop work; to be void, abolish, suspend. With different pointing: to abolish, suspend, dispense with, cancel, deface, neglect; to neutralize an admixture of forbidden food in a certain quantity; to disturb, interfere with; to negate. Suggest inertia-lack of "strength."

גאואל "*Germael* 'Majesty of God'. An angel sent by God to create Adam from the dust. A mission also ascribed to Gabriel." [Davidson, 1971, p. 124.] "Majesty" is connected with Chesed.

גחל burning coals; to burn slowly; carbuncles (skin infection).

חול 1. to twist, to turn, to turn round. to dance in a circle. 2. to be twisted, to be hurled against something. 3. to twist oneself in pain, to writhe, to be in pain. 4. to bring forth. 5. to tremble, causing terror. 6. to be strong or firm.

חגל to go round in a circle. see Key 10, and the letter Kaph (20).

אלוד Night demon of the 1st decanate of Virgo. This decanate is ruled by Mercury and suggest attention placed on wrong images, resulting in unbalanced assimilation.

amor (Lt). love.
fides (Lt). Faith.

dedit (Lt). Gave. Love and Faith gave us strength to pursue union with the Most High. Part of a Rosicrucian saying. see 518.

42

אמא the dark, sterile Mother. Binah as the feminine power of specializing and finitizing prior to manifestation of actual forms. "The Eternal Parent, wrapped in her ever invisible robes, had slumbered once again for seven eternities." [Dztanzz] see 52, 67, 86, 112, 199, 265.

אלוה (Job 19:26). A name of God from the same root as Elohim, the particular Divine Name assigned to Binah.

בלי failure, destruction; no, not, without. Since Binah finitizes, the third Sephirah is the seat of the restrictive power by means of which separation is brought about. Hence is Binah also the Sphere of Saturn.

בהלה dismay, terror, confusion, shock; sudden haste. All these words apply to Binah as the dark, sterile, "terrible" mother. Without balance form the masculine principle, her energy turns upon itself. Inman says the name is derived from בל, Bel and הוה "Bel creates", or Bel moves around us." [Inman, 1942, VI p. 368.]

בלהה terror, horror, calamity. With different pointing: *Bilhah*; Rachel's handmaiden; mother of Dan [54] and Naphtali [570]. Genesis 29:29: "Laban gave his servant girl Bilhah to his daughter Rachel as her maidservant."

חלד What glides swiftly, what is transient. A noun for life, it refers to the personal life of man, considered as being fleeting, ephemeral. *Kheled* is also a special qabalistic name for the "earth" of Malkuth. There is a very definite relationship between Binah, the Mother, and Malkuth, the Bride. In this connection *Kheled* refers to the world of man, including his terrestrial environment, as being essentially transitory, as undergoing continual change.

"The World, Earth of Malkuth. "One of the Seven Earths (corresponding with Tebhel, to Yesod and Malkuth); our own earth." [Godwin, 1999. p. 499.]

חדל As a verb to cease. to desist, to come to an end. As a noun *khedel*, cessation, this world; the place of rest. the abode of dead, a yawning gulf. As an adjective it means forbearing, lacking; ceasing, transient. Translated "frail" in Psalm 39:4 In the Jewish translation of the Massoretic it is translated "short-lived." Compare this with the meaning of חנט (67). מה-חדל, "how short-lived" is the actual wording in the Hebrew text. see 45.

לוו 19th Shem ha-Mephorash, short form. see 57 & Appendix 10.

וול 43rd Shem ha-Mephorash, short form. see 42 & Appendix 10.

chaos (Lt). a yawning gulf. In Latin it is associated with the idea of boundless space and darkness. It designates the confused, formless, primitive mass out of which the universe was made. It is the Great Abyss of Darkness; and because the idea of that darkness is related to Binah, the third Sephirah is colored black in our symbolic scale. Note that chaos is the primitive state of nature. see 67.

"The endless eternity and unsearchable Primum Mobile [130] are represented by the trinity, which produces the Fiat [34] and produces nature in the mode of Prima Materia [112], otherwise chaos." [Waite, 1993, p. 22].

liber (Lt). a book, a rescript, a decree. All these ideas refer to nature, which is the "one, only book" mentioned by Rosicrucians. In Tarot, the Book of Nature is the scroll of the High Priestess.

luna (Lt). the moon, silver in alchemy. Connected with the High Priestess, who is the dark and terrible mother, Hekate, Goddess of the underworld, which is the abode of the dead. The world is חדל, *khedel*. In later alchemical and heraldic use, Luna denotes the metal silver. see 160, 146, 40.

canis (Lt). dog. Recall the dog in Key 18, the Moon. In the Book of Lambspring it says: "Alexander writes from Persia That a wolf and a dog are in the field, Which, as the Sages say, Are descended from the same stock, But the wolf comes from the east, And dog from the west. They are full of jealousy, Fury, rage, and madness: One kills the other, And from them come a great poison. But when they are restored to life, They are clearly shown to be The Great and Precious Medicine, The most glorious Remedy upon the earth, Which refreshes and restores the Sages, Who render thanks to God, and do praise Him." [Waite, 1974, Vol. 1, p. 284]. see 56, 79 (Lt) Note that Key 18, the Moon (Pisces) shows a wolf and a dog.

Ogdoad. 8 pointed star; symbol of the "creative Logos whose name is Alpha and Omega-the radiations of which result in the continuous flow and unbroken circle of manifestation which is ever returning to its source." [Atwood, 1918, p. 2]

43   (prime)

I. The number of orgasm – especially the male. [Crowley, 1977, p. xxv].

אי-כבוד "Where is the..." The son of the priest Phineas, born on the occasion of the capture of the ark. In Samuel 4:21: "And she named the child Ichabod, saying, the glory is departed form Israel, because the ark of God was taken, and because of her father in law and her husband."

גיל to rejoice, delight, to mourn. also tongue of a bell.

גם also, even, too, moreover, yes. The affirmative that the Great glory is within us always. With different pointing: together, as in Psalm 133:1: "how good and pleasant it is when brothers live together in unity." see 65, 6031.

"Every idea of accumulation, agglomeration, complement, height; expressed in an abstract sense by the relations *also, same, again.* The Arabic develops as does the Hebraic root, all ideas of abundance and accumulation. As a verb, it is the action of *abounding, multiplying*; as a noun, and in a restrictive sense, [it] expresses a precious stone, in Latin *gemma.*" [d'Olivet, 1976, p. 315.]

ידידיה One beloved by God. The name given to Solomon at this birth by the prophet Nathan. In 2 Samuel 12:25: "And because the Lord loved him, he sent word through Nathan the prophet to make him Jedidiah."

להח 34th Shem ha-Mephorash. see 58, & Appendix 10.

גדול larger, great. Loud in Deuteronomy 5:22. Root of גדולה, *Gedulah*, greatness, majesty. see 48, 72.

ליז Hazel, almond. Alternative wood used for making the magical wand. Name of the place where Jacob is said to have had the dream of angels ascending and descending a ladder. Also a verb whose primitive meaning is "to turn away, to deviate." Latter ideas include forwardness and perversity, linking it to the path of Gimel--the involution or descent of energy from Kether, the cause of all limitations and "evils." see 404.

ליז Little Bone. Waite is cited by Donald Tyson: "Each man who is born into the world is provided with an imperishable bone in his present physical body, and it is from or on this that his organization will be built up anew at the time of the resurrection-it is like the rib taken from the side of Adam. The bone in question will be to the risen body that which the leaven is to the dough". [Three Books of Occult Philosophy Ch. 20 p. 68]

גדול great-in mass or size (weighty, important); in vehemence (violent); in dignity (authority); in eminence (distinguished). Suggests intense power and value. Symbolically represents the potency ascribed to the magic rod.

חלה Represents the Shekhinah, the "Cohabitating Glory" or divine agency through which God rules the World. The intermediary power between the Primal Will [Kether] and its manifestations. Represented by the Uniting Intelligence of the 13th Path. see 49, 263, 93 and K.D.L.C.K. (p. 346).

חלה to make sick, to mollify, appease. With different vowel points: cake. In Numbers 15:20: "You shall offer of a cake of the first of your bough for a heaven offering..." With different pointing: *Hallah*, name of a tractate of the Talmud.

לביא Lion, Lioness. In Job 4:11: "The old lion perisheth for lack of prey, and the stout lion's whelp are scattered abroad." see 340, 211, 310, K.D.L.C.K. (p.151).

מג. Magus; the Rosicrucian grade corresponding to Chokmah, sphere of the Zodiac. Part of the Supernal Triad of master of the inner school, our spiritual Hierarchy. With different pointing: Persian priest, chief of the Magi. In Jeremiah 39:3: "Then all the officials of the King of Babylon took seats in the middle gate: …a chief officer, Nergal-Sharezer a chief priest [i.e. Magus] and all the other officials of the King of Babylon."

I. "A root not used in Hebrew. The Arabic expresses the idea of a thing which is sour, acrid, bitter, sharp; which irritates, troubles, torments. In a restrictive sense the verb signifies *to be repugnant*." [d'Olivet, 1976, p. 386.]

II. "**מג, מוג**; under these two forms Furst gives a great amount of valuable information, leading us to believe that the origin of the word is to be traced to the Aryan or Sanskrit *magh* or *magha*, which signifies power and riches; or to an old Persian word, *mag* or *maga*, whose meaning is 'might,' 'force,' in a religious aspect. The word was known amongst the Phoenicians, in whose tongue **מגן**, *magon*, was 'a priest or wise man.' In the Greek, we find that Μαγος, signifies, 'one of the priest and wise men in Persia who interpreted dreams,' whilst μεγας, signifies 'big or great.'" [Inman, 1942, Vol. II p. 233.]

Filii (Lt). of the son. The "son" is *Ben* (53), or Tiphareth (1081).

qui (Lt). who. The son, who is majestic is a reflection of its source, *Hu* (see 12, also pronounce "who") in Kether. Part of a Rosicrucian saying. see 518 Latin.

I. The sum of the 9 sides, 14 corners and 21 boundary lines of the vault of the adepts. Combined value of Mercury (37) & sulphur (7).

II. Perimeter of a circle with a diameter of 14. Circumference of the Creative World, Briah.

אליאב "God of his Father."

אם + **אב** Father + Mother. The addition the Hebrew words Father and Mother, referring to Chokmah and Binah. It therefore represents the union of Wisdom and Understanding. These Sephiroth are part of the Creative World.

דם blood. Formed from the word Adam [**אדם**]. The physical organism of Man is condensed from Blood. It is from blood that the substance used in the Great Work is derived-identical with the Lunar (white) and solar (red) currents of prana "congealed" or brought into a solid state by gradual loss of Heat. In the *Fama*, the location of the temple of the Wise men was at Dam-Car, located in Arabia. Dam-Car means Blood of the Lamb. The temple is the initiate's own body. The practices of initiation modify the blood. see 5, 55, 45, 470, 68 and *True and Invisible Rosicrucian Order* for commentary of the *Fama* allegory.

The red water is blood. The blood's chemical condition can be modified by intelligent control of diet, and by the response of the ductless glands to suggestions. This is the means in which changes in cell-structure are brought about to unfold our consciousness to precipitate the Stone of the Wise. The law is no thought without corresponding cell-activity. To think any particular thought it is necessary that our cells are made so that they can transmute the vital principle into specific thought forms. Thus our work is to control of the cell forming functions of the body, to the end that cells may be developed capable of responding to the vibrations of thought and perception beyond the ranges of ordinary human consciousness. In summary learn how to modify the blood so that it will build the sort of cells we need for our interior development.

Blood was the first of the 10 plagues of Egypt. In Exodus 7:19: "the Lord said to Moses, "Tell

Aaron," take your staff and stretch out your hand over the waters of Egypt-over the streams and canals, over the ponds and the reservoirs," and they will turn to blood. Blood will be everywhere in Egypt, even in the wooden buckets and stone jars."

"The roots which, by means of any sign whatever, arise from the roots אב or אם, symbols of active or passive principles, are all very difficult to determine and to grasp, on account of the extent of meaning which they present, and the contrary ideas which they produce. These particularly demand close attention. It is, at first glance, universalized sympathy; that is to say, a homogeneous thing formed by affinity of similar parts, and holding to the universal organization of being.

דם is a broader sense, it is that which is *identical*; in a more restricted sense, it is *blood*, assimilative bond between soul and body, according to the profound though of Moses... It is that which *assimilates*, which becomes *homogeneous*; *mingles with* another thing: thence the general idea of that which is no longer distinguishable, which ceases to be different; that which renounces its seity, its individuality, *is identified* with the whole, *is calm, quiet, silent, asleep.*

The Arabic expresses in general a glutinous, sticky fluid. In particular, as noun, it is *blood*; as verb; it is the action of *covering with a glutinous glaze*. From the later meaning results, in the analogue, that of *contaminating, calumniating, covering with blame*." [d'Olivet, 1976, pp. 323-324.]

Sendovigius comments: Thou hast in thy body the anatomy of the whole world, and all thy members answer to some celestials; let, therefore, the searcher of the sacred science know that the soul in man, the lesser world or microcosm, substituting the place of its center, is the king, and is placed in the vital spirit in the purest blood [דם]. That governs the mind, and the mind the body... [New Light of Alchemy, p. 42]

טלה Aries. a young ram. Aries is a fire-sign. Refers to Christos, Brother C.R. and the brain is under the rulership of Aries, the means whereby man controls the forces of flame used in magic. The sign Aries, as the beginning of the zodiac, is a symbol of the commencement of the creative activities in בריאה which result ultimately in the Life-Power's self-expression in the names and forms of the physical world. The Ram and the Lamb are one, and correspond to the Hindu deity Angi, Lord of Flame (להט).

חול. sand. The root of the noun is a verb spelled with the same letters meaning, "to turn round, to twist, to whirl." [Job 29:18]. The birth of the alchemical 1st matter is in the sand (mineral kingdom). Alchemist call this their Phoenix-a spiral twisting motion directly connected with sound and thought.

With different pointing: to dance, to twist, writhe. To turn in a circle. Note the letter sequence: fence, nail, ox-goad. Suggesting movement within an enclosure, round a pivot (Vav, like the point in the center of a circle), incited by the law of action and re-action of which the letter Lamed and Key 11 symbolizes. As a masculine noun חול means sand, on account of the whirling pillars of sand familiar to all desert dwellers, which are the source of tales about Genies. *Khole*, is also the Hebrew name of the Legend of the Phoenix. In Job 29:18: "and I shall multiply my days as the sand." The Jewish translation is: "and I shall multiply by days as the Phoenix."(וכחול) "And like the Phoenix or sand," is the literal translation. Sands refers to the mineral Kingdom-first substance in the Pythagorean triangle. חול is also the root of the name חוילה (58), "The land of Havilah where there is Gold." [Genesis 2:11] Also: to wait, hope, to fall upon, happen; to be firm, strong. see 127, 395.

להט magic; flame, The flame of light. The art of Life. In relation to בריאה, Teleh and [להט] are technical mystery-terms, referring to the same idea that is expressed in the New Testament mention of the Lamb slain from the foundation of the world. Aries represent the beginning of creative activities in Briah which result in physical names and forms. The Ram and the Lamb are one and correspond to the Hindu Agni, Lord of Flame. With different pointing: magic arts, enchantments; glittering blade, glitter, flashing. As a verb: to flame, consume, to practice magic; to hide, to cover. see 7, 14, 22, 28, 66, 88.

לב אחד One heat, undivided heart. see 89 & Ezekiel 11:19.

אגלי drops (of fluid). A clear reference to blood, also to the heavenly influence which fall in "drops" as in Key 16, 18, 19. see 83.

אגם to gather together; a pool, a pond, muddy water; marsh; uncleared ground containing roots of trees, reedland; sorrow. As an adjective, sad, depressed, despondent, sorrow, "the slough of despond." The pilgrim's progress is an example of the same imagery.

דלי a vessel for drawing water, Aquarius. Refers to the Aquarian age, symbolized by the head of a man, which will perfect the human arts, science and philosophy. In the New Testament, the bucket is a significant symbol, recorded in Mark 14:13 and Luke 22:10. The Greek word one of the many indications as to the real meaning behind the surface narrative. see 296.

I. Paul Case comments on *Ancient Faiths* by Inman, his translation "to emit semen": דלי is Aquarius, the water-bearer." The two pitchers is דליו, which is 50 the number of נ, Scorpio and the two who bear the water [מ] should be easily understood by readers of the book. Aquarius is the distinctive sign of man, and manhood is *virilitas* in Latin and כח (strength, power, 28)"

II. Mark 14:13 "And he sends two of this disciples, and says to them, go into the city, and a man carrying a pitcher of water will meet you; follow him."

גאלי my redeemer. [Job 19:25] It is important for the understanding of the passage cited to know that the fundamental meaning of גאל, *Goale*, redeemer, is a blood relative, or next of Kin. *Goale* is also spelled גואל. see 50.

גולה captivity, exile, banishment; those in exile. Refers to the limitations which are the logical necessities of creation.

בלבי "in my heart." Psalm 119:11.

These words are directly related to the watery nature of Briah.

vir (Lt). a man, a husband. Same as the Hebrew שי [איש]. see 311.

45

I. Σ9 = 45

II. Length of each line of a Hexagram.

אדם Adam. generic humanity, a proper name. It particularly refers to man the microcosm. The verbal symbol for the ALL. Aleph refers to Kether, the Crown, Daleth to Malkuth, the Kingdom and Mem to Binah, Understanding (Zohar). The WORD by whom all things were made, and without whom nothing was made that was made (John). The primordial man is the universal mind looking inward into itself or Chokmah (Wisdom). By its letter is hints of the combination of the Spirit of Rauch (Aleph) in the Blood [דם].

Adam is the primordial man and embraces the essential nature of the whole Tree of Life. Adam is God's image or mental self-representation. this mental image of itself in the universal mind is also the primary being underlying the whole self manifestation of the Life-power. Adam is the Microcosmic philosopher's stone and (the elements) acting thus in concert upon each other, there result from them a harmonious whole, which composes what is called the Philosopher's stone, or the Microcosm. Adam is the "Red Earth," the earth of the sages.
I. Genesis 1:26: Then God said, "Let us make man in our image, in our likeness, and let them rule over the fish of the sea and the birds of the air, over the livestock, over all the earth, and over all the creatures that move along the ground."

II. "And-he-said, HE-the-Gods, (declaring his will) we-will-make Adam in-the-shadow-of-us, by-the-like-making-like-ourselves; and-they-shall-hold-the-scepter, (they shall rule, they, Adam, universal man) in-the-spawn breeding-kind-of-the-seas, and-in-the-flying-kind of-the-heavens, and-in-the quadrupedly-walking-kind,

68

and-in-the-whole-earth-born-life,   and-in-all-moving-thing crawling-along upon-the-earth.

He comments: Adam... I beg those who are reading this without partiality, to observe that Moses does not fall here into the modern error which has made of man a particular species in the animal kingdom; but only after having finished all that he wished to say concerning the elementary, the vegetable and the animal kingdom, he passes on to a kingdom distinct and higher that he names Adam.

Among the savants who have searched for the etymology of the word *Adam*, the majority went no further than its grossest exterior, nearly all of them have seen only red clay, or simple clay, because the word אדום signifies red or reddish; because by אדמה, the earth in general, has been understood; but they failed to see that these words themselves are compounds, and that they can only be roots of words still are compound; whereas the word אדם being more simple cannot come for it.

The name given to Adam signifies not only "homo," *man*, but it characterizes, as the Samaritan word meaning *universal*, that which we understand by mankind, and which we would express much better by *saying kingdom of man*; it is collective man, man abstractly formed of the assemblage of all men. This is the literal meaning of אדם.

This root is דם which carries with itself every idea of assimilation, of similitude, of homogeneity. Governed by the sign of power and stability א, it becomes the image of an immortal assimilation, of an aggregation of homogeneous and indestructive parts. Such is the etymology of the *Adam*, in its figurative sense.

The hieroglyphic meaning, which Moses allows nevertheless, to be understood in the same verse, and to which he makes allusion, by causing the same noun, which is singular, to govern the future plural verb ירדו [let them rule]: quite contrary to the rule which he had followed, of making the noun of the Being of Beings אלהים which is plural, govern always the singular verb. The hieroglyphic root of the name Adam, אדם is את, which composed of the sign of unitary,

principiant power, and that of divisibility, offers the image of a relative unity, such as might be expressed, for example, by means of the simple although compound number 10. The root number being endowed with the collective sign ם, assumes an unlimited development: that is to say, the symbolic number 10, being taken to represent the root את, the sign ם will develop its progressive power to infinity, as 10; 100; 1,000; etc. [d'Olivet, 1976, pp. 56-59.]

III. Adam at its higher aspect is "A symbol of the Divine nature of humanity-the Archetypal Man of the three higher planes." And in its lower aspect, "A symbol of the lower mind, energies from the desire plane, but receptive of impression from the higher nature. This is the fallen mind (Adam)." [Gaskell, 1981, pp. 22-23.]

IV. Issac Myer writes: "The Great androgyne, the Adam Illa-Ah or Adam Qadman, which includes in itself all the ideas, and all the content of all the prototypes of the existence. This (first) Adam is considered as the first distinctive beginning in the finite, and therefore is the sole occupant of the Atzluthic world... in reading the first and second chapters of Genesis, a distinction was made by the learned of the Israelites, between the higher Adam, i.e. the Adam Qadmon, or first paradigmic ideal man, and he inferior (terrestrial) Adam... "The third Adam is the terrestrial Adam, made of dust and placed in the Garden of Eden. This Adam was also an androgyne... it had, when first created, a glorious simulacrum or light body, and answer to the Yetziratic world... The forth Adam was the third Adam as he was after the fall, when he was clothed with skin, flesh, nerves, etc. This answers to the lower Nephesh and Guph, i.e. body, united. He has the animal power of reproduction and continuance of species, and also answers to the Assiatic world, but in him is some of the light of all the preceding (Adams)... together they form the great universal man. The Qabalah names man as the purpose of creation, and the first step in the upper Adam or celestial man." [Qabbalah pp. 114, 401, 418]

V. The Zohar [I:34B. p.130] says: ...the words 'let us make man' [in our image, after our likeness-Genesis 1:26] may be taken to signify that God imparted to the lower beings who came from the side of the upper world the secret of forming the divine name 'Adam', which embraces the upper and the lower in virtue of its three letters, Aleph, Daleth, and Mem final.

VI. F.J. Mayers: Let us return again for a moment to the name Adam and note its hieroglyphic construction. א [Aleph] as we know denotes anything primal-the first cause; potentiality - God . ד [Daleth] is the sign of multiplication, abundance; final ם [Mem] is the sign of unlimited plurality. The name Adam therefore means the one becoming many. But as a spiritual being, Adam was only One. As we said in speaking of the group-souls, a spiritual conception, a species or genus cannot, as such, multiply. It can only multiply in the number of individuals comprised in it, and this multiplication can only take place on the physical plane... We have now, the explanation of Adam being both singular and plural, him and them; and both male and female. In his singular aspect he was the human principle, the soul or essence of humanity. As a spiritual unity Adam was sexless, but sex was a necessity of multiplication in the physical realm-and in the physical realm alone ... [in Genesis 2:7] What we are told of now is still a spiritual act, the formation of a spiritual being in the spiritual realm, but eternal to the essential being of God. The Adam still has no physical or material form of existence. He was formed not of the dust of the earth or of any earthy substance, but from the Adamah [50]-The spiritual elements of humanity, of the qualities and attributes that constitute man a kingdom of being in himself or a link between the sub-human and divinity. [The Unknown God, pp.90, 121] see 390.

VII. "'Adam' is *Aleph immersed in blood,* but this blood is not "all absorbing"; it can become 'cosmically fruitful', which means that the human body can come to radiate cosmic energy. The schema for man *(Adam) is Aleph* (1), *Dallet* (4), *Mem* (40 or 600). The fact that *Mem* final can be 40 (i.e. resistance) and can leap to 600 (i.e. cosmic fertility) indicates the vast range of possibilities in man. The true vocation of mankind is this transfiguration of 40 into 600. The text goes on to say that Adam can be considered as a living shadow, or image, of the Elohim: given the potential of greater power of resistance than any other being, he can become the receptacle of the greatest intensity of life on this planet. (In a certain respect, we can see this

illustrated today wherever men are being trained to withstand the strain of living in rockets, beyond gravitation, on the floor of the oceans, in the Antarctic ice-fields, or to test their physical and psychological resistance in all kinds of competitions.)" [Suraes, 1992, p. 97.]

VIII. "We know that Adam is a schema for the human being. It indicates that *Aleph,* the pulsating creativeness of life-death, is within him, struggling so as not to drown in the absorption of Dam, 4.40. The earth, as *Adamah,* claims that blood as belonging to it. It says, mythically: I, Adamah [אדמה], am your mother and spouse; you, my husbandman, are kin to me: you are earth.

If we accept this proposition and live accordingly, the *Aleph* in us suffers death by suffocation, just as it is buried in *Eretz* where nature continuously repeats its prototypes, each according to its species.

But the Hebraic myth states that YHWH-Elohim has breathed in man the *Sheen* (300) which is the organic movement of the whole universe (Gen. 2, 7). This develops into the well-known dispute between YHWH and the earth as to whom the blood belongs.

YHWH's point contended for in argument is founded on a basic postulate of Qabala: the unity of energy and of its contradictory aspects as spirit and matter, good and evil, high and low, etc. They coalesce in the synthetic formula *Yod-Hay- Waw-Hay* where their two lives fertilize each other." [Suraes, 1992, pp. 114-115.]

IX. The Hebrew word *Adam* derives from the Egyptian *Atem*, the Mother Goddess of Time and Periodicity, hence Adam signifies 'man' (i.e. humanity), as the continuity of existence incarnate. [Grant, 1994, p. 73.]

אדם Edom. Edom is the Kingdom of unbalanced forces. With different pointing: *odem.* "red"; ruby, carnelian or hematite. The first stone of the breast plate of the High Priest, in [Exodus 28:17] "Then mount four rows of precious stones on it. In the first row there shall be a ruby [hematite], a topaz [emerald] and an emerald [marble]." see 98

אמד to appraise, supposition, to estimate, value; conjecture, assessment. Man is above all else, a calculator, a reckoner, an estimator. These meaning all relate to the power whereby man measures and defines.

הוא אביך "He (God) thy Father." Deuteronomy 32:6. Hu, He, is a special title of Kether.

הם abundance, wealth. as a pronoun (name): they, these, who; and various other meanings, all representing what surrounds the EGO, and therefore to be included in what is sometimes called "non ego." Written המה in Psalm 23:4: Even though I walk through the valley of the shadow of death, I will fear no evil, for you are with me; your rod and your staff *they* comfort me.

"הם Universalized life: the vital power of the universe. Onomatopoetic and idiomatic root, which indicates every kind of tumultuous noise, commotion, fracas.

הום Action of *exciting a tumult, making a noise, disturbing* with clamor, with an unexpected crash, every *perturbation, consternation, trembling*, etc. [d'Olivet, 1976, pp. 331-332.]

זזאל The Spirit of Saturn. Godwin spells it זאזל. However, Paul Case spelled *Zazel* as shown.

אגיאל Agiel. Intelligence of Saturn. Binah is the sphere of Saturn, the limiting or finitizing power, which establishes definite limits.

מאד as a verb: strength, might; exceeding, excessively. as a masculine noun: strength, might, vehemence. Root of the rabbinical word for Mars [מאדים], Madim.

מה mah. What? which; why? Used as an interrogative pronoun, as an adjective and an adverb. Used to mark the indefinite-whatever, that which. The prologue to the Zohar contains many references to this word. Rabbi Simeon says: "The heavens and their Hosts were created through the medium of *Mah*." It refers particularly to the Lesser Countenance. Mah is

the secret name of the World of Formation (Yetzirah) see Appendix 9.

Man is associated with the secret nature of Formation. Its substance is Man (Adam). However unknown this essential formative power may appear to be, the object of quest in occult science is the true nature of Man and the subject of alchemical operations in none other than Adam. see 73.

זבול Sacrifice to idols. With different pointing: *zebol*. lofty; heaven of Tiphareth. see 270.

גאולה redemption, liberation.
חבלה She who ruins.

זחל to creep, to crawl, to flow, to run; to fear, be afraid, to be timid [Deuteronomy 32:24]. serpent.

זחלי עפר "serpents of the dust."

ילה 44th Shem ha-Mephorash, short form. see 60 & Appendix 10.

הולד begat.

Deus (Lt) God. It is written Demon est Deus inversus" or the Devil is the reverse of God. see 314 Latin.

Homo (Lt). Man. It is also said Demon est Home inversus - "The Devil is Man upside Down." Therefore God and Man are essentially one. see 510, 1035.

Mens (Latin.) Mind. "...above the rational spirit is the *mens* or concealed intelligence, commonly call *intellectus illustratvs* [enlightened perception], and of Moses the breath of Life. This is that Spirit which God himself breathed into man, and by which man is united again to God." [Thomas Vaughan-Works-*Anthroposophia Theomagica*, p.28] see 116, 145 (Latin.); 214, 18, 23.

demon (Lt). devil, demon; part of a Latin phrase. see 244.

Ipse (Lt). This, this very person, Self. the superlative, Ipsissimis, is used as a title for the

Rosicrucian grade which correspond to Kether. Ipse is the Latin pronoun designating the Ego.

auri (Lt). golden. In Hindu books the SELF, or Ipse, is sometimes call "The golden person in the heart." Tiphareth corresponds to the Heart. As the sphere of the Sun, Tiphareth is related to Gold.

Nox (Lt). night, gloom, darkness, death; a goddess, the darkness of ignorance; figuratively, the subconscious plane, which is occult or hidden form the intellect. see 146. "All things were brought forth out of night." [Vaughan]

valle (Lt). the ablative case of valles, a valley, vale. Used in Rosicrucianism and alchemy to designate the field of the Great Work. Compare this with various details of Tarot symbolism which show the Great Work as being carried on, and especially as beginning, at the level of self-conscious awareness. see 62 (Lt)

vere (Lt). truly, really, in fact, properly, rightly. All implying a standard of measurement, to which whatever is indicated by Vere conforms.

46

Σ46 = 1081, the numerical value of Tiphareth.

אליה a name of God ("Jehovah is God") Elijah (Hebrew Lexicon). see 52.

אביגל Abigail, "Father of Joy, Source of Joy" [1 Samuel 25:13] Now the name of the man was Nabal; and the name of his wife Abigail: And she was a woman of understanding, and of a beautiful countenance." Abigail was later David's wife. see 14, 82, 56 (variant spelling).

לוי Third son of Jacob and Leah; Lavie, of the tribe of Levi [Genesis 35:23] "the sons of Leah: Reuban, Jacob's first-born, and Simeon and Levi..." As the priestly tribe, early in the history of Israel, the Levites became custodians of the sanctuary and its furniture.

אילה doe, hind. In Genesis 49:21: "Naphtali is a doe set free that bears beautiful fawns." (New International) "Naphtali is a hind let loose: he giveth goodly words." (King James). *Naphtali*

[570] is attributed to Virgo and alchemical distillation. see 570.

חובל sailor. The microcosm, as a vehicle with the great sea. Sephir Sephiroth gives: "A ruiner."

טואל In ceremonial magic, one of the Angels of the 12 signs of the zodiac, ruling Taurus and the 2nd astrological house.

ההאל "God in three persons." 41st Shem ha-Mephorash. 201E-205E. Chontaré. April 29, July 10, September 20, December 1. Associated with the 5th quinance (21E-25E) of Aquarius; Angel by day of the 7 of Swords. This represents the influence of Netzach, sphere of Venus, in Yetzirah, the world of mental formation. see Appendix 10.

דמב 65th Shem ha-Mephorash, short form. see 61 & Appendix 10.

אמה handmaid. female slave, tribe, race, people. mother (as the Great Mother, Binah), mother city, Metropolis, measure, or cubit, post, foundation, middle finger, virile member, penis, canal, dike, sewer.

מאה one hundred (100).

יוד יהוה Yod Tetragrammaton. hand of Jehovah. see 20, 26.

הבדלה A dividing sundering or separating, separation, division, to break apart, or in two. Power of Zain, the sword, connecting Binah to Tiphareth. From a root בדל [36].

מו The cry of the vulture. "A peculiar cry is said to issue from the mouth of the vulture. This cry or word is Mu. Its number, 46, is the 'key of the mysteries', for it is the number of Adam (Man). Mu is the male seed, but it is also the water (i.e. blood) from which man was fashioned [Adam was made from the 'red earth', see 45]. The vulture is a bird of blood and its piercing cry is uttered at the time of *sundering* [see above] which accompanies the act of manifestation: 'For I am divided for love's sake, for the chance of union'. (AL. I. 29).

The number 46 also connotes the dividing veil (Paroketh). *Meah* [see above] is the Hebrew for 100, the number of Qoph and therefore of the 'back of the head', the seat of the sexual energies in man. One hundred denotes completion or fulfillment of a cycle of time. The full meaning of the symbolism is therefore that when the vulture opens her wings to receive the phallic stroke in the silence and secrecy of the cloud [Paroketh also means 'a cloud'; a reference to the invisibility traditionally assumed by the male god when impregnating the virgin.], her shrill scream of rapture, is MU (46)." [Grant, 1994, pp. 122-123.]

בדיל   Tin, metal of Jupiter. A copper alloy of tin. Aramaic meaning: "on account of, for the sake of." D.D.

Aesch Mezareph: Bedil, Tin; in natural science, this metal is not greatly used; for as it is derived by Separation, so its matter remains separate from the universal medicine.

Amongst the planets Zedek [צדק = 194 = Jupiter] is attributed to it; a white wandering planet, to which the gentiles applied an idolatrous name, mention where of is forbidden, see Exodus 22:12 and a greater extirpation is promised, Hosea, 2:17, and Zechariah, 13:2.

Amongst the beast, no allegory is better applied to this metal than that because of its crackling, it should be called 'Chazir Mijaar [חזיר מיער], a boar out the wood Psalm 80:14, whose number is 545 which is not only 5 x 109, but in its lesser number shows a quinary, as the Name Zedek 194; which Number being added, make 14: and they make the Number 5, which twice taken is 10, the lesser number of the word *Bedil*, by the two figures of 46 being added together. But 5 x 10 shows the fifty gates of Binah[1], and the first letter of the Sephirah Netzach, which is the Sephirotic class to which this metal is referred.

In particular transformation, its sulphurous nature alone both not profit, but with other sulphurs, especially those of the Red [Mars and Venus] metals, it does reduce thick waters, dully terrificated into Gold; so also into Silver, if its nature be subtilized into a thin water by Quicksilver which (amalgam) amongst others is made well enough by Tin.

But its viscous and water nature may be meliorated into Gold, if it be only pulverized with the calx of Gold through all the degrees of fire, for ten days, and by degrees thrown upon flowing Gold, in the form of the little masses, which also I am taught is to be done with Silver. But no man is wise unless his master is experience. [Westcott, 1997, pp. 27-28]

[1] Westcott add the following footnote: The Fifty Gates of Binah or Understanding (see also Chapter III, paragraph 1) may be referred to the Decad of Potencies acting through the Five human senses, but the phrase has a more arcane meaning: the *Theosophical Glossary* says that 50 is a blind, and that the number is 49.

flos (Lt). flower; suggesting the "rose" symbolism and relates particularly to the microcosm. It has been linked with the Great magical Agent, by Eliphas Levi, who terms it also "Azoth, ether, magnetic fluid, soul of the earth, Lucifer, etc.." One of the faces of the philosophical stone bears its name, along with Adam, Eve, and Azoth. see 683, 36, 252, 315, 154, 224, 314, 29.

Jove or *Iove* (Lt). Jove; the Latin Jupiter, the sky-god, connected with beneficence. King and Father of the Gods. Same as the Greek Zeus.

omnia (Lt). All, everything; symbolizes the universe. (The radius which determines the size of a circle is 23 [חיה], Chaiah, the Life-force seated in Chokmah.) The "field" or "vineyard" of the universe is pervaded by Life, so that no portion of it may be regarded as a dead mechanism. see 506 Greek.

I.N.R.I. Initials of inscription on the cross of Jesus that Pilate wrote. It has many esoteric meanings.

Blavatsky Quotes a Rosicrucian motto: "Igne Natura Renovatur Intergra which the alchemist interpret as Nature renovated by fire, or matter by Spirit." see 270, 1223.

Ordo (Lt) Order. Part of the motto: "A new order of the ages" on the Great Seal of the U.S. see 80, 94, 126, 220, 370 (Lt), 240.

Igneo (Lt). igneous, fiery; of fire. Relates to the "Triangle of Fire." see 134, 88 (Lt).

47 (prime)

I. The yoni as dynamic, prehensile, spasmodic, etc. *Espirit de travail*. [Crowley, 1977, p. xxv].

ביד אל   "by the hand of God." Job 27:11.

יזל   13th Shem ha-Mephorash, short form. see 78 & Appendix 10.

מבה   14th & 55th Shem ha-Mephorash, short form. see 78, 62 & Appendix 10.

אומ   30th Shem ha-Mephorash, short form. see 47 & Appendix 10.

במה   high place, mountain, altar; non-Jewish place of worship. The Lord ascertains who is ready to be "snatched up" by the spirit to "high places".

בביה   a weeping. Part of the divine inebriation.

אויל   fool. The divinely inspired.

אליו   unto, to towards, into, at, by. In Exodus 19:3: "And Moses went unto God, and the Lord called unto him out of the mountain, saying, thus shalt thou say to the House of Jacob, and tell the Children of Israel."

יאל   Angel ruling Virgo, connected with alchemical distillation, and with "the hand." Godwin spelling is ויאל and says it rules the 6th Astrological House [ruled by Virgo].

יואל   Joel. "Jah is God," one of the minor prophets. See 46 and Joel 1:1.

חלט   to snatch up, decide; definitely; to ascertain; to knead with hot water. *Khaylet* as a noun: secretion, humor.

rosa (Lt). Rose A symbol of aspiration, of desire and of the Human soul. The white rose represents purified desire; the red completion of the Great Work through action. see 75, 87, 194, 246 (Lt); 294 (Greek).

forma (Lt). Form Represents the embodiment of life as the "golden rose." see 101 (Lt)

vita (Lt). life. Desire for more Life involves the transmutation of the rose, and the discovery of the true "Gold." In he Rosicrucian allegory, this was the title of a Book, found in the vault and said to have been written by Brother CR, from whence the "relation" in the *Fama* was taken. see 18, 132, 106 (Lt).

aureae (Lt). Of the Golden. Connect with the sun or alchemical gold. Part of the Title, "Brother of the Golden Cross." Golden refers to Tiphareth, seat of the Higher Self in the heart and center of the "Rose." In the microcosm, the liquid or "potable Gold" is the solar Yod-force assimilated from food by the use of Mercury in Virgo. see 701 (Lt), 193, 79.

48

I. (3 x 2⁴)

II. 12x4: The multiplication of the powers of the 4 elements by the 12 signs of the zodiac.

III. מ-ה The "length" of the Pillar of Severity on the Tree of Life.

כוכב   a star or planet. Specifically Mercury. Related to the 8th Sephirah, the sphere of Mercury, and to Key 17 (The Star). כו = 26 = יהוה, Tetragrammaton and כב = 22 = number of letters of the Hebrew Alphabet. see 15, 453, 98, 343, 721 and Numbers 24:17.

With respect of quicksilver or Mercury, *Aesch Mezareph*: And so Kokab[1], a star, is the name of the planet Mercury, under whose government this matter is, with the whole word is 49; which same is the number of El-Chai.

But remember that all quicksilver doth not conduce to his work, because the sorts of it differ even as Flax from Help or Silk, and you would work on Hemp to no purpose, to make it receive the Tenuity and splendor of fine Flax. [Westcott, 1997, p. 38]

[1] Kokab is 48 and add one for the name we get 49

"The word כוכב, vulgarly translated star, is composed of the root כו, which is related to every idea of strength and of virtue, physically as will as morally, and of the mysterious root אוֹב which develops the idea of the fecundation of the universe. Thus according to the figurative and hieroglyphic sense, the word כּוֹכב signifies not only star, but the virtual and fecundating force of the universe. Therein can be found the germ of many ancient ideas, where relative to astrological science, concerning which it is known that the Egyptians thought highly, or whether relative to the Hermetic science. [d'Olivet, 1976, pp. 47-48.] Note that Chokmah is the sphere of the zodiac or stars is the center also of חיה Chaiah, the Life-force. see 73, 23.

גדולה   Gedulah. greatness, majesty, magnificence, a name for Chesed (72). From a root גדל, gadal, meaning: to twist, and therefore connected with the idea of spiral motion. see 37, 43, 440.

חיל   a women, force, power, strength, efficiency; wealth, vigor, health. The word is derived from a root, spelled the same way, meaning "to whirl, to twist." A reference to the spiral motion which is characteristic of the influence descending from Kether, where the whirlings begin, into all the paths of wisdom below the Crown.

חם Ham. warmth, heat, fire, blackness. As a proper noun חם is the son of Noah [5:32, 6:10] see 936, 993, 190.

"Ham... this name is on the whole, the opposite of that of *Shem*. The sign ה which constitutes it, recalls al ideas of effort, of obstacle, or fatigue of travail. The root which result from its union with the sign of exterior action, employed as collective, presents a bending, a dejection, a thing which inclines toward the lower parts: it is the heat which follows a sharp compression: it is the hidden fire of nature: it is the warmth which accompanies the rays of the sun; it is the dark color, the blackness, which results from their action; it is finally, in the broadest sense, *the sun* itself considered as the cause of heat and of torrefaction.

When the name of *Ham* is presented alone and in an absolute sense, it can be taken in a good sense, since it expresses the effect of the sun upon inferior bodies; but if one only sees in it the opposite of *Shem*, it offers only sinister ideas. If

Shem is the sublime, the superior, *Ham* is the abased, the inferior; so if the former is the radiant, the exalted, the infinite, the latter is the obscure, the bending, the limited, etc." [d'Olivet, 1976, pp. 170-171.]

With different pointing: חם Khem. The Egyptians' own name for their country. Through Egyptians influence of the Greeks, the root of our words alchemy and chemistry.

מח clapping, applause, fullness of the body; good humor.

"Onomatopoeic root which depicts the noise that is made in clapping the hands: figuratively, action of applauding; state of being joyous, of having good appearance. *Clapping, applause, fullness of the body; good humor.*

מח The sign of exterior and passive action united to that of elementary labor, or to the root אח, symbol of all equality, constitutes a root to which are attached the ideas of abolition, desuetude; of ravage carried on by time, by the action of the elements, or by man; thence מחה action of *effacing, depriving, taking away, destroying*; of *razing a city*, an edifice; of *washing, cleansing*, etc. [d'Olivet, 1976, pp. 388-389.]

יובל stream, river; trumpet blast (from the sound coming from a stream). Jubal, the name of the son of Lamech (traditional founder of Free Masonry). See Genesis 4:21.

יובל jubile. ram; ram's horn, inventor of musical instruments.

חיל army, rampart; wall.

מאהב Love.

מאז of old. In Proverbs 8:22: "The Lord possessed me in the beginning of his way before his works *of old*." see 3, 12, 21, 30, 39, 57.

ומב 61st Shem ha-Mephorash, short form. see 79 & Appendix 10.

ודואל "God Great and Lofty" The 49th Shem ha-Mephorash. Psalm 145:3: "Great is the Lord and most worthy of praise; his greatness no one can fathom." One should recite the whole Psalm to over come chagrin and when has a contrary spirit. Exacts one toward God, to bless and glorify, when one is touched with admiration. Rules great personages and all who elevate and distinguish themselves by their talents and virtues. Person born: sensible and generous soul: will be esteemed by all good people, will distinguish himself in literature, jurisprudence and diplomacy. Associated with the 1st quinance of Aries; Angel by day of the 2 of Wands. see 965, & Appendix 10.

arbor (Lt). a tree. A word which recurs continually in Qabalistic, alchemical and Rosicrucian texts.

fons (Lt). fountain, spring, source, origin, cause. Literally, a pouring forth. Compare with the doctrine that the 4th Sephirah is the source of supply.

rota (Lt). a wheel. Used in the *Fama Fraternitatis* to designate one of the most valuable Rosicrucian "books." Origin of the artificial noun, TAROT. Key 10 represents the whirling force descending from Chesed.

Tora (Lt). the Torah or the law; the scroll held by the High Priestess in Key 2. see 20.

orat (Lt). speaks. Part of the Latin phrase "The wheel of Tarot speaks the Law of Hathor." the speech is that of intuitive knowledge.
Ator (Lt). Hathor; The Egyptian cow-goddess, who symbolized mother nature.

Nihil (Lt). Nothing. A reference to the No-thing or *Ain*, the 1st veil of the absolute. see 61, 538, 560, 31.

Decus (Lt). Ornament, splendor, glory, honor, dignity. Hod in Latin. Elohim Sabaoth. see 15.

49

I. (7 x 7) or 7^2 Number of the magic square of Venus.

מטה The rod of Aaron. Related to the magical Wand. ט: The Hanged Man, or reversal. מ: the

symbol of Fohat (Kundalini) and its direction (strength). see 404, 43, 470, 175, 1225.

דמה her blood. With different pointing: *dawmaw*. meditated. see 54, and Genesis 1:26.

אל-חי El Chai. The Living God. Divine name of Yesod, Sphere of the Moon. see 363, 80.

הגאל Hagiel. Intelligence of Venus. Intelligence of Venus, when Venus enters the signs of Taurus and Libra [Dictionary of Angels p.132]. This intimates that desire is essential to alchemical congelation and sublimation. see 331, 501.

מואב Moab, Moav. The son of Lot and The ancient land of the Dead Sea named after him. Inman says the word means: 'the seed of the father.' [Inman, 1942, Vol. II p. 816.] See Genesis 29:37.

חמא Chema, Haymah. warmth, heat; fury; fever. To maintain a steady and even heat in the anthanor is a prerequisite of the Great Work. Derived from *khem* (48). With different pointing: hot season. [The Egyptian Khem, root of alchemy, the "Egyptian Art."

מוג solve, dissolve; to melt. One of the two alchemical maxims. also: to cause to melt, melted, soft. see 64 (Lt), 103.

ילדא she bore.

לידה lidah. A bring forth, birth, nativity [Crowley, 1977, p. 7]. This word does not occur in scripture on in the Hebrew Lexicon.

גויל parchment. This suggest the blank page where the "new name" is written, and the "rough ashlar" which is shaped into the "Stone of the Wise."

גולחב Qlippoth of Geburah called "the Arsonist". Suggest imbalance of the Mars force.

חולה a sick person, patient. The process of transmutation is like coming from sickness into full health.

Lux (Lt). Light. The source of all manifested life. Light, is the substance of all material forms. It penetrates every solid thing and overcomes the subtle. As Roman numerals it is written L.V.X. see 116, 364, 207, 73, 122 (Lt), 620, 397.

niger (Lt). Black. the absence of Light. Color of the Black Pillar Boaz. Also refers to the Black Raven, an alchemical symbol of the 1st matter, or unmanifested life. see 126, 87 (Lt), 998.

rebis (Lt). two-thing. Corinne Heline Writes: "In this alchemical process, the Gold (Spirit) which is God, and the base metal which is man have been conjoined and man becomes the Living Stone. The Keystone of the Arch in Masonic phraseology. The androgyne consciousness is represented by the Hermetic cypher REBIS, meaning the two things. The alchemical double Mercury bears the same significance. Albert Pike employs the grand climax of Masonic initiations. He writes: For as birth, life, exaction, suffering in fire and death were, as it were, ascribed to the philosopher's stone in black and gloomy colors, and finally resurrection and life in red and other beautiful colors, so the terrestrial stone (man's body) may be compared with the celestial stone (the Body of Christ)." [Occult Anatomy and the Bible, XII, New Birth Through Regeneration, p. 37]

50

I. The five platonic solids are formed from 3 basic shapes, the triangle (pyramid, octahedron, and icoshedron), the square (cube) and the pentagon (dodecahedron). The triangle is a 3 sided figure, the cube 4, and the pentagon 5. The sum of the squares on the 3 sides of a 3-4-5 right triangle is fifty ($3^2 + 4^2 + 5^2 = 50$). Thus in the construction of the polyhedra we find the Egyptian triangle of Osiris (3), Isis (4) and Horus (5).

II. Note also that 50 is the number of faces of the 5 platonic solids and the number of their points (vertices).

III. The 50 "Gates of Understanding" attributed to Binah.

IV. Of the 50 gates Westcott in the *Aesch Mezareph* states in a foot note to Chapter 4: "The Fifty Gates of Binah or Understanding (see also Ch 3, para, 1) may be referred to the Decad of Potencies acting through the Five human senses,

but the phrase has a more arcane meaning: the *Theosophical Glossary* says that 50 is a blind, and that the number is 49."

V. 10 (Yod):Chokmah x 5 (Heh):Binah

VI. The number of years Sirus A & B take to orbit each other.

VII. The number of oarsman (Argonauts) in Jason's Ship the Argo.

VIII. The number of the companions of Gilgamesh.

IX. The number of heads of Cerberus (guardian of Hades, later myth stories reduce this to three).

X. The number of eyes of Argus, the monster sent by Hera to watch over Io.

ל/כ Kaph/Lamed, Jupiter (Kaph) in Libra (Lamed).

נ; ן Nun. A fish, to sprout, to grow. The powers of growth and transformation represented by Nun and Key 13. Asscoated with the sign of Scorpio and sexual energy and the 24th Path of the Imaginitive Intelligence.

I. As a proper name Nun means perpetuity, eternity, or everlastingness. Jesus is variation of Joshua, the successor of Moses, whose father was name Nun. Nun, as eternity, is associated with reproductive power. Thus the power of Jesus and Joshua is generation and regeneration. Recall that Jesus said that unless you are born again you cannot enter the kingdom of heaven.

II. Nun is associated with Scorpio, which governs the reproductive function. Through Scorpio's associating with the 8th house of the zodiac is attributed to death and inheritance (see Key 13). Inheritance implies something gained or transmitted from parents to children, and this is seen by the meaning to Nun, to sprout, to grow. All this implies that the secret to regeneration is the use of the sexual energy in a way other than procreation. see 1219, 407 (Greek) and Matthew 14:17, 15:34 for the parable of the loaves and fishes.

III. Rabbi Ginsburgh: "The bent over form of the Nun, 'the bent over faithful one,' indicates a sense of poverty and need to receive. This bent over form is the most fundamental (simple) "vessel" form amongst the letters of the alef-beit. In the form of the letter Teth, we envision a vessel filled by (pregnant with) "introverted" light, whereas Nun is a vessel alone." [The Alef-Beit,]

IV. Waite: "If you, my son, wish to prepare this precious Stone, you need not put yourself to any great expense.. you must diligently observe what I do, and remember the worlds of Aristotle (Meteror iii and iv) who says: "Study Nature, and careful peruse the book concerning Generation and Corruption [attributed to Key 13 and Nun]." [Waite, 1974, Vo. 1, p. 131] see 470.

VI. "This character as consonant, belongs to the nasal sound; as symbolic image it represents the son of man, every produced and particular being. As grammatical sign, it is that of individual and produced existence. When it is placed at the end of words it becomes the argumentative sign final ן, and gives to the being every extension of which it is individually susceptible. The hebraist grammarians in placing this character among the *heemanthes*, had certainly observed that it expressed, at the beginning of words, passive action, folded within itself, and when it appears at the end, unfoldment and augmentation..." [d'Olivet, 1976, pp. 394-395.]

אדמה red earth, soil, ground, land, territory. Corresponds to Terra Adamica (86) in Genesis 2:7.

יהוה אלהים The complete divine name of Binah formed the essence of the man [האדם-את, 451], from the dust עפר Aphar (350) of the ground [אדמה] Adamah. Adamah is the earth of Chesed, one of the 7 earths in the diagram of the 4 seas. see 291, 14, 365, 105, 432, 337

האדם ha-adam. Metathesis of Adam. Generic humanity. The Adam. Translated sometimes in Genesis 2 as "The Man" and sometimes by the proper noun Adam. What is indicated is that the Man and the "Ground " are identical in essence. [Genesis 2:25] see 610.

ים the sea; ocean; lake; large basin, reservoir, large river, west, western quarter. One of the many titles of Binah when the Mother is considered to be the great reservoir of substance from which forms are specialized. The "sea" is the radiant darkness of limitless light, the ocean of root-matter (Sanskrit: Mulaprakriti). The Mother (Binah) is the sea wherein swims the fish (Nun), and the fish and the sea are one. The fish and the son are also one. [Book of Tokens] see 52.

ה-זיאל The spirit of Saturn.

ה-הם the abundance.

המה To ferment.

גד גדול great fish. Jonah 1:17. When the great fish (Scorpio) swallowed the prophet Jonah (Dove, 71). The forces of Mars and Venus are conjoined. Note also that Ninevah, the capital of Assyria, where Jonah was sent, is spelled נינוה, so that it combines the letters נון Nun, and יה. [Book of Tokens, p.131] see 121.

חבלי pains and sorrows, throes of birth; suffering, damage, injury. For which the great fish is an emblem. All pain and sorrows are the portals through which man passes to the heart of the Great Mother. see חבל, 40. [Book of Tokens]

אטם to close, to contract, to shut up. Indicates the limiting activity of the specializing process. see 86, 158, 4, 14, 41, 72, 104.

לך to thee. "To thee, O Israel, is the opening and shutting of the Gates." [Book of Tokens]

מי what? which? After many questions the realization of one's immorality is attained. With different pointing: where? and how? Refers to the Gates of Understanding and to the square of the Pythagorean triangle (236). Who?; whoever, someone, anyone. In the prologue to the Zohar, מי is discussed in relation to the initial process of creation and is linked to the no-thing. "מי... is the living water, transmitting life." see 85, 64.

מי water. Singular form of the word usually rendered Mem. מים occurs only as a component of proper names in the Bible. Used also as a euphemism for semen virile, the actual substance which is secreted by organs under the rulership of Scorpio. see 64.

אִיזֶבֶל Izhebel, Jezebel. chaste [1 Kings 16:31]. Considered to mean "without cohabitation", implying virginity; Furst, on the other hand, considers that it is a contracted form of זבל-אבי, Abi-Zebel or "Father enthroned on high." Inman considers the name to mean "Baal is strong", Baal being the deity considered adulterous to Israel. To reach the "Father", one must practice virginity and practice reverence to the one true God of Israel. see 63 (Greek)

ייל 58th Shem ha-Mephorash, short form. see 81 & Appendix 10.

ילי 2nd Shem ha-Mephorash, short form. see 81 & Appendix 10.

אלדיה 10th Shem ha-Mephorash. "God the Propitious". Viroaso. March 29, June 9, August 19, October 31, January 11. 3:00-3:20." Psalm 33:22: Let your mercy and loving-kindness, O Lord, be upon us in proportion to our waiting and hoping for You (Amplified). For those involved in secret crimes, who fear to be discovered. Protects against pestilence, and the recovery from sickness. Person born: Enjoy health, esteemed by their acquaintances. Associated with the 4th quinance of Virgo; Angel by night of the 9 of Pentacles (Yesod of Assiah). see 965, & Appendix 10.

כל kole. all, whole, every. As the fish is hidden in the waters of the sea, so is the ALL shut up within the semblance of the many.

"This root expresses all ideas of apprehension, shock, capacity, relative assimilation, consummation, totalization, achievement, perfection.

That which is *integral, entire, absolute, perfect, total, universal*: that which *consumes, concludes, finishes, totalizes* a thing; that which renders it *complete, perfect, accomplished*; which *comprises, contains* it, in determining its *accomplishment*; the *universality* of things; their *assimilation, aggregation, perfection; the desire* of possessing, *possession; a prison: the consumption of foods*, their *assimilation* with the substance of the body, etc. The action of *totalizing, accomplishing comprising, universalizing, consummating*, etc." [d'Olivet, 1976, pp. 372-373.]

semen (Lt). seed. This designates the reproductive element in the human organism. In alchemical writings, semen has the same figurative meaning as in Virgil, who employed this word to represent the 4 elements as the ground, origin, or cause of all physical forms. see 64 (Lt).

Radix (Lt). root. The part of the plant which draws in nourishment. The plant is the human organism; the nourishment is the Life-power. see 137 (Lt).

Jeus. of Jesus. The seed of Jesus forms the root of the Christos. Part of a saying in the Rosicrucian Fama Fraternatas. "A seed planted in the breast of Jesus. Part of a second saying, which includes the words "in Jesus we die", also in the *Fama*. see 310, 95, 66, 99 (Lt), 683 (Lt).

regio (Lt). A direction, line; a boundary; country, territory, district, sphere, hence kingdom. see 496; 108 (Lt).

51

יהדאל 62nd Shem ha-Mephorash. "Yah is God"-Supreme Being. Oroasoer. May 20, July 31, October 11, December 22, March 4. 8:20-8:40 PM [Psalm 119:159] "Consider how I love thy precepts: quicken me, O Lord, according to thy loving-kindness" To gain wisdom. Rules philosophers, the illuminati and those who wish to retire from the world. Person born: Loves tranquility and solitude; fulfills exactly the duties of his estate, and is distinguished by this modesty and his virtues.

Associated with Angel the 2nd quinance [6E-10E] of Gemini; Angel by night of the 8 of Swords (see King of Solomon, figure 52).. This represents the influence of Hod, Sphere of Mercury, on Yetzirah, the formative world. see 20, 965, & Appendix 10.

אדום Edom. red; Land south east of Palestine; Name given to Israel (variant spelling, see 45, 342). [Isaiah 34:6] "The sword of the Lord is filled with blood, it is made fat with fatness, and with the blood of lambs and goats, with the fat of the kidneys of rams: for the Lord hath a sacrifice in Bozrah, and a great slaughter in the land of Idumea (Edom)." The kingdom of Edom is connected with the unbalanced force. The three letters אדם signify to stamp firmly, man, to be red. There is something mystical about red as a color. In Genesis 25:30: "And Esau said to Jacob, fed me, I beg you, with that same red pottage; for I am faint : Therefore was his name called Edom." see 611, 715.

I. "We therefore presume that Edom means 'the red one.' Furst tells us, s.v. Obed-edom [אדם עבד, 2 Samuel 6:10], that the red was a designation of Mars, like עשר, *esar*, amongst the Phoenicians, to who the ass was sacred (חמור, the red)… But, although "the red one" was a name of Mars, it had another meaning… We can readily understand a citizen of Gath bearing the name of Phallic origin; but we cannot understand how an Israelite, and of the priestly tribe, could bear such a cognomen, except on the supposition that the religion he professed involved, like that of the Gittite, the adoration of the male organ as an emblem of the Creator." [Inman, 1942, Vol. II p. 422.]

II. 513. BEHOLD! this have we learned in the "Book of Concealed Mystery": that the Ancient of the Ancient Ones before that he prepared His conformations[1] (*in the equilibrium and balance*) formed certain kings, collected certain kings, and gave due proportion unto kings; but they only subsisted (*for a time*) until he could expel them; and in that hath He concealed them.

514. This is intimated in those words, Gen. 36: 31: 'And these are the kings which have reigned in ADVM,[2] *Edom*.' In the land of Edom; that is, in the place wherein all judgments exist.

[1] As the Sephiroth proceed each from the preceding one in the series, it is evident that before the counterbalancing Sephira is formed, the force in the preceding Sephira is unbalanced; e.g., the fourth Sephira is Gedulah or Chesed, Mercy; and the fifth Sephira is Geburah or Pachad, Sternness; therefore, till Geburah appears, Gedulah is unbalanced, and this condition is the reign of one of the edomit Kings; but when Geburah appears, his reign is over.

[2] ADVM = 1+4+6+40 = NA = Failure. AN = also 51, and means pain. *Ergo*, also unbalanced force is the source alike of failure and of pain. [Mathers, 1993, p. 174]

III. In the symbolic representation of the Fall the heads of the Dragon bear the names of the eight Edomite Kings, and their horns the names of the eleven dukes: 'And because in Daath was the utmost rise of the Great Serpent of Evil; therefore there is as it were another Sephira, making eight heads according to the number of the eight kings; and for *the Infernal and Averse Sephiroth* eleven instead of ten, according to the number of the eleven dukes of Edom. The Hebrew version of *Tum* or *Atum*, the red or setting sun symbolic of the phallic force illuminating the underworld (subconsciousness), Amenta. The 11 Dukes of Edom refer to the reflections of the cosmic power-zones, including Daath, in the subconsciousness of humanity. [Grant, 1994, pp. 62-63, 263.] See Esau (376).

אן On. an Egyptian god (Genesis 41:45). City of Heliopolis in Egypt, or Beth-Shemesh, the House of the Sun. see 581, 1052, 120 (variant spelling), 57, 707, 701.

"An onomatopoetic root which depicts the agonies of the soul, pain, sorrow, annihilate. און. Every idea of *pain, sorrow, trouble, calamity*. אן. The signs which this root are those of power and of individual existence. The determine together the seity, sameness, selfsameness, or *the me* of the being, and limit the extent of its circumscription.

אן in a broader sense, it is the *sphere of moral activity*, in a restricted sense, it is *the body* of the being. One says in Hebrew, אני *I*; as if one said *my sameness*, that which constitutes the sum of my faculties, *my circumscription*." [d'Olivet, 1976, pp. 295-296.]

נא a primative particle of incitement and entreaty, which may usually be rendered *I pray, now* or *then*. Also tough or uncooked flesh, *raw*. [Strong's Bible Dictionary]

"*No*. Every idea of youth, newness; every idea of freshness, grace, beauty, every idea springing from that which is formed of a new production, of a being young and graceful.

נאה That which is *beautiful, lovable, new, young, fresh*; which is not worn out, fatigued, peevish; but, on the contrary, that which is *new, tender, pretty, comely*." [d'Olivet, 1976, p. 395.]

אים Aim. Goetic Demon #23 by day of the 2nd decanate of Scorpio. In the Tarot Minor Arcana this decanate is assigned to the 6 of Cups. This represent Tiphareth, the central Ego, or sphere of the Sun, in Briah, the place of mental images and creative thinking.

Goetia: "He is a great strong duke. He appears in the from of a very handsome man in body, but with three hears; the first, like a serpent, the second like a man having two stars on his forehead, the third like a Calf. He rides on a Viper, carrying a firebrand in his hand, wherewith he sets cities, castles, and great places, on fire. He makes thee witty in all manner of ways, and gives true answers unto private matters. He governs 26 Legions of Inferior Spirits." [Mathers, 1995, p. 38]

אכל ate, devoured. [Crowley, 1977, p. 8]

lapis (Lt). stone. The mystical stone of the Philosophers. see 53, 104, 126, 216.

Zion (Lt). Refers to the adytum the aspirant builds within the brain. see 216.

52

I. 52 weeks in a year. The path of Gimel is 52 units long (joining Kether to Tiphareth) and is the diameter of the Creative World of Briah and a symbol of what determines the limits of creative activity.

אימא Aima. the Bright Supernal Mother, fertilized into productivity by the influx of the life-force from Chokmah through the path of Daleth. Title of Binah. The Empress, and the queens of the minor trump. The "Mysterious Power" of which Krishna declares: "My Maya is the great womb into which I cast the seed: from this is the birth of all creatures." see 67.

אבא ואמא Father and Mother. Qabalists designate the union of Wisdom and Understanding.

בן Ben. "Son". Special designation of Tiphareth. Ben is the name of the "secret nature" of Assiah, the Physical World. see 45, 80, 311, 1081.

I. אימא, and יוד הה וו הה, or יהוה spelt in full, with the names of the four letters. This is the spelling of the Tetragrammaton is the world of Assiah or physical plane (see Appendix 7). Note that 26 is 1 + 6 + 9 + 10. These are the numbers of the Middle Pillar on the Tree of Life. See C.13

The central Sephirah is Beauty, called בן, the Son. Note that this is 52, or 4 x 13 (the number of unity and love). See **13**

II. *Ben* in the Tarot is the garden of the magician; and the soil of the garden is identical with אבן, the Stone. The stone and the garden are really *Aima* אימא, the mother. Note that *Aima* and *Ben* have the same number. *Binah*, בינה, which is *Aima*, are conjoined the letters בן, and the sum of these (*Ben* and *Aima*) is 14. Key 15 is Temperance, the Holy Guardian Angel and number of the Father. In the Tarot *Ben* is 1 (Beth) and 13 (Nun), whose sum is 14. Note also that Key 14 is the Intelligence of Probation. Nothing can be known until it is tried, and in union, the Holy Guardian Angel effects that union.

All this hangs on the recognition of the fact, that ALL human beings personal activities (even the most menial and debase) is work of what is pictured as Key 14. Every circumstance of any man's life is a particular dealing of God with his soul. The Actor is always superpersonal. For humanity of earth, the Actor is *Ben,* so it is the personal you that watches, yet what of reality has that, apart from בן." see 53, 124 & C.17.

בהמה animal, beast. Applies to the larger quadrupeds. Points to Binah as the source of the organic life of the various forms of animal creation below the human level. From these lower forms the human body has been evolved.

בבל from all, among all, in all things [Genesis 24:1]. The Binah clause of The Pattern on the Trestleboard begins, "Filled with Understanding.." Zohar says בך in בבך is the designation of the "River of the Waters of which never fail."

חמד something desirable, object of delight, take pleasure in. see Song of Solomon 2:3.

יוד הה וו הה Letter name of יהוה spelt in full. The divine name of the Father. see 26, 104 and Appendix 4.

זמה thought, plan, purpose, imagination, meditation; evil device; wickedness, idolatry, incest, shameful seed. In some biblical passages this noun has a good sense and in others a bad one. In itself it is neutral. "Bad" and "good" have to do with the objectives of planning and thinking. They cannot be applied to the thought-force itself. This word is probably the same as the first two words of the mysterious words mentioned by Jesus [Pistis Sophia, Chap. 10] "Zamma Zamma Ozza Rachama Ozai." Probably a transliteration of זמה זמה עזא רחמה עזיה, Thought, thought, the power of the womb (or matrix) of the strength of Yah." The "Strength of Jah" (עזיה) is the Life-force seated in Chokmah. The womb of that power is Binah, the Great Mother. In Binah, the Life-force is specialized as the though-force active in Neshamah (395).

כלב caleb. Dog. Proper name of Caleb, companion of Joshua. Stands for faithfulness (Joshua 14:6). Also forcible [Deuteronomy 1:36] כל (50) is *kole*, the All. לב (32) is *laib*, the Heart. A sign of understanding, connected also with Thoth (Dog-headed God) of Egypt, the Mercury (Kokab) in Hod, and the 12th Path of the letter Beth. The self-conscious mind of man has always been the herald of the Gods because it is the focal point or center for the ALL. see 145, 197, 126 The little dog companion of the fool, who is a reflexion of Jeheshua, or Christ (Joshua).

I. Numbers 13.6: from the tribe of Judah (יהודה), Caleb son of Jephunneh (יפנה145).

II. In the book of Numbers, Moses sent spies to the land of Canaan (כנען, 190). Among these spies was Caleb. Because of his good report Joshua advanced, when other people tried to persuade him not to.

Caleb signifies dog, a name of disrepute in Israel. Yet here is a treasure of wisdom that is part of the lore that Moses was instructed in as a youth in Egypt. For the story of Caleb is a figure, and Caleb the dog stands for faithfulness, but there are deeper things than this. The number of *caleb* is 52 and is a veil for אימא (*Aima*). Fifty-two is בן (Ben), and אבא ואמא *aba ve-ama*, or Father and Mother. This represents the conjoining of Chokmah with Binah. The Path of this conjunction of Father and Mother is the letter Daleth and the Path of the Luminous Intelligence which joins Chokmah to Binah.

The first two letters of Caleb is כל, which spell *kal*, the ALL. And the last two לב spell *laib*, the Heart. Kaph and Lamed add to 50, and these are the gates of Binah, and Lamed and Beth are 32, and these are the Paths of Wisdom. In Caleb is concealed the secret of the ALL, which is a Secret of the Heart. The heart of Adam Quadman, Tiphareth the Son, into which pour all the streams of *Mezla* from above. And this same *Mezla* descends to the Paths below it through the Tiphareth, the Separative Intelligence or Mediating Influence. So Caleb is a sign of understanding, for his name as we have said, is of like number with *Aima*.

The God Thoth is represented as a dog-headed man. It is said that Thoth is Kokab, whom the 'oppressors' called Mercurious. Kokab has its sphere in Hod, and its Path is the letter Beth. Thus the Intelligence of Transparency is figured by Caleb and with this is creation begun. Because the letter Beth is first letter in the word 'in-beginning (בראשית) he-created (ברא).'

The only dog in the Tarot is shown in direct association with man on Key 0. It is the pet and companion of the Fool. He is the letter Beth that follows after Aleph, just as the dog follows the Fool.

Caleb was the son of Jephunnah (יפנה). Note these 4 letters. The first is Yod, phallic, and a symbol of Chokmah and Yesod. The second is Peh, the letter of Mars; the third is Nun, the letter of Scorpio, and the last is Heh, the letter of Aries and relates to vision. Remember that Caleb was a spy, and that the Text plainly refers to the perfection of his masculine vigor. The number of his years is 85, which is the number of the letter name פה, Peh. This is divided into two parts; 40, his age when he served as a spy (Mem, meaning waters, 40); and 45, which elapsed thereafter. Fourty-five is a symbol of אדם, Adam. That is, the dog became a completed man, and this involves the use and direction of the Mars force in accordance with a reversal of ordinary procedure, for the other spies reported unfavorably and caused the people's hearts to melt. But Caleb at 40 stands for the reversal, symbolized by the Hanged Man (associated with the letter Mem).

Caleb was a Kennizite, an outsider by birth, who was adopted into Israel,. But he received his proper reward. This passage is an allegory relating to the fixation of Mercury of the alchemist. That is, the highest use of self-consciousness in a creative function, reversing customary attitudes of mind and the activities they prompt, and leading ultimately to the overthrow of error.

כבל Fetters, chain, as anchor chain, submarine cable [Psalm 105:18, 148:8]. As a verb: to chain and tie. Creative imagination is the tie that binds, as well as the fetters that chain.

יבם Husband's brother; Brother-in-Law. May apply to Ben בן, the Son. (The Husband is אב, the Father). With different pointing: *Yedem*, the 70th Shem ha-Mephorash, short form. see 67 & Appendix 10.

בים Bim. Goetic demon #26 by day of the 2nd decanate of Sagittarius. Attributed, in the Tarot minor arcana, to the 9 of Wands. These represents Yesod, the pattern world of subconsciousness, in Atziluth, the archetypal plane of ideas, or the principles behind the reproductive power of the One Self.

Goetia: "He is strong, great and mighty duke. He appears in the form of a Dragon with three heads, one like a dog, gryphon, and man. He speaks with a high and comely voice. he changes the place of the dead, and causes the spirits which be under him to gather together upon your sepulchers. He gives riches unto a man, and makes him wise and eloquent. He gives true answers unto demands. And he governs 30 Legions of Spirits." [Mathers, 1995, p. 39]

לאויה 11th and 17th Shem ha-Mephorash. As 11th Shem ha-Mephorash "God is to be Exalted" 51E-56E. Ronbomare-Saturn. March 30, June 10, August 20, November 1, January 12. 3:40-4:00 AM. [Psalm 18:47] For obtaining victory. Rules renown, influence, through great personages, savants and all who win celebrity by their talents. Associated with the 5th quinance of Virgo; Angel by day of the 10 of Pentacles. see 965 & Appendix 10.

As 17th Shem ha-Mephorash 81E -85E PHUOR-Sun. April 5, June 16, August 27, November 7, January 18. Order of Thrones 5:00 -5:20 AM. [Psalm 8:2] Against torments of spirits of sorrows and for good repose at night. Rules high sciences, literature and philosophy. Associated with the 5th quinance of Libra; Angel by day of the 4 of Swords.

לכב 31st Shem ha-Mephorash, short form. see 83 & Appendix 10.

נב A priestly city in Benjamin [162]. see 1 Samuel 21:1.

"The mysterious root אוב being united by contraction to the sign of produced existence; gives rise to a new root, whence emanate all ideas of divine inspiration, theophany, prophecy; and in consequence, that of exaltation, ecstasy, rapture, perturbation, religious horror.

נוב Action of *speaking* by inspiration; *producing* exteriorly the spirit with which one is filled: in a literal and restricted sense, *divulgation, fructification, germination*. In this last sense, it is the root אב, which is united simply to the sign נ employed as initial adjunction." [d'Olivet, 1976, p. 396.]

מגוג Magog; the second son of Japeth [Genesis 10:2] According to d'Olivet: "elastic stretching power" for extended explanation see Gog and Magog, (70).

יהואל Yahoel; angle of Kether of Binah (Ace of Cups) and Yesod of Binah (Nine of Cups) [Crowley, 1977, p. 8]. "Yaho, Jehoel, Jaoel… an angle equated with Metatron (Yohoel is, in fact, the 1st of Metatron's many names. He taught Abraham the Torah and was the patriarch guide on earth as well as in paradise. …in the Apocalypse of Abraham, another psenoemgraphic work, Yahoel says to Abraham," "I am called Yohoel… a power by virtue of the ineffable name dwelling in me. As Jehoer, he is the heavenly choirmaster, or one of them." [Davidson, 1971, pp. 317-318.]

אביטל "Father of Dew", i.e. fresh. The supernal "dew" is a product of the union of Chokmah and Binah.

gratia (Lt). agreeableness, esteem, favor, loveliness, grace. This is the word used in the Latin version of the angel's words to Mary (Luke 1:28), "*Ave, gratia plena; Dominus tecum; benedicta tu in mulieribus*", literally, "Hail, full of grace; the Lord is with thee; blessed art thou among women." Here is a key to much of the esoteric doctrine of the Gospels.

sancta (Lt). (fem.) sacred, pure, holy. Directly connected with Binah, since the latter is named "Sanctifying Intelligence."

Humana (Lt). Human.

rosea (Lt). "of the rose."

αιμα hiama (Gr). Blood. In its plural, streams of blood. Its secondary relationship is blood-relationship, kin. It is the substance by means of which the radiant LVX energy of Life is specialized within the physical body. In alchemical doctrines of the Great Work as the means through which states of Higher consciousness are experienced. We are all brothers and sisters in LVX. The letters are the Greek equivalents of those which spells Aima.

Μαια Maia (Gr). The mother of Hermes. Also the name of Gautama, the Buddha. Maya is likewise the "Mysterious power" of which Krishna declares: My Maya is the great womb into which I cast the Seed: from this is the Birth of all creatures."

κακια kakia (Gr). Badness; wickedness, vice, hence evil. Septuagint translation of רע [270] in Isaiah 45:7: "I form the light and create darkness; I make peace and create evil; I the Lord do all these things. see 270, 1977.

53 (prime)

I. Number of degrees in the angle formed by lines constituting the vertical line and hypotenuse of a Pythagorean triangle. Therefore the number 53 defines the union of the Son, Horus, with the Father, Osiris.

II. The yoni as an instrument of pleasure. [Crowley, 1977, p. xxv].

הָ-גְדוּלָה The Majesty, the magnificence. Alternate name of Chesed prefixed by a definite article. In 1 Chronicles 29:11 translates it as "Greatness," and includes the names of Geburah, Tiphareth, Netzach and Hod. It is one of the oldest references to the Tree of Life. [In Chronicles 29:11 the Vav is omitted, giving a short spelling of the word or 47]. see 48, 1389, see 360 ("His Great Fire").

חֵמָה Sun (poetical). The "secret fire" of the alchemist, the radiant energy of the Sun. Figuratively poison due to its inflaming effect. Also alchemical Gold, whose center is Tiphareth, the heart center. It is the "secret fire" of alchemy, the radiant energy of the sun and the quintessence, the substance of all things. Literally heat, also fever; rage; to be hot, to glow, excitement through wine. Heat, anger, burning anger, wrath, fury in Genesis 27:44. With different pointing: khaemaw. (fem noun) to bind or join; to unite, to hold; to enclose, to surround with a wall (see Key 19). Figuratively, to be allied in affinity, to fasten. See חָם, Ham, and שֶׁמֶשׁ.

יוד-הא-וו-הי. Special spelling of יהוה. Since it has the same value as *Khammaw*, it designates the heat and fire which descends through the Tree of Life on the side of Geburah.

גַן Gan. garden, wall enclosure, a placed hedged or walled around, hence an enclosure, mystically the Garden of Eden, perfected state of being which the state of conscious identification of the EGO with the cosmic or Universal Self. In Genesis 3:24 it is Garden of Eden גַן עֵדֶן; in Genesis 13:10: Garden of Tetragrammaton יהוה גַן in Ezekiel 28:13: Garden of Elohim אלהים גַן. see 124, 177.

I. "גַן The organic sign united by contraction to the root אָ or אוֹן, forms a root from which come all ideas of circuit, closure, protective walls, sphere, organic self-sameness.

That which *encloses, surrounds,* or *covers* all parts; that which forms *the enclosure* of a thing;

limits this thing and *protects it*; in the same fashion that a sheath encloses, limits and protect its blade.

The Arabic in general, everything which covers or which surrounds another; it is, in particular, a protecting *shade, a darkness*, as much physically as morally; *a tomb.* As a verb, this word expresses the action of enveloping with darkness, making night, obscuring the mind, rendering foolish, covering with a veil, enclosing with walls, etc. In the ancient idiom has a signified *a demon, a devil, a dragon; a shield; bewilderment* of mind; *an embryo* enveloped in the womb on its mother; and every kind of *armor*; etc. In the modern idiom, this word is restricted to signify *an enclosure, a garden.*" [d'Olivet, 1976, pp. 315-316.]

II. The Garden, or Paradise, is another term expressive of the whole Sephirotic system in Atziloth, the archetypal world. [Mathers, 1993, p. 67]

בטחו ביהוה Trust in the Lord. [Isaiah 26:4] The only way to return to the Garden of Eden and sit upon the "Stone", of Majesty.

אבן ehben. "stone," rock, a weight. From a root meaning: to build. Conjunction of Father and Son. The state of conscious identification of the EGO with the cosmic, or universal SELF. Also known as the Philosopher's stone, the "third eye," the Sanctum sanctorum (Holy of Holies) or pineal gland. The organ of true spiritual vision which enables one to see beyond the limits of the physical plane, and perceive man's perfect union with his divine source. The Stone is identified with the secret fire of alchemy and with the quintessence (spirit). The alchemical Fire is the radiant energy of the sun. With different vowel points: oven, fossil. see 73, 444, 54 (Lt). [Hebrew Lexicon], 532.

I. The stone is the garden, and the garden is the place of delight. That is, אבן (ehben) is גַן (gan), and *gan* is עֵדֶן (Eden). The stone is the union of the Son with the Father, and since *ehben* and *gan* are both 53, the stone is the stone of Eden. The stone and the garden are one, and the stone is the union of Chokmah (אב) and Tiphareth (גַן), so also is the garden that same union; and from union comes delight. There is never delight in separation. Only when Father and Son are conjoined is there delight.

II. Note the double veil. בן (Ben) and אימא (Aima) are both 52, the conjunction of אב (Ab) and בן (Ben) implies the conjunction of *Ab* and *Aima*. *Ben* and *Aima* are identical in numeration, but either *Ab* and *Ben* or *Ab* and *Aima* may be in the perfect union intimated by אבן.

III. This union is גן, Gimel is the Uniting Intelligence, and נ is the Imaginative Intelligence. Gimel (ג) unites Kether to Tiphareth, and נ unites Tiphareth to Netzach. ג is the Moon. נ is Mars in Scorpio. Key 2 (Gimel) and Key 13 (Nun) add to 15, which is Key 15, the Renewing Intelligence that links Tiphareth to Hod. The Path of Nun (נ) links the sphere of the Sun to the sphere of Venus. Thus in *gan* the whirling motion of Kether, descending to the sphere of the Sun, and projecting itself into the sphere of Venus. Venus is The Empress (Key 4), this is the Garden of the Magician. And the soil in the garden is אבן, the stone. The stone and the garden are *Aima* the mother, and אימא and בן are one in numeration. see 52, 124 and **17**.

In *Fama* the memorial tablet was faseten to a stone with a nail (Vav).When the table was removed the stone came with it. This is a verbal symbol that intuition (Vav) follows right recollection (ehben). What we recall is who we are, at the truth we discover is the stone of the wise. That is, the Father (Ab) and the Son (Ben) are one. This truth is brought forth by intuition, the hidden door (0 2ΛΔ∀ ∀<γT(μγ<0, the open door, see 1480) is seen.

אבים Father of the sea. personal noun. Spirit-fire (Father) involving itself in manifestation (the sea). *Ab* אב is Chokmah, the cosmic father; ים yawm is the sea, a title of Binah, the cosmic mother. Here a union of the two is implied. The path that connects them is Daleth, or creative imagination through acts of desire. It is spirit-fire (father) involving itself in manifestation (the sea).

טחול tekhol. the milt or spleen. Associated with Mars is some versions of the Book of Formation. Assigned to the "seed-making" power."

הזיאל Haziel. 9th Shem ha-Mephorash. "God of Mercy." One born under influence: Mercy of God, friendship and favor of the great, execution of a promise made. Governs: Good faith and reconciliation. Positive Influence: sincere in promises, will easily extend pardon. Negative influence: Hate, hypocrisy. Angle of the 2nd decanate (and 3rd quinace) of Virgo attributed to the 9 of Disks. see Appendix 10.

מאהבה Lover. From מאהב, Love.

אבן navah. to speak under divine influence, to prophecy, to inspire, endow with prophetic gift.

מגדו "Place of Troops". An ancient Canaanite stronghold, near which was fought the battle of Armageddon, in with the fortress of light defeat those of darkness in the last great battle. In Zechariah 12:11: "In that day shall there be a great mourning in Jerusalem, as the mourning of Hadadrimmon in the valley of Megiddo." see 958, 1008 (Greek).

ηλε. hyle (Gr). Wood. The gnostic name for the astral light. Wood is an organic substance which absorbs personal emanations of the astral light.

ακακια. acacia (Gr). Innocence; without guile, harmlessness. Wood used to build the Temple of Solomon. Symbol of immorality and initiation. Tree (in Masonic symbols). Makey writes: "The spring of Acacia... presents itself as a symbol of the immorality of the soul being intended to remind... by its evergreen and unchanging nature of that better and spiritual part within us, which as an emanation from the Grand Architect of the Universe, can never die. And as this is the most ordinary, the most generally accepted signification, so also is it the most important... Secondly, then the Acacia [Akakia] is a symbol of innocence. The symbolism here is of a peculiar and unusual character, depending not on any real analogy in the form or use of the symbol to the idea symbolized, but simply on a double or compound meaning of the word. For ακακια, in the Greek language signifies both the plant in question and the moral quality of innocence or purity of life. In this sense the symbolism refers, primarily, to him over whose solitary grave the Acacia was planted [i.e. Hiram Abiff], and whose virtuous conduct, whole integrity of life and purity of life and fidelity to his truths have ever been presented as patterns to the craft..." [p.8]

datum (Lt). given. Used in Secret symbols (p.20) at the close of a preface to an alchemical treatise. The full phrase is "*Datum In Monte Abiegno*," which identifies it as Rosicrucian. see 182.

ecclesia (Lt) . church. The church is the Stone.

Liber M (Lt). "Book M." The book which brother CR translated from Arabic into Latin. It is the "book of the World."

mons (Lt). mountain. A typical Rosicrucian symbol for the Stone and also for the Great Work. See Secret Symbols (p.11).

panis (Lt). bread (lit. the feeding thing). The House of Bread (Bethlehem), the sign Virgo, and the part of the body governed by it (the small intestine), and the Stone which is said in alchemical books to be, life bread, a product of coction-cooking or baking. In the church (eccelesia), the Christ is held to be represented by and mystically present in the Bread of the communion (Panis) and is identified with the Stone.

patebo (Lt). I will open. Part of the Motto on the vault of C.R. "*Post CXX Annos Patebo.*" see 200.

spes (Lt). hope; a goddess in Roman tradition. see 167, 717.

R.C, G., G.G, P.D. The initials of the second group of four who were called by Brother C.R. to complete the work of founding the Rosicrucian order. They raised the 4 to the 8, the square of the perfect cube.

54

I. (2×3^3)

II. נ/ד Daleth/Nun. Venus (Daleth) in Scorpio (Nun).

אגן a bowl or basin; a disk. With different pointing: *ogen*, brim, rim of a vessel, edge; handle. In Key 14 the angel is pouring fire water from two vessels or bowls.

ד A hill, wall, heap, (forming on the water). In Exodus 15:8: "And with the blast of thy nostrils

the waters were gathered together, the floods stood upright as a heap, and the depths were congealed in the heart of the sea." In Joshua 3:16: "That the waters which came down from above stood and rose up upon a heap very far from the city Adam, that is beside Zaretan (צרתן, 740): and those that came down toward the sea of the plain, even the salt sea, failed, and were cut off: and the people passed over right against Jericho" (ירדו, #234, "place of fragrance, City of Palm trees). see Key 20, Judgement for the blast of the trumpet and the sea.

דמי ceasing, still; cutting off, standing still. In silence the personality ceases and man becomes the "image and likeness" of God. With different pointing: *dahmi*, quite, rest; as an adjective: *dawmi*, sanguinary. This word is from the noun דם [44], meaning blood. These meanings are shown in Key 13 plainly enough. Translated tranquility, prosperity in Isaiah 38:10. From the verb דמה.

חן to be burned; blackish; hence as a color, swarthy, blackness, brown, dark. With different pointing: to have pity, spare. see 614.

ילהט It will flame (or burn). The power of God.

כח יהוה Kach Tetragrammaton. Power of God This power is associated with fire and burning is as much as Tetragrammaton is like a devouring Fire. see 493.

In I.Z.Q (p.673): What is understood by Kach Tetragrammation is מזלא קדישא, Mezla Qadisha, the Holy influence called the Concealed with all Concealments. And from the Influence that Strength and That Light depend.

ידיד יהוה The beloved of God. In Deuteronomy 33:12: "And of Benjamin He [Moses] said; the beloved of the Lord shall dwell in safety by him; and the Lord shall cover him all the day long, and he dwells between his shoulders." Note that Benjamin = Sagittarius = alchemical incineration = Key 14. The heart center is between his shoulders. see 9, 18, 27, 36, 45, 63, 72, 81, 90.

מטה rod (of Moses), staff, branch, tribe. As a feminine noun: bed, couch, litter, bier. see 49, 311.

וגדולה Ve Gedulah. and magnificence. Relates of Chesed. see 106, 756, 120, 372, 50, 406, 496, 222.

דן Judge, Tribe of Dan [Scorpio]. Associated with alchemical putrefaction, the 8th stage of the Great Work. Purification is the disintegration of the alchemist own personality. It is effected by turning the Mars-force in a new direction to repudiate one's ignorant interpretation of selfhood. Proper use of mental imagery through meditation daily raises the cross (Saturn center) which carries Mars up to the Sun Center, until the process becomes automatic. The standard of the tribe was a coiled serpent. Genesis 49:16, 17: "Dan shall judge his people, as one of the tribes of Israel. Dan shall be a serpent by the way, an adder in the path, that bits the horse heels, so that his rider shall fall backwards." Note that the horse is an alchemical symbol for Nun. see 95, 30, 570, 501, 331, 7.

"ך. The sign of sympathetic divisibility united to the root א, symbol of the circumscritive activity of being, constitutes a root whose purpose is to characterize, in a physical sense, every kind of *chemical parting* in elementary nature; and to express, in a moral sense, every contradictory judgement, resting upon litigious things. דן Every idea of *dissension*; literally as well as figuratively; every idea of *debate, bestowal, judgment*." [d'Olivet, 1976, p. 324.]

coagulate (Lt). Coagula. In alchemy to solidify, and has to do with heat. But remember that the alchemist say that they "burn with water," and Scorpio is a watery sign ruled by Mars. see 64 (solve).

Ignis (Lt). Fire.

pater (Lt). Father (name of God).

Lapidem (Lt). Stone. The "Stone of the Wise" or EGO. Part of an alchemical phrase in Secret Symbols (page 17). "Visit the interior of the earth, by rectifying you shall find the hidden stone." see 570 (Lt), 53.

55

I. Σ10 = 55

אב אימא Father-Mother. Combines the titles of Chokmah and Binah which intimates that in Malkuth is the balanced manifestation of the male potency of wisdom and the female potency of understanding. Symbolized by the central figure in Key 21, The World.

ואן with (or in) a stone. The stone is the union of Ab the father and בן Ben the son, it represents regenerated personality. See 53 and Exodus 21:18.

גזילה robbery, pillage. Refers to the tendency of the senses, centered in Malkuth, to produce illusion of separate personal existence and thus to induce man to ascribe to himself instead to the One Life, powers and possessions which he cannot rightly administer. This is sometimes called "idolatry".

גנב thief, robber; as a verb: to steal, rob; to steal away.

דומה Silence, stillness; With different pointing: *Dumah*, angel of dead. As a masculine noun: silence.

חוליא knuckle, member, link. In the Biblical allegory, Eve (the Bride) was formed by God from a rib (limb) of Adam.

הן Lo!; whether, if; behold. In Genesis 4:14: "Behold, you have this day driven me out from the face of the land, and from your face shall I be hidden; and I shall be a fugitive and a wanderer on the earth; and it shall come to pass, that whoever finds me shall slay me." Said my Cain to יהוה.

"The sign of life [ה] united to that of individual and produced existence [ן], constitutes a root which characterizes existence and things in general; an object, a place; the present time; that which falls beneath the senses, that which is conceived as real and actually existing.

הּ that which before the eyes and whose existence is indicated by means of the relation, *here, behold, in the place; then, in that time.*" [d'Olivet, 1976, p. 332.]

מיה 48th Shem ha-Mephorash, short form. see 86, 1525 & Appendix 10.

הום to swell, heave; murmur, roar, discomfort. [Micah 2:12] "I will surely gather all of you, O Jacob; I will surely bring together the raiment of Israel. I will bring them together like sheep in a pen, like a flock in its pasture, they shall make great noise (i.e. murmur); the place will throng with people." see הום (#51).

הדום ha-dom. a footstool, a stool, a resting-place for the feet. In Isaiah 66:1: Thus says the Lord, the heaven in my throne and the earth my footstool: where is the house that you build unto me? And where is the place of my rest? Note that Malkuth is the only Sephirah referring to the element of Earth.

כלה Kallah. the crowned one, The bride, (of Melek, the King in Tiphareth). Name of Malkuth. Refers to the New Jerusalem, the holy city or manifested Kingdom. [Revelations 21:9] With different pointing: to be complete, be completed, be finished. see 1006, 543, 496.

הכל all, everything, the All. In the Kingdom are all the powers conjoined, and the Kingdom is the physical body of man to which the name Guph is given. Malkuth represents the sum-total of the influences on the Tree of Life, concentrated into the field of manifestation called the "world"; the world of physical man's sensory experience, the world of his mental impressions of sensations experienced through his body. Bodily contact with this field of sensation is the basis of all human knowledge. Kaph represents comprehension, Lamed symbolizes Justice and is related to action. Heh is the foresight which gives authority and power over circumstance. To grasp the meaning of experience is to act to make the adjustments this comprehension necessitates. The fruit of this is true vision real insight and dependable foresight see 998.

הלך to go, to walk, depart; to follow; to pass away, disappear; as a noun: traveler, flowing. With different vowel points: to swell, heave.

האדמה ground. It is from the same root as אדם, Adam, Man. In Genesis 2:6: "But a mist went up from the earth, and altered the whole face of the ground. see 5, 44, 45.

נגב south, south country, mid-day; to be dry. As a noun: to be dry.

נה ornament, beauty.

I. "This root is the analogue of the root נא and as it, characterizes that which is fresh, young, recent: thence; נוה state of being *young, alert, vigorous, pleasing*; in consequence, action of *forming a colony, founding a new habitation, establishing ones flock elsewhere*, etc.

נה onomatopoeic root which describes the long moaning of a person who weeps, suffers, sobs. The Arabic depicts every king of noise, clamor." [d'Olivet, 1976, p. 398.]

דגדגיאל Dagdagiel. The Sentinel of the 14th Path of Daleth on the inverse Tree of Life.

I. "The 14th tunnel is suffused with the *kala* of Venus represented by the Whore. Her qabalistic attribution is Daleth, meaning 'a door'; the door that permits of access to her house or womb, and egress from it. Her cosmic power-zone is Venus.

This tunnel backs the first Reciprocal Path on the Tree of Life; its infernal counterpart is the base of the pyramid which, when inverted, is balanced upon the point of the *Ain* in the void of the Abyss. The name of its sentinel is Dagdagiel. Her number is 55, which is a mystic number of Malkuth, the power-zone of Earth. Fifty-five, as 5 x 11, resumes the formula of magick (11), set in motion or powered by *shakti* (5). It is also the number of דומה, 'silence', which is the formula of woman (*shakti*) when she becomes pregnant with the child of light produced by the next *kala*. The word HIM, 'to swell', is indicative of this condition; and ידם (a metathesis of הום) means to 'conceive', 'to have sexual intercourse', and 'to create', 55 is also the number of כלה, 'the bride', 'the daughter-in-law', which suggests the cosmic bride Malkuth, the daughter of IHVH, she that is the final term (Heh) of manifestation.

The daughter is the symbol of imminent return; of the incipient reversion of manifestation to its primal state of nonmanifestation; of being re-becoming non-being. In the present Aeon the Son is the Child, but in the coming Aeon of Maat the Child will be the *Daughter*, for at the end of that Aeon Malkuth will once more return to its sleep of dissolution (*pralaya*) prior to a new manifestation.

The title of the Atu of this Path is The Daughter of the Mighty Ones. The theme is repeated by the word MUT (a form of Maat) which also adds to 55 and which signifies to 'shake', waver, 'totter', 'fail', 'decay', 'die'. It derives from the Egyptian word *mut*, meaning to 'end' or 'die'.

The sigil of Dagdagiel shows the letter *Daleth* reversed and in the form of a gallows from which hangs an inverted triangle above the letters AVD. AVD (Od) is the magick light. The triangle is the inverted pyramid set in the Abyss with its apex in the Void (*Ain*), for this reciprocal tunnel is reflected into the gulfs beyond Kether.

The implication is that the pyramid is the magick light or Fire Snake suspended from a gallows in the form of the Woman of Night [A term signifying the 'Elemental Gods'] whose vagina (Daleth = door) is here reversed. This peculiarity shows that she is an initiate of the highest sexual mysteries and that she possesses the special mark [The retromingent vulva] of a Scarlet Woman. Her totems are the dove (the Typhonian bird), the sparrow, and the sow. In a holograph note in his personal copy of *Liber 777*, Crowley notes against this path (column xxxvii): 'The Sow = type of Venus which matches Mars (opposed to romantic and other higher types). Mars = boar. By this he means that as the virgin basks in the idyllic light of romantic or unrealized love, the sow wallows in the sty of sensuality. But the comparison of the Sow of Venus with the Boar of Mars comports another mystery which may be fathomed only in terms of the Draconian Current. The sow (Babalon = whore) is the qlipha [a harlot] or outer shell of the Goddess. Her inner mystery involves the kalas or Kali Herself, for She is the ultimate Mother. In New Aeon terms, therefore, Mars is the cosmic power-zone assigned to Ra-Hoor-Khuit as the child (Har) of the present Aeon, because the blood associated with this zone (of Mars) is not the blood of the male shed in battle, but the blood of the female that embodies the child.

The dove also is attributed to the 14th *kala*. The dove was the bird of blood (feminine source) before it became the bird of air (masculine spirit). First was Mars-Kali-Typhon, then came Venus-Nephthys-Nu-Isis.

The magical power corresponding to this *kala* is, traditionally, the ability to distil love philtres. The phrase is an euphemism for the vaginal vibrations emanating from the virgin in the form of sexual magnetism that attracts the Creative Light into her womb.

In the verse of the grimoire pertaining to this *kala*, it is written: The Virgin of God is enthroned upon an oyster-shell; she is like a pearl, and seeketh 70 to her 4. In her heart is Hadit the invisible glory.

The oyster is the typical aphrodisiac; the virgin is drunk upon its shell and seeketh 70 [i.e. the erect phallus symbolized by the Eye (Ayin = Eye = 70) of the Devil] to her 4 [Daleth, 4, = door, i.e. vagina]. In her heart is Hadit (i.e. Set, the Devil Himself), the invisible glory that motivates her desire. The virgin thus becomes the whore, or, in the language of magical symbolism, the entranced priestess becomes enlightened or awakened; the pythoness becomes oracular, being inspired with the divine spirit. Hence the magical formula of this kala is *Agape*, the number of which is 93, which is the number of desire or will (*Thelema*) and of the Devil (Aiwass) Himself.

All aphrodisiacs and all soft voluptuous odours are ascribed to this *kala*, the presiding deities of which are Hathor, Aphrodite, Kapris Cottyto, and, in the tantric systems, Lalita [The Lilith of rabbinical lore], the sexual aspect of *shakti* (power).

Diseases typical of the 14th *kala* are syphilis, gonorrhea, and nymphomania. The element of nymphomania is evident in the succubi or shadow-women generated from the yoni of the Goddess whose magical weapon is the girdle. The shadow woman is the means of dream control for it is through her magical circle that the dreamer enters dimensions that lie on the nightside of the inverted pyramid which is a projection of the *yantra* of the Goddess. The formula has a sexual basis and all that can be divulged has already appeared in my Typhonian Trilogy." [Grant, 1994, pp. 176-182.]

Αγελεια. Ageleia. Title of Athena. "She who carries off the spoils," or "She who drives off the Spoils." Occult tradition attributes this to the Pythagoreans, in reference to the number 7. Seven and 10 are related, because the extension of 7 is 28, which reduces to 10. The extension of 10 is 406, which reduces to 10. see 406.

Ληθη. Lethe. river of oblivion (in underworld). In Malkuth natural man has forgotten his true identity.

aquila (Lt). Eagle. The bird of aspiration and vision. Connected with Scorpio and the Mars force. In the *Confessio Fraternitatis*, it is said of the brethren "no longer are we beheld by human eyes, unless they have received strength borrowed from the Eagle." Strength is Key 8 in the Tarot and is associated with Kundalini. In K.D.L.C.K. (p. 600) it relates the eagle to Malkuth; and Malkuth when it is raised unto Tiphareth, as in Proverbs 30:19: "The way of an eagle in the air." Binah is called the "Great Winged Eagle"; and its wings the six Sephiroth. By gematria נשר, eagle [550] = סבט ברזל, Rod of Iron and שרים, princes.

Iehova (Lt). Jehovah. Name of God.

mundi (Lt). of the world (possessive). Refers to the Kingdom of the physical plane, the sphere of embodied action recorded by the senses. see 89.

renes (Lt). Reins, i.e. the kidneys, associated with balance and Libra. In later Hebrew kidneys sometimes means the testicles. Therefore כליות refers to the physical primary sources of bodily power and vigor. In the ancient world it was believed that the loins and reins were the seat of the lower mind, called φρην in Greek. The Latin *renes* was derived from the this Greek word meaning kidneys, in English it is called reins.

56

I. Number of minor Tarot Trumps.

II. The length of the 7 vertical lines bounding the vault of brother CR. The crest on the observe on the Great Seal of the U.S.

יום day, light of day, time, season. In Genesis 1:5 gives as God's own name for light, the (Qabalistic symbol of the Manifest (69), as contrasted with darkness, to which the name Night is given, as representing the Unmanifest. With different pointing: *Yoom*: to be warm, or bright.

I. "A day; it is frequently put for time in general, or for a long time; a whole period under consideration, as, in the day signifies in the time when; in that day, at that time. Day is also put for a particular season or time when any extraordinary even happens, whether it be prosperous and joyful, or adverse and calamitous; which day is denominated either from the Lord who appoints it, or from those who suffer in it: Job 18:20, Psalm 137:7; Ezekiel 21:25. 'Day of the Lord' a day of visitation or of judgment. Hosea 6:2, 'two days' two seasons of calamity. All the day, all the day long, is the same as always, continually. Days are put for years: Leviticus 25:29; 1 Samuel 27:7; 1 Kings 17:15. Other peculiarities may be seen and easily accounted for in the several translations: Genesis 1, 5." [Wilson, 1987, p. 109.]

II. "Symbolic of periods of manifestation-cycles of involution and evolution. The six days of Genesis are all periods of involution, not evolution... The light is the consciousness, the spirit-side of being, whilst the darkness is the material, the form-side of nature. Evening and morning are symbolic of the indrawing and the outgoing forces, constituting the first Life-wave." [Gaskell, 1981, p. 254.]

III. "The first and foremost thing to keep in mind is that the 'days' of creation describe a simultaneous, perpetual, and ever-present action of the 3 archetypes *Aleph, Bayt* and *Ghimel,* of their corresponding *Dallet, Hay, Waw* and of *Zayn* the seventh. They describe the autonomous life and movement of the universe." [Suraes, 1992, p. 100.]

אימה dread, terror, fear.

אנה He suffered; to sigh, lament, to mourn, to wrong. With different vowel points: to bring about, cause, to happen, overreach in. see 650.

כול to comprehend, measure, hold, or compromise, to keep in, to contain. In Richardson's Monitor of Freemasonry (p. 43), as part of the Mark Mason's degree, the candidate takes in each hand a small block of white marble about 4 inches square and six inches long, weighing about 11 pounds each. Paul Case has this note: Boundary lines = 24(4x6) + 32(8x4) = 56" = 7x8 = to measure = כול. Note that the weight of the 2 stones = 22. Twenty is the circumference of a circle or cycle of manifestation. see 96, 600 (מלאכה) (ששׁ).

נאה beautiful, comely, becoming, befitting, lovely.

נאה dwelling, habitations, pasture, meadow; to be lonely, be befitted. In the 23rd Psalm: "He makes me to lie down in green pastures."

נאה becoming, well. With different pointing: *naah*. to adorn oneself; to beatify, decorate. The result of the light which shines into darkness.

והם Hoham. "God of the Multitude." King of Hebron (Amorite King). In Joshua 10:3: "Wherefore Adonai Zedec King of Jerusalem sent unto Hoham King of Hebron..." Represents the false notion of deity held by the masses of ignorant persons. Also a symbol of the exclusiveness and of the inequalities of classes which derive directly from the false notion of God. For he King of Hebron, that is, King of the Court, so and of hereditary aristocracy. see 321.

הייאל "God, Master of the Universe." 71st Shem ha-Mephorash. 351E-355E. May 29, August 9, October 20, December 31, March 13. 11:20-11:40 PM. To confound the wicked, and to deliver from those who see to oppress us. Protects all who call upon him. Positive influence: brave. Negative: discord, traitors, infamy. Influences arsenals, fortresses, and all that belongs to the genius of war. Person born: Has much energy; will love military life, and will distinguish himself by his talents and actions. Angel of the 3rd decanate (5th quinance) of Cancer and attributed to the 4 of Cups (Chesed of Briah). see 25, 965, & Appendix 10.

אביגאל Abigail, "Father is Rejoicing"; "Father of Joy", "Source of Joy." variant spelling, see 46, 82, and 1 Samuel 25:3.

נו Nu. An Egyptian Goddess, Hebrew transliteration.

"נו.. the convertible sign ו, image of the bond which unites being and nothingness, which communicates from one nature to another, being joined to that of produced existence, produces a root whose sense, entirely vague and indeterminate is fixed only by means of the terminative sign by which it is accomplished.

The Arabic is an onomatopoetic and idomatic root which depicts the aversion that one experiences in doing a thing, the disgust that it inspires. As verb, it is the action of being repugnnant, of refusing, of being unwilling.

נוה Every idea of a *new dwelling. The point of equilibrium* where an agitated things finds *repose*: action of *resting, remaining tranquil, enjoying peace and calm.*" [d'Olivet, 1976, p. 398.]

כבוד יהוה "The Glory of IHVH." see Exodus 16:10.

angus (Lt). Lamb. Symbol of the mystical Son of God.

terra (Lt). Earth. Refers to the physical plane which holds all times and seasons.

I. "You will never discover anything unless you first enter my workshop, where, in the inmost bowels of the earth I ceaseless forge metals: There you may find the substance which I use, and discover the method of my work." [Waite, 1974, Vol. 1, p. 123]. Paul Case links earth in this sentence to Virgo. see 570 (Virgo, alchemical distillation), 291.

II. "Therefore, beloved brother, let me warn you to have nothing to do with subliminations of sulphur and mercury, or the solution of bodies or the coagulation of spirits, or with all the innumerable alembics, which bear little profit unto veritable art. So long as you do not seek the true essence of Nature, your labors will be doomed to failure; therefore, if you desire success, you must once for all renounce your allegiance to all those old methods, and enlist under the standards of that method which proceeds in strict obedience to the teaching of Nature-in short, the method which Nature herself pursues in the bowels of the earth [Virgo region in human body]." [ibid, pp. 152-153] see 496.

III. "The Sages have written about many waters, stones and metals, for the purpose of deceiving you. You that desire a knowledge of our Art, relinquishing Sun, Moon, Saturn and Venus for our ore [23 Latin] and our earth, and why so? Every thing is of the nature of no thing." [ibid, p. 204]

IV. "The stone is mystic, or secret, because it is found in a secret place, in an universally despised substance where no one looks for the greatest treasure of the world." [ibid, p. 226] (Case: viz, in Virgo, where it is felt, but not seen.)

gloria (Lt). glory. The Light of God which shines on all things. see 74, 126, 136, 237.

turba (Lt). tumult, uproar, disturbance, commotion, especially one caused by a crowd of people. Title of an early alchemical treatise with the Turba Philosophours. Jacob Boehme writes: "And it is highly recognizable by us how the imagination of the eternal nature has the turba in the craving, in the mystery, but not awakenable, unless the creature, as the mirror of eternity, doth itself awaken this, viz. the fierce wrath, which is eternity is hidden in mystery." [Mysterium Pansolphicum, V, p. 161]

metalla (Lt). metal. One of seven interior centers, also known as planets, stars and chakras; a vortice of Life-force connected with an inner body or plane of consciousness in the microcosm. In alchemy, one of the constituents of the stone of the wise.

57

אבדן Abbadon; destruction, ruin, perdition in Esther 8:6: "For how can I endure to see the evil that shall come unto my people? Or how can I endure to see the destruction of my kindred?" (Note the combination of אב, the father and הן,

Dan, Judgement in this word. (Thus "Father of Judgement") One of the 7 infernal mansions depicted on the diagram of the 4 seas. see 337, 911, 99, 1026, 566, 108, 291; 54, 3; 64, 707.

און ability, strength, power, manly vigor [Genesis 49:3]. With different pointing: 1. wealth, riches; bill of sale, deed; 2. *awven*. trouble, grief; sorrow, wickedness; 3. idolatry in Numbers 33:21. Root meaning of these words implies effort. In *own*, the effort succeeds, in *awven*, it comes to nothingness, vanity. wickedness, affliction, pain. see Psalm 90:10.

און to breath, to effect by work, to take pains. [Hosea 12:9]. Note the connection between breathing and working. "Every idea of pain, sorrow, trouble, calamity. [d'Olivet, 1976, p. 296.] see 51 for his commentary on its root אן.

און On. A city in lower Egypt called by the Greeks Heliopolis (City of the Sun). Heliopolis is the sun of the Bible.

און Avnas. Goetic demon #58 by night of the 1st decanate of Scorpio. The 1st decanate of Scorpio is also attributed to the 5 of Cups which corresponds to the operation of Geburah, sphere of Mars and divine volition in Briah, the Word of Creation. see Appendix 11.

Goetia: "He is a great president, and appears at first in the form of a flaming fire; but after a while he pus on the shape of a man. His office is to make one wonderful knowing in astrology and all the liberal sciences. He gives good familiars, and can bewray treasure that is kept by spirits. He governs 36 Legions of Spirits." [Mathers, 1995, p. 59]

ויגא Vine; Vinea. Goetic demon #45 by night of the 3rd decanate of Gemini. see appendix 11.

I. *Goetia*: "He is a great king, and an earl; and appears in the form of a lion, riding upon a black horse, and bearing a viper in his hand. His office is to discover things hidden, witches, wizards, and things present, past, and to come. He, at the command of the Exorcist will build towers, overthrow great stone walls, and make the waters rough with storm. He governs 36 Legions of Spirits." [Mathers, 1995, p. 51]

אלוך Alloces. Goetic demon #52 by night of

the 1st decanate of Virgo. see Appendix 11.

Goetia: "He is a duke, great, mighty, and strong, appearing in the form of a soldier riding upon a great horse. His face is like that of a lion, very red, and having flaming eyes. His speech is hoarse and very big. His office is to teach the art of astronomy, and all the liberal sciences. He brings unto thee good familiars; also he rules over 36 Legions of Spirits." [Mathers, 1995, p. 55]

אנו the pronoun "we." Suggest that by eliminating the illusion of separation one realizes that all spiritual powers of the cosmos find expression in the magical operation.

איום threat, warning; fright, terror, formidable, terrible. see 617

בנה to build, erect; to establish, to raise, to build up. With different pointing: to establish firmly (note this word contains בן, Ben, the Son + Heh, vision or constitution power of the Father, (אב). see 108, 53.

דגים fishes; sign of Pisces, the 12th sign of the Zodiac, attributed to the Letter Qoph, the Corporeal or body-building intelligence. All the above words [אבן, איום, בנה, כלוא] apply in various ways to incarnation. The physical body is continually perishing, yet it is while we are incarnate that it is that which is the means to all wealth and power. It is the basis of all effort, yet if it be separated from the directing spirit it is nothingness and vanity. It is the cause of all our terrors, when we misuse it or misinterpret it. On the Cube of Space Qoph is assigned to the direction south-below, or the operation of the Sun (Resh = south) in subconsciousness or the Moon (Gimel = below). see 259, 389, 186.

דגן dawgawn. corn, grain. In Genesis 27:28: "Therefore God give thee of the dew of Heaven, and the fatness of the earth, and plenty of corn and wine." see 707.

כלוא a prison. In Jeremiah 37:4: "Now Jeremiah came in and went out among the people: for they had put him into prison (Jeremiah means "God is exacted"). And in Jeremiah 53:31: "And it came to pass... that evil Merodach King of Babylon... lifted up the head of Jehoiachin, King of Judah (alchemical digestion), and brought him forth out of prison" (Jehoiakim = Jehovah raises up") see 3, 12, 21, 30, 39, 48, 66, 265 (Jeremiah).

מזבח altar, derived from זבח, to slaughter, to sacrifice. The altar represents truth and conformity to the cosmic order. What is sacrificed or destroyed is the sense of personal separateness. What is killed out is the illusion that one does anything of oneself.

אוכל consuming; he that eats, eater, consumer.

ביטול a breaking down, subversion, destruction, annulment, cessation.

מחבא making secret, the laying by, hiding-place. From חבא, to hide, to conceal.

הבן comprehend. With different pointing: ebony. The metathesis of בנה, to build. Comprehension is the result of building; understanding is the ebony black color of Binah, builder of form. Also can be read: *ha-ben* הבן, the son. see 53, 67, 707.

לויה Levoiah. "God who takes away sins". 19th Shem ha-Mephorash. 91E-95E. SOTIS Venus. April 7, June 18, August 29, November 9, January 20. 6:00-6:20 AM. [Psalm 40:1] "I waited patiently for the Lord; and he inclined unto me, and heard my cry." To obtain the grace of God. Rules the memory and intelligence of Man. Person born: amiable and enjonee, modest in words, simple in his manner of life, supporting adversity with resignation and much patience. Associated with the 1st quninace of Scorpio, Angel by day of the 5 of Cups. see Appendix 10.

וליה "King Dominator." 43rd Shem ha-Mephorash 211E-215E. STOCHNE, Sagittarius. May 1, July 12, September 22, December 3, February 13. 2:00-2:20 PM. [Psalm 87:3] "Glorious things are spoken of thee, O city of God, Selah." Rules peace, influences the prosperity of empires; makes firm the thrones and power of kings. Person born: Loves military state, become celebrated by his feats of arms, and will gain the confidence of his prince by services rendered to him. Associated with the 1st quinance of Pisces; Angel by day of the 8 of Cups. see Appendix 10.

בהן thumb, big toe. Has a distinctly esoteric and phallic significance. In Exodus 29:20: "then thou shall kill the ram, and take of his blood, and put it upon the tip of the right ear of his sons, and upon the thumb of their right hand, and upon the great toe of their right foot, and sprinkle the blood upon the altar round about." The reference is to the consecrating of priests. see 707.

זן species, kind; sort. In Psalm 144:13: "Our barns will be filled with every kind of provisions. Our sheep will increase by the thousands, by tens of thousands in our fields.

I. "זן. The demonstrative sign united to the root א, symbol of the moral or physical circumscription of the being, constitutes a root which develops two distinct meanings according as they are considered as mind or matter. From the view point of mind, it is a moral manifestation which makes the faculties of the being understood and determines the kind, for that of matter, it is a physical manifestation which delivers the body and abandons it to pleasure. Thence:

II. זן Every classification by *sort* and by *kind* according to the faculties: every pleasure of the body for its *nourishment*: figuratively, all *lewdness, fornication, debauchery: a prostitute, a place of prostitution*, etc.

III. זן action of *being nourished, feeding* the body; or metaphorically the action of enjoying, making abuse, *prostituting* one's self." [d'Olivet, 1976, p. 343.] see 707

bonum (Lt). utility, profit, good.

lumen (Lt). light (literally and figuratively). see 570.

rosae (Lt). of the rose, rosy. Refers to the symbol of the human soul, of aspiration. The red rose symbolizes desire, the white purity. see 421 (Lt).

אבידיל "Possessor of Night." variant spelling. also called Abigail. In 2 Samuel 18:25: "...Abigail, the daughter of Nehash." Nahash is the serpent, or the power connected with Scorpio. see 358, 61, 499.

חילי my strength, power, might.

כבוד יהוה Kebode IHVH. "The Glory of IHVH." In Exodus 16:10: "And it came to pass, as Aaron spoke unto the whole congregation of the children of Israel, that they looked toward the wilderness, and, behold, the glory of the Lord appeared in the cloud."

מלידה ruler of water. i.e. the alchemical Water or "Water of Mercury."

דאגן Dagan. Night demon of 1st decanate of Sagittarius. דא means "this"; גן means "garden:.(i.e. the garden of subconsciousness). This decanate is under the rulership of Jupiter and suggest the negative attributes of depression, indetermination and short-sightedness on subconscious levels." also ד+ג = דג, *dag*, fish = Pisces = אן = "where, whither?" see 7, 51.

חן love, kindness, grace, precious. Notariqon for, Chokmah Nesetrah, [חכמה נסתרה], the Secret Wisdom, i.e. the Qabalah. see 111, 53, 788, 60.

נגה Nogah. the sphere of Venus, Netzach; shining, brightness, morning star. Variant spelling. see 64.

נבו Nebo. The planet Mercury worshipped as the celestial scribe by the Chaldean (Isaiah 46:1) and the ancient Arabians. The etymology of the name does not ill accord with the office of mercury; namely נבו for נבוא i.q. נבוא (vowel points omitted) the interpreter of the Gods, the declarer of their will; for the root נבו (vowel points omitted). As to the worship of Mercury by the Chaldeans and Assyrians, we find it attested by the proper names which have this name at the beginning, as *Nebuchadnezzar, Nebushasban* (see them a little below), and also those mentioned by classic writers, *Nabonedus, Nabonassar, Naburianus, Nabnoasbus*, etc. – *Gesenius' Hebrew-Chaldee Lexicon to the Old*

כלה Calah, perfection, also a trunk or pillar; with different pointing: He is firm, or pining with desire. This name was borne by an Assyrian City (according to Inman), and it may have been derived from a word like כלה Calah, adorned, crowned, a bride, equivalent to the virgin , or Ishtar; if so, we may compare it to καλη *kalee*, beautiful . In Genesis 10:11: "out of that Land [Shinar] went forth Asshur, and built Ninevah, and the City Rehoboth, and Calah."

D'Olivet suggest that Calah means the growing wise, old men ruling within: "The word כלה, which signifies literally, *an ancient, an old man*, that is to say, a man whom age and experience have led to perfection. Thence by extension, the idea of a senate, of an assembly of old men, of a wise and conservative institution." [d'Olivet, 1976, p. 284.] see 55.

נח noah. rest, cessation. pleasing, kind. Ark builder. marks a period of parlaya, or rest in cycles of cosmic manifestation. see 936.

This name appears in Genesis 5:29: And he called his name Noah, saying He shall comfort us concerning our work and toil of our hands: because of the ground which the Lord hath cursed"

I. "And he called his name Noah (repose of elementary nature), saying, this shall rest us (our existence) and lighten our labor, and the physical obstacles of our hands, because of the Adamic element which יהוה has cursed.

II. He comments: נה. Noah. The root from which this important name comes, is composed of the sign of produced being נ, image of reflected existence, and the sign of the effort of nature ה, which gives birth to vital equilibrium, to *existence*. This root offers the idea of that perfect repose, which, for a thing long agitated in opposed directions, results in that state of equilibrium where it dwells immobile.

Nearly all the tongues of the orient understands this mysterious expression. The Hebrew and the Chaldaic draw from it two verbs. By the first

נהוה, one understands, *to lead to the end, to guide toward the place of repose*; by the second, נוא, *to repose, to rest tranquil, to be in a state of peace, of calm, of perfect bliss*. It is from the latter, that the name of the cosmogonic personage who saw the end of the world and its renewal, is derived. It is the emblem of the repose of elementary existence, the sleep of nature." [d'Olivet, 1976, pp. 167-168.]

III. "A symbol of the individuality, or the manifested self in evolution-the permanent center of evolution in the soul. It is the Buddhi-manasic principle, or the incarnation of the self as applying to the three lower planes... The Noah principle... is perfection of the soul according to its sage of development. The knowledge it possessed is derived from within (walked with God)." [Gaskell, 1981, p. 538.]

IV. A. Jokej writes: "Noah is the divinely appointed figure, in whom the whole cause of regeneration is set forth, every secret of this great mystery being here drawn for us as God alone could draw it.. Noah, then, is the spiritual mind, for he is only the continuation of Seth's line, and figures the form of life which the spiritual mind takes as this stage in its development, when it has come so far as to know the judgement of the old creation, and the way through that Judgement to a cleansed and better world." [Types of Genesis, pp. 104-105]

להחוה 34th Shem ha-Mephorash. "God the clement." Positive influence: Individual known for their talents and acts, the confidence and fervor of their prayers. Negative Influence: Discord, war, treason. Angle governing the 2nd decanate (and 3rd quinance) of Capricorn attributed to the 3 of Disks. see Appendix 10.

ייאל 40th Shem ha-Mephorash. "God who rejoices." For the deliverance of prisoners, for consolation, for deliverance from one's enemies. Governs: Printing and books, people of letters and artists. Evil influence: on lugubrious spirits and those who flee society. Angel of the 2nd decanate (4th quinance) of Aquarius and attributed to the 6 of Swords. see Appendix 10.

מהד 64th Shem ha-Mephorash, short form. see 89 & Appendix 10.

האבן the stone. see 53.

crux (Lt). Cross. Refers to the golden cross of 6 squares, belonging to the Rosicrucian order "which every brother carries on his breast" [Secret Symbols]. Also see the equal-armed cross of the 4 elements, the cross of Tav on the breast of Key 2. see 109, 246, 66, 62, 47 (Lt), 1274 (Greek).

59   (prime)

I. The yoni calling for the lingam as ovum, menstruum, or alkali. [Crowley, 1977, p. xxv].

חוילה The "land" where there is gold [Genesis 2:11]. From the root Khool, חול, sand (44), connected with the Phoenix, referring to the mineral Kingdom. Said to be the root of חוילה, "a circle, or district (in man)." see 64, 345.

"Hawilah... Here the root חול חל or חול, is related to the idea of effort, of tension, or virtual travail, or trial, etc. This root is used as continued facultative, with the emphatic article Heh. [d'Olivet, 1976, p. 79.]

חול or חיל. Action of *suffering* from the effects of a violent effort being made upon one's self; action *of being twisted, stretched* [see skeleton in Key 13], action of being *confined, bringing into the world*; *being carried* in thought or *action toward an end*; *producing* ideas: action of *tending, attending, hoping, placing faith* in something; action of *disengaging, resolving, dissolving, opening, milking, extracting*, etc. [Hebrew Tongue Restored p. 351] see 65, 571, 100, 739, 259.

אחים brethren [referring to Lilith & Samael].

אחילוד "A brother is born". The father of David's recorder, Jehoshaphat ("God has Judged", 410). In 2 Samuel 20:24: "And Adorah was over the tribute: and Jehoshaphat the son of Ahilud was recorder." Note that David means "beloved". see 14, 305.

גוים foreigner, heathen; nations. See 64.

Goyim is a reference to the Gentiles in the Bible. Esoterically the 'Nations' are the millions of cells not directly concerned with the controlling the functions of the body, as are the more highly specialized cells known as the 12 tribes. The constitution of the human body is the pattern for the proper constitution of the human society. Just as the gross mechanics of the body furnishes the pattern for all machines based on the laws of mechanics, while the subtler structure of the same body provides the patterns for those inventions which utilize the power of electricity. see 65, 671, 100, 739, 259 & C.20.

חומה wall, city wall, enclosure.

נדה gift, wages of prostitution. As a feminine noun: *niddah*, impurity, impure thing, period of menstruation, menstruate woman. The cycles of throwing out the foreign brethren" must be complete before the land of Gold is reached.

נדה name of a tractate of the Talmud. With different pointing: *nuddawh, neiddah*. to remove, thrust out, to be banished, be excommunicated.

Pereat (Lt). "let there consume, destroy, or He shall eat up, devour." In the *Fama* (p. 3): "Our Rota takes her beginning from that day when God spoke Fiat ("Let there be light"), and shall end when he Shall speak Pereat."

magia adamica (Lt). adamic magic or the magic of Adam [humanity]. Title of a treatise by Thomas Vaugnan. Subtitles "The Antiquity of Magic and the Descent there of from Adam Downwards Proved". See 29, 30.

columba (Lt). dove. a symbol of Venus, and of sexual warmth. "In India there is a most pleasant wood, In which two birds are bound together. One is of a snowy white; the other is red. They bite each other, and one is slain And devoured by the other. Then both are changed into white doves, And of the dove is born a Phoenix, Which has left behind blackness and foul death, and has regained a more glorious life. This power was given it by God Himself, That it might live eternally, and never die. It gives us wealth, it preserves our life, And with it we may work great miracles, as also the True Philosophers do plainly inform us." [Waite, 1974, vol. 1, p. 290]. see Key 3, 71, 73 (Lt), 81 (Lt).

clavis (Lt). key. A "key", as to a book or cipher.

60

I. The number of degrees in a vertex of a pentagon.

II. Dodecahedron (attributed to Akasha) has five 12 pentagonal faces (12 x 5 = 60). The Iscohedron (attributed to Water) has 20 triangular faces (20 x 3 = 60). Since Akasha and Water are both represented by 60, or 5 times the number of Fire, we may regard Akasha and Water as being in some sense a fivefold manifestation of FIRE.

III. Carringron, in *The Number Key* calls 60 "differential and human order, completeness of character". And the "actualizing of maturity."

IV. "A might conjunction," the period between the conjunction of Saturn and Jupiter (more correctly 59.6 years).

V. The number of stones in Stonehenge outer circle.

ס   Samekh. Once the letter Samekh was interchangeable with the final form of the letter Mem, but after mankind left the Garden of Eden, he mistook temporary shelter for the final letter of the abode of perfection (Mem). Because of his error, the arm of the tent peg was bent. [Codex Obligitas, XIV:60]

I. Note this letter is similar to final Mem. It is a modification of the circle, and is symbolic of a serpent swallowing its own tail. Note the serpent girdle on Key 1, The Magician. Note that Teth and Lamed are also symbolic of a serpent and the serpent-power. In Samekh it is a serpent swallowing its own tail and also symbolizes the completion of a cycle of manifestation. Since Samekh follows Teth and Lamed, it corresponds to the end of a series of manifestations.

II. "This character as consonant, belongs to the sibilant sound, and is applied as onomatopoeia to depicting all sibilant noises... This character is, in Hebrew, the image of the bow whose cord hisses in the hands of man. As grammatical sign, it is that of circular movement in that which is related to the circumferential limit of any sphere." [d'Olivet, 1976, p. 405.]

בחן tried by fire, to test or try; examine, proved. This has a special reference to the testing of metals by fire. Translated a tried (stone) in Isaiah 28:16: "Therefore thus says the Lord God, behold I lay in Zion for a foundation a stone, a tried stone, a precious corner stone, a sure foundation: he that believes shall not make haste." With different pointing: 1. watch-tower, 2. trial, examination proof; 3. testing, examination; 4. to inquire. The higher self watches our tests from within. see 186

This is not the same word translated "temptation or trial" in the special title of the path of Samekh associated with Sagittarius and Key 14. see Book of Tokens (Samekh).

הנגב the south. See Daniel 11:5.

ב-חן In grace, by grace, by favor. By taking Beth as a preposition "in", and חן as "grace". *Khane* (חן) is an abbreviation (notariqon) for Chokmah Nesethrah [397] the secret wisdom (qabalah). The mystical trial by fire has to do with initiation into the Qabalah. It is by "grace", the "Grace of God" that the "metal" is tested-Key 14. The basic idea is testing by rubbing metals on a Touchstone. See 58, 186.

גאון sublimity, glory. Trial by fire makes visible "the Glory of the Heavenly Sun," or "the Gold of thy Beauty." [Book of Tokens, Mem]. With different pointing: rising, swelling (as the waves in water, or hills on land); highness, excellence, majesty, grandeur, glory, exaltation. These meanings are related to the mountain symbolism in Key 14. Because there is danger that attainment may lead to personal pride, this word signifies also the pride which goes before a fall, and this points toward the kind of test whereby, as the comment of the path of Samekh says, "The Lord God test the devout." Until the dross of egotism is purged out, the "Metal" will not meet the trial of friction (rubbing) upon the touchstone of daily contact with others and environmental conditions.

מחזה vision, apparition; drama. "The vision of thy Lord [shall] be granted onto thee [Book of Tokens, Samekh] With different pointing: 1. theatrical performance, play; 2. window, aperture; vista. [A medieval word with the meaning of "vision, apparition" is מֹחַ. see 310, 120, 536.

כְּלִי Anything completed, prepared or made. Specifically, vase or vessel. Refers to the secret vessels of alchemy, as symbolized by the vase in Key 14. It contains the "fiery, three-fold water" with which the great work is accomplished. With different pointing: article, object, thing; utensil; garment; jewel; ornament; implement, tool; weapon, armor. A ship, just as we speak of a ship as a "vessel". Even dress (of men), and trappings (of animals) are sometimes designated by *keliy*. Something prepared and therefore almost all variations of the ideas of a prepared apparatus or instrument. With different pointing: 18th Shem ha-Mephorash, short form. see 91, 100, 800, & Appendix 10.

הֲלָכָה Traditional law. Practice, adopted opinion, Rule; tradition (opposed to Aggadah). Not to be confused with the Paradosis (666) condemned by Jesus. It is the secret oral tradition. So Qabalists interpret the word. Exoteric Judaism means no more by it than the legalistic "traditions of men" collected in the Talmud.

הָנֵה behold! "The glory of the Heavenly son shall all men behold." [Book of Tokens] With different vowel points: to give pleasure or benefit, to please.

טֶנֶא basket (metaphor for prosperity).

הִיא חַיֶּיךָ She is thy Life. In Proverbs 4:13: "Take fast hold of instruction, let her not go; keep her, for she is thy life." see 540, 12, 18.

נִי lament, wailing. In Ezekiel 27:32: "And in their wailing they shall take up a lamentation for thee, and lament over thee, saying, What city is like Tyrus, like the destroyed in the midst of the sea?"

"Root analogous to the roots נָא [youth, newness], נֶה [young fresh] and נֹ [aversion, disgust] whose expression it manifest. The Arabic word indicates the state of that which is raw." [d'Olivet, 1976, pp. 400-401.]

ילההה Yelahiah. 44th name of Shem ha-Mephorash. Associated with the 1st decanate of Pisces and the 8 of Cups. Meaning: "Abiding forever." Offers protection to magistrates, trials. Protects against armies, gives victory. The individual is fond of travel and learning. All their undertakings are crowned with success; distinguished for military capabilities and courage. Negative influence: Wars.

nitre (Lt). alchemical term as a stage of salt.
Fideus (Lt). of faith, faithful. Part of phrase. see 146.

61 (prime)

I. $5^2 + 6^2$

II. The negative conceiving itself as a positive. [Crowley, 1977, p. xxv].

אִין en or ain. Naughtness, nothing. 1st veil of the absolute. The primal darkness before manifestation. The latent state of cosmic night, containing potencies of the supernal triad. Aleph: pure Spirit or creative power, Unity; Yod: the Formative power of Spirit - The word related to Chokmah; Nun: the reproductive potency of the Cosmic Mother. The absolute as a living mind, the root-source of all substance and energy, protecting, guarding and teaching its manifestations. see 31, 538, 48, 711.

I. Thus לֹא (not, No-Thing) are the usual sign for nothing and for not. This nothing is all. It is the darkness of אִין *Ain* (61), or אֵל increased by 30, and the time shall come when human speech shall show this forth. *Ain* and its numeral value expresses the thought that in the future men would express the idea which is written אֵל, so that a-l-l, the English word, does exactly fulfill this. ALL in English stands exactly for what Qabalists mean by *Ain* (61). see 31, 713, 50, 106 and **29**.

II. The two primal elements as Adam and Eve supply the key also to the magical complex that was reared on the polarity of the sexes. Adam, 45, and Eve, 16, when combined produce *Ain*, 61, which is the source of manifestation as the Eye of the Void. [Grant, 1994, p. 65.]

אדן master, lord, possessor (Psalm 97:5). Root of the divine name Adonai, Lord. However negative may be our ideas of the No-thing (אין) it is the master power, containing all other potencies with itself. The ancient Semitic root appears in the Greek Adonis, the name of the God the Greek borrowed from the Babylonian and Phoenician Mysteries of Tammuz. see 65, 207, 1065.

בטן beten. belly, stomach, womb, the inmost part. It refers to the fruitfulness and power of growth which are inseparable from any true notion of the nature of the One Reality. The "great womb" of the No-Thing is the same as the Mulaprakriti, or root-matter, of Hindu philosophy. It is also that which is inmost in the life of man. Wherever we are, there It is also, with all its limitless supply for every human need. It also suggest that our sense of being in the physical body is largely due to the visceral sensation.

אין (nothing) is the same as אני (I, myself, see below), and בטן, Behten the womb of the Dark Mother refered to in the beginning of the Stanzas of Dzian as the 'Eternal Parent.' Here is the Key to the most potent of magical operations. They who can, may find the lock which it opens into the garden. Remember Adonai in its fullness (אלף דלת נון יוד) is the same number as תרעא (671) the Gate, and this door you will find in Malkuth. see **20**.

אמך ammeka. thy mother (Exodus 20:12). The commandment, "Honor thy mother," is that the human, earthly mother is a symbol and visible representation of the protective, nourishing power of *Ain*. For all that is the perfection of feminine and masculine potencies must be ascribed to the No-Thing.

Ameka is our Mother, and her heart swells with love. *Ameka* is 61, and so is בטן *beten*, the dark womb of creation. As well as אין *Ain*, the Boundless, for there are no limits to the overflowing love, springing like a fountain of Living Waters from the heart of the Mother.

Binah is identified with *Ameka*, our Mother, this is the same as the first veil of *Ain. Ain* is the vast expanse of the dark nothingness which is the womb of creation. Binah is the sphere of Saturn and the Path of Tav. Key 21 associated with Saturn shows the idea of the eternal equilibrium or perfect rest at the center. This rest is is identified with the Waters of Life which are identified with Binah. Key 21 is, in plain sight, a representation of the idea expressed in Hebrew as the word *Ain*, which is both *beten* and *Ameka*. see 67, 400, 713, & C.32.

אילך farther, further, hither, thither, afterwards. Increased distance, or lengthened spatial relation (farther), and also of going beyond previous performance or attainment, the conception of transcendence (further). It serves also to remind us that *Ain*, the First Veil, designates something beyond the range of intellectual definition or perception. Compare these ideas with the symbolism of the Fool, which corresponding to *Ain*.

אליך to thee, toward thee [Genesis 43:9]. Farther expresses the idea of motion away from an observer. Toward thee expresses the idea of motion toward an observer. In relation to *Ain*, however remote the No-Thing may seem, it is omnipresent, nearer than anything else. Man's yearning and striving toward the Infinite is a reaction to the One's earlier movement toward the heart of man. One familiar phrasing of this idea is, "Behold, I stand at the door and knock."

אני I, myself. First person, singular pronoun. There is only one Real Self in the universe. Understood "I" as being essentially identical with that Self, and is the fullness of all being-yet also the *Ain*, because it goes beyond every limitation of Things. 37th name of Shem ha-Mephorash, short form. see 92 & Appendix 10.

הון wealth, riches, capital, substance. as an adverb enough. From a root which means: to be empty; to gain by effort. The nature of the effort has been perfectly expressed by Lao-tze in his admonition: "Having emptied yourself, remain where you are." Our true wealth is within us-the Ain is the true basis of all material possessions. Letter by letter it signifies: Vision (Heh), intuition and the power of correlation (Vav) and imagination (Nun), are the basis of creative power. see 711

םוֹיַה this day (Deuteronomy 9:l). One of the words delusions is that we are somehow separated from the, Ain. Or speech betrays us. The wise live out "this day" with smiling hearts. For the Ain is beyond time, just as certainly as it is free from other restrictions. ALL that it is, it is NOW.

הָלַךְ motion, walking. The root-idea is "a series of steps." Walking is the human function which The Book of Formation associates with the letter Nun and Key 13. The Fool is shown in the act of walking, with one more step ahead of him before he comes to the edge of the precipice. However free from action the Absolute may appear to be, it is Itself the very essence of progress and advancement. It is dynamic being-in-action. It is the Primal Will craving urge (1), towards the production of beautiful results (6). We have difficulty with the idea of a moving Absolute, because motion seems to be the contradiction of all that "Absolute" means.

נָגַח to thrust, or push, as with the horns of an animal, to butt. Figuratively: to make war. *Ain* as the inexhaustible source of a dynamic energy which thrusts itself into manifestation forcibly, and in so doing becomes the adversary of inertia.

נָוַה to abide, to dwell; as a noun: *naven*, home, habitation. The *Ain* is our dwelling place. In it we live, and move, and have our being. To experience it is to realize that the Ain is our home, a haven of refuge and a place of safety. As an adjective: same pointing, beautiful, comely, dwelling, abiding.

דְּמַבְיָה "God, Fountain of Wisdom." 65th Shem ha-Mephorash. 321E-325E PIEBION-Moon. May 23, August 5, October 14, December 25, March 7. 9:20-9:40 [Psalm 90:13] Against sorcery, and to obtain wisdom and the success of useful enterprises. Rules the seas, rivers, springs, maritime expeditions, and naval constructions. Influences sailors, pilots, i.e. ?PCHE?, and all those engage in commerce. Person born: distinguishes himself at sea by his expeditions and discoveries, and amasses a considerable fortune. Associated with the 5th quinance; Angel of 10 of Swords. This represents the operation of Malkuth; sphere of the elements, in Yetzirah, the World of Formation. "Damabiah is an angel of the Order

of Angels with dominion over naval construction." [Davidson, 1971, p. 94.] see 965, 46 & Appendix 10.

זַאגָן Zagan. Goetic demon #61 by night of the 1st decanate of Sagittarius. This decanate corresponds to the 8 of Wands which is the operations of Hod, the lower mind, in Atziluth, the archetypal plane. see 711 & Appendix 11.

I. *Goetia*: "He is a great king and president, appearing at first in the from of a bull with gryphon's wings; but after a while he puts on human shape. He makes men witty. He can turn wine into water, and blood into wine, also water into wine. He can turn all metals into coin of the dominion that metal is of. He can even make fools wise. He governs 33 Legions of Spirits." [Mathers, 1995, p. 60]

II. "זָא: za. Every idea of movement and of direction; noise, the terror which results therefrom: *a dart; a luminous ray; an arrow, a flash*. The Arabic indicates, as onomatopoetic root that state of being shaken in the air, the noise made by the things shaken." [d'Olivet, 1976, p. 339.] And of the last 2 letters see 52.

הֲוִילָה Havilah. Name of a land (where gold is). Genesis 2:11. see 59, 44, 345.

יְיָאֵל 22nd Shem ha-Mephorash, attributed to Psalm 121:5. Associated with the 4th quinance (16E-20E) of Scorpio; Angel by night of the 6 of Cups. This represent the influence of Tiphareth; sphere of the Sun or Central Ego, in Briah, the World of Creation. "Ieiaiel is an angel of the Future, sharing the office with Teiaiel." [Davidson, 1971, p. 148.]

materia (Lt). matter, substance. This extends the conceptions we have been considering in relation to [אָמֵן] and [בְּטֶן]. We must constantly readjust our conception of substance. We must continually we rid ourselves of the false notion that power and wealth are to be sought in the accumulation of things. The world's failures may be traced to belief in external things and to dependence on them. They never fail who rest secure in their reliance on the Ain.

magnum (Lt). great. Refers to the Great Work. see 124.

artis (Lt). of (the) Art. this is the art of alchemy, which transforms the dross personality into the Gold of union with the Higher Self. see 314 (Lt).

coelum (Lt). Heaven. The abode of Spirit, source of matter.

terrae (Lt) . of earth. The vessel of Spirit is every form of "earth", or the physical plane. see 56.

62

The number of vertices, lines and faces on a Icosahedron and Dodecahedron.

בין to understand, discern, know, perceive, to distinguish, separate mentally-part of the discrimination which characterizes illumination. . The root of Binah בינה [67], understanding, which is the finitizing principle. With different pointing: between, among, during. see Genesis 1:4.

"*Beyn*... does not mean 'divide' in Hebrew, but 'between' or rather 'among', and according to the code it has a far greater significance. Its letter-numbers show that 2 [ב] and 10 [י] (containers in existence) unfold a cosmic 700 [ב,ך]which is the first and ultimate principle at stake in the universe: the freedom of indetermination." [Suraes, 1992, p. 88.]

בלל to overflow; to mingle, mix. Note that to mix, mixture is equivalent to the old sense of temperance, the title of Key 14. Also that this word: אסא healing and זנה adultery, false mixture. Other meanings: to confuse, confound; to mix fodder; to stir, knead.

זנה false mixture; to commit fornication, be a harlot, figuratively, to go after strange gods. Also: with different pointing: to commit fornication; also: to be committed (fornication)

בני the sons. Temperance purifies the sons (and daughters) of God. see 52, ?898?

מבהיה "God Eternal." 55th Shem ha-Mephorash 271E-275E. SMAT, Jupiter. May 13, July 24, October 4, December 15, February 25. 6:00-6:20 PM. [Psalm 102:12] "But thou O Lord, shall

endure forever; and thy remembrance unto all generations." To receive consolation, and for those who desire to have children. Rules morals and religion, influences those whom it protects in all their endeavors, and prospers their undertakings through all possible means. Persons born: distinguishes by his good deeds, his piety, and by his zeal to full his [duty] toward God and men. Associated with the 1st quinance of Taurus; Angel by day of the 5 of Pentacles. see 965 & Appendix 10.

ווים "hooks", pegs, nails. Used in the construction of the veil of the Holy of holies, in the Hebrew Tabernacle. [Exodus 38:28] "And of the thousand seven hundred and seventy-five shekels he made hooks for the pillars, and overlaid their capitals, and overlaid the hooks with silver." see 12, 1775 = palace of the body of heaven, i.e. Netzach, sphere of Venus.

ניב produce, fruit. [Malachi 1:12] "But you are profaning it, [i.e. the Lord's name] in that you say, the table of the Lord is polluted and its food (fruit) is contemptible." Also in [Isaiah 87:19] "I create the fruit of the lips [i.e. speech); peace, peace to those who are afar off and to those who are near, says the Lord; and I will heal them."

האון Ability, vigor.
וכול hold.

כהנה behold.

במחזה in the vision of the Lord.

ב/ס Beth/Samekh. Mercury in Sagittarius.

טוב מאד very good. "Not only is 9.6.2 [טוב] the building of shells (or containers, or physical supports) but 40.1.4 [מאד] which qualifies that process could not express more clearly the imprisonment of *Aleph* within two resistances, 40 and 4." [Suraes, 1992, p. 89.]

post (Lt). after. following the discoveries, one becomes an illumined brother. Part of a phrase in Secret symbols. see 717.

sophia (Lt). wisdom. From Greek σοφια [981]. see 73 (Chokmah).

chalybs (Lt). steel. "Our chalybs is the true key of our Art, without which the Torch would in no wise be kindled, and as the true magi have delivered many things concerning it, so among vulgar alchemists there is great contention as to its nature. It is the ore of gold, the purest of all spirits; a secret, infernal, and yet most volatile fire, the wonders of the world... As steel is attracted to the magnet, and the magnet turns toward the steel, so also our Magnet attracts our Chalybs. Thus, as Chalybs is the ore of Gold, so our Magnet is the true ore of our Chalybs. The hidden centre of our Magnet abounds in Salt, which salt is the menstruum in the Sphere of the Moon, and can calcine gold. This center turns toward the pole with anarchetic appetite, in which the virtue of chalybs is exalted by degrees..." [Waite, 1974, vol. 2, pp. 166-167]. Case notes: *chalybs* = 62 = *Sophia*.

valles (Lt). a valley or vale; use in Rosicrucian and alchemy to designate the field of the great work. Compare this with the various details of Tarot symbolism which show the great work as being carried on, and especially as beginning, at the level of self-conscious awareness. Note that in Key 0, the Fool (Aleph-spirit) is descending into the valley of manifestation. see 45 (Lt).

framer (Lt). Brother. The "brethren" are spiritual related through the Heart. see 701, 246.

intacta (Lt). Untouchable. Part of a motto found on the tomb of Brother CR. see 136 (Lt).

63

חן the grace.

כבוד-אל Kabode-AL. the Glory of God. Spirit resides in all manifested form, yet it takes self-conscious work to recognize this. see 32, 67, 73, 833, 124, 419, 430

The Glory of God is the Kabode-El, for God is One and alone and there is nothing else, as it says Isaiah. *Al* is 31, and *Kabode* is 32, so that *Al - Kabode* is 63. Ponder closely. Sixty-three is 9 times 7. On the Tree of Life this is the multiplication of Victory (7) by the power of the Foundation (9). Among the letters it is the multiplication of *Zain* (7) by the power of *Teth* (9). Nore are these different. Because Victory (Natzach) is the Sword of Understanding (Zain),

and the Foundation (Yesod) is the power of the Royal Serpent.

The Path of *Zain* links Binah to Tiphareth, and that *Zain* זין is 67, as is בינה. Right disposition is rooted in Understanding (Binah), and this is the sharp sword of discrimination (*Zain*). There is no love without understanding, and love must be discriminating in the good and constructive sense of this word. Note that *Zain* as 7 must be multiplied by *Teth* as 9 to make the 63 of *Kabode-AL* and though Teth is the serpent-power, the Tarot pictures that power as a red lion (Key 8, Strength), tamed by a woman who represents the feminine aspect of Chesed. Every Sephirah is both male and female. Female, as receiving the descending influence. Male as projecting it to whatever paths are below. The feminine Chesed is pictured as being like the Empress. For the taming of the lion and the serpent, these two being really identical, is woman's work even as it is written in the writings of the Sons of Hermes. This is, if you understand, a practical revelation of the Great Arcanum. See **23**.

אבדון destruction; the angel of the bottomless pit. Abaddon has also been identified as the angel of death and destruction, demon of the abyss, and chief of demons of the underworld hierarchy, where he is equated with Samael or Satan. The Hebrew name for the Greek Apollyon, Απολλυων (1461) in Revelations 9:11.

I. Also the angel (or star) that binds Satan for 1,000 years, as in Revelation 20. In Proverbs 15:11: "Sheol (Death) [the place of the dead] and Abaddon (destruction) [the abyss, the final place of the accuser Satan] both are before the Lord; how much more the hearts of the children of men?"

II. "According to Mathers, *The Key of Solomon the King*, Abaddon is a name for God that Moses invoked to bring down the blighting rain over Egypt. The Qabbalist Joseph Ben Abraham Gikatilla denominates Abaddon as the 6th Lodge of the seven lodges of Hell (Arka), under the presidency of the Angel Pasiel.. Abaddon has also been identified as the angel of death and destruction, demon of the abyss, and chief of demons of the underworld hierarchy, where he is equated with Samael or Satan." [Davidson, 1971, pp. 1-2.]

וכנה and establishes.

בונה builder, founder. All building or creation takes place with the letter Heh (the vision of the prophet) and is accomplished by division (Zain, the Sword) from the unity of the whole. see 68.

זון to feed, nourish. The substance or water of creation nourishes all things.

גלל to roll, roll off, roll away, remove; to roll up a scroll. The scroll is that of memory, which is rolled up upon completion of the creative process.

סבא old, aged; ancestor; grandfather; elder. The race-memory is connected with these. see 189, 604.

נחה to guide or lead; to bring. In Exodus 23:34: "But go now, lead the people where I told you. Behold, My angel shall go before you; nevertheless in the day when I punish, I will punish them for their sin."

סג "Secret" name of the World of Briah. see Appendix 7.

"The circumferential sign united to the organic sign, constitutes a root whose purpose is to depict the effect of the circumferential line opening more and more, and departing from the center: thence all ideas of *extension, augmentation, growth*: *physical possibility*." [d'Olivet, 1976, p. 406.]

דגן Dagon. A fish-god of the Philistines. [1 Samuel 5:2] "After the Philistines had captured the Ark of God, they took it from Ebenezer to Ashdod. (2) Then they carried the Ark into Dagon's Temple, and set it beside Dagon." see 713.

נביא prophet. In Exodus 7:1: "Then the Lord said to Moses, 'see I have made you like God to Pharaoh, and your brother Aaron will be your prophet." One who foretells future events, or who speaks for God.

חימה fervor [Crowley, 1977, p. 10]. Not found in scripture or the Hebrew Lexicon.

opus (Lt). Work. Refers of the alchemical great Work. see 124, 61.

Magnesia (Lt). the first Matter (In Alchemy).

64

I. (8 x 8) or 2^6

דין Deen. Justice, the highest name for the 5th Sephirah, Geburah. It is the square of 8, the special number of the Sephirah Hod, and of the letter Cheth, which is the channel carrying the influence from Binah down to Geburah. The wise see meaning and purpose in the reign of divine law. In human personality are summed up all the forces and laws of the universe. Man is the instrument through which the Life-power brings the Great Work to completion, symbolized by the pentagram, one of the geometrical correspondences to the number 5 and Geburah. see 92, 216, 95, 297, 850.

דני Doni. a twin intelligences of Gemini. The 50th name of Shem ha-Mephorash, short form. see 95 & Appendix 10.

אנחה a sigh, a groan, a deep breathing. The deeper meaning refers to the exercises of volition and of the practice of deep breathing, which is part of the practical technique of every Greater Adept. Superficially, emotional reactions to those who do not understand Divine Justice.

נוגה Nogah. The sphere of Venus (alternate spelling. Netzach on the Tree. External splendor. see 58, 148, [K.V., p. 57]

אדם חוה Adam-Eve/Havvah. Adam and Eve. A Qabalistic verbal symbol for all humanity. "The form of man, says the Rabbi Benjohai [Zohar I: 191, III:144], contains all that is in heaven and earth-no form, no world could exist before the human prototype; for all things subsist by and in it: without it there would be no world, and in this sense we are to understand these words, The Eternal has founded the earth upon his Wisdom."

והאבן "and this stone" (Genesis 28:22). Refers to the Stone of Bethel, which tradition identifies with the "crowning stone" now in Westminster Abbey. The letters of והאבן form הוא בן, and read *Hu Ben* to indicate that *Hu* (Kether) and *Ben* (Tiphareth) are united in the mysterious אבן,

Ehben, Stone. This "Stone" is the Lapis Philosophorum, or Mercurius de Mercurio. *Hu Ben*, moreover, may be read: "He (is) the Son (or "Stone")." see 216. Mark 1:11.

מי זהב Water of Gold, Golden Waters. Concerning which there is much in the works of Alchemist. In Genesis 30:39 This name appears as two words. Mother of Matred and Grandmother of Mehetabel. The first two letters refer to Mercury (מי). see 50, The Greater Holy Assembly (para. 996).

I. The *Aesch Mezareph*, speaking of alchemical Silver: "This wife (or female) is also called Me Zahab, the Waters of Gold, or such a water as sends forth Gold.

If the artist be betrothed to her, he will beget a daughter, who will be the water of the royal bath. Although some would have this bride to be the waters that are made out of Gold; which bride (not-withstanding) poor men leave to be espoused by great men." [Westcott, 1997, pp. 39-40]

מיזהב the mother of Matred; mother of gold.

I. I.R.Q. Para. 996: "'The daughter of MTRD, *Matred*,' the elaborations, on the side of Severity: 'the daughter of MIZHB, *Mezahab*;' that is they have been firmly contempered and intertwined together-namely MI, Me, Mercury (This partakes of alchemical symbolism-Mezahab, the philosophical Mercury.) and ZHB, Zahab, Gold, Mercy, and Judgment."

נוח to include, lie down, rest. The proper name Noah (variant spelling, see 58). Also rest, quiet, resting place in Esther 9:16. As an adjective: pleasing, kind, easy, benign.

מטה to expand, to extend, stretch out. In Isaiah 44:13: "The carpenter selects a piece of wood, and stretches out his rule; he marks it out with a line; he fashions it with planes and makes it into the likeness of man, according to the beauty of man."

סבב to revolve, turn, surround.
ידים hands.

הגוים the nations (Hosts), the gentiles. Hence all of unredeemed humanity (Adam) who are not yet part of spiritual Israel. In the microcosm, the millions of unspecialized body-cells, which have not been transmuted into light-bearers by higher vibratory rates.

הגן Worthy, respectable, suitable, proper. A Rabbinical word. It implies, as does the English "worthy", that what it describes is equal in value to something else, has been weighted and not found wanting, is rightly adjusted to use. Compare theses ideas to Key 11.

החוילה "(Land of) Havilah" (where there is Gold)". [Genesis 2:11]. see 59, 44, 345.

נבואה prophecy, prediction.

יחום sexual excitation; poetical name for Son [יחום], a medieval word. Compare with פחד "Thigh" (92) and פחדים, meaning gonads, testicles (142). Both these words are part of the Gematria of Geburah.

ידיד יהוה Beloved of God [Deuteronomy 33:12; John 13:23].

מידי from my hand.

גונה serenity [Godwin, 1999. p. 505.]. The state of inner peace.

סד stocks (for the feet of a culprit). In Job 13:27: "You fasten my feet in shackles; you keep close watch on my paths by putting marks on the soles of my feet."

חוים Hivites. A petty tribe of Canaan, conquered by the Israelites; a term used to indicate tent-dwellers or "villagers." see Genesis 10:17.

I. "Bestial Life." "The absolute verb חוה, receiving the sign of potential manifestation in place of the convertible sign, becomes the symbol of universal life חיה: But if the first character of this important word degenerates, and is changed into that of elementary existence, it express in חזה only natural, animal, bestial life:

if it degenerated again still further, and if it received the sign of material sense, it becomes the symbol of absolute material life in עיה." [d'Olivet, 1976, p. 288.]

αληθεια. aletheia (Gr). truth. "Not forgetting." Suggest perfect memory. The magician opposes reality to appearance, fact to fancy, order to disorder. "You shall know the truth and the truth shall make you free." For that which is at once liberation and preservation is the understanding and living of truth.

γενεα. genea (Gr). Birth, race, descent; a generation, offspring, age, period, time, nation.

dictum (Lt). a saying; a prediction, a prophecy; an order, a command. The Perfect Law is at once a prophecy and a command.

domus (Lt). abode, dwelling, home, house. The Divine Justice is our true abiding place.

salus (Lt). health, well-being, prosperity, deliverance, preservation.

sal aqua (Lt). salt water (Secret Symbols, page 30). Sal Aqua is called also Matrix Corpus, matrix of the body. The correspondence is to Geburah as the Sphere of Mars. see 674, 82, 156.

solve (Lt). dissolve. The first of two alchemical admonitions. The other is coagula, coagulate. Dissolution comes first. We must remember that the use of creative imagination is concerned with the breaking down of old forms and habits as well as the building up of new ones. You cannot become the New Creature and remain as you are. There is a relation between the highest functions of Geburah and alchemical dissolution.

sperma (Lt). seed. The whole alchemical work has to do with the "seed of metals." The "metals" are the inner centers of the body, the stars or chakras. The power which works through them is the "seed". The Mars energy can bring the 7 psychic centers (metals) into conscious activity. Human beings are sometimes called "metals" by the alchemists. On the same page of THE Secret Symbols where we find sal aqua, we read "Semen Spiriti Sancti," and, in the Latin of the Rosicrucians, semen and sperma are interchangeable terms (ex semen spiriti sancti). see 50 (Lt), 146, 210, 199 (Lt).

Virgo (Lt). A Virgin. Name of the zodiacal sign Virgo, symbolized in Tarot by Key 9, the Hermit, and by the letter Yod. see 10, 20, 515 (Greek).

Paragon. Webster: to compare; to parallel; a mold or pattern. "The true philosophers are far of another mind, esteeming little the making of [physical] Gold, which is but a paragon, for besides that they have a thousand better things..." [R.C. Allegory, p. 7].
Gradus (Lt). Step, grade. Implies a level of consciousness, Part of a Latin Phrase. see 166.

Anima media (Lt). middle spirit. "...figured by the Tree of Knowledge... the only medicine to repair the decays of the natural man..." [Thomas Vaughan].

Δαναη (Danae). Literally "dry earth." See the myth the union of Zeus (Air) and Danae (dry earth). Zeus transformed himself into a shower of gold, and Danae gave birth to Pereus.

65

The number of the units of the pentagon when the length of the sides are 13 units each.

אדני Adonai. Lord. Divine Name for Malkuth, attributed to the element earth [ארצ]. The Haikal, or temple, is for human personality the physical body, and that body is formed from the earth, or physical manifestation of the Life-power's spiritual energy taking form as the "matter" constituting man's body in his physical environment. All activities of man are carried on within the being and body of Adonai. See 671.

דודאים Mandrake. In Genesis 30:14: "And Reuben went in the days of wheat harvest, and found Mandrakes in the field, and brought them unto his mother Leah. Then Rachel said to Leah, give me, I pray thee, of thy son's Mandrakes."

I. Waite: "As I pondered in my mind the marvels of the Most High, and the duty of fervent love to our neighbors, which he laid upon us; I remembered the wheat of harvest, when Reuben [259] the son of Leah, found Dudaim in the field, which Leah gave to Rachel for the love of the Patriarch Jacob." [Waite, 1974, vol. 1, p. 57]

II. Paul Case: *Deodayim = Adonai = haikel.* H*aikel,* according to *Sepher Yetzirah,* is in the midst. Note that mandrakes, are aphrodisiac. The same root is found in דוד = זהב, Gold.

כמה Cama or Kama. to pine, or long for. Name of the Hindu God of love, or desire.

ללה 6th name of Shem ha-Mephorash, short form. see 96 & Appendix 10.

היכל temple, palace. Meeting place for the Shekhinah. Paul Case: *Haikel* is 65. It is "in the midst" according to *Sepher Yetzirah*-the interior center (Tav). *Haikel* may be read ה י כל = The Yod All. The Yod is the point of concentration. "Light and there was Light. These words imply that there had already been Light. This word אור (light), contains in itself a hidden significance.

הס hush! keep silence. In Habbakuk 2:20: "The Lord (יהוה) is in his holy temple [היכל], let all the earth [ארץ] keep silence before him." see 671.

"Onomatopoetic and idiomatic root which depicts silence. The Arabic seems to indicate a sort of dull murmur, as when a herd grazes in the calm of night." [d'Olivet, 1976, p. 332.]

דומיה silence, quietness; the 4th occult maxim (to keep silent). Hence: trusting in silence, hoping, waiting. In Psalm 62:1: "Truly my soul trust God in silence; my salvation comes from him."

גם יחד together in unity [Psalm 133:2]. Important phrase in Masonry. see 2, 13, 22, 1169.

הלל to shine, glory, praise, to commend, sing praises, Thanksgiving. Psalms 113-118 recited by the Hebrews on new moon and festivals. With different pointing: to shine, to be boastful, foolish. Mathers [K.V. Introduction 66] writes: אדני" is the queen by whom alone Tetragrammaton can be grasped, whose exaction into Binah is found in the Christian assumption of the virgin." see 52.

מזוזה door post. A rolled up piece of parchment containing Deuteronomy 6:4-9 and Deuteronomy 11:13-17 fixed on the door post.

מכה stroke, wound, beating, blow; plague, defeat (in war). With different pointing: to deal one a heavy blow. Indicates misuse of the physical plane.

סה Silence. "Root analogous to אס [circumference, tour, circuit, rotundity]. The Arabic indicates the circumference of the buttocks: the *rump.* סהד That which is round in form; *a tower, a dome, the moon; a necklace; bracelets,* etc." [d'Olivet, 1976, p. 407.]

נהי wailing, lament, mourning-song. Notariqon for נצח/הוד/יסוד or Netzach, Hod, Yesod. [K.D.L.C.K. p. 563]

אחים Weasels and other terrible animals [Crowley, 1977, p. 10]. This word does not appear in scripture or in the Hebrew Lexicon. It suggest the quality of guile and deceit which hinders the great work.

L.V.X. (Lt). Lux. Light. The universal radiance which is the essential substance of all manifested things. see 207.

jugum (Lt). yoke. Part of a Rosicrucian motto, Legis Jugum, found in the vault of C.R. related to the Sanskrit yoga or union, and to the throat-center symbolized by Taurus and by Venus. see 113 (Lt), 870 (Greek), 111.

follis (Lt). a leather bag, purse; a pair of bellows; puffed-out cheeks. Follis is a container for Air, or breath. The word fool is derived from the Latin *follis.* In the Tarot Key 0 is the Fool and is also associated with the element Air. Follis also implies the leather wallet of The Fool. The wallet is a symbol of memory, the summary of experience from previous manifestations. In the beginning of a new cycle, the Life-power carries the essence of all its experiences in former cycles. see 82

66

I. Σ11 = 66

II. Perimeter of a circle with a diameter of 21. The circumference of Yetzirah.

III. Mystical number associated with the Sephiroth Daath (The "11th" Sephiroth), the gateway to the Qlippoth, because 66 is the summation of the numbers from 1 to 11 (Σ11 = 66).

IV. The word 'us', in both verses, is qabalistically equal to 66 which is the 'Mystic Number of the *Qliphoth* and of the Great Work'. Here then is a key to the real meaning of the *Qliphoth* which has eluded qabalists and occultists alike, for few have fathomed the function of the *qliphoth* in relation to the Great Work. But when it is realized that the 'world of shells' comprises the reverse side of the Tree it is possible to understand why it has been regarded as wholly evil. The *qliphoth* are not only the shells of the 'dead' but, more importantly they are the anti-forces behind the Tree and the negative substratum that underlies all positive life. As in the case of the Egyptian Book of the Dead, the title of which signifies its precise opposite, so also the Jewish Tree of Death is the noumenal source of phenomenal existence. It is the latter that is false for the phenomenal world is the world of appearances, as its name implies. The noumenal source alone IS, because it is NOT. Once this truth is grasped it becomes evident that the ancient myths of evil, with their demonic and terrifying paraphernalia of death, hell, and the Devil, are distorted shadows of the Great Void (the *Ain*) which persistently haunt the human mind. These mysteries are explained in qabalistic terms by the number 66 which is the sum of the series of numbers from one to eleven. 66 is the number of the word LVL which means 'to twist' or 'go round' (the other side of the Tree). As already noted, humanity is 'booked for a turn round the back of the Tree' during the Aeon of Zain. In the Aeon of Zain humanity will have transcended the illusions of time and space, having understood the noumenal basis of phenomenal consciousness. [Grant, 1994, pp. 30-31.]

אכילה food, something edible. Indicates the source of daily bread as not being in the material world, but in the pattern world.

אלהיב thy God (is a consuming fire). [Deuteronomy 4:24; Isaiah 60:20; Exodus 20:7]. see 546.

בחן an assayer (of metals); a trial, a test. With different pointing: *bakhoon*. a watchtower, observatory.

גלגל literally, "whirl", a wheel, cycle, whirlwind; celestial orb, heaven (As the wheeling of the heavenly bodies- the "beginning of the whirlings" is attributed to Kether). A special name of Shekhinah, the Divine presence ("cognomen scheckinae"). Compare with Rota as the rotary nature of all formative activity (48).

Galgal is used in *Sepher Yetzirah* [2:4] as signifying circle, celestial orb, sphere: "Twenty-two foundation Letters: He placed them in a circle, like a wall with 231 Gates. The Circle oscillates back and forth. A sign of this is: There is nothing in good higher than Delight. There is nothing evil lower than Plague." [Kaplan, 1997, p. 108] see also 3, 21, 12, 30, 39, 48, 57, 75, 116 (and zero).

אניה a ship. Symbolizes the formative world as the connecting medium which carries the powers of the higher worlds down into the external physical plane. Conversely, the means whereby, on the path of return, we may be ferried over from the physical world to those beyond. see 7, 22, 14, 44, 21, 28, 88.

כמו like, as, when. [Exodus 14:5] see 19

דנהבה Give forth judgements. Capital city of Bela, King of Edom. [Genesis 36:32] "And Bela the son of Beor reigned in Edom: and the name of his city was Dinhabah". The kingdom of Edom is that of unbalanced force; compare דן, Dan, "Judgement" = putrefaction = Scorpio = 54.

I. IRQ: 522-527: "…What is Dinhabah? As if it were to be said, 'Give forth Judgment.' Like as it is written, Proverbs: 30:15: "The horse-leech hath two daughters crying, 'give, give.' But when he ascended, so that he may be formed therein, he cannot subsist and he cannot consist.

Wherefore? Because the form of the man is not as yet constituted. What is the reason of this? Because the constitution of man contains all things under this form, and in that from all things disposed. And because that constitution of Adam was not as yet found, they (*the Edomite Kings*) could not subsist, nor be conformed, and they were destroyed. Have they then been abolished, and are all these included in the (the supernal) man? For truly they were abolished that them might be withdrawn from form, until there should come forth the representation of Adam. But when that form is configured, they all exist, and have been resorted in another condition." [Mathers, 1993, pp. 175-176]

II. The name of a City of Edom which is the shadow of the City of the Pyramids (Binah) in the Desert of Set Its pylon, Daath, is the shrine of that Sacred Head (the Eighth) which the Templars adored under the image of Baphomet, the God of the Eightfold Name, *Octinomos*. [Grant, 1994, p. 32.]

גנוז hidden, secret. See "hidden light" (273).

בֶּן-דָּוִד Ben-David. son of David.

I. "The builders of the temple, then, must be 'the Son of David';. ...David is the English from of of the Oriental 'Duad,' which means 'Beloved,' and the Builder is therefore the Son of the Beloved. David is called in Scripture "the man after God's own heart," a description exactly answering to the name; and we therefore find that Solomon the Builder is the son of the man who has entered into that reciprocal relation with "God" or the Universal Spirit, which can only be described as Love." [Troward, 1942, p. 123.] see 375, 52, 14, 771 (Greek).

Aurora (Lt). Dawn. "The Chaldean word for dawn is שפרפר. In Daniel 6:1; this word, prefixed with the letter Beth is translated "in the morning" ["Then the King arose very early in the morning, and went in haste unto the den of lions"] It is written בשפרפרא, the final Aleph indicates that the word is definite, emphatic. There is a mystery here for this is a the Hebrew text is permutated. The first Peh is written much smaller that the other letters; and the second Peh is written much larger than the other letters. This method is call permutation." see 860.

[Giljhnston: Gematria of the Pentagram-compiled]

Biagenos (Lt). A Rosicrucian mountain; life-giving, generating, strength.

granum (Lt). A seed. In the *Fama*, brother CR is called "*Granum Pectori Jesu Insitum*," A seed planted in the breast of Jesus. The inner meaning has to do with Jesus own saying: "The seed is the word." Note that both "dawn" and "seed" imply the first stage of development. see 310, 95, 50, 99 (Lt).

Aurum (Lt). Gold. see 14, 109, 246 (Lt).

67 (prime)

I. The womb of the mother containing the twins. [Crowley, 1977, p. xxv].

בינה Binah. Understanding, the third Sephirah. Sometimes Binah is translated as "Intelligence." This must not be confused with *saykel* (350), which is the more general term for intelligence, or more accurately, for consciousness.

I. The fundamental meaning of Binah is the power of separation, the ability to distinguish truth from falsehood, and the power to adapt means to ends. Thus it is the mental ability to distinguish one thing from another which is the basis for understanding.

Binah is both the dark sterile Mother, אמא *Ama* and אימא *Aima*, the bright, pregnant Mother. This aspect of Reality is the matrix of all possible specialized forms of expression. *Ama* represents this aspect of Being prior to the beginning of a cycle of the Life-power's self-manifestation. *Aima* is the fertile womb from which flow forth all forms made manifest during such a cycle of the Life-power's self-expression.

Binah is called Shabbathai, the Sphere of Saturn, because every appearance of special, particularized manifestation necessitates *limits* of quantity, quality, mass, form, etc. In the astrological terminology of Ageless Wisdom, the contracting, limiting power is called Saturn. Note, in this connection, that the birth of living creatures results from contraction of the womb which carries the body during its period of gestation.

Binah is attributed *Neshamah* נשמה (395), the Divine Breath, the Holy Spirit in Christian symbolism. No matter how gravely a human being sins, this Neshamah is never involved. It is the highest aspect of Soul. The seat of the Divine Life's intuitive knowledge of all that it is, and of all that it must inevitably bring into manifestation because of what it knows itself to be. In man, Neshamah is the source of intuitive knowledge of spiritual truth. It is also the supreme source of guidance in the progress of man toward mastery.

Understand that the Sabbath of the Eternal never ends. How then may man find rest, save in the heart of the Mother? For that heart is the ever virgin Neshamah, and she is one with the Everlasting Heavens. Dark she is, but lovely, as Solomon says. The source of terror to the ignorant, and therefore *Pachad* (Geburah) depends with all its stern judgments from her. Yet is she also אמך *Ameka*, thy Mother, and her heart swells with love. *Ameka* is 61, and this is בטן *beten*, the dark womb of creation, and אין *Ain*, the Boundless, for there are no limits to the overflowing love, springing like a fountain of Living Waters from the heart of the Mother.

Everywhere may you find that heart, Children of Light, and nowhere else shall it be found, save at the center, which is the Holy Temple in the Midst (תם), where Shabbathai has its abode. There all is perfect rest, and thus was the great temple on earth built by Solomon, whose name signifies 'the peaceful,' and set up in Jerusalem the dwelling place of peace. For these outer things are but figures. Until you find the Hill of Zion in yourselves they shall be no more than figures, and dark ones in very truth.

There is a continual recurrence to the idea that the ONE is timeless. That sequence has little or no meaning to the consciousness which is above and beyond all human thought. Thus often there seems to be confusion in their words. For example Binah is identified with Ameka, thy Mother, and immediately this is indicated as being the same as the first veil of *Ain,* and as the vast expanse of the dark nothingness which is the womb of creation. Yet all the while dealing also with Saturn, and with the Path of Tav, and so

with the idea of the eternal equilibrium or perfect rest at the center. Moreover, that rest is by clear implication identified with the Waters of Life. You may remember the saying "To those who labor I will give you rest," and to have told the woman that if she but knew who was speaking to her, that knowledge would be a well of living water. The meaning is not far to seek. Had she known who spoke to her she would have known the central Reality of her own Being, and who knows that, finds eternal life, eternal rest, and perfect peace, for these three are one. What you must take as your clue to the application to most of the Text referring to Shabbathai, is the place of Tav on the Tree. Note that the *Mezla* descends to Malkuth through Tav, is what completes the perfection of Binah." See C.32.

חנט to ripen (as fruit, because ripeness, odor and flavor go together) , to embalm (a body) or preserve, to spice (food). Binah, Understanding, is a preservative and relates to the preservation of a body of wisdom inherited from the past. Binah perfects human personality through complete mastery of the physical organism. It is that which holds the Wisdom of Chokmah. Related to final mastery of the human organism and to the body of C.R. found fair and unconsumed in a sepulcher.

זין Letter name Zain. weapon, sword. The sword symbolizes discrimination gained through trial and error, and understanding is the ripened fruit of discrimination. There is a distinct relationship between the third Sephirah, the Suit of Swords and the Yetziratic world.

I. Mercury rules Gemini, represented in the Tarot by Key 6, and this is the key corresponding to Zain, whose number is 67, the same as Binah. Therefore the Path of Zain is the first channel for the descending influence of Binah, and partakes of her essential nature. She is pregnant with the descending influence from Kether through the Path of Beth." see C.33.

II. The secret of Tiphareth is 7, or Netzach; but since 7 is also Zain, the secret is shown in the Tarot by the Lovers, and their number in the series is 6 [Key 6]. Zain and Binah and to 67, whence the path of the Lovers descends to Tiphareth. 6, 9 and 13 are the Tarot numbers of זין. Not that 6 + 9 + 13 add to 28, the perfect number which is the extension of 7, and 7 is

Netzach. See C.13, 1081, 187, 148, 418, 134 (Lt).

III. Daleth is the path of union of **אב** (Ab, Chokmah) and **אימא** (*Aima*, Binah). Without that union, Binah is **אמא**, dark and sterile; but after that union she is *Aima* and brings forth *Ben*, the Son. The path of Zain carries down the power of Binah, and therefore is there a mountain, symbol of pregnancy, in the background of Key 6. see C.13.

זלל to shake, to tremble, to quake; to pour out, to shake out; motion to and fro. The root idea is vibration-a step downward from the perfection of Kether. To manifest at all, the limitless must enter into conditions of apparent restriction. Vibration is alternating activity, and the vibratory pitch of anything represents certain fixed limits or boundaries. This coincides with Binah as the first Sephirah of limitation and the basis of all form. Saturn is active in Binah because its root meaning is the same limitation and "fixing of boundaries" which is essential to the expression of anything at all. With different pointing: to be a glutton, to be vile, mean. Prodigality and waste, baseness. The product of unrestricted subconscious activity.

נגיד he who is foremost, he who is at the front. a leader, a prince, noble, a prefect (Daniel 9:25). The Hebrew name for the Rosicrucian Grade of Master of the Temple, corresponding to Binah.

בן יה Ben Yah. Son of Jah (God). [Lesser Holy Assembly, 228-229]

אבדן Father of Judgement. See Geburah and the Path of Lamed on the Tree of Life.

אוני Belong to the lobe, lobar. See K.D.L.C.K (p. 57).

וינא Vinah. Night Demon of the 3rd decanate [Saturn/Uranus] of Gemini.

כוליא Kidney; gonad.

יבמה Word which produces all things. 70th Shem ha-Mephorash. 346E-350E. THOPIBUI. May 28, August 8, October 19, December 30,

March 12. Genesis 1:1. Rules the generation of beings, and the phenomena of Nature; protects those who wish to regenerate themselves and establish in themselves the harmony interrupted by the disobedience of Adam, which they accomplish by exalting themselves toward God, and in purifying the elements which compose the nature of man; when he recovers his rights, his original dignity, when he becomes again the master of nature, and exercises all the prerogatives which God gave him in creating him. Person born: distinguished by his genius; consulted by the savants of all nations and becomes one of the first lights of philosophy. Associated with the 4th Quinance of Cancer; Angel by night of the 3 of Cups. This represents the influence of Binah, sphere of Saturn, in Briah, the World of Creation. see Appendix 10.

Jesus. Latin spelling of Yeshua. In Christian esotericism this name is applied to the Son, and we have seen that in the very word **בינה** are to be found the letters **ב** and **ן**, forming Ben, the Son.

Natura (Lt). Nature; Mother Nature. Nature is the Maya-Shakti of Hindu philosophy, the finitizing principle Qabalists name Binah.

unus (Lt) . one; alone, single, sole. Refers to the unity of all life. The actual substance of "all things" is the being of the Logos or Word [Logos = 373, reduces to 13, which is **אחד**, *echud*, one and **אהבה** *ahebah*, love, thus love and unity.] The established order of all things is a unity "all things" are nature. see 215, 39.

crucis (Lt). cross. The "cross" of the 4 elements, constitution the 4 colors of the Sephiroth Malkuth, the manifested universe, or Kingdom of God. see 65, Adonai, 193, 701 (Lt)

centro (Lt). It is in the Secret place within that we make contact with Binah. There, and there only, may we hear the voice. This inner center is the point at the center of the Cube of Space, the point at the innermost center of human personality, associated with Tav. Represents the meeting-place of the axes of the cube, which are 13.

templi (Lt). of the temple. The "temple is regenerated human personality; one who has succeeded in this "building" has become a Master of the Temple. see 84, 151 (Lt).

אבניה The Stones there of (of it). In Job 28:5,6: "As for the earth, out of it comes bread: and under it is turned up as it were fire. The stone of it are the place of sapphires: and it hath dust of Gold." The earth or physical body brings forth the bread of life from the "secret fire". In the passage cited, the phrase translated "stones of it" is אבניה, which broken down is יה אבן, ehban Yah. As *Yah*, is the special divine name attributed to Chokmah, and *ehban* expresses the union of Chokmah and Tiphareth, the son, *ehbawnayaw* is a symbol of that union. (Chokmah, as the sphere of the fixed stars, is the greater whole that includes the special sphere of the sun, or Tiphareth, in as much as the sun is one of the fixed stars. see 78, 536.

חכם Wise. With different pointing: *kawkham*. to be wise, act wisely; *kikkem*. to make wise, teach, wisdom; kukkahm. to be made wise.

הבונה The builder, founder. Wisdom is built upon the foundation of stone. see 63.

חיים life, the living ones; sustenance, maintenance. In Psalm 16:11: "Thou will show me the path of life: in thy presence is fullness of joy; at thy right hand there are pleasures for evermore."

זנוה harlot, prostitute. In Proverbs 23:27: (26) My son, give me your heart, and let your eyes observe my ways. (27) For a harlot is a deep pit; and a strange woman [wayward wife] is a narrow well." And in [Isaiah 23:16] "Take a harp, go about the city; O you harlot that has been forgotten; play sweet melodies, sing many songs, that you be remembered." see 308, 316 (Greek).

וכביאה Vacabiel. Lesser assistant angel of the sign of Pisces in the zodiac [In joint rule with Rasamasa, another Genius in Transcendental Magic]. Pisces is attributed to alchemical multiplication, to sleep, and to the Corporeal Intelligence, which organizes the body cells into the new image.

טין tin. clay. spelled טינא (Aramaic) in [Daniel 2:41] "And whereas thou saw the feet and toes, part of potters clay, and part of iron, the kingdom shall be divided; but there shall be in it of the strength of the iron, for as much as thou saw the iron mixed with miry clay." see 719, 28.

סם transgression; error, sin. Written סמה in [Psalm 101:3] "I will set before my eyes no vile thing. I hate to commit transgression; They will not cling to me."

"A root not used in Hebrew. The Arabic characterizes in general, a vehement, illegal action. The compound Arabic verb signifies literally *to command with arrogance, to act like a despot.*" [d'Olivet, 1976, p. 408.]

הדס Myrtle; considered as sacred to Venus by the ancients. In Isaiah 41:19: "I will put in the desert the Cedar and the Acacia, the Myrtle and the Olive. I will set pines in the wasteland, the fir and the cypress together.

Diabolos (Lt). Devil; slanderer.

I. In Psalms (Chapter 90) this is the number of years of the ordinary span of human life, in contrast to the magical age of 120 years Genesis 6.3).

II. The number of days the ancient Egyptians took to embalm a mummy.

III. the number of days the Star Sirius was below the horizon (in Egypt) to its heliacal rising.

IV. The 70 Elders of Israel (Book of Numbers).

V. the members of Jacob's family that went to Egypt.

VI. The number of day's the Egyptian's mourned Jacob's death.

VII. The number of years the Jews were in captivity in Babylon.

ע Ayin. The eye as an organ of sight, the visible part of an object, the surface appearances of things. A symbol of the phenomenal existance as opposed to the underlying spiritual reality. Ayin appears on the 15th Tarot Key, the Devil, called

The Slanderer. The untrained eye is the great deceiver. In this connection the Devil on Key 15 has the symbol of Mercury to indicate our need to use discrimination to pierce through the veil of outer from to the inner reality. In this connection note that the 26th Path of Ayin connectes Tiphareth (The Sun) to Hod (Mercury). Discrimination (Mercury) must pierce the veil of illusion (Ayin) before we enter the palace of the king (Tiphareth).

I. Rabbi Kushner comments: "The letter Ayin does not speak. It only sees. It is an eye, עַיִן. Close your eyes. Open your mouth. Now try to see. That is the sound of Ayin." [The Book of Letters]

II. Rabbi Glazerson comments: "The name of the letters עַיִן Ayin when rearranged, spells "Poor" עָנִי. The letter Ayin comes after Samekh in the alphabet, to teach us that a man should "support" (ס) the "poor" (ע) before poverty causes them to fall. In its shape also, the letter Ayin, with its one curved leg, suggest a person who has no firm basis; it is bending and unstable." [Letter of Fire]

III. "This character should be considered under the double relation of vowel and consonant. Following its vocal acceptation, it represents the interior of the ear of man, and becomes the symbol of confused, dull, inappreciable noises; deep sounds without harmony. Following its consonantal acceptation, it belongs to the guttural sound and represents the cavity of the chest. Under both relations as grammatical sign, it is in general, that of material sense, image of void and nothingness as vowel, it is the sign ן, considered in its purely physical relations: as consonant, it is the sign of that which is cooked, false, perverse and bad." [d'Olivet, 1976, p. 413.]

אדם וחוה Adam ve-Chavah. Adam & Eve. i.e. Humanity. see 45, 19, 64 (more commentary).

הסה Hush! Be silent! Hold your peace! With different pointing: *hasah*, to be silent; tongues. Compare this with the meaning of pax (35), has to do with the control of speech. Silence is one of the 4 occult maxims. It is the soundless voice of the inner life, expressing itself through thought. Silence intensifies desire. see 474, 346, 131, 815.

הסה means control of speech. It tells us there is something not to be disclosed, except to those qualified. This mystery is symbolized by the wine and its intoxication (both positive & negative). It is a mystery of darkness (ליל), limitation (סובב), and various appearances reported by our senses (see ע & Key 15). It is also a secret (סוד) of renewal and regeneration.

I. Paul Case: "The Hebrew word for silence הסה, claims our attention now. Its first letter is Heh, and so is its last. Our teachers in the Qabalah, tell us that the first Heh is the Heh of the Mother, Aima of Binah, while the last is the Heh of the Bride, Malkuth. The first Heh, therefore corresponds to the creative world and to the faculty of intuition. Thus it reminds us that to receive the interior tuition which reveals to us the mysteries of cosmic law we must learn to keep silent. The inner voice is not heard by those who indulge in needless talk, furthermore, the letter Heh is the letter of sight, and for the clearest, intensest vision, silence is essential. The second Heh may serve to remind us of Lao-Tze dictum the state should be governed as we cook small fish, without much business." When we come to apply whatever magical knowledge we may possess to the actual work of taking our part in the administration of the kingdom, we shall accomplish more work and do it better if we do not have too much to say about our plans and projects. The middle letter of *haseh*, Samekh, hints that in silence there is a supporting or sustaining power. That this is true every practical occultist learns sooner or later. The practice of silence as to what you aim at, as to what you are doing, has two very important practical results. First of all, it prevents other people from leaning of your plans and perhaps setting themselves in opposition to you. Thus silence is over and over again a time-saver and an energy-saver. Secondly, the practice of silence serves to intensity desire-force. Your one aim (the arrow of the archer, represented by the letter Samekh) is something that you must keep religiously to yourself. Not even your closest friends should know of it. This one aim is typified in Revelation by the white stone, upon which is written a name which no man knows, save him that receives it. The one things you have to do in order to fulfill your destiny will be, or perchance has been, revealed to you from within. See that you tell no man. For in silence and secrecy the strength and potency of that aim will be intensified until it dominates your whole life. But if you tell your secret to other people, virtue goes out of you and you are almost certain to incite somebody to acts of open or veiled opposition." (Theory of Magic pp. 166-168) [1925] see 815

כן. thus, so, just so, such, so much; honest. In Genesis 1:7: "So Elohim made the firmament and separated the water under the expanse from the water above it. And it was so." Also in Genesis 42:11: "We are all sons of one man. Your servants are honest [כנים, masculine plural] men, not spies." see 720.

"This root, wherein the assimilative sign is united to the root אן, image of all corporeal circumspection, is related to that which enjoys a central force energetic enough to become palpable, to form a body, to acquire solidity: it is in general, the base, the point upon which things rest.

That which holds to *physical reality, corporeal kind; stability, solidity, consistency; a fixed, constituted, naturalized* thing: in a restricted sense, *a plant*: in an abstract sense, it is the adverbial relatives, *yes, thus, that then*, etc.

The Arabic characterizes the state of that which is, that which exist, or passes into action in nature. This root which, in Arabic, has usurped the place of the primitive root הוה, signifies literally, *it existed.*

כון Action of *constituting, disposing, fixing, grounding*; action of *strengthening, affirming, confirming*; action of *conforming, qualifying* for a thing, *producing* according to a certain mode, *designating* by a name, *naturalizing*, etc." [d'Olivet, 1976, pp. 373-374.]

יין wine. This is word is used in Genesis 9:21: "And he [Noah] drank of its [the vineyard's] wine, and became drunken; and he was uncovered within his tent."

I. "And being steeped with the spirit of his production, he intoxicated his thought (attained ecstasy) and (in his exactation he revealed himself in the center (most secret place) of his tabernacle.

II. He comments: מו-חריין with-what-is-spirituous... The word יין, which is the natural order signifies simply *wine*, designates in the moral order, and according to the figurative and hieroglyphic sense, *a spiritual essence*, the knowledge of which has passed in all times, as belonging to the most profound mysteries of Nature. All those who have written of it, present the mysterious essence as a thing whose profoundness can not be known without revelation. The Kabbalists in speaking of this wine, that he who drank of it would know all the secrets of the sages. I can only offer to the read the grammatical analysis of the Hebrew word, leaving the rest to his sagacity.

I have often spoken during the course of my notes of the root אין [*Ain*], which enjoys the universal privilege of characterizing alternately, being and nothingness, everything and nothing...

It is evident that this root, emerging from the deepest abysses of nature, rises toward being or fall toward nothingness, proportionally, as the two mother vowels אי, enlighten or obscure it. From its very principle, it suffices to materialize or to spiritualize the convertible sign ו, in order to fix its expression upon objects genuine or false. Thus one sees it in און, virtue, strength, valor, and in אין, *vice, vanity, cowardice*, in יון the *generative faculty of Nature*; in יון the clay of the earth.

In the word here referred to, the two vowels are not only enlightened by replaced by the sign of potential manifestation י, image of intellectual duration. This sign being doubled constitutes, among the Chaldeans, one of the proper names of the divinity. United to the final sign ן, it seems to offer the very body of that which is incorporeal. It is a spiritual essence which many peoples and particularly the Egyptians, have considered under the emblem of light. Thus, for example, one finds in the Coptic word for *light* or *torch*. It is in conceiving this essence under the form *of spirit*, that those same peoples, choosing for it an emblem more within the reach of the vulgar, have taken for its physical envelope *wine*, that liquor so vaunted in all the ancient mysteries because of the *spirit* which it contains and of which it was the symbol. This is the origin of these words which, coming from the same root appears so different in signification: אוֹן *being* and ייר *wine*, of which the Greek analogous offer the same phenomenon: ων *being*, and οινοσ, *wine*.

...it is by an almost inevitable consequence of this double sense attached to the word ייר, that the cosmogonic personage called Διονυσος *Dionysus*, by the Greek, has finally designated for the vulgar, only the god of wine, after having been the emblem of spiritual light; and that the same word which we use has become such, only as a result of the same degradation of the sense which was attached to it, a degradation always coincident with the hardening of the mother vowel: for, from the word ייִן, is formed the Teutoic *wein*, the Latin *vinum*, and the French *vin*." [d'Olivet, 1976, pp. 264-265.]

III. "Noah transmutes downward his "Eesh" [איש, 311] quality of fire by becoming Eesh (husband) to Adamah [אדאמה, 50] (the earth). The earth reproduces this fire as wine (the wine as symbol expressed that fact, as the Qabalah well knows).

Genesis 9:21. The strange fruit of the nuptials between Eesh (as man-fire) and Adamah is Yeen [ייִן] a doble existence in the number 700. [Final Nun, ן = 700]... This *Yeen* is a sort of tornado in which anything can happen. The English word wine is the Hebrew word scarcely modified, so also is the Latin (incidentally, it is not generally realized how may of our words derive from, or are, the Hebrew ones).

This verse exemplifies the fact that the symbols of blood and wine belong to the same category. Having drunk, Noah-as is expected if his name נה, is understood-loses his Adamaic quality and sinks unto an unevolved state. The relationship between him and Adamah is all to Adamah's advantage. Noah's consciousness now lapses into the unconsciousness of undifferentiated cosmic life and uncovers the true significance of this Noah whose numbers reveal that he is a life not yet entered into the process of evolution (he falls asleep with his genitals uncovered)." [Suraes, 1992, p. 147.]

ליל night (literally, a twist away from light). A variant of לילה (75). Said in Genesis to be God's own name for חשב *khoshek*, darkness. The symbolism of Key 15, which corresponds to Ayin and 70, is a representation of darkness. It is a picture of the dark night of the soul, and of the adversity.

ילל howling. Deuteronomy 32:10: In a desert land he found him, in a barren and howling waste.

אדניה Lord (i.e. worshiper) of Jah. In 1 Kings 1:5: Now Adonijah, whose mother was Haggith, put himself forward and said, "I will be king"... Jah is a divine name attributed to Chokmah. see 15, 26, 73, 65.

נחבי Nahbi. occult. Numbers 13.14: from the Tribe of Naphtali, Nahbi the son of Vophsi (ופסע, meaning Additional).

מיכ 42nd name of Shem ha-Mephorash, short form. see 550, 101 & Appendix 10.

גוג ומגוג Gog ve-Magog. A name given to a race or people inhabiting some part of the northern region. Gog is used in 1 Chronicles 5:4; Magog appears in Genesis 10:2. The names "Gog and Magog", only appear together in the Greek of the apocalypse of John, where they are used as symbolic terms for the world as hostile to God's people and kingdom. In [Revelations 20:8] "And [the Adversary] will go forth to deceive those nations which are in the four corners of the earth, Gog and Magog, to assemble them together for war; whose number is as the sand of the sea."

I. D'Olivet renders Magog as "elasticity", or "elastic stretching power." "The root of גוה, which expresses a movement being opposed to itself, indicates in the word גוג an extension continued, elastic, pushed to its utmost limits. This word governed by the sign of exterior action מ, characterizes that faculty of matter, by which it is extended and lengthened, without there being any solution of continuity." [d'Olivet, 1976, pp. 273-274.]

סובב circle, ring, circumference.

סוד a council, assembly; secret; to plaster [Crowley, 1977, p. 10]. In Psalm 25:14: "The secret of the Lord is in those who revere him, and he shows forth his covenant to them."

αγνεια. hagneia (Gr). purity, chastity.

filius (Lt). Son.

tartar (Lt). a part of the alchemical salt.

vinum (Lt). Vinum.

71 (prime)

I. A number of Binah. The image of nothingness and silence which is a fulfillment of the aspiration. [Crowley, 1977, p. xxv].

יונה yonah. a dove, a pigeon. Used figuratively as a metaphor for sexual warmth, a marked characteristic of doves. One of the birds sacred to Venus (and is closely connected with Saturn). Refers to the reproductive functions of Venus, and creative imagination. see 70, 400, 406, 601, 378, 486, 700, 801 Greek.

I. Matthew 12:39: "But he answered and said unto them, an evil and adulterous generation seeks after a sign; and there shall be no sign given to it, but the sign of the prophet Jonas"

II. For as Jonah was three days and three nights in the whale s belly, so shall the son of man be three days and three nights in the heart of the earth." See also Matthew 16:14, Luke 11:29. **יונה** = Virgo (Yod) +Taurus (Vav) + Scorpio (Nun) + Aries (Heh) . see 59.

III. This is a symbol of Jonah, who was swallowed by the great fish (Nun, Key 13). Jonah is a symbol of Israel in the Bible. It was also form that the Holy Spirit took at Jesus baptism by John. Also spelled **ינה**, so that contains 3 of the 4 letters used in the spelling of **יהוה** with Nun.

IV. Cited by d'Olivet in Genesis 8:8: "Then he sent forth a dove from the ark, to see if the waters had abated from, the face of the ground." He renders the verse: "And he sent forth Ionah (plastic forces of nature, brooding dove) from him, to see if the waters were lightened from off the face of the adamic."

V. He comments: **היונה** Ionah.... Here again is an emblem famous in ancient cosmogonies; emblem, that the Greek and Latin interpreters have again presented under the least of its characteristics; under that of a dove. It is indeed true that the Hebrew word **יונה** yonah, signifies a dove, but it is in the same manner that the word **ערב** ereb [272], signifies a *raven*; that is to say, that the names of these two birds have been given them, in a restricted sense, in consequence of the physical or moral analogues which have been imagined between the primitive signification attached to the words E*reb* and Y*onah* and the apparent qualities of the raven and the dove. The darkness of *Ereb*, its sadness, the avidity with which it is believed that it devours the beings which fall into its pale, could they be better characterized than by a dark and voracious bird such as the raven? The whiteness of the dove on the contrary, its gentleness, its inclination to love, did not these qualities suggest it as an emblem of the generative faculty, the plastic force of Nature? It is well know that the dove was the symbol... Aphrodite, and of all the allegorical personages to whom the ancients attributed the generative faculty, represented by this bird…

It is evident that the name of Ionia, that famous country claimed equally be Europe and Asia, comes from the same source as the word **יונה**. The Chaladic and Hebrew **יון**, **יוני**, or **יונאי**, always designate Greece, or that which belongs to her: these are the Greek analogues Ιωνια, Ιωνικος. For, if we examining Greece concerning Ιωνικος, we find all ideas of softness, sweetness and amorous languor, which we attach to that of the *dove*. The Greek root Ιοv or Ιωv, contains the ideas of cultivated, fertile land; of productive soil; of existing being in general; of the violet flower consecrated to Juno, etc.

In the Hebrew root **יון** we find in general the idea of a thing indeterminate, soft, sweet, easy to receive all forms, and in particular, a clayey, ductile. In the hieroglyphic sense, and if we examine the signs of which this root is composed, we shall find in **יון**, the mysterious root אוי, where the sign of manifestation י, has replaced the sign of power א: so that, if the root אן designates indefinite being, the root יון will designate the same being passing from power into action.

יונה expresses the generative faculty of nature. In Hebrew, the compound word אביונה, signifies *desire of amorous pleasures*; and that one understands by the words יונה עלם, *a song, tender, melodious and capable of inspiring love.*

The word יונה holds very colely to the history of Nature, the reader may be interested to learn that the name of this soft Ionia, from which we have imbibed all that we have imbibed all that we have which is delightful in art and brilliant in knowledge, is attached on side to the mysteries dove of Moses, so that of Semiramis; and loses itself on the other, in that sacred emblem called *Yoni* by the Brahmans; *Yng*, by the Chinese *Tao-teh*, over which it is necessary that I draw an impenetrable veil." [d'Olivet, 1976, pp. 230-233.]

אמדוך Amdusias. Goetic demon #67 by night of the 1st decanate of Aquarius. see Appendix 11.

I. *Goetia*: "He is a duke great and strong, appearing at first like a unicorn, but at the request of the Exorcist he stands before him in human shape, causing trumpets, and all manner of musical instruments to be heard, but not soon or immediately. Also he can cause trees to bend and incline according to the exorcist's will. He gives excellent familiars. He governs 29 Legions of spirits." [Mathers, 1995, p. 63]

אימך thy terror. "The implications of הידה, riddle, and בכה, weeping." see 27

היון the mud, mire. see 99

אליל nothing, apparition; image; idol; false God; worthlessness, naught, i.e. appearance. see 121

אלם To be dumb, silent; which is also a name of a system of chanting called literally רחקים יונה אלם. "The dove who conceals that which is distant." With different pointing: to bind sheaves (of wheat). see Key 3

אנך To be pointed, to be sharp; an engraving tool; a plumb-line, plummet. In Amos 7:8: "And the Lord said unto me, Amos, what do you see? And I said, a plumb line. Then said the Lord, Behold, I will set a plumb line in the midst of my people Israel: I will not again pass by them anymore."

חזון vision, prophecy, divine revelation. True vision is a higher fruit of the reproductive power (Nun) and imagination (Daleth). see 137, 787

מלא complete, to overflow, to be filled; plentitude, fullness. All these words are connected with that principle which is at once Nahash, the tempter, and Messiah, the anointed, according to the mode of its manifestation. It is that which at once the serpent and the dove, that which is copper, or Venus. see 358.

coction (Lt). cooking or baking (alchemical term).

Annuit (Lt). He hath prospered. Part of the motto "He hath prospered our undertakings" on the great seal of the U.S. see 79, 150, 370 Latin.

72

18 x 4 or the multiplication of the 4 elemental powers through the activity of Yah, Chai, Life. The number of degrees on an arc of a circle inscribed by a pentagram and between 2 points of a pentagram.

חסד Chesed. Mercy, beneficence. 4th Sephirah. The primary meanings of Chesed are: eager, earnest desire, and ardor or zeal toward anything. Also kindness, love, good-will, pity and compassion. The measuring, arresting or receptacular Intelligence. A reservoir of Limitless power and substance of all things needful both spiritual and material. It rises like a boundary to receive the emanation of the Higher Intelligences which are sent down to it. The grade of Chasidim, Masters of compassion and healers which is the consciousness of exempt adept. see 48, 82, 194, 178, 528, 122.

I. Chesed is called Gedulah, [גדולה], Majesty or Magnificence. Chesed is known also as the Measuring Intelligence, for it is the basis of all adjustment, measurement, order & adaptation.

II. The basis of all adjustment and regulation is memory. The whole course of evolution is an orderly development made possible because the Universal Life has perfect memory. Every point of manifested Being is a focus of perfect memory. The One Life remembers perfectly all that it is in itself, and every event in the series of its self-expressions. Nothing is forgotten. Nothing is beyond recall. Human memory is one phase of this cosmic record.

Chesed is the Sphere of Tzedek, or Jupiter. Jupiter is the "sky-father" who was the ancient personification of the principle of Beneficent Regulation.

בסוד in the secret; in the magical language. This word has special reference to the ninth Sephirah, as well as to Chesed. It is connected with the intelligent direction of the force which is concentrated in Yesod. In human personality, this is the reproductive force whereby the race is perpetuated. Note that one of the paths proceeding from Chesed is Yod, which is symbolized by Key 9, the number of Yesod. Key 9 pictures that which is the true Foundation or Basis (Yesod) of all human activity; and the wise man it pictures, besides being a personification of the powers and beneficence of Chesed, is also one who is "in the secret" of intelligent direction of the secret force behind reproduction. Connected with the intelligent direction of the reproductive force concentrated in Yesod. Key 9 pictures a wise man "in the secret" of this force.

יוד הי ויו הי Yod-Hi-Vav-Hi. Special spelling of IHVH in the Archetypal world, Atziluth, related to the 4 of Wands. According to Ibnezra, their value as 72 refers to the 72 letters of Shem ha-Mephorash, the holy name of God. The divided name consists of 72 triliteral names, which by adding יה or אל give 72 angels. see 777 [columns CXXIX, CXXX, CXXXI and CXXXII] and Kabbalah unveiled, p.171. see also 26, 45

עב darkness, dark cloud, cloud mass; thicket, bag, wrapper. This word is used to indicate the "secret nature of the archetypal world" associated with the suit of Wands. To our intellectual consciousness this highest plane of the Life-power's activity is wrapped in clouds and darkness. Note that Jupiter (and also Jehovah) is a deity connected with cloud and storm. (See Key 10, which carries the influence of Chesed down to Netzach). With different pointing: threshold, sill; beam and as an adjective, thick, dense. see 965.

I. "The number of OB, the Serpent (Aub), the negative or feminine aspect of Od (Aud) which is the Magick Light itself; it is also the number of the Chaldean word דביון, meaning 'flux' or 'drop of blood'. The word derives from the Egyptian Typhon or Tefin, the Mother of Set. In the Egyptian Mysteries these twin powers the Ob and the Od were represented by Shu and Tefnut, the former signifying fire, the latter, moisture or blood." [Grant, 1994, p. 35.]

בכן in, so, thus, then; in such a way; and so; therefore. (see בן, masculine, base, pedestal; post, etc and as an adverb, so, thus, yes) see 52.

ויכלו and they are excellent, finished. The Merciful Ones, who are "in the secret."

Kανα. Kana (Gr). Cana, scene of Jesus 1st Miracle. Basically, "A reed used for measuring," connects with Chesed as the Measuring Intelligence. Measurement is suggested in the story of the miracle. See "place of reeds" 155.

η αληθεια. heh aletheia (Gr). the truth. In John14:6: "Jesus says to him "I am the way, the truth, and the life. No man comes to the Father, except by me." see 9, 18, 27, 36, 45, 54, 63, 81, 90.

Natron (Lt). Mineral alkali; nitre.

vacuum (Lt). empty, void, free, clear. Related to the 4 of Wands in the apparent emptiness of the archetypal world in periods between cycles of manifestation. It is connected with the Eternal Supply aspect of Chesed. In Atziluth this source of supply, in relation to the planes below, seems to be without form and sterile, yet all riches, all beneficence, have their origin in these archetypal principles (Sanskrit Pralaya).

Abiegnus (Lt). "of fir-wood". It is the name of the Rosicrucian "mountain of initiation." Kundalini (the Serpent-fire) rises through the seven interior stars or spinal centers to energize the pineal gland (which is shaped like a fir-cone), Mons Abiegnus, "Mountain of Fir-wood". Represents the Mystical ascent in consciousness, leading to a state of exaltation (illumination), often compared to intoxication [Among the Greeks the Fir tree was among the symbols of Dionysus, God of the vine. The Thyrsus, a staff used in the Dionysian Mysteries, was twined with ivy, and surmounted by a pine-cone.] It is an instance of the operation of Divine Grace. Like the Hermetic caduceus, it refers to the same ascent of Kundalini through the spinal centers which awakens the organ of higher vision. Christ is the true vine", The miracle of Cana changed water into wine, to promote joy at a marriage-feast. Wine is used in the Eucharist, as the material base for a true alchemical transmutation. Rosicrucian, Qabalistic and Alchemical literature is replete with symbols relating to the vine and its fruit. see 125, 129, 668, 811, 1035, 182.

verbum (Lt). word. The Latin equivalent for the Greek Logos. Verbum stands for the formative power of the Creative Idea.

Venus (Lt). Goddess of Love and desire, corresponding to the Greek Αφροδιτη, and Key 3, The Empress in Tarot. A most important key to the entire alchemical great work is the power of creative imagination. see 993 (Greek). 434, 3, 1035.

rubeum (Lt). red. The color of Mars. Part of a phrase. see 406.

naturae (Lt). of nature. Part of a phrase. see 132 (Lt), 156 (Lt).

balsamum (Lt) balsam. Concerning the alchemical dragon, or serpent-power, it is said in The Book of Lambspring: A savage Dragon lives in the forest, Most venomous he is, yet lacking nothing: When he sees the rays of the Sun and its bright fire, He scatters abroad his poison, And flies upward so fiercely That no living creature can stand before him, Nor is even the Basilisk equal to him. he who hath skill to slay him, wisely Hath escaped from al dangers. Yet all venom, and colours, are multiplied In the hour of his death. His venom becomes the great Medicine. He quickly consumes his venom, For he devours his poisonous tail. All this is performed on his own body, From which flows forth glorious Balm, With all its miraculous virtues. Here do all the sages loudly rejoice." [Waite, 1974, vol. 1, p. 286]. Case notes: *Balsamum* = 72 = Venus = *verbum*. see 37 (Lt).

73   (prime)

I. The combined numerical values of Mercury (37), Sulphur (7), and salt (29). An intimation that the powers of Mercury and Salt are combined in Sulphur.

II. The feminine aspect of Chokmah in his phallic function. [Crowley, 1977, p. xxv].

חכמה Chokmah. Wisdom, 2nd Sephirah; Wise woman. Corresponds to Yod in יהוה. The sphere of the zodiac or sphere of fixed stars (Masloth). Continuation in the sense carrying the onward or extending the initial impulse symbolized by 1 (Kether). Seat of Chaih, the Life-force. Contains the unmanifested aspects of the 3rd and 6th Sephiroth. The dual (Masculine-Feminine) potency which brings the whole Tree of Life into manifestation. Sulphur is attributed to Chokmah in the book *Aesch Mezareph*. see 15, 7, 693, 168, 536.

I. Chokmah, to which Sulphur is attributed, is said also to be כהמה, kachmah, the power of formation.

II. Chokmah is called משלות Masloth, the Sphere of the Zodiac (Sphere of the Fixed Stars), because the Indivisible One knows itself as light, of which all luminaries (stars or suns) are condensations into physical form. In the cosmos, this light radiates from stars and is reflected by planets. This radiant energy is alive. Therefore Chokmah is the seat of חיה Chaiah (23), the universal life-force, which is latent in the mineral kingdom, and progressively more active in the scale of evolution which extends from the vegetable, animal, human kingdoms and beyond.

אביכם your father. [Isaiah 51:2] A reference to Abraham, also a link between Chokmah and אב Ab, Father. Another name for the number 2.

גמל Letter-name Gimel. Camel. In one sense, the scroll of the High Priestess is the record of past events which becomes the basis of future recompense. What is on the scroll therefore corresponds to what Hindu philosophy calls the Samskaras or impressions which become the "seeds of Karma." These impressions are the "load" carried by the "camel" on its journey from East, the plane of causation, to West, the plane of manifestation. Gimel, the camel stands for the working power whereby all we do is accomplished and whereby all that is done to us is accomplished. Also the universal substance of subconsciousness which unites all things through memory. The High Priestess represents the Lesser Chokmah or feminine aspect of the Cosmic Wisdom. Like the Gnostic Sophia, she stands for the perfect self-recollection and self-knowledge of the one being.

The scroll of cosmic memory is read by the Magus through equilibrated faith by works [ל], dependence on the One Life [מ], and receptivity to Wisdom from above [ג].

גמל   to do, to show, to cause to, to deal adequately with; to bring to an end or limit; to ripen, to become ripe; to give according to desert; to reward, to recompense, to benefit. In human thinking, this relates to the future inasmuch as we think of the end, or ripening, of the cosmic process as being something ahead of us in time.

חסה to seek protection, to take refuge, to trust. To take refuge in Wisdom is the way of the true sage.

יום טוב a day of feast; literally: "day of good."

The camel which bears rich merchandise of the Life-power's knowledge of itself brings us the treasure of divine wisdom. In that wisdom we put our trust. The Hierophant (Key 5) is shown sitting at the gate of a sanctuary. Every day is a feast day, a day of good, for those that partake of this wisdom. Without wisdom there is no good; with it all is good, and all is peace.

כחמה "The power of what?" designates the Power of Formation. Power or substance, (כח) of Mah (מה). Kachmah is a term associated with world of formation, Yetzirah. Kachmah is a power whose essential nature is open to question, or unknown. Yet not altogether unknown, because Mah is furthermore the secret name of the world of formation. Mah (מה) adds to 45, which is also the number of Adam (אדם) man. Qabalists understand that this unknown power

which is rooted in the Wisdom of Chokmah is also a power distinctly human. The object of quest in occult science is the true nature of man. In the knowledge of this true nature lays the secret of the Master Jesus. Alchemically Sulphur (attributed to Chokmah) is the "power of Formation" because it is inherent in the Life-force. The universal Sulphur is said to be the light from which all particular Sulphurs proceed. "For the soule the bodie form doth take-for soule is forme, and doth the bodie make" [Spencer]

כאבן   ka-ehben. "as (or like) a stone." The successful completion of the Great Work combines the powers of Sulphur, Mercury and Salt into the Stone of the Wise (wise is Wisdom or Chokmah). see 53.

נביא   prophetic. a logical consequence of possessing the "stone of the wise".

בליאל Belial. Demon-king of Hod and Goetic demon #68 by night of the 2nd decanate of Aquarius. see Appendix 11.

Goetia: "He is a mighty and powerful king, and was created next after Lucifer. He appears in the form of two beautiful angels sitting in a chariot of fire. He speaks with a comely voice, and declares that he fell first from among the worthier sort, and were before Michael, and other heavenly angels. His office is to distribute presentations and senatorships, etc., and to cause favor of friends and of foes. He gives excellent Familiars, and governs 80 Legions of Spirits. Note well that this King Belial must have offerings, sacrifices and gives presented unto him by the exorcist, or else he will give true answers unto his demands. But then he tarries not one hour in the truth, unless he be constrained by divine power." [Mathers, 1995, p. 64]

בניהו   Benaiah. In 2 Samuel 23:20: "And Benaiah the son of Jehoiada, a valiant man of Kabzeel, who had done many noble acts, slew two lionlike men of Moab. He went down also and slew a lion in the a pit on a snowy day."

The prologue to the Zohar I:6A, p. 25 Comments: ";Benaiah the son of Jehoiada (i.e. son of God, son of knowing God) contains an allusion to wisdom, And is a symbolic appellation which influences its bearer." Because

120

Benaiah contains בֵּן = son = 52, an appellation of Tiphareth, combined with יהו Yaho, the name celebrated in *Sepher Yetzirah*, in connection with the manifestation of the six directions. יהו = 21 = אהיה, the Kether divine name. 52 + 21 = 73 = חכמה, Wisdom.

גליל Galilee, "the rolling sun" [Inman]; District in northern Palestine where Jesus performed the marriage miracle at Cana. In Joshua 20:7: "And they appointed Kedesh in Galilee in Mount Naphtali (Virgo, 570)." see 86 (Greek)

charitas (Lt). charity (see Secret Symbols page 51). Practical wisdom invariably express itself in words of charitable service, and also in that mental attitude of acceptance mentioned by Lincoln: "Charity for all, Malice toward none."

columbia alba (Lt). White dove. This is from "The Chemical Marriage of Christian Rosenkreutz," and occurs also in other alchemical works. Note the symbolism on the shield of Venus in the Tarot.

interna (Lt) inner. A word describing the true source of reality, the "Inner Light". see 122, 49 (Lt); 620, 397.

vista (Lt). visit. Part of the phrase in Secret Symbols (p. 17) "Visit the interior of the earth, by rectifying you shall find the hidden stone." see 570.

favonio (Lt). west, west-wind. The direction of Jupiter, and of manifestation on the Cube of Space. Part of the Rosicrucian saying: "From east to west and everywhere, the good root of David reigns victorious." see 509 (Lt), 72, 20.

nigror (Lt). blackness.

74

למד Letter name Lamed ox-goad; to teach, instruct, to train. With different pointing, a verb signifying "to beat with a rod," hence, "to discipline, to train, to teach." As a noun *limmud*, is used in Isaiah 50:4 to designate prophets, and applies particularly to the Chasidim. As a verb: *lahmed,* to learn, study, to exercise in; to be accustomed

I. "The logic of it is sufficiently simple if we grant the premises on which it starts. It is that man, by his essential and true innermost nature, is a being fitted and intended to line in uninterrupted intercourse with the All-creating Spirit, thus continually receiving a ceaseless inflow of life from this infinite source. At the same time it is impossible for a being capable of thus partaking of the infinite life of the origination spirit to be a mere piece of mechanism, mechanically incapable of moving in more than one direction; for he is to reproduce in his individuality that power of origination and initiative which must be the very essence of the creative spirit's recognition of itself he must possess a corresponding liberty of choice. As to the way in which he will use his powers; and if he chooses wrongly and the inevitable law of cause and effect must produce the natural consequences of his choice." [Troward, 1942, p. 256.]

דין leader, chief, judge (variant spelling). The Life-power (Aleph: Ox) rules all creatures. Spelled דין in Psalm 68:5: "A father of the fatherless and a judge of the widows, is God in his holy habitation."

סביב a circle, orbit, circuit, the place round about, environs, a circuitous course. The instruction of the one teacher is like a Goad (Lamed) which guides one through the long circuit of existence until one returns to union with God. The course traced by a moving body, such as a wheel, hence related to Key 11, the consequence of Key 10. The idea behind the word is the completion of a cycle of activity. In every circle, any point on the circumference may be both beginning and end. This is the idea behind Karma-the idea that any force sent out returns eventually to its point of origin. A fundamental law of manifestation, operative throughout the universe. Note that a circuitous course, is a reference to a form of meditation in which the mind makes a circuit around a central idea.

עד All the way, constantly; the veiled or hidden time; eternity. The ox-goad of Lamed guides man all the way to the ultimate goal. As a preposition and conjunction: to, unto, up to, as far as; till, until, during, while, while yet; instead of; also; ere. *Ade* implies a passing, progress, in space; also duration in time. Hence, perpetual time, eternity. Suggest also the formulation of some problem, based on appearances (Ayin) and the solution of that problem by an act of creative imagination (Daleth). The idea of definite limit is suggested by the meanings of *ade* as a preposition and a conjunction. The scales of Justice imply the notion of comparison. Ayin and Daleth represent the influences of Capricorn (Ayin) ruled by Saturn, which is exalted in Libra, and of Venus (Daleth), Libra's ruler. In another sense *ade*, is the astral light representing duration, everlastingness, eternity. It is from יד‎ה, to pass over, to come upon, to go on, to continue. It has a second meaning: to put on, to adorn oneself, and this agrees with the deeper meaning of *ade* as the universal agent. *Eternity* must be taken into account if we are to arrive at any adequate conception of Justice.

"The sign of material sense, contracted with the root אד‎, symbol of relative unity, image of every emanation and every division, constitutes a very important root, which, heiroglypically, develops the idea of time, and of all things temporal, sentient, transitory. Symbolically and figuratively it is worldly voluptuousness, sensual pleasure in opposition to spiritual pleasure; in a more restricted sense, every limited period, every periodic return. The Arabic signifies: *to count, number, calculate*, etc.; the time which follows the actual time; *tomorrow*.

עד‎ *The actual time*; a fixed point in time or space expressed by the relations *to, until, near*: a same state continued, a temporal duration, expressed in like manner by, *now, while, still*; a periodic return as *a month*; a thing *constant, certain, evident, palpable*, by which one can give *testimony; a witness*.

Continued time furnishes the idea of *eternity, stability, constancy*; thence, the action of *enacting, constituting, stating*, etc." [d'Olivet, 1976, p. 414.]

דכן‎ this, the same, this specifically. An Aramaic demonstrative pronoun suggesting particular identity. It has the connotation of exact and specific identification. This, and no other. Thus it implies definite knowledge.

הגין‎ meditation, intention, musing, gentle murmur, solemn sound, device; thought,

contemplation, resounding music (later Hebrew), reading, recitation of text, logic-one of the 7 liberal arts. Meditation is the device through which we are guided to the divine intention. Meditation requires us to use the goad of attention to hold the mind to the central idea. see 491, 67

Psalm 49:3: "My mouth shall speak of wisdom; and the meditation of my heart shall be of understanding." Meditation is literally "and-utterance-of" and spelled והגות‎ in *The Interlinear NIV Old Testament*. see 724.

הדסה‎ Myrtle plant (sacred to Venus). bride; Esther's former name. Esther is the regular Syrian form of the name Ishtar, the Babylonian Goddess corresponding to Astarte, and associated in Babylonian astrology with Venus. Hadassah, is the Hebrew translation of the Babylonian Hadashatu, "bride," used as a title for Ishtar. The significance of "Myrtle," points to the Venusian correspondence, but may be an occult blind. The theme of the story of Esther, is the triumph of Justice over injustice. But the deeper meaning concerns Babylonian traditions of conflict between the Gods of the Elamites and Babylon. These traditions veil profound doctrines of ageless wisdom. Ayin and Daleth moreover, is the very Venus who is the "Bride", *hadashatu*, or *hadassah*. see 80.

I. Paul Case: "The central figure if Key 3 in Tarot is Venus, named Aphrodite by the Greeks, who also knew her as Astarate, the same as the Babylonian Ishtar, the עשתרת‎, Ashtoreth of the Old Testament. In this connection it is interesting to note that the value of the Greek name *Astarte* is 910, or 13x70, while the value of עשתרת‎ is 1370. Very often we come across little indication like this which show that the wisdom of the eastern world was by no means lost when it was transferred to Europe through Greek. As the New Testament shows, the number-letter system of the Hebrews and Babylonians was adopted by the Gnostics and adapted to the requirements of Greek.

In the Old Testament, the whole book of Esther is a mine of information about the Semitic conceptions of the Great Mother. The well-known orientalist, A.H. Sayce says: 'Ishtar appears as Esher in the Book of Esther, where Mordecia, it may be noted, is a derivation from

Merodach ('the God'). Note that in this Book Esther is the second Queen. The first is Vashti, 'The Beautiful One', who refuses to come forth at the time of the feast, when the common people were assembled at Shushan. Vashti is the high Priestess in Tarot, for she is the hidden one who cannot be drawn forth for display amongst the multitude of ordinary thoughts and perceptions (common people). Esther is the Empress, the 'Starry One'. The scene of the story is laid in Shushan (שׁוּשַׁן), and the place-name is ordinarily translated 'Lily'. But the word Shushan, and its feminine equivalent Sushanah (שׁוֹשַׁנָּה), really signifies 'rose', and is so translated in many Qabalistic books. Roses, it will be remembered, are sacred to Aphrodite. Another plant scared to Venus. Furthermore, הדסה is the number 74, and this is the number of למד, Lamed, the ox-goad, that Hebrew letter which corresponds to Libra, ruled by Venus, and represented in Tarot by the figure of justice. In the story of Esther, Ahasuerus is the unmanifest self, and Mordecai (Marduk or Merodach) is the manifest self. Haman signifies the illusion of separate personality which demands reverence for itself. The Jews are the higher qualities, which were scattered through the lower nature.

Such is the psychological interpretation. There are many other occult meanings in this book, which is recognized by all Qabalists as being packed with esotericism. [Classics of Ageless Wisdom, 1931, pp. 23-24]

יסד laws; to set, place, to found, to appoint; to set laws, to ordain. This verb is the root of Yesod. As a noun יסד, foundation, base, in principle, or beginning. With different pointing: *yesud*; beginning commencement. [Ezra 7:9] "For on the first month they began to go up from Babylon, and on the first day of the fifth month they came to Jerusalem, according to the hand of God which had been good to them."

נכד progeny, hence descendent, grandson. In Genesis 21:23: "So now, swear to me here by God that you will not deal falsely with me, or with my son, or with my posterity, but as I have dealt with you kindly, you will do the same with me and the land in which you have sojourned."

αι διαθηκαι. ai diathekai (Gr). The covenants, divine agreements [Romans 9:4]. In the passage cited it is coupled with Legislation. This makes the connection with Key 11 perfectly clear.

Adytum (Lt). Sanctuary. holy or holies. The "house of God" in any temple. In the human brain, it is the organ through which established contact with the One identity. The functioning of this center comes about when the ego in Tiphareth, links up with the volitional power in Geburah. Lamed carries of influence of Mezla [78], specialized a *Din* Justice [64], between the 2 Sephiroth. see 126, 825, 72 (Abiegnus).

Angus Dei (Lt). Lamb of God. This is the "Lamb" clearly indicated by the initials which are used in the *Fama Fraternitatis* to designate the Founder (compare יסד) of the Rosicrucian order, whose initial are KR, Kar, Lamb. In Revelations, the Lamb is the symbol of Christ. The lamb sits on the throne at the center of the cubical city of the new Jerusalem. The Lamb is said to be both the temple and the lamp of the city. The city itself is a symbol of regenerated humanity, and of a society composed of regenerated persons. see 56, 18, 134 (Lt)

Axiomata (Lt). Axioms. This word is used in the *Fama*, which connects Axiomata with eternal duration [עד], by saying "We are assured that our Axiomata shall immovably remain until the world's end." The axiomata where the most important item in the philosophical library of the order. The same book says the Axiomata were the most important item in the philosophical library of the order. They are also declared to be "true and infallible."

Concordia (Lt). Concord, Harmony. The result of true Justice. The path of Lamed connects the sphere of divine volition (Geburah) with the sphere of beauty and harmony (Tiphareth) Concord is from two Latin words meaning "same-heart", con-cord.

ROTA- יהוה (Latin and Hebrew). The wheel (of) the Lord. Letters inscribed on the Wheel of Fortune, Key 10. see 26, 48 (Lt)

Dei Gloria (Lt). The Glory of God. Part of the Rosicrucian motto: "The Untouchable Glory of God." The "glory" is the "lamb" as well as the "adytum"

Dei is 18, which corresponds to חי (Chai, life), *Gloria* is 56 or 6 less than Sophia (Wisdom). 18 and 56 add to 74, the value of למד (Lamed), but as you can see from Tarot, the power of the Intact Virgin, who is also Sophia, or Wisdom, is in Tarot represented by the woman in Justice, and she is both the Bride and the Queen, and thus she is also אמיא, מאדה, ISIS, EVE, and all the rest of the host of Anima figures, including the Widow and Venus. See **36**, 56, 126, 136 (Lt)

matrix (Lt). matrix, foundation. see 64, 82, 156

mortem (Lt). Death. The mysteries have to do with the overcoming of death. Part of a phrase in Secret Symbols. see 717

75

גבע. Hill.

הלל Brightness, morning star; Lucifer [Isaiah 14:12].

יללה Howling, wailing, lamentation [Jephaniah 1:10].

כימה a Cluster; the Pleiades; the 7 stars [Job 9:9; 38:31, Amos 5:8].   Exoterically, the Pleiades. Esoterically, the 7 interior stars pictured on Key 17.

כהן Priest; one who is a conscious mediator for divinity. see Genesis 14:18 and 657, 1667, 2879, 886

לילה a twist, a spiral turn (away from the light); Night [Genesis 1:5]. Figuratively it means adversity. see 3, 12, 21, 30, 39, 48, 57, 66, 84, 56, 79.

I. "לילה, Night... The formation of the word of demands particular attention. Refer to Radical Vocabulary, root לא, לו and לל. It is the amalgamation of these three roots that forms the word in question. The words naught and knot, holding to the same root as the word night, portray very felicitously the figurative and hieroglyphic sense attached to the Hebrew word לילה... (p. 35).

לא This root is a symbol of the line prolonged to infinity, of movement without term, of action whose duration is limitless: thence, the opposed ideas of being and nothingness, which it uses in developing the greater part of it compounds... (p. 377) לל or לי Every idea of liaison, cohesion, tendency of objects toward each other. The universal bond. The abstract line which is *conceived* going from one point to another and which is represented by the relations, *oh if! oh that! would to God that!*... (p. 379)

לל The sign of extensive movement being opposed to itself, composes a root which gives the idea of circular movement: in the same manner as one sees in natural philosophy, this movement springs from two opposed forces, one drawing to the center, and the other drawing away from it. [d'Olivet, 1976, p. 382.]

II. "A symbol of potential being, or of the cycle of life in the underworld-the planes of the quaternary, where in the Higher Self (sun) is unapparent to the lower consciousness." [Gaskell, 1981, p. 535.]

III. The Zohar (I:16B, 17A) says: "And the darkness he called night, he summoned to issue from the side of darkness a kind of female moon which rules over the night and is called night, and is associated with Adonai, the Lord of all the earth... the left flamed forth with its full power, producing at all points a kind of reflection, and from this fiery flame came forth the female moon-like essence. This flaming was dark because it was from darkness.. 'Night' is 'the Lord of all the earth' from the side of the left, from darkness. It was because the desire of darkness was to merge itself in the right, and it was not strong enough, that night spread from it. When night began to spread, and before it was complete, darkness went and merged itself in the right, and the night was left defective. Just as it is the desire of darkness to merge itself in light, so it is the desire of night to merge itself in day. Darkness abated its light, and therefore it produces a grade which was defective and not radiant. Darkness does not radiate save when it is merged in light. So night which issued form it is not light save when it is merged in day." (pp.70-71)

יהודים the Jews; connected with the seven interior stars. see 1048.

להם to consume, hence, to destroy. see למו, 76, 539.

כנה the stock (of a plant). In Psalm 80:15: "And the vineyard which thy right hand has planted, and the branch (stock) that thou madest strong for thyself." In this passage the word (with the prefix Vav) occurs as copied here with a large Kaph, indicating its importance. Note that the vine as the plant includes the branches. With different pointing: 1. plant, shoot; stand ruler; 2. to give a name, give a title; to surname, nickname; to express by a substitute.

גווני hues, colors, complexions. The alchemical "peacock" or auric rainbow; part of the process of the great work.

יכדיאל Yekadiel. "Vessel of God", an angel whose sigil is depicted in *The Key of Solomon*, figure 53. [Mathers, 1972, p. 79] It alludes to the earthy vessel of the alchemist. see 24.

מלה 23rd Shem ha-Mephorash, short form. see 106 & Appendix 10.

נויט Nuit. Hebrew spelling of the Egyptian goddess of the sky, mother of Isis and Osiris; deity of the firmament and he rain; personification of the morning, one the great gods at Helioplis (City of the Sun).

הדד בן _ בדד Hadad, Son of Bedad. A king of Edom, associated with Tiphareth. In Genesis 36:35: "And Husham died, and Hadad son of Bedad, who defeated Midian in the Country of Moab, succeeded him as King. His city was named Avith." Note that Edom signifies unbalanced force, and that the Qipphoth of Tiphareth are called the "Haggler". see 45, 1081, 725

matrix (Lt). the womb. The whirling inner energy is the womb from which illumination emerges.

membrum (Lt). the phallus. The organ of generation and center of the reproductive energy.

Oblivio (Lt). The river Lethe in the lower world, said to bring forgetfulness. see 55 (Greek).

signum (Lt). A sign. Part of a Rosicrucian saying. Out of the Darkness of oblivion and the womb of night, the stars shine forth, as on Christmas eve. see 518.

artifex (Lt). art; skilled, clever; skillfully made. A worker, a craftsman in a particular art; a maker, master of, expert at anything; creator. To be a builder of the adytum it to follow the admonition of the Great Work expressed in the Emerald Tablet, "Thou shall separate the Earth from the Fire, the subtle from the gross, suavely and with great ingenuity."

sapiens (Lt). wise, thinking. By implication, one who is imbued with the Wisdom, of Life-Force of Chokmah, which is also the fire of mind. see 73

rosa caeli (Lt). rose of heaven; heavenly rose. The rose is a symbol of the Higher Self. "The solar rose in centered in the glory of the sun, and the Christ of Nazareth is centered in the celestial flower. From Geheime Figuren [Secret Symbols, p. 8, subtitled "Harmonious conception of the light of nature, form which you can deduce the restoration and renovation of all things emblematic."] It is the Rosicrucian adaptation of Khunrath's Christ of Glory... in the deep understanding of Rosicrucian doctrine, the Rose is also the soul, and in the marriage life of this union there is no distinction between the soul and the word within the modes of realization." [Waite, 1993, pp. 19-20] see 47, 28 (Lt).

76

סוד sod. secret. In Amos 3:7: "He reveals His secret." Also rendered in Jewish translation "His counsel." see 114.

חביון Hiding place, Hiding (Secret; put away). See plate in "The Universal One," page 11 where there are exactly 19 divisions of a spiral, each subdivided into 4 parts (4x19 = 76).

עבד to work, labor, to till, cultivate (soil); to make; to prepare, to serve; to worship. Used throughout the Bible in a great variety of shades to meaning.

מול to circumcise, to hem, make a fringe. Also spelt מל.

אבני-בהו "stones of emptiness." [Isaiah 34:11]. In Hebrew Massoretic translation, "Plummet of emptiness." Also, "Stone of confusion in the Zohar (p.49).

כהנא Priest [Ezra 7:1, spelt כהן] "Artaxerxes, King of Kings, unto Erza the priest, a scribe of the law of the God of heaven, perfect peace..." *Kahanah* is also the name of the altar mentioned in section 6 of St. Germain's "Most Holy Trinosophia." It is the definite form and in the Book of Ezra it always refers to Erza himself. Erza is עזרא (278), or the material world, [עולם המוטבע]. Thus *kahanah* is this connection, as it refers to an altar, obviously means salt. St. Germain (section 6) describes the altar as yellow with "a pure flame ascending from it, having no other substance for its alimentation than the altar itself. Letters in black were engraved at the base of the altar." In the accompanying illustration the altar is cylindrical, or like a short column. see 961, 693, 372.

למו A poetic form of להם, to consume, hence, to destroy. [Psalm 119:165]. see 75, 539

ניחה rest, peace; to cause to rest.

I. Exodus 32:10: "Now therefore let me alone [i.e. rest, peace], that my wrath may wax hot against them: and I will make of thee a great nation." The fiery Life-power which destroys the sense of separation is what brings ultimate peace.

II. With different pointing: *nihohah*. Erza 6:10: "That thy may offer sweet odors [ניחוחין-things pleasing] unto the God of heaven, and pray for the life of the king, and of his sons.

III. Daniel 2:46: "Then king Nebuchadnezzar fell upon his face and worshiped Daniel, and commanded that they should offer sweet odors [וניחחין, and-incenses] and sacrifices to him." see 370, 376, 539.

אלילה Goddess. This suggest Binah, the Great Mother.

Αθηνη. Athene (Gr). Athene (Minerva), virginal daughter of Zeus. A name for the number 7 given it by Greek philosophers [orginal notes were to degraded to read, this is my best estimation of the spelling].

Apophis (Lt). Typhon, the destroyer. Symbolized by the uplifted arms of the Child (Horus) in Key 20. A personification in Egypt mythology of the destructive principle. His mother is Isis and his father Osiris. The Child represents the rebirth which results from mastering Typhon. One of the Initials (A) of IAO, one of the most Potent "Words of Power" to bring forth dimensional awareness. see 21, 449 (Greek), 358, 162, 86

unius (Lt). one, single. This awareness comes from a single source. Part of an inscription on the altar in the vault of Brother CR. see 475, 87, 106 (Lt)

mundum (Lt). world. Refers to the "small world" or microcosm, which is man. see 179, 103 (Lt)

pectus (Lt). breast. Note that this is the part of the human body governed by the sign Cancer. Within this area is the sun center, focus of the central ego in the microcosm. With a different spelling, is part of the phrase, "a seed planted in the breast of Jesus", a motto mentioned in the Rosicrucian *Fama Fraternitatis*. see 95, 310 (Lt).

77

A rectangle with a: Width = 5, length = 12, diagonal = 13. The perimeter, 2 diagonals, horizontal and vertical dividing lines add to 77 (2x5 + 2x12 + 2x13 +5 + 12).

מזל planet, wanderer. Singular of מזלות (483). Also constellation, destiny, fate, angel of destiny; fortune, luck, influence. "the influence from Kether." [Hebrew Lexicon] see Mezla (78).

עז oz. strength, power, might; courage, boldness. As an adjective *Ayz*, meaning: strong, mighty, fierce, cruel; bright (of color); pungent, acrid, sharp (of tasted). Mathers says *oz* gives the idea of foundational power to this influence (מזל). [Perhaps related to the attributes of the true "Wizard of Oz."]

בעה prayed. With different pointing: *babayeh*. to ask, inquire, to boil, seethe; to eat up (of grazing animal). Variant of יבעה.

זידון overflowing [Psalm 124:5] Note that in the Hebrew text it is (ה)זידונים which is plural (adjective) to match המים which precedes it.

גיחון The name of the 2nd river of Eden, that which compasses the whole land of Cush [Genesis 2:13]. see 326, 702, 142, 446, 1068, 680, 1560, 858.

גיחון "a stream." The name of the 2nd river of Eden, associated with water. see 724.

"גיחון Gihon.. (from the) root גה. This root is employed here in the intensive verbal from which the augmentative syllable ון...(p. 80) גה... The organic sign united... to that of manifestation (Heh), constitutes a root which becomes the symbol of every organization. This root which possesses the same faculties of extension and aggrandizement that we have observed in the root גא, contains ideas apparently opposed to envelopment and development according to the point of view under which one considers the organization. [d'Olivet, 1976, pp. 311-312.]

עז goat, goat hair. Relates to Capricorn and Saturn.

אולם The vestibule or entrance hall to the temple. Suggest preparation for entry into the holy place of this power. see 358, 65, 216, 637.

מגדל tower, turret, elevated stage, pulpit, raised garden bed; cupboard; castle, lighthouse; rook (in chess). Connected with the tower of Babel [Genesis 11:4] "and a tower with its top in Heaven." Wrongly used, this implies the crown of false will-power, struck by lighting as in Key 16. see 988.

H.C. (Lt). (Mystic name of) Fas Ducit "(Divine) Law or Command Draws (or leads) Him."

moralls (Lt). moral. The basis of occult morality is faithful obedience to the actual laws of God, rather than outward adherence to the customs, taboos, or conventions of a particular historical period or those accepted by some group of persons. see 193, 115 (Lt).

vivum (Lt). As spelled in the phrase "Living silver." see 166, 89 Latin.

78

I. Σ12 = 78

II. As the sum of the numbers from 1 to 12, it is symbolic of the 12 labors of Hercules and the completion of the Great Work

III. 3x26 or the 3 fold extension of IHVH.

ב/י Beth/Yod. Mercury (Beth) in Virgo (Yod).

מזלא mezla. to drip, to flow down in drops; holy influence, whirling, radiant energy (which descends from Chokmah). Divine Grace. The conscious energy that flows through all things. Mezla is a whirling force, and in its physical expression is the spiraling electro-magnetic energy, the substance from which the atoms of the physical universe are created, via electrons and protons. The 3 simultaneous projections of this force from Kether are to Chokmah (via Aleph), Binah (via Beth), and Tiphareth (via Gimel). The 3 worlds of emanation proceeding from Atziluth, which is the Limitless Light as spiritual fire, the support of all that is in manifestation. see 483, 620, 111, 507, 578, 876, 536.

I. Note that 78 is the sum of the numbers from 1 to 12, and you have a clue to the nature of the substance that flows through the Tree of Life. It is for this reason there are 78 Tarot Keys.

78 reduces to 15 (7+8 = 15), and this is the number of יה, Jah, which is the name of Chokmah. Chokmah is the Sphere of the Zodiac which is represented by the 12 signs of the zodiac. 15 reduces to 6, the number of Vav, and Tiphareth. Without the Logos in Tiphareth, nothing can come into manifestation. See **14**.

מבול a flood. "'A flood' and therefore *the* flood. The word derives from the Egyptian *mehber*, [*Meh*, 'the abyss of waters'; *ber*, later *bet*, to 'well forth', 'to belly out', 'be ebullient] which contains the actual name of the abyss." [Grant, 1994, p. 48.]

לחם lechem. bread, food, a feast. The host or body of Messiah. It is symbolized by the eucharistic wafer , the Tree of Life, which is the support and sustenance of man. Note that Beth-lechem, "house of bread" where the Christos is born is the Virgo region in the body. With different pointing: 1. to eat bread, take food; 2. to fight, do battle; 3. war. The bread is the wafer used in the Eucharist to symbolize "This is my body" (see Genesis 14:18 where Melchizedek brought forth bread and wine). This body is also the tree as well as the Christos, the support and sustenance of Man. Mezla, the true substance. The birth-place of Jesus ("reality liberates") is said to be Beth-lechem, or Bethlehem, the "house of Bread" or Virgo region of Virgin birth. see 490, 800, 581 (note-parable of loaves and fishes), 671 (Greek), 638, 1110.

I. Psalm 78:25: "Men ate the bread of angels; He [God] sent them all the food they could eat."

II. Rosenroth in K.D.L.C.K. (p. 500) gives: *panis*, and says it commonly refers to Malkuth. He cites 1 Kings 13:19: "The old prophet answered, I too am a prophet, as you are. And an angel said to me by the word of the Lord: Bring him back with you to your house so that he may eat bread and drink water. (but he was lying to him)." Rosenroth says that others say that *lechem* is Vav, which is in Tiphareth. A discussion follows. In Genesis 14:18: "Then Melchizedek King of Salem brought forth bread and wine; he was priest of God most high."

חלם breaker, to bind; to dream, to see visions. Suggests the breaking up of the mental complexes portrayed in Keys 16 and also the awakened inner vision which can emerge from it.

חנך Enoch. Initiated, to initiate; an Old Testament name. Name of the patriarch who "walked with God."

מלח salt; sea, to subsist. From the verb: to flow, to dissolve, to vanish away. Aramaic to subsist. Substance or manifestation is really an eternal flux. Name of the 3rd alchemical principal, or tamasguna.

"The salt [מלח = 78 = מלא] of Saturn [Shabbathai, 713], the universal son of nature,

has reigned, does reign, and will reign naturally and universally in all things; always and every where universal through its own feasibility, self-existent in nature. Hear and attend! Salt, that most ancient principle of the stone; whose nucleus in the decad guard in holy silence. Let him who hath understanding understand; I have spoken it-not without weighty cause has salt been dignified with the name of wisdom [החכמה (The wisdom) = 78 = מלח]: than which, together with the sun, nothing is found more useful." [Atwood, 1918, pp. 391-392]

חמל to spare, have pity, have compassion. Relates to Chesed חסד. With different pointing: pity, compassion. see 72.

יבינו shall understand. The influx of Mezla through Mercy and Severity brings the understanding of all manifestation (Binah). see 52

כדמדי Kadmadi. Angel of the 1st decanate of Taurus. Relates to Key 5 and intuition.

זמאל Zaumael. Angel of Mars. Refers to the Mars force.

היכל אהבה Literally, "Palace or temple of love". Briatic (creative) palace of Chesed. A key to becoming like Enoch.

יזלאל 13th Shem ha-Mephorash. "God glorified by all things." 61°-65°. THÉSOLK. April 1, June 12, August 23, September 3, January 14. 4:00-4:20 AM. [Psalm 98:4] Rules amity, reconciliation, and conjugal fidelity. Persons born: Apprehends all that he desires. Associated with 1st quinance (1°-5°) of Libra; Angel by day of the 2 of Swords. This represents the influence of the zodiacal forces (Chokmah) in the Formative pattern-world (Yetzirah). Appendix 10.

נכח front, in front of, over against. In Ezekiel 46:9: "But when the people of the land shall come before the Lord at the time of the solemn feast, he who enters by way of the north gate to worship shall go out by the way of the south gate; and he who enters by way of the south gate shall go out by the way of the north gate; he shall not return by the way of the gate by which he came in, but shall go over against it. With different pointing: detours, opposite to, in regard to, in behalf. In Ezekiel 14:7: "For every one of the House of Israel, or of the proselytes who dwell in Israel, who departs from me and sets up idols in his heart and puts the stumbling block of his iniquity before his face and comes to a prophet to inquire of him, I the Lord will be a witness against him."

כבן From an unused root meaning: to heap up; hilly [Strong's Bible Dictionary]. A place in Palestine in: Joshua 15:40. Gesenius, thinks that the word signifies a cake , while Furst considers it equivalent to a hamlet or circle of huts.

מבהאל 14th Shem ha-Mephorash. Associated with the 2nd quinance (6°-10°) of Libra; Angel by night of the 2 of Swords. This represents the operation of Chokmah, sphere of the zodiac, in Yetzirah, the Formative world. see Appendix 10.

אומאל 30th Shem ha-Mephorash. Associated with Wands 6th quinance (26°-30°) of Sagittarius; Angel by night of the 10 of Wands. This represents the operation of Malkuth, the physical plane in Atziluth, the Archetypal World of ideas. see Appendix 10.

"Omael is (or was) of the order of Dominations.. Whether Omael is fallen or still upright is difficult to determine from the information available. He seems to operate in both domains (Heaven and Hell)." [Davidson, 1971, p. 212.]

79   (prime)

אמ-גלה when reveals. In Amos 3:17 אם is listed as a conjunction meaning: if, whether, when, on condition. With different vowel points it means: mother, origin, commencement, womb, basic, authority. see 155, 41.

בעז Boaz. "in strength," The black pillar set before Solomon's temple on the left side. Symbolizes the negative, feminine, polarity of the Tree of Life -the Pillar of Severity. For scriptural spelling see 85 and 1 Kings 7:21.

דלילה Delilah. Pining with desire [Judges 16:4]. "unfortunate or miserable" [Furst]. Delilah, the consort of Sampson, who deprived him of his strength by cutting of his hair. Inman says: "From דלי a pail, also "the testicles" as in Numbers 24:7, The sign of the genitive case, and יה, Jah of "the Bucket of Jah.' Compare 'He shall pour the water out of his buckets' and 'His seed shall be in many water' [Numbers 24:7]." Note that לילה means: 'A twist away from the light; night," prefixed by Daleth or Venus (Desire). see 75, 696.

גן יהוה Garden of God (garden of Eden).

עבה to pass over, continue; to adorn self.

עוג see Numbers 21:33. "The usual interpretation of this cognomen is 'long-necked,' or 'gigantic;' but it is difficult to believe that any such name would be given to an infant. It is much more probable that the word is equivalent to עוג, ug, 'he goes in a circle,' i.e. the sun." [Inman, 1942, (page number unknown)]

סיט Sit. 3rd Shem ha-Mephorash, short form. see 110 & Appendix 10.

ומבאל 61st Shem ha-Mephorash. "God above all things." To obtain the friendship of a given person. Person born under the influence: fond of travel and honest pleasures, sensitive heart. Negative influences: Libertines, vices contrary to nature. Angel governing the 1st decanate (and quinance) of Gemini, attributed to the 8 of Swords. see Appendix 10.

coeptis (Lt). (our) undertakings. Part of the motto "He hath prospered our undertakings" on the Great Seal of the US. see 71, 150, 370 Latin.

Fratres (Lt). Brothers. Title given fellow spiritual aspirants belonging to an order, i.e. those who are on the Path of Return. see 193 Latin.

80

As 8 x 10, 80 suggest the alchemical Quintessence (symbolized by the 8-spoked wheel of the robe of The Fool, Key 0) multiplied by the number of manifestation (10, the number of emanations on the Tree of Life). This suggests that the spiritual essence is veiled in manifestation and that the 10 Sephiroth are part of the vesture or veil of that spiritual essence, the *Ain Suph Aur*. See 414.

פ Peh. The alphabetical symbol of Mars (action). see 85, 899.

I. The heart of נפש, Nephesh, is Peh, and this path (see Appendix 13) carries the power of Netzach into Hod. From Geburah, the Sphere of Madim, the Holy Mezla descends into Tiphareth through the path of action, the sharp goad of Lamed. Yet the path of Lamed of the quality of Nogah, because Nogah is the sphere of Venus and Lamed is Libra ruled by Venus.

From Tiphareth the Holy Mezla descends into the Sphere of Nogah (Netzach) through the path of Nun (Scorpio, change). Thus from the Sphere of Madim (Geburah) the channel begins with Nogah or Netzach (Lamed, Libra ruled by Venus and is the Sphere of Netzach), then takes on the form of Madim or Geburah (Nun or Scorpio ruled by Mars) to enter the Sphere of Nogah (Venus). Note also that the first path from Nogah is Peh, a path of Madim. And the mediator between Geburah and Netzach, Mars and Venus or Will and Desire is Tiphareth, the Sun.

On the Tree the paths of Daleth (Venus) and Peh (Mars) are of like nature (both are horizontal paths), though opposite in appearance. Peh is the heart of Nephesh, and Peh is also one with יסוד Yesod, The Foundation, for the number of פ and Yesod is 80. Peh, פ and ל are one, because פ is כ with י, as you see by looking at the characters. Kaph with Yod gives 30, the number of Lamed a goad, and the goad is the power of Madim. In Yesod יסוד is concealed סודי, Sod Yod, the secret of Yod. Yod itself is Kaph, and the Sod Yod is a mystery of the hidden paternal power of Chokmah. See C.10.

II. Rabbi Munk says: "The Peh consists of a Kaph with a Yod suspended inside it; the Kaph stands for practical action, while the Yod represents wisdom. Thus, the letter Peh represents a spiritual quality (wisdom) contained within the proper vessel for its practical realization... It also denotes productivity and accomplishment, which results through mental or physical efforts, unlike Yod, which stands for "hand" indicating power and possession." [The Wisdom of the Hebrew Alphabet]

III. Rabbi Kardia says: "Why is the letter Cheth assigned to "the function of speech," and Peh to "the mouth as the organ of speech?" Words that originate in the mouth can never protect, and only exhibit the negative side of Mars, aggression. Words that originate from the Divine used the mouth to excite grace. [Simple Stories From the Heart]

IV. "This character as consonant, belongs to the labial sound, and possesses two distinct articulations: by the first P, it is joined to the character ב or B, of which it is a reinforcement; by the second PH, it is joined to the character ו become consonant and pronounced V or F. As symbolic image it represents the mouth of man, whose most beautiful attributed it depicts, that of uttering his thoughts. As grammatical sign, it is that of speech, and of that which is related thereunto. The Hebrew does not employ it as article; but everything proves that many of the Egyptians used it in this way and thus confounded it with its analogue ב, by a peculiar affectation of the pronunciation. Perhaps also a certain dialect admitted it at the head of words as emphatic article in place of the relation פה; this appears all the more probable, since in Hebrew, a fairly large quantity of words exist where it remains such..." [d'Olivet, 1976, pp. 422-423.]

גבעה hill. [Exodus 17:9] see 686, 85.

יסוד Yesod. foundation, basis. 9th Sephirah. The Purified Intelligence. The automatic consciousness or the reproductive activity of the Mars force. The subconscious mind, represented also by the letter Gimel. The Anima Mundi, the Soul of the World or Vital Soul in human personality. The working or operative force and basis of every physical form. Yesod is the reflection of Tiphareth (the Sun) through Key 14 (Samekh represent the form-giving power which supports all forms below it). Yesod also carries influences from Netzach (through Key 17) and Hod (through Key 19). Consciousness of Theoricus in Rosicrucian initiation. The procreative organs of Adam Qadmon, the Archetypal Man. Here the powers of Chokmah and Binah are combined. see 87, 220, 363, 430, 581.

I. The full name of 9th Sephiroth is found in Proverbs 10:26: צדיק יסוד עולם , The Righteous is the Foundation of the world"

In יסוד, Yesod is the combination of Mercury (Yod), Jupiter (Samekh), Moon (Vav) and Venus (Daleth); and these are the metals of the alchemists, or the interior stars. Mars impels the upward flow of power on the Way of Return, and this power is combined with Moon and Venus in the work, as it begins in Malkuth and sends the forces up through the path of Tav. In Yesod, Mars and Saturn give place to Jupiter, and the path of Samekh above Yesod is doubly related to Jupiter (Jupiter rules Sagittarius, attributed to Samekh), as you see from the letters ס (Sagittarius) and כ (Jupiter). But the 'matter of the work' is designated by the 23rd path of מ (meaning waters) between 25th path of ס and the 21st path of כ, and this water will not wet the hand; it will not, that is, wet the Yod. For the 'hand' is Yod. see 10 & C.10.

II. There are two stages at the end of their process of the Great Work, the White Work and the Red. White is for the Moon, and Red is for the Sun. The Sphere of the Moon is Yesod, and the Sphere of the Sun is Tiphareth. The White Work transmutes the leaden Guph (89) into the Purified Intelligence of Yesod, for it shows the alchemist what is the real basis of his personal life. see 89, 406 & C.11.

III. Through countless generations the One Life perpetuates Its utterance by means of successive generations of human bodies. That is why the Wise say that in Yesod is the field of renewal through procreation that is why never blasphem the source of Life. Genesis says "be fruitful and multiply," but there is a fruitfulness beyond that of the flesh, and a multiplication of the power of life having children. Thus in the word Yesod, may you read Yod Sod - or Sod, Yod the secret of Yod. Forms are manifest in varying degrees, and when it is your office to bring forth subtle forms, you fail if you miss your opportunity through the false belief that in the bringing forth of forms less subtle there is any essential failure. see 363, 23, 11, 430 & C.27.

IV. Sephira Dtzenioutha Ch. 1 Para. 33: "Yod… is masculine and refers to the path of the Foundation." [Mathers, 1993, p. 55]

V. In Leviticus 4:7: "And the priest shall put some of the blood upon the horns of the alter of sweet incense before the Lord, which is the tabernacle of the congregation; and he shall pour all the rest of the blood of the bullock at the *foundation* of the alter of the burnt offering, which is at the door of the Tabernacle of the congregation." see 430.

VI. The Zohar [IV: 225A, p. 268] Comments: "Observe that when the priest spreads his hands at the time he blesses the people, the Shekinah comes and hovers over him and endows him with power [Literally, fills his hands]. When blessing, the priest raises his right hand above the left, so as to cause the right to prevail over the left. All the grades over which he spreads his hands, are thus blessed from the source of all things, from the well called righteous [i.e. יסוד, Yesod] the source of all is the future world, the sublime source which illumines all faces, whence are kindled all lamps. It has a counterpart in the source and spring of the well whence all the lower lamps and the lower lights are kindled and radiate. So one corresponds to the other. Hence, when the priest spreads out his hands and begins to pronounce the blessing over the people, the celestial benedictions flowing form the celestial source at once kindle the lamps, and faces are illumined, and the community of Israel is adorned with celestial crowns, and all those blessing from down from on high to below."

VII. *Aesch Mezareph*: Yesod, in natural things, contains under itself Quicksilver; because this metal is the foundation of the whole art of transmutation. [Westcott, 1997, p. 38]

יה אדני God of Yesod. Yesod is the Malkuth of Briah, the world of creation. Patterns held in Yesod are formed from the pure substance of Briah. see 15, 220.

היהודים the Jews. (Esther 6:13). One of many hints that the forces represented by the Tribe of Judah (related to Leo, to Teth, and thus to Fohat) are fundamental in human life.

ועד union, a gathering, a meeting or assembly. Refers to Yesod as being a Sephirah in which are conjoined the influences of the paths above it on the Tree. With different pointing: *viade,* to appoint, to designate.

כלל to complete, to finish, to make whole. As a noun: principle, rule, community, total sum; inclusion; generalization, statement of implication. Compare this with the meanings of 9, the special number of Yesod. Root word of the Collective Intelligence of Resh (כללי). see 90, 440.

מי יהודה waters of Judah (Isaiah 48:1). מי is a Hebrew figure of speech for <u>semen virilis</u>. This has a connection with the Qabalistic doctrine that Yesod represents the generative organs of the Archetypal Man.

יע shovel for removing ashes. In the Vulgate translation it is given as Forceps. The letters of this word are the Hebrew equivalent of the initials I.O., designating one of the founders of the Rosicrucian order. The "shovel" purifies by removing waste; the "forceps" helps to give birth to the new creature via hot-house or forcing process. see 8, 10, 11.

כס throne [Exodus 17:16]. The foundation (stone) of rulership.

סוד י Sod Yod. "Secret of Yod." The Life-force or "Living Gold," or "philosophic gold." Also called חיה (Chaiah) or radiant energy. It is assimilated from food in the small intestine and charges the blood-stream to provide strength for the 3rd eye (Ehben) to open. It is the Secret of Wisdom, the secret of *Ab*, the divine fatherhood, and of solar radiance (Prana). This descends from Kether as Living Light or LVX. In Yesod this Light and Life takes form as Nephesh [נפש], the Vital Soul, common to man and to all lower forms of being. The word secret has double meaning-Yod specifically symbolizes the phallus. Another secret is the ability to reason out ideas and destroy them is an aspect of the reproductive energy. see 21

I. Those who know the secret of Yod become the extenders of the paternal Life and Light. Therefore Yesod is called the Sphere of the Moon, which pertains also to Gimel, the letter of Union.

There are those who seek to be spiritual at the expense of the body. They repudiate all that pertains to Yesod because they misunderstand its real significance. The mystery of the 9th Sephirah is a secret of Yod. Yod is the letter of *Ab*, the Father, and dilates upon Chaih. Thus the secret is has to do with the radiance of the stars, that is with Light, which is one with Life. See C.27.

ההע 12th Shem ha-Mephorash, short form. see 95 & Appendix 10.

סך thick mass, "multitude," crowd. [Psalm 42:5] "There I remember as I pour out my soul: how I used to go with the multitude, leading the procession to the house of God, with shouts of Joy and Thanksgiving among the festive thongs." see 560

I. "The circumferential sign united by contraction to the root אך, image of every restriction and exception, forms a root whose use is to characterize a thing which is round, closed, fitting to contain, to cover, thence סך, a *sack, a veil, covering* of any sort that which *envelops, covers, obstructs*. In a figurative sense, the *multitude* of men which cover the earth; *ointment* with which the skin is covered and that which closes the pours.

The Arabic word principle development spring from the onomatopoeic root which depicts the effect of the effort that one makes in striking. Literally it is *striking*, a thing to make it yield." [d'Olivet, 1976, p. 409.]

עי A town near Bethel; heap ruin [Psalm 79:1] "O God, the nations [גוים, 59] have invaded our inheritance; they have defiled your Holy Temple, they have reduced Jerusalem to rubble.

"This root is the analogue of the roots עה and עו, whose physical expression it manifest. It is, in general growth, material development; accumulation. The Arabic indicates an overwhelming burden, a *fatigue; to goad*." [d'Olivet, 1976, pp. 416-417.]

מם Given without explanation in *Sepher Sephiroth*. "Root not used in Hebrew. The Arabic seems to indicate a thing livid, or which renders livid; a thing inanimate, and as dead.

132

Literally *wax, a mummy*: figuratively, *solitude, a desert*." [d'Olivet, 1976, pp. 390-391.]

novus (Lt). new. Part of the inscription "A new order of the ages" on the Great Seal of the U.S. see 220, 46, 94, 126, 370 (Lt).

Initials of the 1st 4 Rosicrucians, who were the basis or foundation of the order:

C.R.C	22	The Self or Christos
G.V.	26	GAV (Hebrew) middle or center.
I.A.	10	Ahyee, where? How?
I.O.	22	Peh, mouth and Yesod, foundation.
total	80	

The basis of practical occultism (I.O) is self-expression or self-utterance. Adequate self-expression requires self-interrogation (I.A) animated by specific purpose. This work of self-expression is to be realized through concentration, which leads to the establishment of equilibrium through finding one's true center (G.V.).

Twenty-two which is the Latin value of C.R.C. and of I.O. has a connection with the paths of the letters on the Tree of Life, and with the number of Tarot Keys. Twenty-six (G.V.) is the Hebrew value of יהוה. Ten (I.A.) suggests the 10 Sephiroth. Thus the whole system of 32 Paths in intimated.

This sequence also suggests: "By his hand (ביוד, 22) Tetragrammaton (יהוה, 26) reveals himself in the Sephiroth (10) and the letters (22). see 8, (וג-note).

81

I. (9^2) or 3^4

II. The number of the Moon whose magic square contains the numbers from 1 to 81.

אנכי "I" (personal pronoun) In Exodus 23:20: "Behold I send an angel before thee, to keep thee in the way (Path), and bring thee into the place which I have prepared."

The Zohar [III: 25A, pp. 84-85] Comments: When the holy one gave Israel the Torah on Mount Sinai, his first word was *anokhi* contains many mysteries; here, however, we are concerned with the fact that it is the first of all commandments, the root of all precepts of the law: I am the Lord." This is the general axiom. The particular is thy God . The same is true of the Lord thy God is a consuming fire. see Deuteronomy 4:24, 9, 18, 27, 36, 45, 54, 63, 72, 90.

טבע to sink; to impress, impression on a coin, character; as a noun: nature. The meanings of this word imply that nature is like the impression made on wax by a signet ring. Closely related is the occult doctrine that nature is impressed with characters written by the Hand of God. This is a figurative way of stating what is strictly true. One needs only pay close attention to events and things in order to read their inner meaning. Root of Motba, [מוטבע] the 28th Path of the Natural Intelligence. see 86.

אים gods, strong; powerful; influential; to do.

ה-מלאה the fullness.

אף anger, wrath, passion. With different pointing: nose, nostrils. As a conjunction: also, even, too. This strength, when unbalanced is also the passion or wrath of God. see 801

כסא throne. The "throne" is the adytum, or the third eye, which is unfolded by intense and prolonged meditation. with different pointing: 1. new moon or full moon 2. *kebe*. time of the full moon. see 332

פא here, hither. [Job 38:11] "And said, hitherto shall thou come, but no further: and here shall thy proud waves be stayed?" The letter name Peh is sometimes spelled פא. see 85

כונה fervor, intention, intent, attention, devotion; intense meditation. A Rabbinical term describing a mental practice akin to Yoga. The means whereby one becomes receptive to the influx of the Holy Influence Mezla מזלא, descending from Kether. Through meditation one is also shown the true nature of the power experienced as Will, as being received from Geburah.

חזיון Vision, revelation. With different pointing: optics; phenomenon; play, drama. In Isaiah 22:1: "The burden of the valley of vision. what ails thee now, that thou art wholly gone up to the house tops?" Has to do with prophetic inspiration. see valley of vision, #95, 745.

In the Zohar :270: "The valley of vision is an appellation of the temple when the Shekhinah dwells in it, and when it was the source from which all drew their prophetic inspiration; for although the various prophets proclaimed their message in various regions, they all drew their inspiration from the temple. Hence the appellation 'valley of vision'. (The term hizayon (vision) has also been interpreted to signify "reflection of all the celestial hues".) The words 'What ails thee now, that thou are wholly gone up to the houses tops?' Allude to the Shekhinah, who at the destruction of the temple revisited all the spots were she had dwelt formerly and wept for her habitation and for Israel who had gone into exile and all those righteous ones and saints that perished there."

אילם rams. Exodus 16:1. see 731, 736, 965.

אועד. I will meet. Exodus 29:42. [G.G. Locks].

בטנך your womb, the belly. In Song of Solomon 7:2: "...thy belly is like an heap of wheat about with lilies." This word also implies the womb in Key 3, The Empress, whose pregnant womb is surrounded by ripe wheat. Lilies are symbolic of self-conscious activity, as in Key 1. Illumination is the ripe fruit of meditation. In Deuteronomy 7:13: "He will bless the fruit of *your womb*, the crops of your land- your grain, new wine and oil-the calves of your herds and the lambs of your flocks in the land that he swore to your forefathers to give you." see 61, 729.

גחנך. your belly. Genesis 3:14.

ו-לילה and by night. Exodus 13:21: By day the Lord went ahead of them in a pillar of cloud to guide them on their way *and by night* in a pillar of fire to give them light, so that they could travel by day or night.

ל-אבל to be devoured, or consumed.

להבדיל to divide. Genesis 1:14: "Let there be lights in the firmament of the heaven to divide the day from the night."

עבדה service, body of servants; work; bondage. What is bondage to some is service to the One Life by its practitioners. see 82

לילא night. vision and meditation succeed best at night, the "womb of Binah."

כאן Kayon; Camio, Caim. Goetic demon #53 by night of the 2nd decanate of Virgo. see Appendix 11.

I. *Goetia*: "He is a great president, and appears in the from of a bird called a thrush at first, but afterwards he puts on the shape of a man carrying in his hand a sharp sword. He seems to answer in burning ashes, or in coals of fire. He is a good disputer. His office is to give unto men the understand of all birds, lowing of bullocks, barking of dogs, and other creatures; and also of the voice of the waters. He gives true answers of things to come. He was of the Order of angels, but now rules over 30 Legions of Spirits Infernal." [Mathers, 1995, p. 56].

איע Aya. 67th Shem ha-Mephorash, short form. see 112 & Appendix 10.

יליאל "Hearer of Cries" 2nd Shem ha-Mephorash. Rules Turkey. Corresponds to the influence of the Genie named ARICAN. 6°-10°. Rules March 21, June 1, August 12th, October 23, January 3. Psalm 20:6: "Now I know that the Lord saves his anointed; he will hear him from his holy heaven with the saving strength of this right hand." Associated with the 2nd quinance of Leo; Angel by night of the 5 of Wands (Geburah of Atziluth).This represents the operation of the sphere of volition in the archetypal world of ideas. see Appendix 10.

יליאל 58th Shem ha-Mephorash. Associated with the 4th quinance [16°-20°] of Taurus; Angel by night of the 6 of Pentacles. This represents the operation of the central Ego in the material world of Action.

Phoenix (Lt). The legendary bird which lived for 500 years, was consumed by fire and was reborn from its own ashes. An alchemical term. The Book of Lambspring says: "In India there is a most pleasant wood, in which two birds are bound together. One is of a snowy white; the other is red. They bite each other, and one is slain and devoured by the other. Then both are changed into white doves, and of the dove is born a phoenix, which has left behind blackness and foul death, and his regained a more glorious life. This power was given it by God Himself, that it might live eternally, and never die. It gives us wealth, it preserves our life, and which it we may work great miracles, as also the true philosophers do plainly inform us." [Waite, 1974, vol. 1, p. 290]

oculus (Lt). eye. Pictured on the reverse of the great seal of the U.S. This is the eye of providence, which corresponds to the letter Ayin and the 3rd eye. see 70, 130, 237 Latin, 100 Latin.

sanctum (Lt). holy. As spelled in an inscription found in the vault of brother CR. One phrase of this reads "Through the Holy Spirit we become alive again." The eye of the I AM is holy and is approached by devotion and intense meditation. see 683, 191, 87 Latin.

anima mundi (Lt). soul of the world.

noster (Lt). our. It is our refuge and strength and is best seen in Christ, our Lord. Our collective body is one in Christ. Part of a Rosicrucian saying. see 166, 85 (Lt.), 518 (Lt.).

82

The crest of the Great Seal of the U.S has 13 stars, 26 horizontal lines, 24 divisions of Glory and 19 clouds which equals 82.

אלהך יהוה Jehovah Elohekah. The Lord thy God. See 26, 66; Deuteronomy 15:4 & 28:58.

ניחוח soothing, tranquilizing, sweet odor or sacrifice, pleasantness, sweetness, delight.

עובד "serving;" Father of Jesse (320), son of בעז (79). With different pointing: *Abeddo.* His

servant. In Isaiah 50:10: "That obeys the voice of his servant."

לבן white; whiteness, white of the eye; silver coin. White is the symbol of purity and innocence in Masonic symbolism, and on the Great Seal of the U.S. With different pointing: *loben.* whiteness; semen. Spelled ויתלבנו and-they-will-be-made-spotless in Daniel 12:10. see 88, 788, 138 and Genesis 30:35.

נבל Fool; something hollow (see Follis, 65). Husband of Abigail ("source of joy", 45) of the House of Caleb ("Dog", i.e. faithfulness). With different pointing: 1. ignoble, senseless person; impious, villainous person; 2. *Nebbeyl,* to cause fading, cause to whither and fall; to be foolish, to be senseless; 3. *Nebeyl,* to despise, blaspheme, disgrace, treat with contumely; to dirty, pollute; to make an animal ritually forbidden by improper slaughtering. The profanation of spirit by the flesh. See 46, 52 and 1 Samuel 25:3.

חסיד Godly man, saint, pious, kind, benevolent, Hassid, of the Hassidic sect. With different pointing: *chesid,* kindly, righteous, holy. A master of compassion or mercy, attributed to Jupiter on the Tree of Life. see 72, 122

אנאל Aniel. Hanael. "Grace of God." the angel of Venus and of Netzach, the number 7. Alternate spelling see 97.

בעי a prayer. Prayer is the invocation of Grace for purity of spirit.

היכל גוגה Briatic palace of Hod. Has to do with intuition as the source in intellectual creation.

corpus (Lt). body. Refers to the body of the manifested world, as when Jesus says "This is my body." see 64, 72, 156, 200, 118 Latin.

Mundus (Lt). World or Universe; World Order. see 600 Greek.

83   (prime)

I. Consecration: love in its highest form: energy, freedom, amrita, aspiration. The root of the idea of romance plus religion. [Crowley, 1977, p. xxv].

חלילה rotation, succession; round about; in turn; pointed. As an adverb: God forbid!

א-ב-י-ע [A-B-I-O]. Sum of the letter which are the initials of the name of the 4 Qabalistic Worlds. *Sepher Sephiroth*: *Addreviatura Qustuor Systematur*, or abbreviation of the four worlds [Crowley, 1977, p. 13]. Aleph = Atziluth, the archetypal world of ideas; Beth = Briah, the world of Creation; Yod = Yetzirah, the world of Formation and Ayin = Assiah, the world of Action or manifestation. see 537, 218, 315, 385, 1377.

עוז ouz, oz. strength, power, might. Alternate spelling is *oz* (77). Relates to Geburah גוברה. see 216, 84.

חנכה inauguration, dedication; Hanukkah, the festival of the Maccebean dedication of the altar; consecration.

גף body, self; height, elevation; wing; dam; bank of river. see 89, 803.

"All ideas to conservation, protection, guarantee: in a restricted sense, *a body*. גוף Action of *enclosing, incorporating, embodying, investing* with a body; that which serves for defense, for conservation." [d'Olivet, 1976, pp. 316-317.]

פג From an unused root meaning *to be torpid*, i.e. *crude*; an *unripe* fig or green fig [Strong's Bible Dictionary].

"That which extends afar, which wanders, is extended, loses its strength, its heat. The Arabic word as a noun means every kind of crudeness, unripeness; as verb, it is the action of *separating, opening, disjoining*, etc.

פוג Action of being *cool, freezing*; or losing movement. [d'Olivet, 1976, p. 423.]

אגלי-טל dew drops , the drops of dew. In Job 38:28: "Has the rain a father? or Who has begotten the drops of dew?" The heavenly dew is light; it falls in widely-scattered "drops" of solar radiance and forms all bodies with its generative power. see 39, 44.

בניהו Benaiah, "Jah has built [1 Kings 4:4] "Benaiah the son of Jehoiada [Jah knows]..."

גימל Gimel. The letter name Gimel. "Camel" is related to memory and subconsciousness. alternative spelling (see 73).

גלים a flowing, wave. suggest the vibratory activity of mental substance.

לכבאל 31st Shem ha-Mephorash. "God who inspires." Rules the acquisition of knowledge. Governs: vegetation and agriculture. Positive influence: love of astronomy, mathematics and geometry. Negative: avarice, usury. Angel of the 1st decanate (and quinance) of Capricorn attributed to the 2 of Disks. see Appendix 10.

כנגדו as his counterpart, for him. In Genesis 2:18: "And the Lord God said, it is not good that the man should be alone [Adam]; I will make a companion [an help meet] for him." Kaph is a prefix meaning "as, like; about; approximate; while, during"; נגד means: before, in front of, in the presence of; over, against, opposite; thus כנגד means: according to ; towards, opposite. see 45 (Aleph, spirit in דם, blood).

Fait Luz (Lt). "Let there be light." Genesis 1:3

84

I. The number of years of sidereal revolution of Uranus about the Sun (84.07 years).

אגף troop, squadron; wing (army), band, bank of a river, rivulet. With different pointing: *awgaph*, to close, shut a door, seal a jar.

בכל לב with all my heart, with my whole heart.

גמולה reward, recompense. Knowledge is the reward of the skill of perception. see 3, 12, 21, 30, 39, 48, 57, 66, 75, 93.

חנוך Enoch. Initiated. Proper name Enoch, the patriarch who "walked with God." see 564.

I. D'Olivet renders Genesis 4:17: "And Kain knew Aisheth (his intellectual companion, his volitive faculty): and she conceived and brought forth (the existence of) Henoch (founder, central energy). Then he built a spherical enclosure (stronghold) and he called the name of this spherical enclosure after the name of his son Henoch. (p. 323)

II. He comments: ...again I urge the reader to give close attention to the proper names; for to them Moses attaches great importance. The greater part of the hieroglyphic mysteries are now in form of these names. The one referred to in this passage, is composed to the two roots חן and אך. The first חן, characterize proper, elementary existence: it is a kind of strengthening of analogous root חַ, more used, and which designates *things* in general. The second אך, contains the idea of every compression, of every effort that the being makes upon itself, or upon another. For the purpose of fixing itself or another. The verb which comes from these two roots: חנוך *signifies to fix, to found, to institute, to arrest any existence whatsoever.*

It is from a composition quite similar, that the personal pronoun אנוכי, *myself*, in Hebrew results; that is to say אך or חַ, *the finished, corporeal being,* אך founded, י *in me.*" [d'Olivet, 1976, pp. 137-138.]

III. "A symbol of the individuality; that part of the soul which survives physical and astral dissolution, or the first and second deaths, and is immortal." [Gaskell, 1981, p. 250.]

ידע to see, to know, to know carnally, perceive, consider. The root of דעת, Da'ath. Its 1st two letter spell יד, Yod (hand) and Ayin which means human eye. Therefore to know means to touch and see. First of the occult axioms: to know, to will, to dare, to be silent. With different pointing: 1. to appoint, assign; 2. to be known, be familiar. In Genesis 4:1 "Adam knew his wife Eve, and she conceived..." see 474, 503, 20, 701, 130, 708

דמם was silent, to be silent, to be still, to wait in silence; to stop, stand still; to be struck dumb. A reminder of the last, and therefore most emphatic of the four ancient occult axioms. To know, will, dare and be silent. "Be still, and know that I am God." see 86

חלום a dream. "Then shall the vision of thy Lord be granted unto thee" [Book of Tokens, Samekh]. Signifies revelation of knowledge in the silence of night.

אלחמה Alchemy; the science of personality transmutation and the art of physical regeneration through union with God. Note that this word is composed of two other words אל (strength, a name of God), and חמה, *Khammah,* the Sun. Note that אלחם *ilkhame,* is the modern Hebrew verb meaning "to alchemize." see 53.

Case: Alchemy is אל-חמה, wherefore, on p. 75 of this work [Hermetic Mystery and Alchemy, by Mrs. Atwood-A Suggestive Inquiry], those who pin the narrow name of Chemia to this science are denounced as imposters. For though this is the science and art which deals with what hearers calls the operation of the sun , it is altogether misunderstood if it be limited to the sun (חמה). Unless אל (31) be conjoined to חמה (53), the art is not truly named. Therefore is אל the symbol of the one manifested through the three, while חמה signifies the manifestation of the three through the five. The ONE is the first matter; the three are the principles, Sulphur, Mercury and Salt; the five are the four elements and the quintessence extracted from them. Therefore does the name alchemy represent that which by the wise is declared to be One which is also three, four and five (since אל = 31 = 4, and חמה = 53 = 8). The 4 may be symbolized as the + of the elements (with the quintessence at the center). The eight is no where better symbolized than by the numeral 8, which discloses the secret of its movement. Finally, חמה + אל = 84 = the conjunction of 8, the number of Hermes or Mercury with 4, the number of Jupiter, of Zeus. Here in may be found the whole mystery of the Tetragrammaton (4) and Christ (8). And the conjunction of the new Jerusalem, and of the ancient Egyptian symbol [3-4-5 triangle] wherein the whole mystery of the art is synthesized;

while there multiplication (8x4) gives 32, the number of the paths on the Tree.

פ-ד Peh-Daleth. These letters Peh (Mars) and Daleth (Venus) suggest action (Mars) and inagination (Daleth). Peh is the mouth as an organ of speech and Daleth is the door or gate between two worlds.

Initials P.D. of the last brother of the 2nd group of co-founders of the Rosicrucian order according to the *Fama*. Brother P.D. was the secretary. A secretary recevies letters and correspondence, and communicates this to the fraternity. He records the minutes of the meetings and keeps the archives. In connection with the letters Peh and Daleth, he must express well the thoughts of the fraternity. In order to understand the problems of others, me must have a good imagination. He must be silent in the face of criticism and in the presence of the unprepared. He must use discrimination to keep silent in the presence of ignorance. The most effective action comes from silence. Silence builts power and prevents people who are contrary to your work from setting up road blocks.

ע-ח-ה-א Aleph-Heh-Cheth-Ayin. The 4 guttural letters of the Hebrew Alphabet. Aleph = spirit; Heh = vision, reason; Cheth = receptivity; Ayin = mirth, renewal.

I. K.D.L.C.K. (p. 71) says that these are the initial letters of Exodus 32:31, חטא (ה)עם הזה אנא "Oh, this people have sinned a great sin."

II. IZQ para. 699: For in the mysteries of the letters of Solomon the King, those four letters, A, H, Ch, O [א, ה, ח, ע] are surrounded by GIKQ [ג, י, כ, ק]." [Mathers, 1993, p. 332]"

אבימאל The Father is God. A son of Joktan in Genesis 10:28.

אחלמה Amethyst; a precious stone; the ninth stone of the breast-plate of the High Priest; corresponding with Sagittarius. In Exodus 28:19: "And in the third row an opal, an agate, and an amethyst." For other stones, see 45, 98, 702, 150, 345, 395, 370, 308, 1210, 350, 85.

I. Isidore Kosminsky writes: "The ninth stone of the breastplate is achlamah, which with few exceptions, is identified with the amethyst-beyond doubt the correct identification. The Midrash Bemiddah gives the color as purple which is the dominant shade of this beautiful gem: purple is also one of the chief colors associated with the planet Jupiter which in Astrology is termed the Lord of Sagittarius, the ninth sign of the Zodiac... in old poets, travelers, publishers, etc. It would strengthen the wisdom, faith and religion of the wearer and aid in prayer and in dreaming. If bound to the left wrist the amethyst enabled the wearer to see the future in dreams; to dream of the stone itself indicated success to a traveler, clergyman, sailor, philosopher, teacher or mystic, also protection, faith and fruitful thought for pains in the head (headache, toothache, etc.) It was recommended that an amethyst be immersed in hot water for a few minutes, taken out, dried, carefully and gently rubbed over the parts affected and the back of the neck. Almost all authorities agree in translating the Hebrew achlamah as amethyst and as identifying it as the ninth stone of the High Priest Breastplate. It was the seventh precious stone which the sage Iachus gave to Apollonius of Tyana as an emblem of piety and dignity." (pp. 129-132)

centrum (Lt). center. The central or middle point in the Tree of Life is *Tiphareth* (Beauty). In Hebrew Vav, is the nail and the connection link. It is numerically the number 6 and is related to the 6th Sphere on the Tree of Life, Tiphareth. Vav is attributed to intuition, which indicates the *centrum* mentioned in the *Fama* is what directs us to our true philosophy. see 6, 12, 1081.

essentia (Lt). essence.

Magister (Lt). Master, leader, chief, superior. He who "Knows" is initiated into the central essence at the heart and this is his reward. He thus merits the above titles. see 314 Latin, 151 Latin.

I. "And Hebrew understand that the will is a spirit, and different from the desirous craving. For the will is an insensitive and incognitive life; but the craving is found by the will, and is the will a being. This the craving is a magia (29), and the will a magus (55); and the will is greater than its mother which gives it, for it is Lord in the mother; and the mother is dumb, but the will is a life without origin. The craving is certainly a cause of the will, but without knowledge or understanding. The will is the understanding of the craving." [Böhme. 1980, II:2, p. 154.]

II. Paul Case notes: 29 (magia-magic) + 55 (magus-mage) = 84 = magister = centrum, i.e. the point = 1 = magus; the circle surrounding it is magia.

cognitio (Lt). knowledge. Part of a phrase. see 474.

seculum (Lt). a generation, life-time; age.

mundus (Lt). world, universe.

85

אֵין סוֹף Ain Suph. These words represent the <u>means</u> whereby *Ain* the No-thing, establishes *Suph* or limitation.

פֵּה Letter name Peh. the mouth as organ of speech; speech, saying, command, orifice, opening; edge (of sword);extremity, end; womb; border, mouthful, portion, part. Peh is associated Mars and with Key 16, the Tower and the 27th Path of Wisdom, the Exciting Intelligence. Peh connects Netzach (desire) and Hod (intellect) on the Tree of Life and is the northern face of the Cube of Space. see 80, 899.

I. Peh represents the Mars force, or the principle of action and is attributed the Mouth as an organ of speech. The No-Thing (Ain Suph) establishes apparent limitation (Key 15, Capricorn place of Mars exaltation) by the utterance of its Creative Thought. Thought. This utterance is the active principle of manifestation and the power which constitutes the framework of creation (Key 4, Mars in Aries). The ground of similarity among all forms of cosmic manifestation (Key 13, Mars in Scorpio).

The paths of Daleth and Teth cross Gimel above Tiphareth, but the third reciprocal path of Peh crosses the path of Samekh below Tiphareth. Now see a subtlety. Peh, is 85, and this goes back to 4 through 13, so that the path of Peh, veils Daleth again. Thus all the horizontal paths are feminine, even though the path of Peh is related to Mars, and the ruling power in the path of Teth is the Sun. see **11**.

Peh is 85, or 5 times 17. It is the sign of the multiplication of goodness by the vision of the Constituting Intelligence which is Heh, or 5. see 89, 10, 17, 170 & C.27.

יְסוֹדָה Basis, foundation. Feminine form of the Yesod. Establishment of seeming limitation is the result of the operation of the feminine aspect of reality, the feminine foundation. Compare *beten*, the womb and *ameka* (61), thy mother.

הִיסוֹד ha-Yesod. the foundation. Refers to Yesod on the Tree of Life. see 80.

הָעַי heap, ruin. As the name a city, it is translated *Ai*. The prefix H perhaps is considered as the definite article.

אָפֵר to clothe, to glorify, steadfast; to bind about, to gird; steadfastness, constancy. The No-Thing establishes apparent limitation within itself by circumscribing a field of manifestation in which to express its infinite potencies.

בּוֹעַז Boaz. The black pillar of severity set before Solomon's temple. A variant spelling referred to in the Sephirah Hod. בעז is the scripture spelling. See 79 and 1 Kings 7:22.

הָמַם to route, to confuse, to impel, to drive, to put into strong action; to disturb; to bring into confusion, to confound. The No-Thing disturbs its own perfect rest in order to manifest its potencies, and sets up intense activities within the field of seeming limitation it establishes in itself. The primary manifestations are chaotic, disturbed and confused, yet order eventually evolves out of the primary chaos.

לֵב־אֶבֶן "heart of the stone" [Ezekiel 11:19]. In the passage ה is affixed to אֶבֶן. A Qabalistic liberty has been exercised here. "And I will take the stoney heart out of their flesh." The "stoney heart" is a symbolic of the sense of separateness pictured by the Key 16, the Tower.

גָּבִיעַ bowl, a goblet; the calyx of a flower. The cup on the Magician's table, and the flowers in his garden. The "cup" is the creative pattern in the Universal Mind. Its connection with Peh intimates that the power of articulate sound has power akin to the Briatic world of cups.

גביע is from גבע, to be vaulted or arched, suggesting the feminine gender. A flower is that part of a plant in which the reproductive organs are located, and גביע is related to the occult meaning of Mars, which is that force active in the reproductive power of both sexes.

מילה Circumcision (Rabbinical word), the sign of the covenant of union and love, in exoteric Judaism. For spiritual Israel, there is the circumcision of the heart by the control of the emotional nature. In Yod the seed of all the letters is the secret of the covenant and this secret is the Peh-Heh, the mouth of the eternal. This is the true occult meaning of the compass in Freemasonry: "Learn to circumscribe their passions and keep their desires within bounds." Notariqon for "Who shall go up for us to heaven?" see 95, 671, 651, 55 and Deuteronomy 30:12.

I. Yod יוד is the seed of all the letters and is the secret of the Covenant, and this secret is the Peh-Heh, for פה is 85, or היסוד, Ha-Yesod, the Foundation, and 85 is also *miylah*, the Covenant which removes concealment from the paternal Yod.

The physical rite of circumcision does unveil the paternal Yod, but the Covenant is not its symbol. What is hidden here goes deeper.

In *miylah* the first letter is מים (Mem), then comes יוד (Yod), then למד (Lamed), and last, הה (Heh). Yod and Mem spells מי, which is the Living Water, transmitting life. Of that life, the letter Y*od* at the end of מי is the sign, for Yod is the first letter of יהוה, the name of the Most High. Thus Yod stands for Chaiah, the life-force in Chokmah, and the letters Lamed and Heh which conclude מילה are referred to Venus (Nogah) and Mars (Madim) respectively.

The Covenant reveals the paternal Yod in Chokmah. Yet is the symbol a clue to a fact, for the cosmic life-force is projected, generation after generation, into manifestation through human bodies, and the power of Mars is combined with that of Venus in the Vital Soul in Yesod. This is, even now, a closely guarded practical secret. Even these words are veiled. See C.10.

II. Peh represents the Mars force and is a clue to the meaning of מילה, circumcision, which refers to the masculine aspects of the Life Power's activity in reproduction. [Paul Case, unpublished notes]

פה here, hither. see 549, 226, 876, 95.

הגבעה the hill. In Exodus 17:9: "Tomorrow I will stand on the top of the hill with the staff of God in my hand." said Moses to Joshua. This is the feminine of the masculine noun, גבע, hill

Dominus (Lt). Lord. Latin word for God as the ruler of the universe. The Latin word used in translating IHVH and Adonai (65) in the Old Testament. What is intimated is that what the human mind formulates in its idea of God is Lord, is no more than the idea of the agency where by the absolute sets up the conditions of name and form, which are the logical necessities for any manifestation whatever. see 26, 65, 518 (Lt).

veritas (Lt). truth. "Truth" has to do with something we must regard as being intermediate between the Absolute No-Thing and the field of seeming limitation which embraces all things having form, quality, mass, and other definable characteristics. see 441.

Zelator (Lt). The zealous one. Corresponds to 1=10 Rosicrucian grade of initiation corresponding to Malkuth on the Tree of Life, and the element of Earth. The "Lord of Earth" is Adonai Melekh. The Zealator is admonished to keep the fire of aspiration burning in the athanor or vessel of light, in this quest for truth. see 103, 100, 142, 656, 662.

Scorpio (Lt). Scorpion; the eight sign of the Zodiac, corresponding to the Hebrew letter Nun, "seed", Tarot Key 13 Death, i.e. change and transformation, to alchemical putrefaction, and to Apophis (Typhon) in the IAO formula. see 50, 106, 54, 81, 861 (Greek); 70 (Lt).

140

86

אלהים Elohim. Creative Powers, Strengths. The 7-fold Life-breath. Creative name attributed to Binah. The "Gods" or 7 spirits of God, the order of angels of Netzach. Refers particularly to Binah as being Amah [אמא], the Dark Sterile Mother. The power which brings actual things into manifestation in the world of name and form. The masculine plural of a feminine singular. One could say that Elohim is a "plural of majesty." א: Rauch (Ether), ל: Libra (Air), ה: Aries (Fire), י: Virgo (Earth), ם: Neptune (Water). see 42.

I. "Elohim.... This is the plural of the word אלה, the name given to the supreme being by the Hebrews and the Chaldeans, and being itself derived from the root אל, which depicts elevation, strength, and expansive power; signifying in a universal sense GOD. It is a very singular observation that the last word applied to the Most High, is however, in its abstract sense only the relative pronoun he employed in an absolute manner. Nearly all of the Asiatic peoples have used the bold metaphor. הוא (hoa), that is to say, HE is the Hebrew, Chaladic, Syriac, Ethopic and Arabic, one of the sacred names of the divinity; it is evident that the Persian word *Goda*, God which is found in all the tongues of the North. It is known that he Greek philosophers and Plato particularly, designated the intelligent cause of the universe in no other way than by the absolute pronoun το Αντο.

However that may be, the Hebraic name *Aelohim* has been obviously composed of the pronoun אל and absolute verb, הוה, *to be being*... It is from the inmost root of this verb that the divine name ה *Yah*, is founded, the literal meaning of which is *Absolute-Life*. The verb itself, united to pronoun אל, produces אלוה (Eloah), *That-HE-who-is*, the plural of which *Aelohim*, signifies exactly *HE-they-who-are: The Being of Beings*.

The Samaritan says *Alah*, whose root אל is found still in the Arabic Allah, and in the Syariac *Aeloha*. The Chaladic alone depicts from this root and translates ייי *Iaii*, the *Eternity of Eternities*, which is also applied to the Ineffable Name of God, יהוה...also of the words שמים, *the heavens*, and ארצ, *the earth*." [d'Olivet, 1976, p. 28.]

II. F.J. Mayers: In the first place it is a plural name. There is a singular form of the name: Eloha , i.e. god (small g). Elohim , therefore literally means Gods ...although it is clearly a plural name, it is invariably used with the singular verb; i.e. it issued grammatically as if it were singular. The significance of this is that although "Elohim denotes, like the Gods of the nations, the various powers, attributes, qualities, and activities of the supreme being, they are all conceived of as a unity; they all work together as one; they express one will, one purpose, one harmony; their activities are the manifestation of the eternal One, the absolute. One might, therefore, explain the name Elohim as "He the Gods or The unity of Gods , or The activities of the Eternal One. i.e. God expressing and revealing himself outwardly in creative activity. How completely this harmonizes with the New Testament: In (the) Beginning was the word and the word was with (literally in) God, and the word was God. All things were made by Him, and without Him was not anything made that is made, etc. Elohim was the creative aspect of God; he was the creator and maker of all things. So was the word. Elohim was the revealer of the Eternal One. So was the Word... He hath declared him. Elohim was the outward expression of God-the divine image or likeness - which was to be formed ultimately, as we shall see later, in universal man. So was the word the two names express the same idea, one in Hebrew idiom, and the other in Greek idiom. Each is, in the language of theology, the second person of the divine trinity. But it will be noticed that the two names belong to different ages, and correspond to different stages in human evolution. The earlier name Elohim corresponds to an age in which man was still dominantly an instinctive being, far from being full self-conscious. [The Unknown God, pp. 14-15]

III. "Elohim has... been explained as being the process through which Aleph becomes Yod and resurrects from that material metamorphosis. Life in its oneness moves up and down, down and up, from infinite to finite, and from duration to timelessness. [Suraes, 1992, p. 87.]

Elohim… is the process through which Aleph (1) by initiating a physiological movement (30) in life (5) comes into existence (10) and acquires the appearance of a metamorphosis (40) which offers resistance to life and therefore gives birth to living beings. [ibid. p. 184]

IV. The Zohar [I:15B] Comments: "When, however it [the house, Beth] was sown with seed to make it habitable, it was called Elohim, hidden and mysterious. The Zohar was hidden and withdrawn so long as the building was within and yet to bring forth and the house was extended only so far as to find room for the holy seed. Before it had conceived and had extended sufficiency to be habitable, it was not called Elohim, but all was still included in the term Bereshith [913]. After it had acquired the name Elohim, it brought forth offspring from the seed that had been implanted in it." (p. 64)

הַטֶבַע- Nature. Referring to nature or everything in the field of manifestation, which is like an impression on a coin or in substance. As a verb, to be set as a foundation. The Talmudic word for nature is הטבע, which also means substance, element, coin, medal, impression on a coin, universe, character, characteristics. see 81, 23, 4, 14, 41, 72, 104, 158

אבל הגדולה "the great meadow." Incorrectly translated in the English Bible as the "Great stone of Abel." Do not confuse Abel with the name of the 2nd son of Adam and Eve. The "Great Meadow" symbolizes the field of cosmic manifestation, relating to Cheth as the field or fence of human personality within the boundaries of the absolute. see 1 Samuel 6:18

בעדי that which concerns me, what surrounds me, i.e. my environment. "What surrounds me" is the "Great Meadow," the field of cosmic manifestation. The field is itself WITHIN the encompassing being of the One Reality. See Psalm 138:8.

עבדי my servants [Isaiah 65:13, Psalm 135:1]. These are the servants of יהוה, the powers which surround us and constitute our environment and represented by אלהם, Elohim (86). The Great Meadow which constitutes what surrounds me contains nothing but the servants of Tetragrammaton, and these are the creative

powers called Elohim in Genesis. The power of specialization corresponding to Binah and the first Heh in יהוה. see 162

לוים Levites, the class of priest among the Jews. In Deuteronomy 18:1: "The priest, who are Levites-indeed the whole tribe of Levi-are to have no allotment or inheritance with Israel. They shall live on the offerings made to the Lord by fire, for that is their inheritance."

נבדל separative. From a verb meaning: to be divided, separated, set apart; similar to the English "to distinguish". The 6th path is the Intelligence of Mediating or Separative Influence. The Separative Intelligence is a mode of consciousness which acts in man as the discriminative power that classifies various objects of experience. A formula for the powers of the Elohim. They manifest through imagination (Nun), self-conscious effort (Beth), desire (Daleth) and action through balance (Lamed). The sonship of man makes him heir for the powers of the Elohim. see 1081, 536, 548, 640, 886.

אהיה אדני Eheyeh Adonai. A name composed of the special names of Kether (אהיה) and Malkuth (אדני), and thus asserting the identity of these two Sephiroth. It is written, therefore that "Kether is in Malkuth and Malkuth is in Kether, but after another manner." It is also the secret of the saying "I and the father are one." In this connection remember that the holy Spirit came as fire. see 21, 65, 386, 620, 496.

סבו pavilion, tent. "His tabernacle," where it is said to be in Salem (i.e. in peace). This brings out the idea that Elohim is the name used in Psalm 76. [The spelling of sukkoh in Psalm 76 is a longer spelling. This is the defective spelling for special Qabalistic emphasis.] see 370, 376, 92

הללו יה Praise be to God. Exclamation of Joy.

כוס cup, goblet, the lot of fate, whether good or bad; also the pelican called כוס, because its throat resembles a cup or bag. The pelican is an important alchemical symbol. In all its meanings this word suggest the concealment, virgin birth, and preservation of the fire through the feminine principle. see 386, 300.

מום From an unused root probably meaning *to stain, a blemish* (physical or moral), *blemish, blot, spot* [Strong's Bible Dictionary]. Paul Case adds: fault, defect, want.

I. Canticles 4:7: "All beautiful you are, my darling; there is no flaw [defect] in you." Also the short form of the 72nd Shem ha-Mephorash, otherwise written מומיה Mumiah (101). see Appendix 10.

II. "Mumiah is an angel who controls the science of physics and medicine and is in charge of health and longevity. His corresponding angel is *Atembu*i." [Davidson, 1971, p. 199.]

מולי plentitude. The fullness of the powers of deity. With different pointing: filling, stuffing.

לאכלה for food. Referring to herbs in Genesis 1:29: "...every tree which is the fruit of a tree yielding seed: to you it shall be for food." The Tree of Life and its powers.

ודעו and know. In Psalm 46:10: "Be still, and know that I am God..." see 514.

מדאל "God, is Sending Forth as Father. 48th Shem ha-Mephorash. Associated with the 6th quinance of of Pisces; Angel by night of 10 of Cups. 236°-240°. SENCINER. May 6, July 17, September 27, December 8, February 18. 3:40 - 4:00 PM. [Psalm 98:2] "The Lord has made known His salvation; His righteousness has He openly shown in the sight of the nations." To preserve peace and union. Protects those who have recourse to it; they will have present merits and secret inspirations concerning all that happens to them. Rules the generation of beings, and influences friendships and conjugal fidelity. Person born: ardent in love; likes walking for pleasure (la promenads) and ??? in general. see 965 & Appendix 10.

בחלום in dream. See Genesis 31: 10.

הנאל Haniel. Geomantic intelligence of Capricorn.

כיון The planet Saturn, Binah, the sphere of Saturn is also the sphere of the Elohim.

Naometria (Lt). Temple measurement. A Latinized from a Greek noun. It was a title of a curious work by Simon Studion. The book itself is negligible. Yet its title shows that Studion might had had some acquaintance with occult writings circulated by the inner school before the publication of the 1st Rosicrucian manifestoes. In these, the word Naometria had to do with right measurement of the field within the boundaries of the pentagon, i.e., nature as the temple of God. I. "The symbolical expression is reminiscent of Kabalistic or pre-Kabalistic tracts on the delineation of the celestial temples, the measurement of diving body, and Rabbi Eliezer's measurement of the Earth Temple; but the immediate allusion is to the Apocalypse, Revelations 11:1: And there was given me a reed like a rod: and the angel stood, saying: rise, and measure the temple of God, and the altar, and them that worship the rein. For this reason the subtitle of the manuscript is termed a naked and prime opening of the book written-within and without-by the key of David and the reed like unto a rod. The book in question is presumable that which was sealed with seven seals, but was opened in heaven by the Lamb, standing before the throne of God; and Naometria is said to be a brief introduction to a knowledge of all mysteries in holy scripture and the universal world. It follows that Simon Studion, by the claim expressed in his title, but received the power which was given to the lion of the tribe of Juda and the root of David." [Waite, 1993, p. 44] see 333 (Lt)

primus (Lt). first (in order). Indicating the idea that the Field must be manifest before the man appears, just as the pentagon must be constructed before the star of 5 points, symbolizing man, may be drawn.

sapientia (Lt). wisdom. The Latin equivalent of Chokmah. see 73, 357 (Lt), 421

simplex (Lt). simple, uncompounded, unmixed. Indicating the undifferentiated state of the field with the area symbolically enclosed by the pentagon (Chaiah, 23), before it is specialized by the Tetragrammaton (IHVH) Elohim.

terra adamica (Lt). earth of Adam [Secret symbols, page 34]. These words are followed by the word Azoth, written with A and Z in Roman characters, Omega in Greek, and Tav in Hebrew. Thus A-Z-Omega-Tav, Azoth means "beginning and end" and is an alchemical name for the Quinta Essentia. see 158, 1223

Typhon (Lt). The Greek name of the Egyptian divinity Set, the personification of the principle of evil. In Greek mythology Τυφων the father of the winds and the son of TYPHOE, with whom he was sometimes confused. As storms were ascribed to the agency of giants, the name came to mean a furious storm, hurricane, typhoon. An appropriate name for unbalanced force before equilibration has evolved order into manifestation. The "age" of giants and dinosaurs. see 2050, 70 (Greek); 23, 52 (Lt); 861 (Greek)

II. Arthor Redman: Typhon is an aspect or shadow of Osiris. Typhon is not the distinct evil principle or Satan of the Jews; but rather the lower cosmic principle of the divine body of Osiris (81, 590), the God of them. The true meaning of the Egyptian myth is that Typhon is the terrestrial and material envelope of Osiris, who is the indwelling spirit thereof. In the Qabalistic system which we call the Tree of Life this quarternaty of lower principles corresponds to the four Sephiroth below Tiphareth... if one remembers that every anthropomorphic creative God was with the ancients the Life-giver and the Death-dealer -Osiris and Typhon.. It will be easy for him to comprehend that Typhon or Apophis (861) as he was also named was but a symbol of the lower quaternary, the ever conflicting and turbulent principles of differentiated chaotic matter, whether in the universe or in man, while Osiris symbolized the highest spiritual triad.

nobiscum (Lt). with us. Part of a Rosicrucian salutation, *Deus Nobiscum, pax profunda.* ("God with us, peace profound") see 131, 251, 329 (Lt).

87

לבנה Levanah, Lebanah. pale or white one, Moon; [Canticles 6:10] The Sphere of the Moon. Lebanah, as white or pale one, identifies the part of the work associated with Yesod with the alchemical "White work of the Moon", wherein is concealed the real secret of building the mystic temple of regenerated humanity. Formed of לב

laib heart, בן *ben* son, and נה *nah* beauty, ornament. All these words are related to Tiphareth, of which Yesod is a direct reflection. The powers of the automatic consciousness of Yesod are reproductions of the powers of the Ego in Tiphareth. Also לב נה: "Beautiful heart." see 80, 220, 32, 175.

With different pointing: 1. *lebanah,* Brick, tile [Genesis 11:3, Ezekiel 4:1]; 2. *laybeynah.* whiteness, clearness; 3. *Leybanh,* frankincense. Incense connected with the sun and Sunday. The first 3 letters spell לבן, white; and the last 3 spell בנה, to build, to make, to erect. Suggesting: 1. The heart of the son (Man) are to be found the source of beauty; 2. That in the aspect of the Life-power identified in Yoga and alchemy as the white work of the moon is concealed the real secret of building the mystic temple of regenerated humanity.

אסוך vessel, flask, cup or pot for holding anointing oil. Refers to Yesod as a receptacle of influence flowing down from above. "*Asvk* (a form of Aossic), meaning 'chalice', 'calyx', 'part of a flower'. The flower is the flow-er or flowing one, i.e. the female in her courses. The chalice of the flowing one is the vagina of the virgin. The chalice in the Mysteries is concealed behind the veil which in its primal and biological sense is the hymen." [Grant, 1994, p. 19.]

בזלל To shake or tremble.
בוין of the sword.

בלי מה literally "not what?" limitation, restraint, enclosure, nothingness, non entity. In Job 26:7: "He it is Who spreads out the northern skies over emptiness and hangs the earth upon nothing [or over nothing]."

זמם to purpose, to think, to devise, plot. As a noun: plan, device, purpose.

כל-כבודה all glorious. Refers to the King's daughter [Psalm 45:13], understanding by Qabalists to be Malkuth. Yesod may be conceived as being within Malkuth, the most external of the Sephiroth.

אבי-עד The Everlasting Father. In Isaiah 9:6: "For unto us a child is born, unto us a son is given, and the government shall be upon his shoulder: and his name shall be called Wonderful Counselor, The Mighty God, The Everlasting Father, The Prince of Peace."

פז Pure gold. In Psalm 21:3: "You welcomed him with rich blessing and placed a crown of pure gold on his head." Mars (Peh) in Gemini (Zain).

Aesch Mezareph [Ch. 2:6]: "Paz [פז, 87], and Zahab Muphaz [זהב מופז,147 *Zahab* meaning shining or yellow and *Muphaz* means pure] are referred to Tiphareth, 1 Kings 10:18; Psalm 21:4; 19:11 and Daniel 10:5. For so Tiphareth and Masloth are compounded in the Golden Throne, 1 Kings 10:18; also when it is called a vessel of Gold Job 28:17; a crown of Gold Psalm 21:3; Bases of Gold Canticles 5:15."

אני יהוה I am the Lord [Isaiah 42:8].

חסידה stork. A large White bird, connected with the Egyptian bird Ibis, the bird of Meditation (see Key 17). The bird, like the fishhook seeks its food in the depths, or water of subconsciousness.

מה חדל How short lived, frail. In Psalm 39:4: "Lord, make me to know my end, and [to appreciate] the measure of my days, what it is; let me know and realize how frail I am-how transient is my stay her."

אמום model, form; shoemaker's last, cap-maker's block, dress-maker block. The moon (Yesod) is the pattern-world for all forms.

בהלמי Behelemay. Angel of the first decanate of Pisces. This decanate is under the combined rulership of Jupiter and Neptune and implies benign, hospitable and philanthropic activities regarding cell-organization during sleep.

גדף to revile, blaspheme. Misuse of the powers of the Moon.

דגלים banners, flags, standards. Note this word contains the letter דג, dag, a fish, meaning: "to multiply abundantly." Multiplication is the alchemical process connected with Pisces. see 7, 57.

ומיאל Vumiel. Angel attributed to Netzach (Venus) and to Binah (Saturn).

אלן Tenth Judge of Israel. Rosenroth in K.D.L.C.K (p.114) says it is the masculine sex in regard to the tree in Isaiah 6:13. "And though a tenth [of the people] remain in it (the land), it will be for their destruction-eaten up and burned; like a terebinth tree or like an oak whose stump and substance remain when they are felled or have cast their leaves. The holy seed [the elect remnant] is the stump and substance [of Israel]."

Animuus Dei (Lt). Life of God. Yesod is the receptacle of the vital soul of all living creatures, including man. see 430.

electrum (Lt). shining substance; amber; an alloy of Gold and Silver.

Rosa coeli (Lt). Rose of heaven. The rose symbolizes desire. Yesod is Pure Intelligence. Purified desire is developed by the spiritual aspirant to reach "Heaven."

sanctus (Lt). holy. Desire is rendered pure by seeing the holiness of life in all things, especially in the nature of the reproductive activity centered in Yesod.

88

I. Number of days of the sidereal revolution of Mercury about the Sun.

חכלל colored. The word "color" is derived from a Latin root, meaning "to conceal." This suggests that the material world is a veil of color, concealing the real nature of the Life-Power. With different pointing: redness, sparkling.

חמם to be hot; to glow, to brood, to hatch. This word is closely related to the old name of Egypt, Khem (חם), whence, by an interesting series of linguistic transmutations, we get our modern word *chemistry*--so that the name of that branch of science which is doing so much to establish the real unity of the material world is, literally, "The Wisdom of Egypt." see 78.

חסך to spare, withhold, be without.

נחל something hollowed out, a valley. The popular idea is that the material world is a vale of tears; but there is a profounder meaning than this. The Fool (Aleph), always descends into a new valley on his adventurous Journey to the next mountain peak. With different vowel points: to take possession, possess, to inherent, to get, acquire. see 108, 7, 21, 14, 44, 66, 28.

לבן whiteness, semen. Refers to purity and innocence. see 82.

מגדיאל Magdiel. A duke of Edom, associated (with Mibzar) with Yesod. "El is renown" (in man). In Genesis 36:43: "Magdiel and Iram. These were the chiefs of Edom, according to their settlements in the land they occupied." Edom is a representation of unbalanced force.

I. "'El is renown.' We may notice here that El and Ilos were Babylonian names for the sun, and the *Ilinos* was another of his titles; and as we have Magdi-el for a prince amongst the ancient Edomites, so we have Magda-elene (Μαγδαληνη) amongst the later Jews." [Inman, 1942, (page unknown)]

חלן Strong. A proper name, the father of Eliab of Zebolon in Numbers 1:9, 2:7. Refers to alchemical separation. see 95

חניך trained person; apprentice; pupil. This word really means initiated. In Genesis 14:14: "And when Abram heard that his brother was taken captive he armed his trained servants, born into his own house, and pursued them unto Dan." Dan = Scorpio = alchemical putrefaction. see 318, 94 & Key 13.

חף pure; innocent. In Job 33:9: "I am pure and without sin; I am clean and free from guilt. (10) yet God has found fault with me; he considers me his enemy." see 808.

I. "Every idea of protective covering given to a thing; a guarantee, a surety. The Arabic is an onomatopoetic and idiomatic root which depicts that which acts upon the surface, which skims lightly over a thing. The Arabic verb characterizes the condition of that which becomes light; anything which shivers, shudders with fear, trembles with fright, etc.

חוף Action of *covering, protecting, brooding, coaxing.* A *roof, nest, shelter, port*: action of separating from that which *harms*; of *combing, appropriating*, etc. [d'Olivet, 1976, p. 353.]

חפ danger; net; snare, trap. In Psalm 119:110: "The wicked have set a snare for me, but I have not strayed from your precepts."

II. "Everything which is drawn in, expanded, as *the breath*; all that which is unfolded in order. To envelop and seize, as a *net*; thence, פחה every idea of *administration, administrator, state, government.*

 The Arabic constitutes all onomatopoetic and idiomatic root which describes every kind of hissing of the voice, snoring, strong respiration, rattling. When this voice is strengthened, it signifies literally, *an ambush; a trap.*" [d'Olivet, 1976, p. 425.]

nike (Lt). Victory. Note that 88 is 8 + 8 = 16 + 1 + 6 = 7, the Sephirah named Netzach (Victory). see 360, 744 (Greek).

Aqua Vita (Lt). Water of Life. "If you would make our substance red, you must first make it white. Its three natures are summed up in whiteness and redness. Take, therefore, our Saturn, subject it to coction in Aqua Vitae until it turns white, becomes thick, and is coagulated, and then again till it becomes red. Then it is red lead, and without this lead of the sages nothing can be effected."

Filius Dei. Son of God. The water of life is the mystical son of God and that son (the rider in the chariot in Key 7) is also the rose itself. see 154, 119.

victoria (Lt). victory. see 224, 360.

Invenies (Lt). You shall find. Part of an alchemical phrase in Secret Symbols (Page 17). "Visit the interior of the earth by rectifying you shall find the hidden stone." see 570 Latin.

trigono (Lt). triangle. The triangle of Fire, which symbolizes spiritual energy or Aleph. see 134, 46 (Lt)

Nascimur (Lt). We are born. You shall find that the son of God is born anew through us by the

146

aid of the triangle of Fire and the water of Life. Part of the phrase discovered in the vault of brother CR, see 683 Latin.

maximus (Lt). great; greatest. Part of a phrase referring to God. see 234.

summmom (Lt). The highest. Part of an alchemical phrase. see 145 (Lt)

89   (prime)

I. A number of sin – restriction. The wrong kind of silence, that of the Black Brothers. [Crowley, 1977, p. xxv].

ט/פ Peh/Teth, Mars (Mars) in Leo (Teth)

גוף Guph. The physical body, person, substance, essence, one of the 4 elements (matter as opposed to spirit), person (grammatical). see 496, 19, 463, 400, 430, 543, 1006, 55, 564, 170, 231, 809.

I. Guph is lowest and most external aspect of personality. Assigned to Malkuth, the fruit of completion of the Tree of life. Gimel in Guph stands for the Uniting Intelligence joining Yekhidah in Kether to the Ego seated in the hearts of men in Tiphareth. It is directly related to the Life-force in Chokmah. Vav stands for the Ego as the inner teacher. The burden of his teaching is that true wisdom must ever find expression in loving-kindness. Peh stands for the destruction of error and represents Yesod (by numeration) and the powers of the automatic consciousness. It is during man's Life in the physical body that he must accomplish the work which overcomes the delusions which seem to limit him. Guph is the starting point for the work which leads to liberation and is also the place where the Great Work finds completion.

The essence of *Guph* is the serpent-fire of which the letter Teth is a symbol. This fire comes forth through the working of the Active Intelligence, assigned to Peh. The number of *Guph* is 89, and this 9 is Teth, and its channel of outpouring is Peh, or 80. Add 8 and 9, and you see the power of Zain (7) coming forth through 1 to bring forth 8, or Cheth.

Through the path of Cheth the power of Saturn or Bonah conjoins itself with the force of Mars or Geburah. This power of Saturn descends also through the path of Tav into Malkuth, and thus gives form to Guph in the World of Assiah, the material world. See C.7.

II. Eighty-nine is its number, and as the numbers are Sephiroth, this reveals Hod (8) as the instrument of Yesod (9). Nine is Yesod, and so is 80, the numeration of יסוד. And 8 the seed of 9, because 1, 2, 3, 4 5, 6, 7, 8 total 36, and 9 is the sum of 3 and 6. Yet see here the Mother, 3, and the Son, 6. Look at Key 8, and see there before you the Mother, and her Son, the Lion of the Tribe of Judah. For ONE is All, and thus is Hod but another aspect of יסוד. There is but one Foundation.

89 is Teth (9), operating through 80, or the spiraling light-power working through the Mouth of the Eternal (Teth through Peh). When lightening flashes, thunder roars, and thunder has been for the ages a symbol for the Voice of God. So is your body far more than a lump of earth. It is the intelligence that unites us with the Crown (Kether). It is the Nail (Vav) that joins us to the Paternal Wisdom. Guph is truly the Mouth of the Lord. For in Guph are the letters ג, ו and פ, and these letters unite us forever with the Kingdom. See C.8.

III. Guph is כלה, Kallah, the Bride, and in her name is shown the perfection of the Kingdom. The Kingdom is 10, and Kallah is 55, or the sum of the numbers from 1 to 10. The Bride, כלה, is also הכל, the ALL. In Guph is the whole creation made manifest. Therefore is Guph, the body, the whole, the holy temple of the Most High. And where is this Temple? It stands in the midst, or center, and in it abides forever Adonai Melek (אדני מלך), our Lord and King, Holy is His Name, Blessed be He!

Guph is really the Kingdom, or the Bride who is the ALL. Can anyone separate even the smallest body from the whole? Through a single atom course all the forces of the universe, and whatever body you may take for an example, whether it be small as an electron or great as a galaxy, this remains true. Whatever body you may consider, that body is the mathematical center of an infinite expanse." See C.9.

דממה silence, whisper, hush; dormancy. The great work goes on in silence but can be delayed by inertia.

חפא to cover, to veil, a cover or case, to protect. Also in a sinister sense, to veil (the true nature of one's intentions).

לטים one enchanted, enchantments. The Illusions of "Egypt." The incarnate life veils the consciousness through the illusion of separation. In Exodus 7:22: "And the Magicians of Egypt did so with their enchantments: and Pharaoh's heart was hardened, neither did he hearken unto them; as the Lord had said." יעט yahat, ya at to clothe. An Aramaic word spelled the same means: to consult. In Isaiah 61:10 this word is יעטני, meaning "He hath covered". The Tarot keys corresponding to yahat (Keys 9, 15, and 8) are clues to its deeper meanings.

נטל to lift up, take up a burden or weight; to impose, to lay upon. A cross is a symbol of the burden (Saturn) and of bearing the burden. yet it should be remembered that the burden borne by those who know the great Archanum is Light, not heavy. In Proverbs 27:3: "A stone is heavy and sand is weighty [i.e. a burden or load]; but a fool's wrath is heavier than both."

פדח to separate, release, to ransom, redeem, deliver. The mystery of redemption, veiled in the new testament depends upon the incarnation, to which the word גוף, through its gematria, affords a clue. "The kingdom of spirit is embodied in my flesh" say the Malkuth statement of the Pattern.
הדף hadaph. to push away; To cast out, to drive out, eject, to thrust, to push. Refers to the purification of the body-cells by elimination of the "shells of the dead" or Qlippoth. This is accomplished by clear vision (Heh), creative imagination and strong desire (Daleth) and the overthrow of the false conception of personality (Peh). See [Deuteronomy 9:4], 809.

חפה to provoke, mock, blaspheme. The result of failure to understand what the word *Guph* really means.

מחיאל "God who vivifies all things." 64th Shem ha-Mephorash. Associated with the 4th quinace of Gemini; Angel by night of the 9 of Swords. 316°-320°. ASTIRO. May 22, August 2, October 13, December 24, March 6, 9:00-9:20. [Psalm 33:18] "Behold, the Lord's eye is upon those who fear him-who revere and worship Him with awe; who wait for him and hope in His mercy and loving-kindness." Against adversities; governs the prayers and wishes of those who trust in the Mercy of God. This Shem ha-Mephorash, and those following to the 72nd, belong to the choir of angels. Protects against rage and ferocious animals; rules savants, professors, orators, and authors; influences printing offices and libraries, and all those established in commerce. Person born under this influence distinguishes himself in literature. see 965 & Appendix 10.

טף "children"; mentioned in the departure of the Israelites form Egypt. In Exodus 12:37: "The Israelites journeyed from Rameses to Succoth. There were abut six hundred thousand men on foot, beside women and children." see 809.

Aula Lucis (Lt). The Temple of Light. Title of one of the alchemical writings of Thomas Vaughan.

Anima Mundi (Lt). Soul of the world. Mother Nature active on the physical plane. see 55

I. "For itself is the universal and sparkling flame of the light of nature, which has the heavenly spirit in itself, with which it was animated at first by God, who pervades all things, and is called by Auicenna, the Soul of the World. [Hermetic Huseum I. p. 78]

II. Waite describes the Mercury symbol as: "The crescent denotes the lunar part, which is feminine, and volatile in nature: This is the spiritus mercurii. The medial circle has no point in the center, signifying the immature state of Mercurial Sulphur Solis: This is the Anima Mundi of Quicksilver. The cross at the base represents the volatile body of the metallic substance." [Waite, 1993, p. 460]

Cibus animae (Lt). Food of the Soul.

Hermetis (Lt). of Hermes, i.e. Hermetic.

pyramis (Lt). pyramid. Classical Latin spelling. "Fire in the Midst." The Fire of Life, which renews and transforms all physical things. Also connected with self-conscious attention and clear vision. see Key 4.

Argentum (Lt). Silver. Metal of the Moon and of subconsciousness. In alchemy it is one of the higher brain centers which have access to cosmic memory. Its highest aspect is Living Silver. see 166, 77 (Lt).

Sal Artis (Lt). Salt of the Art. "The enigma of the wise (the Stone) is the Salt and Root of the whole Art, and, as it were, its Key, without which no one is able either to lock or unlock its secret entrance. No man can understand this Art who does not know the Salt and its preparation, which takes place in a convenient spot that is both moist and warm; there the dissolution of its liquid must be accomplished while its substance remains unimpaired. These are the words of Geber." [Waite, 1974, vol. 1, p. 176] Case adds to note carefully that sal artis = 89 = Argentum = Anima Mundi.

90

I Number of degrees in the angle formed by lines constituting the vertical line and base of a Pythagorean triangle. Therefore the number 90 defines the union of the Mother, Isis, with the Father, Osiris.

II. Sum of the perimeters of the 5 Platonic solids (6, 10, 14, 22, 38).

III. 9x10 = The operation of Yesod through the 10 Lights of Emanation [Book of Tokens].

צ Tzaddi. Fish-hook. Key 17 assigned to meditation, the process whereby the wise attain to conscious union with the Life-power via the Water which is the "Mute, dark mirror." The Zohar (p. 10) states that Tzaddi consist of a nun (Fish) surmounted by a Yod (hand), thus representing together the male and female principles of creation. Using Tzaddi, the fish-hook via meditation, raises Nun, the fish, out of the "Water" or subconsciousness into the region of self-conscious awareness; it also raises the Scorpio force to awaken the higher brain centers. see 20, 106, 477, 104.

I. The letter Tzaddi is looks like a small Kaph, which forms the lower part of the letter, combined with two Yods. Thus the secret value of Tzaddo is Kaph (20) plus two Yods (2x10) or 40. This indicates a connection between Tzaddi and Mem (מ, 40). Note that Aquarius (attributed to Tzaddi) means water-bearer and Mem means water. Note that the function of meditation serves to bring about the changes of personal consciousness which leads to the mental reversal pictured in Key 12 (The Hanged Man), corresponding to Mem. The Letter-name מים adds to 90, which is value of the letter Tzaddi.

Saturn rules Aquarius, and Aquarius among the Holy Living Creatures, wears the face of the man, and that is of Adam. In the Tarot the 12th Key is the suspended Adam, and when meditation reaches its perfection the Stable Intelligence is manifest, and nothing can move it." See C.19.

II. Rabbi Glazerson: "The letter Peh immediately precedes the letter Tzaddi in the alphabet. This is to teach that guarding one's mouth from slander, gossip, foul language, and so on, is the means by which one attains the level of the Tzadik, the righteous one." [Letters of Fire]

III. "This character as consonant, belongs to the hissing sound, and describes an onomatopoeia, all object which have relations with the air and wind. As symbolic image, in represents the refuge of man, and the end toward which he tends. It is the final and terminative sign, having reference to scission, limit, solution, end. Placed at the beginning of words it indicates the movement which carries toward the limit of which it is the sign; placed at the end, it marks the very limit where it has tended. [d'Olivet, 1976, pp. 430-431.]

IV. Paul Case: "The letter Tzaddi means "fish-hook," signifying that which draws the fish (Nun) out of the water (Mem)." [The Tarot]

V. "*Tsadde* is not only an archetype for beauty. It also expresses the construction of forms, the building of structures, beginning with the cell, upwards." [Suraes, 1992, p. 94.]

מים Letter Name Mem. Waters; that which flows. (mute, dark mirror). Alchemical water, microcosmically, is the cosmic fire specialized in the nerve currents and chemistry of the blood. It is purified by the image-making faculty of the Ego expressing through human personality. the purification of this Water must be the first work of the alchemist. Electricity is a fluid, identical with the Mars-force.

I. This is the "fixed water," which is the First Matter when duly prepared. In the Tarot this is the Hanged Man, suspended over a dry water-course. He hangs from a Tav and is centered. The flow is stopped, or suspended, and all personal considerations are eliminated, like the lopped branches of the trees. But the glory is there (around his head), and the perfection, for *Mem* is 90, and 650, if one takes the final ם as 600. Then the water is the "dry water," and the 650 is Adonai (אדני) multiplied by Yod, or היכל (temple) multiplied by Yod. The Lord and His Temple are One, and this is centered in *Guph* (89). All this points straight, if one finds the door. See C.10.

II. Ninty is the number of the right angle or square, symbolizing measurement. The letter Tzaddi is also 90, which suggest a connection between the suspension of personal activity pictured by the Hanged Man (Key 12) and the revelation of the truth about natural law pictured by The Star (Key 17).

דומם a great silence, still, silent, dumb, "in silence". Qabalists say "Mem is mute, like water." It is the mute dark mirror of substance, reflecting deity to itself in a "Great Silence." [Book of Tokens]

מלך Melek. King. One of the names for Tiphareth. As a verb *mawlak*: to administer, to reign, to rule, to counsel. As a noun *meyleyk*: "king, ruler, prince". It refers to Tiphareth as the seat of the Higher Ego or Christos which has dominion over all things. The essential Spirit of Man is the dominant power in creation. The alchemical water is actually the agency whereby the rule or administration of the Life-power is established over all forms and condition of manifested being. see 40, 45, 52, 67, 311, 1081.

I. The King, speaking through that Guph men know by the name of Yeshua. Jesus said, "I am the living water." Note Mem is 90, and so is מלך. Thus Yeshua stilled the waters (seas), for

he knew that *Adonai Melek* (155) is Lord of the Waters. see C.7, 155, 36, & 89

II. The Son is one with the Father, and the King is one with the Seas, and the Man is the symbol of the division of the Seas. For בן (Ben) and אימא (Aima) are both 52, and מלך (Melek), is like מים (Mem, 90) while אדם (Adam) is 45, the half of division of 90. These are the names of Tiphareth. See that *Melek* and Adam are really the same even in number, for though 45 is the half of 90, 4 and 5 total 9. Furthermore the extension of 9 is 45. Thus Adam and *Melek* are essentially one, but since *Melek* is 90, the number of *Mem*, the Seas, the King, like the Son, is one with the Mother, for Aima is also the root of water, and that is the root of *Mem*. *Aima* is named also the great Sea and in this does the royalty of the King have its root. He is one with the Kingdom or Bride, and one with the Mother. Key 12, associated with *Mem*, the Seas, shows the hanged or suspended Adam, thus is his head surrounded with the glory of the sphere of the Sun. He is the *Melek* or King, and his power to rule is the consequence of his utter dependence on what supports him - which is the power at the center corresponding to the letter Tav. Again both *Melek* and *Mem* are related to the letter Tzaddi by the number 90. Tzaddi in the Tarot is the Mother unveiling herself to those who succeed in meditation, as did our Father Abraham according to the Book of Formation. See 45, 52, 434, 400 & C.19.

III. A King is one who exercises dominion, however, to rule nature we must strictly obey her laws.

IV. Leviticus 28:21 'The King' (of Heaven). The fire-king, in whose worship children were made to pass though or between fires, and sometimes were really sacrificed. The deity was extensively worshipped amongst the Phoenicians and the Shemitic races generally. He represented the destructive attribute of the Almighty, and may be regarded as analogous to the Hindu 'Siva the terrible.' Although the god bears this name, he is not generally regarded with fear. On the contrary, nest to Vishnu or Chrisna, he is the most popular of the Hindu deities. [Ancient Faiths, Vol. 2, p. 318-319]

מי to apportion; who? what? a chord. Literally "whatness." *Root appearing in the word man,* moon, month. It is the Sanskrit name for a measure of weight. It refers to man, the measurer, and is directly connected with the 6 of Cups as the seat of the distinguishing, discriminating faculty of the Ego. It also refers to the mysterious food of the Children of Israel during their years of wandering in the Wilderness in Exodus 16:15. The fall of Fire and Water from the Heavens is our true source of Sustenance. The sweet "salt dew of heaven" is the purified body of the adept which actually has a sweet savor and odor. In Exodus 16:15: "And when the Children of Israel saw it, they said one to another, it is Manna, for they know not what it was." With different pointing: *men.* a portion, as in Psalm 68:23. see 786, 899, 395.

"This root, composed of the sign of exterior and passive action, united by contraction to the root אן, symbol of the sphere of activity and of the circumscriptive extent of being, characterizes all specification, all classifications by exterior forms; all figuration, determinate, definition, qualification.

The kind of things, *their exterior figure, image,* that is conceived; *the idea* that is formed, *the definition* that is given to it; their proper *measure, number, quota.*" [d'Olivet, 1976, p. 391.]

פי. mouth of. In Deuteronomy 8:3: He humbled you, causing you to hunger and then feeding you with manna, which neither you nor your fathers had known, to teach you that man does not live on bread alone but on every word from the mouth of [פי]the Lord [יהוה]. [Not on the bread does the man live, but on every thing from the mouth of Yahweh the man lives.] In this connection note that in Revelations 12:15: Then out of his mouth [στοματος] the serpent [ο οφις] spouted forth water [υδωρ] like a flood after the woman, the she might be carried off with the torrent. see 1,181, 780, 850, 1308.

יכין Jakin. the firm or strong one; patron From a Semitic root meaning "unity" and refers to the creative power of the One Thing. The white pillar, the pillar of mercy of the Tree of Life has the same underlying significance as "Yod Tetragrammaton". On the Tree of life, the pillar of the sephiroth whose numbers 2, 4, and 7 add to 13, the number of unity and love. The magic of light or theurgy (God-working) depends on

recognition of the One-ness of all, and is based on knowledge that it is essentially love. The pillar of establishment Solomon set before the porch of the temple, and which is the royal secret (silence) of the life-powers reign. In Masonry Jakin means "He will establish". see 740 and 1 Kings 7:21.

לב האבן the heart of the stone, the stoney heart. In Ezekiel 11:19: "I will give them sn undivided [one] heart, and put a new spirit in them; I will remove from them their stony heart and give them a heart of flesh." The "stony heart" is a symbol of the sense of separateness pictured by the tower in Key 16.

ימם hot springs. incorrectly translated "Mules" in the authorized version of Genesis 36:24. The union of Fire and Water.

כללי Collective; all-inclusive. From the adjective כלל, kellawl, signifying "whole, complete." Resh is associated with the 30th path of the Collective Intelligence, and this has to do with the completion of the Great Work in the production of the new creature, evolved from the natural man by the Life-power, working through the mental, emotional and physical activities of a human personality. The Collective Intelligence is more than a mere aggregate. It does include the sum-total of all modes of conscious life, but it transcends when it includes. see 510, 250, 640, 53.

ה-יסודה the Foundation (fem).

למך Lamek. Powerful. Old Testament patriarch [Genesis 4:18) who, according to Masonic tradition, was the father of that ancient craft. The Greek spelling is 676 the square of 26 (IHVH). Alchemical water is related to all things having to do with creation and construction.

עזון strong, powerful, mighty, majestic. With different pointing: might, force, fierceness. See 333 and Psalm 145:6.

גאלנו our redeemer [Isaiah 47:4]. (The Lord of Hosts is his name). see 127, 525, 961, 1066, 1912.

לב-האבן the heart of the stone, the stoney heart. In Ezekiel 11:19: "And I will give them one heart, and I will put a new spirit within you; and I will take the stoney heart out of their flesh, and will give them a heart of flesh." The "stoney heart" is a symbol of the sense of separateness pictured by the tower in Key 16. see 85, 735, 740

כ/ע Kaph/Ayin Jupiter(Kaph) in Capricorn (Ayin).

סוד הזוג The mystery of sex (technical Qabalistic term). see Mem (40), Tzaddi (90) & 80.

סל wicker basket; basket. Suggest the manna which is collected by the fish-hook from the waters of substance, to establish (Samekh) by the Higher Self to establish balance and harmony through action (Lamed)

"Every kind of movement which *raises, exalts, takes away, ravishes*. The Arabic signifies in a restricted sense, *to draw to one's self. Sal* in a very restricted sense, *a leap, a gambol*; in a broad and figurative sense, the *esteem* or *value* that is put upon things. Also *a heap* of anything; a thing formed of may others raised one upon another, as *a mound* of earth, etc. [d'Olivet, 1976, p. 409.]

פוד Pud. Night demon of the 2nd decanate of Leo. This decanate is ruled by Jupiter and suggest the qualities of unkindness, intolerance and boorishness, the adverse aspect of subconsciousness unguided bye the Sun or Self.

מלך Molech. Moloch; arch-demon corresponding (with Satan) to Kether. The God to whom first-born children of Israel were sometimes offered by followers of the cult. see 570.

יסך to pour, to be poured, as in Key 17. In Exodus 30:32 written ייסך (31) "And say to the Israelites, This is holy anointing oil [symbol of the Holy Spirit], sacred to Me alone throughout your generations. (32) It shall not be poured upon a layman's body, not shall you make any other oil like it in composition; it is Holy, and you shall hold it sacred." see 570.

Arbor aurea (Lt). Golden tree [Secret Symbols, p. 33]. Note that the 6th Path is the Sphere of Sol.

Cyprus (Lt) Cyprus, the island of the Rosicrucian allegory [*Fama*] where brother P.A.L. is said to have "died". Cyprus is associated with copper, Venus and with creative imagination. see 870 (Greek), 111 (P.A.L)

In the Rosicrucian allegory *Fama Fraternitatis*, Brother C.R. began his journey to the Holy Land in company with a certain Brother P.A.L., who died at Cyprus, the birthplace of Venus. The work of transmutation, symbolized by the death of P.A.L., occurs in the Venus or throat center. P.A.L. is a blind for the letter-name Aleph (אלף). Therefore the death of P.A.L. at Cyprus is a alchemical reference to the dissolution of the airy essence represented by Aleph. Aleph is the 11th Path uniting Kether and Chokmah on the Tree of Life.

91

I. Σ13 = 91

II. The 7 lines of a heptagram each of 13 units.

כסאי My throne. According to Isaiah 66:1, the throne is the heaven. Ezekiel 43:7 uses this term in a context which intimates that the place of the throne has suffered defilement by the wicked. The throne itself is Kether, but the place of the throne is the Ego manifesting through human personality and it may be defiled by actions resulting from belief in personal will.

מכלא in all things. In the Lesser Holy Assembly it is written, "The Name of the Ancient One is concealed in all things." Even in those appearances which seem severe and destructive, the Ancient One is awakening His units of expression, human personality.

מאכל Food, meal, fare, mealtime. The Higher Self is the food which nourishes the personality.

מלכא Daughter, virgin, bride, Kore [Crowley, 1977, p. 14]. With different pointing: queen, a title of Malkuth. Compare with *maleawk*, angel, messenger. Paul Case adds to NOTE WELL that

מלאך ,כמאל, מכלא are all written with the same letters. see 259 (Greek), 496, 55

מלאך one sent, angel. A certain type of personality-a conscious "messenger" of the Higher Self. A seer or prophet. In connection with Sarai, in Genesis 16:7: "And the angel of the Lord found her by a fountain of water in the wilderness, by the fountain on the road to Gadar." see 90.

כמאל Kamael. Severity of God. The Archangel associated with the positive aspects of Geburah and the 5 of Cups. He is a symbol of the Life power manifesting as the force we feel within us as volition.

מנא Manna, the divine nourishment of the Israelites in the wilderness (variant spelling see 90).

מנא mene. Numbered. One of the words in the handwriting on the wall described in Daniel 5:26. Metathesis of אמן, amen. Note that in the quotation *Mene* is repeated twice: "And this is the writing that was written: *Mene Mene Tekel Upharsin*." See 131, 231, 35.

סוכה branch, or bough Hebrew lexicon: bush shrub. When one enters into the higher consciousness one perceives one's relation to the great whole, as in Jesus words: "I am the vine, and you (the apostles) are the branches." With different vowel points, *Sukkoh*: a hut, tent, booth.

אמן amen. so be it. A title of Kether. As a verb: to be firm, to be faithful, to support, to rear up, to nurture, to foster; also faithfulness, truth, credibility. As a masculine noun: artificer, artist, master workman. see 155, 620.

Amen is the combination of the divine names יהוה *Jehovah* (26, 2x13) and אדני, *Adonai* (65, 5x13) because 91 is 7x13. The noun נחשת, *nekosheth*, meaning copper has a special relationship to the word Amen. Nekosheth is numerically 758, by adding the last two digits (5 + 8 = 13) and multiplying by the first (7 x 13) we get 91. Please note that the ratio of the width to height of the sides of the vault of Brother C.R. are 5 to 8, and the vault itself is 7 sided.

The summation of the numbers from 1 to 13 is 91 (E13 = 91). Therefore Amen stands for the full expression of the concepts of unity (אהבה, Ahebah) and love (אחד, Achad) because these words at to 13. However, if final Nun is numbered as 700 instead of 50, then the value is 741. 741 is 3x12x19, or The Father Ab (אב, 3) x Unity (אחד, 13) x Eve (the mother of all living, חוה, 19).

Through gematria we see the Amen, meaning faithful, is fundamentally the nature of the Primal Will. The nature of this Will is revealed to us by the symbolism of the vault of Brother C.R., which the *Fama* calls a compendium of the whole universe and in the knowledge that in Amen we see powers of the Divine Mother and Father are unified through love.

כונה fervor, intention, intent, attention, devotion, intense meditation. A Rabbinical term describing a mental practice akin to yoga. The means whereby one becomes receptive to the influx of the Holy influence *Mezla* (78) descending from Kether. Through meditation, we are shown the true nature of the power we experience as Will, which we receive from Geburah (see Kamael).

אב לאבן Father of Fathers. Aramaic text of the Lesser Holy Assembly (Zohar) Chapter 7, section 214 "This Chokmah is the Father of Fathers, and in this Chokmah is beginning and end discovered."

אדני יהוה Adonai Jehovah. Lord God. In Jeremiah 32:17: "Alas, Lord God! Behold, you made the heavens and the earth by Your great power and by Your stretched out arm! There is nothing too hard or too wonderful for You." In Judges 6:22: "And when Gideon perceived that He was the Angel of the Lord, Gideon said, Alas, O Lord God! For now I have seen the Angel of the Lord face to face."

אסל pole; yoke for carrying burdens. Refers to Kether as the supporter of the activities of a whole cycle of the Life-power's self-expression.

אפוד Upper garment; breastplate of the Jewish High Priest of Israel, similar to the chasuble used by Christian priests. It was made of threads of gold, blue, purple, scarlet and fine linen. The gold was a symbol of the sun, blue for water, purple for air, the scarlet for fire and linen for earth. In Exodus 39:2: "They made the Ephod of gold, and of blue, purple and scarlet yarn, and of finely twisted linen."

האלהים ha-Elohim. The Creative Powers (of God), of the Elohim, The God. See Deuteronomy 4:35, Exodus 3:1 and 86, 503, 103.

אילן tree. The Tree of Life.

פאהה extension. Part of a mystic phrase meaning "Light in Extension" or L.V.X. see 65

כליאל "God prompt to fulfill." 18th Shem ha-Mephorash; 86°-90°; JUSITIA. To obtain prompt aid. [Psalm 9:9] "And he shall judge the world in righteousness, he shall minister judgement to the people in uprightness") Makes truth know in law suits, causes innocence to triumph. Just, honest, loves truth, judiciary. negative influence: scandalous trials, base men. Angel of the 6th quinance [26°-30°] of Libra; angel by night of the 4 of Swords. This represents the influence of Chesed or cosmic memory (4) in Yetzirah, the Formative World. see 965, 60 & Appendix 10.

סאל Sael; 45th name of Shem ha-Mephorash, short form. see 106 & Appendix 10.

Stirps (Lt). a race, family.

Flos auri (Lt). Flower of gold [Secret Symbols page 5]. "Salve, soul, gold of the philosophers, and flower of gold." This is the Quintessence. see 131, 231.

Sal et sol (Lt). Salt and Sun. Alchemically salt and gold The word Sal, salt, has a Qabalistic correspondence to 7 because its value is 28, the extension of 7. An instruction of the Freres Chevaliers read in part: "(2) What is truth?-it is the Great Architect of the Universe. (3) What has declared it unto you?-His works, and the work of my hands. (4) How in his works?-all his creatures testify concerning him. (5) How do the work of you hands?-because I have seen the likeness of his creation. (6) Who taught you this work?-our excellent master. (7) What did he teach you?-that in salt and sol we have all things. (8) What is the sun?-it is the work of the philosophers." [Waite, 1993, p. 473] see 78, 231 Greek.

trinus (Lt). triple, threefold. Related to a truth that the essential reality is one, yet in threefold aspect.

92

A complete pyramid with 4 lines of 10 units each for a base and 4 lines of 13 units for its sloping edges.

ב/צ Beth/Tzaddi Mercury (Beth) in Aquarius (Tzaddi). The power of the intellect (Mercury) to dissolve (Aquarius) the delusions inherent in physical existence.

בצ whitish clay, mire, bog. This refers to the ignorant as persons immersed in the illusions of physical existence.

האבי-אר The everlasting father.

ואלהים the Creative Powers.

יהוה אלהיך The Lord our God [Deuteronomy 28:58].

סוכו pavilion, tent, his tabernacle. [Psalm 76:2]. Where it is said to be Salem, i.e. peace. Brings out the idea that Elohim (name used for God in the 76th Psalm) pervades the entire field of manifestation. see 86, 1961

פחד fear, terror, dread, object of fear. One of the names of the 5th Sephirah. It represents the emotional approach of ignorance to the rigid severities of natural law and natural forces. A clue to the deeper meaning of the name Pachad is the plural form, [פחדים], "loins" or "thighs" in the English Bible, in Latin versions it is called *testiculi*. This links with the meaning of Geburah as the Sphere of Mars, for Geburah is held to be the seat of virile strength, and Mars rules the reproductive functions governed by Scorpio. (Pachad is translated "stones" in Job 40:17.) see 64, 95, 216, 142, 297, 850.

חסדך thy loving kindness [Psalm 138:2]. It shows the difference between a wise man's reaction to the power of the 5th Sephirah and that of the ignorant. What the ignorant fear, the wise interpret correctly as loving kindness. Note that the latter is Chesed, the fourth Sephirah. see 72, 216, 64, 572, 725

154

עזיה the "Strength of Yah," the Life-force seated in Chokmah. see 23.

אניאל "God of Virtues" 37th Shem ha-Mephorash. 12:00-12:20 PM. Psalm 80:4. To gain victory and to raise the siege of a city. Rules the sciences and arts: reveals the secrets of nature and inspires wise philosophers in their meditations. Person born: acquires celebrity through his talents and enlightenment, he will be distinguished among savants. Angel of the 1st quinance [1°-5°] of Aquarius; angel by day of the 5 of Swords. This represents the influence of Geburah, sphere of Mars, in Yetzirah, the Formative World. see Appendix 10.

צב litter, covered wagon. [Isaiah 66:20] "And they will being all your brothers, from all the nations, to my Holy Mountain in Jerusalem as an offering to the Lord-on horses, in chariots and wagons, and on mules and camels,' says the Lord."

sigillum (Lt). Seal. Its most important use in the Bible is in the Apocalypse, where it is employed to indicate the seals that closed the book of the Lamb, 7 in number. These seals are the same as the interior stars. An alchemical term to designate the "inner fire of the true sulphur."

93

ג/צ Moon (Gimel) in Aquarius (Tzaddi).

צבא to go forth in a body; to assemble, to mass, to go forth to war. Root of *Tzabaoth* (525, divine name associated with Netzach). Also 3x31, or the value of the divine name AL, attributed to Chesed. The going-forth of the one power is for overcoming every appearance of evil and vanquishing every form of disease, in harmony, and lack. As a noun: army, host, warfare, war, military service, service, fixed time.

בני אל Sons of God.

מגן a disk, shield. Symbol of God as the protector, and especially connected with the hexagram. see 107.

מגן to deliver up, deliver to; defense, protection. In Genesis 14:20: "And blessed be the most high God, which has deliver thine enemies into thy hand..."

לבונה Frankincense. A symbol of aspiration, attributed to the sun, (heart center) and Sunday, Tiphareth.

נחלה torrent, stream, valley, ravine; shaft of a mine. As a feminine noun: inheritance, possession, property, destiny, fate. see 3, 12, 21, 30, 39, 48, 57, 66, 75, 84, 102.

באילים In the powers. see 236.

אהליבמה Tent of the Height. Name of a wife of Esau. "A duke of Edom (associated with Chesed)." [Godwin, 1999. p. 511.] see Ezekiel 23 & Genesis 36:2.

גץ spark; hardened mud. In K.D.L.C.K. (p. 700): the "sparks" are the beginning of individuality, the seeds of Yod planted by the divine in the "mud" or physical plane, to evolve into humanity.

בלאדן Not-Lord or Not-man. "The name of the [evil] lion is Ariel [אריאל, 242] as his face is that of a lion (sun), a dog [Zohar prologue 6.6]. The lion was "slain" by the Lord of hosts and went into the pit, and the dog Baladon was sent by the evil monster there to consume the offerings. The Lion of Moab in this passage refers to one of the temples of the father in heaven, who darkened the light of Israel. Spelled without the Vav in the Bible.

eulogium (Lt). eulogy. see 519 Greek.

luna mater (Lt). "The moon is its mother." From the Emerald Tablet of Hermes.

omnia ab uno (Lt). all is from one. Alchemical and Rosicrucian term.

αγαπη agapeh (Gr). love, spiritual love, brotherly love; charity. Used in the New Testament. Possibly a transliteration of אהבה. see John 15:9-10; 1 Thessalonians 3:12; 2 Corinthians 8:7. Love in general, holy love, without specifying a definite object, e.g. as an attribute of God, in 1 John 4:7. Christian grace in Romans 12:8. see 13.

Mackey writes: "The word used by the apostle [Paul] is in the original [Greek word], or love, a word denoting that kindly state of mind which renders a person full of good-will and affectionate regard toward others." [Encyclopedia of Freemasonry, p. 158]

Θελμα. thelema (Gr). choice, determination; will, decree.

permanens (Lt). permanent, enduring. What is eternal, i.e. the spirit of life. see 129, 36 (Lt).

Sit Lux (Lt). Let there be Light. In Genesis 1:3: "and the Elohim said "Let there be Light", Thomas Vaughan: "...These invisible central artist are lights seeded by the first light, in that primitive emanation, or Sit Lux 'let there be light." [Work: Anima Magica Abscondita, p. 55] see 44, 49 (Lt); 206.

omnia ab uno (Lt). All from one. Alchemical phrase.

94

I. The sum of the top and bottom edges of the trapezoid forming a face of the unfinished pyramid of the Great Seal of the U.S.

אופז A corruption of the word Ophir, a place from whence Solomon got his Gold. In Jeremiah 10:9. see 254, 19, 273.

חזיון The valley of vision. see 17, 81.

גופה body, corpse. The manufacture of gold is in the physical body; without it, the body becomes a corpse. see 89

ילדים Children. From ילד, *eled*, child, son, young man, boy, youth. In the words of Jesus: "Unless you become as a little child, you shall in no wise enter the Kingdom of Heaven."
לבבכם laybawbekem. your hearts. [Deuteronomy 10:16] "Circumcise therefore the foreskin of your hearts, and be no more stiff-necked." Gold is centered in the heart; opening the heart center is the key to success in the Great Work. see 794, 1711.

חניכו his trained men. [Genesis 14:14] Means initiate. see 318, 88.

חלון Window. The meaning of Heh, i.e. clear vision as to how the gold may be obtained.

טפה drop; a drop. The solar radiance or liquid gold is composed of innumerable drops or Yods, which are full of life-energy.

להטים enchantments, secret arts. From להט flame, magic. In Exodus 7:11: "Then Pharaoh called for the wise men [skilled in magic and divination] and the sorcerers-wizards and jugglers. And they also, these magicians of Egypt, did similar things with their enchantments and secret arts." And in Exodus 8:7: "And the Magicians [of Egypt] did so with their enchantments." The secret of alchemy is employed for success in the great work. see 44.

דעך to flicker, go out, be extinguished; to crush. The sense of separation.

מדים "Power of Vehement Strength", i.e. Mars, Godwin's spelling. see 654, 95, 655.

דפי blemish, fault; destruction. In Psalm 50:20: "Against thy Mother's Son thou does allege a fault." The son is Tiphareth; the mother is Binah.

צד side.

"That which is insidious, artful, double, sly, opposed, adverse, deceitful, seductive. The Arabic presents every idea of opposition, defense, the state of quarreling, disputing.

צד in a literal sense, very restricted, *the side*; in a broad and figurative sense, *a secret, dissimulating hindrance; an artifice, a snare.*" [d'Olivet, 1976, p. 432.]

מנד prickley. 36th Shem ha-Mephorash, short form. see 125 & Appendix 10.

חוף coast, shore, harbor. The goal of the voyage or evolution of life.

seclorum (Lt). of the ages; of the aeons. Part of the motto: "A new order of the ages" on the

Great Seal of the U.S. see 46, 80, 126, 220, 370 Latin.

sol pater (Lt). Sun Father [see Emerald Tablet]. The interior "Sun" hidden in the microcosmic "earth" is the Ego.

V.I.T.R.O.L. (Lt) A reference to the Ego. Alchemist call it their vitriol, because the physical substance name vitriol (sulfate of zinc) forms a glassy brilliant crystals which reflect light. It is because the Ego reflects the Light of the One Self rather than being the original Light-source. See Secret Symbols (p.17) and 570.

Monoceros (Lt). Unicorn; one horn. Connected with Hiram the architect of King Solomon's temple, with Hermes-Mercury and with Hod. The horn is a symbol in its higher aspect of aspiration and lofty thought; the single horn refers to the third eye. see 246, 15.

Victrix (Lt). Victory. Latin name of Venus. Aligning our desires with the blessed one gives us the sign of victory.

Benedictus (Lt). blessed. Part of a Rosicrucian saying "Blessed in the Lord our God who gave to us a sign." see 518 (Lt).

alapha et omega (Lt). The first and the last, the beginning and the end. Latin transliteration of Greek, as in [Revelation 22:13] "I am alpha and omega, the beginning and the end, the first and the last." Part of a phrase in Secret Symbols. The name of the Golden Dawn under Mathers in Paris, London, Edindurah and the U.S. see 717, 34, 37 (Lt).

95

מאדים Madim. Mars. "powers of vehement strength". see 655, 92, 216, 297, 850.

דניאל Daniel. A judge from God. Old Testament name, the prophet and astrologer. Combines the words Dan, דין with Al, אל, so that it is a symbol of the expression of the latent powers of Chesed through the activities of the Geburah (דין, Justice).

I. Also the 50th Shem ha-Mephorash, "The giver of mercies", "God is Judge", the angle of confession. [Kircher Oed. eg. V.2 pp. 266-267] 246°-250°. EREGGMO. May 8, July 19, September 29, December 10, February 20, 4:20-4:40 PM. [Psalm 103:8] "The Lord (יהוה) is full of compassion and graciousness, slow to anger and plenteous in mercy." To obtain the mercy of God, and to receive consolation. Rules justice, lawyers, and all magistrates in general. Gives inspiration to those who are embarrassed by too many affairs and do not know exactly how to decide. Persons born: industrious and active in affairs, loves literature, and distinguishes himself by his eloquence. Associated with of the 2nd quinance [6°-10°] of Aries; Angel by night of the 2 of Wands. This represents the operation of Chokmah, sphere of the Zodiac in the archetypal place of ideas (Atziluth). see Appendix 10.

II. "God is my Judge": an angel of the Order of Principalities, according to Waite, *The Lemegeton*. Daniel (as Danjal) is one of a troop of fallen angels, listed in *Enoch I*. In the lower regions he exercise authority over lawyers." [Davidson, 1971, p. 95.]

המים the waters. Its refers to the Waters from which all organic life is spawned. see 90.

המן to be turbulent, to rage. Refers to the restless activity associated with Mars and the 5th Sephirah.

The root הם: "Universalized life: the power of the universe. Onomatopoeic and idiomatic root, which indicates every kind of tumultuous noise, commotion, fracas. The Arabic characterizes, in general, that which is heavy, painful, agonizing. It is literally *a burden, care, perplexity*. As a verb, expresses the action of *being disturbed, of interfering*, of bustling about to do a thing.

הום action of *exciting a tumult, making a noise, disturbing* with clamor, with an unexpected crash; every *perturbation, consternation, trembling*, etc." [d'Olivet, 1976, pp. 331-332.]

זבולן Tribe of Zebulon. "habitation." Cancer. Connected with alchemical separation-the establishment of the personal purpose, the formulation of the particular definition. The subtle is divided from the gross and the distinction between appearance and essence is clearly marked. In Genesis 49:13: "Zebulun shall dwell at the haven of the sea; and he shall be for a haven of ships." This established a clear correspondence the watery sign of Cancer (Key 7) and the 4th House (associated with the home as a "haven") [In the 4th house astrologers seek for indications as to the end of a matter-for indications of what cargo we may expect when our ship comes in]. Compare Domus, (64). Also Deuteronomy 33:19: "For they will suck the abundance of the seas and the hidden treasure of the sand. Compare with the symbolism of Key 7, in which the idea of habitation is strong, by the reason of the walled city in the background. [Links up also with habit, pattern, ritual by virtue of Cancer being ruled by the Moon or sub-consciousness] see 45, 64, 90, 418, 867, 319, 100, 30, 570, 501, 54, 162, 830, 395, 259, 7, 331, 466 and Key 2.

מהלך way, journey, walk, distance, free access. This idea is also suggested by the chariot in the foreground of Key 7. Furthermore, it is implied in the general meaning Zebulun, for a haven for ships is at the end of a voyage or journey.

מלכה Malkah. the bride, a queen. One of the titles of Malkuth. The alchemical queen is connected with whiteness, analogous to Silver and the Moon. She is the bride of the king in Tiphareth, the heart center and sun-power. see 55, 496, 148.

Malkuth is כלה (Kallah) the Bride, and (Malkah) the Queen. *Malkah* is written with the same letters of המלך, the King, and the King is Tiphareth. Tiphareth תפארת is 1081 which reduces to (the seed) 10 which is both Malkuth and Yod. Extending downward Tiphareth is completed in Malkuth. Extending upward Tiphareth itself is the King or Royal Son, one with his Father, and that Father is אב in Chokmah which also is the body of Yod. *Malkah* is 95 and as is letter Peh spelt in plenitude הה-פה. *Malkah* is the Queen and the Queen's daughter all glorious within.

She holds the mystery of union, and thus is she known as אבן גדלה the "Great Stone," that is by interpretation the perfect union in Chesed or Gedulah of the Father *Ab* with the Son *Ben*. See C.26.

המלך The king. i.e. Tiphareth. see 90, 1081.

מנה to appoint, ordain or number.

סלה A word occurring often in the Psalm, the meaning of which is obscure. It indicates the end of a thought. a musical term (in Psalms); for ever [Crowley, 1977, p. 15]. In Psalm 32:4,5: "for night and day your hand was heavy upon me; my strength was sapped as in the heat of summer. Selah. Then I acknowledge my sin to you and did not cover up my iniquity. I said, I will confess my transgressions to the Lord -and you forgave the guilt of my sin. Selah."

פה הה Peh. Letter name Peh spelt in full. The mouth of the eternal and said to be the secret of the covenant with spiritual Israel. see 85, 463.

Peh spelt in plenitude is פה-הה. The first letter, Peh is the mouth of the Eternal. And in the three Hehs is the three-fold vision of the past, present and future. The three Heh's add to 15, and this is יה, Jah, the Holy name of Chokmah and הוד (Hod), the Splendor of the Presence. Note that Peh is Mars and Heh is Aries ruled by Mars. Thus we see a word expressing total martain activity. See **26**.

אבן גדהל The great stone. Refers to the perfect union in *Chesed* or *Gedulah* of the Father *Ab* אב, and son *Ben* בן.

החעיה "God is Refuge." (Dieu Refuge). 12th Shem ha-Mephorash. Associated with the 6th quinance of Virgo; Angel by night of the 10 of Pentacles. 56°-60° ATARPH. March 31, June 11, August 22, November 2, January 13. Psalm 10:1. Rules dreams, and reveals mysteries hidden from mortals. Influences persons wise, spiritual and discrete. Persons born: sweet-tempered, amicable physiognomy, agreeable manners. Angle of 6th quinance [26°-30°] of Virgo; angel by night of the 10 of Pentacles. This represents the influence of the sphere of the elements in the physical plane of action.

"...an angel of the Order of Cherubim, and that his corresponding angel is *Atarph* [אתארפה]." [Davidson, 1971, p. 133.]

גיא חזיון **גיא** Valley of vision. Title heading of Isaiah 22:1. Refers to "breaking down the walls". see 745.

insitum (Lt). planted. Occurs in the Fama, in the motto: *Granum Pectori Jesu Insitum*, A seed planted in the Breast of Jesus. Note that Pectus, the breast, is the part of the human body governed by Cancer.

salvator (Lt). savior. see 158.

morimur (Lt). we die. After the seed is planted, we must die to the old and be "saved" Part of a saying, found in the vault of C.R. in the Rosicrucian allegory, which includes the phrase "in Jesus we die." see 683 (Lt).

confessio (Lt). confession. Part of the title of one of the first Rosicrucian pamphlets, *the Confessio Fraternitatis*. To confess is to acknowledge or make known. see 241 (Lt).

96
I. (2⁵x3)

$I. (2^5 \times 3)$

סוד יהוה Sod IHVH. The secret of the Tetragrammaton. It has to do with the various appearances reported by the senses and is a mystery of renewal and regeneration. In has been preserved generation after generation, in the assembly of the inner school. see 70, 700.

Psalm 25:14: "The secret (counsel) of the Lord is with those who revere him; and he makes his covenant known to them."

מלאכה deputyship, work (never servile). From מלאך "one sent; angel, messenger; prophet, seer.

ללהאל 6th Shem ha-Mephorash. "Praiseworthy God." To aquire knowledge and cure disease. Governs: Love, renown, science, arts and fortune. Positive influence: ambition, fame. Negative: evil ambition, fortune by illicit means. Angel of the 3rd decanate (6th quinance) of Leo; Angel by night of the 7 of Wands. This corresponds to the operation of Netzach, sphere of Venus in the archetypal plane of ideas.

בלטיהם by their secret arts. In Exodus 8:7: "And the magicians did so with their enchantments by their secret arts..." see 94. Check quote.

אלהין Creative Spirits; Builders. Chaldee of אלהים. see 86.

אל אדני God the Lord.

פוי Poi. 56th name of Shem ha-Mephorash, short form. see 127 & Appendix 10.

צו order, command, precept. In Isaiah 28:10: "For precept must be upon precept, precept upon precept; line upon line, line upon line; here a little, and there a little; that they might go, and fall backwards, and be broken, and snared and taken."

occultum (Lt). hidden. Part of an alchemical phrase in Secret Symbols (page 17): "Visit the interior of the earth, by rectifying you shall find the hidden stone." see 570 Latin.

tinctura (Lt). tincture. That which tinges or permeates the entire body, transforming its essential nature. see 193 Latin.

97 (prime)

I. A number of Chesed as water and as father. [Crowley, 1977, p. xxv].

האניאל Haniel. "Grace of God", Archangel of Netzach and is the aspect of the One Force active in the 7 of Cups (Netzach of Briah). The working of the desire nature in Netzach is the manifestation of the Divine Grace which has already prepared for us the good gifts we desire. see 101, 311, 246, 280, 314, 251.

בן אדם Ben Adam. Son of Man. In Psalm 8:4: "What is man that you are mindful of him, the son of man that you care for him?" Refers to man as the means whereby the Divine Grace becomes manifest through correct understanding of the desire nature. see 363.

אמן artificer, master-workman, architect, designer; faith. This corresponds to the 7 and the heptagram as symbols of skill developed through trial and error. To partake of the Divine Grace, we must gain conquest over the desire nature and balance with exactitude the 7 inner holy planets, thus preparing ourselves for Adeptship. With different pointing: *aemon.* faithfulness. Variant spelling of אמן. see 91.

אומן craftsman, artisan, mechanic. With different pointing: 1. *omayn*, trainer, educator; pedagogue; 2. *omawn*, border-bed, straight line. Note that his word is metathesis of the proceeding. The Mem (reversal) and Vav (intuition) have been transposed. Vav gives guidance. The result in both words is Nun, that of transformation. Written in the masculine plural form אמונים in Proverbs 20:6 and translated as "faithful." "Many men are considered merciful; but a faithful man who can find?"

אמן Amon. Goetic demon #7 by day of the 1st decanate of Gemini. In the Tarot minor arcana it corresponds to the 8 of Swords, which is the operation of Hod, sphere of Mercury in Yetzirah, the formative world. see 747 & Appendix 11.

Goetia: "He is a marquis great in power, and most stern. He appears like a wolf with a serpent's tail, vomiting out of his mouth flames of fire, but at the command of the Magician he putts on the shape of a man with dog's teeth beset in a head (simply). He tells all things past and to come. He procures feuds and reconciles controversies between friends. He governs 40 legions of Sprits." [Mathers, 199, p. 30]

הים הגדל the Great Sea. A name of Binah, sphere of understanding and intuition, source of grace and mother of the "son of man". see 52, 67.

זמן appointed time, time; date; fate, luck. "I am he who establishes the time of the decree, who declareth the term of the days of Adam" [Book of Tokens, Samekh] "But to each man there is appointed a last day, and none knoweth the time save he who hath appointed it." [Book of Tokens, Ayin]

חטף to catch, seize; to seize suddenly, rape; to do hurriedly. Action without preparation leads to failure.

טפח span, hand-breath; palm. In 1 Kings 7:26: "And it [the molten sea or laver of purification] was an handbreath thick, and the brim thereof was wrought like the brim of a cup..." [Exodus 25:25] "And thou shalt make unto it [the table of shewbread] a border of an handbreadth round about..." With different pointing: 1. to strike, clap; to be damp, clap, slap; to moisten; 2. vetchling (bean plant).

מבנה structure, build, a building. see 57.

אילן Allon, "The oak or the strong one" [Inman]. In Joshua 19:33: (The children of Naphtais) "And their coast was from Heleph, from Allon to Zaananim..."

יפוא Joppa; port city of Palestine; Beautiful (variant spelling see 96). In Ezra 3:7: "They gave money also to the Masons, and to the carpenters; and meat and drink, and oil, to them of Sidon, and to them of Tyre, to bring cedar trees from Lebanon to the sea of Joppa, according to the grant that they had of Cyrus, King of Persia Related to Tiphareth. Richardson's Monitor of Freemasonry (P. 40) says this is the password of the Mark Mason's degree. see 326, 1081.

מהיטבאל Mehitabel, Wife of Hadar, a King of Edom. see 253.

Connected with alchemical silver, in *Aesch Mezareph*: "And in Genesis 36:39[*] it is called Mehatebel, as though it were *me hathbula* [מי הטבלא], by changing the order of the Letters, i.e. the Water of Immersion, because the King is emerged in them to be cleansed." [Westcott, 1997, p. 11]

Or as though it were the *el hatob*, by a like Change of Letters; the Waters of the good *El*, or Living Silver; for Life and Good have power, as Death and Evil have the same. [ibid, p.39]

[*] "Baal-hanan son of Achbor died, then Hadar reigned; his [enclosed] city was Pau; his wife's name was Mehetabel, daughter of Matred, daughter of Mezahab".

Liber Mundi (Lt). Book of the World or Book of Life. In the *Fama*, it is translated from Arabic, the language of initiated perception, into Latin, the Language of science by Brother C.R. This knowledge includes apprehension of the principles of occult healing and mathematics.

The Liber Mundi, connected also with Book M, is liked to Mem, Key 12, the Hanged Man; the numbers of which when reversed are 21 or Key 21, Saturn, Book T. see 314 (Greek), 30, 42, 55 Latin, 106 (Lt), 220, 444, 366, 264, 230.

coelestis (Lt). celestial, i.e. of the heavens, heavenly. The sphere of the zodiac is Chokmah, seat of the Life-force Chaiah. The interior stars in the subtle bodies of man are focuses for the force of the microcosm. see 96, 193 Latin, 73, 23.

sapientiam (Lt). wisdom. Part of a Latin phrase. see 166.

98

I. (2×7^2)

II. Square on the diagonal of a face of a cube of 7 units.

סגלה a treasure, personal possession. The root of this word is probable [סג] Seg, "secret" name of Briah. See 63, 104 and Exodus 19:5

חסל to consume, eat, to finish off; to finish, end.

צח white, clear, sunny, warm, dry. [רוח צח], dry wind [Jeremiah 4:11]. Dazzling, bright, clear, glowing, brightness.

פחדו his stones [Job 40:17]. The Hebrew text translates this word "his thighs," a euphanism for testicles. see 142, 453.

פטדה Emerald, according to Kosminsky; the second stone of the breastplate of the high priest, in [Exodus 28:17] "And you shall set it in settings of stones, four rows of stones; the first row shall be a red [Hematite], an emeralds, and a marble." For the other stones, see 45, 702, 150, 345, 395, 370, 308, 84, 1210, 350, 85.

Isidore Kosminsky writes: "The second stone of the breastplate is give as Pitdah, variously interpreted as a Topaz, peridot, yellowish-green serpentine, diamond and chrysolite. The Targums agree that a green stone is implied and some authorities seek to clear the mystery by advancing that the stone was of a yellowish-green. The Topaz of the ancients is not the Topaz of today, but is identified with the stone known to us as the chrysolite or Peridot. Traditionally the emerald is associated with the second sign of the Zodiac... The gem needed is therefor a green one, and this is traditionally the correct one for the Sionshor or Taurus in which Nogah or Venus delights and in which Labanah or the Moon exalts. The Emerald was sacred to the period this period of the year. This gem was well-known amongst ancient nations, especially those of Egypt and Ethiopia where the chief Emerald mines were... The tribe Simeon corresponding to the zodiacal Gemini was engraved on the second gem of the breastplate-although it has no connection with it... it should be understood that by Emerald is meant the precious Emeralds as we know it or its varieties Beryl and Aquamarine. It may be noted that the Topaz, a gem most generally favored as the second stone on the breastplate, is traditionally assigned to the opposite sign of the zodiac, Scorpio..." [The Magic and Science of Jewels and Stones, pp. 22-24]

מנהג to drive (a chariot); custom, manner, conduct, usage. The noun *menahig*, "driver," is from the verb *minhag*, "to drive" (as a chariot). Note that the study of the Tree of Life and its relationships is often called "The Work of the Chariot." The 13th Path of Gimel, *saykel menahig ha-achadoth* [Driver of Unities]. Variant spelling, see 108.

הוא אלהים He, the Creative Powers. This indicates the essential identity between Yekidah in Kether (He) and Neshamah in Binah (the Creative Powers) through the path of Beth (Key 1, The Magician). this is the "treasure" which drives the soul to unity.

חמים warm, luke warm. The "new image" is manifested by the "gentile heat" of the alchemist.

יפח breathing, puffing out (Hebrew lexicon). This word and Vav as a prefix is used in Genesis 2:7: "and breathed into his nostrils." The breath of life is the consuming treasure. "Puffing" is connected with intonation of divine words of power.

חסידיו his saints. In Psalm 97:10: "He preserves the soul of his saints." see 82.

אבן אדם red stone; stone of Adam. see 53, 45.

כוכבים The planets or wanderers. Esoterically connected with the 3 higher octave planets, Uranus, Neptune, and Pluto. Connected with "volatile" in some alchemical symbolism. see 48, 343.

מאהבן short form of מאסו הבנים masu ha-bonim, (the stone) "which the builders refused." Literally: what! the builders.

מבון means, instructed, taught.

Paul Case: *Maboin* is the nearest approach I have been able to discover in the Hebrew dictionary to the word, which in a certain initiation is said to be the substitute for another greater word which has been lost. Now we know that the lost word is יהוה, for is regained in a certain higher grade. This word is the Key to most of the mysteries, and its value is 26... In Maboin, taking the Nun as 50, the sum of the letters values is 98 which reduces to 8. Thus by reduction, the word corresponds to מונשה (398), forgetting, or making forget. ישוע (386), Jeshua - God the Savior; עור (296), *Zur*, God, a rock; פורושא (593), *purusha*, the I Am or onlooker; הוא אלהים (98), He is the *Elohim* [PFC Notebook, from day to day, Page 1 October 20 1914].

חצ arrow; lighting; punishment; wound. In Lamentations 3:12: "He drew his bow, and set me a mark for the arrow." Also in Habakkuk 3:11: "Sun and Moon stood still in the heavens as the glint of your flying arrows, at the lighting of your flashing spear." And in [Job 34:6] "Although I am right, I am considered a liar, although I am guiltless; his arrow inflicts an incurable wound." See also Ezekiel 5:16.

"Every idea of division, scission, gash, cut that which act from the exterior, as the adverbial relation חוצ expresses outside. The Arabic signifies *to stimulate*; and *to keep stirring, to agitate*. חצ that which divides by making irruption, passing without from within: *an arrow, an obstacle*; *a stone* coming from the sling; *an axe, a dart*: a *division* of troops; *a quarrel*, etc. [d'Olivet, 1976, p. 354.]

μην. mehn (Gr). a month.

Ηελνε. Helene (Gr). Helen.

nequaquam (Lt). no-where. refers to the Rosicrucian saying "*Nequaqam Vacuum*," Nowhere a vacuum. a negative expression of the truth that all space is filled with the divine presence, which is no-thing in itself. see 61, 170, 72 Latin.

I. (9x11)

אני יהוה הוא   "I, myself, IHVH, He" (mine). Ten letters, combining Macroprosopus, Microprosopus and Tetragrammaton. הוא is also called אבא, the Father; and יהוה is between them. אני (61) and אבא (4) and to 65 or יהוה (26), added to אדני (65) is 91 or אמן, amen. see Isaiah 42:8.

נביאי יהוה   The prophets of IHVH.

ימא הגדול   The Great Sea. Reference to Binah, the Cosmic Mother [Daniel 7:2]. see 254.

הניאל   "Favor of God." Angle of Netzach (variant spelling, see 97).

טיט הין   miry clay, "Clay of Death" [Crowley, 1977, p. 10]. One of the 7 infernal mansions or Qlippothic Palaces - the infernal abode of Geburah [Godwin says Tiphareth]. This indicates an imbalance or misuse of Mars in action. טיט means "clay, loam" and hints at the physical body. הין means: mud, mire (the Heh is the definite article). Translated "the mire clay" in Psalm 40:2: "He brought me up also out of an horrible pit, out of the miry clay, and set my feet upon a rock, and established by goings." With different pointing: Dove, and is related to Venus and the desire nature. [Depicted in the diagram of the 4 seas]. see 71, 28; 337, 57, 911, 1026, 566, 108, 291, 799. [Psalm 90:3]

I. D'Olivet list the root of this word as טב, and says it is analogous to the root בא, and which like it, expresses every kind of reflection as is indicated by the following: "טים [28] that which *gushes forth*, that which *splashes*, as *mud, slime, mire*, etc. Figuratively, *the earth*. The Arabic signifies properly *to bend, to give way*, to be soft." [d'Olivet, 1976, p. 358.]

II. "Tit ha-yaven, Miry Clay; the 4th Hell (corresponding to Tiphareth)." [Godwin. 1999, p. 513.]

חבלי לידה   the pangs of child birth.

חופה   the Vault of Heaven; an inner chamber; wedlock, nuptial.

ידיעה   cognition, knowledge. The birth of the inner Christ requires direct knowledge. see 84, 434.

ακοη. akoeh (Gr). The hearing, i.e. the sense of hearing, as in 1st Corinthians 10:17; the act of hearing in 2 Peter 2:8; Matthew 13:19. What is heard, the thing announced message, teaching, preaching; "report" in Isaiah 53:1; Matthew 4:24. Spelled ακουω [1291] in *Young's Concordance*.

αμην. amen (Gr). So be it. see 91 (Hebrew spelling) and Ephesians 3:21.

interiora (Lt). interior. Part of the phrase in the Secret Symbols (page 17). "Visit the interior of the earth, by rectifying you shall find the hidden stone." see 570 Latin.

rectificando (Lt). rectifying. Rectify means of make or set right, to correct from a false state, as the will, judgement. In chemistry it is to refine or purify, especially by a process of repeated or fractional distillation.   Also: to correct by calculation or adjustment. To convert alternating current in to direct current (electricity).

Section 1

Numbers 100 - 199

100

I. (10×10) or $(2^2 \times 5^2)$

II. The Greek God Hecate name means literally, "100."

כף Letter name Kaph. grasping hand; rock. Grasp is always the result of a balance or equilibrium of ideas. see 986, 448, 194, 20.

חצב to hew out, chisel or cleave.

ק Qoph.

I. Rabbi Kushner: "The bottom of the Qoph is a man calling "Holy (קדוש) Kodosh, so that he can join himself to his Creator. the top line, sheltering and reaching down, is the holy One...ק. is one of the letters made by two marks. Heh is the other. The lower mark of the Qoph is man calling God. With the upper mark of the Qoph HE whispers very softly to see if you are really listening." [The Book of Letters]

II. Qoph is a combination of Kaph, which forms the upper part of the letter, and Vav, which is represented by the descending line. Kaph is 20, and Vav is 6 which total 26, the number of the Divine name, יהוה. Note also that the letter name Kaph (כף) is numerically the same as the letter Qoph. Thus we see that the letter Kaph, is the principle of the letter Qoph. Note that in the Tarot Key 10 is associated with Kaph and displays the name יהוה on the wheel, so we see the name is related to both letters.

III.. Rabbi Ginsburgh: "The Will of God hovers above the soul in its source, and decrees upon it to descend, against its own initial will, into a physical body. The soul's mission below requires it to become totally involved in the process of rectification, clarification, of its body and "portion" in the world." [The Alef-Beit]

IV. Rabbi Kardia: "The form of the letter Qoph can be considered as made from combination of a Vav and Kaph. This shows that man is linked to Divine law on both the physical and spiritual levels. [Simple Stories From the Heart]

V. "This character as consonant, belongs to the guttural sound. As symbolic image it represents a trenchant weapon, that which serves as instrument for man, to defend, to make an effort for him. It has already been remarked, that nearly all the words which hold to this consonant in the greater part of the idioms, designate force and constraint. It is, in the Hebraic tongue, the compressive and decisive sign; that of agglomerative or repressive force. It is the character כ, entirely materialized; the progression of the sign is as follows: ה, vocal principle, sign of absolute life: ח, aspirate principle, sign of elementary existence: ג, guttural principle, organic sign: Kaph, same principle strengthened, sign of assimilative existence holding to forms alone: ק, same principle greatly strengthened, sign of mechanical, material existence giving the means of forms." [d'Olivet, 1976, p. 438.]

כלים vases, utensils; weapons. Forms are as vases into which the Life-power pours its essence. Every vessel (form) is an aspect of life. The Jupiter center is like a vessel that receives or holds the record of individuality from one incarnation to another. Vases, vessels, suggest that each organism is like a vase containing the water of life; the comprehension of this fact being necessary to occult progress. see 95 (Zebulon), 660.

מדון effort, exertion. With different pointing: contest, quarrel, length, height; extension. All outer strife is the play of the light and darkness of God. All semblance of effort and exertion is performed by the one actor. Implied in the symbol of the grasping hand. All other strife is the play of the light and darkness of God. In Psalm 80:6: "Thou makes us a strife unto our neighbors: and our enemies laugh among themselves." see 750.

ימים days, seas, times, a day. [Genesis 1:10]. Reference to the influence (Shefah) or abundance of water, as in the Bible "They shall suck the abundance of the seas." see 66, 450.

I. "ימים seas.... That is to say *aqueous immensity*: for the word which designates seas, is only the word מים, *waters* preceded by the sign of manifestation י. As the word מים itself, the following is the history of its formation.

The root מה, מו or מי contains the idea of passive relation, of plastic and creative movement. The Hebrews as well as the Chaldeans and Syrians, employed the verb מום to express the mutation of things, and their relative movement. The name which they gave for water, in general,... was rarely in the singular, and as if their sages had wished to show in the way the double movement which it contains, or that they know it inner composition, they gave it almost always the dual number מים, *double waters.*" [d'Olivet, 1976, pp. 41-42.]

II. F.J. Mayers: "the name seas, Iamim, is exactly the same as the word of waters with y or ee prefixed, making the word mean manifested, or visible waters. This little point, in itself, is quite sufficient to take the ground from under the feet of anyone who ever thought that the word waters, with which we have made so much to do, referred to water in the ordinary literal meanings." [The Unknown God, p. 42]

III. "A symbol of the astral plane of the desires and passions... and the supreme now directs [In Genesis 1:9, 10] that the waters under the heaven, that is the astral matter shall be centralized and coordinated, so that preparation shall be made for physical matter (dry land) to appear. And the physical matter is named 'Earth,' which term also stands for the lower nature of the soul, -the 'natural man', and the gathering together, of the waters signifies the formation of the astral 'sea' of desires. And all is pronounced 'good', that is, perfect in involution for purposes of forthcoming manifestation through evolution." [Gaskell, 1981, p. 661.]

IV. The Zohar [I:33A]: "And the gathering together of the waters called the seas. This is the upper reservoir of the waters where they are all collected and from which they all follow and issue forth. Rabbi Hiya said: The gathering place of the waters is the Zaddic (Righteous One), because it is written in connection with it, And God saw that is was good, and it is written elsewhere, in the words he called seas, because he takes all the streams and sources and rivers and he is the source of all; hence he is called waters. Hence it says: And God saw that it was

good."

V. A double reference to the fact that what is occultly termed water is the basis of organic development which involves the sequence of time-cycles. [Paul Case, unpublished notes]

מחי טבאל Mitigation of one by another. "All opposites are bound together by the grasp of Kaph so that nowhere in the universe is there any real want or failure." [Book of Tokens]

מחיטבאל Better by God. Name of the daughter of Matred, the daughter of Mezahab [Genesis 36:39]. She was the wife of Hadar, a king of Edom, whose capital city was Pau.

I. Hadar means "Magnificence, propelling, propulsive." Pau signifies "crying out" (as of a woman in Labor). Mezahab means: "Water of gold" or "golden waters." The Zohar interprets Hadar as the supreme benignity, because הדר, Hadar, may be written with a dot in Daleth, doubling that letter, so that the word is really הדדר, 213, the number of חסד עלאה דאל, Chesed Auleah Da-El, the Supernal Mercy of El. The name of the city, Pau, is said to refer to the prayer of the man who is worthy of the Holy Spirit. His "crying out" is heard. Meyhetabel means "Made better by El" [Zohar]. Thus she is the feminine working power corresponding to Chesed. Finally, the name Mezahab מזהב, is made of 2 words, מ: refers to Mercury while זהב is Gold. [Greater Holy Assembly 993-996].

II. "The secret of overcoming the modifications of the mind by their opposite, a secret intimates by the fact that one side of this wheel ascends as the other descends, so that opposite and complementary motions are combined in the revolution." [Paul Case, unpublished notes]

לע gullet, throat. In Proverbs 23:2: (1) "When you sit to dine with a ruler, note well what is before you, (2) and put a knife to your throat if you are given to gluttony."

"Root not used in Hebrew. The Arabic appears to express in general, covetous desire, consuming ardor." [d'Olivet, 1976, p. 383.] Recall that the throat is connected with Venus, desire and creative imagination.

על Yoke, pole of wagon; obligation,

dependence. In Genesis 27:40: "Thou shalt break off his yoke." With different pointing: *ol*, High, Most High, a title of Divinity. See 106, 652, 686.

"The material sign ע considered under its vocal relation being united to that of expansive movement, composes a root which characterizes, hieroglyphically and figuratively, primal matter, its extensive force, its vegetation, its development in space, its elementary energy; this same sign, considered as consonant changes the expression of the root which it constitutes, to the point of making it represent only ideas of crime, fraud, perversity.

על *Material extent*; its progression, its indefinite extension, expressed by the relations *toward, by, for, on account of, notwithstanding, according to* etc. Its aggregative power, its growth by juxtaposition, expressed by *upon, over, above, along with, near, adjoining, about, overhead, beyond,* etc. על or עלל (intensive) that which *grows, extends, rises, mounts*; that which is *high, eminent, superior*; the *aggregated superficial* part of anything whatsoever; that which constitutes *the form, the factor, the exterior appearance; the labor of things; an extension, a heap*, etc." [d'Olivet, 1976, pp. 417-418.]

נ-ן (N.N) Frater N.N. in the Rosicrucian *Fama* who uncovered the brass plate and pulled out the large "nail" (Vav) which revealed the "door" (Daleth) to the tomb of Brother C.R.

גו, יא, יע (I.O., I.A., G.V.) Sum of initials of the first 3 fraters called by C.R. in the Rosicrucian Allegory. see 312, 412.

פך flask, bottle for holding the anointing oil. In 1 Samuel 10:1: "Then Samuel took a flask of oil and poured in on Saul's head and kissed him, saying has not the Lord anointed you leader over his inheritance?" see 580.

"Every distillation which comes from vapor suddenly condensed: *a drop of water*, metaphorically, *a lens*. The Arabic literally *to be dissolved*." [d'Olivet, 1976, p. 426.]

מס a suffering, discouraged one; pining, afflicted one. In Job 6:14: "A despairing man should have the devotion of his friends, even though he forsakes the fear of the Almighty."

With different pointing: *mas*, tribute, tax. In Esther 10:1: "King Xerxes imposed tribute throughout the empire, to its distant shores."

"Every dissolution, literally as well as figuratively: that which enervates, which takes away from physical and moral strength. The Arabic characterizes the state of that which is touched, that which is contiguous. It also means *to suck*; to be fatigued, to lose ones strength, to *be enervated*." [d'Olivet, 1976, pp. 391-392.]

צי Dryness, arid place, desert, wild beast, desert dweller. In Isaiah 13:21: "But desert creatures will lie there [in Babylon], jackals will fill her houses, there the owls dwell, and there the wild goats will leap about." With different pointing: ship, boat in [Isaiah 33:21: "There [in Zion] the Lord will be our Mighty One. It will be like a place of broad rivers and streams. No galley with oars will ride them, no mighty ship will sail them." D'Olivet says this root resembles עא and עה, but develops greater intensity." [d'Olivet, 1976, p. 434.]

נלכ 21st Shem ha-Mephorash, short form. see 131 & Appendix 10.

Justitia (Lt). Justice. Associated with Jupiter.

Liber Domini (Lt). The Book of the Lord. The same as the akashic record. Also called "The Book of Consciences, recorded in the Astral Light." It is furthermore, the "one book" of the Rosicrucians. The Jupiter Center in the human body is each human being's personal copy of the *Liber Domini*. From it may be extracted knowledge of the inner secrets of creation. The unwritten Qabalah.

signatura (Lt). signatures. Refers to what is written in the Book of the Lord. By reawakening the inner centers, access to this past history enables one to project into a better, more awakened, life pattern and to establish Justice. These are the characters which are inscribed on the mechanism of the world and repeated, as the *Fama* says. "Throughout the mutations of Empires." These characters written on the world-machine constitute the "one, only book" from which may be learned all that has been, is now, or will be learned form al other books."

trygano (Lt). triangle. Spelling employed in the *Fama*. The triangle is, especially when equilateral, a symbol of Justice, and of the principles employed in adjustment. see 81, 237 (Lt).

practicus (Lt). One who practices. Grade attributed to Hod. Knowledge and seed-ideas received in study and meditation are verified by actual processes of careful observation. One becomes directly aware of the truth that all events, all objects, all situations are operations of a single identity, a single power. see 85, 193, 103, 142.

Anima Soulis (Lt). Soul of the Sun; Soul of Gold. The truth verified by the Practicus. The foundation of all occult practice is the truth that the animating principle of the Sun is identical with the One Reality designated as Deus Jehova.

Deus Jehova (Lt). God Jehovah (יהוה). This truth is summarized by the Tetragrammaton.

machina mundi (Lt). machine of the world. Knowledge of the cycles portrayed by the letter Kaph gives the observer a vision of the "machinery of the universe" animating by the vital soul (Yesod), the image-making power of God.

101 (prime)

נימא A gut, gut-string [Crowley, 1977, p. 16]. This word does not occur in scripture or in the Hebrew Lexicon.

D'Olivet writes of the first two letters: ני ni. "Root analogous to the roots גא [youth, newness), נה [fresh, young, recent) and נו whose expression it manifest. The Arabic indicates the state of that which is raw." [d'Olivet, 1976, pp. 400-401.]

Of מא he says: "That which tends to the aggrandizement of its being, to its entire development; that which serves as instrument of generative power and manifest it exteriorly. מא characterizes in general, passive matter, the thing of which, with which, and by means of which, all is made. It is in particular, in the Arabic idiom, *water*; anything whatsoever, *all* or *nothing*, according to the manner in which it is considered. This important root, considered as pronominal relation designates the possibility of

all things and is represented by the analogues *what* and *which*; conceived on the contrary, as adverbial relation, it is employed in Arabic to express the absence of every determined objects and is rendered by the analogues *not, no*. As a verb, the Arabic root signifies in general *to go everywhere, to extend everywhere, to fill space,* etc." [ibid., pp. 385-386]

These meanings apply to the gut-string, which is the raw material from which music is produced on the strings of a violin; similarly in the preparation of the aspirant; it is the raw material of experience which produces the heights of spiritual illumination.

יה אלהים Divine name of Daath.

אסם a granary or storehouse. With different pointing: *Osem,* a rich harvest. The great stone is the harvest and storehouse of "secret arts". see 661

בלהטיהם By their secret arts, By their enchantments. [Exodus 7:11]. "Then Pharaoh also called the wise men and the sorcerers: now the Magicians of Egypt, they also did in like manner with their enchantments." see 661, 96, 94.

צוה to order, command, give or lay a charge; to appoint, ordain. With different pointing: 1. to be commanded, be ordered; 2. to set up, to establish. In Psalm 133:3: "As the dew of Hermon, and as the dew that descended upon the mountain of Zion: For there the Lord commanded the blessing, even life for evermore."

אבן גדולה a great stone. see 48, 53 & Jeshua 24:26; 1 Samuel 14:33.

מיכאל Like unto God, House of God, Power of God. The Angel associated with Tiphareth and of the Sun, of fire and of the South. Pictured as the Holy Guardian Angel on Key 14.

I. 42nd Shem ha-Mephorash. "Virtue of God, House of God, Like unto God." For safety of travel and the discovery of conspiracies. Person born under the influence: concerned with political affairs, diplomatic. Negative influence: treacheries, false news, malevolence. see Appendix 10.

II. Angel of the 3rd decanate and 6th quinance of Aquarius and attributed to the 7 of Swords.

מליכה kingship, kingdom, state; "A virgin princess." Figuratively Ecclesia (The assembly of the gathered together). see 91, 294 (Greek).

האבן האזל The stone of Ezel (of departure). The stone of departure is the consciousness which departs from separation. see 1 Samuel 20:19.

יצא to go forth; to finish. Those in darkness go forth to finish the great work of kingship, i.e. the rule of the higher self in Tiphareth.

מומיה 72nd Shem ha-Mephorash. Protects in mysterious operations, brings success in all things. Governs chemistry, physics and medicine. Influences health and longevity. Positive influence: doctor and healing arts. Negative: despair and suicide. see Appendix 10.

Angel of the 3rd decanate and 6th quinance of Cancer, attributed to the 4 of cups (Chesed of Briah). His activity is figured by omega, which designates the end of all things.

ויהי כן and it was so [Genesis 1:9; 1:11].

המון crowd, multitude; abundance; noise, roar; tumult, confusion.

ננא 53rd name of Shem ha-Mephorash, short form. see 132 , 965, 646, 96, 86 & Appendix 10.

מלאכי Malachi, my messenger. The name of the last book of the prophets in the Bible, one of the later Prophets. In Malachi 1:1: "An oracle: the word of the Lord to Israel through Malachi." see 90.

קא vomit. In Proverbs 26:11: "As a dog returns to its vomit, so a fool repeats his folly. "This is the analogous root of קן which characterizes the expression of the sign. As onomatopoeic root it is convulsive and violent efforts; *to spew out, to vomit forth*." [d'Olivet, 1976, p. 438.]

אלע swallowed, destroyed [Crowley, 1977, p. 15]. This word does not occur in scripture or in the Hebrew Lexicon. Suggest death [Nun] swallowed up in victory (Netzach, Venus).

והמן and the manna. Numbers 11:7.

למלא to consecrate Exodus 29:33.

vehiculum (Lt). Car, chariot. Given by the Pythagoreans to the number 7. The triangle symbolizes the higher triad, and the square stands for the lower tetrad, in the occult constitution of man. The figure of a triangle on top of a square is the basis of the composition of the picture of a charioteer and his car in Key 7. see 7.

forma pater (Lt). from the father. We find this Latin term in plate 46 of The Secret Symbols, where the words are shown in connection with a circle containing a solar symbol, and having the additional inscription Sperma Masculls Mundi, "Masculine seed of the world." Its number is 216, that of Lapis Philosophorum, Philosopher's Stone, and of *Sion Philosophorum*, "Zion of the Philosophers." Note that *Lapis* and *Sion* have the same numerical values, 51. Here is a direct connection between the stone and Zion, and Zion is the occult designation of the part of the human brain we call adytum.

catholicus (Lt). universal, catholic. Part of an inscription in Secret Symbols (p. 25). "The water of the philosophers is universal." see 36, 165, 366 (Lt).

corporis (Lt). of the body. Represented the things of the physical plane, or the embodiment of spirit in the Kingdom of flesh. Part of the phrase. see 145.

optimus (Lt). incomparably good; the best. Part of the phrase referring to God. see 234.
compendium (Lt). a condensed summary. Part of a Latin phrase inscribed in the vault of C.R. see 832.

theosopia (Lt). Literally "God-Marks"; title of a treatise by Jacob Boehme, with subtitled "The highly precious gate of the divine intuition showing what Mysterium Magnum [The Great Mystery] is, and how all is from, through and in God; how God is near all things, and fills all.

Mater Jesu (Lt) Mother of Jesus. see 51 (Lt).

punctus (Lt). pierced. Letters inscribed at the center of a hexagram, part of a plate "God known of the heart", in Secret Symbols. It is understood as emblematic of the christhood. That which is born in darkness must die on the cross of suffering. [Waite, 1993, p. 20]

102

אהה אדני יהוה   Ah, Lord Jehovah [Jeremiah 32:17].

אמינה   faithfulness, firmness, steadfastness, trust, faith, religion, confidence. A significant word in the higher grade of Free Masonry. In Deuteronomy 32:4: "For his works are perfect, and all his was are just; he is a faithful God and without iniquity, just and upright is he. And in [Isaiah 25:1] "O Lord, thou art my God; I will praise your name; for you have done wonderful things, and given faithful counsel from afar, amen."

אלהינו   our God [Deuteronomy 6:4]. Part of the Shema. "Hear, o Israel: the Lord our God, the Lord is One."

יצב אמינה   to place, to station; to continue. As an Aramaic noun: to speak truly, truth.

צבי   grace, splendor; glory. With different pointing: stag, deer, gazelle see 3, 12, 21, 30, 39, 48, 66, 75, 84, 93, 111.

קב   a dry measure of capacity; crutch; to curse. In 2 Kings 6:25: "There was a great famine in the city [of Samaria]; the siege lasted so long that a donkey head sold for 80 shekels of silver, and a fourth of a qab of seed pods for 5 shekels."

"The onomatopoetic root קא, united by contraction to the sign of interior activity ב, expresses all rejection, expurgation. Literally, it is an *excavation*; figuratively, an *anathema, a malediction.*

But if one considers here the figure ק, as being contracted with the root אב, then the root קב characterizes every object capable of and containing every kind of measure: Literally, *genitalia muliebra*; figuratively *a bad place.*

The Arabic root expressing every effort that one makes to cut, carve, sharpen. It characterizes, in general, that which retrenches or is retrenched; thence, the idea of a price, a magistrate; of any

man or any thing which operate a line of demarcation. The Arabic designates again, the principal sound of the musical system, *the keynote.*" [d'Olivet, 1976, pp. 438-439.]

בעל   Baal. Lord, Master, possessor, owner, proprietor; husband, the Canaanite God Ball. With different vowel points: to rule over, be married, have sexual intercourse. see 543, 581.

בלע   Bela, a king of Edom. to possess; lands, government [Crowley, 1977, p. 16]. Edom signifies unbalanced force and is associated with the sphere of Daath (474). Note that this word is a metathesis of בעל. see 51 and Genesis 36:32.

אווז לון   The white goose. White is connected with the Moon. see 57.

בן האדם   Ben Ha-Adam. The Son of Man. A Title applied to Christ. throughout the New Testament. Hebrew spelling. see 2960 (Greek).

וילון   veil; the first of seven heavens of the Tree of Life, corresponding to Yesod, the astral and to Malkuth, the physical plane. see 752, 80, 496.

נחמד   concupiscibills; strong sexual desire, covetousness, eagerly desiring, endeavoring after, aiming at [Crowley, 1977, p. 16]. This is the positive attitude of an aspirant on the paths of return. This word does not occur in scripture or in the Hebrew lexicon.

d'Olivet says of the first two letters: נה. "If one considers this root as formed of the united signs of produced existence, and elementary existence, it implies a movement which leads toward an end: If one considers it is formed of this same sign of produced existence united by contraction to the root הא, image of all equilibratory force, it furnishes the idea of that perfect repose which result for a thing long time agitate contrarily, and the point of equilibrium which it attains where it dwells immobile. Thence, נה, in the first case, and in a restricted sense, *a guide*: In the second case, and in a general sense, *the repose of existence.*" [d'Olivet, 1976, p. 399.] Of מד he writes: "The sign of exterior action, being united to that of elementary division, constitutes that root which come all ideas of measure, dimension, mensuration, commensurable extent, and in a metaphorical sense, those of custom, rule, condition. The Arabic word in particular, it is that which extends, unfolds, lengthens." [ibid., p. 386.]

Porta Coeli (Lt). Gate of Heaven.

punctus (Lt). pointed, pricked in.

proteus (Lt). change. From *Fama* "Rota Mundi for that displaying the Greatest Artifice, and proteus the most profitable." Variant spelling. see 110.

103 (prime)

אבן האדם **Ehben ha-Adam.** the Stone of Adam. The Stone of Adam is a verbal symbol for the mystical union of the Father, Chokmah, with the Son, Tiphareth, in Adam, the sixth Sephirah. This is represented in Key 17 by the great star surrounded by 7 smaller stars.

בנאים builders, masons. A name used by the Essenes. True builders are those who share the one secret doctrine which is practical and has much to do with the occult doctrine of the stars. Note that his word is a metathesis of the word for "stones." 108, 220, 1379 (Greek).

Spelled in Ezra 4:1 as בונים. "Now when the adversaries of Judah and Benjamin heard that the children of the captivity were the builders [ones-building] of the temple unto the Lord God of Israel". [Psalm 118:22] "The stone which the builders refused is become the headstone of the corner."

גנן to hedge about, protect, shield, to cover over, surround, defend. Behind the Qabalah is a deep science of the stars, which gives more than adequate protection from every danger. The "Building" is the secret place of the most high. It is called the "adytum" and is within the brain of the illuminated adept.

הוא האלהים He (Elohim) is God. Deuteronomy 4:39: "Know therefore this day, and consider it in your heart, that the Lord he is God in heaven above, and upon the earth beneath: there is none else." Hu designates Kether, the Indivisible Self, Yekhidah (And also IHVH as the "Ancient of days"). Ha-Elohim is a special designation for Binah, relates also to Kether. The absolute unity of what appears to be manifold is curiously veiled Elohim is a plural

noun, meaning "Creative Powers." see 91, 203, 663.

הכוכבים the stars; (Hebrew name for Key 17). *Kokab* [כוכב, 48] is a name for Mercury which is the planet which directs the activity of meditation. In Genesis 1:16: "And God made two great lights, the greater light to rule the day, and the lesser light to rule the night: He made the stars also." And in Judges 5:20: "They fought from heaven; the stars in their courses fought against Sisera." God is Elohim, the 7 Creative Powers, corresponding to the 7 interior "stars" in the microcosm. see 1777 (Greek).

אבן הדאם ehben ha-Adam. The stone of Adam. Verbal symbol for the mystical union of Father (Chokmah) with the son (Tiphareth), in Adam, represented in the 17th key by the Great Star surrounded by 7 smaller stars. see 53.

מגדון Megiddon. rendezvous. The place of the battle of Armageddon in the Apocalypse. We must come to this place of rendezvous, where the peace of illumination during quiet meditation is experience, after the storm and conflict of early awakening have passed. Rendezvous means "render yourself." Its roots is in "surrender." One in meditation surrenders to the indwelling Shekinah, who is the "daughter of the seven." He makes his appointment, and to her faithful lover she unveils. In Zechariah 12:11: "In that day shall there be a great mourning in Jerusalem, as the mourning of Haddad-Rimmon in the valley of Megiddon." see 222, 958, 274 (Greek); 753, [Zechariah 12:11]

מגני my shield [Psalm 119:114]. "Thou art my hiding place and my shield I hope in thy word." Each verse begins with the Letter Samekh in this passage.

אבנים stones. Plural of *ehben* [53]. Same letters as Bonaim, builders. In 1 Kings 5:17: "And the king commanded, and they brought great stones, costly stones, and hewed stones, to lay the foundation of the house." And in Genesis 31:46: "And Jacob said unto his brethren, gather stones; and they took stones, and made a heap: and thy did eat there upon the heap";

געל to abhor, loathe. With different pointing: loathing, abhorrence.

אבימלך Father of the King; A king of the Philistines. see Genesis 20:2.

יצג A primitive root meaning: to place permanently, establish, leave, make, present, put, set, stay. [Strong's Bible Dictionary] In Exodus 10:23: be stayed.

מנחה gift, present; tribute; offering, meal-offering; after-noon prayer, afternoon. see Genesis 4:3.

אבק to wrestle, grapple with; dust, powder. With different pointing: dust, powder (gun-powder; particle; shade of). see Deuteronomy 23:10.

נבאים prophets. see Jeremiah 23:21.

מזון mawzon. food. see Genesis 45:23 & Daniel 4:9.

נגן music. A primitive root, to beat a tune with fingers; to play on a stringed instrument; generally to make music. [Strong's Bible Dictionary]

monoceros (Lt). Unicorn.

vehiculum (Lt). car, chariot. Name given by the Pythagoreans to the number 7. The triangle symbolizes the higher triad, and the square stands for the lower tetrad, in the occult constitution of man. The figure [triangle on top of square] is the basis of the composition of a charioteer and his car, in Key 7. see 2.

theoricus (Lt). One versed in theory. Corresponding to the 2=9 grade of Rosicrucian initiation, attributed to Yesod (Foundation) on the Tree of Life. This is the astral plane of subconsciousness, which must be purified by right knowledge before the "stars" can be activated and further building take place. see 85, 100, 142.

Sulphur (Lt). The second alchemical principle, corresponding to self-consciousness. Depicted in Key 4, the Emperor. see 28, 109.

malneum mariae (Lt). bath of the sea. An alchemical term. "The two [spirit and body] must be united by a gentle and continuous fire, affording the same degree of warmth as that with which a hen hatches her eggs. It must then be

placed in a St. Mary s Bath, which is neither too warm nor too cold." [Waite, 1974, vol. 1, p. 183]

Janua Artis (Lt). Door of the Art, an alchemical term.

fons mundi (Lt). fountain of the world, an alchemical term.

subjectum (Lt). subject, one placed under [test and trial], alchemically speaking.

104

I. (2^3 x 13)

II. Length of 2 diameters of a circle with a radius of 26, forming a cross. Total axes of symmetry of invisible curves of a 3x3x3 cube. Diagonal of rectangle of 40 by 96.

צדי Letter name Tzaddi. fish-hook. Twenty-eighth Path of Wisdom. Associated with meditation, whereby the mind is set in order. Meditation reveals principles which are operative forever (**לעד**). By meditation we reverse our errors, and correct our actions, thus the work of meditation is implied by the injunction "repent ye" (**נחמו**). see 90, 477.

לעד Forever. Lamed is a preposition meaning: for, but also means: to into; at, for, with. **עד** means: duration, in the sense of advance or perpetuity; eternity, ever-lasting [Strong's Bible Dictionary]. see 5, 14, 74.

נחמו repent, comfort ye [Isaiah 40:1]. The Hebrew equivalent of a Greek noun "repent ye." The root meaning is: reversal of mind, change mind; New Mind. This implies recognition of some principle of order violated by the action of which one repents. By restoring order, or complying with it, one secures satisfaction and comfort. With different pointing: *nihum*. consolation, comfort. In Isaiah 57:18: "I have seen her ways [i.e. Jerusalem], and I have healed her and have comforted her, and I have give comfort to her and to her mourners."

נחום "comfort"; one of the minor prophets. In Nahum 1:1: "The wound of Ninevah, which is in the book of the visions, of Nahum the

Alkoshite." Of his prophecy it is said: "The striking pecuniary of Nahum's thought is its fixed gaze on the enemies of God's chosen people. The prophet evidently has no fear for the people themselves. At all events, he alludes neither to their sin nor to any impending wrath to be visited upon them. Presumably, the destruction of Assyria meant to him the deliverance of Israel from a source of distress and a menacing danger." [Standard Bible Dictionary, p.604]

אב המון Father of the multitude or Mob. Unregulated meditation. "The initial efforts to control by one-pointed concentration seems to excite the mind to unwanted activity. As we attempt to concentrate the mind, the more we seen to stir up mental images, or a mob of images." [Paul Case, unpublished notes]

מדין quarrel, dispute. According to Inman, this is probably derived from מי, *mi* water or seed, and דן, *Dan*, the Judge connected with alchemical putrefaction and Scorpio. Thus is signifies "the seed of man".

I. "At first between the old habits of thought and the new one [of meditation], there is stirred up considerable dispute. The old ways fight for their lives and there is no peace." [Paul Case, unpublished notes] see 133, 336, 754.

II. With different pointing: *Midian*; one of the sons of Abraham by Keturah; later one of a number of tribes in NW Arabia. In Judges 8:22: "Then the men of Israel said unto Gideon, rule thou over us, both thou, and thy son, and thy son's son: for thou has delivered us from the hand of Midian." Arabia signifies "sterility" in the Rosicrucian allegory; NW on the cube of Space is the direction assigned to Lamed, "Justice". Abraham (254) means "father of a multitude"; Keturah is "frankincense"; assigned to the Sun].

סגולה personal belongings. "The intensity [of thought in meditation] is directed particularly on the old habits of thought of personal separateness implied in the word *segolah*, possessions or personal belongings; and our thoughts are continually diverted by being related to possessions. This is perhaps the primary reason why people who wish to adopt the contemplative life find it advantageous to live in voluntary poverty. Possessing little or nothing, they are no so easily diverted from their meditations." [Paul Case, unpublished notes] see 98.

סדם Sodom; "burning, conflagration". The Biblical city which was destroyed by God because of its perversity. Samekh (alchemical incineration, 162) added to *dam* [44] blood. In Genesis 18:26: "And the Lord said, if I find in Sodom fifty righteous men within the City, then I will spare all the place for their sake." Note 50 is Nun, the "fish , which is hooked by Tzaddi, and burned by Samekh. It represents transformation, and represents Fire in alchemy.

I. "Meditation burns out the old way of thinking and doing even as the fire from heaven destroyed Sodom." [Paul Case, unpublished notes] see 44, 60 (Samekh) 315, 664, 385.

II. Inman: (Genesis 13:10), Is probably a variant of Siddim. Furst suggest that it means 'an enclosed place.' [Ancient Faiths, Vol. 2, p.747]

סולח giving up, presenting, remitting. "...meditation is successful to the degree that one surrenders himself utterly to the influx of the higher consciousness, presents his whole personality as a living sacrifice, and rids himself of all sense of being anything other than a steward of what the world counts as possessions, mental and physical." [Paul Case, unpublished notes]

ויפח and breathed (into his nostrils). Also יפח "breathing, puffing out." see 98 and Genesis 2:7.

דק fine, slender, lean, see 510.

אבן + *lapis*. This combination of the Hebrew and Latin words for Stone occurs often in secret writings of the western tradition. see 51, 53, 754.

Lux Mundi (Lt). Light of the World. The opening of the third eye brings illumination the radiance around the hanged man's head in Key 12.

Heirophant (Lt). One who expounds sacred things; an initiatory priest. From Greek ιερο-φαντης. Often specifically the chief priest of the Eleusinain mysteries. He was always one of the Eumolpides (sweet-singing, singing well), a family of priestly singers, 9 of whom wee rulers of religious and civic affairs.

Mons Sion (Lt). Mount Zion. Signifies the center of the brain which is aroused by meditation.

Art Notaris (Lt). Universal science. The art of knowing. The art of reading the signs and characters which, says one of the Rosicrucian manifestoes "God hath inscribed upon the mechanism of the world, and which he repeats through the mutations of Empires." These signs may be discerned in every kingdom of nature. To have the Arts Notaria is to be able to read what Rosicrucian texts call "Book M." see 430, 510.

Mater Ecclesia (Lt). Mother church (Binah). It is symbolized by the kneeling woman of Key 17. The interior church (communion of saints) is composed of persons who, by meditation, have reversed the errors of ordinary human thought. (In early stages of this reversal, they are seldom aware of that others are having similar experiences. As they progress, they not only sees some of their fellow travelers on the path of return, but they also enter into an interior communication with persons who may be living in distant lands.) It is identical with the True and Invisible Rosicrucian Order.

Terra Damnata (Lt). Reprobate earth. Refers to the matter of the alchemical work in its unpurified, unsubliminated condition. It is not itself changed by the Great Work, being always *Lux Mundi*, though hidden by veils which the work dispels.

105

I. Σ14 = 105.

II. 1/24 of a "week of times (2520 years).

הפך to turn, to change, to transform, to overthrow; to turn into; to prevent; subvert. Tracing a pentagram is an affirmation of the operator's power to divert the normal course of energy to predetermined channels, thus transforming magically the appearance surrounding him, and over-throwing adverse condition [*haphak*] by realizing the world of form is in a state of flux. The power which takes form as objects constituting the environment is identical with an inner power which is the original creative force of the One Self. see 585.

פכה to flow, to run, to pour forth; to ooze, drop.

With different vowel points: to make sober, sober down.

ציה to glow, to burn, to glitter. From this word is derived the place-name Zion (156). The actual force employed in magical operations, the glowing, scintillating, fiery energy is concentrated in Zion and represented by ציה.

ציה dryness, aridity; wasteland, desert. Corresponds to sandy, desert earth; one of the 7 earths (Earth on Netzach) in the diagram of the Four Seas. see 291, 50, 14, 365, 302, 432, 337.

עלה to go up, ascend, mount; to come up; to depart, withdraw, retreat; to rise, appear; to spring up, grow, shoot forth, to surprise, excel, be superior to; to be reckoned, be considered, counted in; to go up (on the altar), be sacrificed; to be void, be neutralized. In Exodus 19:3: "And Moses went up unto Al-Halhim, and יהוה called unto him out of the mountain." With different pointing: covering, protection. see 512; 456, 561, 702.

אדק to adhere, cohere, connected. With different pointing: 1. *ehbeq*, dropper; brace; 2. *ahdahq*, spray bottle (for perfume).

מסה trial, test, temptation; trouble, despair. With different pointing: essay, thesis. The test of aspiration is perseverance through trouble and despair, and overcoming adversity.

נימה thread, hair; (gut) string. Suggest the sutratma, or thread-soul, which provides continuity in all incarnations.

יהודע "Jehovah knows", Old Testament name [2 Samuel 23:20]

Mea victoria (Lt). my victory; part of the phrase mea victoria in cruce rosea, my victory is in the rosy-cross. see 224, 88 (Lt) & Secret Symbols (p. 35).

genus homo (Lt). human species. The point of departure from homo spiritualis (Spiritual Man). see 184.

Ponticus (Lt). Astringent, sour, binding, contracting. Connected with the "Catholic, pontic water," the "gold" of the sages. These are adjectives Jacob Boehme applies to the first 3 principles i.e. astringency-salt (the other 2 are: compunction-Sulphur, rotation-Mercury. These further correspond to: Ain-Mercury-Kether, Ain Soph-sulphur-Chokmah; Ain Soph Aur-Salt-Binah.

106

I. 2 x 53 or $[5^2 + 3^4]$

II. Number of years on the life of brother C.R.

נון Letter name Nun. fish. As a verb: to grow, sprout or multiply; as a proper name the father of Joshua (Jesus) and means "perpetuity." It is the transmission of the fundamental resemblances, generation after generation, that the sources of Liberation are found. Thus the changeless reaps the harvest of the mutable. see 756, 326.

צחח to glare, to glow, burn, to be bright, to be dazzling white, shining, to be sunny. A reference to the "White Brilliance" of Kether. A correspondence which indicates the mastery of the fiery Mars force which is connected with the letter Nun.

קו thread, a cord, a measuring line, measuring. A rule or standard of conduct; a reference to Chokmah (73). One of the meanings of the number two. Refers to the 24th Path of Nun as the thread or cord of perpetual change (Nun) has a face of life and a face of death but is the changeless life in reality. This is the "Line of the Heavens," for "their line is gone out through all the earth," says the Psalmist. "The mastery [of the Mars-force] makes us conscious of that undying perpetual reality which the Hindus call sutrama, the 'thread soul,'-that particular ray of the one light upon which successive personalities are strung, like beads on a thread, until mastery ends the necessity for reincarnation." [Paul Case, unpublished notes] see 470.

אלהיכם your God [Deuteronomy 4:23]. see 45, 132, 1145, 685, 638, 666.

דבק attained; to cling, to cleave, to adhere, to join, overtake; to bring close together, to paste, glue. As a masculine noun dehbeq: soldering or welding of metals (alchemy). As a verb: to follow close, to pursue, to overtake. also attachment, appendage; paste, putty. Attained because the completion of the great work is the mastery of the force symbolized by Key 13,

Death in the Tarot as death). see 512.

המלוכה The kingdom, the realm, kingship.

והאבן גדלה and a great stone. In Genesis 29:2: "And he [Jacob] looked, and behold a well in the field, and, lo, there were three flocks of sheep lying by it; for out of that well they watered the flocks: and a great stone was upon the wells mouth." see 756

עלאה Supernal. An Aramaic adjective used in The Lesser Holy Assembly in reference to supernal Wisdom (Ch2, sec 56).

עלו his yoke [Genesis 27:40]. refers to the yoke of Jacob upon Esau. see 756, 120, 54, 372, 100, 680

עול Evil, wrong, injustice, inequity, wickedness. Refers to the apparent inequity of some phases of cosmic manifestation.

פלו Antimony. With different pointing: color, to paint, eye-paint (stibium). A Hermetic name for the first matter which is also called "permanent water" and "philosophical mercury." This attainment enables one to differentiate the white light into any color or special rate of vibration. see 160, 586 and p. 18 of R.C. allegory.

סאליה 45th Shem ha-Mephorash; "Mover of all things." 221E-225E. SESME, Sun. May 3, July 14, September 24, December 5, February 15. 2:40-3:00 DUPIOR. [Psalm 94:18] "If I say my foot slips, thy mercy, O Lord (יהוה) holds me up." For confounding the merchants. It relieves those who are humble. Rules vegetation; bring life and health to all who breathe, it influences through the principle agencies of nature. Person born: loves to instruct himself; he will have great means and many faculties.

Angel of the 3rd quinance [11E-15E] of Pisces and angel by day of the 9 of Cups. This is the operation of the Moon or subconsciousness in Briah, the World of Creation. see Appendix 10.

האדומים The Edomites. Written without the Heh in [2 Chronicles 28:17]. "The Edomites had again come and attacked Judah, and carried away prisoners." i.e. these who rule the kingdoms of

174

unbalanced force. Note in this context that Judah is connected with Leo and the heart, as well as the Sun. see 30.

מאניה "Jah is a protector".

מלהאל 23rd Shem ha-Mephorash. "God who delivers from evil." Against weapons and for safety in travel. Governs: Water, produce of the earth, and especially plants necessary for the cure of disease. Positive influence: courageous, accomplishes honorable actions. Negative: All that is harmful to vegetation, causes sickness and plagues. see Appendix 10.

Angle of the 3rd decanate and the 5th quinance [21E-25E] of Scorpio; angle by day of the 7 of Cups. This is the operation of the sphere of Venus or desire, in Briah, the creative world.

Ρεα. Rhea. Earth goddess Rhea (or Cybele). A deification of Earth; producing and sustaining the wild life of nature. see 12.

sapientum (Lt). of the wise. see 221 (Lt), 142.

verbum fiat (Lt). the word "let there be", the divine creative word in [Genesis 1:3] "And Elohim said 'let there be light', and there was light." Jacob Boehme: "As the eternal nature of the essence of external nature renews itself, and abandons that which it brought out of the eternal will into the outward by verbum fiat at creation; so may man also renew that which he makes. If he abandon the earthly, then he may renew that which he has progenerated from the eternal; but if it be not renewed, it remains in the source." [Six Theosophic Points I 24, p.37]

107 (prime)

The sum of Ab (3), Aima (52) and Ben (52), the names of the Qabalistic trinity: Father (Chokmah), Mother (Binah), & Son (Tiphareth).

מגן דוד Mawgen David. Shield of David, or Shield of Love (hexagram). The great star in the Hermit's hexagonal lantern is the macrocosmic star, referring to the Ego in Tiphareth linked by light to the paternal-maternal cosmic forces. see 701, 346, 20.

מני אדם Beni Adam. Sons of Adam; sons of Humanity. In Psalm 90:3: "Thou turns man to destruction, and says 'return you sons of Adam.'" see 713, 1200, 1308.

The *Beni Adam* are identical with the האלים-בני (148). Enosh, אנוש (mankind, 357), is the state of the Sons of God when they suppose themselves to be merely the Sons of Adam, and the return is to the original Angelic condition. In this is the deepest mystery of Saturn closely related to the secret of Mars. The Sons of Adam have forgotten that they are truly Sons of God. For them there is no rest, and in diverse ways they seek relief from the intolerable tension that is produced by the sense of separateness. Only a few members of the human race realize their true status, and live accordingly. The rest are turned to destruction until utter collapse of their supposed autonomy sends them back. Now these deluded ones see death everywhere, are taught survival perhaps, but do not usually really believe it. Thus they seek vicarious immortality in posterity, and surrender themselves to death. They who have come into the peace of the Sabbath are free from this delusion, and know better than to prolong the chain of birth and death. See **31**.

מלאביו you angels of his, angles-of-him. In Psalm 103:20: "Praise the Lord, you his angels [messengers], you mighty ones who do his bidding, who obey his word." see 91, 158.

גלעד Gilead, hill of testimony. In Genesis 31:21: "So he [Jacob] his face toward the Mount Gilead." see 117, Abdiel; 221 (Jair), 317.

אונן "Onan", probably a clan, of Canaanite origin, that lost its identity in the amalgamation of clans incidental to the growth of the tribe of Judah (Sun, Leo). In Genesis 38:4: "She (Shua) conceived again and gave birth to a son and named him Onan." And in Genesis 38:9: "But Onan knew that the offspring would not be his; so whenever he lay with his brothers wife, he spilled his seed on the ground to keep from producing offspring for his brother." Note the power of Spirit (Aleph) linked (Vav) to reproductive force (Nun) in perpetual cycles of its own use, and abuse (Nun). see 757.

The Zohar [II:186B, 187B, 188A] has these comments: "... while the holy soul is still within man's body, it is incumbent of him to multiply the image of the king in the world. There is herein an esoteric thought involved, namely that just as the celestial stream flows on forever without ceasing, so must man see that his own river and spring shall not cease in this world... (p.212) "And raise up seed for thy brother', as that seed is needed for the purpose of putting things right by growing into human shape and form then and thus preventing the stock form being severed from its root. And when all has been put right, then those concerning receive praise in the other world, as the holy one is pleased with them (p.216). Now of all the sins which defile a man, that which defiles him the most, both in this world and in the world to come, is the sin of spilling one' seed (semen). A man guilty of this sin will not enter within the heavenly curtain, and will not behold the presence of the ancient of days." (p.217).

זק chain; flaming arrow. In Proverbs 26:18: "Like a madman, shooting firebrands or deadly arrows, (19) is a man who deceives his neighbor and says, 'I was only toiling.'" And in [Psalm 149:8] "To bind their kings with fetters, their nobles with shackles of iron." Key 15.
"Every idea of diffusion in time or space. *A chain, suite, flux; a drought* of anything whatsoever. That which *spreads, glides, flows* in space or time. Thence, *years, old age*, and the veneration which is attached to it: *water* and the purity which ensues: *a chain* and the strength which attends it; *an arrow*, etc. In a restricted sense, the Arabic signifies a *leather bottle* where in one puts any kind of liquid. It is doubtless the Hebrew word שק or the Chaldaic סק, a sack." [d'Olivet, 1976, pp. 344-345.]

וסיאל Usiel. Angel of Netzach of Briah [Crowley, 1977, p. 16]. Corresponds to the 7 of Cups or sphere of Venus and desire in the creative world. "Uzziel, Strength of God... Usiel is an angel that fell, and is therefore evil; he was among those who wedded human wives and begat giants. Of the 10 unholy sefiroth, Usiel is listed 5th. The Book of the Angel Raziel, Uzziel (Usiel) is among the 7 angels before the throne of God, and among 9 set over the 4 winds." [Davidson, 1971, p. 299.] The spelling may be עזיאל.

ביצה egg [Crowley, 1977, p. 16]. Symbol of the manifested universe.

Christos (Lt). Christ

LUX Domini (Lt). Light of the Lord.

108

I. The number of degrees in a vertex of a pentagon.

II. 20 x 108 = 2160. 1/20 of The Great Age.

מנהיג driver, conductive, From the verb מנהג, minhag, "to drive" (as a chariot). Note that the study of the Tree of Life and its relationships is often called "The Work of the Chariot." The first 2 letters spell: מן a root meaning "to apportion." The first 3 letters spell מנה (Menah): "to ordain, to appoint, to number." The fourth letter Yod symbolizes the Sephirah Chokmah. The fifth letter represent the 13th Path of Gimel. Thus מנהיג signifies: "The apportionment of the power of You, the Father, through Gimel. Part of the name of the 13th path of Gimel, the Conductive Intelligence of Unity. see 88, 424, 419, 532, 536.

Menahig signifies "the apportionment of the power of Yod, the father, through Gimel. Ha-achadoth, the unities. The first letter, Heh is a definite article and the letter of Binah, the mother. The next 3 letters אחד, "one", add to 13, the number of the path of Gimel. The fifth letter is Vav, which is the conjunction, "and" and corresponds to the 16th Path linking Chokmah to Chesed. Vav as the number 6 is used as a sign for Tiphareth (the 6th Sephiroth), the son. The 6th letter Tav is the last letter of the alphabet. Thus this workd means: "the (Heh) first (אחד) (one) "and" (Vav) the last (Tav), or, "The mother is first and last."

באבי הנחל the fruit of a deep valley. The "valley" is the Abyss of the Unground, or Boundless Subsistence.

חיצ a wall. Suggests protection, as does the Magic Circle.

אונים ears.

חמס to be sharp, bold, violent

חנן to incline, to have mercy, to love, to favor,

to bestow. Suggests that the supreme attainment is rather by the grace or favor of God than as the result of the aspirants personal efforts. With different pointing: 1. to love very much, be gracious, pity; grant; 2. to make gracious, favorable; to beg for mercy.

"Yet it must be clearly understood that the grace or favor is not capriciously extended. God does not grant it to some and withhold it from others. It should be realized that this grace inheres in the in most nature of the Life-power. What is here intended to be conveyed it that this particular aspect of the Life-power, rather than personal endeavors of the aspirant, is what brings about the final attainment of the crown." [Case, 1985, p. 299.]

חסם to close, to shut, to hinder

חצי the middle, an arrow (compare with Greek kentron, an arrow-point, hence center). Refers to the "Middle way" between the pairs of opposites. In part this refers to the position of the 13th Path of Gimel on the Tree of Life. With different pointing: half, one half. see 216.

חק that which is inscribed; that which is appointed; revelation, divine (cosmic) law. Suggest the fulfillment of the divine intention by the final stage of the way of return to the supreme goal. With different pointing: 1. a conclusion, an enactment, a decree; 2. to measure out; statue, law; rule, custom; prescribed due; prescribed unit, boundary. see 16, 64, 113.

"Every idea of definition, impression of an object in the memory, description, narration; that which pertains to symbols, to characters of writing. In a broader sense matter used according to a determined mode. The action of *defining, connecting, giving a dimension, deciding upon forms; of hewing, cutting after a* model; *to carve, to design*: a thing *appointed, enacted, declared, constituted*, etc. The Arabic more particularly to that which confirms; verifies, certifies; to that which is true, just, necessary." [d'Olivet, 1976, p. 354.]

בונים Builders. Refers to the Elohim, the cosmic forces working through the manifested universe and in the planetary centers of man. The Essenese called themselves builders. see 103,

142, 273, 86, 220.

גיהנם Gehenna, Gehinnon. One of the 7 infernal Mansions, Hell of Yesod-Malkuth. A subdivision of Sheol (Hades) into a cavern separated by a wall or chasm, occupied by the departed unjust. It means "The valley of Hinnom." A figure of everything suggestive of disgust and abhorrence; a place of punishment for the wicked. Hinnom was the 'valley of (the sons of) Hinnom,' the broad valley which encloses Jerusalem on the west and south. The boundary line between the tribes of Judah and Benjamin [Joshua 15:8, 18:16]. It was the place where children were sacrificed to the God Melek (Moloch) [2 Kings 23:10, Jeremiah 2:23]. Later Jewish abhorrence to this practice caused the name Gehenna to be used as a name for Hell. see 668, 337, 57, 911, 99, 1026, 291 and The Standard Bible Dictionary (p. 223).

עזאל "The lust of God". A giant [Crowley, 1977, p. 16].

I. Godwin: Demon Prince of Water. [Godwin. 1999, p. 515.]

II. "(Asiel, whom God, strengthens")- one of 2 fallen angels (Aza is the other) who cohabited with Naaman, Lamech's daughter, and sired the sedim, Assyrian guardian spirits. Azael, it is reported, is chained in a desert where he will remain until the day of judgement... In *Midrash Petirat Moshen*, Azael is mentioned as one of 2 angels (other being Ovza) who came down from heaven and was corrupted, Cornelius Agrippa, in his Occult Philosophy, list 4 evil angels as the opposite of the 4 Holy Rivers of the Elements; among the evil ones Azael, is included, Schwab in his *Vocabulaire de L'Angelologue* identifies Shamhazai (Semyaza) with Azael (Aziel), guardian of hidden treasures." [Davidson, 1971, p. 63.]

סהגם Sagham. Lesser angel governing triplicity by day of Leo [Crowley, 1977, p. 16]. "According to Levi, Transcendental Magic, Sagham is ruler with Seratiel of the sign of Leo in the Zodiac." [Davidson, 1971, p. 252.] see 155 for Godwin's spelling.

testiculi (Lt). testicles.

illuminati (Lt). The illuminated or enlightened ones. Literally, those filled with light. The truth or reality has dawned in them, and they in turn become light-bearers to the rest of humanity. Their evidence was made possible by those "reservoirs" mentioned above.

Regio Lucis (Lt). Kingdom of Light. The dwelling-place of the illuminati. See also the "region of light", described by Thomas Vaughan as the Birth place of Mercury. see 50, 58.

Terra Sancta (Lt). Holy Land. This phrase implies the perfected "body of Light", for only is such a body is the "holy Land" attained. see 52 (Lt), 56 (Lt).

109 (prime)

אם כל חי   Mother of all living. In Genesis 3:20: "And Adam called the name of his wife Eve (חוה, Nature) because she was Mother of all living things." see 18, 50, 51.

נדנה vigina. עגול circle, sphere. בקן lighting. אהפ air. [Nightside of Eden, p. 121]

מנוחה   rest, quietness; resting place. Numbers 10:33.

לעדה Inman: (1 Chron. 4:21), 'She determines, or she establishes.' [Ancient Faiths, VII, p. 200]

לעט taste (attributed to Teth); to swallow, greedily, gulp. With different pointing: *laoat*, food swallowed.

אחימן Brother of a portion (Ahiman) [Numbers 13:22]. Each brother of light has a portion of the responsibility to extend the light to others. see 372.

סחיאל Sachiel. Sachiel; "Covering of God." [Crowley, 1977, p. 16]. Angel ruling Jupiter and Thursday.

"...of the order of Hashmallim (Cherubim) Sachiel is resident of the first heaven (in some sources, the 6th heaven). He is a Monday (or Thursday or Friday) angel, invoked from the south (also from the west). In addition, he is a presiding spirit of the planet Jupiter. In Goetic lore, he is called a servitor of the 4 sub-planes of the infernal empire." [Davidson, 1971, p. 252.]

קט littleness, hence little, small. In Ezekiel 16:47: "You not only walked in their ways and copied their detestable practices, but, as if that were a very little thing, in all your ways you soon became more depraved than they."

"This root develops the ideas of resistance opposed to that of tension, of extension: Thence in a very broad sense the *Occident*; in a very restricted sense, *a stick*. The Arabic onomatopoetic and idiomatic root which depicts every kind of cut made without effort, as with a knife, etc. This root employed as adverbial relation is represented by *only, only so much, so little*." [d'Olivet, 1976, p. 441.]

אסכוזדאי   Askozdai. Day demon of the 2nd decanate of Aquarius [Crowley, 1977, p. 16].

צדידא Given without explanation in *Sepher Sephiroth* [Crowley, 1977, p. 16]. This word does not occur in scripture or in the Hebrew Lexicon.

Of צד d'Olivet writes: "That which is insidious, artful, double, sly, opposed, adverse, deceitful, seductive. The Arabic presents every idea of opposition, defense; a state of quarreling, disputing. In a literal sense, very restricted. *the side*; in a broad sense, *a secret. dissimulating hindrance an artifice. a snare.*" [d'Olivet, 1976, p. 432.] If we take Yod in this word as signifying the creative hand of God, then the first three letters suggest the secret of creativity.

Of דא: "This root which is only used in Hebrew in composition, is the analog of the root די, which bears the real character of the sign of natural abundance, and of division. In Chaldaic it has an abstract sense represented by the relations *of, of which, this, that, of what*. The Arabic characterizes a movement which is propagated without effort and without noise.

דאה Action of flying with rapidity; of swooping down on something: thence a דאה a kite; דיה a vulture. [ibid., 318-319]

αηρ. aer. Air. This word appears in Revelations 9:2: "And he [the fifth angel] opened the pit of the abyss, and a smoke ascended out of the Pit, as a smoke of a great furnace; and the sun and the air were darkened by the smoke of the pit." see Revelations 18:17; 1 Thessalonians 4:17.

Ηρα. Hera (Gr). Hera, the wife of Zeus (Jupiter). Literally, Chosen One.

aqua spherica (Lt). spherical water. Symbolized in Saint Germain's Trinosophia by a picture of the Bird of Hermes. The fiery solar fluid or mercurial water. see 372, 153.

aurae crucis (Lt). golden cross. The cross of 6 squares, belonging to the Rosicrucian order "which every brother carries on his breast." [Secret Symbols]. see 246, 66, 58, 62, 47 (Lt).

110

I. Sum of the first 10 even numbers from 2 to 20 inclusive.

II. Age of Joseph when he died.

אבן בהן The stone of Bohan (the son of Reuben) [Joshua 15:6]. Place-name Bohan means: The Dwarf. With different vowel points, Bohen: thumb, big-toe.

עלי upper, higher. With different pointing: *aeli*, pestle; pistil in flower.

סיטאל "God, hope of all creatures." 3rd Shem ha-Mephorash. 11E-15E inclusive. Genie: CHONTACR -Sun. Days: March 22, June 2, August 13, October 24, January 4. Invoke against adversities. [Psalm 91:2] "I will say of the Lord (יהוה) He is my refuge and my fortress: my God, in him will I trust." Time: 0:40 - 1:00 AM. Rules mobility, magnanimity, and great undertakings. Protects against weapons and ferocious beasts. One born under this influence loves truth, is true to his word, and goes gladly to help those in need on his services. Angel of the 3rd quinance [11°-15°] of Leo; angel by day of the 6 of Wands. see Appendix 10.

ומטהן Cherubic signs - Scorpio (night house of Mars) replaced by Aries (day house of Mars). The Cherubim are assigned to Yesod-Purifiers of the Foundation.

חבק to embrace, clasp; comprehend, comprise.

מוסד foundation, basis. In Isaiah 28:16: "A costly cornerstone of sure foundation."

אב האמונה Father of Faith.

דמיון resemblance, likeness, imagination, example. Name of the 24th Path of Nun (Intelligence of Resemblance). see 466, 470.

ימין the right hand, the right, the south, the southern quarter. "At the end of the days." South is the direction of the Fire and the Sun (or heart center).

נס A sign, flag, standard, ensign; signal, sign, miracle, wonderful or providential event. The sign of brotherhood in the unity of God is a wonderful event. In Isaiah 49:22: "Thus says the Lord God: behold, I will lift up my hand to the gentiles and set up my standard to the nations; and they shall bring your sons in their arms, and your daughters shall be carried upon their shoulders."

"Every idea of vacillation, agitation, literally as well as figuratively: That which wavers, which renders uncertain wavering. In a restricted sense, *a flag, an ensign, the sail* of a ship: in a broader sense, a movement of *irresolution, uncertainty*; from the idea of *flag* develops that of *putting in evidence, raising*: from the idea of *irresolution*, that of *tempting, of temptation.*

The Arabic describes the noise of a thing floating, as water; consequently, characterizing-literally, that which imitates the movement of waves; figuratively, that which is given over to such a movement." [d'Olivet, 1976, p. 402.]

עם people, populace, nation; kinsman. All are united in resemblance by the foundation stone. With different pointing: *em*: with, together with; by, close to, beside; while, during, as long as. In Daniel 2:43: "And just as you saw the iron mixed with baked clay, so the people will be a mixture and will not remain united, and more than iron mixes with clay." see 1186, 670 and Leviticus 16:33.

"Matter universalized by its faculties: tendency of its parts one toward another; the force which makes them gravitate toward the general mass, which brings them to aggregation, accumulation, conjunction; the force whose unknown cause is expressed, by the relation *with, toward, among, at*. Every idea of union, unction, conjunction, nearness: *a bond, a people, a corporation.*" [d'Olivet, 1976, p. 418.]

עיל height, heaven. see 116.

נין descendant, son. see Isaiah 14:22.

Protheus (Lt). Version of Proteus - A prophet and God of the sea, with the power of changing himself into different shapes. hence, change. "Rota Mundi for that displaying the greatest artifice, and Protheus for the most profitable." [*Fama* p. 5]

unicornis (Lt). Unicorn. "Hear without terror that in the forest are hidden a deer and a unicorn. In the body there is Soul and Spirit" [Waite, 1974, vol. 1, figure 3, p. 281] see 56, 79 (Lt). "If we apply the parable to our Art, We shall call the forest the Body... The unicorn will be the spirit at all times. The deer sesires no other name But that of the Soul... He that know how to tame and master them by Art, To couple them together, and to lead them in and out of the forest, May justly be called a master." [ibid, 280]

crux rosea (Lt). Rosy cross. "The crux rosea, or rosy cross, might simply be a cross of that color- e.g. 'red with precious blood'... This was the general or characteristic sign, adopted when the title of rosy cross was formulated as a symbol. When the brotherhood in one of its revivals or developments became ordo roseae et aureae crucis, the emblem was a golden cross emblazoned with a red rose." [Waite, 1993, p. 102]

111

I. Sum of each line of the magic square of the Sun. see Appendix 8.

אלף letter-name Aleph Ox, bull. The activity whereby the ONE reflects itself to itself, and so produces the number 2. The first out-pouring of spiritual influence into the realm of experience. With different pointing: 1. eleph. a thousand, family, clan, cattle; 2. *illafe*. to teach, instruct, train, to learn, to slip, to guide.

פלא wonderful, admirable, mystical, marvelous, hidden, extraordinary. 1st Path of Kether, the Crown and associated with the Rosicrucian grade of Ipsissimus (He who is most himself). The Admirable or Mystical Intelligence. The reversal of the meaning of Aleph, whereby the limitless light is condensed by a contracting spiral into the first point or the crown. Used in Hebrew Isaiah 9:6 as the first of a series of divine names. With different pointing: to divide, separate, distinguish. Root meaning is that which is set off; miracle. Refers to the initial act of apparent division, or separation, whereby manifestation is begun. *Pehleh* suggest that Aleph's power in the 11th path of Aleph is like a reflection of the power of Kether. see 157, 507, 620, 579, 876, 831, 142, 217, 242, 311, 255, 532, 364

פלא to search, to make special (vows). see 164.

אבן חן A precious stone; stone of grace; jewel. The alchemist's "Stone of the Wise." The realization that the One Ego in Tiphareth is identical to the cosmic Life-Force in Chokmah. In Proverbs 17:8, Chane חן, signifies grace, favor, something precious, goodwill. It forms the initials of *Chokmah Nestawrah*, "The Secret Wisdom," i.e. Qabalah. see 53, 58, 788.
In Proverbs 17:8: "A bribe is like a bright, precious stone that dazzles the eyes and affects the mind of him who gives it; [as if by magic] he prospers whichever way he turns." [Amplified]

The Zohar [IV:1840, pp. 126-127] observes: "The lower world is always in a receptive state- being called 'a good (precious) stone'-and the upper world only communicates to it according to the condition in which it is found at any given time. If it shows a smiling countenance, light and joy from the world above pour down upon it; but if it be sad and downcast, it receives the severity of judgement, as it written 'worship the Lord in Joy' [Psalm 100:2]. That the joy of man may draw down upon him supernal joy. So, too, does the lower sphere affect the upper: according to the degree of awakening below there is awakening and heavenly joy above. Therefore the Israelites hast to awaken the voice of the trumpet, which is compounded of fire, water and wind, and all are made one and the voice ascends and strikes that 'precious stone' [אבן חן = אלף], which then receives the various colors of this voice and then draws down upon itself the attribute from above according to the color which it shows. And when it is duly prepared by this voice, mercy issues from on high and rest upon it, so that it is enfolded in mercy, both above and below."

אחד הוא אלהים One is he, Creative Power is One, The Lord is One. The first word refers to Chokmah, the second to Kether, and the third to Binah. It sums up the powers of the first 3 Sephiroth.

אפל thick darkness, obscurity; gloom. figuratively, misfortune. יהוה said he dwelt in the thick darkness. In Job 28:3, אבן אפל, "The stone (concealed in) thick darkness.

כיפא Aramaic name for Peter; the Rock [Kephas]. see 3, 12 21, 30, 39, 48, 57, 66, 75, 84, 93, 102, 120.

אדמוני red; reddish, red-haired. Described of Esau. [Genesis 25:25]. see 45.

אסן ruin, destruction, sudden death.

מהלל mad; jolly, jovial. see Key 0, the Fool.

עלוה Olvah. Duke of Edom, a hidden reference to Daath. In Isaiah 21:11: "The oracle concerning Edom [Dumah, דומה], One keeps calling me from Sier [reference to Edom, משעיר, from Sier],'Watchman how far gone is the night?' 'Watchman, how far gone is the night?' [literally, what is the time of the night]

עולה a step, a staircase. The graded ascent of evolutionary development. With different pointing: 1. oleh. one going up, a pilgrim, a new settler, immigrant; 2. avela: a burnt-offering, a sacrifice. Refers to the self-offering of the Life-power in the perpetual sacrifice of cosmic manifestation.

ובאבנים and in (vessels of) stone. In Exodus 7:20: "Stretch out thy hand upon the waters of Egypt...that there may be blood throughout all the land of Egypt, both in vessels of wood, and in vessels of stone." With different pointing: vo-baehbanim. Spirits (of Daath). see 671.

סאים a dry measure for grain (1/3 of an epha). In Isaiah 27:8: "In measure when it shoots forth [i.e. the blossoming of Israel], thou will debate with it: he stays his rough wind in the day of the east wind."

יצוה will command.

מסוה. a veil, or face covering [Exodus 34:33].

אנס to commit rape; to take by force, rob. With different pointing: anaws, robber, violent man.

יהויכין Proper name: "Appointed by God."

לעבדה to till it (the Garden of Eden). From עבד awbad, to work, labor; to till, cultivate; to serve, worship.

נכיאל Angle (intelligence) of the Sun. see 666.

"In the Qabalah, the intelligence of the Sun, when the sun enters the sign of Leo. Nachiel's corresponding spirit is Sorath, according to Paracelsus's doctrine of Talismans." [Davidson, 1971, p. 203.]

עולה young girl. The "bride", Malkuth, after being married to the "King", Tiphareth. Aleph, the "eternal youth."

כהני יהוה Priest of the Lord. In Isaiah 61:6: "And you shall be named the priest of the Lord: men shall call you the ministers of our God. You shall eat the riches of the gentiles, and in their glory shall you boast yourselves."

אלוה God, deity. Written as a tetractys:

א	= 1
א ל	= 31
א ל ו	= 37
א ל ו ה	= 42
	= 111

This word is 42 by itself. The Alephs = 4, the 3 Lameds = 90, the 2 Vavs = 12 and the single Heh = 5. This is concealed the formula 4 + 90 + 12 + 5 as well as 1 + 31 + 37 + 42. see אהבה.

οικια. hoika (Gr). House, abode, residence; family. These all describe our relation to the Life-power.

εννεα. enna (Gr). Nine. the number of a complete cycle. see Luke 17:17.

E pluribus (Lt). From many, out of many. Used on the Great Seal of the U.S. Describes the apparent multiplicity of forms of the One Unity.

Trifolium (Lt). Trefoil.

AOM (Lt). Equivalent to AUM, the Hindu Pranava or sacred syllable, commonly written OM.

argent vive (Lt). living silver (Mercury).

gloria mundi (Lt). glory of the world. The Emerald Tablet says: "So thou hast the glory of the whole world; therefore let all obscurity flee thee..."

112

I. (7 x 16) or 7 x 2^4

II. Area of each of the curtains of the tabernacle in Exodus 26:1.

אל אלים God of gods (Daniel 11:36). see 672.

חסידך Thy Holy One; Thy Godly One. (Psalm 16:10).

יהוה אלהים IHVH Elohim. The Lord God. The special Divine Name of Binah, the third Sephirah. This name shows she is the active agency whereby the inciting and masculine power of Chokmah (IHVH) is made manifest in the work of creation. see 42, 52, 67, 86, 199, 265.

I. Genesis 2:4: "These are the generations of the heavens and the earth when they were created, in the day that the Lord God [Jehovah Elohim] made the earth and the heavens."

II. I.R.Q. Para 735: "Jehovah Elohim, is the full name of the most ancient of all, and of Microprosopus; and when joined together they are the full name. But the other forms are *not* called the full name." [Mathers, 1993, p. 202]

III. I.R.Q. Para 795: "The Holy Name, because it is written, Genesis 2:7: 'And יהוה אלהים, *Tetragrammaton Elohim*, created ADM, *Adam, Man*,' with the full Name, which is *Tetragrammaton Elohim*, analogous to him (Adam), seeing that *Tetragrammaton*, nenotes the masculine, and *Elohim*, the Feminine.*"

* "For Elohim, is form the feminie toot ALH, and is really a feminine plural, for while many masculines from their plural in ות, many feminies conversely form theirs in ים. In both these cases, however, the gender of the singular is retained in the plural."

כבד אלהים Glory of God. In Proverbs 25:2: "It is the glory of God (Elohim) to conceal a thing, and the glory of kings is to search out a matter." כבד has connotation of weight and gravitation, as well as "glory". see 32, 672, 619 (Greek).

בינה אדם the understanding of man. The first property of the Life-power, that limits and compresses (Saturn) to produce the frames or forms of all things, is an essential part of the constitution of man. In Proverbs 30:2: "Surely I am more brutish than any man, and have not the understanding of a man." see 672.

בעלי masters.

ואדם אין and no man. In Genesis 2:5: "When no plant of the field was yet in the earth, and no herb of the field had yet sprung up, the Lord God had not [yet] caused it to rain upon the earth, and there was no man to till the ground."

חדק sharpness; brier. With different pointing: to press into, drive in.

דבוק joining, attachment; glue; solder. With different pointing: *dybbuk*, a ghost possessing man's body. As an adjective, joined, attached.

איעאל "God, delight of the children of man." 67th Shem ha-Mephorash. 331E-335E. ABIOU-Saturn. May 25, August 5, October 16, December 27, March 9. 10:00-10:20 AM. [Psalm 37:4] ("Daleth") "Resign thyself unto the Lord (ליהוה) and wait patiently for him; fret not thyself because of him who prospers in his way, because of the man who brings wicked desire to pass." For consolation in adversities, and to acquire wisdom. Rules changes, the preservation of monuments, longevity. Influences the occult sciences. Brings knowledge and truth to those who have recourse to him (the Shem ha-Mephorash) in their works. Person born: Will be illuminated by the spirit of God; loves solitude, distinguishes himself in the transcendent sciences; principally astronomy, physics, and philosophy. Angel of the 1st quinance [1E-5E] of Cancer and angel by day of the 2 of Cups. This represents the operation of Chokmah, sphere of the Zodiac, in Briah, the creative world. see 81 & Appendix 10.

הקבה "A name of God; *notariqon* [acronym] *Ha-Qodosh Baruk-Hu*, 'The Holy One, blessed be He.'" [Godwin. 1999, p. 516.]

omnia ad unum (Lt). all into one. see 46, 61 (Lt).

αγγελο. Aggelo (Gr). angel. Angel means messenger and may refer to illuminated men. see 386 (Greek).

Lac Virginis (Lt). Virgin's Milk. First Matter. An unctuous, oily "water" or chyle-a milky, fatty lymph which is one of the principal means whereby the blood is supplied with the energy derived from food. Formed in the Virgo region of the small intestine and contains compounds of oxygen, hydrogen, carbon, the esoteric fire (sulfur), water (mercury) and earth (salt). The form of the first matter used by adepts to perform the Great Work.

Prima Materia (Lt). First Matter. The substance of all things, the divine spiritual energy or mind-stuff, to be sought by alchemist in the "Bowels of the Earth" (see above). Manifested through subconsciousness.

I. "And thus we understand here the essence of all beings, and that it is a magical essence, as a will can create itself in the essential life, and so enter into a birth, and in the great mystery, in the origin of fire, awaken a source which before was not manifest, but lay hidden in mystery like a gleam in the multiplicity of colors; as we have a mirror of this in the devils and in all malignity. And we recognize also form whence all things, evil and good, take their origin, namely from the imagination of the great mystery, where a wonderful essential life generates itself." [Böhme. 1980, V, p. 160.] Paul Case adds: "Hence for Jacob Boehme 'the imagination in the great mystery' is the Prima Materia, or first matter."

II. Waite: "The endless energy and unsearchable Primum Mobile [130] are represented by the trinity, which produces the Fiat [31] and produces nature in the mode of Prima Materia, otherwise chaos [42]." [Waite, 1993, p. 22]

Sella turcica. Turkish saddle; a protective bone covering the pituitary body, a "skull within a skull". The Pituitary is the focus of the Moon center.

corporalis (Lt). of the body; substance, essence of. see 277 (Lt).

113 (prime)

אבן בחן a tried stone [Isaiah 28:16]. Reference to the mystical lamb with seven horns [Secret Symbols, p. 35]. The lamb is KR (CR), and the 7 horns are the personified powers of the brethren who helped C.R. found the Rosicrucian order. see 137, 220, 314, 1483, 1973.

הבונים the builders. In Psalm 118:22: "The stone which the builders refused is become the headstone of the corner." This is a reference to the Messiah or Christos. see 1389 (Greek), 673.

מה-הבנאי what! the builders! see 45, 108.

מה-הבונה Power of the Builder. Observe that 113 is the result from [what! the builders!], an interpretation accepted by many modern commentators, and that is equivalent numerically to מכבנא (knoll), which closely approximates the continental form. see 311.

הנאהבים the lovers, the beloved. Title of Key 6 [Zain]. In 2 Samuel 1:23: "Saul and Jonathan were lovely [beloved] and pleasant in their lives, and in their death they were not divided: they were swifter than eagles, they were strong than lions." (David's lament at news of the death of Saul, and Saul's son Jonathan). From נאה, "comely, becoming, befitting."

בעולה Beulah, espoused. In Isaiah 62:4: "Thou shall no more be termed forsaken; neither shall thy land any more be termed desolate: but thou shall be called Hephzibah ["my delight is in her, 192], and thy land *Beulah*: for the Lord delights in thee, and thy land shall be married." A reference to the New Jerusalem ["Abode of Peace"] of prophecy.

סליחה forgiveness, pardon; penitential.

נחמיה Nehemiah, "Yah comforts"; name of a

Persian cup-bearer to the king who helped the Jews rebuild the wall of Jerusalem after their return form exile. See Nehemiah 1:1.

פלג a stream brook [Crowley, 1977, p. 16]. The proper name Peleg, son of Eber; father of Reu." In Genesis 10:25: "Two sons were born to Eber: one was named Peleg, because in this time the earth was divided; his brother was named Joktan." Also known as *Phaleg*; Olympic planetary sprit of Mars.

"Ruling prince of the order of angels. Phalec is also the governing spirit of the planet Mars (and hence often referred to, as he is by Corellus Agrippa, as the war lord). Of the 106 Olympic provinces, Phalec has dominion over 35. His day, for invocation, is Tuesday. According to Agrippa, heaven has 196 provinces, with 7 supreme angles governing them, of whom Phalec is one... In white magic, Phaleg is one of the 7 stewards of heaven." [Davidson, 1971, pp. 223-224.]

sepulcrum (Lt). seplchre; tomb, resting-place. The inner light embodied in physical form. Part of a phrase found written on the altar of the vault of Brother C.R. see 122 (Lt).

Dues et homo (Lt). God and Man.

legis jugum (Lt). yoke of the law. The 2nd motto found in the Vault of Brother C.R. in the *Fama* allegory. see 170, 65, 155, 136, 574 (Lt).

The motto was written around a circle enclosing the figure of an ox.The ox is attributed to the sign Taurus which rules the next and the same place the yoke is placed. Yoke is derived from the Sanskrit word *yoga*, which roughly means practice. Thus the yoke of the law is the spiritual practices necessary whereby the seeker of illumination overcomes the bonds of material form. These practices awaken the chakra located near the throat, hinted at in the Fama by the death of Brother P.A.L. who dies in Cyprus (see 870). Yoga kills out the sense of separateness, and thus awaken the realization of union (*jugum*). Then we realize that there was no actual sacrife, for we have given up the illusion of death and have gained the ALL.

Mesericordia (Lt). Mercy. Equivalent to Chesed (72).

propinqua (Lt). now; the present time, i.e.

eternity.

Radix David (Lt). Root of David. see 137, 50 Latin.

spiritum (Lt). spirit. As spelled in an inscription found in the vault of C.R. in the Rosicrucian allegory. It includes the phrase: "Through the Holy Spirit we become alive again." see 683 Latin, 119.

114

גלה סודו he reveals his secret [Amos 3:7]. Written of God's revelation of his purposes to prophets. see 38, 76.

דמע juice (of grapes or olives), wine or oil (literally tears of olives or grapes); tear, the priest's share of fruit. As the metathesis of מרע, this suggest creative imagination (Daleth) impregnating the power of substance (Mem), to produce the "juice" or drops (tears) or radiant Yod force. "Wine" is associated with blood, and this has its implications in the microcosm. "Oil" is connected with the serpent-power (Teth). With different pointing: to shed tears, weep. see 44.

מלמד teacher, tutor (evidently the root is Lamed).With different pointing: 1. ox-goad; 2. *maylumawd*, trained, skilled, learned; scholar, man of learning. Teaching and training is a key to knowledge of "wine" and "oil". see 74.

חנון gracious, merciful; obliging, indulgent. The supreme attainment is by the grace and mercy of God. see 108.

גמליאל Gamaliel. Qlippoth of Yesod [Crowley, 1977, p. 17]. They are called "The Obscene Ones." Also called "Reward of God", "recompense of God."

I. "Levi in his *Philosophie Occulte* rate Gamaliel as evil, 'an adversary of the Cherubim', serving under Lilth (who is the demon of debauchery). In the *Revelation of Adam to His son Seth* (a Coptic apocalypse), Gamaliel is one of the high, holy, celestial powers whose mission is 'to draw the elect up to Heaven.'" [Davidson, 1971, p. 120.] This suggest that when the powers of subconsciousness are purified they are God's reward; unpurified they are keys to hell.

II. "Da'ath was the cosmic moon and the source of the illusion of phenomenlity, i.e. the ego; Yesod was the astral or celestial moon, the moon of magic and witchcraft...Da'ath is to the supernal triad what Yesod is to the infernal triad, and it is significant that the Qilphotic image which the Jews assigned to Yesod was that of Gamaliel, the obscene ass. According to Sharpe the head of the ass is an Egyptian hieroglyphic determinative having the numerical equivalent of 30, which shows its relationship to the lunar current and the month of 30 days divided into three parts, each of ten days... (p. 112) elsewhere he says that "the formula of Gamaliel" is that of the 'obscene woman' whose zoomorphic symbol is the ass which the templars were accused of worshiping." [Grant, 1994, p. 263.]

גיהנום Gehenna; Hell. The valley of the 'sons of Hinnom', near Jerusalem; the place where in ancient times children were sacrificed to the God Moloch. Later Jewish abhorrence of this practice caused the name Genenna, to be used as a name for Sheol, or hell. [Standard Bible dictionary, p. 426]. It was seen as the place of eternal torment, where refuse of all sorts was subsequently cast, for the consumption of which fires were kept constantly burning. [Brewer's Dictionary of Phrase and Fable, p. 392]. see 13, 14, 674.

claustrum (Lt). bar, bolt, bounds, cloister.
In the *Fama* Brother C.R. was placed in a cloister until he was 5. A cloister, indicates the state of limitation and bondage prior to liberation. To be placed in a cloister is to be shut away and separated from the rest of mankind. The soul assumes the burdens of the apparent limitations imposed by its incarnation in human personality. In John: "The Logos (Christos) became flesh, and tabernacle among us; and we beheld his radiance, a radiance as a son one-begotten from a father, full of grace and truth." The spiritual motivation come from the awakening of our desire by an impulse originating in the universal and indivisible self. Unless this eager longing is stirred, the indwelling Christos remains locked in the cloister of the 5-sense life. Thus all mystery rites agrees that the first preparation of a candidate for initiation must be in the heart.

propinqua (Lt). now; the present time. i.e. eternity.

conclusus (Lt). enclosed, confined, shut up.

Implies spirit encompassed within the limitations of form. Part of a phrase. see 204.

115

יעלה went up [Genesis 2:6]. "A mist went up." (אלה to go up, ascend). see 512.

עזאזל Azazel. "God strengthens." Demon, devil. As an interrogation: "to Hell!" לזאול-Hebrew Lexicon. Azazel or Azael is one of the chiefs of the 200 fallen angels. He is the scapegoat of Rabbinic literature.

I. "Demon Prince of Air." [Godwin. 1999, p. 516.]

II. Inman: Scape Goat. (Leviticus 16:8), Azazel. Among all the names I have hitherto examined, there is none which has given me so much trouble as Azazel. There is doubt whether it is the cognomen given by the writer to a being, to a locality, or simply to an animal driven away. Adopting the belief that Azazel is spoken of as antithesis to Jehovah. The cognomen originally stood as עזז אל *azaz El*, which signifies 'the strong El, 'the being who causes misfortune, disease, and death;' in other words, 'the demon of destruction.' [Ancient Faiths, Vol. 2, pp. 704-705]

דמליאל Damlial. Geomantic intelligence of Virgo. The sign is ruled by Mercury. Note the first two letter דם are the word for Blood, and the connection with self-conscious creation. see 44.

הנני Here am I, Here I am. With different pointing: behold. The I AM is everywhere, and everything. see 400, 1973, 2478, 2965, Isaiah 28:16.

חום היום the heat of the day. חם Khem is the root of the words alchemy and chemistry; יום, yom or "day" means the manifest. see 48, 56.

חזק to be strong; be firm, to hold vast, to press, be urgent; to be hard, be severe, vehement, eager.

סנה thorn-bush, thorn.

אלידע "God knows". The father of Rezon ("Prince") or Zabah. In 1 Kings 11:23: "And God stirred him up [Pharaoh] another adversary, Rezon the son of Eliadam." see 263.

פהל 20th Shem ha-Mephorash, short form. see 130 & Appendix 10.

116

גלגלים whirlings, whirling motion. The initial motion which begins every cycle of manifestation, great and small. Galgalim is term for the sum total of the manifestations of the cosmic forces which have their beginning in Kether. The Path of Malkuth in any world is always a receptacle for the total forces and activities expressed by that world. Thus the primal formative forces corresponding to Kether in Yetzirah, and the formative powers of Ruach which express through man as his dominion over all that is below. see 575, 1032.

אפלה darkness [Exodus 10:22]. The "thick darkness" where IHVH dwells. see 444, 328, 126.

יונים doves.
עילאה Primordial.

הללויה praise the Lord. Note, this is a strange spelling, three Lamed's. The Lexicon gives this spelling הללויה ("Praise ye the Lord"). Blessing and praise are transmuting powers. see 86.

ינון Yinnon, symbolic name of the Messiah [Hebrew Lexicon]. Note that it consist of Yod, the "creative hand" + נון Nun, the letter-name for Nun or "fish", the reproductive power. Thus "hand+fish." The early Christians used the symbol of the fish to represent Christ. see 10, 106, 1219 (Greek).

מכון fixed place, foundation; institute, institution; name of one of the 7 heavens; heaven of Chesed. With different pointing: 1. *mekahen* a kind of tool, vise; 2. *mekuawn*, in a line; a corresponding; exact, precise. The benevolent lines of heaven (Jupiter) are connected with the foundation (Moon) of the earth (Chesed and Yesod).

נדיבים The munificent ones. Those who have established the above connection, i.e. the Chasidim. [from נדיבה nobility, nobleness, excellency]. see 71.

בטן האדמה the bowels of the earth. A reference as to where the alchemical first matter may be found in the microcosm. בטן beten = womb = אין ain or nothing. אדם Adam = man or humanity = Aleph = spirit + דם dam = blood or spirit immersed in blood. This is the אדמה adamah or earth of Chesed = 50 = Nun = מי, water. see 61, 45, 50, 44.

האלף Halaph, Halphas, i.e. אלף-ה ("the spirit"); Goetic demon #38 by night of the 2nd decanate of Aries. The 2nd decanate of Aries is also attributed to the 3 of Wands in the Tarot minor arcana. This corresponds to the operation of Binah (Saturn) in the archetypal world of Atziluth. See Appendix 11 & 116.

Goetia: "He is a great earl, and appears in the from of a stock-dove. He speaks with a hoarse voice. his office is to build up towers, and to furnish the with ammunition and weapons, and to send Men-of-War to places appointed. He rules over 26 Legions of Spirits." [Mathers, 1995, p. 48]

המליאל Hamaliel. Archangel of Virgo. "Angel of the month of August, one of the rulers of the order of virtues, and governor of the sign of Virgo-all the foregoing according to Trithemius. In ceremonial magic, the governor of Virgo is Voil or Voe." [Davidson, 1971, p. 134.]

פול Phul. Phur; Olympian Planetary Sprit of the Moon. Also: Pul, a King of Assyria, also known as Tiglath-Pileser III in 2 Kings 15:19: "Then Pul king of Assyria invaded the land, and Menahem gave him a thousand talents of silver to gain his support and strengthen his hold of the kingdom."

"(Phuel) - Lord of the Moon and ruler of 7 of the Olympian Provinces. As a Monday angel, Phul is to be invoked only on Monday. In the cabalistic works of Cornelius Agrippa, Phul's sigil is given. There he is called 'Lord of the powers of the moon and supreme lord of the waters.'"

[Davidson, 1971, p. 226.]

כסלו Kislev, the third Hebrew month, November-December, corresponding roughly to the period when the sun is in Sagittarius. [Zechariah 7:1] "In the forth year of King Darius, the word of the Lord came to Zechariah on the fourth day of the night month of Keslev."

גמיגין Gamigin. Goetic demon by day of the 1st decanate of Taurus. see Appendix 11.

Goetia: "...a Great Marquis. He appears in the from of a little Horse or Ass, and then into Human shape does he change himself at the request of the Master. He speaks with a hoarse voice. He rules over 30 Legions of Inferiors. He teaches all Liberal Sciences, and gives account of Dead Souls that died in sin." [Mathers, 1995, p. 11]

Lux occulta (Lt). Hidden Light. A name for Kether. see 364, 49, 67.

philosophia (Lt). philosophy. In more ancient usage this had to do with occult investigation. see 193 Latin, 100.

lapis solis (Lt). stone of the sun. "I have called it by various names, but the simplest is perhaps that of 'Hyle' [438, Greek], or first principle or all things. It is also denominated the One Stone of the Philosophers, composed of hostile elements, the stone of the sun, the seed of the metals... by these and may other names it is called, yet it is only *one*." [Waite, 1974, vol. 1, p. 186]

117

I. Diagonal of a rectangle (45 x 108).

איננו he (was) not [Genesis 5:24]. Refers to Enoch "for the Elohim took Him". As אש sometimes signifies "to be present, to be near, at hand; so *Ain* is used in the contrary sense, "to be not present, or, at hand." Therefore איננו means: he was not present, or was no more." see 183, 123, 784, 1047.

מלאך יהוה Angel of IHVH [2 Kings 1:3]. In the quotation a Vav precedes the first letter of Malak ("and"). Malak also means: messenger.

see 91, 605, and Exodus 3:2 (burning bush).

קביה Cube. From קוביא, Kebeyah: die, dice. see 119, 147.

אופל fog, darkness. The "thick darkness" of the unmanifest, where dwells the presence of deity. see 116, 126.

אלוף Duke, chief, head of family or tribe; friend, intimate companion; tame, docile; to champion in a game; guide. A metathesis of *aophel*. Note that this word contains the letters of אלף Aleph, the Life-Breath or Spirit combined with Vav or intuition, inserted between Lamed (ox-goad, teaching, balance) and Peh (creative word, Mars). The above meaning all have to do with Aleph. see 837.

זעם to be enraged, to be angry, anger; wrath; to be indignant; to denounce. The cutting power of (Zain, sword, Mercury) through the agency of Ayin (eye, of appearances, Capricorn) affecting Mem (Water, of consciousness). Anger is produced through misunderstanding the appearances of separation and is the result of fear of these delusions. see 677, 743.

עבדיאל "Servant of God." [Book of the Angel Raziel]. According to Milton, the "Flaming Seraph" who routs rebel angels among Satan's Host on the first day of fighting in heaven. Name of a resident of Gilead (גלעד, meaning hard, firm). See 1 Chronicles 5:15.

118

חלף to pass, renew, change, pass away, to pass through, pierce, to came anew, sprout again. With different pointing: 1. *kheleph*. to exchange, to return for; in place of; shoot, reed; 2. *khelaph*. slaughtering knife.

חסן strength; Chassan, ruler of Air.

כהן גדול High Priest, Hierophant. (Serpent Power page 148). see 106, 136, 128.

חמע in alchemy, vinegar, With different pointing: to ferment. see 830.

הנביאים the prophets. In Amos 3:7: "Surely the Lord will do nothing, but he reveals his secret unto his servants the prophets." see 402, 76, 92.

המיגין Hamigin. Hamigin or Gamigin; Goetic demon by day of the first decanate of Taurus. The demon's name suggest faulty vision or reason (Heh), stabilized into reversal of dependence on universal life (reality) (Mem), willing itself (Yod) into patterns of memory (Gimel) which link it to union (Yod) with cycles of reproductive error (Nun). The first decanate of Taurus, ruled by Venus has the qualities of devoted, artistic, sympathetic. The influence of the demon suggest conscious imbalance resulting in the opposite negative qualities. This decanate is also attributed to the 5 of Pentacles, or Geburah, sphere of Mars, in Assiah, the material world. When negatively aspected, as here, it can mean toil unrewarded; loss of money; poverty; and trouble through lack of imagination and foresight. The remedy is to welcome change and desire perpetual transformations instead of embalming oneself in some set form of existence. Personal will must be seen as the instrument of universal will. see 766.

D'Olivet comments on הם: "Universalized life: the vital power of the universe. Onomatopoetic and idiomatic root, which indicates every kind of tumultuous noise, commotion, fracas. The Arabic characterizes, in general, that which is heavy, painful agonizing. It is literally *a burden, care perplexity.* As verb expresses the action of *being disturbed,* of *interfering,* of bustling about to do a thing." [d'Olivet, 1976, p. 331.]

אדם בליאל Adam Belial. Arch-demon corresponding (according to Waite) to Chokmah, Belial means unprofitable or wicked; Adam means man or humanity; thus "wicked Man" or "wicked men". In apocalyptic literature Belial (under the form of Beliar) is personified and identified with the Genius of all evil, Satan, and was formerly of the Order of Virtues, as well as having been created (as Belair) next after Lucifer.

Waite: "When the Adam and Eve of Genesis partook of the forbidden fruit, their fall confounded the good with the evil cortices, that of Adam with the male shells of Samel or Adam Belial...the nations of the world can be destined

only to return whence they came, and Adam Belial is obviously not under the law... to put the position tersely, the souls of the Israelites were distributed in the members of the protoplastic Adam, regarded in his mystical extension through the four worlds, and the souls of the gentiles [i.e. "Nations", גוים, 59] in the members of Adam Belial, belonging to the aversetres." [Waite, 1992, p. 419] see 73, 45.

העם 38th Shem ha-Mephorash. short form. see 132, 133, 678 & Appendix 10.

זימימאי Zimimay. Demon king of the north [Godwin, 1999, p. 351]. see Appendix 11.

"Zimimar (Zimmar) – 'the lordly monarch of the North', a title given him by Shakespeare." [Davidson, 1971, p. 328.]

ριζα. riza (Gr). a root; source from which it comes.

spirituale (Lt). spiritual. see 200.

lapis magnus (Lt). great stone; i.e. the stone of the wise, or philosopher's stone. see 51 (Lt), 52 (Hebrew).

119

I. The vertical axis of a completed pyramid like that of the seal of the U.S.

הוא יבנה לי He shall build me a house. In 1 Chronicles 17:12: "He shall build me a house and I will establish his throne forever." see 12, 67, 40, 107, 1244, 1363.

ויאבק and wrestled [Genesis 32:24]. see 113.

טעם taste, flavor; sense, discretion, discernment; decree, command; reason, cause, intonation, accent, good discernment in [Psalm 119:66.

דמעה Tear. weeping.

כמו אבן like a stone. Refers to pharaoh's chariots and men sinking in the read sea "like a stone." In Exodus 11:5: "The deeps covered them and they went down into its depths like a stone." see 66, 53.

פגול abominable, a foul thing, refuse, an abominated sacrifice. What is rejected in the building of the stone are those elements and negative patterns in personality which are obstructing the free flow of light.

אבן בוחן a tried stone, (variant spelling); Lydian stone; examined or inspector stone. see 113. The stone is consciousness.

בעלזבוב Beelzebub. Lord of the Flies, "Fly-GOD" [Crowley, 1977, p. 18]. "Archfiend" in the Hebrew Lexicon and associated with Chokmah. Chief of the 9 evil hierarchies of the underworld (Qlippoth). From זבוב "to fly".

I. 2 Kings 1:3: "But the angel of the Lord said unto Elijah the Tishbite, arise, go up to meet the messengers of the king of Samaria, and say unto them, is it not because there is not a God in Israel, that ye go to inquirer of Beelzebub the God of Ekron?

II. Originally a Syrian God. "In Matthew 10:25, Mark 3:22, and Luke 11:15, Beelzebub is chief of the demons, 'prince of the devils' (as in Matthew 12:24), but he is to be distinguished from Satan (just as he is in all magic, medieval or otherwise)... In the *Gospel of Nicodemus*, Christ, during his 3 days in hell, gives Beelzebub dominion over the underworld in gratitude for permitting him (Christ) over Satan's objections, to take Adam and the other 'saints in prison' to Heaven... Another of his titles was 'Lord of Chaos', as given in the gnostic writings of Valentinus... " [Davidson, 1971, p. 72.]

חאלף Night demon of 2nd decanate of Leo. This decanate is ruled by Jupiter and suggest subconscious imbalance, resulting in unkindness, intolerance and boorishness. Note that it contains the same letters as חלף to change, renew, with the addition of Aleph (Uranus) between Cheth (Cancer, Moon) and Lamed (Libra, Venus). This imbalance is seen to be the result of the higher octave of Mercury, or spirit. see 118.

בן אוני name given to Benjamin (162, "son of the right hand") by his mother. In Genesis 35:18: "And it came to pass, as her soul was in departing (for she died) that she called his name Benoni: but her father called him Benjamin." **בן אוני** = 52+67, so that it = **בן בינה** (67), and

thus suggest (בן) תפארת and בינה (אימא). see 162, 52, 67, 1081.

fraternitas (Lt). fraternity, brotherhood. see 421 (Lt).

in cruce rosea (Lt). in the rosy cross [Secret Symbols page 35]. All brothers in the rosy cross form the fraternity of spirit. see 224, 88.

natura humana (Lt). Human nature. The first word is 67, corresponding to Binah, and the second is 52, the value of Ben, the son.

verbum vita (Lt). living word [Secret Symbols page 31]. The son, Tiphareth, is the Living Word, or the Logos.

spiritus (Lt). spirit. The son is also the spirit Ruach (214), the human spirit links Neshamah (the Soul of God, seat in Binah) to Nefesh (the Animal Soul, attributed to Yesod). see 132, 175, 214, 496, 243, 60, 64 Latin, 113.

spiraculum (Lt). A breathing hole, a vent. The triad or triangle (equilateral) is like a vent or spiracle, through which the influence of the Life-breath enters and leaves the field of manifestation. In Secret Symbols, the word is connected with both Life and Death. see 251 (Lt).

Saturnus (Lt). Saturn. Builder of form; sphere of Binah, the cosmic mother; one of the seven planetary centers. see 713, 400, 406, 67.

sperma mundi (Lt). seed of the world. "The Philosopher's Stone is called the most ancient, secret or unknown, natural, incomprehensible, heavenly, blessed, sacred Stone of the Sages... In the writings of the sages we may also find it spoken of as the *Catholic Magnesia* [129 Latin], or the seed of the world, and under many other names and titles of a like nature, which we may best sum up and comprehend in the perfect number of one thousand." [Waite, 1974, vol. 1, p. 97] see 64 (Lt), 1000.

120

I. (3 x 5 x 8)

II. Σ15 = 120

III. The number of years which elapsed from the "death" of C.R. until his sepulcher was opened.

The perfected consciousness and life of an illuminated man. See Genesis 6:3.

IV. Paul Case: "This number is contained in the scripture with the seventy years of the ordinary span of life, mentioned by the Psalmist. The difference between 120 and 70 is 50, so that we may say the magical age of 120 years is attained by adding 50 to the 70 years of ordinary human experience. The number 50 and 70 are, of course, symbolic. Fifty is the number of the letter Nun, symbol of the occult power, which, when sublimated, leads to illumination. Seventy is the number of the letter Ayin, whose name means: 1. the human eye, as organ of vision; and 2. "outward appearances", or the superficial aspect of things.

...Now 120 is the theosophic extension, or secret number, of 15-the sum of the numbers from 1 to 15 inclusive. In relation to the 15th key, therefore, it represents the full expression, or complete manifestation, of the power represented by The Devil. So long as we are outsiders, what stands in our way looks like the Devil. But when we overcome our terrors, Key 15 represents the great magical agent, the astral light, truly called Lucifer, the Son of the Morning. This is our adversary, because it is the immediate cause of the manifold appearances which delude the ignorant. But when we strengthen our vision with force borrowed from the eagle, we are able to *see through* those very same illusion, and then we are no longer deluded by them." [True & Invisible Rosicrucian Order, pp. 110, 111]. see 50, 70.

רמיוני Resemblance or Imaginative. Referring to the 24th path on Nun. The first two letters of the name of the path are Daleth and Mem, forming, the Hebrew noun for blood. The rest of the world, יונ, is numerically equivalent to a Hebrew noun [חביון], meaning "hidden treasure." This is a hint that the secret of the 24th path has something to do with valuable occult properties of blood. see 470, 44, 68.

סמך Letter name Samekh. tent-peg, prop, support. As a verb: to prop, to bear up, to establish, hold or sustain, invigorate. The 25th Path of Wisdom, linking Tiphareth and Yesod of the Tree. Representing the purgation and perfection of personality, to become a pure and holy habitation (temple) for the One Spirit. The

Path of Nun and Samekh are essentially the same. With different pointing: to lay (hands); to pack, make close, block.

The 25th Path of Samekh linking Tiphareth to Yesod is doubly related to Jupiter, because Samekh is associated with Sagittarius, ruled by Jupiter. see **10**, 80, 536, 800, 162, 186, 600, 1343.

מף Moph. Memphis; the capital of Egypt. Sometimes used as a name for Egypt itself. Mentioned in Hosea 9:6: "Even if they escape from destruction, Egypt shall gather them and Memphis will bury them. There treasures of silver will be taken over by briers, and thorns will overrun their tents." see 380, 850.

מועד the time of the decree, appointed time; festival (half-holiday, intermediate days of Passover and feast of tabernacles; appointed meeting, assembly; appointed place; temple, synagogue; appointed sign, signal; festival sacrifice. Refers to the time of liberation of Adam by the Life-power. With different pointing: *muahd*: forewarned, an attested danger. see 106, 756, 372, 50 & K.D.L.C.K. (p. 517).

ען On. a name of God. It is the city of Heliopolis in Egypt, or Beth-Shemesh, the House of the Sun. see 581, 1052.

מבין strengthening, renewal. "The fullness of those days shall see the strengthening of thy weakness, O Israel." [Book of Tokens, Samekh]. see 60, 310.

ינין shall be continued. see 770.

מכלל Perfection. see Psalm 50:2.

ימיני yimini. my right hand. see Psalm 110:1.

מסך a covering, a curtain, a hanging. see Numbers 3:16.

מסך mix drink, mixed-spice. In Psalm 75:8: "In the hand of the Lord is a cup full of foaming wine mixed with spices; he pours it out, and all the wicked of the earth drink I down to its very dregs."

I. Water is the basis of the great work. *Mawsak* is 120, the extension of 15. Note that יה, Jah. 15

190

as is אד, meaning 'steam, vapor', and 'fate'. Fifteen is אביב, (derived from אב, Father) the month of the Exodus and the Passover, corresponding to the sign Leo, ruled by the Sun. Fifteen is the extension of 5, and 5 is אד, meaning vapor. The sequence 5-15-120 suggest the gradual condensation of vapor into water. Water is the support (Samekh) and foundation (מוסדי, see below) of all material manifestation. 120 is 30+40+50 = נמל למן, to eat off, to cut off; suggesting the dissoloving properties of water. Note also 30-40-50 is a Pythagorean triangle with each of its units divided into 10 parts.

II. Key 14 shows the mixing of the fundamental waters at the beginning of the Long path which leads to the crown in the background. 120 is 3 x 40, suggesting the triple manifestation of the letter Mem (40). That is, Mem in the 3 worlds below Atziluth produces 120. This is a clue to the alchemical secret.

עמדו stand! In Jeremiah 6:16: "This is what the Lord says: Stand at the cross roads and look; ask for the ancient paths, ask where the good way is, and walk in it. But you said, 'We will not walk in it.'" see 3, 12, 21, 30, 39, 48, 57, 66, 75, 84, 93, 102, 111, 138, 140, 260.

עמוד Pillar, column, that which is stretched out, erect; stand, platform; cylinder around which scroll is rolled. In Exodus 13:21: "And the Lord went before them by day in a pillar of cloud, to lead them the way: and by night in a pillar of fire, to give them light; to go by day and night." see 170, 290, 421, 2521, 2580, 60, 310.

כעל according to. In Isaiah 59:18: "According to their deeds, according he will repay" and Isaiah 63:7 "According to all that the Lord hath bestowed on us."

לין scorner, one-mocking. In Proverbs 9:7: "Whoever corrects a mocker invites insult; whoever rebukes a wicked man incurs abuse." see 930.

עוגיאל Ogiel. "The Hinderers"; Qlippoth of Chokmah." [Godwin. 1999, p. 517.]

כסיל thick one, hence fool. (suggesting Tarot Key 0, related to Aleph and spirit). With different pointing: strong one, giant, hence the constellation Orion (conceived of by the ancients as a giant bound upon the sky.) In Psalm 92:6: "The senseless man does not know; neither does a fool understand." And in Job 38:31: "Can you bind the beautiful Pleiades? Can you loose the cords of Orion (i.e. the Giant).

מוסדי foundation, basis.

מלים words, sayings, decrees, prophetic, to/from water. see Genesis 1:6.

ועלטה thick darkness, and darkness. In Genesis 15:17.

למן for the measure or "hanna". see 90.

נמל to eat off, to cut off. see *mawsak* (above).

פם mouth, tongue. see 80, 474, 680.

I. "By פם is understood the foundation-namely the letter Yod joined with his bride; the speech is the marital influx flowing forth from the bride; for the queen is called the word; but the great things are the inferiors of all grades produced. This tongue (פה) is hidden between Yod and Heh. For father and mother are perpetually conjoined in יסוד, but concealed under the mystery of דעת." [Book of Concealed Mystery 37:37]

II. In Daniel 7:8: "I considered the horns, and, behold, there came up among them another little horn, before whom there were three of the first horns plucked up by the roots [of the beast with iron teeth]; and behold, in this horn were eyes like the eyes of man, and a mouth speaking great things."

צל shadow, shade; shelter, protection. In Psalm 191:1: "The shadow of the almighty."

פלי secret, wonderful. In Judges 13:18: "And the angel of the Lord said unto him, why asketh thou thus after my name, seeing it is secret?"

הסנה the thorn-bush. Refers to the burning bush-the image of God who "spoke" to Moses. In Exodus 3:2: "And the angel of the Lord appeared unto him is a flame of fire out of the midst of a bush: and he looked, and, behold, the bush burned with fire, and the bush was not consumed." see 586.

למים and the waters. [Genesis 1:6]. Refers to the firmament which God placed in the "waters" of creation.

סם spice; dissolved power; medicine, poison. also moth (Lexicon).

כפך hand. Letter name of the Hebrew letter Kaph.

clavis artis (Lt). key of art.

In principio (Lt). In the beginning, principle. The Latin translation of the Hebrew בואשית *Bereshith*, the first word in Genesis. It applies particularly to the construction of the equilateral triangle, from which the measure of a heptagon is derived, in as much as the triangle comes first. It may with equal propriety be translated "in principle"; and this also is a correct rendering of Bereshith. [also John 1:1 in the Latin of the Vulgate]. Relates also to the reality that "beginning and end are One." The process which begins from the higher unity of life ends there as well.

medicina catholica (Lt). Universal medicine.

I. Waite: "Moreover, it [the treasure] is the universal medicine described by Solomon [Ecclesiastes 38]; the same also is taken form the earth, and honored by the wise." [Waite, 1974, vol. 1, p. 132]

II. "The fire of divine love prepared the heavenly Quintessence and eternal tincture of souls from the cosmic cross of the four elements, and... by the medicina catholica the whole human race is liberated from the yoke of hell, delivered from death and transmuted by spiritual regeneration, so that the soul is clothed with the splendor of everlasting being... This is the body of the radiant or resurrection body of adeptship..." [Waite, 1993, p. 459]

pax profunda (Lt). Peace profound. An ancient Rosicrucian salutation.

fons naturae (Lt). fountain of nature. Concerning the philosopher's stone, "it is a pearl without price, and, indeed, the earthly antitype of Christ, the heavenly corner stone. As Christ was

despised and rejected in this world by the people of the Jews, and nevertheless was more precious than heaven and earth; so it is with our stone among earthly things: for the spring where it is found is called the fount of nature. For heaven as though Nature all growing things are generated by the heat of the sun, so also through Nature is our tone born after that it has generated." [Waite, 1974, vol. 1, p. 181] "In the fountain of Nature our Substance is found, and nowhere else upon earth; and our Stone is fire [216, Latin], and has been generated in fire, without, however, being consumed by fire." [ibid, p.213]

121

I. (11 x 11) or 11^2

כסיאל Cassiel. Planetary angel of Saturn (Binah).

נינוה Nineveh [Like 11:30]. capital of Assyria, where Jonah was sent by God. Combines the letters of נון (Nun), and יה (Jah). see 50, 15.

אפס. an end, extremity, fool for God; to cease, disappear.

הגלגלים. of whirling motions.

אצל emanated from.

מלאים consecration.

אין-בם. you do not.
חזק be strong.

אלילים vain idols, false gods. Those contacted by astral visions, where personal subconsciousness colors the true images, and becomes a channel for negative forces.

אצל to lay aside, set apart; to reserve, withhold, withdraw; to influence. The "dew of heaven" is reserved for the enlightened; its influence is the measure of truth. also: With different pointing: by the side of, near, nearby, beside. Its presence in "nearer than hands or feet", for it dwells within.

חזה די לילא nocturnal vision. contact with this "dew" brings inner vision, which begins as the recollection and interpretation of dreams.

אנכים perpendiculars. exactly upright, or vertical, pointing to the zenith; rectitude. Suggest the path of Gimel which extends vertically from Tiphareth to Kether. Gimel is connected with the Moon and with subconscious memory, activated during the dream state.

עבאל Okael. Lesser angle governing triplicity by night of Cancer. This sign is ruled by the Moon.

כעאל Kael. Angle governing the Lesser Night Triplicity of Cancer. [Crowley, 1977, p. 18].

מטבע Coin. Corresponds to the suit of Pentacles in the Tarot minor arcania, to the plane of Assiah, the material world, to the 2nd Heh of IHVH and to the 4th occult admonition-to be silent. This word does not occur in scripture or in the Hebrew Lexicon.

Of מם d'Olivet comments: "This root, composed of the sign of exterior and passive action, united to that of resistance, develops all ideas of motion or emotion given to something; vacillation; stirring; a communicated movement especially downward. מוט. *Action of moving, rousing, budging, stirring, agitating; going, following, happening, arriving*, etc." [d'Olivet, 1976, p. 389.]

Of בע: "Every idea of precipitate, harsh, inordinate movement. It is the root בא, in which the mother vowel has degenerated toward the material sense. בעה. *An anxious inquiring, a search; a turgescence, a boiling; action of boiling*, etc." [d'Olivet, 1976, pp. 306-307.]

revivicatio (Lt) reborn, revivified. Part of a phrase in Secret symbols. see 717.

divine natura (Lt). divine nature. The nature of divinity is to perpetuate itself. see 54, 67, 496 Latin.

perpetuum (Lt). perpetual. The power of perpetuation corresponds intimately with the function of imagination assigned to Nun. see 120, 250, 50, 700.

Non Omn Ibus (Lt). Not for All. Motto of the gate of the inner wall in an illustration of Khunrath's Amphitheatrum Chemicum (1609). The inner wall summarizes the alchemical operations; the motto intimates that entrance into the central mystery is not for everyone.

In this diagram the radiant triangle encloses the letters אבן (53). It is worn by a dragon which is on the top of a mountain. The mountain is in the center of an enclosure is surrounded by the 7-sided wall that has written in the corners: dissolution, purification, Azoth pondus, solution, multiplication, fermentation, projection.

An other wall formed from a 7 pointed star with 14 equal lines surrounds this inner wall. There is a gate flanked by 2 triangular pyramids or obelisks. The obelisk named Faith has a sun over it. The obelisk named Taciturnity (Silence) has a moon over it. Between the pillars is a figure bearing the caduceus of Hermes or Mercury, standing behind a table on which is written "Good Works." Below is the motto: "The ignorant deride what the wise extol and admire."

122

חסדים merciful or beneficent ones, the compassionate. Rosicrucian grade of Exempt Adept. The Masters of Compassion are those who are wholly devoted to realizing their identity with the One Reality. Chasidim are persons who partake of the quality of Jupiter, Chesed, and enjoy continual receptivity to the Hierophant via the 16th path of Vav. For them the fact of eternal being is a direct perception so that they are able to say: "Before Abraham was, I AM". see 508, 72, 48, 528.

אל האלהים unto the Elohim, unto God. In Exodus 19:3: "And Moses went up unto God [the Elohim, on Mr. Sinai] where IHVH called unto him out of the mountain saying..." [אל pointed means "to, unto, at, by." So the name means "unto the Elohim (the seven spirits, or chakras). 122 reduces to 5, the number of Heh, and since it refers to the Elohim, the Heh is the first Heh in יהוה and refers to Binah. see 682.

צלב to hang, crucify, impale. This is spirit embodied in physical forms. Evolution sacrifices or crucifies the lower nature, to be reunited with God. This is accomplished through the power of meditation (Tzaddi) aided by the agency of balanced action (Lamed) and the transparency of self-conscious attention (Beth). With different pointing: *tzelakub*: cross-the cross of the 4 elements: Fire, Water, Air, and Earth. It is equilibrated by the Quintessence.

מיא מיא the glassy sea. A term used in alchemy; suggests the city of pure gold, like clear glass in Revelations 18:21. Implies the illuminated consciousness-when receptivity to the intuitional level of Binah becomes as a "glassy sea" [Binah is the "Great Sea"]

אנוסה an assulted woman. Suggest failure to approach subconsciousness (the woman of Key 2) "suavely and with great ingenuity." Failure is the inevitable result.

ענב grape. Suggest renewal (Ayin) through change (Nun) and self-conscious attention (Beth). see 133, 166, 44, 1431 (Greek), 216, 1336.

אסמודאי Asmodai. Asmoday or Asmodeus. The arch-demon corresponding to Geburah or Netzach; Goetic demon #32 by day of the 2nd decanate of Aquarius. see Appendix 11.

I. "('creature of judgement')-the name is derived from ashma daeva... Asmodeus is a Persian rather than a Jewish devil; however incorporated into Jewish lore, he is there regarded as an evil spirit. According to Furlong, *Encyclopedia of Religions*, Asmodeus is 'the Talmudic Ashmedai, a demon borrowed from the Zend Aeshmadeva', a 'raging fiend' [*The Book of Tobit* 3:8]. It was Ashmadia (Ashmedai), says Furlong, who made Noah drunk, and who, it *Tobit*, slew the 7 bridegrooms of the young Sarah, and who overcome by the angel Raphael, was finally 'banished to upper Egypt.' In Demonology Asmodeus in Hell is controller of all gaming houses. Wierus the demonographer says Asmodeus must be invoked only when the invokant is bare headed, otherwise the demon will trick him... In *The Book of the Sacred Magic of Abramelin the Mage*, we find this report: 'some rabbins say that Asmodeus was the child of incest of Tubal-Cain and his sister Naamah; others say he was the demon of impurity.' Jewish lore charges Asmodeus with being the father-in-law of the demon Bar Shalmon... In Solomonic legends, Asmodeus also goes by the name of Saturn, Marcolf or

Morolf. He is credited with being the inventor of carousels, music, dancing, drama, 'and all the new French fashions.'" [Davidson, 1971, pp. 57-58.]

II. "Asmoday (Ashmeday, Asmodius, Sydney) - a fallen angel 'who has wings and flies about, and has knowledge of the future,' according to Budge, *Amulets and Talismans*, p. 377. Asmoday teaches mathematics and can make men invisible. He 'giveth the ring of virtues' and governs 72 legions of infernal spirits. When invoked, he manifest as a creature with 3 heads (bull, ram, man)... A variant spelling of the name is Hasmoday, who is one of the demons of the moon." [ibid, p. 57.]

III. *Goetia*: "He is a great king, strong, and powerful. He appears with three heads, whereof the first is like a bull, the second like a man, and the third like a ram; he has also the tail of a serpent, and from his mouth issue flames of fire. His feet are webbed like those of a goose. He sits upon an infernal dragon, and bears in his hand a lance with a banner. He is first and choicest under the Power of AMAYMON, he goes before all other. When the Exorcist has a mind t call him, let it be abroad, and let him stand on his feet all the time of action, with his cap or head-dress off; for if it be on, AMAYMON will deceive him and call all his actions to be bewrayed. But as soon as the Exorcist sees Asmoday in the shape aforesaid, he shall can him by his name, saying: "Art thou Asmoday?" and he will not deny it, and by-and-by he will bow down unto the ground. He gives the ring of virtues; he teaches the arts of arithmetic, astronomy, geometry, and all handicrafts absolutely. He gives true and full answers unto thy demands. He makes one invincible. He sows the place where treasures lie, and guards it. He, among the Legions of AMAYMON governs 72 Legions of Spirits Inferior." [Mathers, 1995, p. 43]

זלפה Leah's hand-maden; mother of Gad and Asher. In Genesis 29:24: "And Leban gave his servant girl *Zilpah* to his daughter as her maid servant." see 7, 501

גלגולים revolutiones (Anamarum); rotations or wheeling (of spirit). given by Rosenroth in [K.D.L.C.K p. 236], where he cites the Zohar.

lux interna (Lt). inner light. Refers to Kether. see

620, 397, 49, 73 Latin.

sepulchrum (Lt). sepulchre; tomb, resting-place. The inner-light within physical form. Part of a phrase found written on the altar of the vault of C.R. see 475, 87 Latin.

123

אהה יהוה אלהים   "Oh, IHVH, Elohim." a name of God, implying Kether, Chokmah & Binah. 3, 4, and 5 letters.

מלחמה   war, battle, quarrel, controversy [Exodus 15:3].

נגע a blow, stroke, spot, mark, sore, plague, esp. suspected Leprosy.

ענג pleasure, delight, enjoyment. metathesis of נגע. Gimel (Uniting Intelligence) is now the result of piercing the bonds of ignorance (Ayin) and transforming negative patterns (Nun). Life becomes more delightful. With different pointing: *enneg.* to make soft, make tender, to make pleasant; to enjoy.

פגם defect, blemish; injury, hurt, damages for blemish; the decrease of the moon, decline. This the power of Mars (Peh) which pierces the veils of ignorance in subconsciousness, the Moon (Gimel), affecting reversal of mental substance (Mem), and which can cause pain in the process. With different pointing: *pahgam.* to cut, mutilate; to discredit [laesio aliqualis violatio: an attack on someone, an injury].

כהן הגדול the high priest. In Leviticus 21:10: "The High Priest, the one ordained to wear the priestly garments, must not let his hair become unkempt or tear his clothes." see 75, 43, 773.

124

Length of the 4 sloping lines in a structure required to complete the unfinished pyramid on the reverse of the Great Seal of U.S.

יהוה הוא אלהים   Jehovah (The Lord), He is God. see 129.

גלה סודו he reveals his secret.

עדן ayden. Eden, delight, pleasure. A noun meaning: time. The purpose of human life is to enjoy a "good time." The secret of happiness is in the honest development of our own gifts. We are given the seeds of mental imagery. It is up to us to develop them so that Adam can return to the Garden of Eden. see 703, 179, 129, 53.

The Stone is the Garden, and the Garden is the place of delight. That is, אבן (eben) is גן (gan), and גן is עדן, because the Stone is the union of the Son with the Father. Since *eben* and *gan* are both 53, the Stone is the Stone of Eden, as is the Garden. Eden means delight, or pleasure. Its number is 124 or 4 x 31 or אל multiplied by 4. Four is Daleth, this is the development of the power in Chesed (4th Sephiroth) to which אל is the Divine Name. Daleth is Venus, thus the power of Daleth, which is the power of Netzach or Nogah (the sphere of Venus), is what multiplies the strength of Chesed into delight. The stone and the Garden are one, and as the Stone is the union of Chokmah and Tiphareth. So is the Garden in that same union; and from union comes delight. Never is there delight in separateness. Only when Father and Son are united is there delight.

Gan (garden, גן) is the sign of this union. Because Gimel (ג) is the Uniting Intelligence, which links Kether the Crown to Tipareth the Sun. Nun is the Imaginative Intelligence, which unites Tiphareth to Netzach. Gimel is Key 2, the Moon and Nun is Key 13, Mars in Scorpio. In Tarot they add to 15, which is the sign of the Ayin, the Renewing Intelligence that links Tiphareth to Hod.

In Tarot, 15 is the Adversary, but he is more than this. His number is the same as יה (Divine Name in Chokmah) and הוד, (the name of the 8th Sephiroth). Ayin is the 26th Path and has the same number of Tetragrammaton, which is the special name of Tiphareth. He is the Life in Chokmah, and Adam, the King, in Tiphareth, and he is also the Splendor of the Mercurial Work.

Thus the letters of *ayden*, begins with the Renewing Intelligence, followed by Daleth, the Luminous Intelligence which links Chokmah to Binah. The Delight of *ayden* is completed by the letter Nun, which is also the last letter of אבן and of אין; and a sign of the 50 gates of Binah. Nun links the Sphere of the Sun to the Sphere of Venus. In *gan* you see the whirling motion of Kether descending to the Sphere of the Sun, and projecting itself into the Sphere of Venus.

Ayden is the garden of the Magician (Key 1); and the soil of that garden is identical with *eben*, the Stone. Thus the Stone and the Garden are אימא, the Mother, because אימא and בן are one in numeration. See C.17, 53, & 52.

מלמדי [than all] my teachers. In Psalm 119:99 Mem: "I have more understanding than all my teacher: for thy testimonies are my meditation." The root of the word is למד, lamed. see 114.

ובלך-לבבך with all thy heart. In Deuteronomy 30:2: "And shall return unto the Lord thy God, and shall obey his voice according to all that I command thee this day, thou and thy children, with all thy heart, and with all thy soul." see 604, 1217 (Greek), 32, 50.

עוחנן John; "God the gracious", or "favored by IH Yah." The book of Revelations of John the divine links Eden with the Holy City or New Jerusalem. see 1119 (Greek).

לעיטה leoitah. stuffing with food, fattening.

חוסן an oak; hardness. [Note חום in the Lexicon: to pity, have pity. Perhaps relates to the Tree of Life planted in the Garden]

עיגיאל Oghiel, Gohgiel. The cortex of the Qlippoth of Chokmah.

פגיאל personal noun, masculine. "Accident of God". (From Latin *ad + cadere*, a be-falling). Angel petitioned in ritual prayer for fulfillment of the invocants desires.

bene serviendo (Lt). well in serving. To serve well in the performance of the Great Work is a "delight".

Magnum Opus (Lt). The Great Work. The alchemical operation which transmutes and regenerates the consciousness of man, transforming it into the "stone of the wise" Then are the Father (Chokmah) and Son (Tiphareth) said to be in "perfect union" at the inner center. "The objective (Of the Great Work) is the new birth as one of the sons of the doctrine. Meditation is the process. it is the physiological demonstration of a see-idea." Passion purified (Key 8) becomes compassion. see 61, 63.

The alchemists say the Magnum Opus is "woman's work," and even our speech uses the words "travail" and "labor" for birth. This Work does not have to do with genetics. It is by a second birth within the heart.

The force that is used is the Scorpio power; but in each human personality, for flesh and blood cannot inherit the Kingdom, nor can it be transmitted by genetic processes to posterity. Never will the race evolve into the 5th Kingdom. Every person must transmute his own lead into gold. Evolution is a genetic process. The Magnum Opus goes beyond this.

The Great Work transmutes the Microcosm into the Macrocosm. The Microcosm is illusory. It does not exist. Cosmic consciousness is truly Nirvana, or extinction. Thus the Great Work brings us to the place of God at the Center, that is, Tiphareth - in heart, not in head.

Thus in all alchemical transmutation the genetic process is inhibited, as one may see from all texts of alchemy, magic and yoga. There is no more oft-repeated statement than this. Thus all the Rosicrucians of the first circle were "bachelors of vowed virginity."

Remember that the Sons of the Doctrine are never to be so much suspected as when they write most openly. Remember also, that they said also that some of them had children to whom they could not pass on their mysteries. Evidently "vowed virginity" is not simply celibacy, or else priests and nuns would also be adepts, and they are not.

Understand that if the Scorpio force is used for generation it cannot be used for the Great Work. Used it may be, in several ways; but whatever the special regimen, it always excludes physical procreation. In Tibet this is well-known, as it is in the Western School. The objective is the new birth as one of the Sons of the Doctrine. Meditation is the process. It is the physiological demonstration of a seed-idea, and the names מלך, בן, אדם are the statement of that idea.

196

See C.13.

Omnipotens (Lt). Almighty. see 80, 314 Latin.

125

I. (5 x 5 x 5) or 5^3

מוֹעֵד an appointed time or season. see Exodus 34:18, 1 Samuel 9:24, Daniel 12:7.

עָנָה to answer, reply, respond; to be occupied, to busied with, to sing, speak tunefully; to be low, be humbled, be depressed, afflicted.

עָנָה to humble, oppress, afflict; to violate (a women); to sing, sing in chorus; to detain, postpone; to cause privation, make to fast.

דנמאל Danamel. Night demon of 2nd decanate of Pisces.

מנדאל "God Adorable". 36th Shem ha-Mephorash. 176E to 180E Aphut. April 24, July 5, Sept 15, November 26, February 6 [11:40 to 12:00 Noon]. For maintaining one's employment and conserving the means of existence which one possesses. Psalm 26:8 "Lord (IHVH) I love the habitation of thy house and the place where thy Glory Dwells." (Against Calumnies and to deliver prisoners). Menadel helps exiles to return to their native land. Angel of the 6th quinance [26E-30E] of Capricorn; Angel by night of the 4 of Pentacles. This represents the operation of Jupiter or cosmic memory in the material world of action. see 965 & Appendix 10.

"Menadel - an angel of the order of powers, according to Ambelain; also one of the 72 angels of the zodiac, according to Runes… Manadel keeps exiles faithful or loyal to their native land. His corresponding angel, in the cabala, is Aphut." [Davidson, 1971, pp. 189-190.]

צלה "Shadow", one of Lamech's wives and mother of Tubal-Cain and Na'amah. In Genesis 4:19: "And Lamech took unto him two wives: the name of the one was Adah, and the name of the other Zillah." see 598, 165, 90, 122 (Asmodeus).

Mons Abiegnus (Lt). Mountain of Fir-Wood. Represents the mystical ascent in consciousness leading to a state of exaltation, often compared to intoxication. used in Rosicrucian literature. And instance of divine grace (A gift) or beneficence from Chesed. see 72, 129.

Itinerarium (et Vita) (Lt). Travels. Refers to the Allegorical journeys of C.R.

Formido Maxima (Lt). Greatest Fear, dread. Produced by the illusions created by the eye (Ayin).

fons aureus (Lt). golden fountain. an alchemical term. "For whoever drinks of the golden fountain, experiences a renovation of his whole nature, a vanishing of all unhealthy matter, a fresh supply of blood, a strengthening of the heart and of all the vitals, and a permanent bracing of every limb. For it opens all the pores, and through them bears away all that prevents the perfect health of the body, but allows all that is beneficial to remain therein unmolested." [Waite, 1974, vol. 1, pp. 325-326] see 48.

126

I. Perimeter of a 6 square cross built from a 9 x 9 x 9 cube.

נעבד neobed. Serving, Administrative or Aiding. 32nd Path of Tav. It may be read as perpetual generation (Nun), the fountain or renewal (Ayin) in (Beth) Daleth.

I. Upward on the Tree runs the Way of Return. It begins in Guph, and rises to Nephesh through the path of Tav. This path is named *neobed*, Administrative and its number is 126, and it has close connection with the symbols of the R.C. For 126 is the total length (in feet) of the boundaries of the Vault described in *Fama Fraternitatis*. The Path of Tav is also closely related to all temple symbolism. The word *neobed* also calls attention to Mars in Scorpio (נ), and Mars combined with Saturn(ע), and these are combined with the letters of Mercury (ב) and Venus (ד). Mars in Scorpio, Mars exalted in Capricorn, Saturn ruling Capricorn - these are Nun and Ayin. Mercury is Beth, and Venus is Daleth. Meditate on this, and find out what you have to administer in the Temple of the Body. See C.10.

II. The 32nd Path is שכל נעבד (Saykel Naobed,

Intelligence of Service or Serving), and that it is so called because it governs the motion of the 7 planets and concurs therein to Tav, the letter of this Path, to which the wise declare that the Temple of the Midst pertains, and that this Path is also that of Shabbathai or rest. *Neobed* answers to the number 126, and so does אלמנה (Almanah), or Widow. This refers to Malkuth in her separation from Tiphareth. Thus does the Path of Tav end in Malkuth, but its first letter is the beginning and end of Tiphareth. Its last letter is Vav, assigned to Tiphareth. The Temple of Holiness in the Midst is in the heart of the 6, and there is the place of rest, or Shabbathai. From Shabbathai came forth the other planets, and unto Shabbathai they all returned.

In *neobed* that the first letter pertains to Madim (Mars), and to the perpetuation of life by generation. The 2nd letter is the Fountain of Renewal in which Shabbathai rules and Madim has its chief power. Then Beth, and Daleth, so that you may read it as: Perpetual Generation, the Fountain of Renewal In Daleth, for Beth and Daleth together may be read "in Daleth.".

In describing the vault, its boundaries as given in the *Fama* total 126. There are 7 lines of 5 feet at the top, 7 of 5 feet at the bottom, and 7 vertical lines of 8 feet, and this totals 126 feet. Note that 21 lines establish these boundaries, and 126 is a 6 x 21. It is then אהיה multiplied by Vav, the letter of Tiphareth to which the vault is assigned. The reference to נעבד and אלמנה (widow) may seem obscure at first; the riddle solves itself with a little meditation.

The Path of Tav calls for a total reorientation to the Spiritual East. East is connected with Venus and the Secret Wisdom. Your personal reorientation and your personal victory, are also a work of Venus. Furthermore the dancer on Key 21 is androgyny, see if you can think through to its meaning, remember that the key stands for Shabbathai, and Saturn.

The wreath in Key 21 is an ellipse or a zero sign representing אין (not), אני, that is I, myself, and בטן, the womb. Key is 21, has the value of אהיה, the Divine name of Kether, and יהו, or Yaho, whose permutations establishes the Cube of Space (see Sephir Yetzirah). The Great Work is both personal and social, but it must begin with people. As they achieve it, as they enter the

sanctuary, as they discover for themselves the true secret of Saturn, they progress stage by stage into conscious participation in the New Order. This has gone on for many generations. Since you do not know how many have already achieved the Summum Bonum, it may seem to you it is still far off. On the contrary, it is imminent. See C.36, 474, 61.

אלמנה almahnah. a widow, a desolate place. Said to refer to the "Fall" of Malkuth, the Bride in her separation from the Son, Tiphareth. Contains the mystery of widowhood, which is also one of motherhood, for the bride and the mother truly are one. The widow is connected with the ideas derived from the Egyptian Myth Isis. The Widow refers to Malkuth in her separation from Tiphareth. see 496, 52, 306, 432.

I. But the Widow, is also the Bride, and one with the Mother. In Mizraim was she known as Isis, and her son was Khoor, whom the Greeks called Horus. Horus is בן, the Son who is Tiphareth, and his mother Isis is Binah. It is written "out of Egypt have I called my son," and that son is Ben or Tiphareth. The mystery of Widowhood which separates the Bride from the Son, is a mystery of Motherhood, because the Bride and Mother are one.

II. *Almahnah* first two letters are אל, the Divine Name is in Chesed, The next letters Mem and Nun reveal the hidden Manna. The last letter Heh, signifies sight, and is also the special letter in Tetragrammaton (יהוה) pertaining both to the Mother and the Bride. The Mother is the sphere of Shabbathai, or Rest, and the letter of Tav is Shabbathai itself. From the 32nd Path of Tav depends Malkuth the Bride, who is the Resplendent Intelligence, and her glory comes from Shabbathai, which from the Midst governs and administers all. See C.36.

אפילה darkness. The "darkness" of physical embodiment. In Exodus 10:22 this word is spelled אפלה, and used with חשך. Thus חשך אפלה is "thick darkness." In Rabbinical Hebrew: late fruit, latter rain (the autumnal rainy season). see 711.

האפיל to darken, obscure, mystify, to be late in ripening.

יהוה אדני אגלא Jehovah Adonai AGLA. A talismanic name of God. A notoriqon for: Ateh Gibor le-Olam Adonai, Thou art mighty forever, O Lord or Thine is the power through the endless ages, O Lord. AGLA is the sum of the words יהוה (26), Jehovah; אדני (65) Adonai; and אגלא (35). Note that the heptagon of the vault of Brother C.R. has a perimeter of 35 feet (5 x 7), and its area is 91 square feet. If we consider the vault as a solid 3 dimensional solid, then the boundary lines would add to 21. see 26, 65, 35.

כהן אן Kohen On. priest of On in Genesis 41:45. see 302

לוז A name of a City in Genesis 28:19. Inman: 'To bend or curve, to enwrap, to veil;' 'an almond or nut tree.' It is possible that this word may have been originally לוש, lush, 'the strong or powerful one,' or לוין, luz, 'the wanton, or lose one.'

מלון lodging, inn, night quarters, hospitality.

סוס horse, swallow. Refers to "dung of the Horse," and alchemical expression. see 711, 1059 and Genesis 49:7.

עבד אדמה obade adahmah. (and Cain became) a tiller (or slave) of the earth [Genesis 4:2]. As a verb obade means: to work, to till, cultivate, to serve, to worship. As a noun, Ehbed: worshiper, subject, servant, slave. see 50, 76, 160 (Cain).

נוע to wave, to quiver, vibrate, to stagger, be unstable; to tremble, shake, to wander about; to blow the nose. As a verb: aoon or ahvon. to lie down, to rest, to dwell, to move agitate; marital duty, cohabit. It had the early meaning: to conjure, do magic, act as a soothsayer, but now it is spelt עון for that specific purpose.

עון guilt, sin, iniquity, punishment, crime. In Genesis 4:13: "And Cain said unto the Lord, my punishment is greater than I can bear..." see 16, 826 and Genesis 15:16.

ענו humble, lowly; poor and afflicted, oppressed.

פלאה wonderful, mysteries, miracle, marvel, wonderful deed. In Psalm 139:6 it is spelled with

different pointing and is translated "too wonderful." see 111, 527.

פלאה A personal masculine name, obade "God has done a wonder". One of Ezra's assistants (Ezra was a Jewish scholar, teacher and religious reformer in post-exile times). obade

אדני Adonai. Lord. Divine Name for Malkuth. Written as a tetractys:

א	1
א ד	5
א ד נ	55
א ד נ י	65
	total: 126

see also: 406, 713, 291, 400.

סיון Sivan, the ninth month of the Hebrew year, corresponding to June-July (or to May-June, according to Standard Bible Dictionary), and thus to Cancer and Cheth. In Esther 8:9: "At once the royal secretaries were summoned-on the 23rd day of the third month [i.e. from the vernal equinox], the month of Sivan." As symbol of Cancer, connected also with alchemical separation. see 95, 1360, 776.

י-ו-ו-ל-ע-י J V I O L, the initials of inveni verbum in ore leonis, "Discover the word in the lion's mouth." If taken as Hebrew letters.

"The Lion [ארי, אריה, Arai,, Araiah, which also means the altar] still holds in his mouth the key of the enigma of the sphinx." [Pike, 1992, p. 211.] see 216.

בוק 35th Shem ha-Mephorash, short form. see 141 & Appendix 10.

ענו 63rd Shem ha-Mephorash, short form. see 157 & Appendix 10.

גימיגין Gimigin. Day demon of the 1st decanate of Taurus [Crowley, 1977, p. 18]. This decanate is ruled by Venus and has the qualities: devoted, artistic, sympathetic. The influence of the demon suggest conscious imbalance, resulting in negative aspects of these qualities. In the Tarot minor arcana the 1st decanate of Taurus is attributed to the 5 of Pentacles. This represents the operation of Geburah, sphere of Mars and volition, is Assiah, the material world of action. When ill-dignified, as here, this may indicate toil unrewared; loss of money, poverty; trouble through lack of imagination and foresight. The remedy is to learn to welcome change and become receptive to the voice of intuition.

סנוי Sinui, Senoi, Sanuy.

I. "...Sennoi was dispatched by God to bring Lilith back to Adam after a falling out between the pair in the pre-Eve days. Lilith was evil, but an amulet bearing the name Sennoi was sufficient, when Lilith beheld it, to deter her from harming anyone, particularly infants (in, that is, post-Eden days). For the sigil of Sennoi see *The Book of the Angel Raziel* and Budge, *Amulets and Talismans*, 225." [Davidson, 1971, p. 266.]

II. "On of the three angles invoked against Lilith." [Godwin. 1999, p. 518.]

η ριζα ha riza (Gr). the root [Revelations 22:16] One of the names of Christ. "A root that from which anything springs." Metaphorically, a root, stem, stock of a family. Latin "Stirps", a face, family.

Lapis Chemicus (Lt). The stone of Alchemy. see 53, 51.

Novus ordo (Lt). New Order. Commemorated on the Great Seal of the U.S. has to do with man's altered conception of the physical plane as being the kingdom (Malkuth) of Heaven (Kether). see 224, 370.

sanctuarium (Lt). sanctuary. Tav is the holy temple or sanctuary in the midst. Tav is the temple or sanctuary in the midst. Note that the Shabathai is the day of service and sacrifice for the Jews. See **36**.

Virgo Intacta (Lt). untouched virgin, virgin of purity. The "untouchable Glory of God" [*Fama*]. see 74, 18, 56.

Virgo Sophia (Lt). The Virgin of Wisdom.

aqua mineralis (Lt). mineral water. The microcosm in one stage of its development. The "seed of the world" in all senses. see 74 (Lt).

The mineral water and the microcosm are one. That is, the mineral water is the microcosm in one stage of its development. But be on your guard against a too restricted an interpretation. The Aqua mineralis is the seed of the world. It is the Intact Virgin, or the Untouchable Glory of God. See **36**.

The power of the Intact Virgin, who is also Sophia, or Wisdom, is represented in the Tarot by the woman in Justice. She is the Bride and the Queen. She is also אימא, מאדה, ISIS, EVE, and all the rest of the Anima figures, including the Widow and Venus. The microcosm is the chemical stone, rough, and requiring treatment by art before it is purified and perfected. Yet it is in essence ever pure, and nothing can diminish that essential purity. However, in the field of relative phenomena, the work veiled in the figurative language of the Hermetic sciences must go on. Its outcome makes evident the truth that the mineral waters and the chemical stone are the microcosm. That is the true Adam who is Ben the Son. Hence the substitute word of our Masonic Brethren really signifies what is the Son, and he who knows the answer to this experimentally, finds the Alchemical Stone, the Sumum Bonum, and the place of rest that is Shabbathai in the Midst. Man himself is the Abode of Peace, the place of refuge, the Sanctuary, and the time draws near when here in America they who are true Sons of the Widow will realize in truth the New Order, which is commemorated on the Seal of the United States. See C.36.

intellectus (Lt). understanding, perception. see 261 (Lt), 45.

corvus niger (Lt). The "Black Raven" is an alchemical symbol of the first matter. see 87 (corvus), 49 (niger); 998

127 (prime)

The total number of Sarah's years: "And the Life of Sarah was 120 and 7 years." [Genesis 23:1].

מוטבע Natural. From a verb *Tawbah*, טבע, meaning to press in, to impress, to sink. As a noun it means nature. The meanings of this word imply that nature is like the impression made on wax by a signet ring. Closely related is the occult doctrine that nature is impressed with characters written by the Hand of God. This is a figurative way of stating what is strictly true. One needs only pay close attention to events and things in order to read their inner meaning. In Qabalistic writing there is much emphasis on the numerical identity of הטבה, as this word is usually written, Heh being a definite article, with אלהים, Elohim. The idea suggested is that the creative powers are identically with "nature." To separate nature form God is a fundamental error. Religionist are prone to fall into this false notion as well as materialist. [מוטב good, better; the right conduct] see 477, 86.

מלך הכבוד King of Glory [Psalm 24:8, 9, 10] In verse 1- the Psalmist asks "Who then is the King of Glory?. The Lord strong and mighty, the Lord mighty in battle. Lift up your heads, O ye gates; even lift them up, ye ever lasting doors; and the King of Glory shall come in. The Lord of Hosts, He is the King of Glory." The Lord of Hosts is IHVH Tzaboth, is the divine name assigned to Netzach. Kabode [כבוד] Glory has for its fundamental meaning weight or ponderability. With the definite article Heh, ha-kabode is 37, the value of Yekhidah [יחידה], the One Self, seated in the White Brilliance of Kether. [Kether is the concentration, at a radiant point of the power of Ain Suph Aur , the limitless light] In Psalm 24:8 the King of Glory is also described as "The Lord strong and mighty." see 26, 89, 333, 360, 90, 414, 525.

צוה יהוה the Lord commanded [Psalm 133:3]. This occurs in the psalm celebrating brotherly unity, familiar to Freemasons. The deeper occult meaning has to do with the precious ointment, שמן הטוב (the precious oil) flowing down Aaron's Head, and Qabalists interpret this as being a reference to the Holy influence through the paths of the Tree of Life. That influence is הכבוד, the glory (also named מזלא, Mezla). *Tzevah* means: to command or constitute, may be read צ וה, Tzaddi and Heh. Its meaning: to command, to constitute, is allied to the special mode of consciousness represented by Heh and the sign Aries, the Constituting Intelligence. see 32, 78, 10.

פויאל "God who sustains the universe." 56th Shem ha-Mephorash, Associated with the 2nd quinance of Taurus (6-10°); angel by night of 5 of Pentacles. 276E-280E THEMESO. May 14,

July 25, October 5, December 16, February 26. 6:20 6:40 PM. Psalm 145:14 "The Lord (IHVH) upholds all that fall, and raises up all those that are bowed down." To obtain what one requires. Rules renown, fortune and philosophy. Person born esteemed by all the world for his modesty, his moderation and his agreeable humor; he make his fortune by his talents and his conduct. see Appendix 10.

mysterium (Lt). a secret or mystery.

sapientia vera (Lt). true wisdom. Observe that the first of these 2 words is the number 86, relating it to ALHIM. see 381 (3x127: "I will instruct thee" Psalm 32:8)

Galia Narbonensi. A city in Gaul, for which Gallia Narbonensis takes its name. A place mentioned in the *Fama* without explanation. Gaul is from the root gallus, meaning a waterpot, a pail or round vessel, drinking bowel.

128

I. (2 x 2 x 2 x 2 x 2 x 2 x 2) or 2^7

II. 4x32 The expression of the 32 Paths of Wisdom through the 4 Qabalistic Worlds.

אליפז "God of Gold, Riches". The first-mentioned and perhaps oldest friend of Job ("The Greatly Afflicted One," 19). In Job 2:11: "Now when Job's three friends heard of all this evil that was come upon him, the came every one from his own place; Eliphaz the Temanite..." Teman, a district of Idumaea [Jeremiah 49:20] was noted for its wisdom [Jeremiah 49:7]. Wisdom = Chokmah Life-force. [Note that this was the name used by Eliphas Levi, or Aldolphe Louis Constant]

חלץ to deliver, loose, rescue, tear, cut. Intuition via memory delivers the soul from darkness and ignorance. With different pointing: to prepare for war, draw off. The connection with the Mars-force and "war" should be apparent.

חסין strong, powerful. "*Robustus Gratia*" in K.D.L.C.K. (p. 399). A cognomen, or descriptive name for Chesed, whose divine name is AL El, "strength, power, might." Chesed is the sphere of Jupiter, or cosmic memory, thus employing that strength, an attributed of Mars is linked with

Jupiter to produce the linkage which enables the contact with Intuitional levels of Binah to be made. Note the path of Teth (Key 8-Strength) connects Chesed to Geburah on the Tree of Life. see 73, 216, 419, 31.

יהוה אלהינו   God, the Eternal One. Vav, attributed to the Hierophant (which links Chokmah to Chesed) is the Triumphant and Eternal Intelligence.

אני בינה   I am Understanding [Proverbs 8:14].

אנמיאל   Amnuel. Ruling angel of Aquarius [Crowley, 1977, p. 19].

הכהן הגדול   The High Priest. Refers to the Hierophant, the instructor in the sacred wisdom (Chokmah) of Life (Chaiah). see 118.

פחם   charcoal, soot, coal. With different pointing: *pacham*. Smithy, forge. As a verb: *pepahkam*. to become black, become sooty. These words suggest that personal ignorance causes the external appearance of things to become "black" or "sooty". It is actually the condition of the soul itself. It takes the "forge" of action to remake the "Iron" of will to reflect the divine volition, guided by intuition (the High Priest). It is the divine lightning (Peh) working through personality (Cheth) to produce a change in consciousness (Mem).

אופיאל   Ophiel; Olympic planetary spirit of Mercury. The name suggest a transliteration of the Greek οφις serpent, thus "Serpent of God". "As an angel of the order of powers, he can be invoked. As many as 100,000 legions of lesser spirits are under his command. In Cornelius Agrippa's works, Ophiel's sigil is shown." [Davidson, 1971, p. 213.]

יבוסים   Jebusites; "Son of Canaan"; the ancient inhabitants of Jerusalem and the neighborhood, in early Palestine, mentions in Genesis 15:21. In Zechariah 9:7: "Jebusite" seems to mean "Jerusalemite." The prophecy looks forward to a time when the Philistine remnant shall be incorporated into the purified Jewish commonwealth. see 688.

d'Olivet translates Genesis 10:16: "And (that of) the Jebusite (inward crushing), and (that of) the Amorite (outward wringing), and (that of)

Girgashite (continuous gyratory movement)." [d'Olivet, 1976, p. 344.]

"ואת-היבוסים", and that of the Jebusites... The compound radical verb יבום to tread upon, to crush with the foot, comes from the root בוס, which characterizes that sort of pressure by means of which one treads upon and crushes a thing [i.e. grapes, for the wine press, see 166] to extract liquid and radical moisture." [d'Olivet, 1976, p. 287.]

αιθηρ aether (Gr). the ether or quintessence. A symbol of the highest plane of manifestation, also called spiritual, heaven, light. It is the universe of spirit which precedes the lower universe which is patterned upon it. Called the 5th element by Plutarch-same as the alchemical 5th essence or Quintessence. The ancients considered Aether one of the elementary substances out of which the universe was formed. It was regarded as pure upper air, the residence of the Gods, or creative powers, and Zeus, Lord of Aether, or Aether itself personified. see 214, 86, 300, 600.

129

הוא האלהים יהוה   Hu ha-Elohim IHVH. The Lord He is God. IHVH refers to Tiphareth, the reflection of Kether, designated by Hu and ha-Elohim refers to both Kether and Binah, because Elohim is the special divine name of Binah while the number of ha-Elohim, 91 is the value of אמן Amen, a title of Kether. See Deuteronomy 4:39 & The Greater Holy Assembly (para. 1057).

עדנה   pleasure [Genesis 18:12]. Refers to Sarah asking whether she will have "pleasure," i.e. bear a child.

"The number of Eden is also that of עיטם, meaning a 'Place of ravenous creatures', identical with the Egyptian *atem*, 'to enclose', 'to shut up, 'to annihilate', all equally applicable to the caverns of Choronzon. עדן or עדנה (Eden) means 'pleasure' [Genesis 18:12]. The place of pleasure and of annihilation was the shut place or hidden shrine typified by the womb or garden. And as the solar seed immured in the womb incarnates in flesh, so the Place of Annihilation, or Shrine of Choronzon was similarly a place of transformation for the future life.

The Place of Pleasure (Eden) and the Caverns of Choronzon (the tunnels of the abyss) are the dual polarities of Daath, Eden being the *Tep* or Top of the Garden, the caverns of Set being the Tepth or Depth: Heaven and Hell." [Nightside of Eden, p. 67]

ענג delight, pleasure. This pleasure is of (de) the light or delightful, because the new creature is literally born out of the light in the heart. see 124.

נטע to set in, to plant; to fix, fasten. With different pointing: *netao*. planting, plant, plantation. In Genesis 8:20: "And Noah began to till the ground; and he planted a vineyard." see Isaiah 51:16, 17:11 and Job 14:9.

היכל גונה Place of Serenity; heavenly mansion corresponding to Hod on the Tree of Life. see 65, 15.

F:B:M:P:A (F.B.M.P.A.) Initials of Frater B., listed in the *Fama* as Frater *F.B.M.P.A.*, *pictor et architectus* (painter and architect). [Note: the F in German corresponds to Hebrew Vav]. Divinity paints the artistry of life with mental imagery and is the architect of our salvation. see 2 (Beth).

In Monte Abiegus (Lt). In Mount Abiegnus. In the mountain of Firwood [Secret Symbols Page 20]. see 72, 125.

Lumen Naturaw (Lt). Light of Nature.

Laboratorium (Lt). Laboratory. The human organism, where the alchemical Great Work is performed. see 250, 121 Latin.

materia ultima (Lt). The final or highest substance. refers to the first matter. [Secret Symbols, p. 46] see 61 (materia).

aqua permanens (Lt). permanent water. the universal mercury. see 36 (aqua), permanens (93).

magnesia catholica (Lt) universal magnet (loadstone). "He is the one perfect savior of all imperfect bodies and men, the true heavenly physician of the soul, the eternal light that lights all men [Isaiah 60, John 1], the universal remedy of all diseases, the true spiritual panacea... He is also the true catholic magnesia, or universal seed of the world, of Whom, through Whom, and to Whom are all things in heaven and upon earth- the Alpha and Omega, the beginning and the end, says the Lord that is, and was, and is to come, the Almighty [Apocalypse 1]." [Waite, 1974, vol. 1, p. 98]

130

I. 130 = 13 x 10. 13 = Unity. Therefore "The EYE is the ONE, multiplied through the Sephiroth."

עין Letter name Ayin. eye as an organ of sight. look, face, appearance, color; fountain; visible surface, gleam, sparkle, hole, ring, guide post, cross-roads; substance, being, shade. "Well-spring of outward appearance," and "Darkness is the fountain of existence." [Book of Tokens]. see 708, 780.

עין to look in, to look carefully, search, investigate, to think over, deliberate, contemplate, to read casually, to look up quotations. With different pointing: *unyan*. to be evenly balanced, weighing exactly.

עני humbled, suffering, forbearing, lowliness, oppression, misery, affliction, poverty, destitution, humbleness.

הצלה deliverance. Esther 4:14.

ימינך your right hand [Psalm 138:7]. This is the right hand of Tetragrammaton, and it is taken as an instrument of deliverance - "Thy right hand shall save me." In Psalm 80:17 "And of the plant thy right hand hath planted."

כלף to clap or strike; a hammer. The hammer relates to iron, and to the Mars-force; it strikes the "nail", which is Vav, or interior-hearing, as the grasp **כף** of Lamed, which is Justice, or right action, is accomplished. see 850.

נף Memphis, the capital of Egypt. Egypt is the symbol of the subconscious plane. see 380 and Ezekiel 30:13.

מלאך הגאל Angle of Redemption. The devil becomes Uriel when we see him as he really is -

The Angel of Light, or Lucifer (Light-bearer).

מלין decrees; prophetic sayings; words.

סלם a ladder; staircase. Specifically the ladder mentioned in Jacob's dream, in Genesis 28:12: "And he dreamed, and behold a ladder was set upon the earth, and the top of it reached to heaven; and behold the angels of God were ascending and descending on it." Compare with the Tree of Life which is a ladder with rings, or a staircase with graded steps of consciousness.

I. "A symbol of the soul's path from the lower nature (earth) to the higher nature (Heaven). The 'angels' ascending are the aspiration, and those descending are the divine responses to the soul. 'Jacob' represents the natural man turning to the Lord-the ideal within. He sleeps upon a stone, that is, he relies upon the spirit within." [Gaskell, 1981, p. 439.]

סיני Mountain where Moses received Laws (i.e. the decrees). "From the correspondence of 'ladder' and 'Sinai', we learn that the ladder to heaven i.e. Jacob's ladder-is provided by the law given on Sinai." [Godwin. 1999, p. 518.] see Exodus 19:2.

עמודי Pillars, columns [Job 26:11]. (Jachin and Boaz on Key 2). The Pillar of mercy is that of light. The Pillar of severity is that of darkness. All creation is a mixture and equilibrium of Light and Darkness.

עמד With thee [Psalm 36:9]. In the passage cited, the Psalmist says, "with thee is the fountain of Life," and though he uses another noun for "fountain," the idea expressed is related to the word עין, which means well, spring, fountain, as well as eye, outer appearance. see 780, 358, 830, 17.

פן "lest"; a removing, hence-that not (as a warning). In Genesis 3:22 "Then IHVH Elohim said 'behold, the man [אדם] has become like one of us, to know good and evil; and now, lest he put forth his hand, and take also of the Tree of Life, and eat, and live forever. (23) Therefore IHVH Elohim sent him forth from the Garden of Eden, to till the ground from whence he was taken." see 780.

"The face of anything whatsoever, the front of a thing, that which is presented first to the view: That which strikes, astonishes, frightens: every idea of presence, conversion, consideration, observations, etc. *The aspect* of a person, *his countenance, face, mein, air*, sad or serene, mild or irritated: action of *turning* the face, to turn, expressed by the relations *before*, *in the presence of*, *from before*, etc. Action *causing* the *face* to turn, expressed by *beware! NO! Lest! for fear of!* etc. That which imposes by its aspect: *a prince, a leader; a star, a ruby, a tower*, etc. That which is the cause of *disturbance*, of *hesitation*. [d'Olivet, 1976, pp. 427-428.]

קל swift, light, fleet. In Isaiah 5:26: "He lifts up a banner for the distant nations, he whistles for those at the ends of the earth. here they come, swiftly and speedily.

"The root קו, image of that which is undefined, vague, unformed, united by contraction to the directive sign, ל, produces a root which designates that which is deprived of consistency and form; sound, voice, wind, but, if the same root is conceived as formed by the union of the compressive sign ק, with the root אל image of all elevation and all superior force, it expresses then the action of roasting, parching, etc.

קל Every idea of *lightness, rapidity, velocity*: that which is *attenuated, slender, thin*: without consistency; of little value; *vile, cowardly, infamous*. קול Voice, sound." [d'Olivet, 1976, pp. 441-442.]

נסך to appoint. In Psalm 2:6: "I have appointed my king over Zion, my holy mountain. see 140.

נממ Nemem. 57th Shem ha-Mephorash, short form. see 145 & Appendix 10.

נסך a pouring out, libation. In Numbers 15:5: "And a fourth part of hin of wine for a drink offering shall you offer with the burnt offering or sacrifice, for one lamb." With different pointing: molten image in Isaiah 48:5: "I have made them known to you from of old; before they came to pass I declared them to you, lest you should say, my idols did them; and by graven images and my molten images have saved me."

CR, GV, TA, IO, RC, B, GG, PD (Lt). Initials of the 8 persons who founded the Rosicrucian Order.

Creans tenebras (Lt). "I create the darkness." The Latin translation of Isaiah 45:7.

Primum mobile (Lt). First motion. The Latin for Rashith ha-Galgalim, "The Beginning of the Whirlings," attributed to Kether. see 50, 80.

Sperma solis (Lt). Seed of the sun (or gold). "The hermetic arcanum is this: communicate the male sperma solis to the female matrix of the moon, or in other words turn the light inward and draw out the inward half-circle. The artist who does so kindles an independent fire or light and transmutes Moon into Sun-i.e. Silver into Gold. The true meaning of this emerges in one case." [Waite, 1993, pp. 463-464] Paul Case notes that עדן = primum mobile. see 60, 64.

131 (prime)

סמאל Samael. Arch Demon linked with unbalanced forces (Qlippoth). "Sam" means poison and is therefore the angle of death and order of Seraphim (fiery serpents). By some accounts attributed to Geburah and Jupiter. Applied also to the chief of all evil spirits equalivalant to Satan. Its fundamental meaning is "embroilment", when negative self-conscious produces environmental conditions and human relations adverse to harmony. The cure is to get rid of the delusions of separateness and link oneself with the higher powers, as does the magician. see 141, 626, 2080, 8.

I. "...an 'immortal angel of God.' ... grouped with Michael, Gabriel and other spell-binding angels. [see Dictionary of Angels, p. 256]

II. "Angel of Death; Prince of Demons; Demon Prince of Fire; Qlippoth of Hod; archdemon corresponding to Chokmah (Crowley)." [Godwin. 1999, p. 519.]

III. The God of Assiah [i.e. Satan] is the reversed Sammael of Yetzirah [SMAL - 131 - Pan], who is the reversed Metatron of Briah, who is the reversed Adam Qadmon of Atziluth. In brief, Sammael in Assiah is the reversed Adam Qadomon three times removed; he is the 'dark shadow of the manifestation of the Great Androgyne of Good'. [Grant, 1994, pp. 42-43.]

אמץ courage, valor, strength. One of the 4

occult maxims (to dare). Aleph, the fiery quality of the Life-breath (Rauch) shows that the magician must have a degree of audacity in his psychic make-up-audacity in the face of uncertainty and peril. Mem, daring is the result of a reasoned surrender to life itself. Tzaddi, magical courage is the fruit of conscious possession of internal powers via ceaseless meditation which identifies him with the source of these power. see 346, 474, 70.

ענוה ahnawah. humility, meekness; mildness, gentleness; condescension. The opposite of courage.

עונה marital duty, cohabitation; time; period of 12 astronomical hours; season, period; trouble, suffering, sorrow; sight or affliction of the eye. The metathesis of ענוה. It is the appearance of things (Ayin) modified by intuition (Vav) which brings change (Nun) and clear vision (Heh). This is marred by "embroilment".

נאף to commit adultery with; to worship idols. With different pointing: *nayuph.* adultery, prostitution, misuse of reproductive energy (Nun) perverting spirit (Aleph) in action (Peh).

אנף angry, wraith; to be angry. Spirit (Aleph) working through reproductive activity and change (Nun) in action (Peh). With different pointing: countenance, anger reddens and flushes the face, and produces courage and strength.

סמיא Lesser angel governing triplicity by night of Virgo. This implies a subconscious use of the uniting powers of Yod, by self-consciousness suggestion (Mercury). This involves the industrious use of the powers of discrimination.

אפן to turn the wheel; to systematize, classify, arrange; to break on the wheel, torture. The metathesis of אנף. It is spirit (Aleph) working through activity (Peh) to transform appearance. This may be based on some systematic or painful approach. With different pointing: *ophen.* manner, way, plan, style. The unfoldment of the above.

אפים nose, nostrils; face, anger. The influence of Sammael on the above, reflected in flaring nostrils.

נלכאל 21st Shem ha-Mephorash. "God unique and alone." Against calumniators and spells and for the destruction of evil spirits. Governs: astronomy, mathematics, geography and all abstract sciences. Positive influence: loves poetry, literature, avid for study. Negative: ignorance, errors, prejudice.

Angel of the 2nd decanate and 3rd quinance of Scorpio and attributed to the 6 of Cups. see Appendix 10.

יאמאטע The Sentinel of the 20th Path (Tunnel) of Yod on the Inverse Tree of Life.

I. The 20th Tunnel is under the aegis of Yamatu, his number, 131, is the number of Samael, a name of Satan or Set as Guardian of the Threshold. It is also the number of Pan and of Baphomet, the idol adored of the Templars. מבונה, meaning 'her foundation or fundament', a symbol of the *kteis*, also adds to 131, as well as מאבע. Note that 131 + 535 (the number of *kteis*) = 666, the number of the Beast. This is confirmed by the fact that מאבע, the son [i.e. Set] of Typhon, also adds up to 131.

The sigil of Yamatu is a secret cypher of Set. It exhibits the inverted cross which signifies the downward passage or crossing into Amenta.

The astro-glyph of the 20th Path is Virgo, and its threshold is the kteis of the Virgin guarded by Samael. Its magical formula is that of 'virile force reserved' i.e. Karezza, which comports a build-up of sexual energy for magical purposes but without final release. This is a perfectly legitimate magical formula and one which may be used in connection with the formula described in connection with the previous *kala*.

Immortality in the flesh is one of the aims of the Black Brothers. The idea arose not only from the natural urge to protect the ego from the impact of death, with its consequent disruption of conscious identity, but also from a mis-interpretation of the doctrine of the Death Posture exemplified by the Cult of the Mummy in ancient Khem. In this connection, Michael Bertiaux - writing on Astral Machines -refers to magicians who endeavoured to achieve immorality on the astral plane. He observes:

Instruments like this [an 'the Astral Condenser']

insulate against the changes of time, and it has been known that such instruments have been used by occultists to preserve themselves, or hold themselves on the astral plane against the onward tide of evolution.

The Theosophist Leadbeater deplored this practice as a form of black magic. It is a typical example of the magic favored by occultists who habitually haunt the Tunnel of Yamatu.

Narcissus, the flower ascribed to this tunnel, yields a key to the nature of the formula of sexual magick associated with it, which, in its dark aspect reflects Karezza as a sterile spending of magical force. This is confirmed by the letter Yod being regarded as sacred to Yamatu. Yod means a 'hand' and to this tunnel qabalists ascribe the Order of Qliphoth known as the *Tzaphiriron*, meaning 'The Scratchers'.

The Light, or secret seed, concealed within the body suggests the idea of invisibility and this is the magical *siddhi* attributed to this ray, as also is parthenogenesis [the Virgo-Virgin symbolism]. The work of the Black Brothers thus belongs naturally in the Tunnel of Yamatu where the seed, spilt in a sterile act, renders the body bereft of light and therefore 'invisible'. It was the object of the New Light Sect to retain the light within, thus defying death and achieving immortality in the flesh.

The deity ascribed to this ray is Hoor-paar-Kraat, the Egyptian original of the Greek god of Silence and Strength [i.e. latent sexuality], Harpocrates. He was frequently depicted on the monuments as a child squatting upon a lotus with thumb or forefinger (both emblems of the phallus) pressed against its lips in the mudra of 'not uttering a word'.

The Tarot Trump attributed to this ray is that of the Hermit who carries the lamp and staff symbolic of the hidden light, or the light expressed in darkness. He is the Magus of the Voice of Power, but in his qliphotic reflex he becomes the utterer of the Word of Death imprisoned in the corpse and not permitted to realize its identity with Space (cosmic consciousness).

To be trapped in this tunnel is to suffer the death in life of petrifaction. The typical disease is paralysis, and the inclusion of 'all anaphrodisiacs' among the list of Vegetable Drugs ascribed to this ray again suggests the anti-vital nature of its sterilizing influences. [Grant, 1994, pp. 207-210.]

gluten aqulaw (Lt). Eagle's glue.

Deus nobiscum (Lt). God with us; part of an old Rosicrucian phrase. *Deus nobiscum; pax profunda* (God with us; peace profound). see 251, 120, 329 (Lt) Note that Deus = 45 (אדם) + nobiscum = 86 (אלהים, Elohim) = 131.

κομα. koma (Gr). "has long hair". "Suggest the ideas of joy and richness: fullness of generative power: or productiveness from an underlying or preceding condition. 'Hair', together with its variants 'Wool' and 'Horn' is a widely used symbol, indicating super-vitality or, at times, Divine Intelligence: e.g. the radiant coiffure of the sungods. A synonym for *koma* is *khloephorei*: the word khlo (or phlo) is used by St. Paul ('it was made clear to me things of [my] khole." [1 Corinthians 1:2] with reference to his own super developed psychic powers." [Omikron, 1942, pp. 256-257.]

132

יהוה אלהיכם Tetragrammaton your God [Deuteronomy 4:23, 10:17]. see 106, 26, 1145.

קבל to receive, accept, take. The feminine noun from the verb קבלה, Qabalah. With different pointing: *qabal.* to cry out; to complain. the reaction of the old patterns to the process of regeneration.

חסידים Chasidim. Godly men Merciful or beneficent ones, Saints, "in the congregation of the Saints." Those who have attained the consciousness of Chesed (universal memory, Jupiter) and the Grade of Exempt Adept, also known as Master of Compassion. In Psalm 149:1,5: "Praise the Lord. Sing unto the Lord a new song, and his praise in the congregation of saints... Let the saints be joyful in glory; let them sing aloud upon their beds."

I. Derived from the noun חסד, Chesed, Mercy or benevolence, the 4th Sephiroth. This is the sphere of Jupiter. In astrology Jupiter represents comprehension of natural law, expansiveness, and good fortune. Chesed is attributed to the 4th

Path of the Measuring Intelligence. Thus the Chasidim is one who measures correctly his position in the cosmic order, perceives that human personality rest upon the eternal foundation of the limitless light, and looks upon himself as a channel for inexhaustible benevolence. see 220, 269.

II. Mackey writes: "The name of a sect which existed in the time of the Maccabees, and which was organized for the purpose of opposing innovations upon the Jewish faith. Their essential principles were to observe all the actual laws of purification, to meet frequently for devotion, to submit to acts of self-denial and mortification, to have all things in common, and sometimes to withdraw from society and to devote themselves to contemplation." [Encyclopedia of Freemasonry, p. 160]

בלק to lay waste, destroy. What is destroyed is the false sense of separate personality.

המועא "The bringing-forth one." From the root: מועאה, origin, descent, privy.

נעיב residence, station.

נעיב prefect, deputy, commissioner; military post, garrison; pillar; substance. The pillar of mercy contains the substance of the "bringing-forth", which is the deputy of God, or the inner teacher, the Hierophant. see Key 5.

ננאאל "God who abases the proud." 53rd Shem ha-Mephorash. 261E-265E. Chommé, Saturn. May 11, July 22, October 2, December 12, February 23. 5:20-5:40 PM. [Psalm 118:75] "I know, O Lord (IHVH), that thy judgement are righteous, and that in faithfulness thou has afflicted me." Rules the high sciences; influences eccesiactics, professors, magistrates, and men of law. Person born: melancholy humor, loves a private life, repose and meditation; will distinguish himself by his knowledge of abstract sciences. For success in all things, and brings all experience to completion. Rules chemistry, physics and medicine. Influences to health and long life. Persons born: Distinguished in medicine; becomes famous by his marvelous cures, unveils many secret of nature which promote the happiness of the children of earth, and consecrates his powers and his services to solace the poor and the sick.

Angel of the 5th quinance [21E-25E] of Aries and angel by day of the 4 of wands. This represents the operation of the sphere of Jupiter or cosmic memory, in the archetypal (Atziluth) world of ideas. see 965, 101 & Appendix 10.

עבדון Abdon, "servant" (of On, the Sun-god); the fifth judge of Israel. [Judges 12:13-15] see 782.

Microcosmus (Lt). Microcosm. The idea that man is an epitome of all the forces in the universe, containing within himself, in principle everything included in the constitution of the macrocosm, or Great World. see 175, 119).

balneum naturae (Lt). natural bath or bath of nature. An alchemical term. "The philosophers called the fire their balneum, but it is balneum naturae, 'a natural bath', not an artificial one, for it is not any kind of water, but a certain subtle temperature moisture, which compasseth the glass, and feeds their sun, or fire." [Thomas Vaughan: Writings-Coelum Terrae, p.144] see 60 (balneum), 72 (naturae).

133

גפן the vine, grapevine. A mystical term, used by Jesus ("I am the vine, and you are the grapes"). Also the vine from which comes the "Blood of the Grape." see Judges 9:13, Hosea 10:1 & 260.

גיבכ A synthetic word referred to in I.Z.Q. or The Lesser Holy Assembly Para. 699: "For in the mysteries of the letters of Solomon, the King, those 4 letters א, ה, ח, ע are surrounded by גיבכ." [Mathers, 1993, p. 332]

These 4 letters represent Spirit (Aleph), vision (Heh), receptivity (Cheth) and renewal (Ayin). The 2nd 4 letters suggest memory (Gimel), will (Yod), cyclicity (Kaph) and organization (Qoph).

ים המלח the salt sea. Refers to the Dead Sea.

העמדה "God the hope of all the children of earth." 38th Shem ha-Mephorash. 186E-190E Serucuth. April 26, July 7, September 17, November 28, February 8. To acquire all the treasures of heaven and earth [Psalm 91:9].

"Because thou has made the Lord, which is my refuge, even the most high, thy habitation." Against fever, weapons, ferocious animals, and infernal spirits. Rules all religious cults and all that pertains to God; protects all those who see truth. The angel's name suggest the power within the field of endeavor, (Cheth), welling forth in apparent limitation (Ayin), but resulting in stability (Mem). Corresponding to אגלא [Agla] according to Lenaim's La Science Cabalistique. see 965, 118, 678.

Angel of the 2nd quinance of Aquarius [6E-10E] and angel by night of the 5 of swords. This represents the operation of the sphere of Mars in Yetzirah, or the operation of divine volition in the world of formation. see Appendix 10.

גדעון Gideon, "Hewer" or "Feller". The warriors who delivered the people of central Israel from their enemies. In Judges 8:22: "The Israelites said to Gideon, 'Rule over us-you, your son and your grandson-because you have saved us out of the hand of Midian." Note that מדין Median, according to Inman is probably derived from מי mi, water or seed and דן Dan, the judge, connected with alchemical putrefaction and Scorpio (54). thus is signifies "the seed of Dan." see 104, 336, 396; 783.

נגף plague. Described in the retribution of God upon Egypt [380], during the Passover of Israel [541] in Exodus 12:13: "And the blood shall be to you for a sign upon the houses where you are; and when I see the blood, I will make you glad, and the plague shall not be among you to destroy you when I smite the land of Egypt." see 853.

Lapis Capitalis (Lt). Pinnacle or cap-stone or a pyramid. see 564.

134

אני חכמה I wisdom, I Chokmah [Proverbs 8:12]. "I wisdom dwell with prudence." Prudence in Hebrew Lexicon means: heap, pile, stack.

דלק to burn, to pursue hotly. With different pointing: *deleq*. fuel, burning materials.

מעזיבה plastering, roof-plastering, ceiling. With different vowel points: rampart, floor, pavement.

Trigono Igneo (Lt). Triangle of Fire. A very old symbol of Spirit. The Triangle of Fire is connected with the symbol of the great pyramid, which is called by the ancient Egyptians "the Light" and is considered an eternal flame of spirit. The *Trigono Igneo* is mentioned in the *Fama*, and thus relates to the Lamb symbolism (through Brother C.R.) and *Agni*, the Hindu God of Fire. see 88, 46, 56, 74 Latin and the Great Seal of the United States.

135

ממלכה Kingdom. In 1 Chronicles 29:11: "Yours, O Lord, is *the Kingdom*." In the Hebrew text the prefix Heh is added to this word.

ענה Jah has answered. see Nehemiah 8:4.

ענה destitute female [Crowley, 1977, p. 19].

קהל assembly, company, congregation, community [Deuteronomy 9:10, 10:4, Genesis 49:6]. With different pointing: *qawhal*, to assemble. The assembly of the congregation of the righteous is the body of light, or spiritual Israel.

קלה to roast, parch, to consume, burn. Metathesis of קהל. It is the fire of desire which changes bodies during sleep (Qoph), guides every action (Lamed) and sees clearly the vision of its consuming rulership (Heh).

Rosenroth in K.D.L.C.K. (p. 673) says that written without Vav and with Heh as here, *qawlawh* means voices and refers to Binah, but קול is Tiphareth.

פנה corner; pinnacle, turret. All three letters of this word have to do with the crowning fire: Peh, the Mar-force, or lighting from heaven (Key 16), Nun the reproductive agency which multiplies and transforms (Key 13) and Heh, the result, or sovereign reason, which constitutes the highest good (Key 4). see 636.

פנה to remove, clear, clear away, empty; to free, acquit, transfer. The result of the above. see 530, 1240.

עמיהוד People of Splendor. The father of Elishama, prince of Ephraim [Numbers 1:10]. Ephraim = Taurus = alchemical congelation. see 331.

מלכדיאל Melekdial. Geomantic intelligence of Aries (alchemical calcination, 7). Aries is also connected with Heh, Key 4 and the creation of the stone.

אדם מלך Adam Melek. King of Adam or Adam the King. The One Ego, or the Stone, the Higher Self. To attain this is to become one with the stone.

אפרים Tribe of Ephraim. "a double fruit"; Taurus.

גוסיון Gusion. Goetic demon #11 by day of the 2nd decanate of Cancer. This decanate is associated with the 3 of Cups in the Tarot minor arcana, or the operation of Binah, Sphere of Saturn in Briah, the world of creation. see 785 & Appendix 11.

Goetia: "…a great strong duke. He appears like a Xenopilus. He tells all things, past, present, and to come, and shows the meaning and resolution of all questions thou may ask. He conciliates and reconciles friendships, and gives honor and dignity unto any. He rules over 40 Legions of Spirits." [Mathers, 1995, p. 33]

δοξα. doxa (Gr). Glory. dignity, honor, praise, worship. [Strong's Bible Dictionary]

οδαξ. odax. by biting with the teeth. [Temple, 1987, p. 169]

Ex Deo Nascimur (Lt). "from God we are born." This phrase is part of an inscription which was found in the vault of brother C.R see 683, 25, 22, 88 (Lt).

ignis vivens (Lt). living fire. "The sages call it the living fire, because God has endowed it with His own divine, and vitalizing power." [Waite, 1974, vol. 1, p. 199]

136

I. 34 x 4 = 136.   Σ16 = 136. Summation of the Magic Square of Jupiter and mystic path of Vav (16th Path).

אבדה יהוה בכל-לבי Psalm 9:2: "I will give thanks unto Tetragrammaton with all my heart."

הסמאל Kasmael, Hismael. the Intelligence of Jupiter.

יהפיאל Yophiel, Jophiel. the Spirit of Jupiter.

טוב טעם Good discernment [Psalm 119:66].

ממון wealth, value; money, fines, penalties. The word comes form the root aman, 'to trust' (ma'mon, Aramaic "that which is made secure or deposited")

עוני affliction, poverty, privation.

עניו answering, reply, response; meek.

קול voice. Qabalists refer this particularly to Tiphareth, which is the heart or inmost center. Refers also to the unheard voice-the voice of intuition or of understanding, attributed to Binah, seat of the higher soul, Neshamah, pictured as Key 5, the Hierophant. also קהל kahal, "to call", "an assembly," the voice; time. see 67.

קלו His voice [Deuteronomy 4:36]. With different pointing: call, cry, thunder.

מלאך הגואל The angel of vengeance. The opposite quality of "good discernment," caused by not listening to "His Voice" Goval means redeemer and is so used in Jeremiah 59:20. In Numbers 35:19 it is used to mean avenger (of blood) but spelled גאל. see 4, 16, 34, 340, 440.

כפול double.

מצאה ability, means, to be supplied with

מפיו out of his mouth. In Numbers 30:3: "from his mouth" and in Job 22:22: "I pray thee, instruction form his mouth." see 906.

Corvus niger (Lt). the Black Raven. An alchemical term which The Secret Symbols of the Rosicrucians (page 11) calls the "door of the art." The Black Raven is the first stage of the matter of the Great Work. It is called the "door of the art" because it is the point of entrance through which the power of the Divine Soul enters into the field of manifestation. One clue is the black color, attributed to Binah, and Binah, as the point through which the powers of the supernal triad descend into the 7 Sephiroth of manifestation is the "door of art." Furthermore, In Binah the triad of the supernals is completed, so that Binah is the point at which the triune nature of the Life-power becomes manifest. Behind the veils of appearance is hid the glory of God. We read that the "habitation of God is thick darkness." Black is also the color of Saturn of which Binah is the sphere. Binah is also the Sephirah to which Neshamah, the divine soul is assigned, as is also grace. [Saturn is the lowest and first chakra, to which Tav and the holy city are attributed]. see 273, 272.

Deus Trinus (Lt). the Triune God. A reference to the supernal triad. In Binah this triad is completed and it is the point at which the triune nature of the Life-power becomes manifest.

Dei gloria intacta (Lt) "The untouchable glory of God." The divine soul, Neshamah, seated in Binah (67). The one operator in the Great Work. That spotless, imperishable principle whose purity cannot be soled by even the worst of human beings. The Inner Glory which is the essence of the real man is not only untouched by the outer vehicle of personality and cannot be defiled. Consider a stream with a factory dumping pulltion into the waters. Down stream of the factory the water is polluted, but upstream the source is ever pure. Refer to the first paragraph of the Fama, where it speaks of man's innate nobleness and worth.

One of the Mottos in the vault of Brother C.R. It was written round a circle, one of the 4 engraved on the brass plate at the altar. In the circle was a picture of the head of a man. It represented the sign Aquarius. Aquarius is associated with the element Air, which is an intimation that the inner life of man is associated with spirit and breath.

καρδια. kardia (Gr). heart. A key to all the meanings of 136. The tabernacle of God is the Human "Heart," and the Shekinah, or divine presence in its Holy of Holies, is the untouchable Glory of God. see 144.

137 (prime)

חזון מיהוה Visions from Tetragrammaton [Lamentations 2:9]. The loss of which is lamented in the text.

קבלה Qabalah. "The Reception." Tradition, the ageless wisdom. Applies to 4th Path of Chesed, the Measuring, Arresting or Receptacular Intelligence. The Qabalah, which is from the East, both Literally and Figuratively, is that inner tradition, founded on the sure vision from Tetragrammaton, inspired by the spirit of God. This tradition, moving from the actual and symbolic east to the actual and symbolic west, and becoming universal is what can open the books with 7 seals. see 72, 132.

אופן wheel; circle, manner, way. One of the Ophanim, order of angels assigned to Chokmah; a circuit of celestial forces in both macrocosm and microcosm. Davidson says Ophan is "identified by the ancient sages as the angel Sandalphon." [Davidson, 1971, p. 213.] Sandalphon is connected with Malkuth. Nun = 700, see 137, 280, 187, 787.

אסטומכא belly, gullet, stomach; muscle, cartilage. In K.D.L.C.K. (p.138): Malkuth is called the stomach, because the stomach takes in nutriment and digest it, separation what is useless; moreover chyle is selected and sent to the appropriate place, to the other parts of the body: likewise Malkuth takes into herself the supernal spiritual influences, digesting and converting them into harmonious materials and conforming them so that there foods are vehicles for the "thrones."

In Proverbs 31:15: "She gets up while it is still dark; she provides food for her family and portions for her servant girls."

מצבה an image; pillar, stock, stump of a tree. With different pointing: military post, guard; general assembly (lexicon).

גדעני warlike. From גדע "to cut off, hew down."

Bene Radix Davidis (Lt). The Good Root of David [Secret symbols page 35]. Part of the Latin motto, "From east to west and everywhere the good root of David reigns victorious." see 113, 24, 50.

Spiritus Dei (Lt). Spirit of God. see 18.

בן אלהים Ben Elohim. Son of God. see 148.

צמח branch [Zech 6:12], plant, sprout. Name of the Messiah. see 3, 12, 30, 39, 48, 57, 66, 75, 84, 93, 102, 111, 120, 300, 358, 855.

לבנון Lebanon, the "White Mountain." From the root Levanan [לבנה], the pale or white one, the moon. Combined with לב, heart, as the seat of life, thought, emotions, etc, or "the midst" of anything, with Nun, the fish, or "to germinate," or sprout. see 21, 108, 788, 87, 10, 880, 1006, 96.

Rosenroth in K.D.L.C.K. (p.497) gives: *Libanon*, and says it is the supreme crown, from its surpassing whiteness, and moreover so called, when it sends down its influence.

חלק to divide, apportion; to assign, distribute; to impart, to share; to be smooth, slippery; to create; to separate. The One Ego of all humanity is separated into innumerable personalities. With different pointing: *chawlawq.* smooth, bald; blank space; as a masculine noun: smooth stone. The "stone" is the union of Father and Son. see 53.

חלק part, portion, shore; track of land; lot, fait; smoothness, seductiveness.

לקח instruction, teaching; lesson. metathesis of חלק. It is the goad of spirit (Lamed) multiplying through the body cells (Qoph) and making the personality receptive to the divine influence (Cheth). With different pointing: to take, take in, take away; to receive, accept; to capture, take possession of; to procure, buy; to bring, fetch. This instruction is our true reception and inheritance. see 78, 1831.

חמץ to leaven, ferment; be leavened, fermented; to be sour; to be red; to be ruthless. Recall that Ayin (tribe of Issachar) corresponds to alchemical fermentation. see 830, 130, 948.

חנף to pollute, to be polluted, be profane, to be godless, to flatter, be hypocritical. The influence of Ayin, or Key 15, the Devil.

מחץ He shall smite; to smite through, pierce,

wound, severity; to dip. Metathesis of מצח here reversal (Mem) is put before enclosure (Cheth). With different pointing: severe wound. see 948.

מצח forehead, brow. Seat of memory; or the Moon center.

הכהנה הגדולה The High Priestess; Key 2 in Tarot. To remember is to be united to the source.

מנחם counselor, comforter; name of the Messiah. In 2 Kings 15:17: "...Began Menahem son of Gadi to reign over Israel." Gadi means "the fortunate one." The plural of "comforter" in Hebrew = 188 = "corner-stone". From נחם, to comfort, give. see 207, 7.

הגדול מלך the great king. See 2 Kings 18:19.

Fraternitas R.C. (Lt). Fraternity or Brotherhood of the Rose-cross. The Latin signature at the end of the *Confessio Fraternitatis*.

Mater et virgo (Lt). Mother and virgin.

Perseverantia (Lt). Perseverance. The mystical title of one of the founders of BOTA.

Rex Judaeorum (Lt). King of the Jews.

Valle Josophat (Lt). Valley of Josophat. A mystical term in Alchemy and Free Masonry.

Aurum Potabile (Lt). Fluid Gold. The radiant fludic solar energy which "informs all bodies" through innumerable "drops" or Yods.

audi ignis vocem (Lt). "I hear the voice of fire." From Thomas Vaughan. see 54, 51, 33.

139 (prime)

אחיסמך Brother of Samekh.

הדקל The eastern river of Eden. Alternate spelling, used in the Sepher Dezenioutha. see 122, & Genesis 2:14.

מטיט היון Out of the Miry Clay [Psalm 40:3]. see 605.

גן אלהים Garden of Elohim (Creative Powers). Same as the Garden of Eden (Delight).

The story of which is the earliest recording the birth or creation of the Philosopher's Stone. see 53, 45, 19, 358, 126.

In Ezekiel 28:13: "you have been in Eden, the Garden of God; you were decked with every precious stone, the Sardius, the Topaz and the Emerald, the Beryl, the Onyx and the Jasper, the Sapphire and Pearls; and you have filled your treasures with Gold and your chest with precious stones; you had all these things from the day you were created." In Ezekiel 31:8,9: "the Cedars in the garden of God could not surpass it; the Fir tree in the garden of God like to it in its beauty. I made it beautiful by the multitude of its branches; so that all the trees of Eden that were in the Garden of God envied it."

נטף drop. In Job 36:27: "For if we should number the pillars of the heaven, and bind the drops of rain by themselves, which the skies do drop in their season" (who can understand these things?).

Spiritualis (Lt). Spiritual. see 319, 45 Latin.

Librum Nature (Lt). Book of Nature. Wherein the student learns to read the signatures or "characters" written by the spirit "or, a perfect method of all the arts." [*Fama*]. see 67, 72 Latin.

Epsissimus (Lt). "He who is most himself." A title of the Rosicrucian Grade associated with Kether.

140

מלכים Kings. The "Kings" are an order of angels in Briah (Creation), attributed to Netzach and the number 7. They are understood to be the Elohim, or 7 Spirits of God. In Assiah, the material world, they are attributed to Tiphareth, which is also Melek, King. They include those human beings who have awakened to conscious awareness that the Ego seated in Tiphareth is the angel, or messenger of the Self in Kether. Thus personal man becomes one of the Melakim or "kings" who rule as God rules. Furthermore Tav = Saturn = muladhara (Saturn) chakra, Ayin = Capricorn, ruling the knees and Daleth = Venus]. In Assiah, the "Kings" also refer to the 7 interior metals or 7 principles or forces in the occult constitution of man. Melakim is also associated with the 6 of Swords. see 474, 7, 120.

I. 1 Chronicles 8:9: " By his wife [Shaharaim in Moab] he had Jobab, Zibia, Mesha, Malcam [מלכם]]."

II. Inman: The Queen of Heaven. Ishtar, the Celestial mother (= מלכה and אם, *malcah*, and *em*), equivalent to the 'virgin of the spheres,' 'the mother of all creation.' Cuneiform, Malkat, who was the greatest of the Assyrian pantheon; she was represented as the wife of Ashur, and is the same as Sacti, Saraiswati, Ishtar, Maia, and the Yoni." [Inman, 1942, Vol. 2., p. 244]

חכמה-בינה   Chokmah-Binah.   Wisdom-Understanding. It is through combining the wisdom of Chokmah, the Life-force, with the understanding or defining principle of Binah that the Ego is perceived as being one with the Self. Then the personal man becomes one of the Malakim or "Kings" who rule as God rules.

מטה אלהים   Staff of God, Rod of Elohim. In Exodus 17:9: "...tomorrow I [Moses] will stand on the top of the hill with the Rod of God in mine hand." see 54, 86, 345, 686.

הממלכה   the kingdom. In 1 Chronicles 29:11: "Thine, O Lord, is the greatness, and the power, and the glory, and the victory, and the majesty: for all that is in the heaven and in the earth is thine; thine is the kingdom, O Lord, and thou are exacted as head above all."

עיני   mine eye. In Psalm 32:8: "I will instruct thee and teach thee in the way which thou shall go; I will give counsel, mine eye being upon thee." (or, "I will guide thee with mine eye") see 130, 1379, 1749, 433.

סף   sill; entrance, threshold, entrance. Spelled with prefix Heh in [Judges 19:27] "and her Lord rose up in the morning, and opened the doors of the house; and went out to go his way: and, behold, the woman his concubine was fallen down at the door of the house, and her hands were upon the threshold. see 860, 1096.

"Every idea of summit, end, finish; anything which terminates, consummates, achieves. *The extremity* of a thing, the point where it ceases; *its achievement, consummation, end: the defection, the want* of this thing: *the border, top, summit, threshold*: that which *commences* or *terminates* a thing; that which is *added for its perfection*: also,

reiteration of the same action, *an addition, supplement*; the final thing where many others come to *an end*: a time involving many actions.

The Arabic has preserved of the radical sense the idea of a thing reduced to powder, which is taken as medicine. The Syriac characterizes every kind of consummation, or reducing to powder by fire." [d'Olivet, 1976, p. 411.]

צן   thorn. Plural form in Genesis 3:18: "Thorns also and thistles shall it (ground) bring forth to thee; and thou shall eat the herb of the field." Plural צנים in Proverbs 22:5: "In the paths of the wicked lie thorns and snares, but he who guards his soul stays far form them." see 790.

I. "Symbolic of evils, sufferings, and sorrows. Sins and suffering shall proceed from the lower nature; and the lower mind (Adam) shall subsist through the produce of the sensation nature and the affections." [Gaskell, 1981, p. 755.]

II. Basil Wilburforce: "Each man is the soil in which the hereditary Adam-seed produces thorn and thistle, and the hereditary god-seed produces grape and fig. The two growths in the same individual strive for the mastery, and from the deep contrast between them emerges the perfected life of the child of God." [Problems, p.81] Recall that the rose is surrounded by thorns.

III. "That which conserves, preservers, put in safety. *A dwelling* where one gathers for shelter; *a shield, an urn, a basket*; any sort of defensive *weapon*, etc." [d'Olivet, 1976, p. 435.]

עלם   4th Shem ha-Mephorash, short form.   see 155 & Appendix 10.

מעל   from above, which were above. In Genesis 1:7 "So God made the expanse and separated the water under the expanse from the water *above it* [מעל]. And it was so."

נסיך   libation, drink, offering. Used in the plural form in Deuteronomy 32:38: "The gods who ate the fat of their sacrifices and drank the wine of their drink offerings [נסיכ, drink-offering-of-them, Interlinar Bible]. Let them rise up and help you! Let them give you shelter." Metal images in Daniel 11:8: "He will also seize their gods, their metal images [נסכיהם, metal-

213

images-of-them, Interlinar Bible] and their valuable articles of Silver and Gold; and carry them off to Egypt. For some years he will leave the King of the North alone." see 130.

נץ flower; hawk. In Job 39:26 "Does the hawk fly by thy wisdom, and stretch her wings toward the south?' The south is the direction of Resh, i.e. the Sun on the Cube of Space. Horus, a hawk-headed god was the son of Isis and Osiris, and is associated with an energizing spiral force. Horus is a solar deity, and just like the Masonic hero Hiram, is the son of a widow. see 950 and *True and Invisible*, p.47.

"That which reaches its term, end, extreme point: that which is raised as high and spreads as fast as it can be, according to its nature. The end of every germination, *the flower*, and action of *blossoming*; the term of all organic effort, *the feather* and the action of *flying*; the end of all desire; *splendor*, and the action of being *resplendent, glimmering, shining*." [d'Olivet, 1976, p. 403.]

מק rottenness, putridity In Isaiah 5:24: "Therefore, as tongues of fire lick up straw, and as dry grass sinks down in the flames, so their roots will decay [כמק, like-the-decay, *Interlinear NIV Bible*] and their flowers blow away like dust; for they have rejected the law of the Lord Almighty and spurned the word of the Holy One of Israel."

"That which is founded, literally as well as figuratively. The action of being melted, liquefied; growing faint, vanishing." [d'Olivet, 1976, p. 393.]

סף end, extremity. In Daniel 5:5: "Suddenly the fingers of a hand appeared and wrote one the plaster of the wall, near the lampstand in the royal palace. The king saw the extremity (i.e. the palm) of the hand as it wrote."

פֿס". That which comprise only a portion of the circumference or totality of a thing. *A part, a face, a phase*. Action of *diminishing*, of breaking into pieces. That Arabic word signifies literally to *examine minutely*." [d'Olivet, 1976, p. 428.]

קלי Kallai; a priest [Nehemiah 12:20]

coelum it terra (Lt). Heaven and earth. The entire Universe, or which the vault of C.R. is said to be a compendium, or synthesis. see 56 Latin.

Ordo seclorum (Lt). Order of the ages. World Order. The last 2 words on the reverse of the Great Seal of the united States. Their numeral identity with coelum et terra hints at a deeper meaning for the mottos: "A new order of the ages" is really "A new Heaven and Earth;" a new conception of the meaning of the words "Heaven" and "Earth."

141

נאמן Faithful, firm, loyal, lasting, established, reliable, trustworthy (22nd Path or Lamed).

אמיץ strong, mighty [Job 9:4]; strength, might [Isaiah 40:26]. This indicates the special quality of the influence flowing through the 22nd path, which descends from Geburah.

הקול The voice. see 136.

אסף to collect, gather, assemble, accumulate; put away; store, remove. With different pointing: To gather up, to contract, to take back or away; to take out of the way, to destroy.

אסף gathering, collection; in modern Hebrew: compilation. With different pointing: stores; ingathering, or harvest. These meanings are connected with the time of year corresponding to Libra, and with the symbolism of the scales.

אפס to fail, come to an end; cease, to have an end, As a noun *ehfes*: naught, cessation, coming to an end, and end (as the ends of the earth), an extremity. As an Adverb: but, however.

למינהו after its kind. In Genesis 1:21: "And God created... every living creature... after its kind... and God saw that it was good." see 74, 501.

קמא first, former, previous (Aramaic). The ending of each cycle is the ingathering of the harvest.

זין-למד Zain-Lamed. profuse (spelled in full, of זל); "of blessed memory." The creator is the "profuse giver" of all.

פכיאל Pakiel. Lesser assistant angel of Cancer. Cancer is maternal, receptive, domestic, ruled by the Moon or subconsciousness, suggesting where the ingathering of the harvest is made. see Key 7.

סמיאל Samael. "Venom of God". Angel of Death. alternate spelling, see 131.

בוקיה "God who gives joy". 35th Shem ha-Mephorash. 171E-175E. Aploso, Mercury. April 23, July 4, September 14, November 25, February 5. To regain the grace of those one has offended. [Psalm 71:1] 11:20-11:40 AM. Rules wills, successions, and all that which are based on friendship. It favors peace and harmony in family life. Persons born: love to live is peace with all the world, even at the expense of his own interest; he makes it his business to recognize the fidelity and the good offices of those who are attached to his service. see 965, 126 & Appendix 10.

Angel of the 5th quinance [21E-25E] of Capricorn; angel by day of the 4 of Pentacles . This represents the operation of Jupiter or cosmic memory in the physical world of action (Chesed of Assiah).

מצוה precept, law; the commandments. In Psalm 119:96: "to all perfection I see a limit; but your commands are boundless."

Solve et coagula (Lt). Dissolve and coagulate. The summary of the entire alchemical process. In some versions of Tarot, solve, dissolve, is inscribed on the right hand of the devil in Key 15, and coagula (literally, to curdle) is written on his left arm. In Key 11, the sword corresponds to solve. The sales, for weighing and measuring ponderable substance, stand for coagula. The hidden operation of alchemy is a modification of the blood serum, of its albumin (which is used extensively for clarifying liquids), by coagulation, directed by subconsciousness, under the immediate control of "Mercury."

142

אל האבן הגדולה In 1 Samuel 6:15: Upon the Great Stone. "And the Levites took down the ark of the Lord (IHVH), and the coffer that was with it, wherein the Jewels of Gold were, and put them on the Great Stone."

בליעל Worthlessness, badness, wickedness; nothingness; destruction. Compare this with the negative meanings of the title and symbolism of Key 0. In later Hebrew and in the New Testament, Belial is equivalent to Satan.

בעיני in the eyes (of IHVH). In Genesis 6:8: "But Noah found grace in the eyes of the Lord."

זולל בסבא a glutton and drunkard. In Deuteronomy 21:20: "...this our son is stubborn and rebellious, he will not obey our voice, he is a glutton and a drunkard." see 111, 831, 901.

חדקל One of the four rivers of Eden, said to go "toward the east of Assyria." [Genesis 2:14]. Associated with the 11th path of Aleph (associated by some with the river Tigris).
I. "The name is formed of two words חדד *emitting, propagating*, and קל *light, rapid*. It is used in the intensive form." [d'Olivet, 1976, p. 81.]

I. "A symbol of the astral plane which proceeds from buddhi. The symbol 'Hiddekel' stands for the astral plane on which the personality develops, becoming as it were, a dawn of consciousness-light in the east-precursor of the rising of the Higher Self (Sun) in the soul." [Gaskell, 1981, p. 359.]

II. Swedenburg says: "The river Hiddekel is reason, or the clearness and prespecuity of reason." [Arcana Celestia to Genesis II]

מחמדים desires, delights, precious things (Fire plus Water). Delightfulness in Canticles 5:16: "His mouth is most sweet: yea, he is altogether lovely. This is my beloved, and this is my friend, O daughters of Jerusalem." see 92.

פחדים loins, thighs, testicles. Plural of Pachad (92). Alludes to the seat of virile strength or Geburah as the sphere of Mars, which rules the reproductive functions governed by Scorpio. Translated as dread, terrifying in Job 15:21: "A dreadful sound is in his ears: in prosperity the destroyer shall come upon him." see 1200, 98.

בקלי to my voice. In Exodus 19:5: "Now

therefore, if you will indeed harken to my voice and keep my covenant; then you shall be a peculiar treasure to me above all people..." see 98, 136.

בלעם balaam; a stranger. In the Old Testament he stands for the unavailing curse of the heathen enchanter; in the New Testament he is the type of the tempter to idolatry, especially that part of it in which lust plays a large part. The incongruous qualities of a heathen soothsayer and a man touched by the spirit of the Lord. [Standard Bible Dictionary]. See Joshua 24:9.

אסמודאל Asmodel. Angel ruling the sign Taurus and geomantic intelligence of Taurus.

בעלם Balam. Goetic demon #51 by night of the 3rd decanate of Leo. This decanate of Leo corresponds to the 7 of Wands in the Tarot minor arcana. This is the operation of Netzach, sphere of Venus in Atziluth, the archetypal world, or the drive, the motive behind personal desire.

Goetia: "He is a terrible, great, and powerful king. He appears with three heads; the first is like that of a bull; the second is like that of a man; the third is like head of a ram. He has the tail of a serpent, and flaming eyes. He rides upon a furious bear, and carries a goshawk upon his fist. He speaks with a hoarse voice, giving true answers of things past, present, and to come. He makes men to go invisible, and also to be witty. He governs 40 Legions of Spirits." [Mathers, 1995, p. 54]

Hic est copus (Lt). This is the body.

Sinus Arabicus (Lt). The Arabian Gulf. From the *Fama*, the Latin for the Arabian Gulf. It is a symbol of what our Brother and Father must cross to come to Egypt. Arabia means "sterile" and refers to the purification and sublimation of the Mars-Force during a period of temporary celibacy, before the insight into the secrets of nature (Egypt-the subconscious realm) is realized.

structores (Lt). builders. see 108, 273.

philosophus (Lt) One versed in philosophy; a philosopher. Corresponds to 4=7 Rosicrucian grade of initiation, associated with Netzach (Victory), sphere of Venus on the Tree of Life. The philosophus seeks to develop within himself

a philosophy of life which expresses the unity of all things in his ever day affairs. see 85, 103, 100 (Lt), 148.

aqua sapientum. Water of the Wise. This is the Universal Mercury. see 36, 106.

143

אבן דומם The dumb (silent) stone [Habbukkuk 2:19]. Refers to graven images and idols.

אבן מים The stone of water. In the *Hermetic Museum*, The title page of the tract, The Sophic Hydrolith has the subtitle Water Stone of the Wise, "That is, chymical work, in which the way is shewn, the matter named, and the process described; namely, the method of obtaining the universal tincture." [Waite, 1974, vol. 1, p. 69] see 53, 90, 135.

אבצן Ibzan, the ninth Judge of Israel. [Judges 12:8-10] see 793.

המלך הגדבל The Great King (Emperor).

חליצה Things stripped from the dead, military equipment; untying, pulling off; drawing shoes of the Levirate (elders). [Deuteronomy 25:9].

ונזלים and flowing streams (from Lebanon) [Song of Solomon 4:15]. Note that "fountain" = Ayin, garden = גן = Stone (אבן, 53), Waters = מים = Tzaddi and Yesod [יסוד] (90), Lebanon = white mountain, connected with the Moon; לב heart + נון "fish" or Nun. All this has to do with creativity and building, to establish the dominion of spirit. see 138, 32, 106.

η δοξα. heh doxa (Gr). The Glory, Radiance. Part of the Lord's Prayer. see 135.

Quinta Essentia (Lt). Fifth Essence. The alchemical term for spirit or superconsciousness.

144

I. (12x12) or $2^4 \times 3^2$

II. 144 cubits (196 feet) is a measure of a man in

Revelations 21:17. see 2075.

אבי גבעון "Father of Gibeon."

קדם Ancient days, primordial heavens; Anterius; the East; days first of the first, front (opposite to back). Note the relation to east, the source of light, and **דם** (44) blood, the carrier of consciousness. The connecting agent is Qoph, assigned to the Corporeal Intelligence and to alchemical multiplication. Rosenroth in K.D.L.C.K. (p.670) gives: *oriens seu anterius*, and say the supreme crown is thus called as it is before the created world. A long discussion follows. see 44, 100, 793, 259; 460 (Greek).

קדם to precede, come before, be in advance; to excel, surpass. front. In Deuteronomy 33:15: "And for the Chief things of the ancient mountains, and for the precious things of the lasting hills." With different pointing *qadem*: before, the east; ancient times.

סנדל a sandal, shoe, horseshoe, a flat fish; abortion.

ידעני a wizard, sorcerer; a magician. Also (per lexicon): familiar spirit; soothsayer.

η καρδια. heh kardia (Gr). the heart. see 136.

Θειον. Theion. deity. Theion is neutral of Orlos, the divine being, deity. in epic Greek it meant "Brimstone" (Latin sulfur). Note that in alchemical symbolism Sulphur stands for activity and self-consciousness, and in Qabalah is linked to Chokmah, root of Life-force.

"Daily use, moreover, blunts its indwelling powers, namely sulphur, or its soul, and it is continually becoming mingled and defiled with other things that are foreign to its nature. Hence it becomes daily more and more unfit to be subject of art. You must, therefore, seek to obtain gold which has a pure, living spirit, and of which the sulphur is not yet weakened and sophisticated, but is pure and clear (by passing through antimony, or by the heaven and sphere of Saturn, and being purged of all its defilement): otherwise the first substance, being spiritual and ethereal, will not combine with it." [Waite, 1974, vol. 1, p. 81] see 693, 720.

η εκλογη. heh-eklogeh (Gr). the chosen; the elect of God. [Romans 11:7] "What then? The thing Israel earnestly seeks; this he did not obtain; but the chosen obtained it, and the rest were blinded."

145

מטה האלהים Rod of God (Moses staff).

עלמה virgin maiden, damsel, a young women of marriageable age. In Hebrew scriptures it always implies technical virginity. It never applies to a married woman. see 10, 443.

יפנה "He will be prepared." the father of Caleb (Joshua 15:13). Yod is Chokmah and Yesod, Peh is Mars, Nun is Mars in Scorpio, Heh refers to Aries and to vision. This all has to do with the secret use of the Mars force to produce the son (Caleb). Also: Yod + Peh = 90 or Mem (**מים**, Key 12) and Tzaddi. Reversal and meditation. Nun + Heh = 55 (Nah) or ornament, relating to Malkuth. see 197, 249, 52.

מעלה ascent; inscrutable. The ascent up the Tree of Life. With different pointing: *maelaw*. ascent; stair, step; rise; gradation; superiority, advantage, height; heaven; virtue.

מעלה prominent, distinguished, excellent. see 452.

סעודה a feast, dinner, meal.

מן האדמה out of the ground. In Genesis 2:9: "and out of the ground made the Lord God to grow every tree that is pleasant to the sight, and good for food; the Tree of Life also in the midst of the garden, and the Tree of the Knowledge of Good and Evil."

ממון hidden riches, treasure; hiding place. The "ground" or physical plane; in the microcosm, the physical body.

נממיה "God is Lovable, God Praise Worthy." 57th Shem ha-Mephorash. 281-285. May 15, July 26, December 17, February 27. 6:40-7:00 PM. [Psalm 115:11] "You that fear the Lord, trust in the Lord: he is their help and their shield." To prosper in all things, and to deliver prisoner. Rules great coronals, admirals, generals, and all who fight for a just cause. Person born: loves things military; distinguished himself for his activity, bravery and his grander of soul, and supports those with much courage. see 130, 690, 965.

Angel of 3rd quinance [11E-15E] of Taurus; angel by day of the 6 of Pentacles (Tiphareth of Assiah). This represents the sphere of the sun or central Ego, in the material world of action. The 6 of Pentacles is astrologically associated with the 2nd decanate of Taurus, ruled by Mercury. When well dignified, the influence of this angel can indicate practically and determination, discretion and diplomacy; gain by letters, writing, travel, speaking, teaching, commissions and through advertising, study, books, and all things ruled by Mercury. When ill-dignified, it can mean loss through the same things. see 145 & Appendix 10.

הקם "God who erected the universe." 16th Shem ha-Mephorash, short form. see 160 & Appendix 10.

נצה Blossom; flower. In Isaiah 18:5: "For before the harvest, when the bud has perished and the grapes is ripening in the flower, he shall both cut off the lean shoots with pruning hooks and take away and shake off the branches." And in [Job 15:33] "He shall shake off his unripe grapes, as the vine, and shall cast off his flowers as the olive tree."

Summon Bonium (Lt). highest good "Above all things you must let it be your first object to [dis]solve this substance (or first entity, which the sages have also called the highest natural good). Then it must be purged of its watery and earthy nature (for at first it appears an earthy, heavy, thick, slimy and misty body), and all that is thick, nebulous, opaque, and dark in it must be removed, that thus, by a final sublimation, the heart and inner soul contained it may be separated and reduced to a precious essence." [Waite, 1974, vol. 1, p. 80]

filius Dei roseae. Son of God + Rosy. Christ, (בן) the son, and also the rose at the center of the cross. see 88, 57 (Lt).

Αβρααμ. Abram (Gr). Abraham, the father of Israel. In Hebrews 11:8: "In faith Abraham was obedient, he being called to go forth into the place which he was in future to receive an inheritance; and he went forth, not knowing where he was going." see 248.

146

סוף end, close, to limit, to perish. In the Chaldee (Aramaic) signifies "to be fulfilled." These nouns are derived from a verb meaning to erase, or to perish. Thus the strict meaning of Ain Suph is "not perishable," or "never ending."

בבא קמא the First Gate [K.D.L.C.K. p.184]. The primary activity which begins the creative process is the establishment of the field of apparent limitation. The entrance of the No-Thing into the Something is through the fixation of a field in which to manifest itself. Relates to the meanings of Key 1.

עולם something hidden; time immemorial; antiquity, hidden times (the past); eternity; the world. The true nature of this field is a mystery, but one which is somehow related to our conceptions of time and duration. The field is the field of eternity, and this eternal arena of the Life-power's self-expression is the true "world." Signifies primarily, hidden times, time long past; but has the same meanings as the Greek word Aeon, the Latin *Mundus*, and the English "world." Here it is the "universe", which better indicates the whole cycle of manifestation as a space-time continuum. With different pointing: means long duration; futurity, forever, always, continuous everlasting; the here and now. In Genesis 9:12: "And God said to Noah, this is the sign of the covenant which I make between me and you and every living creature that is with you, for perpetual (*olahm*) generations." In Ecclesiastes 3:11: "He has made everything beautiful in its time; he has also made the world dear to man's heart, so that no man can find out the works which the Lord has done from the beginning to the end." Translated "of old" in Deuteronomy 32:7 and everlasting to everlasting in Psalm 90:2. see 207, 706, 536, 1192, 632, 861 (Greek), 1577.

יוסף Joseph. As spelled in Deuteronomy 33:17.

יהוה נסי the miraculous or marvelous. In Exodus 17:15: "(And Moses built an altar and he called its name) IHVH the miraculous/marvelous."

חמה ולבנה Sun and Moon. see 53, 87.

147

I. (3 x 7 x 7) or [$6^2 + 11^2$]

II. Area of a square on internal diagonals of 7 cube (exact).

רמדונע חכה The setting of the Sun. A hint that the "beginning" of a cycle is also the "end" of another. "End and beginning are one." Qabalists knew, long before Copernicus, that the Earth was a globe, and that sunrise and sunset are only appearances.

זהב מופז Pure Gold. *Aesch Mezareph* [Ch. 2:6]: Paz (87), and Zahab Muphaz are referred to Tiphareth... For so Tiphareth and Malkuth are compounded in the Golden throne.... For so Tiphareth and Malkuth are compounded in the Golden Throne; also when it is called a vessel of gold; a crown of Gold, Bases of Gold. see 14, 133 and Paz (87) for full quote.

יהוה אדני אהיה אגלא IHVH Adonai, Eheyeh, Agla. four names in the ritual of the Lesser Pentagram as ordinarily written.

148

בני אלהים Sons of God, Sons of the Elohim. The angelic choir or order of angels associated with Hod, in Assiah, the material world. The same choir is attributed also to Hod in Briah, the creative world.

נצח Netzach. Victory, eminence; juice of grapes, to shine; eternity [1 Chron. 29:11 and Isaiah 25:8]. Seventh Sephirah. Overcoming ignorance. Opposite and complement of Hod. The original signification of this noun is brightness, clarity. Sometimes translated as splendor, glory, sincerity or truth. Occasionally it has the connotation of perpetuity or everlastingness. Often it conveys the idea of completeness or perfection, its use in this sense being comparable to the English "clear," which has the same basic meaning of brightness. The most usual meaning of Netzach is Victory. In 1 Chronicles, 29:11, in that Prayer of David which

is a brief summary of the main points on the Tree of Life. In Isaiah 25:8 Netzach is translated victory. "He will swallow up death in victory." Furthermore, the pronoun "He" in this passage refers to Jehovah Tzabaoth, the Lord of Hosts, specially assigned to Netzach in Qabalah. As the Occult or Hidden Intelligence it suggests the idea that the one life is a power that is perfectly successful and cannot fail, as a whole or in any detail. The victory for man has to do with the control and direction of reproductive (Mars) force, by the practice of meditation and then applied to definite forms of cultural activity transforming appearances of failure into evidences of victory, by control of desires, conserving physical energy and supplying the bloodstream with strength to manifest the higher powers. Tzaddi = Fishhook, that which lifts the fish, Nun, from the water, raises the reproductive power from subconsciousness to self-consciousness-meditation. Cheth = field, enclosed by a fence; limitation of a specific area for purposes of cultivation. Ojas, literally "the illuminating, the brilliant" is the root meaning of Netzach. Ojas is "the highest form of energy attained by a constant practice of continence and purity. see 710, 525, 93, 64 and *True and Invisible Rosicrucian Order*, [pp.203-212].

In the cube בן, מלך and אדם are conjoined. These are the names of Tiphareth, which add to 187 which reduces to 7, and this is its essence. The secret of Tiphareth is 7, or Netzach. The letters of Victory are Nun, Tzaddi, and Cheth. This is the Power, the Method, and the Result. The power of Scorpio, raised by the meditation (Tzaddi) which unveils Truth, brings about the consciousness that personality is the vehicle, or Chariot (Cheth), which is also the lodge, and the house, temple, or palace of influence. See **13**.

נצח to shine, sparkle; to be victorious. With different pointing 1. *netzachah*: to superintend, act as overseer; to lead in music, glorify, make illustrious. 2. *nutzach*. to be defeated, be vanquished. 3. to be.

אהיה יה יהוה אלהים A Divine Name which combines the names of God ascribed to Kether, Chokmah and Binah. Thus it stands for the Supernal Triad of Sephiroth, and by its correspondence to נצח, intimates that in some sense the 7th Sephirah is a synthesis of the powers of the Supernal Triad. Therefore 148 is a numerical symbol of the divine powers concentrated in the Primal Will, Wisdom, and Understanding. The concentration of these forces produces the eternal victory of the Life-power. The victory is related to the fact that the Life-power does nothing, it is always withdrawn from activity. This is the most difficult doctrines, for it seems to contradict the teaching that the Life-power the cause of all activity.

אלהא עליא The Most High God. (Daniel 3:26). Aramaic. Eloha is 37, the number of **יחידה**, Yekhidah, the Supreme Self. Elyah adds to 111, the number of the letter-name Aleph. Here is a suggestion that the 7th Sephirah partakes of the combined powers of Kether, focused in Yekhidah, and of the path of Aleph, which links Kether to Chokmah.

מאונים balances, scales; sign of Libra; in later Hebrew, horizontals. The later meaning is a clue to the significance of the term "horizontals" in Masonic symbolism. Note that it is derived from the horizontal position of the beam of a balance when the weights in the pans are equilibrated. see 158, 302.

נחץ to press, to urge; to be urgent, to require haste. This word is a rearrangement of the letters of **נצח**, is related also to the 7th Sephirah as the seat of desire and passion.

חבק to enclose, encompass.

חסף clay. In Daniel 2:33: "His legs of iron, his feet part of iron and part of clay." Part of the image revealed in the king's dream. With different pointing 1. *khoseph*: revelation; laying bare. 2. *khahsaf.* to lay bare, reveal; draw water. see 868.

סחף to withdraw, retire. With different pointing: to sweep, or scrape, away; to bear down, to cast down. In Proverbs 28:3: "A poor man that oppresses the poor is like a sweeping rain which leaves no food." In Jeremiah 46:15: "Why are thy valiant men swept away? They stood not, because the Lord did drive them." Compare with the symbolism of Key 16 which represents the primary projection of desire-force from the seventh Sephirah.

פסח Literally, "a skipping over", the technical term translated Passover in the English Bible. The Passover festival, Passover sacrifice. With different pointing: to limp, hobble.

קמח flour, meal. With different pointing: to pound, grind. The relation of this word to Netzach, the seat of desire, is an important clue to the inner meaning of Jesus' parable of the leaven, which a woman took and hid in three measures of meal. The three measures may be understood to be the three Sephiroth immediately below Tiphareth on the Tree. These three are the seats of the principles of personal consciousness, and it is they which must receive the "leaven" which comes from above. see Genesis 18:6, 656 (Greek), 507, 1379, 889, 1919, 1969.

אדם מאבין Man of Understanding. In Proverbs 28:2: "For the transgression of a land many are the princes thereof: but by a man of understanding and knowledge the state thereof shall be prolonged." see 45, 102.

אמאימון Amaimon. Demon King of the element of Earth and the North. According to the *Goetia*, the Demon King of the east [Godwin, 1999, p.18]. see 798 & Appendix 11.

אנסואל Ansuel. Angel ruling the 11th house of Aquarius.

Soiriti damnati (Lt). reprobate spirits [Secret Symbols p. 30]. This refers to spirits under condemnation because of uncontrolled activities of the desire nature and misuse of the intellect. Yet these aspects of human personality when brought under right direction from above are released from condemnation, that is, from automatic response to deluded self-consciousness.

149 (prime)

אלים חים the Living Gods [Deuteronomy 5:26]. see 154.

הספד a beating of the breast; a noisy striking.

הספד mourning; funeral oration, obituary.

Serpentarius (Lt). The serpent. Mentioned in the *Confessio Faraternitatis* "God, indeed hath already sent messengers which should testify his will, to wit, some new stars which have appeared in Serpentarius and Cygus, the which powerful signs of a great council show forth how for all things which human ingenuity discovers, God calls upon his hidden knowledge."

Serpentarius or Ophiuchus is a constellation associated with the 1st decanate of Scorpio due to its position on the elliptic. It is shown as a man wrestling with a serpent, symbolizing the part of the Great Work which has to do with the transmutation of the forces of reproduction associated with the letter Nun (50). Cygnus is associated with the forces of Ayin (70).

Ipsissumus (Lt). He who is most himself. I my very self. The Rosicrucian Grade of consciousness corresponding to Kether and *Yekhidah* יהידה, the One Self. It represents the highest possible realization of the meaning of I AM. In this connection note that יהידה is the feminine form of יהיד, Unity. Although the I AM is One and Alone, it is the vehicle or receptacle for *Ain Soph Aur* אין סוף אור, the Boundless Limitless Light, and as a receptacle, by definition it is feminine. see 7, 620, 111.

Αριηλ. Ariehl. Ariel, "Lion of God"; a poetic name for Jerusalem. Septuagint Translation of אריאל (242) in Isaiah 29:1: "Woe to you Ariel, Ariel, the city were David settled! Add year to year and let your cycle of festivals go on." see 242, 586, 216.

ακριβεια. akribeia (Gr). exactness, strictness, extreme accuracy. Refers to instructed in all the exactness the precise discipline and observance of the traditional law. see Acts 22:3.

οικημα. oikehma (Gr). a dwelling, house or building. In the New Testament, a prison. written οικηματι in Acts 12:7: "And behold, an angel of the Lord stood by him, and a light shone in the building; and striking Peter on the side, he awoke him, saying, 'arise quickly'. and his chains fell from his hands." see 1672.

150

The number of days the waters prevailed over the land during the Biblical flood.

אדם עלה the heavenly man. Of which God is said to have used it as a chariot (מרכבה) Mercavah to descend [Zohar] the divine idea of man is the vehicle whereby God enters into the apparently separated forms of creation [John 1]. see 151, 267, 373.

על-האדם the man. In Genesis 2:16: "And the Lord God commanded the man, saying, of every tree of the garden thou may freely eat" (but not of the Tree of the Knowledge of Good and Evil). על is here translated "the", but has the usual meaning height, upper part, above. This seems to imply that Adam here is the supernal Adam, of archetypal humanity, before the "fall" from above.

אלהא עליא Most High God.

מלך הנגב King of the south. See Daniel 11:5.

עינך thine eyes [Deuteronomy 19:13, 15:9]. Refers expressly to the divine beneficence, which prospers all human undertaking. see The Greater Holy Assembly (para. 652).

בסחף to scrape away.

בחסף in clay.

פ/ע Mars (Peh) in Capricorn (Ayin).

קים stable, enduring, lasting; path of Mem variant spelling. see 160, 710.

קן cell, chamber; nest, bird in a nest; bird offering, the couple of sacrificial birds. In Leviticus 12:8 "...She shall bring... two young pigeons; the one for the burnt offering, and the other for a sin offering..." The "chamber" refers to the "upper room" or brain center where contact with the "eye" of God is made. The sacrifice of birds suggest that intellect, an airy quality, must be stilled for this to happen. see 800.

I. In Job 29:18: "I thought, 'I will die in my own nest (קני, i.e. house), my day as numerous as the grains of sand." Plural קנים in Genesis 6:14: "So make yourself an ark of Cypress wood; make rooms in it and coat it with pitch inside and out."

II. "This has two sources whose expression are blended in one. By the first, it is derived from the root קָ, image of the blind force which moves matter, united to the augmentative sign ן; by the second, it springs from the compressive sign ק, contracted with the root אָ, symbol of all corporeal circumscription; thence,

קָן that which *tends* with ardor toward a thing, that which is *envious, usurping, vehement, covetous* of gain and possession; thence: That which is *centralized, concentrated* in itself. From these two root קִין [Cain] if formed, in which are assembled the opposed ideas of *appetent tension* and *compression, vehemence* and *closeness, power* and *density*. It contains *the central force, profound basis, rule* and *measure* of things; also *the faculty* which *seizes, usurps, agglomerates, appropriates* and *assimilates with itself.*

The Arabic verb which partakes most of the radical sense, signifies literally to *forage* the iron, to strike it while it is hot; *to solder* metals, to unite them by means of the forge.

קָן or קָנוּ (intensive) is a literal and restricted sense *a nest, a center, a cane, a measure, reed; an abode, a possession, an acquisition, conquest; a possessor, envious person, rival; envy, hatred, jealously, an affair, property, wealth,* etc." [d'Olivet, 1976, p. 443.]

כַּלִמֻּדִים as they that are taught. In Isaiah 50:4: "The Lord God has given me the tongue of the learned, that I should know how to speak a word in season to him who is weary: he awakens morning by morning, he awakens mine ear to hear as the learned."

יִדְעֹנִי wizard, sorcerer, magician; soothsayer, familiar spirit. In K.D.L.C.K. (p.53): "Ariolus [is a] name for one of the outer shells which are Qlippoth or the pair of impure shells." Note: the root of this word seems to be יָדַע "to know, learn to know; to perceive, consider." It is interesting to know that the heads of the dragon (Qlippoth) extend as far as דַּעַת Da'ath or Knowledge. see 474.

נָעַל to bolt, bar, lock; to lock up, close. Suggests closing the mind to impure thoughts. With different pointing: 1. to put on sandals, shoes. 2. sandal, shoe, boot. Those used for treading the magic circle.

עָמַם "Covered in Darkness." 52nd Shem ha-Mephorash, short form. With different pointing: *Amam.* to darken, dim. Written יוּעַם [lost-luster] in Lamentations 4:1: "How the gold has lost its luster, the fine gold becomes dull." To bear (a load); to lay upon, to load. Genesis 44:12: "... then they all loaded their donkeys, and returned to the city." see 165, 710 & Appendix 10.

"Every union in great number; *a multitude*: action of *gathering, covering, hiding, obscuring, heating* by piling up.

Of its root: עַם hum. Matter universalized by its faculties: tendency of its pares one toward another; the force which makes them gravitate toward the general mass, which brings them to aggregation, accumulation, conjunction; the force whose unknown cause is expressed, the relations *with, toward, among, at.* Every idea of union, junction, conjunction, nearness: *a bond, a people, a corporation.*" [d'Olivet, 1976, p. 418.]

יָסַף to add. In Leviticus 22:14: "And if a man eats of the holy thing unwittingly, then he shall add a fifth part thereof to it and shall give it to the priest with the holy things." Also in Isaiah 38:5: "Go and say to Hezekiah, King of Judah, thus says the Lord, the God of David your father: I have heard your prayer, I have seen your tears; behold, I will add fifteen years to your days." see 870.

Salvator Mundi (Lt). Savior of the world [Secret Symbols page 7].

Jehova Salvator (Lt). Jehovah Savior. Intimates the identity of the Logos with the supreme reality designated as IHVH. see 26.

Annuite coeptis (Lt). "He hath prospered our undertaking." "He" is IHVH, symbolized by the all-seeing eye on the Great Seal of the U.S. see 71, 79, 370 (Lt), 632.

occultum lapidem (Lt). hidden stone [Secret Symbols page 17]. see 570, 57, 164, 94.

Omnia in omnibus (Lt). all in all.

Jesus mihi omnia (Lt). Jesus is all things to me. A Rosicrucian motto [*Fama*]. The actual substance of all things in the One Being. The inscription was found engraved on the circular altar in the tomb or C.R.

"The name Jesus signifies 'self-existence liberates'. Thus the *Fama* by connecting this word of freedom with the word *omnia*, signifying 'everything' intimates the characteristic Rosicrucian point-of-view, which is that everything contributes to liberation. The nature of things is to set free, rather than to bind. Thus the motto is the affirmation of the inherent tendency to liberty, at the very heart of the cosmic order. ...

Jesus promised to those who would pray 'in his name'. For whosoever truly prays <u>in</u> that name prays in the recognition of the idea the name represents, and he prays effectively who is thoroughly imbued with the thought that the nature of things is liberative, rather than restrictive. [Case, 1985, p. 121.] see 67, 373, 46 (Lt), 326, 1480, 2368 Greek.

Ναθνιλ. Nathanel (Gr). Gift of God [John 1:49]. Greek spelling of a Hebrew name.

151 (prime)

אדם עלאה adam e-lo-oh. the heavenly man. (variant spelling, see 150).

מקוה meqeveh. collection, gathering together (of water), a place where water flows together (confluence), pool; reservoir; ritual bath of purification; with different pointing: hope, confidence.

I. In the *Sepher Sephiroth* "The Fountain of Living Waters" [Crowley, 1977, p. 21]. However, in this usage the word is translated as "hope".

II. Jeremiah 17:13: "O Lord, the hope (מקוה) of Israel, all who forsake you will put to shame. Those who turn away from you will be written in the dust because they have forsaken the Lord, the spring of living water (מקור מים חיים)."

קומה qomah. a standing upright, stature, height, man's height; floor, story. The true measure of a man is the extent to which he has been able to raise his consciousness in daily life.

קנא qna. jealous, zealous; zealot, fanatic. As a verb: to be jealous, to be zealous; to be envious.
נקא neqa. clean, pure.

אנק awnaq. to shriek, cry, groan.

נאק nawahq. to groan (growing cry). The change (Nun) of Spirit (Aleph) in the bodily organization (Qoph). This implies less resistance than above for positive results.

אלף הה יוד הה Aleph-Heh-Yod-Heh. Eheieh (I am) spelled in plentitude. The goal of the quest. see 21, 111, 10, 20.

מאלף Malaph; Malphas. Goetic demon #39 by night of the 3rd decanate of Aries. see Appendix 11 & 871.

Goetia: He appears first like a crow, but after he will put on human shape at the request of the Exorcist, and speak with a hoarse voice. He is a mighty president and powerful. He can build houses and high towers, and can bring to thy knowledge enemies' desires and thoughts, and that which they have done. He gives good Familiars. If thou makes a sacrifice unto him he will receive it kindly and willingly, but he will deceive him that does it. He governs 40 Legions of spirits." [Mathers, 1995, p. 48]

חן חן לה khane khane lah. grace, grace unto it. In Zechariah 4:7: "Who are thou, O great mountain? Before Zerubbabel; thou shall become a plain, and he shall bring forth the headstone thereof with shoutings, crying, grace, grace unto it."

I. "These considerations bring out into a very clear light one meaning of Daniel's prophecy of 'the stone' cut out without hands, which grew until it filled the whole earth. It is the same 'stone' of which Jesus spoke, and is bound by the inevitable sequence of evolution to become the chief corner-stone; that is, the angular or five-pointed stone in which all four sides of the pyramid find their completion. It is the headstone capping the whole, of which it is written that it shall be brought forth with shoutings of 'grace, grace unto it.'" [Troward, 1942, p. 141.] see 58.

יהוה אלהים יהוה אחד IHVH Elohim IHVH Ehad. "The Lord (Tetragrammaton) of the Gods, the Lord (Tetragrammaton) is one." See Deuteronomy 6:4; 410, 951.

η καθηδρα. heh Kathedra (Gr). God's seat (Cathedral). [original text degraded, this is my best guess]

Λαοδικεια. Laodikeia (Gr). Laodicia. In Colossians 4:15, one of the 7 churches (interior stars) in Revelations 1:11.

Μαρθα. Martha (Gr.). Probably of Caldean origin. meaning mistress. [Strong, 1996, p. 655.] Sister of Mary. In Luke 10:38-42: "(38) Now while they were on their way, it occurred that Jesus entered a certain village, and a woman named Martha received and welcomed Him into her house. (39) And she had a sister named Mary, who seated herself at the Lord's feet and was listening to His teaching. (40) But Martha (over-occupied and too busy) was distracted about much serving; and she came up to Him and said, Lord, is it nothing to You that my sister has left me to serve alone? Tell her then to help me-to lend a hand and do her part along with me. (41) But the Lord replied to her by saying, Martha, Martha, you are anxious and troubled about many things; (42) There is need of (but a few things, or) only one. Mary has chosen the good portion-that which is to advantage-which shall not be taken away from her." Martha represents devoted service, which is apparently slower, but which leads to the same goal.

Magister Templi (Lt). Master of the Temple. corresponds to the Grade 8=3 and to Binah. Implies that the adept is in control of all of his vehicles of consciousness. see (84.

152

נקב to hollow out; to perforate; to cut asunder; to designate, to pierce, bore, perforate; to designate, distinguish, specify, to curse, blaspheme.

ויסעו That they set forward.

ויכל אלהים And God finished. see Genesis 2:2.

צביים Zeboiim. "Place of Hyenas." One of the 5 cities in the vale of Siddim, two of which are Sodom and Gomorrah in Genesis 14:8. In Hosea 11:8: "How shall I give thee up, Ephraim? How shall I deliver thee, Israel? How shall I set thee as Zeboiim? My heart is turned within me, my repentings are kindled together." Hyena suggest forlorn wailing. see 354, 104, 315, 50, 287.

בנימן Benjamin; "Son of the Right Hand". The name of the tribe of Israel related to Sagittarius and alchemical incineration (variant spelling). In Genesis 49:27: "Benjamin is a ravenous wolf; in the morning he devours the prey; in the evening he divides the plunder." see 162, 812, 802.

המוציא the bringing-forth one [Crowley, 1977, p. 21].

נציב residence, station [Crowley, 1977, p. 21]. Garrison, outpost in 1 Samuel 13:3: "Jonathan attacked the Philistine outpost at Geba, and the Philistines heard about it..."

Μαρια. Maria (Gr). Mary.

153

בצלאל Bezaleel. the skilled workman who made the greater part of the fittings of the Mosaic tabernacle. Son of Uri (217). [The Zohar termed it Betzel El, "in the very shadow of God.". Bezaleel typifies the alchemical operation-the building of the tabernacle of the regenerated personality. This is accomplished by control of the vibrations of atmospheric air through sounds and words, and the chanting of divine names and sentences (words of power). In Exodus 31:2,3: He was filled with the spirit of God, (Rauch Elohim) in Wisdom (Chokmah) and in Understanding (Tebunah, the Special Intelligence), and in Knowledge (Da'ath), and in all manner of workmanship (Melakah). see 217

בני-האלהים Sons of the Elohim, Sons of the God. Those who have followed a path of return back to their father's palace in the midst. Order of angels attributed to Hod and the Grade of Practicus. Refers of the descent of Tiphareth into Malkuth through Yesod. In Genesis 6:2: "That the sons of God saw the daughters of men that they were fair, and they took them wives of all which they choose." Mark 12:25: "For when they shall rise from the dead, they neither marry nor are given in marriage; but are as the angels which are in heaven." [i.e. Beni Elohim] see 148,

713, 268.

עגלים calves. In Malachi 4:2: "But unto you that fear [revere] my name shall the sun of righteousness arise with healing in his wings; and you shall go forth, and grow up as calves [בעגלי, like-calves-of] in the stall." A full-grown calf has developed intuition (Taurus, the Bull, Vav) and has the super-consciousness of the "ox", which is Aleph. The stall is Cheth, the fence or field of personality. The "sun" is the higher self in Tiphareth.

אני יהוה אלהיך I am the Lord thy God. [Isaiah 41:13, 43:3].

על-אבן upon this stone. [Judges 9:5]

בינה אלהים The great Supernal Mother. "The "Lord our God" is mother as well as father. see 67, 86

חדקיאל Chadaliel. Angel governing the sign of Libra, the balance.

געף Gaaph; Goap. Goetic demon #33 by day of the 3rd decanate of Aquarius. Demon King of the South. see Appendix 11.

I. "Gaap (Tap) - Once of the order of potentates (powers), now a fallen angel, Gaap serves in hell, as a great president and a mighty prince. As king of the south, he rules 66 legions of infernal spirits... pictured in the form of a human being with huge bat wings." [Davidson, 1971, p. 117.]

II. "Formally an angel of the Order of Power; now fallen and in hell. *Goap* is one of the infernal region's 11 presidents. He is also known as *Gaap* and *Tap*... That *Goap* was once of the Order of Powers was proved after infinite research, reports Spence, *An Encyclopedia of Occultism*. According to Demonologist, *Goap* was 'Prince of the West .'" [ibid, 1971, p. 125.]

III. *Goetia*: "He is a great president and mighty prince. He appears when the sun is in some of the southern signs, in a human shape, going before four great and mighty kings, as if he were a guide to conduct tem along on their way. His office is to make men insensible or ignorant; as also in philosophy to make them knowing, and in all the liberal sciences. He can cause love or hatred, also he can teach thee to consecrate those things that belong to the dominion of Amaymon his king. He can deliver familiars out of the custody of other magicians, and answers truly and perfectly of things past, present and to come. He can carry and re-carry men very speedily form one kingdom to another, at the will and pleasure of the exorcist. He rules over 66 legions of Spirits, and he was of the Order of Potentates." [Mathers, 1995, p. 44].

154

אלהים חים Elohim of Lives, Living God. In Deuteronomy 5:26: "For who is there of all flesh, who has heard the voice of the living God speaking out of the midst of he fire, as we have, and lived?"

Writing about alchemical silver the *Aesch Mezareph*: "To this place [Pau, פַּעָר brightness, 156] belongs another surname, i.e. Elohim Chaiim, as though it were called Living Gold, because Elohim and Gold denote the same measure. [Pau is the royal city of Tiphareth, the King] but so this water is called, because it is the mother and principle of living Gold: for all other kinds of Gold are thought to be dead; this only excepted." [Westcott, 1997, p. 40] see 158, 504, 149.

יהוה אלהוו יהוה Jehovah, our God Jehovah. In Deuteronomy 6:4: "Hear O Israel: the Lord [IHVH] our God is one Lord-the only Lord" (Amplified). "Hear O Israel! the Lord is our God, the Lord is one!" (New American Standard).

עולם הבא the world to come, future world. According to some, means the same as Gan Eden, the Garden of Eden. It is called "the world to come" in relation to the idea that man in his dream of separation must consider his restoration to the paradisiacal state as an event which is in the future, or "to come." The world to come is the New Heaven and Earth. see 52, 124, 177, 714.

לחם ויין Bread and wine. In Genesis 14:18: "Melchizedek brought forth (made manifest) bread and wine..." The bread symbolizes the Life-power as substance. The wine is the same as "Blood of the Grape," and is the animating energy. Both the substance and the animating energy are expressions of the Life-power, which is Jehovah, our God Jehovah." see 683, 36, 252,

315, 224, 314, 29, 714, 1364, 1352 (Greek), 1346.

האופן הגד   The wheel of fortune. Note that גד is the Babylonian name of Jupiter, meaning "good fortune." see 47.

אביאסף   Father of Gatherings.

חמה אין לי   fury is not in me, I am not angry.

Isaiah 27:4: "I am not angry, if only there were briers and thorns confronting me! I would march against them in battle; I would set them all on fire." [Kohlenberger, 1987, Vol. IV, p. 51.]

II. "If we once realize the great truth stated in Psalm 18:26 and 2 Samuel 22:27, that the divine universal spirit always becomes to us exactly the correlative of our own principle of action and that it does so naturally be the Law of Subjective Mind, the it must become clear that it can have no vindictive power in it, or as the Bible expresses it, "fury is not in me."". [Troward, 1942, p. 236.]

III. Psalm 18:26: "With the pure you will show yourself pure; and with the crooked you show yourself shrewd." 2 Samuel 22:37 is identical except it uses the word "unsavory" for "shrewd". See Ezekiel 18:29-32.

In centro solis (Lt). in the center of the sun. In the Rosicrucian Confessio, in a context which promises "all the goods which nature hath dispersed in every part of the earth" to those who are willing to cooperate in the Work of God. He who cooperates conforms his desire with the Great Center, and "all that the Father hath is mine" expresses this consciousness.

rosa Jesus est (Lt). The rose is Jesus. "Jesus" is to be understood as meaning the same as in Jesus Mihi Omnia (150). The rose is the flower of Venus, and when it s centered on a cross of 6 squares, formed by the opening-out of a cube, we have the true emblem of the rose-cross. It is a symbol of the perfect coordination of the desires of man (the rose) with the basic pattern of creation. Essentially, this is what is meant also by: In centro solis. see 67, 47 Latin.

Vicarius filii Dei. Vicar of the son of God. Jesus is the earthly representative of the Solar Logos. [This numeration is by Latin Cabala simplix, see

666]. see also 326 for esoteric meaning of the name Jesus.

Γαβριηλ. Gabriel (Gr). "The Divine Messenger to Earth. The hermeneia of the word suggest the strength of man and of God. As herald his nature is akin to that of Iris, the Messenger of Promise." [Omikron, 1942, p. 251.]

155

קנה   cana. a reed, a measuring rod. In the Hebrew dictionary: reed, stalk, cane; beam of scales; arm, shaft (of lamp stand); windpipe (Talmudic). The Hebrew name of the City, Cana, where Jesus performed the miracle of changing water into wine. As a verb it means to purchase, to buy, to possess, to acquire possessions by a symbolic act. Also proper name of a brook between Ephraim and Manasseth [Joshua 16:8] and a City in Asher [Joshua 19:8]. see 72 (Greek).

אדני מלך   Adonai Melek. Lord King, The Divine Name attributed to Malkuth. see 90, 65, 671, 496.

I. In Malkuth is the power of our Lord and King Adonai Melek. The number of Adonai Melek is the same as דודנאמן, the faithful friend, for our Lord King is our friend. See 26, 31, 386, 90, 89.

Adonai Melek is Lord of the Waters, and waters is Mem מים, which is 90, the same as מלך (King) and the King Yeshua stilled the waters (seas). Adonai Melek is 155 or אל Al 31 x 5. This relates to man's body and his five senses and the pentagram, which in magic is directly connected with Malkuth. see C.7.

אם גלה סודו   He reveals His plan [secret] In Amos 3:7: "Surely the Sovereign Lord does nothing without reavealing his plan [secret] to his servants the prophets." The initial אם is usually omitted in considering this gematria. But since אם-גלה is a hyphenated word, meant to be considered as one word, it is included. Its value 79 is also the number of בעז, Boaz, the black pillar also spelt בועז (85). see 79, 70, 41, 715.

דיד נאמן   faithful friend. see 14, 91.

226

צ-נ-ט-ו Vav-Teth-Nun-Tzaddi. the fixed signs of the zodiac. Symbolized by the living creatures which are shown in the corners of Keys 10 and 21. see 564 Latin.

ינהלני yanheleni. He leads me. In Psalm 23:2: "He leads me beside the still waters…" Paul Case adds this note in the margin: he leads me = he reveals his secret = secret of secrets = the faithful friend. see 55, 654.

קימה rising, raising, erection.

עלמיה "the concealed and saving." 4th Shem ha-Mephorash. Associated with the 4th quinance of Leo; angel by night of the 6 of Wands [Tiphareth of Atziluth] or the central Ego on the archetypal plane. see 140 & Appendix 10.

"One of the 8 Seraphim of the Tree of Life in the *Book of Yetzirah* [Book of Formation], an angel (one of 72) bearing the mystical name of God Shemhamphorae. Elemiah rules over voyages and maritime expeditions. His corresponding angel is Senacher." [Davidson, 1971, p. 104.] see 700.

צח ואדום "(my beloved is) white and ruddy." [Canticles 5:11]. An alchemical allusion to the white and red stages of the great work. see 715, 1706 (Greek).

סנהם Sanahem. Lord of triplicity by day for Leo. the guardian support (Samekh) of the seed of change (Nun) constituted (Heh) into stability (Mem). Godwin Spelling, see 108 for S.S. spelling.

דקנא the beard

I. S.D.: "The beard of truth. (That is, now follows a description of the beard of Macroprosopus, and its 13 parts, which are made fully described in the Idra Rabba)."

["The beard is the influx which descends from the first sephira through all the others. Macroprosopus is of course… the first Sephira, Kether, or the crown: also called the Ancient One."] [Mathers, 1993, p. 66]. see 78.

arcanum arcanorum (Lt). secret of secrets. "The Kingdom (Malkuth) is here, though it is truly the Kingdom of the skies, and its secret has to do with embodiment, that is to day, with the right knowledge of what bodies are, and what they are for." [Secret Symbols page 20]. see 564.

aureum seculum (Lt). the Golden Age. Part of the title of an alchemical treatise included in Secret Symbols (page 20).

libertas evangelii (Lt). the liberty of the Gospels. In the *Fama Fraternitatis* written round the circle containing the picture of an eagle, or Scorpio-water (see 564).

"…it refers to the 'good news of freedom' which is the burden of the New Testament. That 'good news' has for its essential principle the idea represented by the name Jesus, which means 'the nature of reality is to set free'. Jesus and Joshua are two forms of the same name, and the Old Testament tells us that Joshua, who succeeded Moses as leader of the children of Israel, was the son of Nun. That is, his father's name was the same as the name of the letter connected by Qabalists with the sign Scorpio. Just as the leadership of Joshua follows that of Moses, so does the fulfillment of the ancient law by Jesus succeed its earlier manifestations of sacrifice. similarly, after preliminary purifications of yoga and alchemy (The yoke of the Law, [see 113]) comes the liberation of the good news which is heard by the initiate through the transmutation of the Scorpio energies. Thus the Rosicrucian allegory tells us that when brother C.R.C. had overcome the feebleness of his body during his stay of Damascus [444] he heard of the wise men at Damcar [264], went to their temple, and received from them good news, not only as to the significance of events that had happened while he was yet in the closter of the sense-life, but also concerning the true meaning of the world of nature. This good news is associated with the eagle, as a symbol of the regenerated activities of the Scorpio force, connected with the element of water, always a symbol of purification. Hence we find the alchemist directing their pupils to wash the matter many times, and then, say they, the great wonder will appear to you. Similarly, when this purification is accomplished we have borrowed strength from the eagle, and have eyes with which to see and recognize the great truth that every thing in our environment works for liberty, and not for human bondage." [Case, 1985, p. 125.] see 326, 106, 700, 50.

The perimeter of a right angle triangle whose sides are 39, 52 and 65 and the area of 104.

אבן אחד ולא אבן One stone and no stone. Alchemical description (reference) of the first matter.

אדם עלאי High Man. The celestial or ideal man. The Life-power's perfect image of itself. see 150, 151, 161, 1496.

אהל מועד Tabernacle of the Congregation. In Exodus 33:7 translated "tent of meeting." In Leviticus 1:1 as the place where Tetragrammaton called to Moses. Refers also to the fact that he who finds the hidden stone enters the Holy of Holies or Adytum. Where he becomes aware of his affiliation or communion with the congregation of those who know. see 570, 36, 120.

אפעה a hissing reptile, adder, viper. [Job 20:16 and Isaiah 30:6, 59:5]. Refers to the serpent-power, but whose activity without control is poison to those who use it.

יוסף Joseph. Multiplier, addition. . Refers to the alchemical doctrine that the stone has powers of multiplication. In Genesis 49:26: "The blessing of your father have prevailed abode the blessing of my progenitors unto the utmost bound of the everlasting hills: they shall be on the head of Joseph, and on the crown of the head of him that was separate from his brethren." Yesod as the generative power of Tiphareth is one meaning; it is the dwelling place of the "multiplier". The separated brethren are multiplied into unity. Note: The correspondence of יושף and to עוף, both representing the positive aspects of the North, just as מלכות ערפל and שקוץ שמם are terms relating to the negative aspects.

כמיץ Kamotz, Kamauts. Angel of 1st decanate of Scorpio. This decanate is ruled by Mars. see 45, 270.

הסניאל Hasaniel. Angle of Hod in Briah. Has to do with the power of intellect (self-consciousness) in creative imagery.

נעול enclosed; shut up. See Song of Solomon 4:12, where this adjective is combined with the word גן, Garden and גל, spring, water-source. גן refers to Binah, the mother, and to Malkuth, the Bride. The garden is the same as עדן כבוד, the Eden of Glory.

עדן כבוד Eden (paradise) of Glory. Applied to the 16th Path of Vav, "called the Triumphant and Eternal Intelligence because it is the delight of glory, the glory of *Ain* [61], the no-thing, veiling the name of him, the fortunate one, and it is called also the Garden of Eden, prepared for the compassionate." [Text on the 22 Paths].

עין יהוה the Eye of Jehovah. In Psalm 33:18: "Behold, the eye of the Lord is upon them that fear him, upon them that hope in his mercy." Refers to the 3rd eye which it is the purpose of alchemy to rouse to full activity (see Zion below & Job 28:2).

ציון Zion. The Holy of Holies. The mountain top in Jerusalem (abode of peace) where contact with God is made. This refers to the awakening of the Brain center around the Pineal Gland (Mercury inner holy planet) to experience a higher mode of consciousness. [ציץ, 105, "to glitter, to burn, to glow: the power from Kether. Note Zion in Assiah is the seat of Yekhidah (Kether in the physical body)] With different pointing: dryness, sigh-post, monument, quote. The east hill of Jerusalem on which the temple stood. (Mt. Moriah, sometimes mentioned as the site of the temple, is simply a peak of the hill to which the name עיין is given). Thus Zion was the foundation supporting the temple. Hence the Zohar (Lesser Holy Assembly, page 743) identifies Zion as the feminine aspect of Yesod, the Foundation. It says "this is the feminine secret part, and in the bride (Malkuth) is called the womb. Also parched ground, desert. see 158, 750, 513, 569, 1060 (Greek), 74 (Lt).

In Psalm 110:2: "The Lord shall send the rod of thy strength out of Zion: rule thou in the midst of thine enemies." Psalm 50:2: "Out of Zion, the perfection of beauty, God has shined."

צלול clear, lucid. In Judges 7:13: "a round loaf." It is used as a symbol in a dream. Sepher Sephiroth: limpid blood [Crowley, 1977, p. 21].

קיּוּם permanence, duration, existence, confirmation. Relates of alchemical Water. see 184, 744.

עוֹף to cover with wings, to fly, fly away; to flicker. With different pointing: fowl, bird, winged creature. In Genesis 1:20: "And Elohim said 'let the waters bring forth abundantly the moving creature that has life, and fowl [birds] that may fly, above the earth in the open firmament of heaven."

I. "Fowl... this expression, which depends still upon the verb יִשְׁרְצוּ, *shall spring forth*, and which is connected with the substantive הַמַּיִם, *the waters*, proves that Moses regarded the waters as specially charged with furnishing the first elements of vital movement to reptilian and flying animals. The root רָץ, of which is spoke above and the one now in question, are both linked to the same motive principle designated by the root שׁר; but whereas, by רָץ, should be understood, a laborious movement attached to the earth, by עוֹף, should be seen, an easy, soaring movement in the air. The one is heavy and rapid, the other light and swift. Both receive existence from the vital principle brought forth by the waters." [d'Olivet, 1976, p. 50-51.]

II. According to Westcott, this is one of three names for 'bird' [עִית and צִפּוֹר the other two] in alchemy, which generally means sublimations. *Aesch Mezareph: "And he shall have four Wings of a Bird upon his Back*, the four Wings are two Birds, which exasperate this Beast with their Feathers, to the intent he may enter and fight with the Bear and Lion; altho' of himself he be volatile and biting enough, and venomous like a Winged Serpent and Basilisk. And the Beast had four Heads; in which Words are understood four Natures lurking in his Composition, i.e., white, red, green, and watery.

And power was given him over the other Beasts, i.e., the Lion and the Bear, that he may extract their gluten or Blood." [Westcott, 1997, p. 25] see 376, 480.

פָּעוּ screaming. Name of King and City of Edom (Genesis 36:34). In the Zohar, Edom is connected with unbalanced forces.

I. *Aesch Mezareph:* "But that thou mayest know,

that Tiphareth, of the degree of Geburah, is understood; know thou, that number being added to the whole, is also contained in Isaac [208], which is like manner is of the classis of Gold.

The City of that King [Tiphareth] is called Pegno [pau], Brightness, from its Splendor, according to Deuteronomy 33:2 which name, and the name Joseph (by which Yesod is meant, have the same number, 156). That you may know that Argent vive is required to the Work; and that the Royal Beauty doth reside out of this Splendid City." [Westcott, 1997, p. 40]

II. Deuteronomy 33:2: "And he said, the Lord came from Sinai, and rose up from Seir unto them; he shined forth from mount Paran, and he came with ten thousand of saints: from his right hand went a fiery law for them."

באבאלען Babylon. "confusion"; name of the city in the Apocalypse, connected with the fallen woman. Variant spelling; see 34, 1285. The native name means "gate of God."

I. The title of the Scarlet Woman or consecrated priestess used in the rites of Draconian magick. Her number is 156, which is the number of shrines in the City of the Pyramids. Babalon means, literally, the Gateway of the Sun, or solar-phallic power. But Babalon is not only the medium of the solar force, she is the inspirer of its energy. At the height of her Rite she becomes oracular and endowed with magical *siddhis* (powers). [Grant, 1994, p. 259.]

centrum naturae (Lt). center of nature. Refers to Tiphareth as the seat of the human ego. The Ego is the Center of every person's universe. With the opening of the third eye, the centrum naturae becomes for man what it is for God. It is if the centers of 2 circles where make to coincide. Then the personal circle corresponds perfectly to the divine. The radius of the personal circle is finite; that of the divine circle is infinite. Their centers are one.

I. "I have sought; I have found; I have often purified; and I have joined together; I have matured it: then the golden tincture has followed, which is called the Center of Nature (hence so many opinions, so may books, so may parables). It is the remedy, I openly declare it, for all metals, and for all sick persons. The solution of the God." [Waite, 1974, vol. 1, p. 55]

II. Jacob Boemme writes: "Further, we are to inquire concerning to other will of the eternal father which is called God, which in the center of its heart desires light and the manifestations of the triad in wisdom. This will is set or directed towards the centrum naturae, for through nature must the splendor of majesty arise." [Six Theosophic Points, I 50, p.25]

III. Case: *centrum naturae* = 156 = עיון ועף = עין יהוה.

157 (prime)

מופלא Admirable or Wonderful. The 1st Path of Kether. Variant of *Pehleh* פלא. see 111, 507, 589, 620, 876.

דמדומי חמה the setting of the sun. A hint that the end of one cycle is also the beginning of another.

נזק nizzak, nizaq. to suffer loss. In relation to the Ace of Cups this refers to the limitation that the perfection of the One Life must suffer in order to begin a cycle of manifestation. It is referred to in the Bible as the "Lamb, slain from the foundation of the world." Why the perfect should enter such limitations is beyond human reason. In Esther 7:4: "For we are sold, and my people, to be slain, to be put to the sword, and to perish. But if we had been sold merely as bondsmen and bondswomen, would not have held my tongue, but the enemy would not hesitate to cause loss [בנזק] to the king."

נקבה female, yoni. Here is a reminder that behind all masculine representations of the Life-power is hidden the feminine aspect also. The feminine aspect is the "Nature" which Boehme calls the wrath or fire-spirit. [The masculine is נקב pipe, hole, perforation and plural נקבים, orifices, organs of elimination]. In Genesis 5:2: "Male and female he created them; and Elohim blessed them, and called their name Adam, in the day when they were created."

זקן the beard; lingam. The influence (Mezla) which descends from the first Sephirah through all the others. It is called "the beard of truth" in Sephira Dtzenioutha 2:1. With different pointing: an old man; elder; scholar; grandfather.

זעף anger, wrath. "God created all things..out of eternal nature, the fury or wrath, and out of his love. By means of which the wrath or nature was pacified. The wrath (Fire) is the root of all things and the origin of all Life. In it is the cause of all strength and power, and from it are issuing all wonders." [Jacob Boehme]. This seeming contradiction between wrath and wonderful indicates the transformation made in the force (Chaos) as it passes through it points of Primal Will (Kether). *Zahaef* is one of the alchemical names of the red stone, also called גפרית אדם (Gophrith Adam), etc. It is also called Ram, Mars (red-fire, red sulphur, etc.) With different pointing: 1. angry, irritated, ill-tempered; 2. to cry, cry out, call; 3. to be angry. see 785, 738, 693.

קנז A duke of Edom [Crowley, 1977, p. 22]. Associated with Netzach [*777*, Table CIX). This is related to Venus and thus to unbalanced desires and emotions. see Genesis 36:15.

ענואל 63rd Shem ha-Mephorash. "God, infinitely good." For the conversion of nations to Christianity. Protects against accidents, heals the sick. Positive influence: subtle and ingenious, industrious and active. Negative: folly and prodigality. see Appendix 10.

Angel of the 2nd decanate and 3rd quinance of Gemini, attributed to the 9 of Swords.

matrix corpus (Lt). mold of the body, or womb of the body [Secret Symbols page 27]. Refers to the first path as the womb of forms, containing the archetypal molds or patterns of all forms of embodied existence. Related to the Ace of Cups.

quinta essentia (Lt). Quintessence [Secret Symbols page 27]. The alchemical Quintessence is one with the Stone, and is none other that the true Self, seated in Kether. The whole work of the inner school aims at the discovery of one's identity, which is Yekhidah see 37, 1032.

158

נצח triumphant, eternal, enduring, sure. The 16th Path of Vav. This adjective is derived from the noun נצח, Victory, the 7th Sephirah. The Hierophant represents a mode of consciousness which invariably results in triumphant or victory. This is because, in dealing with every problem of human experience, it provides those who open their interior hearing to the Voice of the Master an absolute certitude based on eternal principles. The addition of a hand (Yod) to Netzach suggest the practical application of a ripened philosophy. That state of consciousness is open to those who have mastered their own personal instrument.

מים חיים living waters. Waters of Life. "The fountain of Living Waters" [Song of Solomon 4:15]. Used in the Song as a reference to the Bride, who is also the sister. The Living waters are the fludic, vibratory energy substance we find in "Zion"; and they are the beginning and end of all things, the alchemical AZΩתּ. [In its first state AZΩתּ, which is also Terra Adamica (Adamic Earth) is the first matter. This is said to be the "father of metals."] A name for the first matter identified with IHVH. Jesus used it as a symbol of the Life directed from within by guidance from the Hierophant.

בציון In Zion. In Isaiah 28:16: "Therefore thus says the Lord God, behold, I lay in Zion for a foundation a stone, a tried stone, a precious corner stone, a sure foundation: he that believes shall not make haste." Refers to the center of human personality, the point within, where man makes contact with the One Reality, designated, but not defined by the name Jehovah. It is the place in the midst, which we call the adytum, or holy of holies. Zion is a Qabalistic name for the feminine aspect of Yesod. see 156.

חצים arrows. Symbols of the direct, concentrated application of the Life-force, the entry of intuitive ideas into the mind. Thomas Paine refers to certain thoughts "entering my mind like arrows shot from outside", and says he made it a practice to always pay particular attention to such mental states. Note that the ancient form of the letter Beth was an arrow head. The arrow suggest penetration and the directness of the concentrated magical will.

חנק to encompass, to choke, strangle, threaten. The verb "to suffocate" refers to the mystical death of personality. Death (Nun) by the construction of the throat (Vav). The total eradication of the sense of separate personality before the true Self can be made manifest to effect the great conjunction "and" (Vav).

Please note that the Norse god Oden hung himself to receive wisdom. Also note that the throat is associated with the sign Taurus (and the letter Vav) which rules the throat associated with intuition. What is suggested is the death of the sense of a separate personality must be eliminated before the True Self can manifest. see 6, 331, 506, 12.

מאזנים scales, balances, Chaldee (Aramaic). Name of the sign Libra and Justice in the Tarot. Intuition enables one to establish this balance of Key 11 (Justice). Libra is under the same planetary rulership as the sign Taurus, which corresponds to the Vav and intuition. Intuition enables one to establish this balance of Key 11. eEuilibrium is the basis of the Great Work. see 148, 108, 520, 30, 74.

In Isaiah 40:15: "Behold, the Nations are as the drop of a bucket, and are counted as the small dust of the balance: behold, he takes up the isles as every little thing." Intuition enables one to establish the balance of Key 11. Libra is under the same planetary rulership (Venus) as Taurus, which corresponds to the 16th Path. Note the meaning of "Nations" and that "bucket" suggest the sign Aquarius (44) and alchemical dissolution. Meditation and equilibrium are thus implied.

Jehovah Salvator (Lt). Jehovah Savior. see 150.

Quinta Essentia (Lt). Quintessence. 5th essence. Akin to Azoth and the Hindu Akasha. It stands for the all pervading spirit. This is the more common Latin form. The quintessence and the "Living Waters" are one and the same. see 157, 168.

Κιρκη (Circe , Greek) The Entrantress in the Greek Odyssy. Circe island was the plance were Orion died.

159

בוצינא. surpassing whiteness. Refers to Kether.

נקדה point. Part of a title of Kether. The simple point.

בזקים in fetters. In Job 36:8: "And if they be bound in fetters, and be held in cords of affliction; (9) then he shows them their work and

231

their transgressions that they have exceeded."

קטן small, young, unimportant. A synonym for man, the microcosm. In Genesis 9:24: "And Noah awoke form his wine, and knew what his younger son [Canaan] had done unto him." Recall that Noah (58) means "rest, cessation"; that wine (70) is connected with the bloodstream and Venus, or desire, and that Canaan is related to wrath and Mars. see 190, 305.

ופגע and chance. In Ecclesistics 9:11.

ανηρ. aner (Gr.). man. refers to Adam and to Christ. see 229 Greek, 45.

"husband. The *aner* is greater than the Ανθρωπος (Man, 1310) *anthropos*. For *aner* means, par excellence, someone who is distinguished for a certain virtue, while *anthropos* means someone who is not distinguished for anything in particular. The word *aner* indicates the hero, the leader, the expert, it is said to be akin to ανυω, I complete, while the noun ανυσις means directing, a leading-up to the Above. Both the words *anthropos* and *aner* may be of the common gender." [Omikron, 1942, pp. 249-250.]

Lux, Crus Rosea (Lt). Light, the Rosy Cross.

Lux ex Tenebris (Lt). Light out of Darkness.

160

I. Number of years of the period of captivity of the Jews, from 747 - 587 B.C. (destruction of Jerusalem and the temple).

קיּם Stable, lasting, enduring. This is a special spelling of the adjective for stable, using two Yods instead of the one which appears in the commoner spelling קים. Thus the basic meaning of *qayam* is found in its feminine verbal root קימה signifying: to rise up, raising, erection. The secondary sense includes such ideas as "to stand out, to endure, to confirm, to establish," and it is from these that the adjective which designates the path of Mem is taken. see 150, 510, 650, 90 and Key 12 (The Stable Intelligence).

אנטימן Antimony [Rabbinical Hebrew]. Metal of the earth. Perhaps the reason for Basil Valentine's emphasis on Antimony in his alchemical writings. Alchemists say that their Antimony is identically with the permanent water and the celestial water. It is therefore the same as the philosopher's Mercury. It is a cleansing and purifying agent. See 106.

אנכי אלהי אביך I (am), God of the Father see Exodus 3:6.

כסף silver (alchemically the Moon). The sphere of the moon is Yesod, seat of the animal soul (311, 80). Silver refers to the reflective, mirroring power of subconsciousness. By means of this may be perceived the basic truth that "I" and "The God of my Father" are only two different ways of saying the same thing. *Kehseph* refers also to the idea or reversal, associated with Key 12, because silver is reflecting and reversed what it mirrors (as does water).

I. *Aesch Mezareph*: "Cheseph, silver is referred to Gedulah on account of its whiteness which denotes mercy and piety. In is it said that by 50 Silver Shekels, Deuteronomy 22:29 is understood Binah, understanding, but when from 50 portals it inclines to the side of Gedulah...

Chesed, in the metallic Kingdom is Luna, *Nemine Contradicente* [no one contradictions]. And so the lesser number of Gedulah is as that of Sama, or Sima [סאמא; 102, lesser number 3, סימא = 111, lesser number 3]. Silver is referred to in Proverbs 16:16 and 17:3, and also in Psalm 12:7, and Job 28:1. Silver, is also found allotted to each one of the Sephirotic decad, thus see chapter 38 of Exodus, 5:17, 19, where silver forms the chapiters of the pillars representing Kether or the summit. While silver is compared with Chokmah, in Proverbs 2:4, and to Binah in Proverbs 16:16.

Gedulah is manifest out of the history of Abraham, where silver is always preferred Genesis 13:2, 23:15,16; 24:35,53].

Geburah is shown, when Silver is put in the fire, Proverbs 17:3 and Numbers 31:21; Psalm 66:10, Proverbs 27:21; Isaiah 48:10; Ezekiel 22:22; Zechariah 13:9; Malachi 3:3.

Tiphareth is the breast of the statue, in Daniel 2:32. Netzach is a vein of silver, in Job 28:1.

Hod are the silver trumpet Numbers 10:2. Yesod

is found in Proverbs 10:20, and Malkuth, in Psalm 12:6." [Westcott, 1997, pp. 20, 22]

מנע to keep back or withhold, restrain. Indicates the work peculiar to the 23rd Path. The same thought is expressed by the title of Key 12. In French it is, Le Pendu, and in Italian L'apposo, which means Literally, "The apprehended", or "the caught". The idea of suspended, or arrested, action - in direct contrast to the fundamental thought of incitement suggested by Lamed, the letter proceeding Mem.

נעם delight, sweetness, grace, beauty, loveliness, splendor. All these words are used by mystics to describe the experience pictured by Key 12. In Zechariah 11:7: pleasure, beauty.

נפל to fall or fall upon; to cast down, to be prostrated; to fall out, to happen, to waste away. This is the verb used in Ezekiel 11:5, where the English says: "The spirit of the Lord fell upon me." With different pointing: 1. to fall down, lie entranced, to cast lots, to allot; 2. to be strong, vigorous; 3. birth, but generally premature birth, miscarriage.

סימן mark, sign, omen; symptom, paragraph, token. See *Sefer Yetzirah* 2:4.

סלע Rock; a crag or cliff; weight, burden, to be heavy, scales on body of snake. This is the special rock identified [Numbers 20:8, 10, 11] as a water source. From a root meaning to be high, to be lifted up, which exactly describes the mental state of a person in samadhi, the condition depicted by Key 12, the Hanged Man.

עיניך thine eyes. In Isaiah 30:20. Also spelled עינך (150). see also 61, 90, 650, 1000.

עץ a tree, wood, firmness, a gallows. The feminine form of עצה, etzah means trees or timber, also the human spine which gives firmness to the body. Related to Mem as the Stable Intelligence, implying immutability, soundness, vitality, coherence, solidity. With different pointing: stem, stock, shaft; wood as a material. The old alphabetical symbol for the letter Mem was two trees, standing side by side. Wherever there are trees, in desert countries, there are either springs or water-courses. Thus there is a close connection between tree, wood

and water.

פניך thy face; thy presence. [Ezekiel 3:8]. The reward of the suspended mind.

צלם an image; a likeness; shadow. God's image (Adam) or mental self-realization. This is the macrocosm-the manifest universe-as well as the microcosm, or man. The primary being underlying the whole self-manifestation of the Life-power. The essential humanity or Primordial man. With different pointing: a shade, shadow, an illusion, an image, a likeness (as in the shadowing forth of anything). From the use of this word in Genesis, where man is called the "Zehlem of the Elohim". It is particularly applicable to human personality. Composed of Tzaddi (Key 17) mediation or Aquarius; Lamed (Key 11), action, changes and adjustments in man's world or Libra; Mem (Key 12) or Binah, the reflecting mirror which turns God's idea of himself outward into the world of relative manifestation, thus seeming to reverse it. Keys 17, 11, 12 add to 40 or 0 (the Fool) manifesting through 4 (the Emperor), who is a man, אדם, a husband, איש and a king, מלך. "Man is God's image of himself"
see 45, 52, 80, 311, 1086.

By gematria we can see an intimate relationship of the following words: qayam, kehseph, nawfal, sehla, etz and tzelm. Qayam, means stable and in this association the lunar current symbolized by silver kehseph; which brings the descent of the cosmic energy into form (nawfal); of the weight of physical manifestation (sehla); of the organic expression of the life-power, symbolized by a tree (etz); and of the reflection of the ideas of the universal mind in forms or images (tzelm).

קין Cain; a lance or spear, that which is pointed. Name of the first murderer. Refers to the false crown of will-power (Key 16) that is shattered by divine illumination. In Genesis 4:1 the etymology of the name is explained as though it were derived from the verb קנה, qahnah, to get, to gain, to obtain. see 37, 155, 220.

In Genesis 4:1: "And Adam knew Eve his wife: and she conceived, and bare Cain, and said, 'I have gotten a man for the Lord.'"

In Genesis 4:8: "And Cain talked with Abel his brother: and it came to pass, when they were in the field, that Cain rose up against Abel his brother, and slew him."

I. "And Kain declared his thought, unto Habel his brother; and they were existing together in productive Nature: and Kain (violent centralizer) rose up (was materialized) against Habel (gentle, pacific liberator) his brother, and slew him (conquered his forces)." [d'Olivet, 1976, p. 322.]

II. He comments: קִן-אֶת, *the self-sameness of Kain*... Need I speak of the importance that the people of the orient have attached to proper names, and of which deep mysteries their sages have often hidden beneath the names?... Moses is the one of the writers of antiquity, who has developed most subtly the art of composing proper names... Moses has often been obliged to throw over them a veil, that I ought and wish to respect. Although I might perhaps give the literal word, I shall not do so. I inform my reader of this in order that he may be watchful: for if he desire it, nothing shall prevent him from knowing.

The root of the name Kain is קִן, which is composed of the eminently compressive and trenchant sign ק, and that of produced being ן. It develops the idea of strongest compression and of most centralized existence: in the proper name under consideration, it is presented animated by the sign of manifested power: thus קִן, Cain *signify the strong; the powerful, the rigid, the vehement*, and also *the central, that which serves as basis, rule, measure; that which agglomerates, appropriates, seizes, comprehends, assimilates with itself*. It is in this last sense that Moses appears to have represented it in the verb which follows." [I did center, קָנִיתִי]. [Hebrew Tongue Restored, pp.122-123]

III. "A symbol of the center of the personality-the I am I feeling in the lower mind, which causes the illusion of separateness, and represents the lower self... The sense of self and separateness supervises the growth of the lower desires which spring form the lower nature... and the lower self, the personal 'I', now gains the power necessary for its evolution, and contrives to obscure the love element in the soul. The 'death of Abel' occurs when the higher general motive of live gives place to the dawn of individuality on the astral and mental planes." [Gaskell, 1981, p. 18, 136.]

IV. Swedenborg: "By 'Cain' is signified faith separate from love. A 'tiller of the ground' is one who is without charity, whatever pretensions he may make to faith which when separated form love is no faith." [Arcana Coelestia].

V. Jacob Boehme: "Cain, whereby is understood in the language of nature, a source out of the center of the fiery desire, a self-full will of the fiery might of the soul." [Mysterium Magnum, p.166]

VI. The Zohar [I:54A]: "Cain was the nest (qina) of the evil habitations which came into the world from the evil side." (P.172)

VII. "Qaheen, being YHWH itself, incarnate but in a state of amnesia, worships an image of itself, which he projects, thereby creating a distance between himself and himself. Since this form of worship reflects a lack of self-knowledge, it is rejected.

This drama is at the core of human experience. We are told that Christ is within, or that there is an Atman, immortally soul or essence within us. Instead of plunging into that living life, what do we do? We worship a picture of what we supposes it is, which cannot be but a projection of its shell or container. [Suraes, 1992, p. 137.]

[Then] Qaheen understands its message. He becomes the container of timeless life; and, as such, he goes toward Hevel-man conditioned according to his time and location-and speaks to him, although their separation has already taken place. But Hevel cannot understand; he cannot even hear Qaheen's parable, and he dissolves into what he essentially is: a bladder of blood. This blood is drunk by the female, earth. The text does not say that Qaheen slays Hevel: it says that he is yaqam, meaning elevated, raised, exalted above him.

So YHWH and Qaheen look for Hevel and do not find him. There is only that pool of blood, which Adamah [50] the enormous female-to-be-conquered, is drinking. And it is the curse of this female which is upon Qaheen. It is preposterous to think that he is cursed by 'God'. On the contrary, it is written: Therefore, whosoever slays Cain, vengeance (of IHVH) shall be taken on him sevenfold [Genesis 4:15]. Qaheen will always re-emerge seven times more strongly: his number is 7: קִן, it is an intense life, terrifying to whoever curses it. Qaheen, as life-death, life-death, is the ceaseless, intermittent pulsation that will always triumph over the female element of resistance forged with blood. He is here, now, present, as he was present always, although more often than not unidentified...

During all this time, while "Cain" (misinterpreted) is forever cursed by mankind's unending fratricide, Qaheen, who cannot prevent Hevel being killed by his own conditioning, is in deepest mourning in the land of Nod (Nod means sorrow.) This land is east of Eden, there where the tree of life is. This "land of Nod" is none other than the Land of Yod, where the N is brought to life in N (50): נוד [Nod] instead of יוד [Yod].

It is not surprising that for the conditioned mind Cain is a killer, whereas he is the very action of IHVH." [ibid, 1992, pp. 140-141.] see 37.

נינטיאל Niantiel. The Sentinel of the 24th Path (Tunnel) of Nun on the Inverse Tree of Life.

I. The 24th Tunnel is under the influence of Scorpio and sentinelled by Niantiel whose number is 160. קין (160), the 'nucleus of impurity' mentioned in connection with the previous tunnel. It is also the number of לנסך, 'for a drink offering', which indicates the sacrament associated with the formula of Niantiel. But a lesser or subsidiary formula is implied by the name מנע (160), which means 'to restrain' or 'keep back', implying the technique of Karezza. Other relevant concepts are Otz, 'tree', the Tree of Life, and יקים, a 'setter up', from the Egyptian *Khem*, meaning 'ithyphallic'; also יפע, 'he shone forth', from the Egyptian *Af*, which denotes the sun in the lower hemisphere. This idea is confirmed by the verse from 231 which reads:

Also Asar was hidden in Amenti; and the Lords of Time swept him with the sickle of death.

The Lords of Time are represented in the tunnel of Niantiel by the infernal waters of Scorpio which imply the alchemical formula of purification via putrefaction. The 'infernal waters' are the 'nucleus of impurity.' They suggest the symbolism of the rainbow as the seal of the deluge from the abyss of space.

160 is that of צלם, 'an image', and this is depicted in the sigil of Niantiel as an image of Death with a five-rayed crown bearing a cross-handled scythe beside the Cross of Set. It is an image of death because the water of purification is the blood that negates life in manifestation, while at the same time affirming it in the Abyss where the blood is sucked [ינק, 160] in as a 'drink offering' The five-rayed crown is the circle or cycle of the five *kalas* typical of the feminine phase of Negation: the lunar period that eclipses 'life' in the form of מפלי [160], which means literally 'flakes of flesh'. The symbol of *Pente*, Five, and of the Pentagram as the Seal or Star of Nuit (Not), has been explained in *The Magical Revival*.

The animals prowing in the shadows of this tunnel include the wolf and hound. This is the hound Cerberus who guards the Abyss. He is the 'great Beast of Hell ... not of Tiphereth without, but Tiphereth within' meaning the infernal sun in Amenta, the phallus in anus [unnatural congress] as distinct from the supernal sun.

Also ascribed to this 24th *kala* are the scorpion and the beetle, both symbols of the Dark Sun.

The typical disease connected with Path 24 is cancer, which links up with the beetle symbolism which preceded that of the crab as the sign of the midnight sun, the traverser of the backward path in the widdershins world of the Abyss. The god-forms appropriate are Typhon, Apep, Khephra, the Merti Goddesses [i.e. the goddesses of death], and Sekhet, the sun of sexual heat, the 'savage' sun in the south as opposed to the great Cat-headed Goddess, Bast, the 'gentle' mother of the north.

In *The Book of Thoth*, Atu 13 is attributed to this ray and its title is Lord of the Gate of Death.

Necrophilia also belongs here as that aspect of meditation on Dissolution that leads the adept to the portal of the Ultimate Mystery of Non-Being. The specifically sexual nature of the formula is made apparent in the attribution to this tunnel of the energies of Scorpio which rule the genital chakras. In a marginal note in his personal copy of *Liber 777*, Crowley wrote: 'In the New Aeon, Scorpio is the Woman-Serpent'. This means that the initiator of the adept is hidden in the image of Death with a five-rayed crown [i.e. woman] the symbolism of which has already been explained in connection with the feminine number, five.

In the African pantheon, the goddess of the rainbow, Aidowedo, pertains to this current. Here, however, the bow is not manifest but latent in the depth of the abyss. The opposite and fructive formula is where the rainbow appears in its full splendor in the heaven of Nu. But here, in the hell of Hecate all is dark, and the serpent Dangbe - the Black Snake - leaves in its wake a trail of slime that indicates the presence of the *Necheshtheron*, the Brazen Serpents, that haunt the tunnel of Niantiel.

Since the Mysteries of Death concern the 24th *kala* it is necessary to understand the kind of magic practiced by the Atlanteans of the Black Temple. It is well known to occultists that at the moment of sexual orgasm the Adept is able to launch a creative thought-construct which penetrates the astral envelope of his *psyche* and reifies in matter at a time appointed by the magician. A similar mechanism operates at the moment of death. When the soul quits its earthly vehicle, the Adept of the Death Cult can direct it to any given location. A black magician could be this means capture the soul of individual and make it subservient to his will. This is the method of creating zombies. But the original Atlantean version of this sorcery involved elements of sexual magick. A consecrated priestess was slain in a special manner and the Adept copulated with her shade to produce a zombie on the astral plane. This was also, if required, incarnated via a living woman through the natural process of birth. The zombie produced in this way was not a soulless mechanism - as in the case of a zombie produced by Haitian Voodoo - but a highly intelligent though automatic entity combining the vividness and plasticity of astral consciousness with the magical qualities of the Adept himself. It was literally a child of the dead, yet equipped with magical powers and with all the faculties of humanity except that of the Will. Bertiaux correctly observes: 'Voudou and witchcraft' came 'from the same mystical parent, i.e. the old religions of Atlantis'.

This highly complex 24th *kala* comports therefore various kinds of sexual magick. For the sake of convenience the elements involved are all related to the backward path of the Sun in Amenta; to the formula of Scorpio (purification via putrefaction); or to the necromantic and necrophiliac sorcery associated with the *Mystere du Zombeeisme* and the *Cult of the Dead*; and to the retention of the sun-seed in the practice of Karezza. It is therefore not surprising that to the path, of which Niantiel's cell is the tunnel are attributed lamiae, stryges, and witches. [Grant, 1994, p. 219-225.]

הקמיה 16th Shem ha-Mephorash. "God who erects the universe." Against traitors and for the deliverance from those who seek to oppress us. Governs: crowned heads, great captains. Gives victory. Negative influence: treachery.

Angel of the 2nd decanate and 4th quinance of Libra, attributed to the 3 of swords. see Appendix 10.

Interiora Terrae (Lt). Interior of the Earth. Part of the alchemical phrase in Secret Symbols (page 17). The interior of the earth "is the inner, Life of Man. When one follows the alchemical admonition, and visits this region, he enters into the state of consciousness the Yogis call Samadhi. In Sanskrit this word has affinities with the ideas of burial and self-immolation. The practices whereby it is attained are all directed toward arresting, or suspending, the flow of mental images. They are also aimed at abstracting attention from sensory perceptions.

Deus Lux Solis (Lt). God, light of the Sun. From the "Chemical Marriage of Christian Rosenkreutz." Here is a very definite statement of the occult doctrine that radiant energy, or light, is one with the Life-power.

161

אדם עילאה the heavenly man; lit. the 'primordial' or 'exalted' man.

קהל יהוה the Congregation of the Eternal.

פנאל Peniel. "The Face of God." Name of the "angel" Jehovah (יהוה), the dark antagonist who wrestled with Jacob in Genesis 32 (variant spelling). The Zohar identifies the antagonist as Samael. In the Qabalah generally, Peniel is a Friday angel, resident of the third heaven, and curer of human stupidity. In Genesis, Peniel is a place-the hollowed place where God revealed himself to Jacob face to face. see 171 and

Dictionary of Angels [p.222].

foemina satacissima (Lt). nature's wanton.

via, vita, veritas (Lt). Way, Life, Truth [Secret Symbols, page 52]. Part of a diagram. see 676, 167, 174.

162

I. (2 x 9 x 9) or 2×3^4

בנימין   Tribe of Benjamin. "son of the right hand" [Genesis 49:27]. Related to Sagittarius and alchemical incineration, the 9th stage of the Great Work. Attributed to the letter Samekh, the direction west above, the mental state of zeal or wrath. Incineration is accomplished through the knowledge and conversation of the Holy Guardian Angel. It is the purging and refinement of the desire nature, which then becomes the great medicine. Incineration is the process which consumes the dross of erroneous thinking. It rids subconsciousness of the subtle residue of the thoughts, feelings and action of former lives, leftover from the stage of putrefaction. The sense of separate personality is reduced to absolute nothingness of blackness. Then the idea is substituted that what ever goes on in the field of personal expression is really the reflection of the one reality. Then events in the field of personal experience are found to be direct operations of the one identity. In Jacob's blessing, the words addressed to Benjamin bear on hunting, a characteristic of Sagittarius. Hunting and inquiry are akin. To hunt for clues, to seek for evidence, to examine, to study, to consider-all these are part of the process of verification and experiment of which Key 14 is the Tarot symbol. Jupiter, which rules Sagittarius is connected with research. see 536, 830, 395, 259, 466, 54, 95, 30, 670, 501, 331, 7.

כל-עבדי יהוה   All ye servants of God [Tetragrammaton] [Psalm 134:1]. In this Psalm, the "servants" are those who "stand by night" in the House of the Lord. Elsewhere in the Old Testament, the "servants of IHVH" are identified with angels. עבדי, Abedey, Servants is 86, the number of אלהים, the creative powers called "God" in Genesis 1. The word is plural, and in Revelation 4:5 they are called the "seven spirits of God." They are also the "planetary" powers of the 7 interior stars. see 86, 2112.

ליהוה המלוכה   The kingdom is God's [Psalm 22:28]. The Kingdom is the cosmic order.

קול יהוה   The Voice of God [Psalm 29:3, Deuteronomy 15:5]. In the passage in Deuteronomy, the children of Israel are cautioned to "Harken carefully" to the voice. It is the voice of the Hierophant in Key 5, and 5 is the reduction of Key 14. Every seeker for truth hears that still, small voice. Not all of them know what they hear; but their successes depend of careful listening. see 186, 800, 120, 600.

גלאס-לבול   Goetic demon #25 by day of the 1st decanate of Sagittarius. see Appendix 11.

Goetia: "He is a Mighty President and earl, and shows himself in the from of a dog with wings like a gryphon. He teaches all arts and sciences in an instant, and is an author of bloodshed and manslaughter. He teaches al things past, and to come. If desired he causes the love both of friends and foes. He can make a man to go invisible. And he has under his command 36 Legions of Spirits." [Mathers, 1995, p. 39]

Corpus Christi (Lt). The Body of Christ; A day of festival, commemorated on the first Thursday after trinity Sunday. It has special significance in certain Rosicrucian circles. The "Body of Christ" is not by any means limited to the consecrated host. It is the whole company of the truly devout.

lapidem angulorum (Lt). A corner-stone. That which is essential to all building. Refers to Chokmah, the eternal impersonal wisdom which directs the temporal, personal lives of men who hear the voice of understanding (Binah) in the Heart. The cornerstone is the "Voice of Tetragrammaton," the Word which is in our hearts, and in our mouths, that we may do it. see 136, 67, 73. See Vulgate version of Isaiah 28:16.

percussion magna (Lt). The great sound. A reference to "incineration" through "the voice of IHVH". see 272.

In cruce mea victoria (Lt). In the cross is my victory.

Typhon-Apophis (Lt). Typhon is the serpent of destruction, a monster of the primitive world, described sometimes as a destructive hurricane, and sometimes as a fire-breathing giant. The child's uplifted arms in Key 20 give the sign of Typhon, or Apophis, the destroyer. the child represents Vav, the voice of the hierophant which brings rebirth as a result of mastering Typhon-Apophis.

caput mortuum (Lt). A death's head or skull. In alchemy, the residuum after distillation (570) or sublimation (501); hence, worthless residue. see 55, 107.

163 (prime)

עבץ Handful. Refers to the Yod, meaning hand.

נוקבה woman, wife.

164

I. The approximate circumference of a circle surrounding a Hexagon having a radius of 26.

מעמיד ma'amiyd. firm, erect; constituting. (15th path of Heh). The adjective *ma'amiyd* is derived from a verb meaning "to rise, to stand erect." The dominant power in the 15th path is the Mars-force which is the active generative principle in nature. The universal creative force, Chaiah, is identical with the procreative power of living organisms. *Mem*, waters and *Od*, eternity is concealed in this word. One is at the center of a boundless ocean (Mem) of a eternally creative mind. Creation is the apparent self-limitation of the Life-power. It is connected with the restrictive materialistic influence of Saturn (Ayin). The aspirant must pass though the 16th path where in the last vestige of false personality is eradicated (Mem). To do nothing for self, but all for the Self, is the test of "sacrifice." To be a conscious channel for the cosmic creative impulse is to know the state of isolation (Yod). One then creates according to the patterns of the universal desire (Daleth). See Appendix 12.

I. The commentary on the 15th Path of Heh, the Constituting Intelligence states that *it constitutes the substance of creation in pure darkness.* In the New Testament John states: "That which has been made was life in him (the Logos, Christ), and the life was the light of men. And the light shines in the darkness, and the darkness

overcome it not." The substance of creation is light, and in this connection note that the Hindu God Agni is a God of Fire who is sometimes shown holding a lamb. A lamb is a symbol of sacrifice, because the infinite potential of the Life-power must sacrifice or limit itself for the sake of manifestation.

הדבקם you shall cleave. The constituting Intelligence is one of close union with the Life power. see 724.

יחצון you shall divide. Exodus 21:35.

אבן אלף the first stone, because Aleph is numerically 1. see 884.

אבן אפל the concealed (hidden) stone, a stone concealed. Black ore in Job 28:3: "Man put to the end darkness; he reaches the farthest recesses for ore in the blackest darkness." In Rosicrucian texts Christ is identified with the "hidden stone." see 150, 570.

אבן פלא the wonderful stone. Wonderful is an adjective applied to Kether and to Christ. In Isaiah 9:6: "And his name shall be called, wonderful, counselor..." In all true Rosicrucian texts Christ is identified with the "hidden stone of the alchemist". When man rectifies his conception of the life he finds within himself, he discovers this hidden stone. To ask, "What am I?" is the beginning of the way which leads within. see 111. [פלא pillae, means "to search, to make special (vows)"] see 814.

חיצון outer, external, exoteric, secular, civil (as opposed to sacred). The manifested cosmos is seen as external to the Self and as proceeding for that Self at the heart of all being. In Tarot the Emperor symbolizes civil authority, as contrasted to the Hierophant as spiritual authority. He suggests material matters-the successful business executive, the result of an orderly use of the mind and directed and focused will. See 814 and K.D.L.C.K. (p.342).

עמדים the pillars (Jakin and Boaz). It is the state of perfect equilibrium, understood as the support or pillars of existence. The pillars of Solomon's temple were placed outside the entrance. In 1 Kings 7:21: "And he set up the pillars in the porch of the temple: and he set up he right pillar, and called the name thereof Jachin: and he set up the left pillar, and called the name thereof Boaz. The magus realizes in himself the union of positive and negative, mercy and severity.

semen metallorum (Lt). Seed of metals. The alchemical term is connected with the planet Mars, ruling Aries, and with the Sun, exalted in Aries. Note its masculine connotation. Both Mars and the Sun are said to be electric and fiery.

165

I. The sidereal revolution of Neptune about the Sun in years (164.8 years actual).

עצה feminine form of עץ, it means not only trees, or timber generally, but is used also to designate the human spine which gives firmness to the physical body.

נקודה a point. see 159

עממיה "God elevated above all things." 52nd Shem ha-Mephorash. 256E-260E. SAGEN. May 10, July 21, October 1, December 12, February 22, 5:00-5:20 PM. [Psalm 7:17] "I will praise the Lord according to his righteousness; and will sing praise to the name of the Lord most high." To destroy the power of enemies and to humiliate them. Rules all journeys in general: protects prisoners who have recourse to him (the angel); inspires them with the means of creating their liberty; influences all those who seek truth in good faith, and departs from their errors in a sincere return to God. Person born: strong and vigorous temperament; supports adversities with much patience and courage; loves to work and executes all that he attempts with frugality. see 965, 150, 710 & Appendix 10.

I. Angel of the 4th quinance [16-20°] of Aries; angel by night of the 3 of Wands (Binah of Atziluth).

II. "Imamiah-in the cabala, an angel of the order of principalities, or rather an ex-angel of that order, since he is fallen. In Hell he supervises and controls voyages, and destroys and humiliates enemies, when he is invoked to do so, or is so disposed. He was once one of the 72

Shemhamphorae. His sigil is pictured in Ambelain, *La Kabbale Pratique*, p. 289." [Davidson, 1971, p. 149.]

קללה curse. In Deuteronomy 30:1: "When all these blessing and curses I have set before you come upon you and you take them to heart whenever the Lord your God disperses among the nations."

נעמה Nemah. A queen (princess) of demons; Archdemon of Malkuth. see 777, Table IV, Row CVIII [Crowley, 1977, p. 23].

הזקים strength. In Ezekiel 3:8: "Behold I have made your face strong against their faces, and your forehead strong against their forehead."

להודיעם to make them know [Crowley, 1977, p. 22]. In Psalm 25:14: "The Lord confides in those who revere him; he makes his covenant known to them."

philosophorum (Lt). of the philosophers. see 193, 28 Latin.

lapis metallorum (Lt). stone of the metals. "I have called it by various names, but the simplest is perhaps that of 'Hyle' [428 Greek], or first principle of all things. It is also denominated the One Stone of the Philosophers, composed of hostile elements, the Stone of the Sun [117 Latin], the Stone of the Metals... by these and many other names it is called, yet is only *one*." [Waite, 1974, vol. 1, p. 186]

166

דם-ענב blood of the grape. The mystical wine of initiation. See Deuteronomy 32:14, & 44, 260, 133.

מעון dwelling place, temple, lair, den, residence. Relating to more particularly to Malkuth, because of the words in Psalm 90:1. "Lord, thou has been our dwelling-place in all generation." Adonai, Lord, is the special divine name of Malkuth. *Sepher Sephiroth*: Heaven of Geburah, the 5th Heaven [Crowley, 1977, p. 22].

עליון the Most High; the Supreme. A title of Kether. In truth the Kingdom and the Crown, the outermost manifestation and the innermost reality, are one. Thus the "dwelling place" is the "most high." The ground is which the vine grows is the very being of the One reality. Vine, vinedresser, and vineyard are all one. see 140, 220, 260, 197.

עמנו with us. In Psalm 46:11: "Tetragrammaton Tzabaoth (divine name of Netzach) is with us."

פני יהוה the face of the Lord. In Psalm 34:16: "The face of the Lord is against them that do evil, to cut off the remembrance of them from the earth." The verse is credited to Peh.

עיני יהוה the eyes of the Lord. In Psalm 34:15: "The eyes of the Lord are upon the righteous, and his ears are open unto their cry." This verse is credited to the letter Ayin. Not that "eye" is plural. So the eyes of the Lord and the face of the Lord, are equivalent. see 156.

עוץ the native land of Job. In Job 1:1: "There was a man in the land of *Uz*, whose name was Job; and that man was perfect and upright, and one that feared god, and eschewed evil." see 976.

נפול Goetic demon #60 by night of the 3rd decanate of Scorpio. The Tarot minor arcana attributes this decanate to the 7 of Cups. This represents the operation of Netzach, sphere of Venus, in Briah, the creative world.

Goetia: "He is a duke great, mighty, and strong; appearing in the from of a lion with gryphon's wings. His office is to make men knowing in all handicrafts and professions, also in philosophy, and other sciences. He governs 36 Legions of Spirits."

"נף: Every idea of dispersion, ramification, effusion, inspiration; of movement operated inwardly from without, or outwardly from within: distillation if the object is liquid, a scattering if the object is solid." [d'Olivet, 1976, p. 403.]

חיב ממון Rosenroth in [K.D.L.C.K. p.498] gives *reus mulctae* [defendant of the milk-pail?, my best Latin translations], and says it pertains to the grade of justice, and it can be said that six are the orders of its inferior powers, under the mystery of the Tree of Good, which is Metatron,

and evil, i.e. Samael.

בעל חנו "Ba'al was gracious". Variant spelling of a King of Edom, its 7th King, in Genesis 36:38. see 210.

argentum vivum (Lt). living silver. The alchemical Mercury, the fludic metal which is the first matter of the Great Work. This "matter" in its white state is "argentum vivum." In its red state, it is דם-ענב, the "blood of the grape," The mystical wine of initiation. see 260, 89, 77 Latin.

"Basil Valentine says that Azoth and fire alone are needed in the work of wisdom, and according to Arnold [of Villanova] water is Azoth, which water is argentum vivum. In his figurative language Eliphas Levi calls it the efficient and final principle of the great work. Here is one aspect of the universal medicine in the light of the Rosy Cross." [Waite, 1993, p. 22]

in Jusu morimur (Lt). In Jesus we die. A motto in the *Fama*. The is the mystical death of the "old" man. The phrase is one of the inner keys to the mystery of the Eucharist, where the wine stands for the occult "blood of the grape," which brings the exaltation of consciousness, to the awareness of our true dwelling-place, and to the knowledge of our essential identity with Yechidah, the One Self in Kether. This state of consciousness is often described in Sufi poetry as "intoxication". see 260, 683, 21, 50, 95 Latin.

Dominus Noster (Lt). Our Lord. see 81, 85 Latin.
gradus ad sapientiam (Lt). the stair to wisdom. see 64, 97, 638.

167 (prime)

אסימון Asimon. The unnameable one; a demon [Crowley, 1977, p. 23]. Associated with the north-west. On the Cube of Space this direction is attributed to Lamed, and thus to Justice in Tarot, and to alchemical sublimation. The demon suggest unbalanced force, unexpectedly changing and destroying (Aleph) the support from within (Samekh) and creating through personal will (Yod) a mental reversal away from the source of all (Mem), uniting itself instead (Yod) with unending reproduction of error (Nun). See 501, 309, 767, 817.

I. "An angel listed in *Malache Elyon* (Angels on High), where reference is made to *The Zohar*." [Davidson, 1971, p. 57.] see 817

II. d'Olivet writes on אם: "A root but little used in Hebrew where it is ordinary replaced by אש (fire). The Arabic presents all ideas deduced from that of *basis*. In several of the ancient idioms the very name of the earth has been drawn from this root, as being the basis of things; thence is also derived the name of *Asia*, that part of the earth which, long considered as the entire earth, has preserved, notwithstanding all its revolutions, the absolute denomination. The Chaldaic אסי has signified in a restricted sense *a physician*; no doubt because of the health whose basis he established..." [d'Olivet, 1976, p. 297.]

מסוביאל Mesvkiel. Archangel of Da'ath.

עין הלב the inner eye [Hebrew lexicon]. Literally "eye of the heart."

Fedes, Spes, Charitas (Lt). Faith, Hope, Charity [Secret Symbols page 52]. Written of a diagram. "And now abideth faith, hope and charity (love), these three; but the greatest of these is charity." see 41, 53, 73 (Lt), 676, 167, 174.

Η Ανηρ. Ho Aner (Gr.). The Man. Refers to Christ, or the Messiah, the re-born savior. see 744, 159.

168

חפף to cover, protect; to enclose, surround. In Deuteronomy 33:12: "And of Benjamin (162) he said, the beloved of the Lord shall dwell in safety by him; and the Lord shall cover him all the day long, and he shall dwell between his shoulders." see 888.

לכל-חסדיו of all his saints. In Psalm 148:14: "He raised up for his people a horn, the praise of all his saints, of Israel, the people close to his heart. Praise the Lord. "Horn" symbolizes strength, honor, prosperity, and was used for storing or carrying oil. see 390.

Pater metallorum (Lt). Father of metals. Refers to the alchemical first matter, which is also Azoth and Terra Adamica. The metals are the 7

inner holy planets. Waite, referring to the plate Mons Philosophorum in Secret Symbols writes: "A healing is administered to the fallen soul by a medicine which is Jesus Christ, but there is also a thing 'sorry in appearance' which insures 'bodily health' to those who attain in the spirit. In it 'the greatest part of the kingdom which the Lord Jehovah has set forth for us in nature': it is called *pater metallorum*, and is said to be hidden in this picture." [Waite, 1993, p. 22] see 86, 158, 1223.

Βενιαμιν. Benjamin (Gr.) "Son of the Righthand." Septuagint translation of בנימין (162) in Genesis 49:27. "Benjamin is a ravenous wolf; in the morning he devours the prey, in the evening he divides the plunder." The tribe of Israel associated with the zodiacal sign Sagittarius and with alchemical incineration.

169

I. 13^2

λιθον. lithon (Gr.) stone.

העמדים the pillars. see Exodus 27:10.
אצבעו his finger. see Leviticus 4:6.

170

צלם image, which has special reference to meditation, and relates also to the sign Aquarius. God's Image [tzelem] or mental self-representation, it must be that this mental image of itself in the Universal Mind is also the primary being underlying the whole self-manifestation of the Life-power.

גמל-וו-פה Gimel-Vav-Peh. Guph, the physical body, spelled in plenitude. "This is thy body is truly the heavenly vision of the goodness of the eternal" [Book of Tokens]. see 17, 89.

מקל Wand, rod, stick, staff. Instrument of the magical directing power of self-consciousness held by the Magician. The wand equates to the archetypal world or Atziluth. see 576.

מלק to wring off, pinch off; to nip, nip off the neck of a bird, wring. In Leviticus 1:15: "And the priest shall bring it unto the altar, and wring

241

off his head, and burn it on the altar; and the blood thereof shall be wrung out at the side of the altar." Metathesis of מקל wand (Mercury). Suggest the dedication of the "head", seat of Mercury to sacrifice impurities in the subconsciousness (blood and altar). Note that Lamed (directing-power, goad) comes before Qoph (sleep, Pisces, organization of body-cells). See also Leviticus 5:8.

לעיני. To the eyes, in their eyes. see Genesis 23:11.

מעין fountain, spring; source, origin. In Song of Solomon 4:12: "You are a garden locked up [enclosed], my bride, my sister, you are a spring enclosed, a sealed fountain." (גל spring, is also used Ayin = Eye, fountains, outward appearance.) see 1496, 53, 70.

ענן Cloud, a cloud (as covering the sky), thundercloud. In Exodus 13:21: "By day the Lord went ahead of them in a pillar of cloud to guide them of their way and bynight in a pillar of fire to give them light, so that they could travel by day or night." With different pointing: 1. to brings clouds, cover with clouds; 2. to use enchantments; to practice magic.

יפיע the bright one, the beautiful one [Joshua 10:3]. Amorite king of Lachish ("the invincible") conquered and slain by Joshua. Typifies the external shows of materialism, and is ruler of the kingdom which believes material wealth and power to be invincible. see 370, 935, 56, 321, 170, 216.

כסילים thick ones, hence fools. Also strong ones, giants, hence the constellation Orion [the hunter], conceived of by the ancients as a giant bound upon the sky; constellations generally, as in Isaiah 13:10: "The stars of heaven and their constellations will not show their light. The rising sun will be darkened and the moon will not give its light." see 730.

נעמי Naomi, mother-in-law of Ruth. In Ruth 1:2: "And the name of the man was Elimelek, and the name of his wife Naomi ["my pleasantness"]..." This is the derivative of נעם Noam, beauty, loveliness, pleasantness. see 160.

ספל bowl, dish, cup. The cup is the magical instrument symbolizing the purifying qualities of "water" or mental substance. In Judges 6:38: "And that is what happened. Gideon rose early the next day; he squeezed the fleece and wrung out the dew-a bowlful of water."

פסל idol [bull] in Exodus 20:4. Inman: The word signifies 'to shape, or form'; also any image 'graven or molten,' but principally an idolatrous figure. A vast majority of these were phallic emblems; and the organ of the bull, which formerly was used to inflict punishment, as the bamboo and cat-o'-nine-tails are now, goes by the name 'pizzle.' [Inman, 1942, Vol. 2., p. 472]

עמודים pillars, columns; perpendiculars (i.e. balances). see 120

פלס balance, scale. In Isaiah 40:20: "Who has measured the waters in the hollow of his hand, and meted out heaven with the span, and comprehended the dust of the earth in a measure, and weighted the mountains in scales, and the hills in a balance?" And in Proverbs 16:11: "A just weight and balance are the Lord's: all the weights of the bag are his work."

מיסן Nisah, the first month of the Jewish calendar [or seventh, if counting from the new year]. Corresponding to March-April and is similar to the time period ruled by Aries in the zodiac, and thus to alchemical calcination. In Nehemiah 2:1: "And it came to pass in the month of Nisan... that... I took up the wine and gave it to the king." Also mentioned in [Esther 3:7] called חדש האביך, "month or ears" in the Pentateuch.

בעל החוטם Master of the Nose. Connected with smell, with discrimination and with Gemini, ruled by Mercury. the path of the Tree of Life (Zain) links the sphere of Saturn (Binah) and Sun (Tiphareth). He who is master of discrimination will change Jacob into Israel, will direct the regenerative current from Saturn to Sun, and will not rely on the comforters of the flesh-he will allow the beloved (David) to send his "servants" (Elohim or forces) to search the city (microcosm) for the corner-stone, which is the "pinnacle", or Mercury center.

Nequaquam vacuum (Lt). nowhere a vacuum, not at all a void. The first of four mottos on the altar in the vault of Brother C.R. was written around a small circle containing the figure of a lion, corresponding to Leo and the element Fire. "Nowhere a vacuum" denies that space is empty. Quamtum physics says that space is filled with a sea of virtural particles and energy. And the Cabalistics state that all space is filled with the Divine Presence. The Bible states that God is Love and a consuming fire. Both of these qualities is represented by the Leo the Lion and the element Fire.

The element fire is attributed to the Mother Letter Shin ש, because Shin is 300, as well as רוח אלהים, *Ruach Elohim,* Spirit (Breath) of God (Creative Powers). Thus *Nequaquam vacuum* indicates the fullness of the divine spirit, that all-pervading fire fills every point in space. See 98, 72, 113, 155, 136, 300, 574 Latin, 1059 Greek.

171

I. Σ18 = 171

גבעה האלהים "Hill of the Elohim," an ancient Hebrew name for Bethel, "The House of God," where Jacob had his dream of the ladder. This ladder is another symbol associated by Qabalists with the Tree of Life. see 731.

מאציל the beginning of emanation. The 10 distinguishable aspects of reality on the Tree from *Ain Soph Aur*, the Limitless Light.

נאצל emanating from. The Tree of Life is a diagram of the progressive emanation of the ten distinguishable aspects of Reality from Ain Suph Aur, the Limitless Light. With different pointing: to be withdrawn, narrowed.

פניאל Peniel. "The face of God".

"Peniel is the angel Jehovah [יהוה], the dark antagonist who wrestled with Jacob [Genesis 32]… *The Zohar* identifies the antagonist as Samael. In the cabala generally, Peniel is a Friday angel, resident of the 3rd Heaven, and (like Penemue) a curer of human stupidity. In Genesis, Peniel is a place-the hallowed place where God revealed himself to Jacob face to face." [Davidson, 1971, p. 222.] see 161.

פלאין Pelain. Lesser angel governing the triplicity of night of Aquarius. The name suggest the power of action (Peh) breaking out of old forms (Aleph), meditating the divine will (Yod) into an eternal pattern of light-bearing, which is the brotherhood of man (Vav). see 821.

172

מקבל Cabalist [Godwin. 1999, p. 525.]

צלם ההבא Golden Image [ibid, p.525].

יעצב He affected.

אלופיהם their chiefs. Genesis 36:19: These were the sons of Esau (Edom), and these were their chiefs.

עקב Jacob. heel; foot-print, footstep; rear, hinder part, posteriors; the remains (in a vessel), to be high, hill-shaped, to be cunning, to mislead. . The remains of sin and sorrow are to be cast off in the return to deity. see 172

E Pluribus Unim (Lt). One out of many. One of the 3 mottoes on the Great seal of the U.S. see 61, 220, 150 Latin.

173 (prime)

אנכי יהוה אלהיך Anoki IHVH Eloheka. I am the Lord thy God. "I am the Lord your God, who brought you out of Egypt, out of the land of slavery." These words are the preface to the ten commandments. see 653.

גל עיני lighten mine eyes [Crowley, 1977, p. 23].

ויקנאו and they envied. Genesis 26:14.

גפנם their vine. Deuteronomy 32:32: Their vine comes from the vine of Sodom, and the fields of Gomorrah.

174

לפדים torches. [Crowley, 1977, p. 23]

לספד to mourn. Genesis 23:2: Abraham went to mourn for Sarah…

Amor Meus Crucifex (Lt). My crucified Love; Love crucified me [Secret Symbols page 52 as part of a diagram]. see 676, 167.

Iesus Christus (Lt). Jesus Christ.

lapis fugitivus (Lt). The flying stone. This is the sperm or seed (Yod) of the alchemical metals, the first matter. [Thomas Vaughan] see 51, 254 (Lt).

Poraios de rejectis (Lt). "Brought from among the rejected ones." Relates to Theoricus Grade and to Yesod.

175

I. Constant summation of the lines of a magic square of Venus.

דיוקנה Phantom, shadow-image, likeness, replica. The Zohar says: "At the time of accomplishment of the union below, the Holy one, blessed be he, sends a phantom or shadow image, like the likeness of a man. It is designed in the divine image [צלם, Tzelem]…and in that Tzelem the child of man is created…in this Tzelem he develops, as he grows, and it is with this Tzelem, again, that he departs from this life."

הלבנה לאבן brick for stone [Genesis 11:3]. In the story of the Tower of Babel, the word לבנה, bricks, is spelled exactly the same as the word for moon. This refers to the functions of the automatic consciousness in Yesod, and in contrast to אבן, stone, a verbal symbol of the union of the Ego in Tiphareth with Chokmah. "Brick for stone" means the substitution of the irrational desires of the animal nature for the impulses from above. The result is what is pictured in Key 16 and the disaster related in the Biblical allegory. see 87.

יכין בועז Jakin-Boaz. The two pillars, which were set up in front of Solomon's temple. A symbol of the balancing of the pairs of opposites, or polarities. see 90, 85, 169, 825.

יניקה young shoot, sapling. With different pointing: suction, absorption, sucking. The growth of the soul is as a young shoot, absorbing its building material form life.

מכפלה duplicity, deception. As a proper name, the field where Abraham's cave was. Carries the same idea of substitution as "brick for stone." see 890.

"She [machpelah, nature] lives in gardens, sleeps in the double cave of Abraham, in the field of Hebron, and her palace is in the depths of the red sea, and in transparent caverns" [Waite, 1974, vol. 1, p. 58]

נפילה a falling, slipping, defeat; a quantity of seed required for a field. The seeds of "bricks" should be replaced by that of "stone".

עקה pressure, trouble, constraint, oppression. The result of imbalance.

קדמאל Kadmael. The Spirit of Venus. The "shadow-image" of God is perfected in man by being receptive to his true desires and perfecting them through mental imagery. see 90, 85, 169, 49, 1225.

קל אדם the voice of Adam. Metathesis of קדמאל. Here the "voice" of intuition in man is linked to his powers of linkage through creative imagination. In Daniel 8:16: "And I heard a man's voice between the banks of Ulai, which called, and said, Gabriel, make this man to understand the vision." see 28, 7, 70, 700, 735.

ויפגעו and they met. see Genesis 32:2.

למינהם after their kind, according to their kinds. In Genesis 1:21: So God created the great creaturesof the sea and every living and moving thing with which the water teems, according to their kinds…

למעלה on High. In Exodus 25:20: "And the cherubims shall stretch forth their wings on high, covering the mercy seat."

הענן the cloud (Shekinah). see Exodus 13:22 & Deuteronomy 5:22.

consummatum est (Lt). It is finished. The

traditional seventh utterance of Jesus on the cross.

Microprosopus (Lt). Lesser Countenance, Little face. A title of Tiphareth [זעיר אנפיל].

minutum mundum (Lt). little world. In the *Fama Fraternitatis* this designates a mysterious object discovered in the vault of C.R. In certain Rosicrucian societies a term applied to various colored diagrams of the Tree of Life. Closely related to man as the microcosm. see 132.

176

I. (11 x 16) or 11 x 2^5

עונן soothsayer, magician. The renewer (Ayin) through inner guidance (Vav), death (Nun) and change or transformation (Nun). With different pointing: *aoon*, to conjure, do magic, soothsay. see 126, 826.

נסיון trial, temptation, test, experiment, experience. The intelligence of Samekh, the 25th Path of Wisdom. see 536, 186.

לעולם Throughout the eons of eons; throughout endless ages, forever. Refers to the power of the One Self, acting through the 10 Sephiroth. see 736.

יועץ counselor, advisor, a divine name emphasized in Isaiah 9:6. see 986, 1492.

אבן החכמים stone of the wise or philosopher s stone. *Chaekawmim* is the plural of חכם wise man, scholar, wise, skillful, and from it Chokmah, wisdom is derived.

פסול illegitimate. With different pointing: 1. trimming, cutting or branches-whatever is opposite to truth; 2. defective, blemished, disqualified-by test and trial; 3. blemish, flaw, disqualification.

פוץ to be scattered, be dispersed; to be spread, dispensed; to overflow. A metathesis of צוף. Here Peh is the initiating force and Tzaddi is the result. Action (Peh) through intuition (Vav) brings revelation (Tzaddi).

עמינרב liberty, or the divine kinsman gives. The ancestral head of a family or clan of Judah in I Chronicles 2:10: "And Ram beget Amminadab; and Amminadab beget Naishon, prince of the children of Judah."

צוף honeycomb, overflow. In Lamentations 3:5: "Waters flowed over mine head; then I said, I am cut off."

Fons Miraculorum (Lt). Fountain of Miracles. On plate 13 of Secret Symbols is shown a blue water triangle, marked Fons Miraculorum. In it are rooted a red rose, representing the "red word" of alchemy, and a white Lily, which symbolizes the "white work". The Lily stands for the lunar current. Yet both are rooted in the water triangle which is the fountain of miracles. The element of Water is the "One Thing", which is the primary substance for all miraculous manifestations. From the *Turba Philosophorum*: "The ignorant, when they hear us name water think it is the water of the clouds, but, if they understand our books, they should know it to be a permanent water, or fixed water, without which its sulphur, to which it hath been united, cannot be permanent."

177

גן עדן garden of delight, Garden of Eden. Refers to the Vav, 16th path of Wisdom. It is the garden in which grow the lilies and roses at the Magician's feet and the Empress sits. Both *gan* and *ehben* are numerically 53, intimating that the both stand for the state of conscious identification of the EGO with the cosmic, or universal SELF. They represent the state of Consciousness from which human personality is driven when it falls into the delusion of separateness resulting from eating the fruit of the Tree of Knowledge. It is a state of being preceding individualized consciousness, a state of ignorance of good and evil. see 53, 124, 508, 122, 315.

In Genesis 2:15: "and IHVH Elohim took Adam, and put him into the Garden of Eden, to dress it and keep it."

"And-he-took, IHOAH, He-the-Gods, that-same-Adam (collective-man) and-he-placed-him in-the-temporal-and-sensible-sphere, for dressing-it and-over-looking-it-with-care." [d'Olivet, 1976, p. 81.]

אל עולם The everlasting God. In Genesis 21:33: "And Abraham planted a grove in Beersheba, and called there on the name of the Lord, the everlasting God." Abraham means "Father of many nations"; Beersheba means "seven wells." The path of Vav is the Triumphant and Eternal Intelligence. The Garden of Eden is in the eternal now. see 248, 575.

זעק to cry out for help, to cry, cry out, call. To return to the garden one must invoke the highest.

עקבה subtility. One "ascends again to heaven, suavely, and with great ingenuity." [Emerald Tablet]

מלוי המלוי plenitudes of plenitudes. The fullness of the indwelling spirit.

סגדלעי Sagdaloy. Lesser angel governing triplicity by day of Capricorn. This is the zodiacal sign where Mars is exalted, and "day" indicates acts of self-conscious attention. *777*, Table IV, Column CXLIV [Crowley, 1977, p. 26]. see 224 (Godwin's spelling), 70, 130, Key 15.

אדון האדונים God of Gods. Rosenroth in K.D.L.C.K. (p.27) gives: *Dominus Dominorum* and cites Deuteronomy 10:17: "For the Lord your God is God of Gods and Lord of Lords, the great, the mighty, the terrible God, Who is not partial and takes no bribe."

178

קבוע qubboah, quvuah. receptacular (receptive), cohesive, measuring. With different pointing: fixed, constant, permanent, regular. The Intelligence of the 4th path of Chesed. See Appendix 12.

בן אלמנה The widow's son. In 1 Kings 7:14: Hiram Abiff. "He was a widow's son of the Tribe of Naphthali [Virgo = distillation], and his father was a man of Tyre, a worker in Brass: and he was filled with wisdom, and understanding, and cunning to work all works in brass. And he came to King Solomon, and wrought all his work." see

254, 273.

חלצים Loins, lower part, strength, vigor. see 738.

חפץ khahphatz. desire, love; longing, good pleasure. With different pointing: to delight, take pleasure, to be pleased, being willing, desirous, purpose, choice, decision, will, wish.

כסף חי Living silver; quick sliver, the Mercury of the sages. Also called the first matter of the Stone, *Ehben* [53] Attributed to the 4th Sephirah, Chesed, beneficence or Mercy, sphere of Jupiter or cosmic memory, an aspect of the Moon, attributed to silver. It also implies Yesod, sphere of the Moon. Memory helps to dedicate the forces of generation to making the stone.

Aesch Mezareph: "And as the name of El [אל], doth insinuate the nature of Silver, because both belong to the class of Chesed, (but here to that Chesed, which is inferior viz. Yesod). So the name of El Chai [אל חי], is the same as it were, Cheseph Chai, i.e. quicksilver." [Westcott, 1997, p. 38] see 570, 949.

centrum in circulo (Lt). center in the circle. The symbol of the point within the circle.

tria sunt mirabilia (Lt). three are the marvels. Part of a Latin motto inscribed in a circle and symbol heading of "The Golden Age Restored," an alchemical treatise included in Secret Symbols (Page 20) and in *The Hermetic Museum*, I, page 51.

179 (prime)

אבינעם Father or possessor of Grace; the Father (God) is pleasantness [Standard Bible Dictionary]. Father of Barak [302, Lightning, brilliancy] in Judges 5:12: "Awake, awake, Deborah; awake, awake, utter a song, arise, Barak, and lead thy captivity captive, the son of Abinoam. Deborah means "bee" and is connected with the Moon and Venus. Chesed, sphere of Jupiter and cosmic memory is the center of compassion and grace-connected also with lighting: Jupiter was the sky God in mythology. see 443 (note), 217, 302, 173.

עקדה bonded, striped. With different pointing:

aeqaydawh, binding the sacrifice for the altar; the story of the attempted sacrifice of Isaac ("He laughs", 208) What is sacrificed is the illusive personality, as in the path of Ayin (Key 15-mirth). Tiphareth is the "beloved" attributed to Vav. The hierophant is attributed to this letter and the path of Vav is called "the garden of Eden, prepared for the compassionate." The "great voice" is that of intuition, the inner teacher. Vav means "the nail" "I make myself known as the bond of union between creature and creature, and between the creatures and their creator. The creator is myself, and I am the nail which joineth thee to me." [Book of Tokens, Vav]

Rosenroth in K.D.L.C.K. (p.632) gives: *ligatio*, and says it is Malkuth with respect to Geburah, because it is Geburah which binds and constrains.

minutum mundum (Lt). small world. The microcosm or human personality, it is a fabricated and is considered a work of a art rather than a product of nature. The vault in the *Fama* is considered a symbol of the microcosm or regenerated personality of an initiate.

Fama Fraternitatis: "Concerning minutum mundum, we found it kept in another little altar, truly more finer than can be imagined by any understanding man, but we will leave him undisturbed until we shall be truly answered upon this our true-hearted Fama." see 103, 76 Latin.

crux salvotoris (Lt). cross of the savior. The name of a star in heaven, according to the Reportorium of Simon Studion. see 58 (Lt).

180

I. 180 degrees or a semicircle. A symbol of the "day" or incarnating period of a personality.

קף Letter name Qoph. Back of Head. Variant form, normally spelt קוף. Note that Key 18 pictures a shower of 18 Yods (10). 10 x 18 = 180, the number of degrees in a semicircle. 180 is a symbol of a "day," or incarnation period of a personality, because the sun traces a semicircle through the day. see 186, 100, 739.

נע ונד a fugitive and a wander. In Genesis

4:12: "When thou tills the ground, it shall not henceforth yield unto thee her strength; a fugitive and a vagabond shall thou be in the earth." Said of Cain. The illusion of personal separateness prevents the higher powers from developing. see 160.

מעיין "fountain"; variant spelling of מעין, in [Canticles 4:15] "You are a garden fountain, a well of flowing water, streaming down from Lebanon."

propitiatorium (Lt). a cover, a lid. Used in the Vulgate to describe the cover of the ark (the mercy-seat) containing the mosacial tablets of divine law. see 700, 779 (Greek).

181 (prime)

פסולה vicious, faulty. Imbalance of Mars.

קפא to skim, take off foam. From a primitive root meaning: to shrink, i.e. thicken, congeal, curdle, With different pointing: to freeze; float on the surface. Coagulation is the 2nd stage of the alchemical process. see 331.

ειρηνη. peace. "A condition of concord, or a having-been-woven-together: harmony as a state transcending monotone. The Rainbow (*Iris* or *Toxon*) in its blending of seven colors suggest symbolically, a full number of parts whose resultant is bliss: all of the words-*toxon*, *iris* and *eirene* - convey the idea of a putting-together, or of a building-up. To attain to the state of *Eirene* is – to attain to the full complement of Being under the Creative Plan, that is, to possess the full number of parts. The symbol of the outcome of this ripened growth is a boy-cherub – frequently included in the Horn of Earth's Fruits, as depicted in ancient art. He is the Divine Child of Ploutos, or Panspermia. In Greek Myth, Iris was the messenger of the gods; and her wand, made of two intertwined serpents, was the sign of Union, or of a future bliss. See Gabriel (154)." [Omikron, 1942, p. 254.]

182

יעקב Jacob. Old Testament name. layer of snares, supplanter; Jacob [Crowley, 1977, p. 23].

I. Micah 7:20 "You will show Your faithfulness

and perform the sure promise *to Jacob* [ליעקב], and loving-kindness and mercy to Abraham, as You have sworn to our fathers from the days of old."

II. Book of Concealed Mystery [I:39, p.59] "Because it is written [Isaiah 44:5] "That man shall say, I am of the Tetragrammaton." (the word אני, *ani*, י, when the discourse is concerning judgements, pertains to the queen. But whenever mercy is introduced it refers to the understanding, as in this place, in order that the sense may be: the supernal path, which is called I, or the understanding in act of conjunction with the father, is for the purpose of the formation of the Tetragrammaton, and this is one conjunction between the father and the mother for the constitution of the six members). And that shall be called by the name יעקב Jacob. (to call by name is to preserve; and another conjunction of father and mother is introduced for the purpose of preserving the Microprosopus, which is called Jacob). And that man shall write with his hand, 'I am the Lord's. (to write belongs to the written law, or the beautiful path, and the same also signifies to flow in.) 'With his hand' בידו beyedo [22], is by metathesis ביוד be-Yod, that is, through the foundation, in order that the sense may be, it may be formed from his influx, so that the Tetragrammaton may be written with Yod, as we have above said. And by the name of Israel shall he call himself. He shall call himself thus in truth. For the conception of the Microprosopus is more properly under the name of Jacob, whose wife is Rachel; and his cognomen, as it were, is Israel, whose wife is Leah." see 172

מלאך האלהים Melakh ha-Elohim. Messenger of God.

האקאלדמא "field of blood", field purchased by Judas, who perished therein. In Acts 1:19: "And it was known to all those dwelling at Jerusalem, so that the field is called in their own language Aceldamach, which is, a field of blood. In Acts 2:19: "And I will give prodigies in the heavens above and signs on the earth below; blood and fire, and a cloud of smoke." see 102 (Greek).

זעקה outcry, clamor. From זעק "to cry, cry out", the old blood cells holding negative patterns are disturbed in the microcosmic "field" (Cheth).

מנא מנא numbered, numbered. In Daniel 5:25: "And this is the writing that was written (on the wall), mene, mene, tekel, upharsin" (26) "This is the interpretation of the thing: mene; God hath numbered thy kingdom, and finished it."

מקביל passive (as opposed to מתקבל = active); opposite, parallel. It is reversal of mind (Mem) working in sleep (Qoph) and in waking attention (Beth) to be receptive to assimilation of the divine will (Yod) and guidance (Lamed) of all acts.

Monoceros de astris (Lt). Unicorn from the stars. Connected with Hiram, the Architect, Hermes, Mercury, and Hod. see 94 Latin, 246, 15, 254.

Datum in Monte Abiegno (Lt). Found of Mt. Abiegno (RC symbol).

183

החפץ to bend or curve. The English "bent" has the same connotation. Relates to the 21st path of Kaph, the "Inclination to Seek." see 636, 892.

Λογοι. Logoi (Gr.). Words. A technical mystery term identical with the Sanskrit Mantra, the "Word of Power." see 214.

184

I. (8 x 23) or 2^3 x 23

כח-קום The power of permanence. The second part of the compound word may be rendered as "duration" or "existence." It also means "confirmation." Refers to the power of Mem (in all the Sephiroth), the 23rd Path. see 510, 744, 156.

נקדל ancient time; eastward [Crowley, 1977, p. 24].

Homo Spiritualis (Lt). Spiritual Man. see 105.

185

עינהם their eyes. see Genesis 37:25.

פניהם their faces. Leviticus 9:24.

מקלטו his refuge. Numbers 35:25:

186

קוף Letter name Qoph. back of head; ape, eye of a needle. For alternative spelling. Associated with the Corporal Intelligence and Key 18 of the Tarot. The medulla oblongata is located in the back of the head which controls the must fundamental functions of our body like respiration and body temperature. Therefore the Corporeal Intelligence is the consciousness that shapes bodies and rearranges our structure. In this connection remember the importance of breath control during meditation. see 180, 739.

מוסף an increase, an addition; additional service, offering prayer; attachment, ruin. The idea behind this is that through testing and experiment man adds to the means at his service for the mastery of circumstance.

אבן אחד ואין אבן One stone and no stone. see 53, 156.

אבן בגף A stone of stumbling; a rock to fall over. In Isaiah it refers to Tetragrammaton of Host [יהוה צבאות] as a sanctuary. In the New Testament [1 Peter 2:8], the "stone of stumbling" is identified with the foundation stone which is the pinnacle stone. It is the identification of the son with the father. This is the basic meaning of Key 14. All tests and trials afford experimental evidence of this identity. The stumbling-block to right thinking about this one identity is to be sought in misinterpretations of sense-experience.

I. Isaiah 8:14: "and he will be a sanctuary; but for both houses of Israel he will a stone that causes men to stumble and a rock tham makes them fall…"

II. "Corporeal Intelligence is the aggregate cell-consciousness of the physical body. This is often a stone of stumbling to those who do not know the objective of physical existence." [Paul Case, unpublished notes]

מקום place, locality, dwelling-place; stand, existence, substance. This is directly related to the meaning of the letter name Samekh, a tent peg (120). Misunderstanding of the function of the corporeal intelligence is a great cause of error, which has its roots in a misconception of the significance of "place" or "locality," and of the true inwardness of what seems to be increase or addition. As Jacob said, "surely the Lord is in this place, and I knew it not." Body-consciousness is the Life-power self-knowledge of form. In Exodus 21:13: "And if a man lie not in wait, but God's deliver him into his hand; then I will appoint thee a place whither he shall flee." See 1Kings 8:30.

I. *Maqom* a place, is a reference that the great work has definite location in time and space. It is the utilization of an energy which is out of time-space. It is by bringing the powers of that which is now the unknown, into specific, localized expression that adeptship is attained. But few there be who do not stumble over this 'stone' of material existence, and even the builders have sometimes rejected it. [Paul Case, unpublished notes]

II. The Book of Concealed Mystery: "the balance hangs in the מקום ([place]-a place on which something stands or exist, a location) which is אין (not)."

III. Note that by this is hinted that *maqom* = Ain (61). This is the same as what St. Peter is reported as saying in the Cleminine Homilies: "The place of God is that-which-is-not." *Ain* is the unmanifest point or the center. [see Isaac Myer, The Qabalah, p.118] Itself is a needle. Jesus said that is was easier for a rich man [i.e. materialistically inclined) man to enter the kingdom of heaven than for a camel (Gimel) to pass through the eye of a needle. The "back of the head" is like to *Ain* [see Book of Tokens]. The practice of habitual imagery through concentration to bring about body responsiveness to higher frequencies of light is hindered by the inertia of the "monkey" mind, which will not be still, but persistence brings results.

ניסוני probation, trial, testing, proving by experiment. The adjective is derived from נסיון, nisawyun, meaning "trial, temptation, test, experiment, experience." Probation or trial, signifies the testing of the ideas and innovations suggested by the imagination. see 60, 176, 536.

I. The 25th Path of Samekh which joins Beauty (Tiphareth) to Foundation (Yesod), because only by experiments, trials and tests can the harmony of Tiphareth become actualized in term Foundation.

II. Samekh is associated with Sagittarius, whose symbol is the arrow. This suggest the test and trials necessary to gain the skill to "hit the mark." The fundamental test is that every thing we think, feel, speak, and act (consciously and subconsciously) is the operation of the One Self through our personalities. No act originates in the personal organism, everything originates from the One Life which flows through our personalities.

ממונים perfects, magistrates, directors. The One Ego seated in the hearts of man. This is a veiled reference to chakras, the interior stars or the alchemical metals. Each has jurisdiction over a particular group of organs and functions, and each is capable of manifesting a certain higher type of consciousness. These magistrates or prefects must be awakened from their sleep, and aroused to a full exercise of their powers.

פעלו His work. The context relates to God, under the symbol of הצור, ha-tzoor, the rock. see 296 and Deuteronomy 32:4.

צאן אדם flocks of men. see Ezekiel 36:38.

אלקנה "God has possessed". Name of the Father of Samuel ("Name of God"). In 1 Samuel 1:1: "Now there was a certain man of Ramathaim-Zophim, of Mt. Ephraim, and his name was Elkanah..." see 890.

Γολγοθα. Gilgotha (Gr.). A skull; The hill of crucifixion. There is an occult correspondence here to the letter chi (600). In the life of Jesus the crucifixion was the final, inevitable experiment, whereby the truth of his doctrine was verified. But here is a still deeper meaning, because it is actually in the skull of man that the final stage of the Great Work is completed.

"Gr. kranion, Heb. golgotha, Lat. clavaria, Eng. "skull." The 'crucifixion' takes place in the brain. The Fire, or electric force, rises to the vertex of the skull, where is the opening called mystically the 'door of Iesous' (thura tou Iesou); at the highest centre in the brain, called the 'third eye' (the *conarium* of the anatomists), it is intersected by the Water, or magnetic force, forming a cross in the brain. The strain of the two forces at the point of intersection throws out a spiral, which coils about the head. The physical body is then in a deep trance, seemingly dead, and the consciousness is in the sidereal body. The man is thus 'born form above', 'born of Water and of Breath,' but this is possible only for the purified ascetic who has reached the androgynous state and is thus 'self-born' (*monogenes*). This noetic action in the brain of the seer is expressed by the symbol ⊕ ; that of ordinary man being [circle with cross without top + bar] and of the woman [circle with cross without bottom + bar]. In this sacred trance the light about the head has the appearance of a sun; hence the aureole and cross shown about the head of Iesus. The "thorny crown', of a golden color, represents the radiation of the fire; and the 'purple mantle', the hue without the radiance (*doxa*) takes from the magnetic force or water... the 'crucifixion' is an allegory of spiritual regeneration, not an historical record of a physical death." [Pryse, 1967, p. 200.]

εννοι. ennia (Gr). A thought, idea, intent, design, notion.

Frater Crucis Roseae (Lt). Brother of the Rosy Cross. The cross is the 4 elements of personality (Fire-desire, Water-intellect, Air-emotion, and Earth-physical body). The rose is purified desire. One who has equilibrated the elements of his own nature is said to be Rosi-crucian (Rose-cross) brother, he is turn helps to bring about the brotherhood of all mankind.

187

אופנים Wheels Choir (order) of angels of Chokmah, suggesting mobility. The Ophanim are the circuits of the celestial forces, and they are also the circling of the vital forces in the human body. Control of this vital energy from Chokmah within is what enables one to develop the perfected, transparent vehicle of adeptship. the two Chariot wheels in Key 7 refer to the Ophanim. see 73, 137.

חגוי-סלע clefts of the rocks. See the third degree teaching of free-masonry. The voices of the three ruffians were heard issuing from the rocks by a fell-craft who had just discovered a sprig of acacia on the brow of a hill.

חיי העולם הבא *vita mundi ventural*. the Life-breath of the world. [K.D.L.C.K. p.342]. "For Chokmah is also called 'the Life-breath of the world" because it is the life of the Sphere of Binah, which is called the soul (or breath) of the world

מלך + **אדם** + **בן** [Ben + Adam + Melek). The Son + Adam + The King. These are three title of Tiphareth, Sphere of the Sun and 6th Sephirah. see 52, 45, 90, 67, 1081.

The sum of 187 reduces to 7, and the extension of 7 is the perfect number, 28, and this takes you back through 10 [Malkuth] to 1 [Kether]. Man (**אדם**, 45) is the Son (**בן**, 52), and because he is the Son, he is the King (**מלך**, 90). He stands at the Center (**תם**, 440) at the point of absolute rest. Man's is the core of all, and the core is the heart. A cube has a face of 4 sides, and the angles formed by its diagonals are angles of 45 degrees the number of Adam. The angles at its corners are 90 degrees, Melek. The interior corner-to-corner diagonals are the square root of 3 (1.732). Therefore these 4 lines inside the cube are analogous to such lines on the Tree of Life as Daleth. The square root of 3 x 4 is 6.928 or 7 in whole numbers. And this hides Ben, because Ben is 52, which reduces to 7. See **13**.

פאימון Paimon. "tinkling sound"; demon king of Fire. Goetic demon #9 by day the 3rd decanate of Gemini. Corresponds to the 10 of Swords (Malkuth, sphere of the elements, in Yetzirah, the formative world). see 837 & Appendix 11.

Goetia: "...a great king, and very obedient unto Lucifer. He appears in the from of a man sitting upon a dromedary with a crown most glorious upon his head. There goes before him also a host of Spirits, like men with trumpets and well sounding cymbals, and all other sorts of musical instruments. He has a great voice, and roars at his first coming, and his speech is such that the magician cannot well understand unless he can compel him. The spirit can tech all arts and sciences, and other secret things. He can discover unto thee what the Earth is, and what holds it up in the waters; and what Mind is, and where it is; or any other things you may desire to know. He gives dignity, and confirms the same. He binds or makes any man subject unto the magician if

he so desire it. He gives good familiars, and such as can teach all arts. He is to be observed towards the west. He is of the Order of Dominations. He has under him 200 Legions of Sprits, and part of them are of the Order of Angles, and the other part of potentates. How if you call this spirit Paimon alone, you mist make him some offering; and there will attend him two Kings called *Labal* and *Abalim*, and also other Sprits who of the Order of Potentates in his Host, and 25 legions. And those spirits which be subject unto them are not always with them unless the Magician do compel them." [Mathers, 1995, p. 32]

סופיאל Sophiel. "Thing of God." In *The Key of Solomon the King*, (figure 52), Sophiel is said to be the angel of the 4th pentacle of the moon: "This defendenth thee from all evil sorceries, and from all injury unto soul of body. Its angel, Sophiel, giveth the knowledge of the virtue of all herbs and stones; and unto whomsoever shall name him, he will procure the knowledge of all." [Mathers, 1972, p. 77]

"Sophiel-angle of the 4th pentacle of the moon. In Jewish Cabala, Sophiel is the intelligence of Jupiter. (the corresponding angel here being Zadykiel)." [Davidson, 1971, p. 277.]

188

חצי הלילה midnight.

אבן פ(נ)ח corner-stone. [Abbreviated form] In Job 38:6: "On what were its footings [**ארניה**, footings-of-her] set, or who laid its cornerstone?" Pinnah, means corner, pinnacle, turret. Thus the corner stone is really the pinnacle stone. Note-here the letters **פה**, both of which have to do with the liberating Mars force. see 53, 588, 1185 (Greek).

"The top stone of a pyramidal structure. Mackey writes: "The corner-stone does not appear to have been adopted by any on the heathen nations, but to have been the ehben pinah peculiar to the Jews, form which it descended to the Christians. In the Old Testament, it seems always to have denoted a prince or high personage, and hence the evangelist constantly use it in reference to Christ, who is called the 'chief cornerstone'. In Masonic symbolism, it signifies a true mason, and therefore it is the first character which the apprentice is made to represent after his initiation has been completed." [Encyclopedia of Freemasonry, p. 187]

189

נסבא דסבין. The Ancient among the ancient [Crowley, 1977, p. 24].

190

I. Σ19 = 190

פ-מ-ע Peh-Mem-Ayin. Refers to the sum of the 3 paths proceeding from Hod on the Tree. see 456.

פעם to strike, to beat, an anvil, tread, step, pace.

כנען Canaan, flat, low. the son of Ham (חם, warmth, heat) and the original name of the Land of Palestine, home-land of Israel. May be related to קין, Cain (smith, artificer, appointed spear). see 58, 160, 840, 993.

נקם vengeance; revenge. See Romans 12:19, Proverbs 24:29 and 370, 477 (Greek).

Do not give yourself to vengeance, this leads to wrath. In Deuteronomy 32:35 "It is mine to avenge, I will repay…" You need Light, just as as you need food or money. Spirit supplies all those needs, and Divine Law differs from human legislation in one respect. Ignorance does mitigate the penalties. Not that you can violate cosmic law without reaction, even if you do so ignorantly; but their is no vengeance in Love, and man's duty is to forgive. The Bible also states"I will repay." The payment is Shalom, (שלם) 370, or the number of יחידה Yekhidah (37), multiplied by 10, or the perfect manifestation of the ONE through all 10 aspects. The perfect expression of that Will-to-Good is perfect fulfillment. Love condemns nothing, and, because it never seeks its own, inflicts no lasting penalties for the failures of ignorance. Pain comes through ignorance, but the inflictor of pain is that ignorance, and pain is the goad, Lamed, which teaches and equilibrates (Key 11).

Naqam is 190, or 10 x 19, or , ten times חוה, the perfect manifestation of the Mother who initiates the sin of Adam, but through that, brings forth the Son, the Redeemer. Misdirected Nun, and Qoph becomes the vehicle of suffering; but Qoph climbs the Way of Return, and Mem completes the Work, as these letters in the Tarot show. See C.16.

פנימי inner.

פנין Pearl; one of the titles of Malkuth, the Kingdom. see 190, 840.

"A symbol of experience with its outcome, the *gnosis* or knowledge of the soul-process. The Gnosis is ultimately found first through the awakenment of the Ego by the clamor of this kama-manasic [desire-mind, or animal soul] nature, for it is through this desire side of his nature, that he first begins to function as a truly human entity, and its is from this mentality, therefore, that the germ of *experience* which from this viewpoint is another expression for the "pearl," is collected and transferred to the higher plane of the beings consciousness. It must be remembered that all experience is only the reflection, piecemeal, upon the lower plane of that compete Gnosis which is above; the ideal actualizing, as it were:
Acts of Judas Thomas. The divine parents enjoin- 'If thou, our son, journeys deep down into the domain of illusion, and carries forth from thence the 'pearl' of experience giving control of the lower realms and bringing intuitive knowledge-the gnosis-which 'pearl' is in the astral keeping, betwixt the lower emotions and the desire of the flesh, hard by the passions and animal sense, wherein experience and power to control is gained; then shall thou arise and assume for thyself thy higher vehicles causal and buddhic, and with our brother, thy causal self, thou shall inherent the heavens." [Gaskell, 1981, p. 565.]

קצ the end, the time of redemption, messianic age. see 660, 1000, 305.

I. Daniel 8:17: "So he came near where I stood: and when he came, I was afraid, and fell upon my face: but he said unto me [Gabriel], understand, O Son of Man: for at the time of the end shall be the vision.

II. Daniel 12:13: "As for you, go your way till the end. You will rest, and then at the end of the days you will rise to receive your allotted inheritance."

צלע rib; slope, side of hill; side chamber; plank, board; leaf of folding door. With different pointing: *tzelah*. limping, stumbling, fall; sin, decline.

מצבה אבן a pillar of stone. In Genesis 35:14: "And Jacob set up a pillar in the place where he talked with him, even a pillar of stone: and he poured a drink offering thereon, and he poured oil thereon." This suggest the middle pillar of the Tree of Life, the pillar of consciousness. [spelled **מצבת** is used in this passage].

ציץ plate; shining plate of gold. In Exodus 39:30:"And they made the plate, the sacred diadem [crown], out of pure gold and engraved on it, like an inscription on a seal: HOLY TO THE LORD." With different pointing: 1. blossom, flower, bud, wing, feather; filament, tread, fringe; to shine, gleam; to bloom, blossom, flower; 2. to chirp, twitter; to provide with fringes.

I. According to the Zohar [IV:217B, 218B] *tzeetz* was so called "because it was a reflector, mirroring the character of any man gazing at it. For in that plate were engraven the letters of the divine name and when a righteous man appeared before it the letters so engraved bulged out and rose luminous from their sockets, from which light shone on the man's face with a faint sparking." (no such effect on the face of an evil doer). "All the arrogant of Israel, when they gazed on the plate, became contrite of heart, and looked inwardly into their own deeds."

II. Rosenroth in K.D.L.C.K. (p.664) gives: *corona florida prominens*, and refers it to Binah, and cites Exodus 28:36: "Make a plate of pure gold and engrave on it as on a seal: Holy to the Lord." He says holy refers to the first 3 Sephiroth; to the Lord, to Tiphareth, but since the crown is above the great priest; Binah is also above Chesed.

מנק 66th Shem ha-Mephorash, short form. see 221 & Appendix 10.

קמטיאל Devil of Ain [61]. *Ain* means not or nothing.

I. "The Crowd of Gods" Qlippoth of *Ain* [61]". [Godwin. 1999, p. 527.]

II. "First Devil. V *Porta Coelorum*, figure 16." [Crowley, 1977, p. 24]

191 (prime)

פאבץ Pakatz. Night demon of 1st decanate of Aries. This decanate is ruled by Mars and suggest lack of this energy, leaving individual timid, lackadaisical and lethargic.

Sanctum Sanctorum (Lt). Holy of Holies. A cubical room in the Bible, containing the ark of the covenant, upon which rested the Shekhinah, or divine presence. In the tabernacle, the Holy of Holies measured ten cubits in length, breath, and height. In Solomon's temple it measured twenty cubits in each dimension.

ad gloriam rosae crucis (Lt). to the glory of the rosy cross. Full inscription from initials A.G.R.C., written in circles of the altar table of Brother C.R. in the Rosicrucian *Fama*. see 808 (Lt).

regnum Dei et christi (Lt). The kingdom of God and Christ.

192

I. (3 x 8 x 8) or 3 x 2[6]

הפצי-בה my delight is in her. In Isaiah 62:4: "No longer will they call you Deserted, or name your land Desolate. But you will be called Hephzibah [my delight is in her], and your land will be called Beulah [married]; for the Lord delights in you, and your land will be married."

בטן הסוס the horse's belly or womb. The horse's "dung" is the serpent fire working in darkness; the belly refers to physical embodiment. in alchemy it suggest the Virgo area, where the Christ-child is born. see 711, 383.

זלעפה zahlayawpaw. poisonous wind; Simoon; raging heat, zeal. The great work is performed by even and moderate heat in the athanor. This word suggest imbalance and excess.

חדבקים ביהוה You that shall cleave in the Lord. In Deuteronomy 4:4: "But all of you who held fast to the Lord your God are still alive today." see 26, 220, 189. variant spelling.

Μαριαμ. Mariam (Gr). The name of the 6 Christian women named Mary [Strong's Bible Dictionary]. see 656, 744 (Greek).

193 (prime)

I. [7x7 + 12x12] or $7^2 + 2^4$ x 3^2

בעל אמן Master of verity or Master of knowledge. Title of Rosicrucian Grade of Practicus (3=8). One proficient in the sphere of Hod. Suggests that the object of practice is to confirm or verify knowledge gained in earlier grades, in order to establish that intelligent faith which links personal consciousness to the higher planes of perception. One verifies by direct experience the essential unity of all things in the midst of diversity by separating "the subtle from the Gross" with the aid of Mercury. see 15.

זין יוד נון Zain-Yod-Nun. The value of the letter-name Zain spelled in full. Faithful practice of 3=8 ritual which makes one a 'Master of Verity' is, in effect, the result of the fullest possible use of the powers of discrimination, which are represented by the occult meanings of the letter Zain. These powers, it should be noted, are held to be under the rule of Mercury; and Mercury's sphere of action is the Sephirah Hod, to which the Grade of Practicus is attributed. see 7, 67, 100 Latin.

Frateres Aureae Crucis (Lt). Brothers of the Golden Cross. All persons who really fulfill the ideals of the Grade of Practicus are entitled to be so called; and it is partly on this account that these ideas are associated with the solar or golden cross of 13 squares is associated with the Grade. see 79, 47, 67 (Lt).

Philosphia Moralis (Lt). Moral philosophy. The main object of study in this grade. Here it must be understood: 1) That in more ancient usage, 'philosophia' had the do, primarily, with experimental investigation; and 2) that the basis of occult 'morality' is faithful obedience to the actual laws of God, rather than outward adherence to the customs, taboos, or conventions of a particular historical period, or those accepted by some group of persons. see 116, 77 (Lt).

Sal Philosophorum (Lt). Salt of the Philosophers. He who is Master of Verity acts from knowledge of principle, and the deposit of this knowledge within him is the true salt of the philosophers.

"Know that the salt of which Geber speaks (89) has none of the special properties of salt, and yet is called a Salt, and *is* a Salt. It is black and fetid, and when chemically prepared, assumes the appearance of blood, and is at length rendered white, pure, and clear. It is a good and precious Salt which, by its own operation, if first impure and then pure. It dissolves and coagulates itself, or, as the Sage says, it locks and unlocks itself. No Salt has this property but the Salt of the Sages." [Waite, 1974, vol. 1, p. 176] see 28, 165 (Lt).

Tinctura Coelestis (Lt). Celestial Tincture. It is also true celestial tincture premeating all his vehicles with the heavenly wisdom. see 96, 97 (Lt).

194

I. [5x5 + 13x13] or 5^2 x 13^2

צדק Tzedek. Jupiter, The sky father. As a verb Tzedek means: to be just, be righteous, to be in the right; be justified, be just, prosperity. The 21st Path of Kaph. Rosenroth in K.D.L.C.K. (p. 656) gives: *Justita* and cites Isaiah 1:21. צדק Tzedek.: "See how the faithful city [i.e. Jerusalem] has become a harlot! She once was full of justice; righteousness used to dwell in her-but now murderers!" see 986.

הוא אל קנא Hu El qana. He (is) a jealous God [Deuteronomy 4:24]. The esoteric meaning rests on what amounts to a pun. In Hebrew *qana*, jealous and with different vowel points it means: to own, to possess, to set a measure to are almost identical in sound, and are also related in derivation. The Divine jealousy is like that of all strong powers in the universe. The more truly we measure the forces with which we are working and the more completely we comply with the principles and laws revealed by such measurement, the more perfect is our application. The powers of God and the powers of nature are the same powers. Perfect obedience to the way things really are is the price we must pay; and when we do pay it we get full measure in return-- pressed down and running over. see 72, 48.

פגעיאל Pagiel. God has harmed me. Numbers 1.13: From Asher (אשר, 501, happy): Pagiel the son of Ocran (עכרן, 340, Muddler).

η εννοι. ha ennoia (Gr). a thought, intent, design. The faculty of thinking. see 259 Greek.

oculus universale. the Universal Eye [Secret Symbols page 9]. This is the eye of providence, which is part of the symbolism of Freemasonry and is included in the symbolism of the Great Seal of the U.S. The notion of providence is directly connected with the fourth path and with the sphere of Jupiter.

Rosa Christus Est. The Rose is Christ. A Rosicrucian motto, found in various unpublished manuscripts, and in one or two printed books. "...of human nature in the manifested state, and in that which is called attainment humanity becomes the rose, that is to say, the Christhood. Rosa christus est Herein also is the incarnation understood mystically." [Waite, 1993, p. 634] see 47, 107 (Lt), 154.

Ruoto Della Foruna. Wheel of Good Fortune.

195

נפטון Neptune.

נקמה vengeance, punishment; revengefulness, vindictiveness. [Jeremiah 20:10] "For I heard the evil intentions of many, who were gathering from every side inquiring of my peace with their mouth, but hating me in their heart, saying, point him out to us; we will stand against him; perhaps we can win him over and we shall take our revenge on him." see Psalm 149:7 & Ezekiel 25:15.

פקודה visitation [Crowley, 1977, p. 24].

מקנה a flock.

196

I. (4x7x7) or 2^2 x 7^2 or 14^2

עולמים ages; worlds.

קץ thorn. crown, summit, point. Metathesis of **ציק**. It is organization (Qoph) by listening to the inner voice (Vav) through meditation (Tzaddi). With different pointing: 1. *qotz*, thorn, thornbush; title, jot, apex, piece; 2. to loathe, abhor; to feel a sickening dread, shrink with fear; 3. *qawahtz*, to shrink, be dried up; to curl; *yiyatz* to clear of thorns, to weed out; *qahawtz*, curly head, fruit drier.

צוק constraint, distress; peak, precipice; troublous. In Daniel 9:25: "Know therefore and understand, that from the going forth of the commandment to restore and to build Jerusalem unto the Messiah the prince shall be seven weeks, and three-score and two weeks (62): the street shall be built again, and the wall, even in troublous times." Jerusalem is the "abode of Peace"; Messiah is the Christos in the heart center; 7 weeks refers to the cycle related to the 7 interior stars or alchemical "metals"; 62 = "the tabernacle of IHVH". see 586, 358.

ימסוף the boundless sea. In K.D.L.C.K. (p.435) Malkuth is called the "sea" here, which the paternal light of Chokmah illuminates it; it is limitless on every level and denotes what is "below", rather than simply being the sea.

לפני יהוה in the presence of Jehovah; before the Lord. In Genesis 18:22: "And the men turned their faces from thence, and went toward Sodom: but Abraham stood yet before the Lord." Note that Sodom means "burning or conflagration", and Abraham means "Father of Many nations". see 104, 248, 59.

סטן עו Satan; the adversary, "father of lies", variant spelling. see **שטן** (#359). Satan is the illusion of appearances. The origin of "troublous" times.

קמון Camon, the city where Jair was buried. Linked with Mars & Sun. see 221.

197 (prime)

בן יפנה Son of Jephunna [Numbers 13:6]. Refers to Caleb (52). Intimates Tiphareth manifested in the meditation process, which gives to the mercurial aspect, or consciousness, its full power and perfected humanity. see 145, 52.

In Jephunna Yod and Peh add to 90, the full spelling of Mem (מים), and the number of Tzaddi (צ) and Meditation, which perfected, leads to the state pictured by Key 12. Note that the extension of 10 is 55 which is the numeration of the last two letters. Fifty-five is the number נאה, ornament, as well as Kala (כלה), the Bride. Both these words relate to Malkuth. Thus Ben Jephunna, son of Jephunna, intimates Tiphareth manifested in the meditation process which gives to the mercurial aspect, or consciousness, its full power and perfected humanity. See **33**.

אל עליון Most High God. *Elyon* means high, higher, upper, uppermost, highest, and refers to Kether, the Crown Rosenroth in K.D.L.C.K. (p.92) gives *Deus supremus*, and says that Kether is so called because it has its highest place in Atziluth. see 166, 294, 376.

הע אה אנא חטא עם הזה "The guttural letter הע, which appear in the initial words of Exodus 32:31 ("And as He passed over Penuel, the sun rose upon him, and he halted upon his thigh") [K.D.L.C.K. p.71]

עמנואל God with us, with us (is) god. A typical name of Isaiah's son. [Strong's Bible Dictionary]

αγοραζει. agorazei (Gr). buys, purchases.

198

נצחים victories [Crowley, 1977, p. 24].

κορη. kore (Gr). maiden, virgin. "The name given in Greek Myth of *Phersephone*, the Missing Daughter of *Demeter*. The word indicated a certain age or stage amongst the Pythagoreans, who, after great cultivation of the 'Humanities' sought premature unfoldment of mystic faculties. The word *parthenos* is a synonym. The root-meaning of *kore* appears to

be – a beautifying and a purifying: a ripening and a building together." [Omikron, 1942, p. 257.] see 1776.

199 (prime)

אמונה אמון Creation of Faith, Firmness of Faith, Basis of Faith. Title of Binah. The responsiveness of subconsciousness to suggestion is the psychological truth behind this designation. Binah is the ground in which the suggestive power of true perception sows the seed of faith.

הצדק the righteousness, the equity; figuratively, the prosperity. Closely related the Hebrew name for the planet Jupiter. see 194.

יהוה מסיני בא God (Tetragrammaton) came from Sinai [Deuteronomy 33:2]. יהוה came with 10,000's of saints -relating to the third path of the Sanctifying Intelligence (Binah). Derivation of סיני is unknown. It may have connection with sin, the Babylonian moon-god and with Luna (42). see 130.

צדקה righteousness (fem). In Malachi 3:20: שמש צדקה, Shemesh Tzedaquah, "Sun of Righteousness." This is the same as הצדק, except that the letters are in a different order. The same root-word appears in the name of the Mysterious King-priest מלכי-צדק, King of Salem, מלך שלם. see 294, 90, 370.

Section 2

Numbers 200 - 299

200

I. (5 x 5 x 8) 5^2 x 2^3

ר Resh. Head, face, countenance. Attributed to the 30ᵗʰ Path of the Collective Intelligence because man is a synthesis of all cosmic activities. Human intelligence gathers together all the various threads of the Life Power's self-manifestation and carries that manifestation beyond anything that can be created by nature.

I. "This character as consonant, belongs to the lingual sound. As symbolic image, it represents the head of man, his determining movement, his progress. According to Beohme the letter R draws its origin form the igneous faculty of nature. It is the emblem of fire. ...in his book [Boehme] of the Triple Life of Man, that each inflection, vocal or consonantal, is a particular form of central nature. "Although speech varies them by transposition, nevertheless each letter has an origin at the center of nature. This origin is wonderful and the senses can grasp it only by the light of the intelligence."

As grammatical sign, the character ר is the sign of all movement proper, good or bad. It is an original and frequentative sign, image of the renewal of things, as to their movement." [d'Olivet, 1976, p. 446.]

II. "*Raysh* (200): As 2 multiplied by a hundred, *Raysh* represents the totality of the Universe, of interstellar space, of the myriads of stars and all the planets; all is conditioning of life and the life of conditioning. This is a great cosmic dwelling of life, which retains life manifested in accordance with its capacity (200). It includes the totality of nature, all existence: the myriads and myriads of water-drops, of blades of grass, of living cells, and the infinite myriads of elements living in the living elements of algae. *Raysh* (spelt *Raysh-Yod-Sheen)* gives birth to *Sheen,* the great cosmic breath that is everywhere and in everything." [Suraes, 1992, p. 65.]

עצם bone, body, substance, essence, life, self, wealth, livestock. In Psalm 139:15: "My substance was not hid from thee, when I was made in secret, and curiously wrought in the lowest parts of the earth." The human body and the earth are identified. The "substance," is the universal radiant energy. The word *etzem* is closely related to the word עץ, tree [also might, force], like the Hyle of the Gnostics, its primary meaning is wood. Here the human body is likened to the Tree of Life, whose essence is that Life. see 423, 160.

כנפים wings. In Malachi 4:12: "But unto you that fear my name shall the sun of righteousness rise, with healing in his wings." Note the direct reference to the Sun.

מים יוד מים Mem-Yod-Mem. the letter-name Mem, spelt in plentitude. One of several intimations that Light is fluidic.

סליק finished; the end. Used in Rabbinical writings as we employ the Latin *finis* to mark the end of a book. The more recondite meaning has to do with the idea that the manifestation of suns, or luminaries, is the final step in the condensation of the Limitless Light into physical forms.

קדמון Ancient, old; archetypal. Epithet of God. Its correspondence with Resh intimates that the primal or archetypal substance is the universal radiance. see 86 (Greek).

In Daniel 3:6, 7:9: "Whoever does not fall down and worship will immediately be thrown into a blazing furnace"; as I looked, thrones were set in place, and the Ancient of Days took his seat. His clothing was as white as snow; The hair of his head was white like wool. His throne was flaming with fire, and its wheels were all ablaze."

עגלים calves [Matthew 4:2]. The newly "reborn" as shown as the children in Key 19, attributed to Resh. see 713.

המלכה הגדולה The great queen. see Key 3, The Empress.

נעלים sandal, shoes, boots. Containers of the motive power.

קסם magic, divination. Accomplished through the essence of light or radiant energy.

קיץ belonging to the spring, vernal (Case). also summer.

ענף branch, bough. Connected with the Tree and body. see 589.

קלע slinger, archer, marksman. see 800, qesheth (קשת).

pereclinus de faustis (Lt). "proven by the hand" or "growing form the hand". Relates to the Rosicrucian grade of Zelator. In Latin, *periclitatio* has the meaning of trial or experiment; periclitor means to try, test or prove. see 135 (Greek).

in noblis regnat Iesus (Lt). Jesus rules in us; variant reading of the Rosicrucian password. I:N:R:I, suggesting by Franz Hartmann. see 299, 287, 46 (Lt). note: Jesus = 67 = natura.

201

אמעץ center, midst, middle. The direction attributed to the letter Tav the Cube of Space.

אר light (Chaldean). As a place name *Ur*, the birthplace of Abraham. What is collected at every center is light. Hence the cube of space is sometimes know as the cube of light, or "the flaming cube, light of the Chaldees." The "palace of holiness in the midst" (Tav) is referred to Saturn, and the Sphere of Saturn, Binah. see 406, 207, 713, 291, 400, 813, 1271 (Greek).

202

בר corn, grain, son, chosen, pure, empty With different pointing: 1. *rab,* multitude, abundance; 2. *rawb* many; much; great; abundant; mighty; old, older, ancient; noble, dignified.

"The sign of movement proper, united to that of interior activity, or by contraction with the root אב, image of all fructification, constitutes a root which are developed all ideas of multiplication, augmentation, growth, grandeur; it is a kind of movement toward propagation, physically as well as morally. The Arabic word in general means, that which dominates, augments, grows, usurps, possesses, gathers together, governs, etc.

רב and רבב (intensive). That which is *large, broad, increased,* whether in number or in volume; *augmented, multiplied;* that which is expressed by the adverbial relations, *much, more, still more, many;* ideas of *multitude, numbers, quantity, strength,* or *power* which is drawn form number, etc." [d'Olivet, 1976, p. 447.]

סאיציאל Saitziel. Lesser assistant angel of Scorpio. This is related to mastery and to Daniel. see 54.

בקק to empty, to make waste, to plunder; to make void. In Isaiah 24:1: "See, the Lord is going to lay waste the earth and devastate it; he will ruin its face and scatter its inhabitants."

נקבים apertures [Crowley, 1977, p. 25].

זקיפה lift. Rosenroth in K.D.L.C.K. (p.328) gives: *elevatio,* and says it pertains to Tiphareth. He cites Psalm 146:8: "The Lord gives sight to the blind, the Lord lift [זקף, lifting] up those who are bowed down, the Lord loves the righteous."

Il Papa (Lt). the father, the pope (the old Key 5 name).

torrentes aquarum (Lt). torrents of water.

203

אבר limb, organ, wing; strong.

ברא to cut out, to separate, to select, to create [Isaiah 45:7, Genesis 1:1]. Hides all mysteries of darkness and evil. The presence of seeming evil in the universe is a necessity, because manifestation itself must come through limitation, and limitation is the root of pain. All misery is rooted in ignorance; but ignorance can be cured, and when it is cured, there is an end to misery. We may use the mind we now have to such advantage that we may correct our errors and bring ourselves into a living experience of truth. see 15.

I. "The potential and unmanifest, becoming the actual and manifest in a scheme of being in which the spiritual and mental precede the astral and physical."

258

'What creation is to god, that is thought to man. Creation is in fact the thinking out of a thought.' Alice Gardner, John the Scot, pp. 128, 38.

The Zohar [I:1,2]: 'The deity began (the creation) by forming an imperceptible point; this was its own thought; then it turned itself to construct with its own thought a mysterious and holy form; finally, it covered this (ideal) form with a rich and shining (visible) garment; that it, the entire universe, of which the name necessarily enters into the name of Elohim."

The Zohar also says: 'All that which is found (or exists) upon the Earth, has its spiritual counterpart also to be found on High, and there does not exist the smallest thing in this world, which is not itself attached to something on High, and is not found in dependence upon it.; The basic element … is the *idea* of a of a perfect invisible universe above, which is the real and true paradigm, or ideal model of the visible universe below…

The idea of the Upper ideal but *real* and *true*, and the lower <u>apparently</u> real, but in truth *changeable* and untrue, goes through the entire Apocalypse of St. John, is in St. Paul, and in the Epistle of the Hebrew.' Isaac Myer, Qabbalah, pp. 108, 109. [Gaskell, 1981, p. 182.]

II. "Barah: creation. Creation, violent triumphant affirmation of the creative immanence. The surging-or revolving-action of perpetual creation gives birth to its own containers: bara, bar-Aleph means: Son of Aleph...

Creation! Vertiginous movement, immeasurable movement, movement that transcends all conception. In the hidden depths of movement is the secret of existence. And this movement is he custodian of all possible possibilities. Existing, projection of life, negation of existence (everything that exists must cease to exist). Apparent betrayal of life. Revelation! Life-death is one. And the collision, the shock of passive resistance of the mass, the hard, the dry, the stones: blessed resistance! Without resistance there could be no birth, this is the becoming." [Suraes, 1992, p. 78.]

באר well, spring; pit. A title of Malkuth. With different pointing: to make plain, distinct, to explain, elucidate. Aleph is now placed in the middle-it is the eternal mediator who explains

the true meaning of creation in darkness. see 575.

אבר Lead. The metal attributed to Saturn, the 32nd path, and to dominion and slavery. The alchemist had much to say about transmuting this "base metal" into gold. Relates to the physical plane of manifestation. In Rabbinical Hebrew *ehbar* is a limb, part, organ; and "to be strong, hard". Hence "Pillar of fruitfulness" [is] related to יסוד, the sacred foundation.

In K.D.L.C.K. (p.22) gives: *penna, ala: it membrum, et quidem genitale.* (""limb, wing: that is, a member, indeed the genital [or reproductive organ]". Referring to the Zohar, prologue [3B, p.14] "What was hitherto sealed up and unproductive in the word *bara* has by a transposition of letters become serviceable, there has emerged a pillar of fruitfulness: for ברא has been transformed into אבר (organ), which is the sacred foundation on which the world rests."

א-ב-ר initials of the trinity: אב (Ab), the father, בן (Ben), the son, and רוח (Rauch), the life-breath or spirit.

ארב to lie in wait, to lie in ambush, to lurk. With different pointing: 1. *ambuscade*, ambush; 2. groin. Note that Resh is placed between Aleph and Beth instead of following them, as above. The spirit lies in wait, ready to bring its transmuting power from groin to heart.

באמצע in the midst; in the center. *Sepher Yetzirah* 4:4: "Seven Doubles: Up and down, East and west, North and south And the Holy Palace precisely in the center and it supports them all." [Kaplan, 1997, p. 163]

אלה מעזים The God of forces (a fortress), i.e. Mars.

גר stranger, foreigner; proselyte; exotic, foreign. With different pointing: *gar*, dwelling; to abide, dwell, sojourn, remain. In Isaiah 11:6: "The world will dwell with the lamb, the leopard will lie down with the goat, the calf and the lion and the yearling together; and a little child will lead them."

צדיק just, righteous.

דר pearl.

אברא Beginning of the name Abra-melin. Composed of אב Ab, the father, or Chokmah, and רא ra, which when reversed, reads אר Aur, light. Thus "Father of Light". Also אב, Ab and Resh = Sun + Aleph = super-consciousness or Uranus. Reversal of negative, counter-evolutionary patterns, associated with Yesod and the Moon, brings the Sun and "light". see 3, 201.

קדמני Kadmonite; signifies a dweller in the east, and is synonymous with 'sons of the east'. It refers to the Arabs of the Syrian desert. [Genesis 15:19] "The Kenites, and the Kenizzites, and the Kadmonites."

205

הר/ Heh/Resh. Sun (Resh) in Aries (Heh).
הד har. mountain. Genesis 10:30.

ה-קדומן the Archetypal man.

ה-סליק the end, finished.

וצדקה and the righteous. Deuteronomy 6:25.

ויהוה מסיני בא and the God from Sinai.

אדר Adar, the 6th Hebrew month, February-March, corresponding roughly to the period when the sun is in Pisces. See Esther 3:7.

אגאר Agar. Agares; Goetic demon by day of the 2nd decanate of Aries. The 2nd decanate of Aries is ruled by the Sun and has the qualities: exacted, enthusiastic, loyal. The influence of the demon suggest conscious imbalance, resulting in negative aspects of these qualities. In the Tarot minor arcana this decanate is assigned to the 3 of Wands. It represents the operation of Binah, sphere of Saturn, in Atziluth, the archetypal world of ideas. When ill-dignified, as here this can indicate conceit, arrogance and insolence. The remedy is to be receptive to power form higher levels, while at the same time being able to apply that power to various subconscious or personality planes, in a saintly manner. see Appendix 11.

I. Davidson gives *Agreas* and says this demon was "once of the order of virtues... now a duke in Hell, served by 31 legions of infernal spirits. He manifest in the form of an old man astride a crocodile and carrying a goshawk. He teaches languages and can cause earthquakes... According to legend, Agares was one of the 72 spirits Solomon is reputed to have shut up in a brass vessel and cast into a deep lake (or banished to 'lower Egypt')." [Davidson, 1971, p. 10.]

II. D'Olivet writes of אב. "This root characterizes and active thing which tends to be augmented. The Arabic expresses *ignition, acrimony, intense excitation.* [p.288] Of אר: That which belongs to the elementary principle, that which is *strong, vigorous, and productive.*" [d'Olivet, 1976, p. 299.]

III. *Goetia*: "He is under the power of the East, and comes up in the from of an old fair Man, riding upon a Crocodile, carrying a Goshawk upon his fist, and yet mild in appearance. He makes them to run that stand still, and brings back runaways. He teaches all Languages or Tongues presently. He has power also to destroy Dignities both Spiritual and Temporal, and causes Earthquakes. He was of the Order of Virtues." [Mathers, 1995, p. 28]

206

הפעולות Spiritual activities. Refers to Teth, and the 19th path of Wisdom. The great secret has to do with control of the Mars vibration through the agency of the Venus power of desire. see 1702, 667, 409, 380, 358.

ברד hail.

דבר word, saying, statement; report, news; thing, matter, affair; occurrence, event; order, command; cause, case, something, anything. Daleth as to do with the emotional nature (Venus). The beginning of every word or thought is a feeling. It is the primal feeling of *Ain*, the No-thing. Beth, that feeling is rationalized into self-conscious awareness. When spirit feels itself alive it must also experience a further modification of consciousness (Resh), the consciousness of being a center of positive self-directive energy is manifested. It is the secret of the "Word" made flesh.

I. *Sepher Yetzirah* 1:9: "The Voice [קול] of Breath [Spirit, רוח], and speech [דבור]: and this is the Holy Spirit [Breath]." [Kaplan, 1997, p. 68]

II. With different pointing: *deber*: Murrain, destructive, pestilence, plague; the 5th of the ten plagues of Egypt. In Exodus 9:3: "The hand of the Lord will bring a terrible plague on your livestock in the field-on your horses and donkeys and camels and on your cattle and sheep and goats." According to Case, Debir is the root of Deborah, a bee (217) and means in one sense, to arrange or regulate, suggesting the industry of the bee. see 443 (note), 24 (note).

פעל יהוה   The work of IHVH. [Isaiah 5:10] Has to do with the manifestation of spirit through the word.

בני-קדם   Children of the east. In 1 Kings 4:30: "Solomon's wisdom was greater than the wisdom of all the men of the East, and greater than all the wisdom of Egypt." The Zohar [II:133B, p.33] says: "Herein is an allusion to the descendants of the very children of Abraham's concubines, who... inhabit the mountains of the east, where they instruct the sons of men in the arts of magic and divination." see 766, 52, 144.

ראה   to see, observe, perceive, consider. Also the 69th Shem ha-Mephorash, short form. see 237 & Appendix 10.

207

אין סוף   Ain Suph. No-Limit, Boundless, not perishable, never ending. The Second Veil of the Absolute. As the 2nd Veil it intimates that the Absolute has within itself the potencies of creation, formation, reproduction, maintenance, coordination and expression.

אגראב   a scorpion. Name of the sign Scorpio, linked with death, change, the reproduction force and transformation. see Key 13, 50, 106, 700.

אדון עולם   Eternal Lord of the Universe, eternity. Lord of the Hidden Mystery; Lord of Eternity. The No-Limit, or Boundless, is the Master Principle of the Universe, the Lord of Time and Eternity, the Hidden Ruler of the Mystery of Absolute Being. see 61,146.

הבר   to divide, to cut apart, divide out; that which cuts; to pronounce, enunciate. Root of a noun which designates an astrologer, one who divides the heavens. The basic idea is that of the subdivision of space, and it is allied in meaning to what is suggested by גדל and סוף.

ברה   to cut, to cut asunder. Root of the noun ברית, covenant. With different pointing: to make manifest, to choose, to select. Thus it indicates *Ain Suph*, the limitless, as the source of a division within itself by means of which the Life-power becomes manifest in a cycle of creative activity.

גדר   to wall in, to inclose, fenced. With different pointing: *gadaer;* enclosure, form; to enclose; a wall, a boundary. The Limitless Being, Lord of the Universe, Source of all existence, encloses or surrounds the entire field of the manifest, which field is contained within the Limitless Being of the Boundless One. In order to manifest, it must establish within itself a field of operation, an area which is limited or enclosed.

אור   aur. light, fire, enlightenment With different vowel points: the direction East. The Lord of the Universe, the Boundless, is the One Light we all seek, the One East, or Orient, toward which we turn our mental gaze, and toward which we "travel" as we make our way along the Path of Return. It is the One Source of our existence, and of all other existences, past, present, and to come. Also the place-name Ur, אר, where Abraham was born. see 65, 217, 602 & Genesis 1:3.

Chaiah חיה is אור. *Aur* is 207 or 9 x 23. Twenty-three is the number of Chaiah, and 9 is the number of Yesod (the 9th Sephiroth). Chaiah is in Chokmah, thus the power of life is one with the Father, *Ab* (3). Life and Light are one. Light is always pure and Holy, and the extension of

Light is its multiplication through forms. See **27**, 363, 23, 73, 80

I. "אוֹר, light… I cannot repeat too often that all words of the Hebrew tongue are formed in such a way as to contain with in themselves the reason for their formation. Let us consider the word אוֹר *light*: it is derived directly from the word אוּר *fire*. The only difference between them is, that in the word which designates fire, it is the universal convertible sign וּ which forms the link between the sign of power א, and that of movement proper: whereas in the second, it is the intelligible sign וֹ. Let us proceed further. If, from the words אוּר and אוֹר, one takes away the median sign וּ or וֹ there will remain in the elementary root אר, composed of power and movement, which in all known tongues signifies by turns, *earth, water, air, fire, ether, light*, according to the sign joined there unto." [d'Olivet, 1976, pp. 32-33.]

אר This root and the one which follows [אש] are very important for the understanding of the Hebraic text. The signs which constitute the one in question here, are those of power and movement proper. Together they are the symbol of the elementary principle, whatever it may be, and of all which pertains to that element or to nature in general. Hieorglyphically אר was represented by the straight line, and אש by the circular line. אר, conceived as elementary principle, indicated direct movement, rectilinear; אש relative movement, curvilinear, gyration.

אר that which belongs to the elementary principle, that which is *strong, vigorous, productive*. The Arabic word signifies ardor, impulse in general: in a restricted sense, amorous ardor; action of giving oneself to this ardor; union of the sexes.

אר or יאר That which flows, that which is fludic: *a river*. The Chaldaic אר or אוּר signifies *Air*.

אוּר *Fire heat*; action of *burning*.
אוֹר *Light*; action of *enlightening, instructing. Life, joy, felicity, grace*, etc.." [d'Olivet, 1976, pp. 298-299.]

II. "אוֹר expresses the copulation of Aleph and of its physical support Resh... it is a living energy, both outer and inner. The Qabalist have always laid great stress on that symbol, both in its physical and in its metaphysical significance...

אור, which we call light, is essentially a love in a self-creative twofold mode of being... אוֹר and אוֹר: inner light and outer light.

Inner light and out light. Whether intuition and perception, or heart and mind, or soul and body, whatever their names, when they come to mean something to us, inside us, when there joint action is fruitful, the Revelation is here.

Why has this twofold energy, deriving from the action of the universal life-force upon its cosmic container, been translated as 'light'? The answer is that the universe, considered as a space-time continuum, is set into motion at the maximum speed of which it is capable. According to a very ancient tradition, Genesis 1:3 says that maximum speed is the speed of light...

Some day it may be found that the highest speed of which the universe is capable is not only alive but that it *is* the throbbing of life throughout the entire cosmos. This speed has a number, a measure, which defines the mass, space and time of the universe as well as its duration.

In other words, the infinite movement of *Aleph* imprints in the mass of *Resh* the greatest speed of which *Resh* is capable. It can be inferred that in absolutely all components the universe yields to the mighty power of *Aleph*, or again that the universe is totally permeated by *Aleph* to the point of perpetually generating it, so that *Aleph* indefinitely becomes its own son.

To reiterate in plan and simple language, Genesis 1:3 states that as a consequence of the interplay between the pulsating *Aleph* and the continuous existence of *Yod*, *Aleph* is copulatively (*Vav*) projected into the universe (*Resh*). This living process is therefore expressed in the sequence *Aleph-Vav-Resh*, which spells the word אוֹר (pronounced *Or*), which is what we call light." [Suraes, 1992, pp. 84-86]

III. "A symbol of Truth, Wisdom, and Knowledge, and of the consciousness which apprehends reality or relativity in each.. and that

262

primordial light is 'a symbol of truth as consciousness in the union of spirit and matter at the commencement of manifestation... the supreme wills 'light', or the union of spirit and matter, to be effected; and so consciousness, self-illumination, thereupon occurs." [Gaskell, 1981, pp. 451-452.]

IV. Isaiah 60:1: "Arise, shine, for your light has come, and the glory of the Lord rises upon you."

זקק to melt; to fuse; to strain, filter (as wine); to refine, purify; to bind. Also applied to metals, and in relation to melted metals has the meaning of "to pour, to flow." its relation to *Ain Suph* has to do with the idea of the boundless as the actual source of material for manifestation.

זר a border, wreath, collar, crown, necklace. The crown of the ark of the covenant. A noun which brings to the fore the same idea of limitation or circumscription, which is part of the meaning of , סוף, and גדר. With different pointing: 1. frame, edging; 2. stranger; alien, foreigner; strange idolatry.

ז/ר Zain/Resh. Sun (Resh) in Gemini (Zain).

זקנים the Elders. In Deuteronomy 21:19: "His father and his mother take hold of him, and bring him to the elders at the gate of his twon." This term has a mystical significance in Qabalah. it refers to the states of being prior to the Life-power self-manifestation in a cycle of creative activity. see 767 and Psalm 107:32.

רבה to grow, to be in abundance, to multiply, to increase, to grow great. This One Reality, the Limitless, is the cosmic principle of growth, increase and development. Growth is a fundamental law of manifestation. With a different grammatical structure, ורבו, "and multiply," used in the first divine command recorded in Genesis 1:22. "And God blessed them, saying, be fruitful, and multiply, and fill the waters in the seas, and let fowl multiply in the earth". It intimates that the boundless, *Ain Suph*, is to be understood as a limitless power of growth and development. It is a cosmic principle of increase. With different pointing: 1. to become many, to be large, be great; 2. *ribaw*, to make large, increase; to bring up, raise; to lend or borrow on usury; to make profit; to include by implication; to widen the scope of a law; 3.

rubaw; to be numerous, be manifold. 4. *Rahbawh,* much, exceedingly.

רהב to be or become wide, large, spacious. With different vowel points: 1. to boast, act proudly, arrogance, to be haughty, to urge, importune; to submit too, acknowledge ones authority; 2. pride, arrogance, a sea-monster; epithet of Egypt; fear; 3. proud, defiant. 4. pride, haughtiness.

רז a mystery, secret. The limitless is the essence of all mystery. Although the Aramaic form רזא, appears there, in connection with the forgotten dream of Nebuchadnezzar in Daniel 2:18. "That they would desire mercies of the God of heaven concerning his secret; that Daniel and his follows should not perish with the rest of the wise men of Babylon." It is noteworthy that this dream of has mystical interpretations, handed down for generations through the secret schools. These interpretations have to do with the esoteric doctrines concerning both time and space. The Limitless is the essence of all mystery. It is beyond intellectual comprehension. Therefore we need not try to grasp it. It is to be known after another manner.

מזיקים "Demons; injurers." [Godwin. 1999, p. 529.] The letters of the name suggest a negative reversal of mental substance (Mem) which causes separation and discrimination (Zain), a false sense of personal will (Yod) embodying itself during the sleep state (Qoph) and creating for itself (Yod) a continuous cycle of stability and inertia (Mem).

208

I. (13 x 16) or 13 x 2⁴

ארבה locusts. A pest in years of famine and drought. The 8th of the ten plagues of Egypt. In Exodus 10:12: "And the Lord said to Moses, 'stretch out your hand over Egypt so that locusts will swarm over the land and devour everything growing in the fields, everything left by the hail."

ארבה lattice, latticed windowed; chimney; orbit of the eye; opening panel in wall or door. With different pointing: 1. *awrebawh*; artifice, tricky movement. 2. boat.

חד to be white, hence, to be shining, noble. The father of Uri (217). Refers to Tiphareth and the Ego. In alchemy, its connection with the sun associates it with the metal gold, which is exceptionally lustrous, and is called the most noble mental. Variant in spelling. With different vowel points: hole. see 210, 153, 314.

יצחק Isaac. He laughs, one that mocks. The proper name Isaac, son of Abraham. see 418 and K.D.L.C.K. (p. 266)

הגר Hagar. flight, fugitive. The Egyptian wife of Abraham. She was given a promise by the angel, and her son, Ishmael was the fulfillment of the promise.

בור a cistern.

גהר bowed. With different pointing: 1. gawhar; to bend, crouch; bowed; 2. gahar; bending, prostration; exhaled warm breath.

גרה to excite, provoke, stir up; to make strife, contend. Also: Part of the body from the neck to chest; a female proselyte; the pit or seeds in St. John's bread; cud, spittle. With different pointing: gerah; small coin, the twentieth part of a shekel. Metathesis of גהר.

הרג to kill, slay. With different pointing: 1. horahg; to be killed; 2. hereg: killing, slaughter, massacre; execution by decapitation with a sword; 3. hawrawg: murder, highwayman. Metathesis of גרה.

רוב Multitude. All these ideas are implicit in the promise of the angel to Hagar, through her son, Ishmael. [Coptic-see 828]

אברה wing-feather, pinion.

זרא loathing, abominable.

פענח to reveal, discover; to discover.

רזא the secret. In Daniel 2:27: "The secret which the king has asked can neither wise men, enchanters, magicians, nor astrologers declare unto the king but there is a God in heaven, אלה בשמיא (389) that reveals-secrets גלה רזין (305)." [In the Aramaic Aleph affixed to a word is the definite article "the", ה is the Hebrew] see 694.

Inhabitans aeternitatem (Lt). Abiding eternally, or dwelling in eternity. see 450.

209

הדר Magnificence; King of Edom. Godwin associates this word with Malkuth. Note the prayer to David in 1 Chronicles 29:11: "Thine O Lord, is the greatness, and the power and the glory, and the victory, and the majesty: for all that is in the heaven and in the earth is thine; thine is the kingdom O Lord, and thou art exalted as head above all." The total value of the 24 words in this verse is 5856.

Aesch Mezareph: "The husband of Mehetabel ['God benefit', 97] is that Edomite King, and King of Redness, who is called Hadar, Glorius; viz., the Beauty of the Metallic Kingdom, which is Gold Daniel 11:20-29. But such Gold as may be referred to Tiphareth. For Hadar represents 209, which number also the Tetragrammaton, multiplied by 8, produces (which is the number of circumcision and Jesod) is the whole word by added as one." [Westcott, 1997, p. 40]

הדר to adorn; to honor, pay respect to. With different pointing: *hidder*: to be zealous in religious observance.

בואר Bovar. Goetic demon #10 by day of the 1st decanate of Cancer. According to *Aurum Solis*, demon of the 1st quinance of Scorpio. see Appendix 11.

I. "He teaches Philosophy, both Moral and Natural, and the Logic Art, and also the virtues of all Herbs and Plants. He healeth all distempers in man, and giveth good Familiars. he governeth 50 Legions of Spirits, and his Character of obedience is this, which thou must hear when to callest him forth unto appearance" [Mathers, 1995, p. 33].

II. In the Tarot minor arcana this decanate is assigned to the 2 of Cups. This represents the operation of Chokmah, sphere of the Zodiac, in Briah the creative world of ideas. see 207, אור, for d'Olivet comments on א.

אדר behind, after.

גור whelp. In Genesis 49:9: "Judah is a lion's whelp: from the prey, my son, thou art gone up: he stooped down, he couched as a lion, and as an old lion; who shall rouse him up?" Judah is connected with Leo and with alchemical digestion. see 30.

גור to sojourn, dwell; to stir up strife, quarrel; to gather together (for war); to be afraid, fear, stand in awe. It is the holy guardian angel or higher self which stirs up the personality. see Key 14.

רבבה 10,000; myriad. This word in the plural רבבות, is used in Deuteronomy 33:17 and is translated myriads. Refers to the tribe of Ephraim, son of Joseph. see 331, 156, 615.

בזר scattered, strew. With different pointing: *bizzer*, to scatter. In Psalm 68:30: "Rebuke the company of spearmen, the multitude of the bulls, with the calves of the people, till every one submit himself with pieces of silver: scatter thou the people that delight in war." Ephraim = Taurus = bull. The moon is exalted in Taurus. Moon = silver. Spearmen and warriors = Aries. The alchemical process must be scatted throughout the microcosm to find the treasure of understanding. see 7.

ארח way, path; mode, manner, procedure. "Thou shall separate the earth from the fire, the subtle form the gross, suavely and with great ingenuity." [Emerald Tablet] With different pointing: *awrah*:. to travel, journey, go though.

ארח to lodge, accommodate, entertain a guest. the indwelling presence with us on the path of return. see 277, 1769.

210

II. Σ20 = 210.

נפלים Nephilites, distinguished, illustrious nobel men. Translated "giants" in Genesis 6:4: "There were [the] giants in the earth in those days; and also after that, when the sons of God came in unto the daughters of men, and they bare children unto them, the me became mighty men [heroes] which were of old, men of renown."

And in Numbers 13:33: "And there we saw the giants, the sons of Anak, which come of the giants: and we were in our own sight as grasshoppers, and so we were in their sight." Note that in this passage giants is spelled הנפילים (225) the giants. See 225 and 220.

ענק the land where the giants (Nephilim). The land of the Giants is the astral plane. See Numbers 13:33 and 210 and 225.

I. The Zohar I (p.138): "There were sixty on the earth, corresponding to the number above, as it is written, "three-score mighty men are about it."

II. The Book of Concealed Mystery [IV:18, p.100] says: "They [i.e. the giants] were in the earth in those days, but no in the following time, until Joshua came. That is, they are applicable to the path of the bride [Malkuth, 496], which is also called the land of Canaan, were Joshua found the giants. For the ward נפלים, occurs not fully: except when it is used in the incident of the spies. see 210.

III. "And the Nephilim (elect among men, noble illustrious ones) were upon the earth in those days: and also after than, sons (spiritual emanations) of Aelohim has come in into (mingled with) daughters (corporeal faculties) of Adam (universal man) and they had produced through them those same Ghoborim (might men, those famous Hyperboreans) who were of old, corporeal man (heros) of renown." [d'Olivet, 1976, p. 329.]

"נהפלים then-the-Nephilites... That is to say, men distinguished from others by their power or their strength; for the *giants*... that the Hellenist and Saint Jerome have seen here, have existed only in their imagination, at least if these translators have understood by this, what the vulgar ordinarily understands, that is, men of greater stature than others. If the Hellenists in other instances, have copied the Samaritan translation, had given attention to this one, they would have see that the word by which this translation renders נפלים is... used alike in the Hebrew גברים, and which is placed precisely at the end of the same verse, as synonymous epithet; for this word is nearer than one imagines to the epithet which the Υπερβορεοι bear: those famous *Hyperboreans*, whose origin has so troubled the savants.

These savants had before then, the Latin word *nobilis*, which comes from the same root as the Hebrew נפלים, and presents the same characters with the sole difference of the *b*, which, as in numerous derivative words, has taken the place of *p*, or of *ph*. They have not seen that the Latin word *nobilis*, have passed from Asia into Europe, was the real translation of the word נפלים; and that consequently, in the *Nephilites* of Moses must be seen, not giants, nor men of colossal stature, but *Great Ones*; illustrious, distinguished men, *Nobles*, in fact.

The root of the word is פל which always develops the idea of a thing apart, distinguished, raised above the others. Thence the verbs, פלוא or פלה, used only in the passive movement הפלה or נפלא, *to be distinguished, illustrious*; of which the continued facultative נפלה or נפלא, *becoming distinguished, illustrious*, gives us the plural נפלים which is the subject of the note.

... the articles פלא or פלה, are the root of among others, נפלאים *marvelous, wonderful things*; נפלאות, *unheard-of exploits, astonishing things, miracles*; נפלאת, *a profound mystery*, etc. [ibid., p. 178-180]

IV. "Early human physical forms; mostly Lemurian, some Atlantean. In these rugged forms mind is first aroused... These Nephilim are the monsters which are pre-human and semi-animal. They correspond to soul life to the early attempts at self-realization, which are possible only through the agency of such clumsy modes of expression as are appropriate to the sub-human kingdoms of nature. The ideals of the minds, or spiritual egos (sons of God), conjoined to the processes of the lower planes, give rise to the 'children of men', the progeny of mind, or mental-astro-physical forms. It is as the cosmic forces work though the personality while guided from the individual, that the 'sons of men' are born, that is, the successive incarnations are engendered." [Gaskell, 1981, pp. 529-530.]

V. The Giants or 'Fallen Ones' (*Nephilim*), also called the 'Abortions', were glyphed by the Ape. The *Nephilim* were the builders of the Tower of Babel, known also as the 'confusion of tongues', a way of describing the perversion and ultimate loss of the Word. Masonic and mystical symbolism, with emphasis on the rediscovery of the Word is a mode of re-membering Osiris, and thereby of re-constituting the subtle body in the Amenta, which means, in psychological terms, the reanimation of subconscious strata of the *psyche*.

The correspondences between the Tower, Babel, and Babalon, it is necessary to note that the number of *nephilim* is 210. 210 is the number of NOX (Notz) the 'Night of Pan' or the Veil of the Abyss; it is also the number of reversal through its equation with BQBVQ, 'a bottle', from the Egyptian Baakabaka meaning 'upside down' or 'topsy turvy'. 210 is the number of ADHR, the 'First Adam.' Most significantly, 210 is the number of three words denoting the other side of the Tree, viz: AChAR, the 'back or hind quarter', a name for the hidden passages or tunnels of Set; ARChA, 'way'; and ARChA (Orach), the 'feminine period' [in Genesis 18:11] (whence oracle), or 'tears of the left eye', the backward looking or inner vision. In Sanskrit the word *Arksha* means 'regulated by the stars', and *Arke* in the Greek Mysteries was the Mother of the Gods. Compare the symbolism of Nuit *arched* over the earth or crouched on all fours in an attitude of bringing to birth. Finally, HRH, 'to conceive' also has the value of 210 [The number of NBT-N-PT (Nebet-en-Pet), the Queen of Heaven and thus the Void itself]. [Grant, 1994, p. 93-94.]

VI. Enoch Chapter 7, Section 2: "1. It happened after the sons of men had multiplied in those days, that daughters were born to them, elegant and beautiful. 2. And went the angels, the sons of heaven, beheld them, they became enamored of them, saying to each other, Come let us select for ourselves wives from the progeny of men, and let us beget children." Verse 9: These are the names of their chiefs: Samyaza, who was their leader, Urakabarameel, Akibeel, Tamiel, Ramuel, Danel, Azkeel, Saraknyal, Asael, Armers, Batraal, Anane, Zavebe, Samsaveel, Ertael, Turel, Yomyael, Arazyal. Verse 11. And the women conceiving brought forth giants, 12. Whose stature was each 300 cubits (a cubit is 17-22 inches). These devoured all which the labor of men produced; until it became impossible to feed them; 13. When they turned themselves against men, in order to devour them.

Chapter 15, Verse 3. "You being a spiritual, holy and possessing a life, which is eternal, have polluted yourselves with women; have begotten in carnal blood; have lusted in the blood of men; and have done as those who are flesh and blood do. Verse 6: But you from the beginning were made spiritual, possessing a life, which is eternal, and not subject to death for all the generations of the world."

Verse 9: the spirits of the giants shall be like clouds, which shall oppress, corrupt, fall, contend, and bruise upon earth.

מלפני   From the presence. Genesis 4:16: So Cain went out from the Lord's presence and lived in the land of Nod, east of Eden.

צדיק   just, lawful, righteous (man). [Strong's Dictionary]

ורד   rose, rose-tree. A symbol of the human soul, of desire and spiritual aspiration. With different pointing: *vawrod*: rose-colored. A proper name used in a literal and figurative sense. In the literal sense, it denotes a mythological sea-monster of the same class as the dragon, and is probably connected with the Semitic myth of Tiamat, the destroyer of God's order in the universe. In Isaiah 51:9: 'Awake, Awake, put on strength, O arm of the Lord; awake, as in the ancient days, in the generation of old. Art thou not it that has cut Rahab, and wounded the dragon?' In the figurative sense, it is a name given to Egypt In Psalm 89:10: 'Thou has broken Rehab in pieces, as one that is slain; thou has scattered thine enemies with thy strong arm." see 368, 380, 220.

רהב   proud. In Job 9:13: "If God will not withdraw his anger, the proud helpers do stoop under him."

רהב   breath, width, extent. With different pointing: 1. *rahab*: breadth, broad expanse; 2. wide, broad, spacious, roomy.

חרב   Horeb, the mountain on which the law was given to Moses, also called Sinai. Literally means: "He is high, or firm"; "dry and burnt up" [Inman] In Exodus 17:6: "Behold, I will stand before thee there upon the rock in Horeb; and you shall smite the rock, and there shall come water, out of it; that the people may drink. And Moses did so in the sight of the elders of Israel."

Metathesis of רחב. Note that Cheth (receptivity, will) is placed before Resh (face, head).

חרב   to be dry, be dried up; to be waste, be desolate. With different pointing: 1. *korab*: to be dried; 2. *karehb*: dry; waste, desolate, ruined; 3. *korehb*: dryness, drought; heat, desolation, waste.

חרב   swords; knife, sharp tool blade of plough. Has to do with the continence of the Mars forces. see 215.

דער   generation; period, age. With different pointing: to dwell, lodge; to pile up, heap up; circle, rim. Suggest the movement around a center, as pictured in Key 10.

רגז   raging, rage, commotion, wrath; noise, turmoil; trouble, disquiet; excitement; zeal Effect of the Mars force when unbalances. With different pointing: to quake, to be excited, to perturbed; to be disquieted; to rage, be wrath; to be agitated. Variant spelling, see 216.

גזר   to cut, divide in two; to cut down, cut off, destroy; to decide, decree; (with על) to prohibit; to circumcise; to derive (etymologically). Metathesis of רגז. Here the power of memory (Gimel) cuts apart what is valid form what is not (discrimination = Zain) and leads to the birth of the new creature (Resh).

גזר   piece, part, cut; log of wood; carrot. With different pointing: *gozehr*: 1. decision, verdict, judgment; 2. *gzahr*: decision, decree, sentence.

הרה   to conceive, to join together, to be coupled. With different pointing: 1. to be conceived; 2. a pregnant woman.

אדר   Adam Primus; the first Adam, or archtypal humanity Notariqon for אדם הראשון Adam ha-rawshon. see 607, 45.

בזאר   Bazar. Day demon of 1st decanate of Cancer. This decanate is ruled by the Moon and indicates lack of receptivity to subconscious memory.

קינן   Son of Enos and father of Mahalaleel; great-grandson of Adam, lived 910 years (325-1235 after creation); spelled Kenan in R.S.V. In

Genesis 5:9: "And Enos lived ninety years, and begat *Cainan*. Cainan = קין Cain (160) + Nun. Inman: "This word is probably a variant of כנן Chanan, or Kanan, meaning: he stands upright, he is set up, equivalent to a Hermes." (i.e. bust of Mercury set up at a crossroads) [Ancient Faiths, V1, p.382] see 860, 910.

בעל חנן "Baal was gracious." The seventh king of Edom (45), associated with Yesod; according to Waite, an arch-demon, corresponding to Netzach, sphere of Venus and desire. In Genesis 36:38: "And Saul died, and Baal-hanah, the son of Achbor, reigned in his stead." see 860, 166.

מסין Misin. Angel of the first decanate of Capricorn ruled by Saturn and indicates qualities of: cautions, judicious and executive. In the minor tarot arcana it corresponds to the powers of Chokmah, wisdom functioning in Assiah, the material world. These powers are those of conscious life, which begin all cycles of creation, great and small. The fist decanate of Capricorn is ruled by Saturn, Showing a connection between the false appearances of things (Ayin, attributed to Capricorn) and the consciousness which makes all things new (Saturn). It is associated with the stage of the alchemical great work called fermentation (830, 1112). The angel here corresponds to the black work of alchemy wherein the physical body is made fitting channel for the wisdom of Chokmah, and recognizing every activity of personal existence as part of the motion of the universe. When well-developed, this can bring harmony in the midst of change; alternation of gain and loss; change of occupation, and ups and downs of fortune. Negative alignment intimates discontent; foolishness in the management of resources and restricted condition of material affairs. The angel's name suggest the power of mental substance (Mem) strengthened by experience (Samekh) of reproductive energy (Nun), alignment with the divine will (Yod) to transmute this energy into its highest use on the physical plane (Nun). see 860.

הרה pregnant. Genesis 16:11.
עצמי my bone. Genesis 29:14.

נכסף desires, longs. Genesis 31:30.
חרב drought. Genesis 31:40.

בבור in the pit, dungeon. Genesis 37:29.
לקללך to curse you. Deuteronomy 23:5.

211 (prime)

גבור gebur. strong, mighty, large, great. Root of Geburah גבורה, strength. Formed by suffixing the letter Heh. see 216.

ארי lion.
יאר Jeor, a flood, canal, river, the Nile.

איר The 8th Hebrew month, April-May, corresponding roughly to the period when the sun is in Taurus.

212

זהר Zohar. splendor; title of Qabalah text.

זרה stranger, alien (feminine), harlot. Proverbs 5:3 "For the lips of a strange woman drop honey (as an honeycomb, and her mouth is smoother than oil". Remember the connection between Gimel, depicted as a woman in Key 2 and חכמה Chokmah, wisdom. see 73.

מעקב cubic. The secret knowledge concerning which the hierophant discourses may truly be called "cubical", for the symbolism of the stone pertains to universal truth, and to the union of father (Chokmah) and son (Tiphareth).

אין מקוה no abiding. In 1 Chronicles 29:15: "For we are strangers before thee, and sojourners, as were all our fathers: our days on the earth are as a shadow, and there in none abiding." Paul Case: no expectation; a spring of gathering. In the Hebrew Lexicon מקוה is translated collection, gathering together (of water), reservoir, pool, hope; ritual bath of purification. Purity leads to the pool of wisdom.

חרד fearful, trembling; god-fearing, reverent; orthodox. To "fear" (revere) the Lord is the beginning of wisdom.

חרד to tremble, quake; to be anxious, be uneasy, to come or go trembling, hurry.

רבי my master, rabbi, teacher. The inner teacher is the "rabbi". see 115, 185 (Greek), 613.

האור Haoor; Haures. Goetic demon #64 by night of 1st decanate of Capricorn. see Appendix 11.

Goetia: "He is a great duke, and appears at first like a leopard, might, terrible, and strong, but after a while, at the command of the Exorcist, he puts on human shape with eyes flaming and fiery, and a most terrible countenance. He gives true answers of all things, present, past, and to come. But if he not commanded into a triangle, he will lie in all these things, and deceive and beguile the Exorcist in these things or in such and such business. He will, lastly, talk of the creation of the world, and of divinity, and of how he and other Spirits fell. He destroyed and burns up those who be the enemies of the Exorcist should be so desire it; also he will not suffer him to be tempted by any other Spirit or otherwise. He governs 36 Legions of Spirits." [Mathers, 1995, p. 62]

213

הדרד Magnificence; supreme benignity.

חסד עלאה דאל Supernal Mercy of God.

אביר strong, mighty; violent, steed, strong bull, gallant knight, heard. This word is applied to God, the "Mighty One".

אצטגנין astrologer. One who interprets the cycles of universal manifestation, relating it to the microcosm. see Key 10, 619.

הרגה slaughter. In Jeremiah 12:3: "But thou, O Lord, knows me: thou has seen me, and tried mine heart toward me: pull them out like sheep from the slaughter, and prepare them for the day of slaughter." What must be killed out is the sense of separation, and this is done with the aid of memory, or Chesed, the "Mighty and Magnificent".

גיר to make a proselyte. With different pointing: *gir, giyr*: lime, chalk, plaster. In 2 Chronicles 2:17: "And Solomon numbered all the strangers [proselytes] that were in the land of Israel, after the numbering where with David his father had numbered them; and they were found an hundred and fifty thousand and three hundred thousand and six hundred." The "strangers" are raw material, or lime and plaster for the great work. 150 = the heavenly man = "thine eyes" (the divine beneficence) = "They that are taught"; 306 = "Father of Mercies", "And the spirit of God"; "the Lord is my shepherd". Solomon is connected with the Sun, David means "beloved"; Israel means "he shall rule as God". see 128, 28, 935.

הרה 59th name of Shem ha-Mephorash, short form. see 244 & Appendix 10.

ענן גדול immense cloud. Nubes [a cloud] Magna [great] [Crowley, 1977, p. 25]. In Ezekiel 1:4: "I looked, and I saw a windstorm coming out of the north-a great cloud with flashing lighting and surrounded by brilliant light."

214

אזור a girdle, belt or band, zone, region. A girdle is a symbol of Venus and suggest control and support. As an adjective, girded, girt.

דקדוק nicety, fine point, detail, precision, minuteness; accuracy; subtlety. A rabbinical word which has for its primary meaning accuracy; from a root implying minute discrimination. In later Hebrew means grammar; and is related to Ruach and Tiphareth because one of the principle functions of Adam, the Ego consciousness, to give name to things. Mastery of subconsciousness levels depends on accuracy of speech. see 687.

זזר Angel of the 1st decanate of Aries.

חור whiteness, pale; Old Testament name. Father of Uri ("fiery, lustrous") A reference to the white light of Kether. With different pointing: 1. to grow pale, white; 2. to make clear, evident; 3. leprous, leper. see 208 (variant spelling), 217, 254, 240, .

ירד to descend, go down; to move from higher to a lower level. Old Testament name Irad, son of Enoch ("initiated"). Also means to bring down, to make something descend. Expresses a key law which apples to all human use of the Life-power. In using electricity, however it is applied, the energy must always pass from a higher to a lower potential. This holds good for all works of magic.

יָרֶד Jared; the sixth in the series of descendants from Adam. In Genesis 5:18: "When Jared had lived 162 years, be became father of Enoch."

I. "And Mahollael (mighty, exaltation, splendor) existed five and six tens of cycles (of ontological mutation), and he produced Ired (steadfastness, perseverance, either upward or downward."

He comments: יָרֶד Ired... here among the descendants of *Sheth* is the same *Whirad*, that we have seen figuring among those of *Kain*; but who is presented now under a form more softened. In losing its initial sign עָ, which is that of material sense, it has left its passionate and excitative ardor. The natural sense which it contains is now that of perseverance, of steadfastness to follow an imparted movement. It is true that this movement can be good or evil, ascending or descending as is proved by the two verbs springing from the root. רוה: the one רדוה means to govern, to dominate; the other, ירוד, signifies to sink, to descend." [d'Olivet, 1976, pp. 160-162.]

מֵעֲדָנִים delicacies, delights, pleasures, bonds, fetters. see 640, 1081, 45, 52, 90, 311, 478, 536, 548.

מֵעֲדַנֵּי מֶלֶךְ royal dainties. In Genesis 49:20: "out of Asher his bread shall be fat, and he shall yield royal dainties."

רוח Ruach. life-breath, Spirit, Mind, Air, Imagination. Attributed to the path of Aleph. The specialized force of the Primal Will as imagination assigned to Tiphareth and to Yetzirah. Considered as thought-power or creativity from the universal mind stuff. Also manifested as psychic force. Note that Resh (sun) Vav (and) and Cheth (moon) reads "Sun and Moon," of which with the aid of Mercury is the operation of the Great Work. Resh, sunlight transformed by the brain into sensations, emotions, and thoughts is the cause of the operation of this principle. Vav, it is the connecting medium which joins every human being to all other things and creatures in the universe. Cheth, it is a power which can be motivate by means of mental imagery, and especially as expressed in sound vibrations or "words of power". Rauch is the metathesis of the Egyptian Hor (us), indicating a close correspondence. see 1081, 52, 111, 565, 1708, 37.

I. With different pointing: 1. to be wide, spacious; to spread, extend; 2. space, wide space, interval; relief; respite; profit, gain. 3. roomy; wide; Case adds: subtle air; human spirit.

II. Psalm 18:15: "Thy valleys of the sea were expose and the foundations of the earth laid bare at your rebuke, O Lord, at the blast of breath [רוח] from your nostrils." In Job 32:8: "But it is the spirit [רוח] in a man, the breath of the Almighty, that gives him understanding [תבינם, she-gives-understanding-to-them]."

III. "רח In the same manner as the roots אר and הר, considered as rays of the elementary circle, are related to light and fire; in the same manner, as the root רו is related to water, thus we see their analogue רח being related to air and depicting all its effects: we shall see further on רי and רע, related equally, the one to ether and the other to terrestrial matter.

רוח Every idea of expansion and aerial dilation: *wind, breath, soul, spirit*: that which *moves, stirs, animates, inspires, transports*." [d'Olivet, 1976, pp. 449-450.]

IV. "A symbol of the spiritual essence, the Divine Spark, atma-buddhi, which is immortal." He cites Genesis 2:7 'And (God) breathed into this nostrils the breath [spelled נשמת] of life; and man became a living soul.' And into this lower mind, or astro-mental body, was projected the Divine spark, and thence the *man* (manasic being) became a creature capable of responsible, independent existence." [Gaskell, 1981, p. 126.]

V. Genesis 7:15: "Pairs of all creatures that have the *breath of life* [רוח חים] in them came to Noah and entered the ark."

VI. The Zohar [IV:175B, p. 109] Refers to Ruach as "wind" in the following passage: "We have learnt that wisdom beat against the stones of the 32 paths and caused the wind to gather many waters into one place. Then fifth gates of understanding were opened. From the paths emanated ten luminous crowns, and there were left 22 paths. The wind whirled down those paths and fifty gates of understand were opened, and

270

the 22 letters were engraved upon fifty gates of the jubilee and were crowned with the seventy-two letters of the holy name. These opened out sideways in their turn and were crowned with the 22 crowns of compassion which are contained in the ancient of days, who bestowed light upon them, to each according to its place. Fifty engraved letters also were crowned with 42 supernal letters of the holy name, by which heaven and earth were created. And eight gates were opened, which are the eight significations of mercy..."

VII. Ruach (Heb.): Spirit. The Egyptian root of Ru*ach* is *Ru*, the emanating mouth or womb, thus showing that the nature of Spirit was originally conceived of as feminine, and ascribed to water, or blood. In later times, Ruach was given a masculine connotation and assigned to air as the wind or breath of creative spirit, hence the gust or ghost that became the Holy Ghost symbolized by the dove, the beast of the air. In yet later phases of its symbolisms, the Ruach came to be identified with the Reason. [Grant, 1994, p. 276.]

זור Angle of the 1st decanate of Aries.

succus lunaw et solis (Lt). juice (or sap) of the sun and moon. Occurs in the text accompanying a plate on page 13 of Secret Symbols. The commentary tells us that the sap must be fixed before it is transformed into fog or smoke. It says also that the two fogs or smokes are the roots of the hermetic art. "I am the sap which maintains and makes alive everything in nature, and I come from the above into the below. I am the dew of heaven and the oiliness of the Earth. I am the fiery water and the watery fire. Without me nothing can have temporal existence and Life. I am near all things, yes, and through all things, yet unrecognized."

215

אגורה something gathered, bound. Refers to the unity of Life. With different pointing: to gather together, accumulate.

אדיר excellent, worthy, gallant, lordly, glorious, good, noble, principal, worthy. Conveys the notion of superiority or pre-eminence.

ארוח a path or narrow way. A path, a narrow way. Given as a correspondence to Sephiroth. Can also be read: אור-ח (aur-Cheth), "light-field."

ו-ט-נ-צ-ס Vav-Teth-Nun-Tzaddi-Samekh. Letters corresponding to: Emerald-Taurus-Bull-Vav; Diamond-Leo-Lion-Teth; Agate-Scorpio-Eagle-Nun; Sapphire-Aquarius-man-Tzaddi; carbuncle-fire-Samekh. These numbers reduce to 8, an alchemical number. Thus the 4 Fixed signs and Common fiery sign.

הדרב the sword. In Genesis 3:24: "So he [the Lord] drove out the man [Adam] and he placed at the east of the garden of Eden Cherubims, and a flaming sword which turned every way, to keep the way [path] of the Tree of Life." see 259, 310, 53, 124, 272, 1493 (Greek).

זרח to irradiate, to rise (as the sun), shine, to come out, appear. With different pointing: *zerah*, rising, shining. Father of Jubab, and a king of Edom. See Genesis 36:17.

טור row, line; course of building stones; encompass, surround, line in script; column of page. In the Aramaic, same pointing, it means mountain. Suggest the path to attainment.

אחור back, rear; west; buttock, posterior, the reversed part. West is the direction attributed to manifestation, completion-"west-ward the course of empire takes its way."

הנפלים the giants. In Genesis 6:4: "There were [the] giants in the earth in those days; and also after that, when the sons of God came in unto the daughters of men, and they bare children unto them, the me became mighty men which were of old, men of renown." see 210.

חרבה to horeb In Exodus 3:1: "Now Moses kept the flock of Jethro-his father-in-law, the priest of Median: and he led the flock to the backside of the desert, and came to the mountain of God, even to Horeb." With different pointing: 1. pruning-knife; 2. *hawraybah*: waste, ruin; desert land. Note חרב Horeb (210) is masculine and has the same meaning: dryness, drought; heat, desolation, waste. Compare this with ציון Zion (156) parched ground, desert = ציון

monument; land-mark, signpost [from ציה to burn, to glow, to glitter] . In Genesis 7:22: Everything *on dry land* [בחרבה] that had the *breath of life* [חיים רוח] in its nostrils died." see 210, 542, 317.

הדי 15th Shem ha-Mephorash, short form. see 246 & Appendix 10.

εις. hise (Gr). One. Refers to the unity of all life. see 13, 67.

216

I. (6 x 6 x 6) or 2^3 x 3^3

II. [$3^3 + 4^3 + 5^3$]

גבורה Geburah. Strength, severity. Hebrew title of Key 8 and the 5th Sephirah. The resistance necessary for manifestation. All personal notions of will are derived from feelings caused by the resistances to the flow of the Life-force through us. Consciousness of the Greater Adept in Rosicrucian Initiation. see 64, 92, 211, 1200.

I. Geburah has three names. 1. Pachad, פחד, Fear, and represents the emotion induced in many minds by the presence of individuals in whom the will-force flows powerfully. The same emotion is aroused by law in the hearts of law-breakers.

II. Geburah, גבורה, Strength, though it is often translated "Severity." Title of Key 8 and the 5th Sephirah. The resistance necessary for manifestation.

III. Deen, דין Justice. This represents the highest aspect of Law and of Volition. It gives us a standard. No unjust regulation is a real law. No unjust volition is true will. Thus he who exercises what he supposes to be "will" in disregard of the rights of others, deludes himself and demonstrates to wiser men that he is actually a slave to his own delusions.

אריה Arieh. lion, name of the sign Leo. Associated with Key 8, strength. The same power is the source of all our strength. Standard of the tribe of Judah. Symbol of the whole range of the Life-power's activity below the human level. In the Tarot the lion is associated with

Kundalini.

I. The lion represents the highest forms of development in the kingdoms of nature below man. He is the ruling principle of the animal nature. And is the alchemical symbol of the transmutation of natural humanity into the Stone of the Wise, perfected man.

II. In alchemical books there is he Green Lion, the Red Lion and the Old Lion. The Green Lion is the unripend and unpurified animal nature. The Red Lion is the animal nature brought under the control of man's spiritual being. In Key 8 in the Tarot the Red Lion is shown with yellow eyes to symbolized the intelligence at work behind the Great Magical Agent (Key 15). The Old Lion represents the state of consciousness after the work of purification has changed the Green Lion into the Red Lion. The Old Lion symbolizes the state of consciousness where one senses directly the eternal, radiant, mental energy, which preceded the manifestation of name and form.

ראה sight; evidence, proof. Sight is attributed to the letter Heh, and the sign Aries. Vibration is the fundamental nature of the fiery power that makes sight possible.

חבור joined, linked; Place name in 2 Kings 17:6. [spelt ובחבור, and-of-Habor, Interlinar Bible] With different pointing: 1. connection, junction; composition, treatise, essay; addition (arithmetic); 2. company, party; association.

דם ענבים Blood of grapes. see 44.

מורא Mountain.

נקיון cleanliness, innocence. Psalm 26:6.

לך יהוה הממלכה thine, kingdom. Thine, O IHVH, is the kingdom [1 Chronicles 29:11].

עמק profound, deep [Psalm 92:6]. Corresponds to the quality of comprehension derived from the mediational work associated with the path of Teth.

פלמוני numberer of secrets, the wonderful numberer. As translated in the Authorized Version of Daniel 8:13. In the Hebrew dictionary it is given "a certain one" and "anonymous"

Refers to the name of Teth (Secret of all Spiritual Activities) to the basis of vibrational correlation, to the comprehension of the "signatures of nature," to the Measuring Intelligence of Chesed and the Geometry of God.

רגז quivering, trembling, vibration, commotion, restlessness, disquiet, anger, rage. This noun is particularly connected with the letter Samekh. This is the path of Temptation or Trial, and it is because the tests of our faith and devotion, when misunderstood by ourselves and others, appear to be manifestations of the Divine Wrath. The "wrath" is for our good, for our growth and development. Thus those who understand it see in the "wrath" of God the expression of His Perfect Law. Vibration is the basis of manifestation is essentially like sound-fluctuating motion, undulation, pulsation, alternation, taking wave-forms. see 536.

אקקיה acacia. Found in Rabbinical Hebrew and ties up with the Masonic symbolism of the acacia. see 731.

בבא מציעא the Middle Gate (Aramaic). Compare with the symbolism of the number 5, representing mediation. Name of a Talmudic treatise of the order N'zikin.

דביר oracle, shrine, adytum, inner temple, Holy of Holy; yoni. The apparent sexual teaching is really alchemical, for both *Yesod* (80) and *debir* are only symbolized by the bodily organs mentioned. see 156, 586, 301 for esoteric significance.

King of Eglon (the calf-like, one who gambols). The name of this king is derived from the Hebrew noun which means "word" (דבר word, saying, statement; report, news, thing, matter, affair; occurrence, event; order, command; cause, case, something, anything.) Debir is a symbol of worldly wisdom based on outward show and appearance. He rules a kingdom described as "calf-like" in reference to the same notion of immature conduct symbolized elsewhere by he golden calf. The kingdom of Eglon is a symbol of the puerility which characterizes the conduct of those whose only standards of action conform to worldly, materialistic wisdom. Joshua, who overcame these kings, is the realization that the nature of the one reality is eternally on the side of liberation. The five kings, on the contrary, represent the psychological basis of very tyranny. The killing of the kings and their armies is really transmutation. see 159 Eglion and 259 Adonai Tzedek, King of Jerusalem. see 358.

חורב Another name for Sinai, the mountain where the Law was given to Moses. see Exodus 33:6.

יראה fear, reverence, awe. Closely akin in meaning to Pachad, a name for the 5th Sephirah.

רחדב a wide place, breath; an open place; a street. The letters of this word also make up the word Horeb (see above).

אוראוב Auraob; Orobas. Goetic demon #55 by night of 1st decanate of Libra. see Appendix 11.

Goetia: "He is a great and mighty prince, appearing at fist like a horse; but after the command of the Exorcist he puts on the image of a man. His office is to discover all things, past, present, and to come; also to give dignities, and prelacies, and the favor of friends and of foes. He gives true answers of divinity, and of the creation of the world. He is very faithful unto the Exorcist, and will not suffer him to be tempted of any Spirit. He over 20 Legions of Spirits." [Mathers, 1995, p. 57]

Auxiliante Deo et Natura (Lt). aiding God and nature [Secret Symbols, page 5]. This expresses the consciousness of the grade of Greater Adept connected with the fifth Sephirah. The most perfect attunement to this grade is symbolized by the 5 of Wands. A Greater Adept, as self-conscious agent of the perfect Law, uses will power to further the purposes of the Divine and bring nature to perfection.

Faciens pacem et creans malum (Lt). I make peace and I create evil [Isaiah 45:7, Vulgate]. What the unenlightened call "good" and "evil", ascribing them to opposing powers. The wise perceive as originating in the One Life.

Lapis Philosophorum (Lt). Philosopher's Stone, the Stone of the Wise. The stable, unalterable consciousness of a Greater Adept who knows himself to be in perfect union with the Father (Chokmah). Out of this consciousness comes the Greater Adept's power to make nature obedient to his will.

sion philosophorum (Lt). Zion of the philosophers. Same as *lapis philosophorum*. Zion is the adytum in the human brain which we work to build. see 156.

Mercurius de Mercurio (Lt). Mercury from Mercury (Secret Symbols, p. 48). This is one of many names for the *Lapis Philosophorum*, and has the same meaning.

sperma masculus mundi (Lt). Masculine seed of the world. The force of all mighty works of creation. see 64, 97, 55.

217

אויר   air; atmosphere; space, vacuum. *Eveer*, the atmospheric air or wind, is the same as the Vayu of the Hindus. In the yoga classification of the elements, Vayu means literally "the vibrating." To it is attributed the property of locomotion, or movement from place to place, and the subtle principle manifest in the sense of touch. see 471.

אורי   fiery, lustrous. The proper name equivalent to the Greek Photinos, "lustrous, bright" derived from phos, light. Uri was the son of Hur, who was the son of Caleb by Ephrath. Uri's son was Bezaleel (1 Chronicles 2:20). Caleb means "dog" and symbolizes the self-conscious mental activity. Ephrath is a designation for subconscious activity. Uri is the Life-breath manifested in Malkuth, where it is the body-building power following and executing patterns received from above. see 153, 8, 208, 214.

בהיר   transparency, clear, bright, brilliant, lucid. Title of Beth and the 12th Path of Wisdom. There is a basic identity between the 11th (Aleph) and 12th (Beth)-both originate in Kether. Bawhir is closely related to Aur (207), Light. Beth is used in Hebrew like the English "in" and "into." Its very sound is a concentration of breath and all the ideas associated with Beth and Key 1 imply penetration.

חרט   magic; to engrave. God engraves the patterns of light on all the "signatures" of nature [*Fama*]. see 257, 525.

בירה   castle, fort; royal residence. In Mishnaic or Talmudic, temple, sanctuary. Similar in meaning to Beth as a house or abode. The place where the highest cosmic development can dwell.

בריה   Human being; creature; creation. Self-conscious awareness is the capacity which distinguishes human beings from all other creatures on earth. see 218.

בריה   food. The Life-power as light nourishes all creatures.

דבורה   Deborah. a bee; Old Testament name. In Judges 5:12: "Awake, awake, Deborah: awake, awake, utter a song, arise Barak [302, lighting, brilliancy] and lead thy captivity captive, thou son of Abinoam [אבינעם = 109, father, or possessor, of grace]."   see 206, from the root דבר.

I. Deborah, meaning 'a bee' which is the specific symbol of Sekhet, whose name means a bee. She is the goddess of intoxication and sexual passion, hence her connection with honey and with *sakh*, or *sakti*, 'to inflame or inspire' and with 'fermented drink'. The bee, which is the copula between the male and female elements in flowers, was a type of the soul which is represented in Egyptian ideographs as the *Ba* or *Aba-it*, which guides the souls of the dead *en route* for the Sekhet-Aahru, the Fields ot Heavenly Mead or money. Ba, the astral or double is also a word meaning 'honey' and Shu and Tefnut are said to dispense honey. The goddess Sekhet as Sakti is a lunar force, and, together with her attributes of love and sweetness, a fit symbol of the honeymoon, which indicates the sexual nature of the force in question. [Grant, 1994, p. 35.]

II. Sekhet: The fierce lioness-headed goddess of the South. Her ferocious qualities typify sexual heat and the fire of fermented drink. Her counterpart in the North is the gentle Bast, or Pasht, the lunar cat-headed deity of the cool of night, as Sekhet is solar and of the furnace-heat of day. From the name Sekhet was derived the Indian word *shakti*, meaning power, with special reference to the magical power of creation as typified by the Fire Snake. [ibid., pp. 277-278]

וירא   and saw. In Genesis 1:4: "And God was the Light, that it was good."

I. "**וירא**, And-he-did-ken... Moses continues to make the being of beings, the universal creator, speak in the future by turning the expression of his will into the past by means of the convertible sign. The verb **ראות** which is used by Moses on this occasion, signifies not only to see, but to ken, by directing voluntarily the visual ray upon an object. The root **רו** or **רי** composed of the sign of movement proper united to the convertible, or to that of manifestation, develops every idea of a stroke, ray, or trace, of anything whatever, being directed in a straight line. It is joined to the root **או** or **אי**, expressing the goal, the place, the object toward which the will inclines, there where it is fixed, and forms with it the compound **ראה, ראי**, or **ראות**, that is to say, the vision, the act of seeing and the very object of this action." [d'Olivet, 1976, p.34.]

II. F.J. Mayers: "As a man may look in upon himself and consider the capabilities and qualities of his own mental powers, so we are told, did God look in upon himself and 'considered carefully'-(that is the meaning of the Hebrew word which our English version translates by 'saw ') 'the intelligence' he had willed into being. He saw that it was 'good'-suited to carry out his purposes and powerful for the task." [The Unknown God, p.30]

טבוה what is piled up or accumulated, highest point, a height, summit. With different pointing: *tibbur*, navel [Mishnaic or Talmudic]. Transparency (Beth) is the result of the greatest accumulation of the treasures of wisdom.

ריבה pleading a cause, controversy; a young women, maiden.

רוי secret; the path of Daleth is the "essence of time immoral which is the instructor in the secret foundations of Holiness and perfection." see 703.

מויעסאל Mviosael. Angel ruling Sagittarius. Key 14 is the path linking the higher Self (Sun) sphere of Mercury, or self-consciousness to the sphere of the automatic pattern world (moon) or Yesod.

סהקנב Sahqneb. Lesser angel governing the triplicity by night of Scorpio.

בריאה Briah. Creation. creature, world, cosmos. The World of Creation attributed to the 1st Heh in **יהוה** and to the 3rd Sephirah Binah.

I. Briah is the world of creation and associated with the Element Water. It is an invisible and all pervading sea of perfect power, wisdom and intelligence. From this invisible sea of pure spirit all things come into manifestation.

In the world of Briah the indivisible One works through the archangelic forces. The archangelic beings are the creative forces which specialize Atziluthic, abstract will-ideas into specific creative imagery.

II. Briah is the Creative world of the mental plane. The cosmic mental energy is associated with water because it flows in streams, has currents, vibrates like waves, has tides, and is like a mirror or reflector.

ריח smell, odor, scent, savor. The sense of smell is attributed of Zain, corresponding to Gemini, ruled by Mercury. It is the separative mental activity whereby we discriminate between good and evil. Intellect is the discriminating function of the Ego, which corresponds to smell. Mythologically, Mercury is associated with the Egyptian Thoth, pictured with A Jackal's Head in allusion to that animal's keen sense of smell. see 7, 67, 108 and Genesis 8:21.

בורי perspicuity, clearness. Indicating the definiteness which is the outcome of astute intellectual discrimination.

זהור clearness, perspicuity. With different pointing: *Zohar* splendor (see 212, variant spelling). "Chokmah is called the "splendor of unity", spelled **האחדות זהור**. *The Zohar* or Book of Splendor is the archetypal text of Qabalah, along with the *Sepher Yetzirah*.

קול עבדו voice of his servant. In Isaiah 50:10: "Who is among you that fears the Lord, that obeys the voice of his servant, that walks in darkness, and hath no light? Let him trust in the name of the Lord, and stay upon his God." see 640, 82.

חסף טינא miry clay. In Daniel 2:43: "And whereas thou saw iron mixed with miry clay, they shall mingle themselves with the seed of men: but they shall not cleave one to another, even as iron is not mixed with clay." Iron has to do with Mars; clay has to do with the instability of physical existence.

אוירא ether [K.D.L.C.K. p.55]. The letter Yod in IHVH Tetragrammaton implies the word *aur*, light. see 217.

חסד עולם The benignity of time (or Microprosopus). In IRQ para. 871: "But the benighty of Microprosopus is called Chesed Olahm the benighty of time." [Mathers, 1993, p. 219] Microprosopus is Tiphareth, the central Ego of humanity.

ירח the moon. With different pointing: *yehrech*, month, a lunar month. see 87.

I. *Aesch Mezareph*: "Jarach, the moon or Luna in the history of natural things is called the 'Medicine for the White', because she hath received a Whitening Splendor from the Sun, which by a like shining illuminates and converts to her own Nature all the Earth, that is the impure metals.

And the place of Isaiah 30:36, 'the moon shall be as the Sun', may be mystically understood of this, because the work being finished, she hath a solar Splendor: but in this State, the place of Canticles 6:10 belong to her,- 'fair as the moon'.

By the same Name the Matter of the Work is called: and so indeed it is like to the crescent Moon, in the First State of Consistence; and like to the Full Moon in the last state of Fluidity and Purity. For the words Jarach, the Moon, and Razia, secrets, also Rabui, a multitude, have by gematria the same numbers, because in this matter are found the secrets of Multiplication." [Westcott, 1997, p. 43]

II. Westcott: "Rosenroth adds here: 'She is the Shekinah and whether in decrease or at the full, she is a mystery to the student. This increase and decrease are suggested by the name. Irach is referred to the waning moon, and the name לבנה Lebanah [87], to the full moon, when it resembles pure incense, as in Exodus 30:34. Levunah zakan, לבונה זכר, and also the full

moon hath a white color, but it accepts which the light from the sun. And six Sephiroth are called the moons' [Sohar, Jethro 34, c. 139]. This Levunah means Frankincense, and the root is לבו, meaning white Zalah is 'consumed by fire.' Irach also means 'scent' and 'smelling' as well as moon and thence 'month'.

III. Inman: (Genesis. 38:9), i.e., 'that which makes a circuit, or walks majestically;' she is also called האנאבחל, לבנה, 'the pale shiner,' to distinguish her from the burning sun. [Ancient Faiths, Vol. 2, pp. 324-325]

רבוא multitude; increase, plenty; extension of scope, amplification; plural (grammar).

רזיא arcana.

עצבון pain. In Genesis 3:18: "To the woman he said, I will greatly increase your pains in childbearing; with pain you will give birth to children...."

I. "And harsh and rough (imperfect and disordered) productions shall germinate abundantly for thee; and thou shalt feed upon the bitter and withered fruits of elementary nature."

He comments: עצבון, the-woeful-natural-hindrances... The word עצב employed twice in this verse merits a p1articular attention. It springs from the two contracted roots עץ-צב. The first עץ is the same one which forms the name of that mysterious substance whose usage was forbidden to intellectual man. It is not difficult to recognize in it, sentient, corporeal substance, and in general the emblem of that which is physical, in opposition to that which is spiritual. The second עב contains the idea of that which is raised as hindrance, swells with wrath, arrests, prevents a thing opposes with effort, etc.

Moses employs first, the word עצבון, after having added the extensive syllable ון, wishing in indicate the general obstacles which shall be opposed hence to the unfoldment of that will of intellectual man, and which shall multiply its conceptions, forcing them to become divided and subdivided *ad infinitum*. He then makes use of the simple word עצב, to depict the pain, the torment the agony which shall accompany the least creations. This hieroglyphic writer would have it understood, that the volitive faculty shall no more cause intellectual conceptions to pass from power into action, without intermediary; but that it shall experience, on the contrary, deviations without number and obstacles of all sorts, which resistance it shall be able to overcome only by dint of labor and of time.

In the first place, it is not true that Moses made the being of beings say, that he will multiply the sorrows and the conceptions as the Hellenist translate it, but that he will multiply the number of the *obstacles and the conceptions*, as Saint Jerome adhered to the Chaldaic targum as more comfortable with the Hebrew: עצריך וערואיך.

Now, I ask, in the second place, who the being of beings could have said to the corporeal woman that we would multiply the number of her conceptions of her pregnancies, as one understands it, since it would in such a manner shorten her life? Would he not rather have said that he would diminishes the number, by rendering them more and more painful and laborious? But the Hebraic text is as clear as the day. There is strong evidence that the Hellenist only abandoned it to follow the Samaritan version, because they plainly saw that it exposed the spiritual meaning, as indeed it does. For, which it is in accordance with reason and experience, to think that the volitive conceptions increase in proportion to the obstacles which are opposed to their realization and which force them to be divided, it is absurd and contradictory to affirm it of the pregnancies of physical woman which are necessarily diminished with the pains, maladies and suffering which accompany and follow them." [d'Olivet, 1976, pp. 111-113.]

II. F.J. Mayers: "The word 'Itzebonech', translated 'thy sorrow' is the word 'etzeb', extended and made more general in meaning by the affix 'on' [עַ]. It is a contraction of the two root 'etz' and 'צב'. The first is familiar as meaning 'tree' or 'organic substance' etc. The second denotes anything in the way of 'obstacles', difficulty', opposition', prevention.' Combined in tzteb' the meaning is 'physical obstacles', 'difficulties of all kinds', 'anxieties', and so on. In realizing one's conceptions, desires and purposes. So long as will was exercised only in the spiritual realm it was free and efficient.

Whatever was willed in ipso facto realized. In spirit every one is free. We can think, feel, create mentally, anything we wish, and no earthly power can prevent us. But when we try to realize our conceptions in the physical realm and have to adapt ourselves to physical conditions, we are at once hedged about with obstacles and difficulties of a thousand kinds, and many of our conceptions prove to be absolutely impossible of realization. That is exactly what God explains to Aisha, that 'she' will inevitably find in physical conditions 'she; could be no longer free, and her powers would be greatly curtailed." [The Unknown God, pp. 201-202]

בצלמנו image. literally, in-image-of-us [Interlinar Bible] in Genesis [1:26] "And God [אלהים] said, 'Let us make man in our image, in our likeness...'"

I. "The first thing we are told about man is that he is made in the image and likeness of God, the Spirit of Life; therefore capable of manifesting a similar quality of Life. But we must note that words 'image' and 'likeness'. The do not impart identity but resemblance. An 'image' implies an original to which it conforms, and so does 'likeness.'" [Troward, 1942, p. 270.]

II. Paul Case: "in our image" (218) = ירח, the moon and *Briah*, the creative world, which is the second world, reflecting Atziluth.

219

וירא and he created. Genesis 1:21.

הטהר clean. Leviticus 11:47: You must distinguish between the unclean and the clean…

אריח I will smell. Leviticus 26:31. Smell is associated with Key 6, the Lovers with discrimination and the occult sense of smell. The method of determining the clean from the unclean.

220

I. Circumference of a circle having a radius of 70, symbolizing the horizon established by our limits of vision (Ayin).

III. 220 was considered a amiable or friendly number by the Pythagoreans. Amiable numbers come in pairs, where the sum of the numbers that divide evenly into the a number is equal to the value of the other number in a pair. For example the multiples or aliquot parts of 220 are: are 1, 2, 4, 5, 10, 11, 20, 22, 44, 55, and 110. The sum of these numbers is 284. The aliquot parts of 284 are 1, 2, 4, 71, and 142. The sum of these is 220.

IV. "Now in Greek gematria 284 is the number *agathos*, 'good', of *hagios*, 'sacred, holy', and of *Theos*, 'God'". Really, the three words are simply different ways of saying the same thing. Thus that to which 220 is amiable, or friendly, is God himself. And since the parts of 284 add up to 220, which the parts of 220 add up to 284, we have here a numerical symbol of just what is implied in the union of the hypotenuse with the vertical line of the Pythagorean triangle, and just what is implied by the coalescence of the words *Father* and *Son* in the Hebrew for *Stone*". [Case, 1985, pp. 60-61.]

טהורא Clean, pure, purified Intelligence of the 9th Path. The reproductive functions of the automatic consciousness are not evil potencies. Formed by Teth, the alphabetical symbol of the serpent power or astral Light-spiritual energy manifested physically as the radiance of stars or suns. Heh, the function of sight, both physical and mental vision. What we see determines the response of automatic consciousness. Vav, hearing, or brain activity which puts one in touch with super-consciousness, via telepathic communications through subconsciousness. Resh, the sun, the forces of automatic consciousness are reflections of solar force-the vibratory energy of cosmic electricity-the power of pure spirit made manifest on the physical plane. The adjective *tahoor* means primarily clean. It gives the lie to all those false notions which put the stigma of impurity and uncleanness on those powers of organic life which are truly basic in evolution. see 80, 87, 570.

אחאראט brother of Light-Magic. Mystical name of Cagliostro, the adept. אח means brother, member of the same unit, kinsman, friend. אר in Chaldean (also אור) means light. אט means: magician, soothsayer, secrecy. "Brother of the magic of light or hidden light." see 207.

כר a male lamb. initials of founder of the Rosicrucian Order. Also symbolizing the One Ego, the CRistos and for all associated names: The Egyptian Khoor (Horus), the Freemason's KhuRun Abiv (Haram Abiff), the Hindu KhRishna and the Rosicrucian "Father and Brother" C.R. (the founder of the order). All of these refer to the Holy Guardian Angel, in Tiphareth, the soul of all Humanity. A white lambskin apron is the distinguishing badge of the Masonic fraternity, a symbol of innocence and purity. In Revelations, Chapter 21 a lamb sits on the throne in the midst of the New Jerusalem, ruling and illuminating all things from a central position. With different pointing: battering ram, meadow, pasture. see 19, 440, 208, 68.

Inman says this word signifies 'he shots around, he encloses' כר car signifies 'a fat lamb, or sheep, or ram; but it also, as כר signifies 'piercing through', 'a peircer'; the root כרר carar, signifies 'to be strong, firm, powerful, or fruitful." [Ancient Faiths, V1, p.391]

לקץ at the end, or at the limit. לקץ הימין, le-quaetz haiamein, "at the end of the days." In the Hebrew dictionary this phrase is rendered "the messianic age." לקץ, in the Massoretic text of the Hebrew edition it is translated "till the end be." קל in the Hebrew dictionary has the meaning "the end, the time of redemption, messianic age." In Daniel 12:13: "But go thy way till the end be: for thou shall rest, and stand in thy lot at the end of the days." see 335.

מוסד מוסד a sure foundation (literally "foundation-foundation". In Isaiah 28:16: "Behold I lay in Zion for a foundation a stone, a tried stone, a costly corner stone of sure foundation." Refers to a precious corner stone. see 53, 1973.

מכלל-יפי the perfection of beauty (out of Zion). See Psalm 50:2. see 416.

כ/ק Kaph/Qoph, Jupiter in Pisces.

בחור one of the elect, to select; to choose, one chosen. Psalm 89:3: As in "I have made a covenant with my chosen." Refering to the spiritual Israel who are characterized by compassion and their natures described by the *tahoor*, meaning ,clean, pure, elegant. see 540.

מאסו הבונים Refused by the builders [Psalm 118:22]. One of the most important phrases in occult terminology. In the Rosicrucian allegory, it refers to brother C.R. in the New Testament it is expounded as a reference to Christ. It has also a Masonic meaning. "The stone which the builders refused is become the head stone of the corner." see 103, 53, 273.

נפץ to break to pieces, to break, shatter; to disperse scatter. As a noun: *nehpetz*, cloud burst, storm, bursting explosion. Compare with Key 16 and its relation to the Mars-force and to Yesod. "Destruction is the foundation (Yesod) of existence [Book of Tokens]." Also: to be pulverized. Part of the preparation of the alchemical "powder of projection".

רך tenderness, delicacy; gentle, bland. Deuteronomy 28:56: "The tender and delicate woman among you, which would not adventure to set the sole of her feet upon the ground for delicateness and tenderness..." Genesis 18:7: "And Abraham ran into the herd, and fetched a calf tender and delicate... The Hebrew equivalent of the initials R.C., which is the seal, mark and character as described in the *Fama*.

"R.C. were the initials of the brother who founded the Rosicrucian order, as well as those of one of 4 other brethren, who represented the elements required to complete the establishment of the work. Thus brother 'roke' or compassion.

Tenderness must come first and foremost in work of this kind. Sympathy with human suffering, understanding of human problems through ability to put oneself in another's shoes, unselfish desire to lift the heavy burden of ignorance from the minds of the unenlightened - these are primary requirements." [Case, 1985, p. 93.] see 2, 6, 19, 84, 312.

קמיע kamea. a magic square; an amulet. The origin of the word "cameo".

ורדי of a rosy, rosy. A Rabbinical Hebrew word of particular importance because of its connection to the fraternity, which was known, from its first manifestoes, as the fraternity of the Rosy Cross. see 260.

נע alienated. [Ezekiel 23:18, 28] Note: in the Hebrew of the passage cited it is written thus:

אשר-נקעה. "So she discovered her whoredoms, and discovered her nakedness: then my mind was alienated from her, like as my mind was alienated from her sister"; "For thus says the Lord God; behold, I will deliver thee into the hand of them whom thou hates, into the hand of them from whom thy mind is alienated."

ספלים cups. The suit of cups in the Tarot minor arcana corresponds to Briah, the world of creation, and the first Heh of יהוה. Psychologically, the cups are symbols of the powers of imagination. The universal subconscious substance is directed and given pattern through mental imagery, and the whole suit of cups is receptive to universal principles initiated in Atziluth.

ריי riyi. 29th name of Shem ha-Mephorash, short form. see 251 & Appendix 10.

ענק t he progenerator of the giants (Nephilim), the land of the giants. A Canaanite – Anak whose descendents are called Anaqiy (ענקי). A primitive root meaning to choke, with different pointing, a necklace (as if strangling, chain), to collar, i.e. adorn with a necklace, compass about as a chain, furnish liberally (Strong's Dict.). See Numbers 13:33 and 210 and 225.

Christus, Deus et Home (Lt). Christ God and Man [Secret Symbols, page 36]. A clear indication as to what the *Fama Fraternitatis* means when it speaks of C.R. as the foundation of the order.

Novus Ordo Seclorum (Lt). New Order of the Ages. or, New order of the Aeons. One of the 2 mottos on the reverse of the Great Seal of the U.S.

ignis philosophorum (Lt). fire of the philosophers. "This is the fire of the Sages which they describe in such obscure terms, as to have been the indirect cause of beguiling may innocent persons to their ruin; so even that they have perished in poverty because they know not this fire of the Philosophers. It is the most precious fire that God has created in the earth and has a thousand virtues-nay, it is so precious that men have averred that the Divine Power itself works effectually in it." [Waite, 1974, vol.

221

מנקאל "God who seconds and aids all things." 66th Shem ha-Mephorash. 326-330E. "TEPISATRAS. May 24, August 4, October 15, December 26, March 8. 9:40-10:00 PM. [Psalm 38:21] "Forsake me not, O Lord: O my God, be not far from me." Serves to appease the anger of God, and to heal epilepsy. Rules vegetation and aquatic animals, influences through sleep and dreams. Person born: combines all the good qualities of body and soul. He will conciliate the friendship and the benevolence of all good persons by his amiability and the sweetness of his character. Angel of the 6th quinance [26-30°] of Gemini; Angel by night of the 10 of Swords [Malkuth of Yetzirah]. see Appendix 10.

יאיר Jair, the Gileadite. (Note that this is a metathesis of (יאי). In Judges 10:3,5: "And after him [Tola] arose Jair, a Gileadite, and judged Israel twenty and two years... and Jair died, and was buried in Camon." גלעד Gilead (107) means, "hard, firm; hill of testimony." Camon (196) means "the erect on", [from קים com, "to be erect" and אן, city of Heliopolis, connected with the Sun], according to Inman. He also says Jair means "enlightener", for יאי means 'he shines, glitters, blooms, sprouts, flows, etc. Jair was the Greek form Ιαειρος, in which the Jair is united with Epos, Eros, divine love.

In Mark 5:22: "And behold, there comes one of the rulers of the synagogue, Jairus by name; and when he saw him, he fell at his [Jesus] feet." Note the connection between Peh, Jair the Judge (Key 20) and (Key 11), 22 years = complete cycle, hardness and erection linked with Mars; and light, which connected with Camon and the Sun. The place where Mars "dies" (i.e. nun = Death) is the center of divine love (Eros) in the heart, or sun.

פנאץ Phenetz. Goetic demon #37 by night of the 1st decanate of Aries, corresponding to the 2 of Wands. see Appendix 11 & 1031.

Goetia: "He is a great Marquis, and appears like a bird phoenix, having the voice of a child. He sings many sweet notes before the Exorcist, which he must not regard, but by-and-by he must bid him put on Human shape. Then will he speak marvelously of a wonderful sciences if required. He is a poet, good and excellent. And he will be willing to perform thy requests. He has hopes also to return to the seventh throne after 1,200 years more, as he said unto Solomon. He governs 20 legions of Spirits." [Mathers, 1995, p. 47]

ארך a City in Ancient Babylonia (on the boundary of Persia), founded by Nimrod, and a center for the worship of Ishtar, the Semitic Venus. In Genesis 10:10: "And the origin of his [Nimrod's] kingdom was Babylon, Erech, Akhar, and Caliah, in the land of Sinar." Elsewhere this is referred to as a city in the vicinity of Ephraim, the tribe associated with Taurus, ruled by Venus. see 331.

"וארך, and-Arech... The root רך or רק whose effect is to depict the relaxation, the dissolution of things, literally as well as figuratively." [d'Olivet, 1976, p.282.]

222

I. 6 x 37, the powers of the One Self multiplied by the Ego in Tiphareth.

אוריה Light of Wisdom. A compound of אור, Light, with the divine name יה, Jah, attributed to Chokmah. Uriah is the husband of Bath-Sheba, "Daughter of the Seven." The "seven" are the 7 spirits of God (Elohim) assigned to Binah. Bath-Sheba is the mother of David (love). David's son is Solomon (peaceful or perfected one). He is the type of complete enlightenment, a symbol for the rising sun (Ego in Tiphareth). see 86, 103, 15, 14.

יהיד illuminating. Name of the 2nd Path of Chokmah [variant spelling see 262]. The letters of this word form four of the doctrine of the grade of Magus, as follows: "Zain, The Lovers. A magus is a man of circumcision. He is free from the influence of the pairs of opposites, because he has sharply distinguished between the positives and negatives. By keen discrimination between the various polarities of differentiation, a magus is able to combine them, neutralize them, and transcend them. His liberation comes through knowledge, not through ignorance... Heh, The Emperor. In consequence of this accurate discrimination, which is largely an exercise in perceptive power, a magus gains the ability to measure al experience correctly. Thus the illumination intelligence is largely mercurial, or discriminative. One must watch before he can reason. A magus takes correct measures because he has watched, and because he has watched, he has learned to see. Yod, The Hermit, illumination, of which the magic of light is at once the consequence and the expression, comes about through subtle chemical and psychic transformations. A magus does nothing of himself. He is an embodiment of the will of God. Thus nothing can withstand him. All things obey him... Resh, The Sun. There is no self-importance in a magus. He has become the 'little child'. Free from care, free from the burden of false responsibilities, free from the limitations of human conventions and opinions. He extracts the nectar of wisdom from the experience of the eternal now. Thus it is written that he has access to the fruition of all desire whatever, at one sweep, being one with all-seeing self.

Note that *Zohir* is 6 x 37. Six is the number of beauty (Tiphareth), and represents the perfection of the cosmic order, which 37 is the number *abel*, which means a fleeting breath or spirit. Thirty-seven is the value of the angle in a Pythagorean triangle which expresses the relation of the ascending hypotenuse to the base. Thus *zohir* intimates that the Illuminating Intelligence is the perfect relationship of the personal organism of the magus to the fundamental laws of life. A Magicians thoughts and words are beautiful, since action and environments are reflections of thought and word, the Magician is continually surrounded by beauty. This is why they are always healers and teachers.

אל-המקום unto the place. In Exodus 23:20: "Behold, I send an angel before thee, to keep thee in the way (on the path), and to bring thee into the place with I have prepared."

הוורה whiteness? from רישא הוורה resha havurah, the white head, a title of Kether, the place from which the light emanates or flows. see 736

הר טוב goodly mountain. Mt. Zion, analogous to Kether in Assiah, or human personality. In Deuteronomy 3:25: "Let me go over and see the good land beyond the Jordan-that goodly mountain and Lebanon." see 156.

ראיה I will chase. The quest for IH the father, with which this word ends.

ברך to kneel; to bless. an epithet of God. With different pointing: to praise; to thank; to greet. Reverence aids in attainment.

In 2 Chronicles 6:13: "For Solomon have made a bronze platform ...[5x5x2] in the midst of the court; and he [Solomon] went up and stood upon it, and knelt down [ויברך] upon his knees in the presence of all the people of Israel and spread forth his hands in prayer toward heaven."

The knee is ruled by Capricorn. In Isaiah 45:23: "By myself I have sworn, my mouth has uttered in all integrity a word that will not be revoked: before me every knee will bow; by me every tongue will swear."

לידעימחן men of skill, i.e. adepts of grace- Qabalists. In Ecclesiastes 9:11: "I return and saw under the sun that the race is not to the swift... not yet favor to men of skill; but time and change happens to them all." It takes work to develop skill.

רכב chariot, chariots; team; riders, troop; upper millstone; branch for grafting. see Key 7, assigned to Cheth, the intelligence of the house of influence. The chariot is the personality and the "branch". It is ground into the new image by the "millstone" or Binah. With different pointing: charioteer, driver, horseman, rider. The higher self. With different pointing: to ride (an animal).

יריב One who contends, adversary. see Isaiah 49:25.

רבך to be mixed, mingled; to dip, soak (into oil). Written מרבכת in 1 Chronicles 23:29: "They [the Levites] were in charge of the bread set out on the table, the flour for the grain offerings, the unleavened wafers, the baking and the mixing, and all measurements of quality and size." Note that the mixing is also depicted in older versions of Key 14, Temperance. see 702.

בכר a young male camel. Recall that Gimel = camel = subconscious memory, Moon. In Isaiah 60:6: "herds of camels will cover your land, young camels of Midian and Ephah. And all from Sheba will come, bearing gold and incense and proclaiming the praise of the Lord."

כבר a river in Mesopotamia. See Ezekiel 1:3.

כבר to make heavy; to make many, multiply. In Job 35:16: "So Job opens his mouth with empty talk; without knowledge he multiplies words."

ו־גבורה ve-Geburah. In the Lord's prayer it is "and power". However, in the Greek of the New Testament, the Lord's prayer ends with "but deliver us from evil" (The remainder was added in a later English translation-about the time when the Rosicrucian manifesto was published). "And strength relates directly to the 5th Sephirah, as the preceding word ["the kingdom"], by its Qabalistic meanings, relates to he 4th Sephirah as well as to the tenth. see 496, 54.

223 (prime)

קבצאל gathering of God, God has gathered. In the Zohar [Prologue 6A-6B], this word is said to represent the concentration of the Limitless Light in the first Sephirah (Kether). In 2 Samuel 23:20: "And Benaiah the son of Jeholada, the son of a valiant man, of Kabzeel, who had done many acts, he slew two lion like man of Moab: he went down also and slew a lion in the midst of a pit in the snow."

I. Benaiah בן יה, Ben Yah, "son of God" is also a metathesis of בינה. Jehoiada ("Jah knows") = 100 = Qoph and כף, also כלין vessels; meaning "Jehovah known" [Zohar] "Contains an allusion to wisdom" Case: "Because בניהו contains בן, son = 52, and appellation of Tiphareth, combined with יהו = 21 = אהיה, the Kether divine name. 52 + 21 = 73 = חכמה, wisdom" [Zohar] "Kabzeel, from the highest and hidden grade where 'no eye has ever seen, etc.'" In Isaiah 64:3: "When thou did terrible things which we looked not. For, thou came down, the mountains flowed down at thy presence."

II. Zohar (1:, p.24): "A grade which contains the whole and which is the focus of the supernal light and from which everything issues." Thus קבצאל is the central point which is called אבי [Leviticus 19:30] "Upon which rests the unknown, the most high, the unrevealed one

which is יהוה, both being one."

III. This point is the palace of holiness in the midst, referred to in *Sepher Yetzirah* to Tav = the place of God, described in the Clementine Homilies as 'that-which-is-not', or in Hebrew אין, the metathesis of אני. see 271 (Greek). In Leviticus 19:30: "Therefore shall you keep my ordinance, that you commit not any one of these abominable customs, which were committed before you, and that you defile not yourselves therein: I am the Lord your God."

היה ברא to be, to create. The inner meaning is "the essential characteristic of being is creativeness."

כבד אבן ונטל החול "A stone is heavy, and the land weighty", (but a fool's wrath is heavier than them both") see 873, Proverbs 27:3.

הבריאה ha-Briah. the Creation. Refers of Heh, the 15th Path as the "essence of creation" see 423.

אב רך Father of tenderness; Father R.C.

אברך abreach. tender father [Genesis 41:43]; young married man. Refers to the founder of the Rosicrucian order "Father R.C.", which in Hebrew, would be אב רך.

אין עוד מלבדו none else beside him. In Deuteronomy 4:35: "Unto thee it was showed, that thou mightiest know that the Lord He is God; there is none else beside him." see 878.

224

I. (7 x 32) or 7 x 2⁵

דרך way, path; manner of life; occasionally a metaphor for worship, or religion. In Psalm 110:7: "He shall drink of the brook in the way: therefore shall he lift up the head." This "head" is the serpent power, which is transmitted into the head or face (Resh) of the higher self. see 314, 1024.

עבדי צמח my servant the branch [Zechariah 3:8]. Understood to be a prophecy relating to the messiah.

282

יָרִחוֹ Jericho (alternate spelling). According to Inman it means: reverencing Yah (IH). "Place of fragrance" [Standard Bible Dictionary]. see Deuteronomy 34:3 and 234.

חִקּוּקִי engravings, carvings, image, likeness. The pattern of the Tree is carved like an engraving in the consciousness and subtle vehicles of man. Rosenroth in K.D.L.C.K. (p.338) gives: *principia emananoi* [first emanation], and relates them to Chokmah and Binah, the father and mother of the other Sephiroth.

סנדלעי sandali. The Lord of Triplicity by Day for Capricorn. Godwin's Spelling. see 177 for S.S. spelling.

in centro solis et lunae (Lt). in the center of sun and moon. An expression of perfected adeptship. The sun is Tiphareth, and when the Ego is identified as a ray from Kether, the consciousness is *in centro solis*. From, here one purifies and reeducates the automatic consciousness in Yesod, sphere of the moon. Then he shares the prerogatives of the "twice-born," expelling all which darkens knowledge and hinders action [Confessio]. see 154.

mea victoria in crue rosea (Lt). My victory is in Rosy-cross [Secret Symbols. page 35]. see 88, 119, 154.

Nitre - Tartar – Vitriol (Lt). Three kinds of the one salt. In alchemy, the term nitre is used to designate a certain stage in the preparation of 'salt'. Case: "There is, properly speaking, only one salt in nature, but is divided into three kinds to form the principles of bodies. These are *nitre*, *tartar*, and *vitriol*, all the others are composed of them."

הנפילים. The Giants.

225

I. (5 x 5 x 3 x 3) or $5^2 \times 3^2$

II. The sidereal period of revolution of Venus around the Sun in whole numbers. (224.7 days actual).

כנפים + דבא Destruction & Wings. The destruction of the illusion of personal separation leads to the wings of the higher self raising the soul to conscious union with the divine. see 25, 200.

קדמון + יוד + בבא Qadom + Yod + Babah. The ancient or eastern + the creative hand + the gate. The gate is a verbal symbol of transition from one stage to another, or raising of consciousness. This is done with the aid of the creative hand, or Mercury in Virgo, in the microcosm. The alchemical "aid of Mercury" or addition of solar force brings one back to the mystic east, which is an epithet of God. see 5, 20, 200.

כונה + קדם The east + fervor, intense meditation. The means whereby one becomes receptive to the influx of holy influence מזלא mezla, descending form Kether, or the "east". see 78, 144.

ολεθια. destruction (Gr). "The hermenia of this word implies 'To suffer fully.' It probably suggested to the neophyte of the Mysteries, certain trials and sufferings connected with premature progress: or some orderly measure of Undoing and Redoing comparable with the scientific idea of metabolism: or the travails of regeneration." [Omikron, 1942, p. 260.]

226

דברך thy word. In Psalm 119:105: "Thy word is a lamp unto my feet, and a light unto my path." The connection with Peh (85), mouth, is obvious. In Psalm 119:101: "I have refrained my feet from every evil way, that I might keep thy word." see 80, 549, 876, 95, 706, 749.

צפון north, dark, hidden, profound, north wind. The face on the cube of space attributed to Peh or Mars; the place of greatest symbolic darkness, from where Uriel ("Light of God") comes forth. The direction of the letter Peh and the 27th Path of the Exciting Intelligence. According to the Qabalists, Job 37:22 should be read: "Gold comes from the North." The AM translation renders it "From the North Golden Brightness Comes." This agrees with Ezekiel's description of the whirlwind (549). But Jeremiah 1:14 says: "Out of the North shall trouble be blown upon all the inhabitants of this land." And the symbolism of Key 16 is a representation of this.

Rosenroth in K.D.L.C.K gives *septentrio* [relating to the number 7], *reconditum* [conceal]; who says also that the second of these names is occasionally applied to the Elohim, for with the living, beneficence flowing form Chesed, which is always open, the enriched wealth of good is drawn out. A long discourse follows.

צפון treasure, store; hidden; kept stored. Basically the hidden region.

וירדו And let them have dominion. In Genesis 1:26: "And God {Elohim} said, let us make man in our image, after our likeness: and let them have dominion over the fish of the sea, and over the fowl of the air, and ... over all the earth, etc." The "fish" are connected with the reproductive power of Nun (50). Dominion is connected with Saturn, represented by Tav (400, 406). see 713, 106, 700.

Ego dominus faciens omnia haec (Lt). "I Lord (IHVH) do all these things." Here is a direct connection with the idea of the exciting intelligence, and with Peh, the mouth, as the uttering Logos which fashions everything in the manifested universe.

227 (prime)

ברכה blessing.

זכר male; remembrance.

I. "to remember, to be remembered; applied to a male child, because the memory of the father was thereby preserved in the genealogy of the family; which genealogy was confided wholly to males." [Wilson, 1987, p. 265.] see Genesis 1:27, Exodus 17:14.

יאירו they shall give light. Leviticus 8:2.

זקניכם your elders. Deuteronomy 29:9.

I. In Blavatsky's Secret Doctrine (1st Ed. volume 3, p.467) it says: "In the philosophumena we read that Simon [magus] compared the aeons [divine emanations] to the 'Tree of Life'. Said Simon in the Revelation: "It is written that here are two ramifications of the universal aeons, having neither beginning nor end, issued both

from the same root, the invisible and incomprehensible potentiality. One of these (series of aeons) appears from above. This is the great potency, universal mind [or divine ideation...]; it orders all things and is male. The other is from below, for it is the great (manifested) thought, the female aeon, generating all things. These two (kinds of aeons) corresponding with each other, have conjunction and manifest the middle distance (the intermediate sphere of plane), the incomprehensible air which has neither beginning nor end." This female 'air' is our ether, or the Kabalistic Astral light." Thus the masculine and feminine meanings of the word are reconciled.

הרכב the chariot. Exodus 14:28.

כברה in alchemy, a furnace. see 656, 372.

מלכים גדלים great kings. See Psalm 136:17.

228

עץ חיים Tree of Life, Tree of the Living Ones. see 406, 160, 68, 223.

Proverbs 3:18 "She is a Tree of Life to those who embrace her; those who lay hold of her well be blessed."

Etz Chaiim is 228, and the reduction or seed of 228 is 3. Gimel (ג) is the Number 3 as well as Ab (אב), the Father in Chokmah. This is secret of life, and its expression through embodied form. Gimel is associated with Key 2, The Moon and the sphere of Yesod because it is the Sphere of the Moon. Gimel is the 13th Path which is the channel of the descent of influence from Kether to Tiphareth, which continues down the Tree through the path of Samekh, into Yesod and to Malkuth through the path of Tav. See **11**.

כרוב Kerub. Ruler of Earth; one of the Kerubim. The Cherubim are an order of angels ("the strong ones") assigned to Yesod of Assiah. see 278.

בכור first-born. In Genesis 35:23: "The son of Leah; Reuben, Jacob's first born." [Reuben = Pisces = alchemical multiplication. see 259]. And in Deuteronomy 33:17: "His glory is like the first-born of his ox, and his horns are like the horns of unicorns: with them he shall push the people together to the ends of the earth: and they are the ten thousands of Ephraim and they are the thousands of Manasseh." [Manasseh = Aquarius = 395; Ephraim = Taurus = 331]

בני עליון sons of the most high. In Psalm 82:6: "I have said, you are Gods, and all of you are children of the Most High. see 878.

קול יהוה אלהך The voice of the Lord your God. In Deuteronomy 15:5: "Only if you carefully listen to the voice of the Lord your God, to observe to do all these commandments which I command you this day." (The Lord shall greatly bless you).

אלהי יעקב God of Jacob. Note that Jacob received both the blessing of his father, Isaac, instead of Esau; and the blessing of the angle that he wrestled (ברוך = blessed = 228).

כרוב Genesis 36:8.

ברוך blessed.

229 (prime)

והירח and the moon. Genesis 37:9 "…Listen, he said, 'I had another dream, and this time the sun and moon and eleven stars were boding down to me [Joseph].'"

הדרך the way, the road. see Genesis 38:21.

באורך in your light. Psalm 36:9.

230

ירך the thigh but used as a euphemism for phallus. This is linked closely to Qabalistic ideas which are associated with the 7th Path having to do with the activity of the generative and reproductive powers of the One Life. The forces at work in those parts of the human body which are the seat of man's strongest desires are the ones which must be controlled in order to win the victory of which the reward is liberation. The Hebrew lexicon gives: thigh, lion, side, flank; base; leg of a latter. In the Apocalypse (19:16),

the Greek noun μηρος mhros (418) has the same esoteric meaning.

In Genesis 46:26, meaning to be descended from: "All the persons that came with Jacob into Egypt, who came out of his loins, besides Jacob's son's wives, were 66 persons in all." Translated "side" in Exodus 40:22: "And he [Moses] put the table in the tent of the congregation on the side of the tabernacle northward, outside the veil." And in Leviticus 1:11: "And he shall kill it on the north side of the altar before the Lord; and the priest, Aaron's sons, shall sprinkle its blood round about upon the altar. see 335.

נצץ to sparkle, gleam, to glitter, to bloom or to flower. Refers to the intelligence of Malkuth. see 676.

נציב מלח a pillar of salt. In Genesis 19:26: "But his [Lot's] wife looked back from behind him, and she became a pillar of salt." Salt is a symbol of the element earth.

עקודים striped, ring-streaked. In Genesis 30:36: "And he [Jacob] removed that day the he-goats that were ring-streaked and spotted, and all the she-goats that were speckled and spotted and every one that has some white in it, and all the brown among the sheep, and gave them into the hands of his sons." "striped suggest encircling. The periphery encircles the inner light vice-versa.

K.D.L.C.K. (p.632) gives *fasciata*, and says these are lights which are conceived from Adam Qadomon, in which are first manifested what will be the ten lights of Sephiroth. A long discussion follows concerning the order in which the Sephiroth are produced.

צפין thy hid treasure. In Psalm 17:14: "(Deliver my soul) from men which are thy hand, O Lord, from men of the world, which have their portion in this life, and whose belly thou fills with thy hid treasure: they are full of children, and leave the rest of their substance to their babes."

חרבך by thy sword. In Psalm 17:13: "Arise, O Lord, disappoint him, cast him down: deliver my soul from the wicked, which is thy sword." By numeration discrimination (Zain, sword) is equivalent to the "treasure" of the life-force. see Key 11, #23.

יגלפזק   Hod, 42-fold name in Yetzirah [777:Colume 90, p.18]. Suggest the formative power of intellect or Mercury. Mercury rules Gemini (Zain). 31st through the 36th letters of the 42-letter name of God.

בחורי   mine elect. In Isaiah 65:9: "And I will being forth a seed out of Jacob, and out of Judah an inheritor of my mountains: and mine elect shall inherit it, and my servants shall dwell there." Judah = Leo = Sun. see 30.

יד הארי   the paw of the lion. In 1 Samuel 17:37: "David said moreover, the Lord that derived me out of the paw of the lion, and out of the paw of the bear, he shall deliver me out of the hand of this Philistine. And Saul said unto David, go and the Lord be with thee."

231

I. Σ21 = 213.

יראך   Irak. An artificial word, suggesting Iraq, but conceals a profounder meaning. Part of a "limerick."

"There was a young man from IRAK, Whose face was exceedingly black, From his feet to his head, He wore nothing but red, Strange creatures, these men of IRAK."

Twenty-one is the value of אהיה or I am, the divine name of Kether. A young man is the type of the Son who comes forth from Kether through the path of Gimel. He is the personifications of that Son the Egyptian Osiris, of whom it was said: "He is a black god" The face of the Son is black because the Son (בן) is one with the Mother (אימא), because mother and son are both 52. He wears nothing but red because all the manifestations of Binah are veiled or clothed in the operations of Geburah. IRAK is י (earth, Yod in a earth sign Virgo), ר (The Sun, or solar fire), א (Air) and כ (Jupiter, the god of rain and Water). So we see the young man is Ben, one with his black Mother, working through the Perfect Law, and embodied in a vehicle formed of the four elements. Note also the phrase, "from his feet to his head," that is, from Pisces to Aries and this is Guph (89). see C.7 & 89.

כדברה   as she spoke. see Genesis 39:10.

αλς. hals (Gr). salt.

aurora philosophorum (Lt). dawn of the philosophers.

aurum philosophorum (Lt). Gold of the philosophers.

spiritus corporalis (Lt). Embodied spirit.

232

עד עדי עד   Forever and ever. A phrase used at the end of a section 4, chapter 1 of the Book of Formation, which says "The only Lord God, the Faithful King, rules over all from his holy habitation, for ever and ever." the same book declares also that the "holy habitation" is in "the midst," and is symbolized by the letter Tav. This is Tav at the interior center of the cube of space, as the living spirit pictured in Key 21. see 46, 36, 260, 315, 154, 224, 314, 29, 400, 406, 713.

אראל   Aeriel. Archangel; ruler of Fire. Ariel, "Lion of God"; used by Jewish mystics as a poetic name for Jerusalem. Possible alternate spelling of אריאל. see 282, and 242.

יהי אור   let there be light.

אמניציאל   Amnitzial. Geomantic Intelligence of Pisces. Also called Amnixiel, one of the 28 Angels that rule over the 28 mansions of the moon [Dictionary of Angels, p.16] Thus he suggest the idea of reflected light.

233 (prime)

עץ-החיים   Tree of Life. In Genesis 2:9: "And IHVH Elohim made to grow out of the earth every tree pleasant to the sight and good for food; the Tree of Life also in the midst of the garden, and the Tree of Knowledge of good and evil." see 228.

זכור   remember. In Exodus 20:8: "Remember the Sabbath day, to keep it holy." The prologue to the Zohar [5B, p.23] comments: "The highest Sabbath does not come under the injunction of shamor (keep) but is under that of zakhor (remember), which is used in the first version of the 10 commandments [Exodus 20:8], since the supreme king is hinted at in the word zakhor (remember). For this reason he is called 'the king with whom peace dwells', and his peace is within the injunction of zakor (remember). And this is why there is no contention in the supernal realm." see Key 2, #3, 83, 1513. See Exodus 13:3.

234

דכאודאב Goetic demon #69 by night of 3rd decanate of Aquarius. see Appendix 11.

Goetia: "He appears in the form of a star in a pentacle, at first; but after, at the command of the Exorcist, he puts on the image of a man. His office is to discover the virtues of birds and precious stones, and to make the similitude of all kinds of birds to fly before the Exorcist, singing and drinking as natural birds do. He governs 30 Legions of Spirits, being himself a great Marquis." [Mathers, 1995, p. 64]

ואברכה and I will bless. In Genesis 12:3: I will bless those who bless you, and curse those who curse you...

ויחרדו and they trembled. Genesis 42:28.

QUOD erat demonstrandum (Lt). "which was to be shown", traditionally mark the end of a mathematical proof.

235

צדקיאל Tzadqiel. "Righteousness of God", the Archangel of Chesed attributed to the 4 of Cups. Tzadqiel is the One Power manifest as the universal memory in Chesed. The Life-power's perfect recollection of Itself and of all of Its manifestations is founded.

הכיר the laver. Exodus 30:28. With different pointing: acknowledge. see Deuteronomy 33:9.

הירך the thigh. Genesis 32:33.

236

באילים יהוה מי כמכה "In the powers of IHVH how shall there be defeat?" Motto engraved on one side of the pommel of the magic sword. the powers of magic sword are primarily those of Chokmah, the Father. They are really the vibrations of the cosmic light manifested through the zodiac. see 93, 26, 50, 67, 261.

קומץ The hand as a weapon (Latin *pugillus* = pugilist, Kabbala Denudata). It is Yod, the hand or Chokmah (Yod, of IHVH), which may be resolved into 5 fingers, i.e. Binah, since to Binah is referred the first Heh (5) of IHVH, and the fifty gates (10x5). Denotes the powers collected and hidden in the supernals prior to manifestation, whose extension (the opening of the fist) is effected in Binah.

צפוני Tzaphoni, Zephooni. the Northern One; Lilith.

אל-הד the mountain of God. In Exodus 3:1: "Now Moses kept the flock of Jethro his father in law, the priest of Midian: and he led the flock to the backside of the desert, and came to the mountain of God, even to Horeb." see 205.

בהר יהוה Into the mountain of IHVH. In Psalm 24:3: (3) "Who shall ascend into the mountain of the Lord? (4) And who that shall stand in his Holy Place? He that hath clean hands and pure heart." see 552, 310, 2795 (Greek).

ספעטאוי Saphotaui. Lesser angel governing triplicity by night of Aries.

סנסנוי Sansenoy. One of the three angels invoked against Lilith. "The three angels credited with bringing Lilith back to Adam after their separation (in the pre-Eve days). The other two angels who assisted in the reconciliation were Sanuy (or Sennoi) and Samangaluf. Sansanui is now a potent prophylatic against the deprivations of Lilith and her minions." [Davidson, 1971, p. 257.]

237

אלף יוד נון En, Ain. First Veil of the Absolute spelled in full. The "Essence of Glory" is really the No-thing, the rootless root of all

287

manifestation. see 61.

עצם הכבוד essence of glory, referring to the 13th path. The gravitational force of the radiant energy concentrated in Kether. see 37, 200.

גמל מים למד Gimel-Mem-Lamed. Letter name Gimel spelt in full. see 882, 73.

קפאון Dark. In Zechariah 14:6: "And it shall come to pass in the day (of the Lord) that the light shall not be clear, nor dark." The Gnostic adoration says God is "Lord (IHVH) of the light and of the darkness. Day indicates manifestation dark is here the light is formulated, i.e. in the Ain Suph Aur (Limitless Light).

לאור the light. In Genesis 1:5: "and God called the light day."

ראהאל "God who sees all." 69th Shem ha-Mephorash. 341-345 CHRONTARE-Jupiter. May 27, August 7, October 18, December 29, March 11. 10:40-11:00 PM. [Psalm 16:4] "Their sorrows shall be multiplied who hasten after another God: their drink-offering of blood will I not offer, nor take up their names unto my lips." To recover things lost or stolen, and to discover the person who took them. Rules renown, fortune and inheritance, influences jurist, magistrates, barristers, advocates and notaries. Person born: distinguishes himself at the bar, and by his knowledge of customs, usages and sprit of the laws of all nations. Angel of the 3rd quinance [11-15°] of Cancer, Angel by day of the 3 of Cups (Binah of Briah), or Saturn in the creative world of desire. see 965, 206 & Appendix 10.

יחודה + ר Resh + Yekhidah. The solar face (the Ego) + the I Am (the Self). see 200, 37.

פרזים Perizzites; one of the races in Canaan which the Israelites were expected to displace. Also: hamlet-dwellers, villages in Esther 9:19: "Therefore the Jews of the villages [הפרזים], that dwelt in the unwalled towns…"

סויסאל Suiosal. Angel ruling 9th house of Sagittarius. see 800, 162, 320, 19, 322, 941, 271, 15.

ענואנין A'ano'nin. The Sentinel of the 26th Path (Tunnel) of Ayin on the Inverse Tree of Life.

I. The 26th Tunnel is under the aegis of A'ano'nin, whose number is 237. This tunnel underlies the 26th path which transmits the 16th *kala* in the series of microcosmic *kalas* commencing with the 11th path. The Cosmic power-zones constitute the ten sephiroth, Daath being not a *kala* in the strict sense of the term but a Gate of Ingress and Egress of Aiwass (78) via Kether.

The 22 Paths are reflections in human consciousness of the power-zones of cosmic consciousness. The aeons may also be considered in relation to the cerebral centers in man, and the *kalas* in relation to the sexual centers. The psychosexual mechanism of the 16 *kalas* in humanity (8 in the female; 8 in the male) is reflected from the aeonic centres or cosmic power-zones into the cerebro-spinal fluid and endocrine system. The 16th *kala*, in a macrocosmic sense, is equated with Path 16, the Path of the Har or Child (Horus). He is born of the Goddess represented on Path 15 as The Star whose mystical emblem is the 11th zodiacal sign, Aquarius.

The reflection of Horus in the 16th microcosmic *kala*, which is numbered 26, is The Devil, or Double, of Horus, i.e. Set. A perfect fusion and balance of forces in the macro and micro-cosms is thus attained in this 26th *kala*, which is ruled by the energies of Capricorn. The Goat is the astroglyph of the Scarlet Woman whose EYE (Ayin) is attributed to this path via the symbolism of Atu 15, The Devil. This *ain*, or eye, reaches its fullest extent in the name of the Sentinel of this tunnel, i.e. A'ano'nin. His number is 237, which is also that of Ur-He-Ka, the Magick Power of the Goddess **שפחה** (Sefekh, 393). 237 is also the number of IERAOMI, 'to be a priest or priestess', which confirms the sacred nature of this number.

The sigil of A'ano'nin shows the Ur-heka surmounted by the head of the priest and surrounded by the letters **בכרן**, which add up to 272. This is the number of *Aroa*, 'Earth', and of *Bor*, 'to consume', 'to be beastly', 'brutish', etc. It is' also the number of *Orb*, meaning 'the evening', or an Arab, i.e. a person living in the West. The West is the place of Babalon. Her totem, the goat, is the glyph of earth in the west as the place of the setting sun. *Obr*, a metathesis of *Orb* denotes 'tears, 'myrrh-dropping', from the

Egyptian word *abr*, 'ambrosia, 'ointment', and from *aft*, meaning 'exuding', 'distilling'.

The magical powers of Path 26 relate to the Witches Sabbath and the Evil Eye. The Evil Eye is the Eye of Night (i.e. the moon), and the ointment, unguent, or myrrh-dropping is the *Vinum Sabbati* prepared at sundown in the cauldron of the Scarlet Woman. Capricorn is the Secret Flame whereon the cauldron seethes, hence its connection with Vesta.

The disease typical of this *kala* is priapism, and the animals sacred to it are the oyster, the goat, and the ass. The latter is the specific totem of the female and of the *qliphoth* associated with the Moon of Yesod, the *Gamaliel* or 'Obscene Ass'.

The tunnel of A'ano'nin is haunted by satyrs, fauns, and panic demons, and the Order of Qliphoth associated with it is the Dagdqgiron, meaning 'the Fishy', which denotes the feminine nature. The corresponding Magical Weapon is the Secret Force represented by the shuttered lamp, which is an allusion to the eye concealed in the buttocks of the goat.

The Tarotic attribution of this Path 26 is the trump entitled The Devil, The Lord of the Gates of Matter; for the lunar current is the menstruum of reification which seethes within the Cup of Babalon. She is the Bride of Choronzon for he is in truth Lord of the Gates of Matter. According to *Liber 231*:

> The Lord Khem arose, He who is holy among the highest, and set up his crowned staff for to redeem the universe.

This means that Set or Pan erects the phallus to redeem the universe. The Black Diamond is the secret symbol of this operation which involves the gross powers of generation, for the diamond glitters in the darkness of matter as the Eye of Set. [Grant, 1994, pp. 228-232.]

oculus, trygono, gloria (Lt). eye, triangle, glory. Pictured on the reverse of the Great Seal of the U.S. The No-thing finds expression as appearance (the eye), as the three supernals (the triangle), and as the radiant energy which is the substance of all things and, at the same time, the gravitation of weight which holds together the world of name and form (the glory). see 81, 100, 56.

גלה + ר The head (Resh) of man + the word meaning "to lay bare, to denude, to strip of concealment; to open a book." Enlightenment opens the head of man to an influx of radiant energy from the heart, connected with Resh.

"Then shall the vision of thy Lord be granted unto thee, and seeing him shalt thou behold the shining one, who is thine own true self". [Book of Tokens, Samekh]

"Yea, in that day, shalt thou sing unto the Lord a new Song, A song of rejoicing in his beautiful countenance, the face of thine own true self." [Book of Tokens, Resh]

רחל Rachal. Wife of Jacob and mother of Joseph and Benjamin. The Standard Bible Dictionary (pp.759-760) states that "In the patriarchal narrative 'Rachel' undoubtedly has a tribal as well as personal significance, for about her are grouped five northern tribes-Ephraim, and Manasseh (= Joseph), Benjamin, Dan and Naphtals." These correspond respectively, in alchemy to Taurus and coagulation, Aquarius and dissolution, Sagittarius and incineration, Scorpio and putrefaction and Virgo and distillation. Inman says Rachel means "a nursing mother". This is appropriate, for she is associated with a cycle of 7 and with processes that nurture the soul towards illumination. Jacob means "supplanter". see 182, 331, 395, 162, 54, 570.

239 (prime)

ברזל Barzel. Iron, metal of Mars. *Aesch Mezareph*: "Barzel, Iron; in the Natural Science, this Metal is the middle Line, reaching from one extreme to the other. This is that male and Bridegroom, without whom the Virgin is not impregnated. This is that Sol, Sun or Gold of the Wise Men, without whom, the moon will be always in Darkness. He that know his Rays, works in the day, others grope in the night...

And this is that mystic thing, which is written Daniel 7:5, 'And behold another Beast, a second like unto a Bear, stood on its one side, and it had three Ribs standing out in his Mouth, between his Teeth; and thus they said unto it: Arise, eat much Flesh.' The meaning is, that in order to constitute the Metallic Kingdom, in the second place, Iron is to be taken; in whose Mouth or Opening (which comes to pass in an Earthen Vessel) a threefold Scoria is thrust out, from within its Whitish nature." Westcott adds: "from בר, bright, and נזל, to melt, hence cast iron." [Westcott, 1997, pp. 23-24]

יבסגנוץ Yakaysaganutz. Angel of the 3rd decanate of Taurus. This decanate has rulership of Saturn and suggest qualities of : stoical, persevering, firm. see 331 for alchemical significance.

גאה + יהודה + סליק The end + "praised, celebrated" (name of Tribe of Israel = Leo) + to be lifted up. the end of the great work is to lift up the Mars energy from Saturn to Sun or the heart. There the celebration of the mystic bridegroom takes place. see 300, 30, 9.

אזראל Azrael. Angel of death and northern side of heaven [Peh = Mars = North]; one of the chief angels of destruction. Paul Case: "Verily destruction is the foundation of existence and the tearing down thou seest is but the assembling of material, for a grander structure." [Book of Tokens, Peh]

Recall that Peh (80) = Yesod, the foundation of the Tree of Life. Note that 60, the myriads of spirits commanded by Azrael = Samekh, prop, support and בחן, bawchan, "tried by fire".

240

רם the high one, lofty, elevated, exacted. A title of Kether and the spirt of Brother C.R. Part of the name חורם, Khurum (Hiram, 254), which combines the 2 words חור (214), Khoor, meaning white and רם (240), meaning high. see Job 32:2.

ככר a circle, district, surroundings. With different pointing: a talent (weight = 3000 shekels); round loaf of bread, cake; round weight. From a Asyriac root meaning: to surround, which is spelled כרך, meaning: "a circle."This relates it to Kether, the Crown because Kether is derived from a Hebrew root also meaning to surround. See 620 and 220.

על-פני on the face of. In Genesis 1:2: "And the spirit of God [Elohim] moved upon the face of the waters." With different pointing: on the surface of, in the presence of, in the life-time of. The waters are those of Binah, the great mother.

מר Myrrh, perfume attributed to Binah, sphere of Saturn. With different pointing: 1. bitter; embittered, gloomy, sad; violent, cruel; a drop; bitterness care, worry; 2. hoe, rake; 3. sir, master, Mr.

נצנים flowers, blossoms. In Canticles 2:12: "Flowers appear on the earth, the season of singing has come, the cooing (voice) of doves is heard in our land."

In K.D.L.C.K. (p.591) gives: *prima gemina* [first twin] and says these are Chesed, Geburah, and Tiphareth, when they first ascend in thought; for that voice denotes the beginning of germination. He cites Canticles 2:12.

פקודים numbering, mustering; precepts, orders, commands. Spelled פקודין in Psalms18:8: "The statues of the Lord are right, rejoicing the heart, rejoicing the heart; the commandment of the Lord is pure, enlightening the eyes"; And Psalm 103:18: "To such as keep his covenant and to those that remember his commandments to do them"; Psalm 119:4: "Thou hast commanded us to keep thy precepts diligently." *Sepher Sephiroth*: cash, counted down, paid out [Crowley, 1977, p. 29].

נגעי ונ אדם plagues of the sons of Adam. Refers to the succuba, or night demons, who seduce men with lascivious acts under female form, and excite them to nocturnal pollution, i.e. impure thoughts. This a result of not following the precepts of God. נגע means stroke. see K.D.L.C.K. (p.563).

עמלק Amalek; the Amlekites, a very ancient people. see Genesis 14:7; Numbers 24:20.

ספק to smite, to strike upon the thigh a sign of indignation and lamenting.

כרך C.R.C.. The initials of the brother who founded the Rosicrucian order. see 340, 220, 320.

Rota Taro Orat Tora Ator (Lt). The Wheel of Tarot speaks the Law of Ator (Nature).

241 (prime)

זרבבל offspring of Babylon, sown in Babylon, grief of Babylon. One of the leaders of the exile who returned to Palestine. In Zechariah 4:6: "Then he [the angel] answered and spoke unto me saying, this is the word of the Lord unto Zerubbabel, saying, not by might, nor by power, but by my spirit, says the Lord of Hosts. see 546.

אמר to say, word, command.

ארם highland, mountain; Aramea, Syria. Illumination takes place where consciousness is raised to the top of the head. Metathesis of אמר here Mem comes before Resh.

מרא obstinate, rebellious; to fly; to feed, to stuff. [variant of מרה marsu, bitterness]

זה הדרך zeh ha-derek. this is the way. In Isaiah 30:21: "And thine ears shall hear a word behind thee, saying, this is the way, walk ye in it, when ye turn to the right hand, and when ye turn to the left."

אפקיים horizontals. Suggest balances, as depicted in Key 11 or Libra, Justice is equilibrated action, which brings the waters of consciousness from feet to head. see 191.

אלברה Literally, "no flying". Note אלברה is one of the alchemical names for the quicksilver (Mercury) of the sages, which is also called "lamb", אמר.

סמקיאל Samquiel. Lesser assistant anger of Capricorn. Mars is exalted in Capricorn -Ayin is the Renewing Intelligence.

רם a family name in Job 32:2: "But Elihu son of Barakel the Buzite, of the family of Ram became very angry with Job for justifying himself rather than God."

242

I. (3 x 11 x 11) or 3 x 11²

אל גבור the mighty God. Isaiah 9:6: "...and his name shall be called wonderful (111), counselor, the Mighty God, the everlasting father, the prince of peace (896). see 216, 211, 1492, 31, 2279.

אריאל Ariel. Angel of the element air, ruler of Air. Identified with the 11th Path of Aleph. It also means "hero," "the lion of God," and is a poetic name of Jerusalem. ארי is one spelling of the Hebrew for "Lion." see 232.

Davidson quotes Agrippa as saying that "Ariel is the name of an angel, sometimes also of a demon, and of a city, whence called Ariopolis, where the idols is worshiped. In Heywood, *The Hierarchy of the Blessed Angels*, Ariel ranks as one of the 7 princes who rule the waters and is 'Earth's great Lord'. Jewish mystics used Ariel as a poetic name for Jerusalem. In the Bible the name denotes, variously, a man, a city (Isaiah 29), and an altar. In occult writings Ariel is the '3rd archon of the winds'. Mention is also made of Ariel as an angel who assists Raphael in the cure of disease... in the Coptic *Pistis Sophia*, Ariel is in charge of punishment in the lower world... *In The Testament of Solomon* he controls demons. In Gnostic lore generally, his is a ruler of winds and equated with Ialdabaoth as an older name for the God. In practical Cabala he is regarded as originally of the Order of virtues. According to John Dee... Ariel is a conglomerate of Anael and Uriel... Sayce sees a conglomeration between Ariel and the Arelim... the Valiant Ones spoken of in Isaiah 33:7, an order of angels equated with the order of Thrones." [Davidson, 1971, p. 54.] see 282.

והוכן בחסד כסא And in mercy shall the throne be established. In Isaiah 16:5: "And in mercy shall the throne be established: and he shall sit up it in truth in the tabernacle of David, judging, and seeking judgement, and hasting righteousness The "thrones" in Binah established in Chesed, indicate that the outflow of fire from the supernals, has reached the level of cosmic memory, the highest for human evolution. ." The "thrones" are attributed to Binah; their establishment in Chesed indicates that the outflow of fire from the supernals has reached the level of cosmic memory (Jupiter), the highest level of human evolution of the physical plane. see 282, 892.

זכרה recollection. Literally, "Yah has remembered". Name of the prophet *Zechariah*. Refers to the cosmic memory, an inherent quality of the Life-force, Chaiah in Chokmah.

יהוה יראה God (IHVH) will see [Genesis 22:14]. The name Abraham gave to the place where he was delivered from sacrificing his son, Isaac, by the substitution of the Ram. ("And it is said to this day 'in the mount of IHVH it shall be proved'".) Also Adonai Jireh. see 255, 449.

יראבך thine adversary. In Isaiah 49:25: "...for I will contend with those who contend with you, and your children I will save." The adversary is none other than the Life-power. see 1418 (Greek).

מצוחצח Fiery, Scintillating. The 11th path of Aleph. From the verb צחח to glare, to reflect brilliantly, the light and heat of the sun, to be dazzling white (the white sun above the fool is Kether, the White Brilliance). As an adjective: brightness, clearness, splendor. see 106, 111.

קו לקו line upon line [Isaiah 28:10]. This is the power emanating from Chokmah, of the One Life. see 106.

243

I. (3⁵)

נצח + הוד + יסוד Netzach + Hod + Yesod. Victory + Splendor + Foundation. Names of the three of the four personality sephiroth corresponding to the desire nature or emotions (Venus), the lower mind or intellect (Mercury), and the astral body or automatic consciousness (Moon). These 3 must be purified, balanced and integrated with the physical body (Malkuth) before the birth of the higher self can take place.

מארב Marbas. Goetic Demon #5 by day of the 2nd decanate of Taurus. Attributed to the 6 of pentacles. This represents the operation of Tiphareth, sphere of the sun and central ego, in Assiah, the material world of action.

Goetia: "He is a Great President, and appears at first in the form of a Great Lion, but afterwards, at the request of the Master, he puts on Human Shape. He answers truly of things hidden or secret. He causes disease and cures them. He gives great wisdom and knowledge in mechanical arts; and can change men into other shapes. He governs 36 legions of Spirits." [Mathers, 1995, p. 29]

גרם bone. A primitive root meaning skeleton-like. From to bone, i.e. denude the bones.

Domus Sancti Spiritus (Lt). House of the Holy Spirit. In the Rosicrucian allegory (*Fama*) the meeting place of the order, built by brother C.R., which shows the real nature of the undertaking announced by the manifestoes.

"In the last paragraph of the *Fama Fraternitatis*: 'also our building, although 100,000 people had very near seen and beheld the same, shall forever remain untouched, undestroyed and hidden to the wicked world... Let it be ours to affirm that it is a real building, though unseen; more marvelous than any of this world's other wonders. The way to it stands open today, as in the past, and none shall fail to find it who seek diligently, *in the right direction* (italics added). See the path on Key 18 if the Tarot.

The notion that the house of the Holy Spirit is open but on one day of the year would be far from true. Those who know the way to it may visit it as easily in January as in June. Yet it may not be saying too much to declare that the hundredth day of the astrological year is actually a date of special importance, on which Rosicrucians from all over the world do "meet" in the house of the holy spirit. This they can do through their physical bodies may be separated by thousands of miles." [Case, 1985, p. 101.] see 220, 119, 60, 64 Latin, 867.

fraternitas roseae crucis (Lt). brotherhood of the rosy cross; i.e. the True and Invisible Rosicrucian order. see 119, 124, 238 (Lt)

244

מרד to rebel, revolt; to run, discharge, matter. With different pointing: *mered*; rebellion, revolt. It is the power of Mem or Water of mind, which initiates revolt, for the mind can wander. Resh, the higher self, initiates the mediation effectively; here, it is the agency only of action initiated by Mem. The results are apparent in the desire-nature or creative imagination (Daleth) in both cases.

הדראל "God who knows all things". 59th Shem ha-Mephorash. 291°-295° . ISY , Sun. May 17, July 28, October 8, December 19, March 1. 7:20-7:40 PM. [Psalm 113:3] "From the rising of the sun unto the going down of the same the Lord's name is to be praised." Against barrenness in women, and to render children tractable and respectful toward their parents. Rules treasure, the agents of change, public funds, archives, libraries, and all rare and precious connections; influences printeries, libraries, and all engaged in commerce. Person born: Loves to instruct himself in all the sciences in general; will have much to do with the stock market, speculates, to advantage, and distinguishes himself by his probity, his talents, and his fortune. Angel of the 5th quinance [21°-25°] of Taurus; Angel by day of the 7 of Pentacles (Netzach of Assiah). see 965, 213 & Appendix 10.

דרך way of. See Genesis 3:24.

Demon est Deus inversus (Lt). the devil is God reversed.

245

מרה bitter. The name of a well in Exodus 15:23: "When they came to marah, they could not drink its water because it was bitter. (That is why the place is called Marah) (24) So the people grumbled against Moses, and said 'What are we to drink?' (25) Then Moses cried out to the Lord, and the Lord showed him a piece of wood, He threw it into the water, and the water became sweet." see 250, 290, 440.

אדם קדמון Adom Qadom. the archetypal or archetypal man. see 45, 200, 101.

רוח אל Ruach El. Spirit of God. What is in the heights is behind Adam Qadmon, both bitter and sweet and "adorned with glory". In Job 33:4: "The Spirit of God hath made me, and the breath of the Almighty hath given me life." see 214, 31.

כל-פני האדמה The whole face of the ground. In Genesis 2:6: "But there went up a mist form the earth, and watered the whole face of the ground."

F.J. Mayers: Whatever it was that 'emanated' from the earth (אד, 5) it was something that had to make its influence felt in the 'Adamah'-something of a spiritual nature; it was something that had to take part in preparing the spiritual element from which 'Adam' was to be formed. We have already seen that Adam was created as a universal spiritual being, and also as a human kingdom of individuals of a physical plane. It was necessary then that Adam should be first formed in the spirit world, of spiritual 'human' elements, and then attracted to the physical plane to be 'formed' into physical individual men and women... At the point which our study of the narrative has reached a connection had to be formed between the physical plane 'earth' and the Adamah, so a 'force' or 'influence' 'emanated' from the earth and ascended into the spiritual plane, contacted it and was absorbed by it. The earthly and the spiritual (to use the suggestions conveyed by the word Ishekah) embraced or kissed one another, inclined themselves to one another so that a mutual attraction linked or kissed one another, inclined themselves to one another so that a mutual attraction linked them together. [The Unknown God, pp.118-119]

הנצנים the blossom. In the Prologue to the Zohar [I:p.3] "Rabbi Simeon opened his discourse with the text: The blossoms appeared on the earth, etc. 'The blossoms', he said 'refer to the work of creation. Appeared on the earth: when? On the third day, as it is written, "and the earth brought forth" They thus then appeared of the earth.'"

Sapiente et doctrinae Filis (Lt). Wise men and sons of the doctrine [Secret Symbols, page 20].

246

גבריאל Gabriel. Man (warrior, strength) of God. Procreative Power of God, Might of God. Archangel of the sphere of the Moon and the 9 of Cups. Gabriel is the angel of annunciation. His name stands for the Life-power's manifestation in the processes of reproduction and signifies the strength, virility and procreative force of God. Gabriel is also the Archangel ruling Water and the West and the manifest. It thus corresponds to the Jupiterian good fortune assigned to West on the Cube of Space. In Daniel 9:21 he is called the man Gabriel (האיש גבריאל). In Daniel 8:17-26, Gabriel explains a vision having to do with the end of a time-cycle. Thus he corresponds to the symbolism of the West, as representing the end of the day or completion. Gabriel is associated with the last trump of Judgement day. In Luke 1:19-20 Gabriel appears to the Herald of the Birth of John the Baptist. He announces to Zechariah a new thing, something seldom heard of (חדש, new, fresh). He also appears to Mary, to announce the coming of the Fountain of Jacob (עין יעקב), that her son is to reign over Jacob's house forever, and that his reign will have no end. Finally, the son announced by Gabriel is to be the fulfillment or end of one dispensation, and the beginning of another. Note: Jacob's name means "supplanter". Gabriel is from the root גבר to be strong, mighty; to conquer. With different pointing: man, male; warrior; cock; penis. see 205, 154 (Greek).

"Gabriel ('God is my strength')- one of the 2 highest-ranking angles, in Judeao-Christian and Mohammedan religious lore. He is the angle of annunciation, resurrection, mercy, vengeance, death, revelation... Gabriel presides over paradise, and although he is the ruling prince of the 1st heaven, he is said to sit on the left-hand side of God... Mohammed claimed it was Gabriel... of the 140 pairs of winds' who dictated to him the Koran... to the Mohammedans, Gabriel is the spirit of truth...Cabalist identify Gabriel as 'the man clothed in linen' [Ezekiel 9, 10] In Daniel 10:11 this man clothed in linen is helped by Michael. In Rabbinic literature, Gabriel is the prince of justice. Origin in De Principlis 1:18 calls Gabriel the angle of war... the name Gabriel is of Chaldean origin and was unknown to the Jews prior to the captivity." [Davidson, 1971, pp. 117-118.]

מור to alter, to change; to exchange, to remove; to barter. All these meaning are in basic agreement with חדש (new, renew, fresh). As a noun, it is one of the Hebrew spelling for "Myrrh." In the New Testament, Myrrh is mentioned as one of the gifts of the Magi, and is understood to be a symbol for sorrow. Also spelled מר, see 240.

מראה mareh. mahrayaheh. the act of seeing, sight, aspect, view; mirror, picture. With different pointing: 1. *mareaw;* vision, revelation; an appearance, looks; 2. *murewh;* crop, gizzard (where revelations are digested).

רום height, pride, loftiness; apex. A title of Kether, translated "on high" in Habakkuk 3:10: "The mountains saw thee, and they trembled: the overflowing of the water passed by: the deep uttered his voice, and lifted up his hands on high." With different pointing: *room.* a verb meaning: to rise up, to raise, to be high, uplifted; to exalt oneself; be proud, haughty; 2. Unicorn, *monoceros* (also spelled ראם, re'em). see 94, 100, 241, 103, 190, 182 Latin, 194, 636, 806, 254.

מדבר wilderness, mouth, speech. In Exodus 19:1: "In the third month, when the children of Israel were gone forth out of the land of Egypt, the same day came they into the wilderness of Sinai." And in [Psalm 29:8: "The voice of the Lord shakes the wilderness; the Lord shakes the wilderness of Kadesh." קדש kadesh or qadesh means "holy". With different pointing: speaker; the anterior part of the tongue; 1st person singular (gram.) see 650, 376, 206, 248, 404.

מרגג Given without explanation in *Sepher Sephiroth*. This word does not appear in scripture of in the Hebrew lexicon. [Crowley, 1977, p. 29]

Of מר D'Olivet writes: "The sign of exterior and passive action being united to that of movement proper, constitutes a root whose purpose is to characterize the which gives way to its impulsion, which extends itself, usurps or invades space: but when this same sign is linked by contraction to the root אר symbol of elementary principle, then the root which results is applied to all the modifications of the same element. That which is extending and rising, affects *the empire, the dominion*; as a *potentate*: that which exceeds the limits of one's authority; as *a tyrant, a rebel*; that which is attached to the idea of elementary principled, as *an atom, a drop*." [d'Olivet, 1976, p.393.]

Of גג he adds: Every idea of elasticity that which stretches and expands without being disunited. *The roof* of a tent, that which extends to cover, to envelop." [ibid, p.311]

הדיאל "God is Aid." 15th Shem ha-Mephorash. Associated is Psalm 94:22: "But the Lord has become my fortress, and my God the rock in whom I take refuge." Angel of the 3rd quinance of Libra; angel by day of the 3 of swords [Binah

294

in Yetzirah]. see Appendix 10.

"Hariel is also known as Harael and Behemial, and is an angel with dominion over tame beast. Hariel is invoked against impieties. He rules science and the arts and is of the Order of Cherubim." [Davidson, 1971, p. 135.]

Frater Rosae et Aurae Crucis (Lt). Brother of the Golden and Rosy Cross [Secret Symbols]. A plate showing the golden cross of the order, with the explanatory text written on the cross: "That is the Golden Rosy Cross, of fine gold, which every brother carries on his breast." see 62, 47, 58, 109 Latin.

247

מאור light, luminary; window.

אלהי העולמים The Living God of the world, or, of the ages. עולם olahm has among its meanings "something-hidden, time immemorial, eternity". see 146.

אלויד Lesser angel governing triplicity by night of Capricorn. Recall that Mars is exalted in Capricorn and is a means to enlightenment. Capricorn is connected with the material world, being a cardinal earth sign.

ראום Goetia demon #40 by night of 1st decanate of Taurus. In the tarot minor arcana this decanate is attributed to the 5 of Pentacles. It represents the operation of Geburah, sphere of Mars and volition, in Assiah, the material world. see Appendix 11 & 807.

I. "Raum (Raym)- before he fell, Raum was one of the Order of Thrones. In Hell he is a great earl and manifest in the from of a crow. His mission or office is to destroy cities and subvert the dignities of men. He commands 30 legions of infernal spirits... Raum also answers to the name of Haborym and is pictured.. with three headsman, cat, viper." [Davidson, 1971, p. 242.]

II. *Goetia*: "He is a great earl; and appears at first in the from of a crow, but after the command of the Exorcist he puts on human shape. His office is to steal treasures out of king's houses, and to carry it whither he is commanded, and to destroy cities and dignities of men, and to tell all things, past, and what is, and what will be; and to cause love between friends and foes. He was of the Order of Thrones. He governs 30 Legions of spirits." [Mathers, 1995, p. 49]

זרם A gush of water, to carry away as with a flood, pour out, overflowing shower, storm, tempest [Strong's Dictionary]. In Psalm 77:17: "The clouds poured down [זרמו, they-poured-down] water, the skies resounded with thunder, your arrows flashed back and forth."

248

I. The sidereal revolution of Pluto about the Sun in years (247.8 years actual).

אברהם Abraham. Old Testament name; father of many nations. Formed from the original אברם, Abram (high father), by interpolating of the letter Heh (5), between אבר (word meaning: wind, pinion, but interpreted as meaning: membrum, phallus), and the letter Mem, which signifies the feminine substance (water) of Binah. A definite relation between the occult meaning of Abraham and the idea of the perpetuation of the species connected with Nun. see 50, 250.

אוריאל Auriel. Light of God. Archangel associated with Northern quarter of the Heavens and the Earth. He is the Light-bearer (Lucifer) or manifestation. The light carried is that limitless light of the Ain Soph Aur. Composed of *Aur* (207), Light, followed by Yod, the hand and אל, the might (of God). Thus Uriel may be read "The Light is the hand and strength of God." Angel of the element Earth. Corresponds to the animal soul, or body-consciousness, nephesh. "Light of the Creative Powers." Angel of Netzach. Some sources say the planetary angel of Da'ath.

נודע ביהודה אלהים in Judah is God known. Psalm 76:1: "In Judah is God [Elohim] known: his name is great in Israel." Judah is connected with Leo an with alchemical digestion. see 30, 932, 1180.

במראה in vision. Rosenroth in K.D.L.C.K. (p.553) says the metathesis of the phrase is Abraham.

"Then shall the vision of thy Lord be granted unto thee, and seeing him shalt thou behold the shining one who is thine own true self. In the fullness of that blessed vision shalt thou be restored, and as a young lion trampleth upon his prey, so shalt thou conquer all the phantoms of delusion." [Book of Tokens, Samekh]

גמרה teaching, tradition. Probably from the Aramaic גמרא, gemara: teaching, study, tradition; the Amaraic portion of the Talmud.

רחם rawkham. A primitive root meaning to fondle, thus implying to love. With different pointing: 1. *rikhame*: to pity, to have compassion with; 2. rekhem: womb (as cherishing the fetus). 3. poetically: maiden, woman. [Strong's Dictionary]

רמח spear, lance.

חרם to make a net; to swear; to shut in. With different pointing *khaerem*: thing devoted, banned, forbidden; destruction, net; fishpond; curse, excommunication.

חמר to seethe, to foam; to burn; parch; to pile up, to coil up. With different pointing: *khomer*: loam, clay, mortar, sealing wax; material; heap; pile; a dry measure; seventy; stringency.

חמר red wine. With different pointing: *khammawr*: ass driver. The ass is a symbol of the alchemical first matter.

רזיאל Raziel. "Secret of God", "Angel of Mysteries". Archangel associated with Chokmah. The personification of Chokmah, one of the 9 archangels in the Briatic world, chief of the Order of Aralim. Godwin's spelling, see 331 for Case's spelling.

לקטו אבנים gather stones. In Genesis 31:45, 46: "And Jacob took a stone and set it up as a memorial pillar. And Jacob said to his brethren; gather stones; and they took stones, and made an heap: and they did eat there upon the heap."

במדבר In the wilderness. Also the title of the Book of Numbers. see Genesis 16:7 & 246.

אדם + ברא + Adam + beraw. Humanity plus to create. "The three that bear witness, above and beneath, respectively. אדם the spirit, the water and the blood; א being air (spiritus), ד standing for דם blood, and מ being both water and the initial of מים, water." [Crowley, 1977, p. 29] see 45, 203.

249

גמור Goetia demon #56 by night of the 2nd decanate of Libra. see 501 & Appendix 11.

Goetia: "He is a duke strong and powerful, and appears in the from of a beautiful woman, with a duchess's crown tied about her waist, and riding on a great camel. His office is to tell of all things past, present, and to come; and of treasures hid, and what they lie in; and to procure the love of a women both young and old. He governs 26 Legions of Spirits." [Mathers, 1995, p. 58]

מגור sojourning, dwelling-place. Note that this word is a metathesis of the proceeding. The dwelling place of deity is found through reversal and receptivity (Mem), by listening to the teachings of the inner voice (Vav) after recalling, through memory (Gimel) that the spiritual sun is the source of regeneration (Resh). With different pointing *mawgor*: "fear", terror in Jeremiah 6:25: "Do not go out to the fields or walk on the roads, for the enemy has a sword, and there is terror on every side."

אדזיאל Araziel. Lesser assistant angel of Taurus. The Moon = memory is exalted in this sign, which is connected alchemical coagulation. see 331.

אצבע אלהים finger of God. In Exodus 31:18: "And he gave to Moses, when he had finished communing with him on mount Sinai, two tablets of testimony, tables of stone, written with the finger of God." see 86, 569.

250

I. (2 x 5 x 5 x 5) or 2×5^3

II. Total length of the lines of a pentagram when each line is 50 units.

III. **ר/נ** Resh/Nun, Sun (Resh) in Scorpio (Nun).

אור גדול a great light. In Isaiah 9:2: "The people that walked in darkness have seen a great light."

באברהם by or through Abraham, for the sake of Abraham. The Zohar says that "it is Abraham who hath established the ends of the earth." Abraham refers to the 4th Sephirah (Chesed). His birthplace, Ur, is the same as **אור**, Flame, Light, thus relating him to the creative aspect of the Life-power. see 248.

"According to another view, the holy one, blessed be he, took **מי** and joined it to **אלה**, so that there was shaped **אלהים**; similarly he took **מה** and joined it to **אבר** and there was shaped **אברהם**. And thus he made the world unfold itself, and made the name complete, as it had not been hitherto. This is meant by the verse 'these are the generations (i.e. unflodings) of the heaven and of the earth **באברהם** (when they were created). That is, the whole creation was in suspense until the name of Abraham was created, and as soon as the name of Abraham was completed the sacred name was completed along with it; as it says further, 'in the day that the Lord God made Earth and Heaven.'" [Zohar I: 4B-5A, pp. 14-15]

בהבראם When they were created. In Genesis 2:4: "These are the generations of the heavens and of the earth when they were created." This may be read **בה בראם** (Beh bawreahm), "with (or by) Heh (**בה**), he created them, **בראם**, or "He created them with Heh." Heh is raised as if to hint that it represents the second Heh of **יהוה**, which is always called "the upper, or superior Heh." This corresponds to the Sephirah Binah, to the element Water, and Briah, the creative world. In the Massoretic Hebrew text of this passage the letter Heh is always written smaller than the others in this word.

I. The Zohar [I:25A] says: "It is in this way that God created worlds and destroyed them, viz. those who do not keep the precepts of this law; not that he destroys his own works, as some fancy. For why indeed, should he destroy his sons, of whom it is written: behibar'am (when they were created) in this passage, which may be analyzed into behe'beraam, 'He created them by means of Heh.' (symbolizing the attributed of mercy)?"

II. The Rabbinical Hebrew, **אבר**, ayber, signifies "limb, part, organ, wing, pinion." **אבר**, awbare, means: to be strong, hard. Hence "Pillar of Fruitfulness," associated with Yesod. The symbolism is phallic, but they who materialize it, and on this account reject it, are in error. see 248, 810, 5000, 26, 4, 14, 104.

דרום south, south wind. Understood to mean both south and midday, because at noon the sun is in the south. It also refers to Chesed, which corresponds to the same ideas as Abraham. As an adjective, *dawroom* means: attacked or killed by wild beasts or birds of prey. Suggest Leo (Key 8) and Scorpio (Key 13).

מדור dwelling, compartment, habitation. Creation takes place in the dwelling of the vital soul (Yesod).

אל חי העולמים Living God of Ages. Refers to Yesod. Whose divine name is "Almighty Living God". see 810.

נר A candle, lamp, light. As a figure of speech, hope, prosperity. In the Hebrew text of Exodus 34:7, the first word begins with Nun written larger than the other letters, thus **נצר**, and the 14th verse of the same chapter, the fifth word in the Hebrew text (**אחר**, translated "other" in the authorized version) ends with an extra large Resh, as shown here. Qabalists say that these two large letter, because they form the word **נר**, light, are so written to show that in the section of the text they mark off is to be found the light which is intimated. This is all has to do with the covenant between Israel and Tetragrammaton, and he who understands the real inner meaning of that **ברית**, Beriyth, is one who has grasped the inner meaning of the 30th Path of Wisdom. Note letters **נר** corresponding to Keys 13 and 19. The power which results in illumination is related to Nun. The consequence of its right direction in the Great Work is related to Resh. see 510, 90, 640, 53, 200, 260, 920.

In Jeremiah 25:10 "Moreover I will take form them the voice of mirth and the voice of gladness, the voice of the bridegroom and the voice of the bride, the sound of the millstones and the light of the lamp." And in 2 Samuel 21:17: "But Abishai the son of Zoraiah succored him and smote the Philistines and killed him. Then the servants of David swore to him, saying you shall go out no more with us to battle, that you may not quench the lamp of Israel." And in Job 29:3: "When he put his worship high upon my head, when his lamp shone over me; and when by his light I walked through darkness."

קלעים slings; curtains, coverings; excavation. [Abramelin p.184] The singular form (קלע, see 200) is directly related to Resh. In The Book of Concealed Mystery the "excavations" of the creative process are related to the emanation or Sephiroth. There is a sense in which divine creativity is covered or veiled from human [i.e. personality level) understanding.

צנינים thorns (in your side) [Numbers 33:55, Hoshua 23:13]. See אטד (14) which is another name for thorn and relates to the creative process. Also connected with the spine and its energizing with the "light" of the serpent power to create the "stone" of the wise.

מרי mari. refractoriness, harshness, rebelliousness. From מרר marar, to make bitter, to be embittered, and as a noun gall, bitter, herbs, etc. With different pointing: to flow, to run, to ooze out. It is connected with the alchemical first matter. see 440, 290, 245.

רן shout, rejoicing; ringing cry. Plural in Psalm 32:7: "Thou art my hiding place; thou shall preserve me from trouble; thou shall compass me about with songs (i.e. cries) of deliverance. Selah." see 900.

דרך יהוה the way of the Lord. In Isaiah 40:3: "The voice of the one calling in the desert: 'prepare the way for the Lord; make straight in the wilderness a highway for our God.'" see 224, 26; 1344 (Greek).

Laboratorium Perpetuum (Lt). Perpetual laboratory [Secret Symbols, p. 7]. A direct reference to the pentagram as a symbol of the human organism, and as representing the microcosm. The use of "perpetual" subtly hints at the nature of the Great Work, which has to do

with controlling the power of perpetuation corresponding to Nun.

251 (prime)

מאיר Illumination, Luminous, shining. Associated with the 14th Path of Daleth. The adjective, *mowayir*, indicates a derived luminosity. The 14th path of Daleth originates in the Illuminating Intelligence of Chokmah, and Chokmah is the source of its light. Chokmah is the dynamo, and the Luminous Intelligence is the light-bulb glowing with incandescence. see 601.

A rabbinical adjective derived from אור, Light. Imagination, the eye of the soul, the adept learns to use the cosmic imagination by surrendering himself to the direction of the Higher Self, holding the personal mind in suspension (Mem). The aspirant must be ready consciously to assume his share of the burden of creation-to become a partner with the Cosmic Self (Aleph). Detachment is necessary-identification with the illusion of appearance must be eradicated (Yod). The intensity of the initiate's consciousness that he is truly the eternal child of the eternal father is the measure of his understanding and the root of his wisdom (Resh).

אמרי words (either vocal or mental) [Genesis 49:21]. The verb אמר, *ahmar*, whence this is derived, means: to say, but includes also the meaning "to think". Thus words are not uttered syllables only. They include the silent speech of thought; and this is one clue to the inner meaning of Key 3 and the 14th Path. With different pointing: summit, top (of tree); upper branch.

אר הבבליא light of the Babylon (Chaldees). see 257, 297.

ארן the pine, a fir or cedar; strength. A slender fir or cedar from which masts were made, carrying the suggestion of uprightness and strength. Variant spelling of the ark of the covenant. see 257, 901, 448 (Greek).

המדבר the Wilderness [Deuteronomy 32:10]. This word also means speech. see 206, 376.

וריהל Uriel. Light of God. Variant spelling or Uriel. Compare with Buliver-Lytion's Coming

Race. see 248, 548 (Greek).

מורה teacher, master, instructor. By consciously turning-over the production of mental images to guidance from the Hierophant, they begin to come into accord with truth and right action. With different pointing: master; early rain; rebel, archer; shot.

חלקי אבנים smooth stones. In 1 Samuel 17:40: "And he [David] took his staff in his hand, and chose him five smooth stones out of the brook, and put them in a shepherd's bag which he had, even in a scrip; and his sling was in his hand: and he drew near the Philistine." see 604

רייאל 29th Shem ha-Mephorash. "God prompt to aid." Against the impious and enemies of religion; for deliverance from all enemies both visible and invisible. Positive Influence: virtue and zeal for the propagation of truth, will do his utmost to destroy impiety. Negative: fanaticism, hypocrisy.

Angel of the 3rd decanate and 5th quinance (21E-25E) of Sagittarius; angel by day of the 10 of Wands. This represents the operation of Malkuth, the material world of action in Atziluth, the archetypal world of ideas. "An angel of the Order of Dominations…" [Davidson, 1971, p. 245.] see Appendix 10.

Frater Rosae et Aureae Crucis (Lt). Brother of Rose and the Golden Cross.

Deus nobiscum, pax profunda (Lt). God with us, peace profound. "The password of the grade [I N R I] is formulated with the response thereto, and these are Deus nobiscum, pax profunda. It is the old Rosicrucian salutation: "peace profound, my breathern: Immanuel [78], God is with us.'" [Waite, 1993, p. 430]

Lumen et Spiraculum Vitae (Lt). Light and spiral of life. Used in the Secret Symbols in a context which relates it directly to the descending influx of the "Water of Light."

Accipe mihi Petitione O Domine (Lt.) Accept my petition, O Lord. Written on the back of Aggripa's Talisman for Saturn.

מאורה . Light-hole. The stream of energy flows into the field of human personality from its source in the Life-power.

המארד the lights. In Genesis 1:16: God made two great lights-the greater light to govern the day and the lesser light to govern the night.

לברך to bless. Genesis 27:30.

נבר Naberius. Goetia demon #24 by day of the 3rd decanate of Scorpio. Attributed to the 7 of cups. This represents the operation of Netzach, sphere of Venus in Briah, the creative world of feelings, or the power of desire in creative thought. see Appendix 11.

I. *Goetia*: "He is a most valiant Marquis, and sows in the form of a black crane fluttering about the circle, andwhen he seaks it is with a hoarse voice. he makes mencuning in all arts and sciences, but especially in the art of rhetoric. He restores lost dignities and honors. He governs 19 Legions of Spirits." [Mathers, 1995, p. 39]

II. D'Olivet writes of נב: The mysterious root אוב being united by contraction to the sign of produced existence, gives rise to a new root, when of emanate all ideas of divine inspiration, theophany, prophecy; and in consequence, that of exaltation, ecstasy, rapture; perturbation, religious horror. The Arabic indicated in *general a shudder*; exterior movement caused by interior passion. As onomatopoetic and idiomatic root the Arabic denotes the sudden cry of a man or animal keenly roused. Literally, *the bark* of a dog. Figuratively express the action of the one who announces the will of heaven, who prophecies." [d'Olivet, 1976, p. 396.]

253

I. Σ22 = 253

הרחם carrion bird; vulture. Leviticus 11:18.

גרים stranger, foreigners, proselytes. Those subject to new ideas. Exodus 22:20.

רגן to murmur, rebel. Implies the division of

unity, as in the path of Zain, descending form the Briatic level of Binah into the multiplicity of personalities overshadowed by the Ego in Tiphareth.

חרם the devoted. Leviticus 27:21. With different pointing: utterly destroying. see Deuteronomy 3:6.

החמר the ass, to donkey. see Exodus 4:20.

254

I. (2 x 127)

ימא רבא yammah rabah. Great Sea. In Daniel 7:2 this expression is "upon the Great sea," and ימא, is prefixed by Lamed, which would be 284. see also 99.

חורם Khuram, Huram. Hiram Abiff . used in Masonry. In 1 Kings 7:13: "And king Solomon sent and fetched Hiram out of Tyre." Personification of the Christos in the Rosicrucian allegory. Analyzed as חור, Hur, whiteness, and R , Ram, Height. Thus (C)Hiram, the Christos, is seen to be a reflection of the white height of Kether, just as the Ego is Tiphareth is a reflection of the Self, in Kether. The first two letter חו, as to 14 (David, beloved), the third is Sol, and the last is water. See 130, 19, 273.

ברוך יהוה blessed be IHVH. In Genesis 9:26: "And he [Noah] said, blessed be the Lord God of Shem; and Canan shall be his servant." Shem was the ancestor of the Semites, including the tribes of Israel; Cain means "lance, spear" and refers to the false crown of will-power (Canaan is the land of Cain); Noah means "rest, cessation." see 340, 160, 58.

מטרה a mark, aim, target; purpose, prison, dungeon.

חמור an ass, donkey, jackass.

נדר a solemn promise, vow, thing vowed, votive offering or sacrifice; Nadar: to vow.

נרד spiknard, nard. In Canticles 4:13: "Thy plants are an orchard of pomegranates, with pleasant fruits; camphor, with spikenard." From Latin *Spika*, a spike, and *narous*, an aromatic root. A fragrant oil or ointment derived from the roots of this plant. Used in India as a perfume for the hair, also the plant itself, Nard.

רחום merciful, compassionate. With different pointing *rawchum*: beloved, dear, favorite. Chesed is the sphere of the merciful ones. In Exodus 34:6: "And the Lord passed by before him, and proclaimed: 'The Lord, the Lord, the God merciful and compassionate, long suffering, and abundant in goodness and truth' (and Moses fell down and worshiped). And in Joel 2:13: "And rend your heats and not your garments, and turn to the Lord your God; for he is gracious and merciful, patient and of great kindness, and he averts disaster."

רומח a spear. Note connection between Cain (pointed, spear), which is the delusion caused by the lower mind (Mercury, sphere of Hod, path of Ayin) when it is not connected to cosmic memory (Jupiter, sphere of Chesed) by the path of Yod, or divine will.

זוריאל Zuriel. Geomantic intelligence of Libra. Archangel of Libra. This sign has rulership of Venus and is connected with equilibrium and alchemical sublimation.

"Zuriel (my rock is God')- prince of the order of principalities, ruler of the sign Libra..., and one of the 70 childbed amulet angels; also a curer of stupidity in man. When equated with Uriel, he is angel of September. In Numbers 3:35 Zuriel is 'chief of the house of the father of the families of Merari." [Davidson, 1971, p. 331.] see 501.

בעליהקבלה Master of the Qabalah. The great mystics who are able to attune themselves to the Christos though receptivity to the "Great Sea". see 137, 244.

לעולם חסדו His mercy endures forever. In Psalm 136:1: "O give thanks unto the Lord; for he is good; for his mercy endures forever." Chesed is the Sephirah of mercy and is associated with the grade of master of compassion (exempt adept). These are those Chasidim who are receptive to the 3rd order from Binah, across the "abyss" separating Binah from Chesed (72). Note that this phrase occurs 6 times in Chronicles, once in Ezra, 3 times in Psalms, once in Jeremiah, 42 (6x7) in all. Note the implication as to חסד.

צדיקים the righteous. In Psalm 34:15: "The eyes of the Lord are upon (toward) the righteous, and his ears are open unto their cry." Note that צדק Tzedeq is Jupiter, the sphere of Chesed. [This verse in the Psalm is assigned to Ain, the eye, or outward appearance] see 166, 728; 715 (Greek).

גרודיאל Garudiel. Angle of the 3rd decanate of Aquarius. This decanate is ruled by Venus (or creative imagination and desire), and suggest the qualities: brotherly, humane, polite. Loving and friendly qualities in humanitarian and social work are needed to raise intellect into larger areas of remembrance.

אלהי יצחק God of Isaac. In Exodus 3:6: "...I am the God of thy father, the God of Abraham, the God of Isaac, and the God of Jacob. And Moses hid his face; for he was afraid to look upon God." The God of Isaac ["He laughs"] is the God of laughter, also of preservation (Isaac saved from sacrifice). Isaac, moreover, is especially the son. Note that the God of Isaac was merciful to both Isaac and Abraham. [רחום = 254 = merciful] see 208, 294, 228.

255

מזרח east; eastern quarter of the heavens; sunrise. Assigned to the 11th path of Aleph and the direction assigned with the letter Daleth (both the Fool and the Empress have yellow hair bound by a green wreath). East is the place of sunrise, where a cycle of activity (day) begins. see 111.

מריה seen of Yah [Genesis 22:2 and 2 Chronicles 3:1]. The name of a hill in Palestine, the site of Solomon's Temple. The "Land of Moriah" is the place Abraham was directed to take his son, Isaac, for the sacrifice. see 471.

Inman: מריה or מוריה (Genesis. 22:2). The origin of the word is most probably from מרה, marah, and יה, Jah, signifying "Jah is strong,' or form מורי יה, 'my lord Jah.' In the Greek, we have some words which suggest other ideas;

μορια are 'the sacred olives,' which call to mind 'the Mount of Olives in Jerusalem; Ζευς Μαριος is 'one of the names of Jupiter,' and μοριος = 'the pudenda;' and these organs, hills or eminencies were frequently compared. The celebrated Mount *Meru*, the seat of the Gods in the Hindu theology, has a name singularly like *Moriah*, its signification is 'excellent,' a name given by the Psalmist to the hill of Jerusalem, which he also says is 'the joy of the whole earth.' [Ancient Faiths, Vol. 2, p. 337]

נהר a stream, river; to flow. The river with four heads which went out of Eden. In Genesis 2:10: "And a river went out of Eden to water the garden; and from thence it was parted, and became into four heads." Also used figuratively to denote prosperity. As a verb: to flow, to stream, to shine, beam, to sparkle, to be cheerful. see 1826.

רמיה deceit, treachery; deceitfully. From a root meaning: to hurl (downward), to cause to fall. Its ordinary signification is: slackness, slothfulness, deceit, guile. A veiled reference to the idea that the creative process is, in a way, the result of a progressive series of slowing down. The intense vibrations of the higher aspects of the Life-power are made to become less and less rapid, and in so doing, the actually cool off and solidify. The objects which are by this cooling-off process made to appear are the source of illusions which deceive the mind of man, and lead it into all the negative attitudes which are covered by the word "guile."

רנה shout, cry, rejoicing, singing. The inward result of orienting the consciousness to the "east", source of the rivers. With different pointing: *wheeze*, rattle. K.D.L.C.K. (p.690) gives: *cantatio elata* [a lifting song] and says it refers to justice, (according to Psalm 33:1: "Sing joyfully to the Lord, you righteous; it is fitting for the upright to praise him.)" since the influx belongs to Geburah.

אנדר Goetia demon #63 by night of the 3rd decanate of Sagittarius. see Appendix 11.

Goetia: "He is a great Marquis, appearing in the form of angel with a head like a black night raven, riding upon a strong black wolf, and having a sharp and bright sword flourished aloft in his hand. His office is to sow discords. If the Exorcist have not a care, he will slay both him and his fellows. He governs 30 Legions of Spirits." [Mathers, 1995, p. 60]

גברים mighty men. In Genesis 6:4: "The Nephilim [נפלים, see 210] were on the earth in those days-and also afterward-when the sons of God went to the daughters of men and had children by them. They were the heroes of old, men of renown." see 815, 210, 770.

I. "And the Nephilites (distinguished, illustrious, noble men) were in-the-earth by-the-days thoses: and also after-that-so (happened) that they-were-comem, the sons (spiritual offspring) of of-HIM-the-Gods, near-the-daughters (corporeal faculties) of-Adam (collective man) and-that-they-had-beggotend-through-them those-very Ghiborites (mighty men, lords) who were of-old-old, corporeal men of-renown." [d'Olivet, 1976, p. 179.]

II. He comments: "And the Nephilim (elect among men, noble illustrious ones) were upon the earth in those days: and also after that sons (spiritual emanations) of Aelohim had come into (mingled with) daughter (corporeal faculties) of Adam (universal man) and they had produced through them those same Ghiborim (mighty men, those famous hyperboreans) who were of old, corporeal men (heros) of renown." [ibid., p. 329.]

III. "הגברים, the Ghiborites…. This important word is composed of two roots which usage has contracted, גב-בור. the first גב, develops literally the idea of a thing placed or happening above another, as a boss, an eminence, a protuberance. Figuratively, it is an increase of glory, strength, honor. The second בור, contains the idea of distinction, of splendor, of purification. it must not be confused with the root word ברוא to create. The latter is composed of the signs of interior action ב, and the elementary root אר: the one now under consideration, unites to the same generative sign ב, the modified root אור, which, applied particularly to fire, develops all ideas attached to that element. It is from this that the following words are derived. בר, wheat, בור to elect, to choose, to distinguish; בחור, that which is white

and pure; בחור that which is selected, put aside, preferred, etc.

Observe that vowel which constitutes this root, undergoing the degradation forms the verb בעור, to inflame, to fill with burning adore; to make passionate, furious, etc.

From this etymological knowledge, that the word גברים signifies very distinguished, very remarkable, very noble men. The first root גב, meaning very, and rendered by the ancient Greeks by υπερ above. The second root בור, has been preserved in the plural Βορεοι, Boreans: meaning, the illustrious, the powerful, the strong, in short, the Barons: for the Celtic word baron, is the analogue of the Hebrew גברון, written with the extensive final ון; the Greek word Υπερβορεοι, is no other than the high, arch-barons. And thus, confusing constantly the name of a caste with the name of a people, as they have done with regard to the Chaldeans, these same savants have been greatly troubled to find the fixed abode of the hyperborean nation.

The word גבור, here referred to, constitutes the fourth name that Moses gives to man: the second, that this hiergraphic writer, makes this superior man descend, by the union of divine emanations with natural forms, that is to say, in other terms, spiritual faculties joined to physical faculties.

The element from which he must draw his passive nature substance, is named after him, Adamah. Soon the divine spirit is united to his elementary spirit; he passes from power into action. The being of beings individualizes him by detaching from him his efficient volitive faculty and makes him thus, free, susceptible of realizing his own conception. The intellectual man, איש, exists.

The covetous passion, universal incentive of elementary nature, inevitably attacks thenceforth this volitive faculty, now isolated and free. Aisha, [306] seduced and believing to take forth this possession of his active nature principle, gives way to the natural principle. Intellectual man is corrupted. His volitive faculty is changed into elementary existence, Hewah [Eve, 19]. Universal man, Adam, is decomposed and divided. His unity, passed first to number three in *Kain* [160], *Habel* [37] and *Sheth* [700] goes to number six through *Kain*, and to number nine through *Sheth*. The corporeal faculties succeed to elementary existence. Corporeal man, *AEnosh*, [357] appears upon the cosmogonic scene.

In the meantime, the divine emanations are united to the corporeties born of the dissolution of *Adam*, and corporeal man gives place directly to superior man, *Ghibor*, [211], hero, demi-god. Very soon this *Ghibor*, this superior man, abandons himself to evil, and his inevitable downfall brings about the repose of Nature.

Thus, in the profound thought of Moses, these four-hieroglyphic names succeed one another: Adam אדם, *universal man*, איש, *intellectual man*, אנוש, *corporeal man*, גבור *superior man*. And these four names so different in form and in signification, employed by Moses with an art more than human, have been rendered by the same word as synonyms!" [d'Olivet, 1976, pp. 181-183.]

2. The Zohar [I.25B] comments: "The Gibborim (mighty ones) are those whom it is written: 'they are the might ones...men of name' [Genesis 6:4]. They come from the side of those who said 'come, let us build a city and make to us a name' [Genesis 11;4]. These men erect synagogues and colleges, and place in them scrolls of the law with rich ornaments, but they do it not for the sake of God, but only to make themselves a name, and in consequence the powers of evil prevail over Israel, (who should be humble like the dust of the earth) according to the verse: 'And the waters prevailed very much upon the earth' [Genesis 7:19]." (pp.99-100)

הרר parched by the sun; a noble or fat man [Inman]. A city in Chaldea, center of the worship of the moon-god Sin; temporary home of Abram. In Genesis 12:4: "So Abram departed, as the Lord had spoken to him; and Lot went with him: and Abram was 75 years old when he departed out of Haran." see 905.

חומרא burdensome, with difficulty [Crowley, 1977, p. 30]. d'Olivet writes of the first 3 letters: חום. Action of *enveloping*, *seizing* by a contractile movement, exercising upon *something a compressive force; heating, rendering obscure*. In a restrictive sense, *a wall*,

because it *encloses; a girdle*, because it *envelops*; in general, *every curved round figure; simulacrum of the sun*, etc." [d'Olivet, 1976, p. 352.]

Centrum mindi, granum fundi (Lt). Center of the World, see of the foundation. This is a free translation of the personal motto of the author of "The Golden Age Restored, an alchemical treatise included in Secret Symbols, page 20. *Sapiente et doctrinae filis* (Lt). Wise men and sons of the doctrine [Secret Symbols, page 21].

Sub umbra alarum tuarum IHVH (Lt). Under the shadow of the wings, Tetragrammaton. In some versions of the *Fama*, the closing motto is so written, with the Hebrew for Tetragrammaton, instead of Iehova. When Iehova is used the motto adds to 284.

Verba secretorum hermetis (Lt). The words of the Hermetic secrets, or more freely, the Hermetic secret discourse. Title of page 17 in Secret Symbols. The rest of the text on that page is a German translation of The Emerald Tablet illustrated by a diagram having round its circumference the words "Visita interiora terra, rectificando invenies occultum lapidem." see 570.

256

I. (16 x 16) or 2^8

נור fire (Aramaic and Chaldee form). Nun is Scorpio, governing the organs of sex. Vav is Taurus, and rules the neck, ears, and throat. It is the polarity and complementary opposite of Scorpio. Resh is the sun, ruling Leo and governing the heart, back and spinal cord. It is exalted in Aries, ruled by Mars and governing the Head and Brain. These are all important parts in the Great Work of Alchemy. see 301, 662.

אהרן Aaron. "Lofty". Elder brother of Moses. In the Bible he is the mouthpiece of Moses and like Hermes he has a rod which buds and becomes a serpent and swallows up the serpent-rods of the opposing priests. He stands between the living and the dead with a censer, and thus stays a plague. Ancient Faiths [Volume 1, pp. 176-179] links Aaron with אור aur or light and הור hur. see 262, 206, 221, 642, 906, 891, 952 (Greek).

אמירה Tidings; a saying speech; proclamation;

dedication.

I. In K.D.L.C.K. (p.128): Under this title the 'parents' are recognized to be under these words: there are various meanings, however, referring to Malkuth [Psalm 68:11] 'the Lord gave the word (referring to Geburah): great was the company of those that announced it." (Amiriah here refers to Tiphareth).

II. I.R.Q. para. 352: "… 'Amirah' is, as it were (*simple*) speech, wherein is required no special uplifting of the voice; 'Debur' is public speaking, wherein is indeed necessary (*considerable*) elevation of voice and (*loud*) proclamation of words." [Mathers, 1993, p. 150] This refers to the control of creativity through "speech".

בני צדק The sons of the righteous. Those who control and direct the secret "fire". see 194, 52, 62.

מפולמין Dampness or darkness. In Job 28:3: "Man puts an end to the darkness; he searches the farthest recesses for ore in the blackest darkness." see 705 and K.D.L.C.K. (p.20)

רוכל Trafficker, trader; seller of spices; peddler, hawker. We sell all we have for the "pearl of great price". K.D.L.C.K. (p.683) gives: *Aromatarius* [provide arms]. This refers to Yesod, since within it are mingled every kind of influx.

לי גבורה I have strength. Proverbs 8:14: "Council is mine, and sound wisdom: I am understanding; I have strength." The reward of the master of fire.

דברים "words"; Hebrew title of Deuteronomy in the Bible, so-called from its first word. In Deuteronomy 1:1: "These are the words Moses spoke to all Israel in the desert east of he Jordan..." Deals mostly with an expansion of the Mosaic code of law to Israel. This book seeks to combine the teaching of prophesy with traditional practices of religious and social life, all attributed to Moses. see 816.

Κλεις. Key (Gr).

חרטם magician, sage. Written plural in Daniel 2:2: "The king commanded to call the magicians, and the astrologers, and the sorcerers, and the Chaldeans, to show the king [the interpretation of] his dreams." . see 217, 525 and Genesis 41:8 (plural).

ארון ark.

אורים the east, illuminations, festival lights. lights. The *urim* or "lights, used for purposes of divination with the *thummim*. [Exodus 28:30] see 817, 480, 753, 207.

מעל לבנה the white wand. Note that מקל means wand; rod, stick; staff, walking stick. לבן is the adjective meaning white. Paul Case adds this word is the feminine word for brightness, לבנה. This word also means moon and brick (and in the masculine, birch). see 87. This seems to suggest a union of masculine and feminine powers. The "white head" is Kether, ultimate aim of the "wand".

נורא fire; fiery. Daniel 3:6, 7:9: "And who so falls not down and worships shall the same hour be cast into the midst of a burning, fiery furnace."; "I beheld till the thrones were cast down, and the ancient of days did sit, whose garment was white as snow, and the hair of the head like the pure wool: this throne was like the fiery flame, and his wheels as burning fire." see 850 (Greek).

K.D.L.C.K. (p.568) gives: *terribilis* (frightful, dreadful), and says it is Tiphareth in all concord or harmony, with respect to Geburah; the middle way is so called since it contains benevolence (mercy) and severity. He cites Genesis 28:17 where the mystery is declared by Jacob: "He was afraid and said 'how awesome is this place! This is none other than the house of God; this is the gate of heaven."

נאור enlightened; illumined, splendid, glorious; enlightened, cultured.

ויאמר and said. Genesis 1:3: "And Elohim said, let there be light: and there was light". This word stands for the formative word. In 2 Samuel 21:16 this is translated "and thought" (And Ishbibenob, which was of the sons of the giant, the weight of whose spear weighed 300 shekels of brass... he being girded with a new sword, thought to have slain David"). The word = the thought = the Logos. The light was formed by thought.

"*Va-Yomer*: expresses an emanation (6) which projects *Yod* (10) and Aleph (1) in the basic attribute of matter, *Mem* (40) included in the universal container *Raysh* 9200). *Yomer* is not a verb as part of speech attributed to Elohim's predication but an action, an exertion or projection of energy, a doing. The two "players" are here said to be thrust into the sphere of appearances." [Suraes, 1992, p. 84]

אבני-צדק just weights. Leviticus 19:36: "just balances, just weights, a just Ephah, and a just hin [a liquid measure], shall ye have: I am the Lord your God, which brought you out of the land of Egypt." see 685, 302, 259, 194.

Institutrix arcanorum (Lt). Establisher of the mysteries. From a Latin commentary of the 14th path of Daleth (the Luminous Intelligence). Refers to Kashmal (copper). see 165, 92 Latin.

258

חורם Hiram, King of Tyre; architect of the Temple of Solomon. [2 Samuel 5:11 and 1 Kings]. see 634.

מזהר Illuminating, radiant. 2nd Path of Chokmah. [Godwin. 1999, p. 537.]

יחרם shall be utterly destroyed. Exodus 22:20.

259

ראובן Tribe of Reuben. "see, a son". Associated with Pisces (Godwin says Aquarius). The ensign of the Tribe of Reuben, according to the Talmud, bore the symbol of a mandrake, in allusion to the story in Genesis 30:15. Mandrakes were reputed to be aphrodisiac, and thus they relate to the very basis of incarnation. Moreover, they are plants sacred to the Semitic goddess corresponding to Aphrodite, or Venus. here is a connection between the Tribe of Reuben and the sign Pisces, because Venus is exalted in Pisces. Also assigned to alchemical multiplication, the 12th and last stage of the Great Work. Reuben mean: "see, a son." Multiplication is the act or process of increasing in number or quantity. Here the alchemist augments his elixir by repeated, or iterated fermentation. The whole body is tinged with the consciousness of the Stone. Through the Corporeal Intelligence a body is built suitable to the Life-power's expression in any environment. Subconsciousness is the active agency of the process during the sleep of the body, and the principle changes occur in the bloodstream, the endocrines and the interior stars. Then the adept can, by mental imagery alone, utilize currents of the universal energy through his body, to heal and to effect other changes in his environment. This leads to projection, the ability to change personality, physically, mentally and morally, and to turn or transmute base metals, "the refuse of the earth" into Gold and Silver. see 7, 54, 95, 30, 100, 162, 395, 466, 570, 501, 331, 739, 830 and Genesis 29:32.

Inman: Now ראה, *raah*, אר, and בן, in the Assyrian language, would signify 'the son of the All-seeing,' or 'the sun's son,' in which case it would not be very unlike our own 'Benson.' We may also trace it to *rab*, Hebrew רב, and *on*, און, and thus find 'great strength,' or 'my great strength,' for its signification. It is tolerably clear that the writer of Genesis 49:3 had some idea, when he designated Rueben 'my might, the beginning of my strength.' [Inman, 1942, Vol. 2., p. 569]

אדני צדק righteous Lord. Old Testament king

of Jerusalem [Joshua 10:3]. see 186, 389, 57.

טמיר   hidden, mysterious, secret.

יהוה זכרו   The Lord is his memorial [Hosea 12:5]. *Zikero* means: memory, resemblance; memorial. With different pointing "male."

נטר   to keep or guard; to bear grudges. "Keeper" in Canticles 1:5: "Do not look at me because I have dark skin, because the sun has tanned me; my mother's sons contended with me; they made me the keeper of the vineyards; but my own vineyard I have not kept. In [Nahum 1:2] "God is zealous, and the Lord is avenging; the Lord is avenging and is furious; the Lord will take vengeance on his adversaries, and he keeps wrath for his enemies."

Sepher Sephiroth: nitre [Crowley, 1977, p. 30]. Nitre is potassium nitrate or saltpeter, and ingredient in gunpowder, otherwise called natron. In earlier times it was supposed be the an nitrous element in the air or in plants. Written נתר in Jeremiah 2:22: "Although you wash yourself with *soda*, and use an abundance of soap, the stain of your guilt is still before me, declares the sovereign Lord." see 650.

להט החרב   The flaming sword [Genesis 3:24]. Understood to be a symbol for the holy influence (Mezla, 78), descending from sephirah to sephirah through the Tree of Life. It has the same basic meaning as the flash of lighting of Key 16. Note that להט = 44 = דם (blood). החרב = 215 = ארח (a narrow way) = זרח (to irradiate, to rise [as the sun]). The magical force is in the blood. It is called the flaming sword in the story of the fall of man, because that story refers to the descent of consciousness from higher and inner planes to the physical. The sword "turns every way" because it is the fire force in the blood-stream, circulating through our bodies, and therefore turning every direction. It keeps us out of Eden, for the time being, so that we may gain knowledge of the physical plane. Yet this same force in our blood is what we must learn to use in order to overcome the delusions which cause all our difficulties.   Lawhat, (flaming) means

also magical, or the force of enchantment.

גרון   throat; neck [Crowley, 1977, p. 30]. Site of the Venus center. In Isaiah 3:16: "The woman of Zion are haughty, walking along with outstretched neck, flirting with their eyes, tripping along with minking steps, with ornaments jingling on their ankles."

Βασιλεια. Basileia (Gr). Kingdom; Also queen.

οι θεμελιοι. hoi themelioi (Gr). the foundations. This occurs in Revelation 21:9. The foundations are stones, bearing the names of the 12 apostles who correspond, like the tribes of Israel, to the 12 zodiacal signs. See 2590 Greek.

260

I. Constant summation of the Magic Square of Mercury.

II. the Number of days in a Mayan cycle of a "sacred year."

צמצם   to contract or draw together; to be exact. With different pointing: to compress, to condense, to reduce, stint, to be united, be restricted. Designates the process which initiates a cycle of the Life-power's manifestation, at the interior center (Kether). Thus it makes the field, or vineyard, wherein the universe is established. This is the technical Qabalistic term indicating the fundamental process of manifestation-the contraction of אין סוף אור into Kether being the first stage. Compare with eastern doctrine of privaton as method of manifestation. see 166, 46, 36, 252, 315, 154, 224, 266, 314, 29, 700.

ורדים   Roses. Flowers of Venus and symbols of desires, which, woven together intelligently, as shown in Key 8, may be used to control and direct the Lion-force of volition. see 220.

טיריאל   Tiriel. Intelligence of Mercury. Designates the consciousness of the divine order which is the consequence of man's use of his objective mind as an instrument whereby he may link himself to the powers of super-consciousness. This angelic name means encompassed about by God and reminds us of Paul's quote: "In him we move and breath and have our being."[From the root מור, toor, to encompass, surround, commonly found in angelic names. מור in the Mishnak period, and in Talmudic usage, means mountain. Mountain in Aramaic is מורא. Thus the meaning of this name would be "encompassed about by God." אל as a suffix relates to the number 4, and the ideas of order, rule and beneficence. see 2080, 8.

כרם vineyard. An important mystical term. The vineyard is the "field" wherein Gepen, גפן, the vine is grown, from which comes the "blood of the grape" [Deuteronomy 32:14]. כרם conceals CR Kar, Lamb and רם, Ram, literally, "the High One." see 220, 166.

סר rebellious, sad, sullen, heavy, ill-humored, declined. The testing and trial of the higher Self (Samekh) reacting on the personality, to bring about regeneration (Resh).

"The circumferential sign joined to that of movement proper, constitutes a root whence issue all ideas of disorder, perversion, contortion, apostasy; also those of force, audacity, return, education, new direction, etc... סר and סור (comp.) That which is *disordered, rebellious, refractory*; which leaves its sphere to cause *trouble, discord*; that which is *vehement, audacious, independent, strong*: that which *distorts, turns aside* takes another direction; *is corrected.*" [d'Olivet, 1976, p.412.] see 700.

גרזים "The mountain where 6 of the tribes of Israel stood to bless." [Godwin, 1999, p. 537.] see Deuteronomy 11:29; Josh. 8:33.

ה-מרה The Moriah (i.e. Jerusalem, G.G. Locks). The land of Moriah was said to be the site of the sacrifice of Isaac, upon which the Temple of Solomon was later built (2 Chronicles 3:1).

מעננים soothsayers.

רכיל tale bearer.

הגברים the mighty men. [From גבר, Aramaic for man, male; warrior; phallus; rooster.] Also, the men of renown. See 255 and Genesis 6:4.

לפסילים *ineptos it profanos*. the inept and profane ones [Crowley, 1977, p. 31]. The inner meaning has to do with body cells which are unable to respond to the new pattern being cultivated.

טמירא the concealed. in Qabalistic texts, such as the Zohar, Kether is often given the title of the concealed (with all concealments), thus indicating that its working, through subconsciousness are occult, or hidden.

י:נ:ר I:N:R The first 3 initials of I.N.R.I the Rosicrucian (Lt) phrase represented by the four letters; one of whose meanings is alchemical: "the fire of nature (entirely) renews." see 270.

ירים exaltabitur, according to Rosenroth in K.D.L.C.K. (p.455) the meaning is: "shall be exalted", and he says it refers to Binah, since it is built above all the other sephiroth, among the supernals.

ניר lamp, light. 1 Kings 11:36: "And to his son I will give one tribe, that there may be a light (lamp) to David my servant always before me in Jerusalem, the city which I have chosen for myself to put my name there." Translated "lamp" in the *Interlinear NIV Bible*.

ברטחיאל Baratchial. Sentenial of the 12th Path of Beth on the inverse Tree of Life.

I. The 12th path or *kala is* attributed to the planet Mercury and its shadow masses in the form of Baratchial whose number is 260, which is also the number of Tiriel, the Intelligence of Mercury.

We expect to find a very precise reflection and inversion of this entity in the depths of the abyss where the path becomes a tunnel transmitting infernal influences. And this we do in fact find, for 260 is also the number of טמירא, the 'concealed' or 'hidden', and of כמר, 'a priest', not of the Light but of the Dark, for כמר means 'blackness', its root being the Egyptian *Kam*, 'black'. Although the 12th path is that of the Magician or Magus, the black or hidden priest should not be identified with the black magician, but with the Black Brother.

This is the *kala* of the Sorcerers, the *Monnim* (260) who transmit the light direct from beyond Kether to Saturn *via* the formula of duality [*Beth* and both being synonymous, implying duality]. Duality is expressed zoomorphically by the twin serpents Od and Ob, and by the ape - the shadow of the Magus who, according to tradition, distorts and perverts the Word of the Magus thus making a mockery of his work, as do the Black Brothers with their formula of duality.

This is evidenced by the symbols of Baratchial: two swords with inturned blades, suggesting intense concentration on the ego as opposed to the Self of All, flanking a ghostly face (mask) surmounted by a crescent moon. The sigil is a glyph of falsity and illusion reflected in the current of duality that reveals the Shadow of Thoth in the image of his ape or cynocephalus. This doctrine is expressed in the second verse of 231: The lightnings increased and the Lord Tahuti (i.e. Thoth) stood forth. The Voice came from the Silence. Then the One ran and returned.

The One is Kether, and it returned to its own power-zone because the vibration of this *kala is* illusory and cannot transmit truth. Its vibration duplicates that of the previous *kala,* thus creating a mere simulacrum of the creative spirit.

The Black Brother is double tongued, as the serpent, the magical power ascribed to the obverse aspect of which this path is the tunnel, is the Gift of Tongues, the Gift of Healing, and a Knowledge of Sciences. The healing here however is the healing of the ego, which merely aggravates with illusion the disease of false identity creating thereby a chain of endless suffering. Likewise, the Sciences of which knowledge is given are the sciences of darkness. Yet it must not be supposed that these are necessarily evil, it is merely that in the hands of a Black Brother they necessarily tend to sterility because directed towards the fulfillment of wholly personal ambitions. The dark sciences of this path contain the secrets of the *kalas* of the void.

The witches and wizards of this tunnel speak with 'voices' that are reflected into the aura of the Adept by the mechanism of unnatural acoustics associated with the mysterious ventriloquism of *Bath Kol,* the Voice of the Oracle. The *beth is* the house or womb of the supreme *kala,* and of the source of that ventriloquism that was primal in the myths of man, for the Word was endowed with flesh and issued from the belly of the mother. Here again the number of Baratchial, 260, corroborates the doctrine of this path of *beth* for it is the number of מינמען, 'pleasures', 'delights', and of ירכיך, 'thy thighs', which reveals the sexual nature of these pleasures.

The disease typical of this path is Ataxaphasia which here refers specifically to disorders of the faculty of speech, typified by the bestial howlings; or cachinnations of the prehuman creation and by that 'monstrous speech' *(mentioned in Liber 7)* that thrills beyond the veil of the void.

The dangers attendant upon the use of this *kala* are extreme, yet the advantages that may be gained would seem to outweigh them in that the Adept is able to transcend the merely conceptual transmission of imagery. He is thus able to maneuver specific atavisms at a level deeper than those he could penetrate as a Magus. This is because the silence of the outer spaces, like the music of the spheres, may be apprehended only when the ape-like chattering of the Magician's vehicle [his senses] has been subdued by contact with the transcosmic forces that sweep through this tunnel from the pathways of the Great Inane. The latter is the *Ain,* or Void, the unwinking eye which emits invisible rays that reify within the innermost sanctuaries of the Adept's non-being. He then becomes *The Magus of power* [The title of the tarot trump equated with the obverse path] in a true and totally different sense to that in which this power has been understood in any previous aeon. For that power *(shakti) is* primal and *does not exist* apart from the shadow, the solidification of which is the entified Magus whose Word is but falsehood and glamour. [Grant, 1994, pp. 162-165.]

μηρον. mehron. thigh (Gr). A euphemism for the phallus. [Apocalypse 19:16]. Closely associated with the 7th Path, which have to do with the generative and reproductive powers of the One Life. These forces in the human body which are the seat of strong desires must be controlled to win the victory whose reward is liberation. see 230, 710.

Benedictus Dominus Noster (Lt). Blessed be our Lord. Represents the total sum of the lines of an equilateral triangle (3x40 = 120) and the line of a heptagon (7x20 = 140). The triangle symbolizes the 3 supernal sephiroth, the heptagon the 7 subordinate sephiroth. Linked together by a circle surrounding them, which is 22, represents the letters of the Hebrew alphabet, the figure is a glyph of the 32 Paths of Wisdom, just as is the Tree of Life. see 140. A variant of a familiar Rosicrucian phrase. (Blessed is our Lord, who gave us a sign).

261

מוריה seen of Jah; a mountain on which Hiram died, and on which the temple of Solomon was built. This implies that the temple is erected on a foundation of fire. Mount Moriah signifies 'the hill of divine vision.' Jah (יה), is the divine name attributed to the Chokmah, which is the 'Root of Fire.' see 255.

אדם + חוה + קין + הבל Adam + Chavah + Cain + Habel. The first father (humanity) + the first mother (nature) + the false crown of will-power (Cain) + "a fleeting breath" (volatility of Mercury). see 1471, 45, 19, 160, 37.

יבלא + יבלע + יבלום Jubela, Jubelo, Jubelum. Three brothers and men of Tyre, wild formed part of the conspiracy to murder Hiram Abiff, architect of King Solomon's temple. Part of the third degree of Freemasonry. The gematria is certainly significant. see 194.

לראיך Goetia demon #14 by day of the 2nd decanate of Leo. This decanate corresponds to the 6 of wands, which is the operation of Tiphareth, sphere of the sun or higher self, in Atziluth, the wold of archetypes. see 741 & Appendix 11.

Goetia: "He is a Marquis great in power,

showing himself in the likeness of an archer clad in green, and carrying a bow and quiver. He causes all great battles and contests; and makes wounds to putrefy that are made with arrows by archers. This belongs unto Sagittary. He governs 30 legions of Spirits." [Mathers, 1995, p. 35]

דראון aborhance, abomination, loathsome. Isaiah 66:24: "And they will go out and look upon the dead bodies of those who rebelled against me; their worm will not die, nor will their fire be quenched, and they will be loathsome of all mankind."

Vince in Hoc, Deo duce, comite ferro (Lt). "I conquer in the (sign), with God my guide, my sword my companion." Motto engraved on reverse of pommel of magic sword [Eliphas Levi]. "I conquer in this sign" refers to the cruciform shape of the sword. Designates the letter Tav, the vibration of Saturn, and the crystallizing, specializing power of human activity. This is the secret of magical victories. "Deo Duce." We do so as conscious instruments of the Life-power. "Comite Ferro", the sword is our companion, our agency, our aid. It is the equlibrated use of the Mars force to overcome all errors. Vav or IHVH symbolizes the magical sword. To wield it is to make use o the potencies of sound-vibration, which is the basic power in all production of forms. see 236, 93.

262

חדרים secret places, chambers, rooms, conclaves.

K.D.L.C.K. (p.334) gives: *conclavia*, and says six parts are given, which are in Binah. He says it refers to the secret of the hidden places of Da'ath as well, and cites Proverbs 24:4: "Through knowledge [דעת, da'ath] its rooms are filled with rare and beautiful treasures." Da'ath (knowledge) is called the secret places of the Garden of Eden, and Binah [67] is the Garden of Eden.

מזהר Illuminating. The 2nd path of Chokmah. see 612.

עין בעין eye to eye. The Zohar says this means the perception of those who "see" God when they are filled with the Spirit of Wisdom.

I. I.R.Q.: Para. 645: Also it is written in Numbers 14:14: 'By whom thou, O Tetragrammaton! art seen eye to eye: and then the opening of the eyes is toward good.' [Mathers, 1993, p. 190]

II. This occurs in a discussion of the eyes of Microprosopus, i.e. Tiphareth. And in Isaiah 52:8 'Listen! your watchmen lift up their voices together they shout for joy, when the Lord returns to Zion, they will see it eye to eye [i.e. with their own eyes]." see 2500 (Greek)

אהרון Aaron. lofty; name of Moses brother and spokesman. The Biblical type of illuminated persons who are the "secret places," the localized, incarnate human expressions of the divine wisdom, see "eye to eye" with the One Reality. see 256, 73, 23, 15, 536, 912.

גבוראן Severities.

I. I.R.Q. Para. 668: "Also we have learned that there are 5 GBVRN [severities] in the conformation of Microprosopus, and they ascend in 1,400 GBVRN [severities], and they are extended in his nose, and in his mouth and in his arms, and in his hands and in his fingers [the 5 parts of the Microprosopus]." [Mathers, 1993, pp. 193-194]

II. Para. 672: "And all those powers, Geboran, commence to descend from the nose. And from it depend a thousand times a thousand and four hundred myriads in their single (forms).*

* This formidable sounding arrangement is only our previous 1,400, considred on another plane of operation, in the material world. [1,400 is its most material forms in Asiah]" [ibid, 1993, p. 194]

III. Later in the text the cause of the severities is said to be obtained out of the heavens. I.R.Q. Para. 685: "And whence is this obtained? Because it is written (Genesis: 19:24)" MN HShMim, *Men Ha-Shamayin*, out of heaven. (But the word השמים, *Ha-Shamayin*, it equivalent to) אש ו-מים, Ash Ve-Mim, fire and water, Mercy and Judgement, in the antithesis of that (condition) wherein no Judgment is found at all." [ibid, 1993, pp. 195-196] Note that Chokmah is the sphere of the fixed stars, the source of the Life-force which flows into Geburah. see 912.

הנורא terrible. There are preliminary adjustments that must be accomplished before the perception implied by "eye to eye" can take place. They are accomplished by painful tensions and conflicts between the various vehicles.

נזדר to admonish, warn. see 405

263 (prime)

ברכיאל Barkiel. "Lighting of God", Geomantic Intelligence of Scorpio. Archangel of Scorpio.

"One of the 7 Archangels, one of the 4 ruling Seraphim, angel of the month of February, and prince of the 2nd heaven, as well as the order of confessors. A ruler of the planet Jupiter and the zodiacal sign Scorpio and Pisces. With the angels Uriel and Rubiel, Barakiel is invoked to bring success in games of chance)." [Davidson, 1971, p. 69.]

אורון Auron. Angel of the 2nd decanate of Pisces. This decanate is ruled by the Moon and suggest the qualities of: pious, retiring, mediumistic. Pisces is connected with alchemical multiplication. see 259.

גרס to learn, study; to be crushed, be broken; to make grits; to accept a variant reading in a text. One learns from "geometry" and is nourished to become the perfect red stone.

אבדרון Abdaron. Angel of the 2nd decanate of Aquarius. The decanate is ruled by Mercury and suggest the qualities: independent, cultured, sociable. Aquarius is connected with alchemical dissolution. see 395.

264

גמאטריא gematria.

דם-כר Dam-Car. Blood of the lamb. In the *Fama*, the mystical "place" in "Arabia" where brother C.R. found the wise men who initiated him. Dam means blood, and Car or KR or C.R. means lamb. Thus blood of the lamb and a reference to Christ as the head of the True and Invisible Rosicrucian Order.

In Damcar Brother C.R. learned about medicine and mathematics. Initiation is based on occult mathematics, specifically the geometric proportions governing the manifestation of all forms in nature.

And medicine because initiation has to do with control of forces whose first awakening is represented by the friendliness of the Turks at Damascus. see 16, 444, 44, 220, 30, 824; 2863 (Greek).

ירדן descending; that which flows down. Jordan, the river of Palestine. Associated by qabalistic alchemist with the "Water of Minerals", that is, the fludic energy which takes form as minerals (as well as everything sense). Esoteric interpretations associate the Jordan with the blood stream of man. In the Rosicrucian allegory temple of Damcar is a place were C.R gained knowledge of the mystic fludic energy. "That which flows down"-down into the dead sea. The symbol of the mystic river of manifestation, flowing down to death- the stream of Maya, the illusive power of manifestation. See K.D.L.C.K. (p.455), Genesis 13:10 and 253, 914; 243 (Greek) *and True and Invisible Rosicrucian Order* [p. 75].

I. *The Aesch Mezareph*: "Jarden denotes a Mineral Water, useful in the cleansing of Metals and Leprous [i.e. impure metallic ores] Minerals. But this Water flows from two sources, whereof one is called Jeor [יאר] i.e. a fluid having the nature of the Right Hand, and very Bountiful ['Jamin' ins the right side]. The other is called Dan [דין, judgement, severity; referred to דן Dan, the name of the tribe], Rigorous and a very sharp Nature.

But it flows through the Salt Sea, which ought to be observed, and at length is thought to be mixed with the Red Sea; which is a Sulphurous Matter, Masculine, and known to all true Artists.

But know thou, that the name Zachu, i.e. Purity [זכו, 33], being multiplied by 8, the number of Yesod, produces the Number Seder [סדר, 264 = 33, zachin x 8], i.e. Order, which is 264. Which Number is also contained in the word Jarden; thus you may Remember, that at least Eight Orders of Purification are required, before the true Purity follows." [Westcott, 1997, p. 38]

II. Rosenroth in K.D.L.C.K. p.338: *Jarden*, and says it denotes a mineral water, etc.

חקוקים emanations. C.R. came into more direct contact with the emanations of the Life-power. K.D.L.C.K. (p.338) says that Chokmah, Binah, and Tiphareth are the first emanations.

מדרך footsteps, a space trodden upon; footprints, vestiges. C.R. recovered the vestiges of past experiences at Dam-car. Deuteronomy 2:5: "Meddle not with them, for I will not give you to their land, no, not so much as a foot breath..."

סדר to arrange, order, a straight row. C.R. established logical sequence and order (a straight row) in his ideas. In K.D.L.C.K. (p.455) it is spelled סדור and means: arrangement, order; offering, present; prayer-book, emanation; system, plan; setting up type. Rosenroth states in the above quotation from *Aesch Mezareph* that the word purity, multiplied by 8, the number of Yesod, produces the number 264: seder, order, thus at least 8 orders of purification are required before true purity follows.

רהטים gutters, troughs, channels, pipes. Human beings are channels of the Universal Life.

265

ק/פ Qoph/Peh. Mars (Peh) in Pisces (Qoph).

אור ה-חמה Light of the sun. (Isaiah 30:26). It has a bearing on certain facts of super-physical experience which are related to Binah.

ים הקדמוני the Primordial sea. Sphere of Saturn. Refers to Binah as being the Great Deep, or Abyss of Chaos, whose root is in the אין Ain or unmanifest. In Genesis 1:2: "And the earth was without form, and void; and darkness was upon the face of the deep. And the spirit of God moved upon the face of the waters." see 52, 67.

מחבא רוח a hiding-place from the wind. In Isaiah 32:2: "Behold, a king shall reign in righteousness. And a man shall be as a hiding-place from the wind, and a covert from the tempest; as rivers of water in a dry place, as the shadow of a great rock in a weary land." A prophecy referring to Jesus Christ. The Christ, or Messiah, the Anointed One, is represented by the sixth Sephirah, which is not only Ben, the Son, but also Ish, the Man. Thus we may understand that [איש], in the passage from Isaiah, refers to Tiphareth. see 311; 3493 (Greek).

ירמיה Old Testament prophet Jeremiah. Literally, "going up to the height of God", "God is exalted". Refers to the spiritual experience of those who have attained to the Rosicrucian grade corresponding to Binah (Master of the Temple). It is because of this experience that they are deserving of the Title, נגיד, Nagiyd, prince, leader. (Spelled ירמיהו on the text of Jeremiah.) see 67, 221 (Greek).

צעקה prayer; cry, shout, call, complaint. typical expression of all prophets and sees who call to the Great Mother and receive guidance form the intuitional level. *Sepher Sephiroth*: a cry of the heart, anguish, anxiety [Crowley, 1977, p. 31].

אדרכל architect [Crowley, 1977, p. 31]. This word does not occur in scripture.

הרס to pull down; broke down, tear down. In Job 12:14 "What he [God] tears down cannot be rebuilt; the man he imprisons cannot be released."

Μαριαμ + η αληθεια. Mariam + heh aletheia (Gr). Mary plus the truth. Mary, the mother of Christ means 'seas' and is related to the "Great Sea" Binah, or the cosmic mother. The truth is the key to many mysteries, including that of the center, to which Saturn is related in the Cube of Space. Recall the occult correspondence between Saturn and Venus in Libra and follow this clue. see 64, 72, 86, 172, 441.

Christian Rosencreutz (Lt). Mythical Founder of Rosicrucian Order.

et acceperunt viri pro omine (Lt). "and the men took as an omen, See Kings 20:33.

266

צמצום contraction.

ירון Termination of Qlippothic names for the 12 signs of the zodiac, has to do with imbalance of will (Yod = Mercury in Virgo), the regenerative force of solar radiation (Resh), intuition (Vav) and change (Nun).

אבן + ורדים by means of + roses. By means of roses, which are flowers of Venus and symbols of desires, man learns to depart form evil, and form a new combination, with the spirit of the mother. see 6, 260.

כמראה an appearance. Leviticus 13:43. In Numbers 8:4: according to the pattern. Numbers 8:4.

קולילפי Qulielfi. The Sentinel of the 29th Path (Tunnel) of Qoph on the Inverse Tree of Life.

I. Tunnel 29 is under the influence of the moon and is the haunt of the witch typified by Hekt, the frog-headed goddess and Lady of Transformation.

Qulielfi is the sentinel; her number is 266. The sigil shows 22 inverted lunar crescents; for Qulielfi represents the termination of the qliphoth of the 12 zodiacal signs. The central three crescents surmount a blind eye raying downward. This symbolism refers to the three viable days of the five-day lunar flow when the phallus turns a blind eye to the Eye of the Moon as she shreds her menstruum of astral creation. Hence the magical power attributed to this 29th kala is that of Casting Illusions and Bewitchments generally. As it is written:

'It is from the excrement of Choronzon that one takes the material for the creation of a God.'

The title of the tarot trump ascribed to Path 29 is *The Moon*, its alternative title being the 'Ruler of Flux and Reflux', and the magic mirror is the sole item of equipment in the lunar temple when Qulielfi is evoked. The mirror denotes the crepuscular state of consciousness peculiar to some regions of the astral plane. It is in this state that successful astral working is achieved, for at the borderland of sleep and waking are the 'liers in wait' [The Tunnel of Qulielfi leads to the city of Chorazin and the liers-in-wait are the Qliphotic ring-pass-not without the City. The Liers in Wait may equate with the *Ghagiel* (The Hinderers) listed in *Liber 777* as the Order of Qliphoth (column 8) associated with the Masloth or Sphere of the Fixed Stars.], those elementals that assist in the reification of the inherent dream.

The secret Symbol Of this tunnel is a dreaming woman performing in her twilight state the manual magick veiled beneath the symbol of the VIII° O.T.O. The number of Qulielfi confirms this symbolism for 266 is סור, meaning 'olla', 'a pot' or 'vase', a glyph of the vulva in its passive and solitary phase.

But the formula of this tunnel comports another element that is by no means as passive. It is under the sign of the Frog, the transformer from the waters. This totem typifies the evolution of consciousness from the amphibious to the terrestrial state. The frog is the leaper or jumper, which implies a specific formula in connection with the 'other side' of the Tree of Life. In the Cult of the Black Snake this formula is referred to as that of the *Voltiguers*, the vaulters or leapers.

Frater Achad who 'jumped' from Yesod to Binah by what he termed 'an unusual method', had recourse to the secret paths alluded to by Bertiaux. The deeper significance of Achad's magical leap from Yesod to Binah is resumed by the formula of the leapers as it applies to the tunnel of Qulielfi.

It may now be understood in which sense the tunnel of Qulielfi is equated with the Magic Mirror, the 'twilight of the place', for the moon that illumines this tunnel is of Daath, not of Yesod. Hence, in *Liber 231* we read:

> By her spells she invoked the Scarab, the Lord Kheph-Ra, so that the waters were cloven and the illusion of the towers was destroyed.

Khep-Ra is literally the backside of Ra (the Sun), i.e. the Moon. The waters refer to *Mv*, the water of the Abyss. The towers are those of the Black or Dark Brothers. This points to a mystery concerning the true meaning of Black Magic, for the Dark Doctrine is that of the Dark Brothers who appear upon earth (i.e. on the hither side of the Tree of Life) as Black Magicians.

Frater Achad himself approached very nearly to an under standing of this mystery of true Black Magic, but, like many occultists before and after him, he was blinded by assuming that Universe 'B' is 'evil' whereas it is - like Satan - merely the adversary of the sense of individuality that is generated in man by illusory egoidal consciousness. In Universe 'B' occurs the 'dissolution ... in the kisses Of Nu' (i.e. the waters of the Abyss) that Hadit promises. This also explains the nature of the *qliphoth*, the *Nashimiron* or 'malignant women' that are said to haunt the tunnel of Qulielfi. [Grant, 1994, pp. 239-244.]

267

מרכז center.

מרכבה the Chariot. see key 7. The vehicle of personality through which the divine life functions. see 150, 373.

Rosenroth in K.D.L.C.K. p.553 gives: *currus, vehiculum thronus, sella curulus*. He says one source attributes the higher vehicle to Gedulah, Geburah and Tiphareth, and the lower one Netzach, Hod and Yesod. Another correlates the higher chariot to the 4 cherubim: Chokmah of Aquarius (the man); Binah to the eagle; Gedulah to Leo, and Geburah to Taurus. Whereas the lower vehicle comprises Netzach (Leo), Hod (Taurus) and Yesod (Eagle) and Tiphareth as the man. Still others called Malkuth the Chariot.

אסור prisoner. suggest that illusion of separateness in each chariot of God. With different pointing: 1. forbidden, prohibited; 2. *ehsur*: bond, chain; 3. *issur*: forbidden thing; prohibition.

גרן אטד threshing-floor of Atad. Genesis 50:10: "And they came to the threshing floor of Atad, which is beyond Jordan (264), and there they mourned with a great and very sore lamentation; and he (Joseph) made a mourning for his father seven days." אטד is a symbol of union and is related to Briah, the creative world of Water, where archetypal ideas are combines with each other. It has the same value as words for: gold, beloved; a sacrifice; to show the way; a gift; strength. see 14, 264.

ורכיאל Urakiel. Geomantic intelligence of Leo; Archangel of Leo.

Davidson says the name is Verchiel or Zerachiel and says he is "angel of the month of July and ruler of the sign of Leo in the Zodiac... Verchiel is also one of the rulers of the Order of Powers. Budge, *Amulet and Talismans*, equates Verchiel with Nakiel. According to Papus. Verchiel (here called Zerachiel) is governor of the sun." [Davidson, 1971, p. 305.]

חרטמי magicians, of-magicians. see Genesis 41:8.

יראון see, they-see. see Deuteronomy 4:28.

268

רבוני my Lord. Hebrew form of epithet given to Jesus by Mary in John 20:46: "Jesus said unto her, Mary. She turned herself, and said unto him, Rabboni; which is to say Master." The passage cited took place at the Resurrection. Recall that Daniel (God the Judge, 95) was called the Master of Magicians (*Dan* = 54 = Judgement = Scorpio = Nun). see 50, 106, 700.

בידון Biron. Angle of the 3rd decanate of Gemini. see 918.

ירחים months, moon. Exodus 2:2.

269 (prime)

ארחין by-ways. The path of spirit (Aleph) in regeneration (Resh) works through its field of expression (Cheth), which are as by-ways in the evolution of will (Yod) through change (Nun).

כרוביאל Kerubiel. Angel of Binah or Briah (3 of Cups). This implies limitation, or form-building on the plane of mental creativity.

"Eponymous head of the Order of Cherubim. According to 3 Enoch, Kerubiel's body is 'full of burning coals... There is a crown of holiness upon his head... and the bow of the shekinah is between his shoulders.'" [Davidson, 1971, p. 166.]

חי אנכי לעלם I live forever. In Deuteronomy 32:40: "For I lift my hand to heaven, and say, I live forever." see 829.

נדריה she has vowed, vows-of-her. Numbers 30:5.

סמנגלוף Semangeloph. On of the three angels invoked against Lilith.

270

רע evil [Isaiah 45:7]. In all senses, including human wickedness as well as natural misfortunes. The evil that the eye (Ayin) sees under the sun (Resh). With different vowel points: friend, companion; thought, aim, purpose, desire; noise, shout. When Heh is added, רעה, it becomes a verb meaning to feed, graze a flock, as a shepherd leads his sheep. see 45, 367, 311, 160, 479, 288.

I. "We have seen the movement principle, acting from the center to the circumference, modified in turn, by light, fire, water, air, ethereal fluid, according to the roots רא, רה, רו, רי: Now, where is the same movement departing form the root רו and degenerating more and more toward the material sense, to become in the root רע, the emblem of that which is terrestrial, obscure and evil. This is worthy of the closest attention.

רע and רעע (intens.) That which is bent, bowed down; that which is brought together to be made compact; that which becomes fragile, brittle; that which breaks and is reduced to powder: physical and moral evil; misery, malignancy, misfortune, vice, perversity, disorder." [d'Olivet, 1976, pp. 452-453.]

סטרא side, border, power, influences (usually adverse); limit, limit of the sun. Aramaic origin. As a rule sitra is used to designate adverse or evil influences. Its basic meaning is one which implies limitation.

Zohar I. (p.50): "The adverse influence (רע סטרא sitra ahra, evil power of demonry = 480 = לילית Lilith, the Qlippoth of Malkuth) which brings suffering and chastisement is therefore necessary in the world, since it rouses in man fear from through chastisement a man becomes filled with the true fear of God, and does not harden his heart; for it he does then "he that hardens his heart shall fall into evil [Psalm 28], to wit, into the hands of that 'adverse influence' which is called 'evil'". Thus we have a love which is completed in both phases, and from this results a true and perfect love."

אלף-למד-פה Aleph. full spelling of Aleph. Signifies the complete manifestation, or extension, of the powers of רוח, Rauch, of which Aleph [א] is the alphabetical symbol.

נכר strange, different. The appearance of endless mutation (Nun), the turning wheel of change (Kaph), the appearance of limitation (wall in fairy ring in Key 19, Resh). But when the Wheel becomes the fairy ring (under foot) then the land in no longer strange. In Psalm 137:4: "How shall we sing the Lord's song in a strange land?" see 262.

Paul Case: "The Lord song (verse 4) is שיר יהוה = 536 = the world of making, Assiah, the material world עולם העשיה. 'In a strange land' is the field of appearances produced by the serpent power, which is pictured in Key 8 as the lion. When we are 'in' that land we are deceived by the appearances of separateness. Thus נכר, strange = רע, which is created [Isaiah 45:7]. It is the - רע darkness. Yet אדמה נכר, strange land = 319 = life forevermore חיים על-עולם, the blessing of Psalm 133. The clue is in נכר, 'strange', from a verbal root meaning to differentiate, to make distinctions. If we are in the state of consciousness where we are preoccupied with the differentiated appearances of multiplicity, we do not perceive that the world of Assiah, the world of making or construction, is really the song of Tetragrammaton, i.e., the harmonious concord or all the manifestation of the Life-power. The song seems to be a discord, and the discord is evil, or רע. Note too, that אדמה 'land' is a metathesis of Adam האדם = 50 = the letter Nun, and also the gates of Binah, the mother, which are always represented by 50. Furthermore, the word for blood דם is probably a contraction of Adam, and certainly is derived form the root אדם, to be red. Here we have an allusion to the earthy, or carnal consciousness. While we are in this, we cannot sing the song of Tetragrammaton, that is, make our own personal 'making' in unison with the song of Tetragrammaton... But "except Tetragrammaton build the house, they labor in vain that build it" [Psalm 127:1]. The builder is Tetragrammaton,

and all our building is clumsily unless our hands are conscious working as instruments of Tetragrammaton, and unless or conception that material world is that is truly the song of Tetragrammaton."

ר/ע Resh/Ayin. Sun (Resh) in Capricorn (Ayin).

כנען flat or low. As a proper noun, the name of a son of Ham and grandson of Noah. Genesis 9:22: "And Ham, father of *Canaan*, saw the nakedness of his father [Noah], and told his two brethren without." Canaan was the progenitor of the Phoenicians, and the people living west of the Jordan (the previous to the conquest by Israel). Canaan, the promised land. The name is found on Phoenician coins, and it is probable that it was known also to the Carthaginians. see 840, 160.

כוכב מיעקב A star out of Jacob. Numbers 24:17: "I shall come a star out of Jacob, and a scepter shall rise out of Israel, and shall smite the corners of Moab, and destroy all the children of Sheth." Jacob means "to supplant", the star suggest the hexagram, symbolic of Tiphareth; Sheth means "replaced, compensation". see 182, 620, 700, 494.

בריחם bars, boots, latches; axes; clavicles, shoulder-blades, levers. The Ego or higher self resides in the heart center, between the shoulder-blades. It is barred from the profane, who are unprepared. The same letters may be read to mean: flying serpents. In the Old testament this second meaning is associated with the "crooked serpent" and also called "Leviathan." There is a whole body of secret doctrine behind this reference which connects it with נחש (358).

י:נ:ר:י Hebrew equalivant of Latin *I:N:R:I* The abbreviation of sentence nailed on the cross of Jesus when he was crucified, *Jesus Nazareus rex Judaorum.* "Jeusus of Nazareth, King of the Jews." *Ingi natura renovata interga* "whose love nature (or passion) renews the whole"; *Intra nobis regnum Dei* "interior (among us) kingdom of God"; *Isis natura regina ineffabilis*, "Isis, the ineffable, Queen of Nature." *Ignis*, translated "love", is defined in the Latin dictionary as meaning: fire, brightness, glow of passion. see 46, 908.

Aσενεθ. Asenath (Gr). wife of Joseph

(Septuagint Greek). The Hebrew is אסנת, aw-se-nath (511) "dedicated to Neith," and daughter of Potipherah, Priest of On, whom the King of Egypt bestowed in marriage upon Joseph. Scholars have speculated that the name Asenath as representative of a Coptic compound assheneit means, "she who is of Neith." Note the correspondence between "Isis, the ineffable, Queen of nature," and Asenath "she who is of Neith' (Isis-Neith). In the Old Testament, Joseph is never refereed to as a tribe, although he was a son of Jacob. Instead, his two sons are referred to as each a half-tribe, Ephraim and Menasseh.

271 (prime)

אסרי binding, tethering-of. In Genesis 49:11: He will tether his donkey (Capricorn) to a vine (Tiphareth), his colt to the choicest branch…

לאמר saying. to say. see Exodus 6:10.

272

כרבים The Mighty Ones (the *Cherubim*). The order of angels associated with Yesod. These are the beings associated with the formative, reproductive powers of Yesod [80]. Written כרבים in Genesis 3:24: "After he drove the man out, he placed on the east side of the Garden of Eden Cherubim and a flaming sword flashing back and forth to guard the way to the Tree of Life." see 351, 278, 1227.

"הכרבים, *that-self-same-Cherubim*... The root רב, which contains the idea of all multiplication, of all infinite number. It is used to the plural and governed by the assimilative sign ב." [d'Olivet, 1976, p. 120.]

עבר to cause to be pregnant, to be with child; to transgress repeatedly. This correlation connects the Kerabim with the reproductive aspects of Yesod. With different pointing *aybahr*: to become pregnant; to be intercalated, to be disfigured, be spoilt;

עבר region beyond; region across, side. With different pointing *awbahr*: to pass, pass over. Deuteronomy 9:1: "Hear O Israel, thou art to pass over Jordan (264) this day, to go in to

possess nations greater and mightier than thyself, cities great and fenced up to heaven. see 278.

ערב Evening, the close of the Day. Sometimes the direction west. With different vowel points: Raven. Also the progenitor of the Hebrews, mentioned in Genesis 10:24. see 998, 278.

I. *Orb*, meaning 'the evening', or an Arab, i.e. a person living in the West. The West is the place of Babalon. Her totem, the goat, is the glyph of earth in the west as the place of the setting sun. *Obr*, a metathesis of *Orb* denotes 'tears, 'myrrh-dropping', from the Egyptian word *abr*, 'ambrosia, 'ointment', and from *aft*, meaning 'exuding', 'distilling'. [Grant, 1994, p. 229.]

II. "ערב. *west-eve*... This name famous in all the ancient mythologies, is the Erebus which we have drawn from the Greek ερεβος. Its signification is not doubtful. It always recalls to the mind something obscure, distant our of sight. The Hellenists who have rendered it in this passage by εσπε α and the Latins by *vespere*, 'evening', making visibly weakened the meaning. It signifies the Occident, and all ideas which are related to it, not only in Hebrew, but in Chaldaic, Syriac, Ethopic and in Arabic. The name of the last-mentioned people is derived there from therefrom." [d'Olivet, 1976, pp. 35-36.]

III. He also sites Genesis 8:7 and translates: "And-he-let-out what-constitutes *Ereb* (westerly darkness) that-issued-forth by-the-issuing and-periodically-repairing, till-the-drying-up of-the-waters from-off-the-earth." [p.231]

"And he sent forth Ereb (western darkness) which went to and fro (with periodic movement) until the drying up of the waters upon the earth." [ibid., pp. 335-336]

IV. And comments: הערב. *Ereb*... I am well aware that the Hellenist and after them, the author of the Latin vulgate, have seen in *Ereb*, that famed *Ereb* of ancient cosmogonies, only a simple raven: transforming thus a vast and mysterious idea into an idea petty, and ridiculous: but I am also aware that there same Hellenist who worked upon the version which bears the name of the Septuagint, Essences and consequently initiates in the Orallaw, penetrated the hieroglyphic meaning of the sepher deeply enough not to be the dupes of such a metamorphosis. One cannot read them with any kind of attention without discovering their perplexity. Not knowing how to disguise the periodic returns of the alleged bird, and fearing that the truth might shine forth in spite of them, the decided to change completely the original text and be delivered of the Ereb which perturbed them, by saying that the raven being sent forth returned no more. But in this instance, everything betrays their pious fraud. The Samaritan text agrees with the Hebraic text and makes it unassailable; the Samaritan version and the Chaldiac Targum say alike that *Ereb*, given liberty, takes an alternating movement of going forth and coming back; finally Saint Jerome, forced to recognize this truth, can only weaken the force of the phrase by saying, without doubting the first verb and changing their temporal modification of it, *'qui egrediebatur et revertebatur.'*

It must be remembered that to reveal the depth of this hieroglyphic expression, the Ereb was not set at liberty, and did not take this periodic movement until after the release of the nocturnal light [the moon] referred to in the preceding verse." [ibid., pp. 229-230.]

V. The Raven of Noah returns not again is: "A symbol of the lower mind, which goes forth to the things of the world." [Gaskell, 1981, p. 613.]

VI. A. Jukes writes: "The dove and the raven are sent forth, figuring (for they are birds of heaven, and the heaven is the understanding) certain powers or emotion of the understanding, both pure and impure. In the action of these is shown the working of the good and evil which to the last remains with us. The raven, finding its food in carrion, figures these inclinations with feed on dead things." [Types of Genesis, p.120]

רעב to be hungry, to be famished. Metathesis of ערב and עבר. Note that Resh comes before Ayin.

בער consume, kindle, injure; brutish. The power of Beth (Key 1) through the agency of Ayin (Key 15) resulting in Resh (Key 19).

רבע to be square, to be stretched out, lie down; to lie with, mate (of animals), to have connection with a beast; to commit sodomy; to fructify the ground. With different pointing: 1. *ribeyah*: to do something for the fourth time; to make a quadrilateral; to water the soil; 2. *rubah*: to be

square, have four sides; 3. *rebah*: lying down; a forth part; one side of a four-sided figure; rain, fructifying showers; 4. *robah*: one fourth; fourth of a kab; 5. *raydeh*: descendant of the 4th generation.

רינו Goetia demon #27 by day of the 3rd decanate of Sagittarius. see Appendix 11.

Goetia: "He appears in the from of a monster. He teaches the art of rhetoric very well, and gives good servants, knowledge of tongues, and favors with friends or foes. He is a Marquis and great earl; and their be under his command 19 Legions of Spirits." [Mathers, 1995, p. 40]

273

I. 21x13 = 273 = number of 13s on the great seal of the U.S.

אבן מאסו הבונים the stone which the builders refused. (Masu is from מאס: to despise, reject, refuse.) A reference to the philosopher's stone. The principle of human equality, founded upon the presence of the mystical Christos with the temple of every personality. The syllables of the "substitute" of the lost word is concealed in these 3 words. see 108, 142 Latin and Psalm 118:22.

אור גנז the Hidden Light. Transmitted from generation to generation through the mystery schools. see 203.

חרם אביו Hiram Abiff. the name of the central figure in the legend of Freemasonry. One of the three original Master Masons. Haram was the son of a widow who was of the tribe of Naphtali (Virgo). In the Egyptian mysteries Khoor or Horus, the Hawk-headed God, was the probable derivation of the name Hiram. Note that Horus, Hiram, Krishna, Christ and C.R. all have the sound (KHR). see 19, 80, 254, 640, 465, 751 [Greek], 1378, 833 (Greek).

"Among the manuscripts of Dr. Sigismund Bacstron, the initiated Rosicrucian, appears the following extract from Von Welling concerning the true philosophic nature of the Masonic Chiram: 'The original word חרם, Chiram, is a radical word consisting of three consonants Cheth, Resh and Mem. (1) Cheth, signifies *chamah*, the sun's light, i.e. the *universal*, *invisible, cold fire of nature* attracted by the Sun, manifested into *light* and sent down to us and it every planetary belonging to the solar system. 2. *Resh*, signifies *Ruach* [214], i.e. *spirit, air, wind*, as being the vehicle which *conveys* and *collects the light* into numberless foci, wherein the solar rays of light are agitated by a circular motion and manifested in *heat* and *burning fire*. 3. Mem, signifies *majim, water, humidity*, but rather the *mother of water*, i.e. *radical humidity* or a particular kind of *condensed air*. These three constitute the universal agent or fire of nature in one word CHiram, not Hiaram.'" [Hall, 1994, p. 78.]

ארבע   four. The principle of equality symbolized by the 4 equal lines of a square, incorporated into the pyramid of the Great Seal of the U.S. Also the four elements, balanced in human personality. The sign of the cross or crossing, and of the four directions of space.

"ארבע, four... its root רב involves every idea of strength, of solidity, of greatness, resulting form extent and numerical multiplication... formed of the sign of movement proper Resh, and that of generative action, contains all ideas of grandeur and multiplication. If the last character is doubled, as in רבב, this would acquires an endless numerical extent; if it is followed by the sign of material sense, as in רבע, it becomes the expression of solidity, of physical force, and of all ideas attached to the cube. It is in this state that it represents the number four." [d'Olivet, 1976, pp. 78, 153.]. For other numerals, see 13, 400, 636, 348, 600, 372, 395, 770, 570, 441.

גער   to rebuke, scold; to curse. With different pointing: reproach, reproof. The refusal of Hiram Abiff to reveal the master Mason's word. The Declaration of Independence rebuked the tyranny and oppression of the British crown, to establish a "new order of the ages".

גרע   To scrape off by implication: to shave, remove, lesson, or withhold, to withdraw, diminish, to restrain, to subtract; to form kernels (of fruit). In his death Hiram takes away the secret-the hidden light of Freemasonry.

רגע   Primitive root meaning to toss violently and suddenly. The Declaration of Independence set in motion a series of political changes which have transformed the world. It analyzed the

fundamentals of natural law. The hidden light sets in motion changes in human personality. With different pointing: a wink of the eyes, i.e. a very short space fo time; instant, moment, space, suddenly [Strong's dictionary].

I. רגע is connected with square in Chapter 1 of the 3rd book of Abra-melin (first square, 2nd column), in connection with יראגע. [Mathers, 1976, p. 165]

אוראניה   Uraniah. Urania, Greek muse of Astronomy.

אליפז לוי צהד   Elphas Levi Zahed. Pseudonym of Alphonse Louis Constant. see 128, 46, 99.

αθανασια. Anthanasia (Gr). immorality. The Declaration of Independence based its doctrine on the principal of immorality, familiarized in the Masonic Legend of Hiram Abiff. This is the stone which the builder rejected and the "hidden light".

Written αθανασιαν in 1 Corinthians 15:53, 54: "For this corruptible must be clothed with incorruptibility; and this moral must be clothed with immorality. (54) and when this corruptible shall be clothed with incorruptibility, and this mortal, shall be clothed with immorality, then will that word be accomplished which has been written, 'death was swallowed up in victory.'" Also with reference to the king of kings, Christ, in 1 Timothy 6:16: "The only one possessing immortality, inhabiting light inaccessible; whom no one of man has seen, nor is able to see; to whom be honor and might everlasting. Amen."

η κλις. heh kleis (Gr). the key. Literally "A thing to close the door with" from the outside (as well as what opens the door, i.e. Daleth-creative imagination, to the inside). This is the key of the Gnosis or Knowledge, which Jesus accused the scribes of having taken away in Luke 11:52. In Isaiah 22:22 it mentions the Key to the House of David מפתח בית דוד [954]. see 954, 528 & Revelation 3:7.

274

בעבר   near to. see Genesis 50:10.
ריחנו   stench, our stench. see Exodus 5:21.

רעד trembling. see Exodus 15:15.

275

רעה   shepherd, to graze a flock; friend, companion; evil.

רהע   39th name of Shem ha-Mephorash, short form. see 306 & Appendix 10.

יאר דין   River of judgement; *fluvius iudicum* [K.D.L.C.K. p. 177]. *The Aesch Mezareph: yar din* is the river of judgement flowing out of the north. [Westcott, 1997, p. 9] On the Cube of Space, the northern face is attributed to Mars; the path of Shin (Key 20, Judgment) connects the northern (Mars) and southern (Sun) faces. The Mars force must be directed to the Sun via transformation and resurrection (Shin) to avoid "evil".

אחוריים   On the rear, hindmost, backward posterior. K.D.L.C.K. (p.72) "Which pertains to Malkuth, and it is so-called because it is last (in order) from the Atziluth plane."

דירה נאה   *domicilum pulchrum*; beautiful dwelling [K.D.L.C.K. p.395]. A reference to the 2nd Heh of IHVH, which pertains also to Malkuth, and is one of the names for the divine presence, Shekinah, who is moreover called the stone, דר (pearl) and the beautiful dwelling; that is, when she departs form her archetypal home in Binah to dwell in the kingdom of God. The divine presence brings the friendship of the father.

סרטו   scripture [Crowley, 1977, p. 32]. This word is not found in scripture.

Of סר d'Olivet: The circumferential sign joined to that of movement proper, constitutes a root which issue all ideas of disorder, perversion, contortion, apostasy; also those of force, audacity, return, education, new direction etc... That which is *disordered, rebellious, refractory;* which leaves its sphere to cause *trouble, discord;* that which is *vehement, audacious, independent, strong*: that which *distorts, turns aside,* takes another direction; *is corrected* etc. Of טו he says: That which arrest, which opposes resistance." [d'Olivet, 1976, pp. 412, 357.]

צדקנו יהוה   Jehovah (IHVH) our righteousness. Jeremiah 23:6: "In the days Judah shall be saved, and Israel shall dwell safely: and this is his name whereby he shall be called the Lord of righteousness." Recall that Judah is connected with the sign of Leo = heart or Sun = alchemical digestion. Israel means "he shall rule as God". Righteousness is linked with Chesed, Mercy, the sphere of cosmic memory, or Jupiter. see 30, 1801 (Greek).

סיהרא   the Moon. Chesed is the sphere of the cosmic moon, wherein the waters of memory are gathered. see 87.

כנור   a cithara; harp, lyre; violin. Connected with the physical body.

"So this thy body is the instrument whereon may be played the song of life. Nay, it is more than this; for on this harp of ten thousand strings, the wind of the spirit moveth ever, and soundeth night and day the melodies and harmonies of the eternal song. Yet few there be with ears to hear, for that hearing is too often dulled by the noisy clamor of the world's illusion." [Book of Tokens: Epilog - Malkuth]

אחודראון   Achodaraon. Lesser angel governing the triplicity by night of Libra. Note that Libra corresponds to the letter Lamed, the ox-goad, whose primary meaning is "to teach, instruct." The one teacher is life, helping its creation through recollection. see 74, 926.

אריטון   Ariton. Demon king of water and the west. Water indicates receptivity; the west is the direction of manifestation. Note also by adding Heh to ארי, the first three letters of this word, we obtain אריה lion (216). The final three letters, טון = 65, the value of הס, hush, keep silence. The lion is the animal nature; silence is one way to conserve energy for constructive work. Demon suggest subconscious imbalance, resulting in negative aspects of these qualities. In the Tarot minor arcana this decanate is assigned to the 5 of Wands. This represents the operation of Geburah, sphere of volition or Mars, in Atziluth, the archetypal world of ideas. When ill-aspected, as here, this can indicate cruelty, violence, lust and prodigality. The remedy is to learn to identify personal will with the one will manifest in the cosmic order, and so free oneself from the delusion of separateness. see 926.

רעו name of one of the descendants of Shem in Genesis 11:21: "And after he became the father of Serug, *Rev* lived 207 years and had others sons and daughters."

כרוכל Crocell. Goetia demon #49 by night of the 1ˢᵗ decanate of Leo. see Appendix 11.

Goetia: "He appears in the from of an angel. He is a duke great and strong, speaking something mystically or hidden things. He teaches the art of geometry and the liberal sciences, he, at the command of the Exorcist, will produce great noises like the rushing of may waters, although there by none. He warms waters, and discovered baths. He was of the Order of Potentates, or Powers, before his fall, as he declared unto the King Solomon. He governs 48 Legions of Spirits." [Mathers, 1995, p. 53]

277 (prime)

זרע seed, fruitfulness, sperm. One of the pairs of opposites (creativity, fertility) assigned to the letter Resh. "Seed" is also connected with the power of the letter Nun (to sprout, to grow). see 200, 385, 785.

למרבה for multiplying.

רעוא grace, benevolence; will, pleasure [Aramaic].

גימטריה gematria; geometry (variant spelling).

סהיבר Sahibar. Angel of the 3ʳᵈ decanate of Leo. This decanate is ruled by Mars, and suggest the qualities: fearless, outspoken, animated.

הכרבים The Cherubim. Genesis 3:24: "So he drove out the man; and he placed at the east of the Garden of Eden Cherubims, and a flaming sword which turned every way, to keep the way of the Tree of Life. see 272, 678.

כימאור Goetia demon #66 by night of the 3ʳᵈ decanate of Capricorn. The last three letters of this name suggests אור aur, light. In the Tarot minor arcana this decante is assigned to the 4 of

Pentacles. see Appenidx 11.

Goetia: " He is a Marquis, mighty, great, strong and powerful, appearing like a valiant warrior riding upon a goodly black horse. He rues over all spirits in the parts of Africa. His office is to teach perfectly grammar, logic, rhetoric, and to discover tings lost or hidden, and treasures. He governs 20 Legions of Infernal." [Mathers, 1995, p. 63]

278

עורב raven. an alchemical term. related also to Binah, Arabia, sterility or agreeableness. Alternate spelling [Strong's Dictionary] see 272, 136 (Lt).

כרובים Cherubim; "the strong" or "the mighty ones". Angelic Choir associated with Malkuth (some sources Yesod) and of Binah of Briah, the sphere of Saturn of form-building in the world of creation. Variant spelling, see 272.

עולם המוטבע Natural World. The material world. The physical plane.

עזרא Ezra. The biblical prophet. see 76.

בעור Beor; the father of Bela, the first king of Edom. Genesis 36:32: "Bela, son of Beor became king of Edom. His city was named Dinhabah." According to Inman: "possibly a variant of Peor. Gesenius translates it 'torch', and furst, 'a shepherd'. A torch, a piece of pine wood, or other straight thing, burning at the end, was an euphemism. Hogarth, in his curious engraving 'before' and 'after' has symbolized the same idea by a sky-rocket. It is, of course, well known to all, that Cupid (or desire) bears a torch as an emblem with the flame burning upwards; at death, or at funeral ceremonies, the torch hands down, extinguished, or effete." [Ancient Faiths, Volume 1, p. 346]

עובר Variant spelling of עבר to pass over. see 272.

ארבעה four (variant spelling, see 273).

ערוב wild beast, the fourth of the 10 plagues of Egypt. Written עוב in Exodus 8:21: "If you do

320

not let my people go, I will send swarms of flies (i.e. עוב) on you and your officials, on your people and into your houses. The houses of the Egyptians will be full of flies, and even the ground were they are."

279

אלף-למד-פה + גו Aleph or spirit, spelled in full + middle, center. It is the working power of spirit in the center of all things which completes the operation of the sun in man. Note that 279 reduces to 9, which represents attainment or a goal or cycle of manifestation. see 111, 270, 9, and Key 9.

גן אלהים + מלכים Garden of the Elohim or creative powers plus kings. The garden is the place of birth or creation of the philosopher's stone of alchemy. The "kings" are attributed to Tiphareth in the material world, and are the seven interior stars (chakras). As above = Elohim; so below = alchemical metals. see 139, 140, 52, 86, 90.

סבידו Leprosy. Rosenroth in K.D.L.C.K. (p.458) cites Exodus 4:6. "So Moses put his and into his cloak, and when he took it out, it was leprous, like snow."

וינזרו and they must respect. see Leviticus 22:2.

280

סנדלפון Sandalphon. The Archangel of Malkuth, symbolizing the passive, receptive, feminine aspect of God, the basis of the manifest. 280 reduces to 10, Kingdom. "Then name of the angle Sandalphon, the angel or of the wood of the world of Assiah, since the greatest part of it are sterile trees." [Book of Concealed Mystery V:28] see 101.

פר bull; victim; offering. A bullock, as breaking forth in wild strength [Strong's Dictionary].

רעי my shepherd [Psalm 23].

הערה to make naked, uncover, to pour out, to have sexual contact; to mix liquids. See Leviticus 20:18.

יסיר he removed (the veil). see Exodus 34:34

יער a forest. see Joshua 17:18.

מפנינים more than rubies. see Proverbs 8:11.

עיר From a city (a place guarded by waking or a watch), city, court, town [Strong's dictionary]. Anger, wrath in Hosea 11:9: "I will not carry my fierce anger, nor will I turn and devastate Ephraim. For I am god, and not man-the Holy One among you. I will cone *in wrath* [בעיר]." A messenger, angel in Daniel 4:13: "I saw in the visions of my head upon my bed, and, behold, a *watcher* and a holy one came down from heaven."

עדי 46th Shem ha-Mephorash, short form. see 311 & Appendix 10.

רכס to bind, to chain, fasten; to button up [Exodus 28:28]. With different pointing: 1. to stamp, trample over wetted grain; 2. mountain ridge; rough ground [Isaiah 40:4].

צ + פ + נ + מ + כ Kaph + Mem + Nun + Peh + Tzaddi. Sum of the five letters having a final form. These five letters denote the severest of judgements. "Five kings (which are the roots of the judgements) betake themselves into swift flight before four (the 4 letters of the Tetragrammaton, which bear with them the influx of benignity). They cannot remain (since the judgements and rigors cease and flee)." [Book of Concealed Mystery V:28]

יער Yaear. Angel of the wood of the world of Assiah [Crowley, 1977, p. 32]. In Canticles 5:1: "I am come into my garden, my sister, my spouse: I have gathered my Myrrh with my spice; I have eaten my honeycomb [יערי, honeycomb-of-me] with my honey; I have drunk my wine with my milk."

דגדגירון Dagdagiron. The snakey ones, The Qlippoth of Capricorn [Crowley, 1977, p. 32]. Kenneth Grant: "'the fishy', which denotes the feminine nature." [Grant, 1994, p. 230.] The derivation is from *dag* (7), fish; to multiply abundantly. Note that Capricorn is symbolized by a goat with the tail of a fish.

281 (prime)

פאר to be radiant, to gleam, to shine, to glow, to bloom, to explain, to make clear, to adorn. With different pointing: 1. to explain, to make clear, to beautify, glorify; to go over the bough, glean; 2. *pawar*: Head-ornament, diadem, turban, headdress. Root of Tiphareth, which is the seat of mental activities whereby ideas are clarified.

אפר ashes.

ערוה nakedness; genital organs; unchastity, loudness, obscenity, sexual intercourse. The opposite of fruitfulness is the misuse of the same powers that lead to liberation. see 783.

מאמר creative utterance; decree, commandment. Daniel 4:14: "He called [i.e. decreed] in a loud voice: 'cut down the tree and trim off its branches; strip off its leaves and scatter its fruit. Let the animals flee from under it and the birds from its branches" The Zohar [IL31B, p.119] comments: "We reckon Bereshith ["in the beginning". Genesis 1:1] as a *maamar* (creative utterance) and six days issued from it and are comprised in it, and bear the names of those others." See Esther 1:15.

πας. πas (Gr). all. see 506 Greek, 46 Latin, John 8:2.

282

אראלים Thrones. The choir of angels associated with Binah. The angelic forces or formative forces are those particularly related to the Yetziratic world. The thrones are 12 because 282 reduces to 12. These are the thrones of the "Breath of Lives."

רוח חיים Breath of Lives. Twelve always refers to the 12 zodiacal types and thus the Aralim correspond to the action of the finitizing, limiting power of Binah as it expresses through Ruach or the human spirit. It is that which individualizes, that which effects the differences which distinguish one human expression of the Life-force from another. see 14, 428, 630, 140, 86, 272, 351.

ערבי Arabian. In the Rosicrucian allegory, brother C.R. is shipped across the Arabian gulf (sinus Arabicus) to Egypt. It refers to the termination of the period of celibacy represented by Arabia. Egypt represents the psychic powers of the subconsciousness plane (Yesod), controlled by the power of Arabia. It is the extension of Tiphareth to Yesod through the path of Key 15 (Samekh). see 60.

עברי Hebrew; name given to the Israelites as descendants of **עבר** *Eber*, in Genesis 10:24: "Arphaxad was the father of Shelah, and Shelah the father of Eber. Or in allusion to the immigration of their ancestors from the other side of the Euphrates. Referring to Joseph in Genesis 39:14: "She called her household servants. 'Look', she said to them, this Hebrew has been brought to us to make sport of us! He came in here to sleep with me, but I screamed."

בעיר A colloquial term for beast, cattle. Genesis 45:17: "Pharaoh said to Joseph, 'Tell your brothers, do this: Load your animals and return to the land of Canaan.'"

283 (prime)

ארון יהוה The ark of the Lord. Joshua 3:13: "And it shall come to pass, as soon as the soles of the feet of the priest that bear the ark of the Lord, the Lord of all the earth, shall rest in the waters of Jordan, that the waters of Jordan shall be cut off form the waters that come down from above, and they shall stand upon an heap." The ark of the Lord is the body containing the 'shut-in gold'; i.e. the desire to bring forth seed in the heart, unfolding the higher self. Jordan refers to the descent of consciousness from above to below; the new cycle of evolution begins with the sense of separation. The Quest for self-consciousness, or consciousness of the self. This involved alchemical changes in the bloodstream. see 264, 407, 690, 2610 (Greek).

זכרון Memory, power of remembrance memorial, remembrance, record, memento. The power of memory is attributed to Chesed (72). The influx of memory form Chesed descends to Netzach through the path of Kaph. see 20, 100, 964 and Key 10.

רגלים That goes on foot. Recall that the feet are attributed to Pisces, which is connected with the letter Qoph. The path of Qoph descends from Netzach, the desire nature, to Malkuth, the physical body. Qoph is attributed to the function of sleep and is the Corporeal Intelligence. "The kingdom of spirit is embodied in my flesh" though desire. see 100.

חדרי-בטן Chambers of the bell; depths of the heart, i.e. the inner parts of the body. Proverbs 20:27: "The spirit of man is the candle (lamp) of the Lord, searching all the inward parts of the belly." see 933.

284

I. An amicable number, whose aliquot parts are 1, 2, 4, 7, & 142. The sum of these is 220, another amicable number. see Appendix 6.

אמבריאל Ambriel. Archangel of Gemini.

עיד fugitive. "I am the eternal fugitive." [Book of Tokens, Heh]

באר אלים well of the Gods. In Isaiah 15:6: The waters of Nimrim are dried up and the grass is withered; the vegatation is gone and nothing green is left." The waters of consciousness are fruitful when the green of creative imagination becomes the "well of the Gods"; reflecting the divine will.

כי לעולם חסדו for his mercy endures forever. In Psalm 136:1: "Give thanks to the Lord; for he is good. His mercy [love, kindness] endures forever." Mem = 600, see 284.

I. "The keynote is the <u>mercy</u> of God. This is the very opposite of the conception of God which looks on him as always seeking vengeance, and this therefore is the true ideal of God. We realize our idea... "gleichst dem geist dendu begreifst" says Goethe, and that is the Alpha and Omega of the whole matter. [Troward, 1942, (page unknown)]

Θεος. Theos (Gr). God. see 703 Greek, 740, 592, 785, 373 and John 1:1.

αγιος. haglos, hagios (Gr). Holy one; saint, sacred, holy. A reference to Christ. Also means: 1. devoted to the Gods, pious, pure; 2. worthy of respect, reverence, veneration. Revelation 4:8: "And the four living ones, having each of them six wings apiece, round about and within are full of eyes; and they have no rest day and night, saying 'Holy, holy, Lord God the omnipotent!

The one who was, and the one who is, and the one who is coming." Also in Revelations 6:10: "And they cried with a loud voice, saying 'how long, O sovereign Lord! The holy one and true. Dost thou not judge and take vengeance for our blood from those who dwell on the earth?" see 592, 524 (Greek). see 703, 720.

αγαθος. agathos (Gr). Good.

These three word are simply different ways of saying the same thing. Thus that to which number 220 is amicable or friendly, is God Himself. This word has a number of shades of means: A) distinguished for good and eminent qualities and character-of persons and things; B) in a physical sense, good as opposed to bad; C) in a moral sense, good, well-disposed, upright-of persons, things, actions; D) good things, right virtue, good in respect of operation, doing good; E) good, in respect to the feelings excited, i.e. glad, joyful, happy. Also in Matthew 12:35: "The good man out of his good treasure produces good things; and the evil man out of his bad treasure produces evil things." see 2357.

Sub umbra alarum tuarum Iehova (Lt). Under the shadow of thy wings, Jehovah. see 255.

285

רעה friend, beloved. To arrive at the city in the heart is to unite oneself with the beloved friend. Then one knows that all men are friends and brothers, made one in love. Note this word is a metathesis of העיר; the letters Heh and Resh have been transposed. The city is sought via clear vision (Heh); the friend is recognized via the process of regeneration (Resh). Both require edrei, or strength. see 320.

אדרעי Strength, force, mighty. Edrie is the name of two places in Palestine [Strong's Dictionary] Inman says "The word is probably a variant of אדר adar, which means 'to shine, be splendid, renowned', etc. Also 'great, swelling, inflated, magnificent, large' [Ancient Faiths, Volume 1, p.470]. The word אדר also means "to glorify". see 205 and Numbers 21:33.

פרא Inman: (Joshua 18:23), 'She brings forth,' 'she is fruitful,' 'a heifer,' 'a pit, or hole.' The word clearly has reference to the Yoni, the symbol of the celestial Virgin.' [Ancient Faiths, Vol. 2, p. 449]

הפר void, to-nullify. see Numbers 30:13.

פרה fruitful, producing. see Deuteronomy 29:17.

עירד fugitive.

286

קול + עינך his voice (i.e. Tiphareth) + "thine eye" (i.e. the divine beneficence). The heart or inmost center is connected with interior vision, which prospers all human undertakings. see 136, 150.

מרום high, lofty [Sephir Sephiroth].

מרום *Murum. Murmus, Murmur*. Goetic demon #54 by night of the 3rd decanate of Virgo. The decanate is linked with the 10 of Pentacles, which is the operation of Malkuth, sphere of the elements, in Assiah, the world of physical action. see 846 & Appendix 11.

I. "Before he turned into a fallen angel, Murmur was partly of the Order of Thrones and partly of the Order of Angels. This 'fact was proved after infinite research', reports Spence in *An Encyclopedia of Occultism*, p.119. In hell, Murmur is a great Duke with 30 legions of infernal spirits attending him. He manifest in the form of a warrior astride a gryphon, with a dual crown upon his head. He teaches philosophy and constrains the souls of the dead to appear before him for the answering of questions." [Davidson, 1971, pp. 199-200.]

II. *Goetia*: "He is a great duke, and an earl; and appears in the form of a warrior riding upon a gryphon, with a ducal crown upon his head. There do go before him his ministers with great trumpets sounding. His office is to teach philosophy perfectly, and to constrain souls deceased to come before the Exorcist to answer those questions which he may wish to put to them, if desire. He was partly of the Order of Thrones, and partly of that of Angels. He now rules 30 Legions of Spirits." [Mathers, 1995, p. 57]

אופף Fine Gold. The place where Solomon got his gold for the temple. Variant selling. It is אור, with the letter of Mars. see 291, 1210, 207, 297, 302.

זעיר little, small. The city into which Lot escaped at the destruction of Sodom and Gomorrah. Genesis 19:23: "The sun was risen upon the earth when Lot entered Zoar." The passage which refers to Lot's escape specifically mentions fire and brimstone [A name for alchemical sulfur], while Lot's wife is turned in a pillar of salt One of the 5 cities in the vale of Siddim, also called Bela. . see 693, 78, 104, 315, 354.

מוריאל Muriel. Geomantic Intelligence of Cancer. Archangel of Cancer. "From the Greek 'Myrrh'; Angel of the month of June and ruler of the sign of Cancer. One of the rulers of the Order of Dominations, invoked from the south. One of the chief angelic officers of the 3rd hour of the day." [Davidson, 1971, p. 199.]

חכמה רוח Chokmah Ruach. Spirit of Wisdom. The life-breath or spirit is concentrated as the life-force in Chokmah. It becomes "gold" as it descends through the Tree of Life. see 73, 214.

ופאר Goetia demon #42 by night of the 3rd decanate of Taurus. The 3rd decanate of Taurus in the Tarot minor arcana is assigned to the 7 of Pentacles. This represents the operation of Netzach, sphere of Venus, in Assiah, the material world of action. see Appendix 11.

Goetia: "He is a duke great and strong, and appears like a mermaid. His office is to govern the waters, and to guide ships laden with arms, armor, and ammunition, etc. and at the request of the Exorcist he can cause the seas to be right stormy and to appear full of ships. Also he makes men to die in three days by putrefying wounds or sores, and causing worms to breed in them. He governs 29 Legions of Spirits."

יובב בן זרח Jobab, son of Zerah; A king of Edom associated with Chesed. Edom signifies unbalanced force. In Genesis 36:33: "And Bela died, and Jobab, the son of Zerah of Bozrah reigned in his stead." Zerah means to irradiate, to rise (as the sun), shine. According to Inman, the name Jobab seems to be a variant of another word meaning cherished, beloved. see 51, 937.

288

I. The total length of the 13 boundary lines of the double cube altar of Malkuth (13x13x36).

רעה אחד one shepherd. Ezekiel 34:23: "And I will set up one shepherd over them, and the shepherd shall feed them, even my servant David." see 270, 744.

חרף winter; harvest-time, autumn, freshly gathered fruit. Zechariah 14:8: "And it shall be in that day, that living waters shall go out form Jerusalem, half of them toward the former sea, and half of them toward the hinder sea: in summer and in winter shall it be." see 1008.

זאפר Goetia demon #16 by day of the 1st decanate of Virgo. This decanate corresponds to the 8 of Pentacles. This represents the operation of Hod, sphere of Mercury, in Assiah, the material world of action. see Appendix 11.

I. *Goetia*: "He is a great duke, and appears in red apparel and armor, like a solder. His office is to cause women to love men, and to bring them together in love. He also makes them barren. He governs 26 Legions of Inferior Spirits." [Mathers, 1995, p. 35]

289

פרט to detail, specify, to distinguish, to particularize. With different pointing *perawt*: 1. single thing, detail, explicit, statement, individual; *pawrat;* 2. to play a musical instrument, to do one by one, do singly, to change into small money, to detail, single out, specify; 3. *peret*. Single grapes; grape gleanings which belong to the poor.

פטר to break through, to liberate, to open; break open; to set free; release; dismiss; to escape; to cause exemption; to divorce. Both words (payrate and pawtar), designates the quality of activity represented by the pentagram, as well as the actual purpose of the pentagram ritual, which

seeks to bring about a particular manifestation of the Life-power's energy, and comprehends that energy as working in a five-fold manner. With different pointing *pehter*: opening, firstling, first born.

I. An 'aperture', 'hole', or 'void'. The ideas suggested by the numbers of the verse may therefore be resumed by the symbol of the womb and its ophidian emanations. This is confirmed by the curious word, or name, Coph Nia. Coph or Koph means the 'daughter'. It is a name of Proserpine or Persephone, the goddess of destruction. She is called Koph because, as Payne Knight expresses it, she represents the 'Universal daughter, or general secondary principle; for though properly the goddess of Destruction, she is frequently distinguished by the title *Soteira*, Preserver, represented with ears of corn upon her head, as the goddess of Fertility. She was, in reality, the personification of the heat or fire supposed to pervade the earth, which was held to be at once the cause and effect of fertility and destruction, as being at once the cause and effect of fermentation; from which both proceed'. [Grant, 1994, pp. 35-36.]

ברא אלהים God [Elohim] created. Genesis 1:1: "In the beginning the Elohim created the heavens and the earth."

טרף to tear to pieces, rend; to declare unfit for food; to seize forcibly; to knock, strike, shake; to mix, confuse.

פרט particular; part, particle. see The "three measures of meal" (889). Rosenroth in K.D.L.C.K. (p.647) gives: *particulare*, and says this name evidently pertains to Malkuth; however others attributed it to Kether, said generally and universally: Tiphareth specially and particularly, and to Malkuth in general. Moreover, the sense is that in the crown in general are contained mildness, and mercy; specially exhibited in Chesed, Geburah, and Tiphareth, and generally repeated in Malkuth.

אחירע "Brother of wrong". A prince of Naphtali [Numbers 1:15]. Naphtali is connected with Virgo and with alchemical distillation. see 570.

Granum pectori Jesu insitum (Lt). Seed planted in Jesus' breast.

מרים   Mary, sister of Moses. Signifying rebellion, perversity, antagonism. These meanings are mental states having close association with strong, but unfulfilled desires. Christian tradition gives the virgin (Latin: *Maria*, seas), who is also the holy mother (Binah, the Great Sea) the same name as the Magdalene who was forgiven because she loved much. Paul Case: "Now, the name מרים is מרי, with the termination of Mem. Thus it really signifies "Bitter Water." see 7, 140, 250, 440, 245, 441.

In Exodus 15:21: "*Miriam* sang to them: 'Sing to the Lord, for he is highly exalted. The house and its rider he has furled into the sea"

צר   Tyre, Rock. Name of Tyre, city of Phoenicia. Ezekiel 26:4: "Then will destroy the walls of Tyre, and pull down her towers; I will scrape away her rubble and make her bare rock."

This word is spelled צור in Deuteronomy 32:4: "...your are to pass through the coast of your brethren.. which dwell in Seir.." God and the adversary are one and the same. see Key 15, #258, 624, 296.

עמד ענן   A pillar of cloud. Exodus 13:21: "And the Lord went before them by day in a pillar of cloud, to lead them the way; and by night in a pillar of fire, to give them light; to go by day and night." Numbers 12:5: "And the Lord came in the pillar of the cloud, and stood in the door of the tabernacle, and called Aaron and Miriam: and they both came forth." [The Beth prefixed to עמד is omitted. With the Beth, "in", the value is 292] see 2528, 2580 (Greek); 421, 120, 170.

רמים   wild-oxen; unicorn (plural), "one-horned." Refers to spiritual illumination-the Mercury center of third eye. see 1286, 696.

מימר   Word, equivalent to (Logos) in later Hebrew. Thus, "word of God". see 511.

פרי   fruit; offspring; product, result; profit, interest.

ערך   To set in a row, i.e. arrange, put in order (in a very wide variety of applications), put (set) (the battle, self) in array, compare, direct, equal, esteem, estimate, expert [in war] furnish, handle, join[battle], ordain, (lay, put, reckon up, set) (in) order, prepare, tax, value. With different pointing: a pile, equipment, estimate, equal, estimation, order, price, proportion. [Strong's Dictionary]

רמן   pomegranate. Symbol of feminine fruitfulness and of memory. see Key 2.

רץ   piece. Connected with silver and the Moon in Psalm 68:30: "Rebuke the wild beasts (oppressors) of the marshes, the multitude of the wild bulls, the idols of the gentiles which are covered with silver [i.e. pieces of silver]; scatter the people who delight in war." see 1100.

אפיקי מים   torrents of waters. Compare with the idea of Water as the substance of all physical forms. (Latin: Torrentes Aquarum). Rosenroth in K.D.L.C.K. (p.143) says they are Netzach, and Hod, and so-called since both together receive the supernal waters from Binah, through Tiphareth. When therefore they reside above Yesod, then they the torrents of waters, when their influence descends into Yesod. see 851.

אפיר   The place where Solomon got much of his gold [1 Kings 10:11]. Intimates that the field of concentration in which growth takes place is the alchemical gold, or transmuting agency. In the alchemical treatise, *Aesch Mezareph*, Ophir is referred to Malkuth, because Ophir is the name of a land or Earth derived from a Hebrew noun signifying ashes (Ayper, אפר-also: dry and loose earth; soil, dust, powder, debris). see 287, 297, 311.

אצר   to lay up, store up, to store treasure. With different pointing: stay, strength, help, dominion, rule; *aytzer,* to treasure, preserve. Refers to the wound-up kundalini energy (Saturn) as our treasure. The greater concentration of force which brings up more problems is truly our greatest treasure. Also a personal masculine name used in Genesis 36:21. Ezer, "A leader or prince."

ארץ   earth. One of the 4 elements; attributed to the letter Tav. The temporary fixation of Fire,

Air and Water. One of the 7 earths corresponding to the Supernals. From a root meaning: "low, inferior." Stands for the inferior term of the first opposites, that which is below It is essentially Life (Aleph). It is manifest in the dynamic energy of suns and stars (Resh). Alchemical earth is the root of human existence-giving the Aquarian age impulse to unfold the higher powers of man (Tzaddi). . see 390, 800.

I. Paul Case: This alchemical earth is attributed to the supernal triad and especially to Chokmah ["And the earth was without form and void". I conclude that the mosnacal earth was the virgin sulphur, which is an earth without form, for it hath no determined form". - Thomas Vaughan]. It is also linked to Malkuth, the end of the path of Tav (Saturn). At the beginning of the Christian era, a person we now describe as belonging to the "lower Classes" was called by the Jews: Am ha-*eretz*, "Man of Earth." Thus Earth stands for "that which is below." *Eretz* though particularly attributed to Malkuth, is also, in the system of the 7 palaces, attributed to the supernal triad, and more especially to חכמה, where it is associated with אופנים, Ophanim (Wheels), and with חיה, the Life-force. It is, possibly, to this aspect of *Eretz* that Vaughan refers in his address to the reader in Magia Adamica when he says (page 84), that the earth is invisible. Note that *Eretz* is 291, or 3x97, which is also 3 times הים הגדל, "the Great Sea." But the Great Sea is Binah, is also the number 3. Thus הים הגדל maybe symbolized in a double blind as 3x3 = 9 (יסוד). Note Vaughan's quotation from Hermes: "O Holy Earth, that thou are ordained to be the Mother of All." For mother is אימא. see 50, 14, 365, 105, 302, 432, 337.

II. "The name of the so-called earth, which is Eretz, begins with *Aleph*. The *Aleph* (1) is creative immanence, timeless and immeasurable, like an intermittent spark, which our thinking cannot grasp. Were we to imagine it, we should consider the *Aleph* as a succession: being, non-being, being, non-being--or life-death, life-death, life-death. The *Aleph* appears in the first verse as one of the given elements in this Revelation. But we repeat that while the *Bayt* (2) and the *Raysh* (200) are containing elements, or containers, and accessible to our thinking, the *Aleph* (1) is only an idea in the succession of

Bayt Raysh Aleph Sheen Yod Tav, composing the first sequence in the Bible: *Bereshyt.*

Bayt and *Raysh* are understandable, but not so *Aleph. Aleph* is buried in Eretz. To allow it to spring forth alive in us is *the* absolute function of every human being. In whomsoever the *Aleph* lives and functions is the very Revelation itself. *Aleph is* buried in all the containing elements-in the cosmic container-forms, the stars and the planets, etc., as well as in the container-forms of individuals. The word encompassing every variety of container is Eretz, which all translators have reduced to one word, earth.
What, then, is the aspect of these container-elements in which *Aleph is* buried? The life in them simply swarms, uncontrolled, in a state of (says the verse) "Tohu and Bohu", which is a jumble, a confusion, a hurly-burly, a chaos. It is a fantastic whirlpool of life, not limited to the planet earth, but cosmically including all that exists in the Universe. And, at "the face of its very self", in its very "deepness", that chaos is totally fecund, abundant, prolifically fertile. Such is the "darkness" referred to in the accepted translation. And such is the true meaning of the first part of the second verse concerning Eretz, the so-called earth; that in which *Aleph is* concealed." [Suraes, 1992, pp. 80-81.]

דרך בינה the way of understanding [Proverbs 9:6]. Through trials and problems, and depending on the intensity of the field of expression one has developed, is the way to greater understanding and even higher levels of perception. Since this refers by gematria to the element Earth, it may be compared with the words of Paul, an initiate in the secret wisdom: "Ever since the creation of the world, his invisible nature... his eternal power and divine character... have been clearly perceptible through what he has made." [Romans 1:20]

הר אלהים Hill (or mountain) of God (Elohim). Psalm 68:15: "The Mountain [hill] of God (Elohim) is the Mountain [hill] of Bashan (בשן הר). Bashan means soft, rich soil. see 848, 352, 126, 201, 713, 406, 400, 581, 451.

הרפו be still. Psalm 46:10: "Be still and know that I am god: I will be exalted among the heathen, I will be exalted in the earth." God is revealed when the 'waters' are still. see 1407

(Greek).

זרע דוד seed (posterity) of David. Notice that דוד is 14, and is equivalent to זהב, Zahab, Gold. Here is an alchemical hint.

זרעו בו Whose seed is in itself [Genesis 1:11]. The Zohar says: "Instead of Zareo (whose seed), we may read זרע-ו, zera Vav, "the seed of Vav', which has literally been cast upon the Earth." the "seed of Vav" is the seed-power of Tiphareth, which is represented in יהוה by the 3rd letter Vav. Tiphareth is Sol or Gold.

מימרא Word, Logos, thought. Used by Onkelos for IHVH throughout his Aramaic translation of the Pentateuch. Also: Word, of God, Command.

נמרא a leopard ["Spotted, striped"]. *Aesch Mezareph*: "The third beast [the lion and eagle are the other two] ... which is as it were a leopard i.e. water not wetting, the Garden of the Wise Men; for Nimra a Leopard and Jardin in their lesser Number, make the same Sum, viz., 12. Such also is the Quickness of this Water, that is not unlike a Leopard on that account." This beast is said to have 4 wings (i.e. sublimations) to fight with the bear and lion that he may extract their gluten or blood, and 4 compositions-white, red, green and watery. Nimra was a place in Gilead ('the sun; the witness')." [Westcott, 1997, p. 25]

סירכא to adhere to, to cleave to; prince, chief, general, ruler.

Rosenroth: *adhaesio* [cling to], *adhaerens*[hang to], *princeps* [first, formost]. He says thus is called the Qlippah, when it adheres to Shekhinah from the judgements exposed by the sins of the Israelites. Then she becomes the ruler. He cites Proverbs 30:23: "An unloved woman who is married, and a maid-servant who displaces her mistress." [K.D.L.C.K. p.604]

טבמקיאל Tzakamquiel. Lesser assistant angel of Aquarius [Crowley].

אמרים Amorites; the early inhabitants of Palestine. see Genesis 14:7.

אליך יהוה אדני עיני mine eyes are fixed on you, O Sovereign Lord. Psalm 141:8: "But my eyes are fixed on you, O Sovereign Lord; in you I take refuge-do not give me over to death."

כה-אמר יהוה Thus says the Lord.

בצר gold (in dust). precious ore; support. Job 22:24: "Then shall thou lay up gold as dust, and the gold of Ophir as the stones of the brooks." With different pointing *bawtzor*: to fortify, entrench; to cut off grapes, gather. *Aesch Mezareph*: "Batzar, gold, referred to Chokmah, as though laid up in strongholds, Job 22:24, 25; 36:19]" Job 36:19: "Will he not esteem thy rights? No, not gold, nor all the forces or strength." [Westcott, 1997, p. 13]

צבר to heap, pile up, accumulate. Psalm 39:6: "Surely every man walks in a vain show: surely they are disquieted in vain: he heaps up riches, and knows not who shall gather them." Metathesis of בצר; here Tzaddi (meditation) precedes (Beth) concentration.

צבר heap, pile. With different pointing *tzawbahr*: prickly pear; cactus.

צרב to burn, scorch, singe; to cauterize. The power of meditation (Tzaddi) through the agency of the solar fire (Resh) penetrates the veils of ignorance (Beth).

רפואה healing; remedy, medicine; prayer for health, the eighth benediction of the Amidah prayer. The gathering of 'gold' is true healing.

ארצא land, earth, ground, fill. The 'earth' is the physical body.

זמרדיאל Zamradiel. The Sentinel of the 17th Path (tunnel) on the inverse Tree of Life.

I. The 17th Path transmits the influence of the *Lovers*. Its tunnel is sentinelled by Zamradiel, his number is 292, בצר which signifies 'gold', the metal associated with the twins Set-Horus, Set's totem being the black bird and that of Horus the golden falcon. The earlier twins, however, were Set and Anubis, the golden jackal who, with his dark shade, haunted the desert of mummies, i.e. the astral shells left by those who had made the crossing and transcended the abyss.

The sigil of Zamradiel is composed of a lunar crescent pierced by an arrow shot from a bow, both ends of which terminate in the letter G. The transfixed moon is the crucified flesh. The 'crucified' are those who have made the crossing of the Abyss. The letter G (*gimel*) signifies the 'camel', the ship of the desert, the vehicle by which the crossing is achieved. It is the letter of the High Priestess.

This tunnel concentrates the influence of Set *via* the Black power-zone (Binah) that receives its light from the Stellar Sphere (Chokmah) and rays it downward through the abyss. The 17th *kala* is thus strongly charged with the atmosphere of Daath and of Death, both of which have close affinity with the Lovers.

The number 292 is also that of Chozzar which, as suggested in *Cults of the Shadow*, is probably connected with the name Choronzon, a corrupt form of it, The symbol of Chozzar resembles the astrological sign of Neptune and according to Blavatsky Chozzar is called Neptune by the uninitiated. It is the symbol of Atlantean Magic and its attribution to the second power-zone, Chokmah, is highly significant because Chokmah receives an influx direct from Pluto (Kether).

This is the energy that powers the *Lovers* of the 17th Path, but, in the tunnel beneath it, it has been transformed into the רפואה (292, a drug and אפרוה, a metathesis of רפואה, means 'a young bird') or 'drug of death' that is represented by the black bird of Set and the black pig of Typhon. Chozzar means 'a pig'. This creature was adopted as a symbol of the Great Work by the Typhonians because it was the only animal known to devour human excrement. The pig is symbolic and so is the excrement, for it is not anal refuse that is veiled by this totem, but the blood of the moon, the human female flux in its dark phase. The symbolism was carried over into the solar cults of later ages, and at the time of the vernal equinox the god Khunsu is depicted in the orb of the full moon bearing in his arms the sacrificial pig. The imbibition of the black wine of the moon prepared the initiate for the disintegration, or crucifixion, at Easter time, and this made possible the crossing over into the world of spirit or Nonbeing.

The Gnostics depicted Chozzar in the form of a Serpent whose stellar representative was Draco. The undulation of the serpent was an image of the periodic feminine flow.

The mystery of this tunnel is glyphed by the sigil of its sentinel with the lunar crescent transfixed by the arrow. In Zamradiel's sigil the moon is young and has not yet attained the fullness of gestation which occurs after the lovers have emerged from the City of the Pyramids (Binah) into the desert of Set.
The relevant verse from 231 reads: Here then beneath the winged Eros is youth, delighting in the one and the other. He is Asar [Osiris] between Asi [Isis] and Nephthi (Nephthys).

Osiris is the mummy, the dead one who is reborn in the spirit world, having been conceived by Isis and brought to birth by Nephthys.

The magical *siddhi* of this *kala* is - understandably –bilocation, here symbolized by the mummy (Osiris) and the risen youth (Asi). This dual deity sometimes appears as *The Brothers* and sometimes as *The Lovers*.

It is from this tunnel that dark forces emerge and seep from the abysses of non-being, permeating the power-zones of manifestation with the shadows of their absence. This doubling or dappling with light and shade is typified by symbolic hybrids such as the magpie, the penguin, the piebald, the parrot, the zebra; in fact, all dappled and chameleon-like creatures that have the apparent power of transformation.

The Order of Qliphoth ascribed to this realm is the *Tzalalimiron*, 'The Changers'. The supreme totem of this tunnel is the hyena and this realm is haunted by votaries of the *Bultu*, or Spectral Hyena. Its cult is known to have existed in the paleolithic age. It brought its totem out of Africa and spread it secretly, all over the earth. It had its astral source in the tunnel beneath the Path of the Twins (The Lovers) and was reflected on to the earth plane at a place in Africa named *Kabultiloa*. The name means literally 'the shadow (*Ka*) of the specter or spirit (*loa*) of the hyena (*bultu*)'.

This Cult of the Spectral Hyena persisted when all other forms of its god had perished, and certain magicians and dreamers have received intimations of its existence through the centuries. Dr. John Dee and Aleister Crowley called it Choronzon, while H. P. Lovecraft sensed it as the monstrous and amorphous slime known as Yog-Sothoth [an amalgam of the god-names Set and Thoth].

According to a secret grimoire 'the Beast was called down not from known spaces but *from cells between them* [i.e. the Cells of the Qliphoth], while the *bultu* drums beat off-beat rhythms. Similarly, in the later Petro rites of Voodoo - in which the Cult survived under another name - 'the alignments of the secret *vevers* flowed between the cardinal points, not through them.

The tunnel of Zamradiel is under the aegis of the forces of Shugal-Choronzon in their voodoo forms of Baron Samedhi and Guede-Nibho. The Baron represents the Saturnine aspect. Another of his names is Cimitirere, the place of the dead or of *those who make the crossing into non-being*. Hence, Baron Samedhi is also known as Maitre Carrefour or Carfax, Master of the Crossroads, for at the junction of the four Ways [The center of the cross represents the intersection of the plane of being and non-being.]. The spirits of the living cross over into the realm of non-being, and vice versa.

The dual nature of the symbolism associated with Zamradiel accords with the nature of the *Bultu* which, being of another dimension, is neither flesh nor spectre, white nor black, human nor beast, but a combination of hybrid entities.

The hyena is symbolic of all half lives, all twilight and crepuscular states of consciousness, all crossed breeds interweaving, coiling, worming their ambiguous images into flesh and branding with the mark of the *Bultu* the myriad forms it chooses as its vehicles. Primordial atavisms are unsealed by the beat of the *Bultu* drums and, if used in connection with the tunnel of Zamradiel.

This accounts, in a phenomenal sense, for the 'ominous appearances' and 'banshees', the legendary beings ascribed to this path in *Liber 777*. [Grant, 1994, pp. 190-197.]

293 (prime)

טוב ורע good and evil. Genesis 2:17: "The Tree of Knowledge of Good and Evil." see 479.

בארץ in the earth, on the earth, land. see Genesis 2:5.

ויזרע and he sowed, and he planted seed. see Genesis 26:12.

יזרעו they sow. Hosea 8:7.

כרגע in a moment, at once. Numbers 16:21.

294

מלכי צדק Melchizedek. Old Testament priest king of Salem, [Genesis 14:18]. He brought the bread and wine to Abraham and blessed him. Melchizedek means "King of Righteousness and refers to the Chasidim, the Master of Compassion, the true "Measures of Mercy." he head of the essence order was a "Teacher of Righteousness." See the path of Yod on the Tree connecting the King, or Melek (Tiphareth) with righteousness (Gedulah or Chesed). The King of Salem (peace) is spoken of in the Epistle to the Hebrews as being "without father, without mother, without descent and without beginning or end of days." The priesthood of Melchizedek (after the order of Melchizedek) is not an outer order, like the masons. It is identical with the True and Invisible Order. The interior church or Eckharts-Hausen is another name for the same company of men and women who are liberated from the illusion of physical descent, who know they never began to live, and that their lives will never end, who are, in short, free from the delusion of mortal, temporal existence. These men and women relate themselves neither to the past not to the future. They live out the present, the now with smiling hearts. Thus is it true that the course of empire takes its way westward, but the west to which it leads is the mystic west corresponding to צדק, Jupiter, the planet or center, or western face of he cube. see 100, 312, 314, 194, 246, 636, 746 (Greek), 919 (Greek), 2020, 1494, 1345, 4896.

המאור הגדל the greater light (luminary) (to rule the day). See Genesis 1:16.

אלהי אברהם the God of Abraham [Exodus 3:6]. Note that Abraham in the Bible is directly connected with Melchizedek. see 248, 254, 228, 854, 782, 1199, 1342.

אַרְגָּמָן purple, purple cloth. A "royal" color, connected with Jupiter and the Moon. Red purple is connect with Pentecost, symbolizing the giving of the written law, consisting of 2 sides, of the right and of the left [Zohar III:135A]. Note that purple was a mixture of blue (Chesed) and red (Geburah) and that it figured prominently in the building of the tabernacle, and the covering of Solomon's chariot [Song of Solomon]. Note that reddish-purple is similar to the traditional Venusian rose.

חֹרֶף pertaining to autumn.

צָרַד to be cool, fresh, (unused root).

נִמְרֹד Nimrod. Founder of Babylon. In Masonic tradition Nimrod is considered one of the founders of the craft.

I. Genesis 10:8: "Cush was the father [founder] of Nimrod, who grew to be a mighty warrior of the earth."

II. Inman: This word has never yet been satisfactorily explained, and the following attempt may probably be considered as faulty as any of the extant interpretations… the meaning of *nimrah* [נמרה]… is an euphemism for the 'Yoni.' … עַד, *ad* signifies 'eternity,' or, as we often use the word indefinitely, 'time.' עֹד, *od*, for עוֹד *od*, also signifies 'continuance,' 'duration.' עוּד *ud*, signifies 'to circle,' 'to repeat,' 'to increase,' 'to surround,' etc. … I think, a sensible signification to Nimrod, e.g., 'the Eternal Mother,' 'the womb of time,' 'the perpetual mother,' 'the circling mother,' 'or the teeming womb.' [Ancient Faiths VII, pp. 384-385]

III. "*Nimerod...* The verb נמוֹד, of which this is here the contained facultative, passive movement, signifies literally *to give over to one's impulse, to shake off every kind of yoke, to behave arbitrarily*. It is formed from the root רד, which develops every idea of movement, proper and persevering, good and evil, ruled by the sign of exterior action מ." [d'Olivet, 1976, pp. 280-281.]

IV. The Zohar [I:73B-74A] comments: "He was a mighty hunter before the Lord; wherefore it is said: like Nimrod a mighty hunter before the Lord. Truly he was a man of might, because he was clad in the garments of Adam, and was able by means of them, to lay snares for mankind and beguile them. Rabbi Eleazar said: 'Nimrod used to entice people into idolatrous worship by means of those garments, which enabled him to conquer the world and proclaim himself its ruler, so that mankind offered him worship. He was called 'Nimrod', for the reason that he rebelled (marad = rebel) against the most high king above, against the higher angels and against the lower angels.' Rabbi Simeon said: 'Our colleagues are acquainted with a profound mystery concerning these garments.'" (p.251)

רָצַד to totter, to tremble, (unused root).

αγιοις.. agiois (Gr). saints.

η καλη παραθηκη. heh kale parathekeh (Gr). The good deposit. In 2 Timothy 1:14: "That good thing (deposit) which was committed unto thee by the holy ghost which dwelleth in us."

ομολογια. omologia (Gr). profession, confession; agreement, compact; in war, terms of surrender; an assent, admission.

οθονη μεγαλη. othene megaleh (Gr). a great sheet; fine white linen, a fine linen veil, a garment or cloth, a sail-cloth, sail, sheet.

εκκλασια. ekklesia (Gr). Church. Literally, "They who are called out." An assembly brought together for oral instruction. (The congregation of the righteous, the merciful, the true chasidim, the only true church, the inner church or school, the true Rosicrucian order, the "White Lodge," composed of the "Master of Compassion," said to be Triumphant over death and the grave). see 53 Latin.

ροδον. rhodon (Gr). Rose. The flower sacred to Venus, used to designate the interior church of persons who hear and obey the inner voice.

he akademia (Lt). the Academy (Pythagorean).
η σκηνη. he skene (Gr). the tabernacle. Used in Greek version of the Old Testament.

צהר noon.

מארים + כנפים‎ powers of vehement strength (i.e. Mars) + wings (i.e. Sun). It is the Mars energy which must rise and be transmuted into the sun. see 200, 95.

מלכה + סליק‎ The bride (one of the titles of Malkuth) + finished. The physical plane, i.e the human body is finished when the great work if transmutation is accomplished.

מנרה menorah. lampstand, candlestick. see 301 and Exodus 25:32.

נמרה Nimrah. Inman: (Numbers 32:3), "she is indented, cut in, or notched;' an altered from of נמרה. This epethet, which appears to refer the celestial goddess under the from of the Yoni, conveys precisely the same idea as the word נקבה, n'kebah. By a figure of speech, the stripes or spots of the tiger, or leopard, or antelope are said to be 'cut in;' hence striped or spotted creatures, נמרים, nimrim, (nimrah being the singular), were adopted by the hierarchy as symbols of the female creator.' [Inman, 1942, Vol. 2., p. 383]

צהר roof, a light. see Genesis 6:16.

הפעמנים the bells. see Exodus 39:25.

פריה her fruit. see Leviticus 25:19.

הצר the adversary, the enemy. see Numbers 10:9.

296

צור rock. The fundamental meaning of the root is "to press, to confine, to render compact." see Numbers 25:15.

אחיעזר "Brother of Help". A prince of Dan (Scorpio, putrefaction). see 54 and Numbers 1:12.

כורע K.D.L.C.K. (p.473) gives: incurvans se, curved or bent upon itself, and gives several

references to the Zohar. Gesenius gives of כור, bore dig, hew. The word כורע does not appear in scripture.

d'Olivet writes of כו: Every assimilating, compressing, restraining force: the natural faculty which fetters the development of bodies and draws them back to their elements. Root analogous to the root כא (formation by contraction), but modified by the presence of the convertible sign ו." [d'Olivet, 1976, p. 370.]

Of רע he says: ... the emblem of that which is terrestrial, obscure and evil. That which is bent, bowed down; that which is brought together to be made compact; that which becomes fragile, brittle; that which breaks and is reduced to powder: physical and moral evil; misery, malignancy, misfortune, vice, perversity, disorder. [ibid., 453.]

כדבריכם according to your words. Genesis 44:10.

רמון a pomegranate. Inman: (Joshua 15:32), The shape of this fruit resembles that of the gravid uterus in the female, and the abundance of seeds which it contains makes it a fitting emblem of the prolific womb of the celestial mother. [Ancient Faiths, Vol. 2, p. 612]

297

אלהים גבור Literally, "Creative Powers of Strength", Almighty God, God the Strong, God of Battles, God Almighty. Divine Name of Geburah, the 5th Sephirah, and associated with the 5 of Wands (Geburah in Atziluth). The special seat of the Mars-force and of will power on the Tree of Life. The name indicates the descent of the power of Binah into Geburah through the path of the letter Cheth. see also 211, 86, 5, 14, 41, 104, 64, 92, 95, 216, 850.

אבצר treasure, treasury; storehouse. The Venus center is a storehouse of creative imagination.

צואר the neck. Refers to the Venus center as a key to the work of transmutation.

אופיר fine gold, red (alchemical sulphur). A

place (or country) from which Solomon (Sun) and Hiram (also associated with the Sun) brought fine gold [1 Chronicles 1:23, 29:4 and 2 Chronicles 8:18, 9:10]. Ophir is another name for Havilah, from whence cometh gold. In Alchemy, Gold is a synonym for the Sun. Thus the archetypal reproductive will-force of Geburah is one with the gold of illumination. There is no essential difference between the force which manifests as will and that which manifests as the self identification or "I" reference associated with the Sun, Tiphareth and the Cardiac Ganglion. The first part of this Divine name Elohim Gebur further identifies the reproductive power of Geburah with the finitizing power of Binah. Geburah is the recipient of the powers of Binah through the path of Cheth. In 2 Chronicles 9:10: "And the servants also of Hurah, and the servants of Solomon, which brought Gold from Ophir, brought Algum trees and precious stones."

אַרְמוֹן   fortress, castle, citadel. Also the inner citadel of a King's House. Isaiah 32:14: "Because the palaces shall be forsaken; the multitude of the city shall be left; the forts and towers shall be dens forever, a joy of wild asses, a pasture of flocks."

כֻּרְסְיָא   throne. Aramaic name used in Qabalistic works as one of the appellations of Binah. Geburah receives the power or influence of Binah via the path of Cheth. *Sepher Sephiroth*: a name of Briah [Crowley, 1977, p. 34].

"כֻּרְסְיָא is an immediate emanation from the world of Atziluth, whose ten Sephiroth are reflected herein, and are consequently more limited, though they are still of the purest nature, and without any admixture of matter. [Introduction to Kabalah Unveiled, #58].

נוּרִיאֵל Nuriel. "Fire. Angel of hailstorms in Jewish legend. According to the Zohar, Nuriel governs Virgo. He is 300 parasangs tall and has a retinue of 50 myriads of angels 'all fashioned out of water and fire'. The height of Nuriel is exceeded only by the Erelim; by the watchers; by Af and Hemiah; and of course by Metatron, who is the tallest hierarch in heaven-excepting perhaps Hadraniel and Anafiel. In Gnostic lore, Nuriel is one of the 7 subordinates to Jehuel, prince of fire... As a charm for warding off evil,

Nuriel is also effective. His name is found engraved on oriental amulets, as noted by Schrire, *Hebrew Amulets*." [Davidson, 1971, p. 209.]

298

רַחֲמִים compassion, a title of Tiphareth.

עַכְבּוֹר "Mouse"; name of the father of Baal-Hanan, a king of Edom. see 560, 1860 and Genesis 36:38.

בִּיפוֹר Goetia demon #46 by night of the 1st decanate of Cancer. In the Tarot minor arcana this decanate corresponds to the 2 of Cups. This represents the operation of Chokmah, seat of the Life-force, in Briah the creative world. see Appendix 11.

Goetia: "He is an earl, and appears in the from of a monster; but after a while, at the command of the Exorcist, he puts on the shape of a man. His office is to make one knowing in astrology, geometry, and other arts and sciences. He teaches the virtues of precious stones and woods. He changes dead bodies, and puts them in another place; also he lights seeming candles upon the graves of the dead. He has under his command 60 Legions of Spirits." [Mathers, 1995, p. 52]

חֲמֹרִים asses, donkeys. see Genesis 45:23.

צֹחַר Zohar. In Genesis 23:8: "Ephron son of Zohar…"

רֹצֵחַ manslayer, one slaying. see Numbers 35:11.

299

רַהֲדֵץ Rahadetz. Angel of the 2nd decanate of Cancer.

הִפְרִיד separated. see Genesis 30:40.

יִטָּרֵף be torn to pieces. see Exodus 22:12.

לִנְדֵרֶיהָ to her vows. see Numbers 30:13.

Section 3

Numbers 300 - 399

300

I. Σ24 = 300.

ש Shin. tooth, fang. Refers of cosmic fire (prana). One of the three "Mother Letters" attributed to the Element Fire. The sound of the letter, "sh!" is an admonition to silence and the 4th occult maxium "Be Silent." see 360, 814, 24.

I. The character of Shin is composed of three tounges of flame (Yod) rising from a firery base (Vav). Thus the secret value of Shin is 36 [3 Yods (30) and Vav (6)]. Thirty-six is the extension of 8, and 8 is Cheth (ח, see Book of Tokens meditation on Cheth. Key 20 depicts the liberation described). The Egyptian hieroglyph for the sound 'sh" is an undulation garden. Compared with the symbolism of Key 20 & Key 8.

II. The power of liberation is compared with a venomous serpent, because the tooth (Shin) breaks down forms to begin the process of assimilation. The old must die before the new man may be born. Thirty-six is also 6 x 6 or the magic square (see Appendix 6) of Tiphareth. What is born anew is the Son (Sun) in Tiphareth.

III. "The form of the letter Shin reminds one of a mouth full of teeth. Unlike the letter Peh which is turned to eat whatever it finds on its level, the Shin is turned upwards to receive nourishment from on high. It is thus the higher octave if what is represented by Peh. [The Idiot Speaks, Caleb Folis]

IV. "HE caused the letter Shin to reign in fire." [Sephir Yetzirah 3:5]

V. Rabbi Glazerson: "According to the Zohar, the letter Shin is called "the letter of truth." The three branches represent the three aspects of the truth about man: (1) he possesses a spiritual soul (Neshamah), (2) a spirit (Rauch), and (3) bodily soul (Nefesh)." [Letters of Fire].

VI. "This character as consonant belongs to the sibilant sound, and depicts in an onomatopoetic manner, light movements, sounds durable and soft. As symbolic image it represents the part of the bow from which the arrow is shot. In Hebrew, it is the sign of relative duration and of the movement attached thereunto. It is derived from the vocal sound י, become consonant by joining to its expression the respective significations of the consonants ו and ס. As prepositive relation, it constitutes a sort of pronominal article and is placed at the head of nouns and verbs, to communicate to them the double power that it possesses of movement and of conjunction." [d'Olivet, 1976, pp. 455-456.]

VII. "Sheen (300): Prodigious cosmic motion. Movement of everything that exists. All organisms live through Sheen (300), either through or against its action, because Sheen is similar to a powerful breath which vivifies and carries away. Only the most extreme weakness can elude or oppose it." [Suraes, 1992, p. 66.]

רוח אלהים Ruach Elohim. the Life-Breath of the Gods (Creative powers). The breath on the Mighty Ones, the Spirit of God, Holy Spirit. Maybe understood as the Life-breath has seven aspects, its motion (in and out = 2) is 2x7 or 14. see 360, 86 and Genesis 1.3.

יצר formation, to form, to mold; create, concept. Shin is the "fire of Formation" by which atonement, or union with God is made. Root of יצירה, Yetzirah, World of formation. With different pointing: yatser, conception, formation, imagination, device, purpose, form, framing, pottery; idol; impulse, inclination, desire. אצר to be predestined, preordained. see 315.

יצר to mould into a form; especially as a potter, figuratively to determine (i.e. form a resolution):- earthen, fashion, form, frame, potter, purpose. [Strong's Dictionary] "I stand not aloof, unmoved, watching my handiwork, as a potter watcheth the clay upon his wheel. Nay, not so, for I am the clay, the wheel, and the potter too. I am the work and the worker, and the means of working." [Book of Tokens, Cheth]

צרי balsam, balm. metathesis of יצר.

כפר atonement (at-one-ment), expiate. Literally, to cover, to condone, to placate, to cancel. With different pointing: to atone, procure forgiveness, pacify, propitiate. As a verb to be atoned for, be forgiven, to be made void. see numbers that reduce to 3.

פרוד separation. Shin is said to appear as a flame of separation [Book of Tokens].

בעבורך for thy sake, because-of-you. Genesis 3:17: "To Adam he said, Because you listened to your wife and ate of the tree abut which I commanded you, You must not eat of it, Cursed is the ground because of you; through toil you will eat of it all the days of your life." This was done so that the evolution (of fire) may take place.

מעמקים depths. Psalm 130:1: "Out of the depths [ממעמקים, from depths, *Interlinear NIV Bible*] I cry to you O Lord..." The fire of the father is hid within the depths of the waters of the mother (Binah). see 840.

Paul Case: "'Out of the depths' means out of the innermost or deepest principle of his individuality, the central I AM. (see לב עמק "the heart is deep", in Psalm 64:6: "They search out iniquities; they accomplish a diligent search: both the inward thought of every one of them, and the heart, is deep."

אור בפאהה light in extension (Khabs Am Pekht).

ערל uncircumcised; unpruned.

נמרוד Nimrod. a son of Cush.

מצפץ God of Chesed, of Hod and of Briah. A Temurah permutation of IHVH. see 1399, "two great lights"

רק Only, but, nothing but, save, except. 2 Chronicles 5:10: "There was nothing in the ark except the two tablets that Moses had placed in it at Horeb, where the Lord made a covenant with the Israelites after they came out of Egypt." With different pointing: thin, lean in Joseph's dream in Genesis 41:20: "After them, seven other cows came up-scrawny and very ugly and lean. I had never seen such ugly cows in all the land of Egypt." Also *roq*: saliva in Isaiah 50:6: "I offered my back to those who beat me, my cheeks to those who pulled by beard; I did not hide my face from mocking and spitting."

"Every idea of tenuity, rarity, expansion, giving way. That which is *attenuated, rarified*; which *gives way*, physically as well as morally: in a figurative sense, *time*. [d'Olivet, 1976, p. 454.]

אלף למד הי יוד מם Aleph Lamed Heh Yod Mem. Elohim, spelled in full; i.e. the creative powers of God. see 86.

יהוה צדיק יבמן The Lord tests the righteous. Psalm 11:5: "The Lord tests the righteous and the wicked, and the one who loves violence His soul hates." The Zohar [II:140A, p.48]: For what reason? Said Rabbi Simeon: "Because when God finds delight in the righteous, he brings upon them suffering, as it is written: "Yet it pleased the Lord to crush him by disease" [Isaiah 53:10] ...God finds delight in the soul, but not in the body, as the soul resembles the supernal soul, whereas the body is not worthy to be allied to the supernal essences, although the image of the body is part of the supernal symbolism. Observe that when God takes delight in the soul of a man, he afflicts the body in order that the soul may gain freedom. For so long as the soul is together with the body, it cannot exercise its full powers, but only when the body is broken and crushed again, 'He trieth the righteous,' so as to make them firm like 'a tilled stone,' the 'costly corner-stone' mentioned by the prophet [Isaiah 28:16]."

סכסכבסלים Saksaksalim. The Sentinel of the 25th Path (Tunnel) of Samekh on the Inverse Tree of Life.

I. The 25th Ray illumines the Tunnel of Saksaksalim whose number is 300, which is the number of *Shin* [ש], the letter of Spirit. It is the triple fire-tongue symbolic of Chozzar [Neptune], the disintegrating principle of antimatter. אור בפאהה (*Khabs Am Pekht*, 'Light In Extension') also has this number. It is the False Light, the Great Lie, which is the Word of Choronzon mirrored in the Abyss. Hence, כפר, 300, is a substance used for covering with pitch or ashes. It derives from the Egyptian word *Khepr*, 'to transform', 'reverse', or *regenerate the dead'. The dead are the swathed or bound mummies, and סמר means 'horror', 'as if bound with fear', 'horripflation' (see Job 4:15), from the Egyptian *smar*, 'to bind or enswathe for slaughter', The concepts of reversal, transformation, and annihilation are also implied.

The sigil of Saksaksalim shows the figure of a priest (with arms extended in the form of a cross) hanging upside down in an irregularly bound void in which appear the letters סבר (280) and an inverted figure 7. The void is sealed by the image of a black lunar crescent emitting streams of blood. This sigil resumes the ideas relating the magical *siddhi* of the 25th path, i.e. Transmutations and the Vision of the Universal Peacock. The peacock is a symbol of Shaitan and comports the rainbow symbolism previously explained, thus showing the feminine nature of the transforming fire of this *kala*.

The number 280 is that of רפ, meaning 'terror'. It is also the number of squares on the side of the Vault containing the body of Christian Rosencreutz in the Golden Dawn symbolism of the 5° = 6° Grade, which should be studied in connection with the symbolism of this tunnel. The relevant verse from *Liber 231* reads: And a mighty angel appeared as a woman, pouring vials of woe upon the flames, lighting the pure stream with her brand of cursing. And the iniquity was very great.

The Angel as the woman cursing represents the feminine current symbolized by Nephthys, the sister of Isis. Nephthys is the reifier or transmitter of perfection; the art of transforming raw (i.e. virgin) nature into the image of fulfillment or motherhood.

The Order of Qliphoth associated with this process is the *Nechashiron*, or Snakey, and the Atu of Tahuti attributed to *Kala* 25 is appropriately entitled The Bringer Forth of Life.

In the African pantheon, Aidowedo -the rainbow goddess - is the cognate deity. Her coming is likened to the lightning-flash. This is the Sagittarian influence manifesting in the form of the female current. 'Her fetish is a large serpent that appears only when it wants to drink. It then rests its tail on the ground and thrusts its mouth into the water. It is said that 'he who finds the excrement [menstrual] of this serpent is rich forever'. [Grant, 1994, pp. 226-227.]

301

אש   fire. With different pointing *Ish*: entity. existence, being, man, there is [2 Samuel 14:19;

Micah 6:10]. The secret alchemical fire is the entity with all things, and the foundation of all life and form. Aleph is the Life-breath or Spirit and Shin corresponds to the element fire and has the same numerical value as the "Life-breath of the Creative Powers." Both Aleph and Shin are mother letters. see 53, 44, 444, 256, 471, 360, 300.

I. "This root is symbol of the elementary principle whatever it may be. It is the root אש, what the circular line is to the straight line. The signs which constitute it are those of power and of relative movement. In a very broad sense it is every active principle, every center unfolding a circumference, every relative force. In a more restricted sense it is fire considered in the absence of every substance.

The Hebraic genius confounds this root with the root אם, and considers in it all which is of *the basis* and *foundation* of things; that which is hidden in its principle; that which is *absolute, strong, unalterable*, as the appearance of *fire*. The Arabic designates that which moves with *agility*, vehemence. This idea ensues necessarily from that attached to the mobility of fire." [d'Olivet, 1976, p. 299.]

אש   foundation (Aramaic).

אדני המלך נאמן   "Adonai, the faithful king". The divine name representing God as the master power, ruling over all things from his holy habitation in the center.

אלף למד הא יוד מים   Alohim [אלהים] spelled in full.

הצור   the rock (a divine name). The English of Deuteronomy 32:4 prints this with a capital "R" to show that it is a divine name. This is the rock "that begat thee (360). The inner meaning is that the life of the personal man is essentially one with the prototypical life of the Cosmic Self. The inner man is begotten, not made, being of one substance with the father, by whom all things were made. He shares in the divine nature whence he proceeds.

מנורה   menorah. a candlestick. Specifically the golden candle-stick described in Exodus 25:31-39. It was a symbol of the 7 heavenly bodies and the 7 interior stars or chakras.

צדק ילין בה justice abides in her [Isaiah 1:21]. The authorized version reads: "Righteous lodged in it." Has a recondite meaning, explained in I.Z.Q. But note: the explanation is itself a veil it depends on one occult understanding of ציון (Zion, 156), ירשלם (Jerusalem, 586), and of דביר (Debir, 216). see 961, 1779 (Greek), Isaiah 1:26, & The Lesser Holy Assembly (para. 541).

צורה A rock, appearance, creature, picture, form or shape (of a temple or house, as used in Ezekiel 43:11). A technical term in Qabalah, designating the prototypical spiritual Self. In a sense what is meant by *tzurah* is higher even than Yekhidah, the Self seated in Kether. It is the Self-hood of *Ain* (61), the no-thing, persisting throughout all successive cycles of manifestation and withdrawal. see 696, 492.

קרא to call, summon, proclaim, announce, to call upon, invoke; to convoke, assemble, invite, to call by name; to read aloud; recite; to meet; to happen; befall; to read the scriptures. As a noun: Biblical scholar, Bible teacher. see 464, 360, 300 and Genesis 1:10.

הרמון Hermon. Mountain in Palestine; sacred mountain, "the prominent on." From הרם "to be high or prominent" (Inman). On is connected with the Sun ("the most high God"). It was viewed from ancient times as a sacred locality, with numerous shrines. see 343, 345.

שׂא to drive, to push away; to lift up. A Metathesis of אשׂ and conceals within the name Saul. see 331.

I. "destruction." [Godwin, 1999, p. 543]

II. "The sign of relative movement united to that of power, constitutes a root which is heiroglypically characterized by the arc of a circle inscribed between two radii. The character ס is designated by the arc deprived of its radius or arrow, and closed by its cord. The character ו is designated by the radius or arrow indicating the circumference. The portion of the circle represented by the root שׂא, can be considered in movement or in repose; thence, the opposed ideas of tumult and of the calm which it develops." [d'Olivet, 1976, p. 456.]

κρανιον. kranion (Gr). Skull. In Luke 23:33: "To that place called 'skull,' there they crucified him."

Σεληνη. Seleme (Gr). the moon, a lunar month.

302

ארקא Fertile soil (Aramaic); Earth. One of the 7 Earths corresponding to Hod. see 291, 50, 14, 365, 105, 432, 337.

כהן לאל עליון priest of the most high God (Genesis 14:18). Refers to Melchi-zedek. see 320, 126.

קבר has protected. With different pointing: 1. *qeber*. grave, sepulcher; womb, uterus containing an embryo; 2. *qahbar* to bury.

קרב inward part, bowels intestines; midst, interior. With different pointing: 1. *qahrab*. to come near, approach; to be offered as a sacrifice; to come before a court; 2. *qayrub*. to befriend; to be near, to bring near, approaching; 3. *qerahb*. battle, war. All these meaning of קרב refer to the physical plane and the microcosm.

בקר morning, early day. Suggesting the mystic east, direction attributed to Daleth on the Cube of Space. With different pointing: to inquire, seek, examine, test; to distinguish; differentiate; to visit, attend; or to criticize, review, censure.

I. "בקר, *east-dawn*... This word, produced form the root קר, governed by the sign ב, indicates a thing whose course is regulated, and which presents itself ever the same; a thing which is renewed unceasingly. The Arabic word is found sometimes used to express light. The Syriac contains often the idea of inspection, of exploration. The Hellenist in restricting its signification to the word προι, *morning*, have followed purposely the literal and vulgar sense. The Samaritan version was less restricted; it translates ערב and בקר... that is to say, that which lowers, falls, and that which rises, begins, signals. The Chaldaic Targum says that same thing: רמש and צפר. The English word *over and back*, hold to the same roots as the Hebrew words; and vividly express the figurative sense."

II. East; The Sunrise is an "Emblem of the direction in which the Self appears in the soul. The source of Life, and the light of knowledge is the self (sun) rising in the mind... from the east, or along the celestial path of the self, to which the rising of the sun in the heavens is comparable, was the Divine Ego or Spark sent forth of the Spirit in the Buddhic vestores which clothed it with the full powers of the soul." Dawn daybreak and dayspring, is "a symbol of the commencement of manifestation-the period of the self forthgoing. To establish the planes of nature. This is typified in the approach of the sunrise when the sun (the Self) appears." [Gaskell, 1981, pp. 201, 239.]

בקר   cattle, herd, oxen; cattle driver. Note that Aleph is the "Ox". see 1052, 1265.

רקב   to rot, decay, to putrefy. With different pointing *rahqeb*: rotten; *rahqahb*,. rottenness, putrefaction, decay, decayed flesh or corpse mingled with soil. Observe the last four words are metathesis of 3 letters: Qoph attributed to Pisces and alchemical multiplication (259); Resh, attributed to the Sun and Beth, the letter of Mercury. The following word is also a combination of these letters:

ברק   lighting, brilliancy. A person cited in Judges 5:12 "Awake, awake Deborah: Awake, awake, utter a song; arise Barak and lead thy captivity captive, thou son of Abinoam" ["Father or possessor of grace") see 443 (note), 179, 217, 58.

סראיאל   Sarayel, Saraiel, Sariel. Angel of Gemini. Assisted by another "Genus" (Angel) called Sagras, the ruler of Taurus (ruled by Venus, seat of intuition-connect with alchemical congelation, 331). see Dictionary of Angels, (p. 258).

והארץ   and the earth [Genesis 1:2:. "... was without form and void, and darkness was upon the face of the deep."

מאזני צדק   Just balances. Leviticus 19:36: "... Just weighs, a just Ephah, and a just Hin, shall you have: I am the Lord your God, which brought you out of the Land of Egypt." see 194,

צופליפו   Tzuflifu. The Sentinel of the 28th Path (Tunnel) of Tzaddi on the Inverse Tree of Life.

I. The 28th tunnel is sentinelled by Tzuflifu, whose number is 302. 302 is the number of בקר, 'to cut open', 'inquire into', 'dawn', 'dawning of light', from the Egyptian *beka*, meaning 'to extend', *pekai*, 'to flower'. Its anagram, ברק means 'to lighten', 'send lightning', as applied to the Great Serpent (of the Gnostics), from the Egyptian *buiruka*, meaning 'fulgurant', 'glittering'. A further metathesis, קבר, signifies 'a cave', 'hole in the earth', 'tomb'. These three letters therefore constitute the type-name of a place of divination founded on the oracle of the womb.

The sigil shows a Priest or King wearing a crown in the shape of a phallus with its 'eye' protruding. This is an image of the Great Serpent extended or 'flowering', its eye signifying the dawning or opening power of the phallus.

The Atu pertaining to Path 28 is that of *The Emperor*, who is also called 'Sun of the Morning and Chief among the Mighty'. In the Tunnel of Tzuflifu this dawn assumes an almost deliquescent state of heat that resembles a fluid fire-ball.

The disease typical of Path 28 is apoplexy, and the demons which haunt the tunnel are the furies born of the blood of Uranus who was castrated for crimes against the ties of kinship. The furies (or Erinyes) are depicted in Greek myth as winged women girt with snakes, thus revealing their affinity with the lunar current.

Uranus is the planet assigned to Daath, with its symbolism of reversion to the source of Non-Being, hence the crime of incest associated with this tunnel. The relevant verse of *Liber 231* reads:

Transformed, the holy virgin appeared as a fluidic fire, making her beauty into a thunderbolt.

The thunderbolt typifies the swastika, the whirling or spiral force that restores the world 'ruined by evil'. In this tunnel 'evil' (or chaos) emerges in its raw state through the Gate of the Abyss in the form of lightning (ברק). In an article entitled 'Life, Death and Antimatter' there appears the following:

Antimatter seems mostly or possibly always to penetrate the world of physical matter through spirals, especially geometric spirals, at the center of which the threshold between time and antitime apparently exists. Energy appears to move both ways across this threshold.

Later on in the same article it is claimed that the 'human body is composed of three major spirals oriented around the cerebral aqueduct and the fourth ventricle'. If the reader will refer to Cults of the Shadow (chapters 1 and 4) he will see the force of these remarks in relation to the *kala* that charges the tunnel of Tzuflifu.

Path 28 is under the influence of Aries (ruled by Mars), which is represented by the fiery aspect of Chango and the god Ogoun with his flaming darts, or *manamana* (literally 'chains of fire', i.e. lightning). The martial symbolism of violent heat, and super-abundant energy, denotes the feminine power that reaches its peak in the Tunnel of Qulielfi. [Grant, 1994, pp. 237-238.]

303

שאב to draw (water). Genesis 24:13: "Behold, I stand hereby the well of water; and the daughters of the men of the city are coming out to draw water." And in [Deuteronomy 29:11 "Your little ones, your wives, and the stranger who is in your camp, from the gatherer of your wood to the drawer of your water." (Stand this day before the Lord your God). See also Joshua 9:21.

שבא A region and people in southern Arabia, abounding in spices, gold and precious stones. 1 Kings 10:1: "And when the Queen of Sheba heard of the fame of Solomon and the name of the Lord, she came to test him with proverbs." And in Isaiah 60:6: "A multitude of camels shall cover you, the dromedaries of Midian, and Ephah; all those from Sheba shall come; they shall being gold and frankincense, and shall announce abroad the praises of the Lord." see 793.

באש in fire Exodus 3:2.

וירא אלהים va-ya-re Elohim. and God saw. Genesis 1:18.

304

I. (16 x 19) or 2^4 x 19

זרזיף showers. In Psalm 72:6, where the context shows clearly that these showers water the earth. They are the fructifying showers which promote the growth of vegetation, and since the same context associates them with the manifestation of the powers of the "King's Son," it is clear that here we have a Qabalistic allusion to the descent of the secret power of the "Son of Fire" who is also the "Son of the Woman," personified in Freemasonry as Hiram Abiff.

כאמבריאל Kambriel. Geomatic intelligence of Aquarius. Archangel of Aquarius. Note that the Path of Tzaddi, attributed to Aquarius, links Netzach, sphere of Venus, with Yesod, sphere of the Moon, or automatic pattern consciousness. The function attributed to Tzaddi is meditation, or revelation, and this becomes evident as the Venus and Moon centers are linked in the microcosm by this activity. Davidson gives Cambiel and cites Trithemius as saying it is ruler of the sign of Aquarius and angel of the 9th hour. [Davidson, 1971, p. 80.] see 148, 80, 90.

קדר qahder. cranium, brain-pan, skull; pot, contents of the pot. The cranium is the place where the "dew of heaven" is collected, and where the yellow grains of gold fuse into the adytum of the most high. With different pointing: *qidder.* to cut through; figuratively, to estimating the level distance of places separated by mountains; to make pots;

דקר to stab, to starve, pierce, strike (thrust) through, wound. With different pointing: *qawdahr.* to be dark, be black to be turbid; to be gloomy, be dark; to perforate, cut out. With different pointing: Kedar. Name of a nomadic time of Arabs. *Sepher Sephiroth*: white [Crowley, 1977, p. 34].

רש Green. The color of Venus, which is the desire nature, as well as creative imagination. see 434. also: lapel. The place where a flower is buttoned-the white rose symbolizes purified desire. see 111, 434 and Key 0.

שד breast. Job 24:9: "The fatherless child is snatched from the breast; the infant of the poor is seized for a debt." With different pointing shed: demon, devil in Deuteronomy 32:17: "They sacrificed to devils [לשדים, to-the-demons], not to God; to gods whom they know not, to new gods that came newly up, whom your fathers did not fear." And in Psalm 106:37: "Yes, they sacrifice their sons and daughters to devils."

305

זה הדרך לכו בן This is the way; walk in it. Isaiah 30:21: "Whether you turn to the right or the left, your ears will hear a voice behind you, saying, 'This is the way; walk in it.'" see 241; 3384, 1061, 2323 (Greek).

דשא grass. Genesis 1:11: "And God [Elohim] said, let the earth bring forth grass, the herb yielding seed, and the fruit tree yielding fruit after his kind, whose seed is in itself, upon the earth: and it was so." Note that this word is a combination of דש or "green", suggesting Venus and Aleph, the letter of spirit. The "earth" is the physical body; the grass represents the shoots of the neophyte or new plant, which is the regenerated consciousness. With different pointing: green herbage, tender herb. דשא dawshaw. to sprout, grow grass, grow green with grass.

עולם קטן small world; microcosm. An epithet of man. see 146, 159.

יצרה Yetzirah. The world of formation (variant spelling, see 315). [From יצר: imagination, device, purpose impulse, inclination, desire; form, framing; pottery, idol] The connection between Venus or desire and formation should be apparent.

I. In Jewish mysticism, Paroketh or Parakah was the veil that divided the Temple. Its number, 305, is that of Yetzirah, the World of Formation, and as the Veil of the Abyss divides the World of Emanations from the World of Creation, so the Veil of Paroketh divides the World of Creation from the World of Formation. The Veil of the Abyss conceals Daath; the Veil of Paroketh obscures Yesod, and these two power zones generate the glamour and illusion that constitute the world of appearances. [Grant, 1994, p. 54.]

אור צח dazzling white light. [Note that צח means dazzling, bright, clear; glowing, brightness] the light from on high, or Kether, reveals all secrets of formation.

"That dazzling whiteness, too brilliant to be borne by mortal eyes,
lighteth the path of every blessed one who attaineth to immorality." [Book of Tokens, Nun]

שגב to be high, strong (of a fortress). In Deuteronomy 2:36: "From Adoer, which is by the brink of the river of Arnon, and from the city that is in the valley, as far as Gilead, there was not one city too strong for us; the Lord our God delivered all to us." To rise high, to be exalted, in Job 5:11: "To shut up on high those that are lowly; and the meek shall be exalted by salvation." With different pointing: siggeb. to set up on high, to make strong in Psalm 107:41: (The Lord) "He strengthens the poor and he multiplies their families like a flock." To set up against, in Isaiah 9:11: "Therefore the Lord shall set up the adversaries of Rezin against him [Jacob], and join his enemies together." With different pointing suggahb: to be strong, safe in Proverbs 29:25: "The fear of man brigs a snare: but whosoever puts his trust in the Lord shall be safe."

ערלה foreskin; connected with Israel's covenant with God. In Jeremiah 4:4: "Circumcise yourselves to the Lord, circumcise the foreskins of your hearts, you men of Judah and people of Jerusalem, or my wrath will break out and burn like fire because of the evil you have done, burn with no one to quench it." see 794 and Genesis 31:14.

כריעה A curving, bending [Crowley, 1977, p. 34]. This word is not found in scripture.

הקממנע Haqamano. Netzach, 42-fold name in Yetzirah. Netzach is the sphere of Venus.

הש Given without explanation in Sepher Sephiroth [Crowley, 1977, p. 35]. The combination of letters suggest the power of vision or reason (Heh) united with that of the fire of resurrection (Shin) or Mars in Aries combination with Mars in Vulcan.

"Root not used in Hebrew. The Arabic signifies literally to soften, to become tender. As onomatopoetic root indicates a tumultuous concourse of any kind whatsoever." [d'Olivet, 1976, p. 333.]

306

אשה fire (feminine), woman. It suggest that fire is the womb of manifestation from which all things are brought forth. Also האש the Fire. see Deuteronomy 5:22.

I. See 301 for d'Olivet comments on the root אש.

II. "The name of this woman [אשה]*Esha*, is the feminine element of cosmic fire, inasmuch as she springs from *Esh* [אש] fire. Notice the spelling of *Eesh* for man: [איש]. Adam discovers this, his new name. (The addition of Yod to the name of fire indicates that this 'fire' comes into existence in man). A remarkable feature of this ideograms is that *Esha* does not really exist although she is alive (she has no Yod but has the Heh of Life). This fire, *Esh*, from which she proceeds, has neither life nor existence. It is a pure archetype שא. As to *Eesh*, the man, he has the Yod of existence but no Heh: he in not really alive. When we deeply investigate the notions, existence and life, we can discover that these schemata [words] are an excellent and well-observed description of what our humanity actually is. [Suraes, 1992, p. 113.] see 311.

III. "A symbol of the emotion-nature of the soul, which is to be transmuted from the astral [emotional] to the buddhic [intuitive] state... and the love-wisdom within the soul [In Genesis 2:21-21] cause a state of latency to overtake the mind (man), so that it was for a time unable to carry on its activities. And on the mind plane, one of the higher sub-planes (rib) was specifically selected in accordance with the divine scheme, as the abode of the higher soul related to buddhi, and thereon was the emotion-nature (woman) evolved; and this new factor was brought into relation with the lower mind. And the mind acknowledges the better half of itself to be now of its own substance, and recognizes the mind-emotion that which is apparently dual within the mind itself." [Gaskell, 1981, pp. 821-822.]

IV. Swendenborg assets that "by the woman' is

signified man's own, may be known from the fact that it was the woman who was deceived; for nothing ever deceives man but his own, or what is the same, the love of self and of the world. The rib is said to be 'built into a woman', but it is not said that the woman was 'created' or 'formed', or 'made', as before when treating of regeneration. The reason for this is that to 'build' is to raise up that which is fallen; and in the sense it is used in the Word, were to 'build; is predicated of evils, to raise up of falsities; and to 'renew', of both... 'bone of bones and flesh of flesh', signify the OWN of the external man; 'bone', the OEN not so much vivified, and 'flesh', the OWN that is vivified. Man (vir) moreover, signifies the internal man, and form his being so coupled with the external man... the OWN which was before called 'woman', is here denominated 'wife'". [Arcano Coelestia, pp. 72, 74]

ורוח אלהים ve-Ruach Elohim. and the Holy Spirit. Genesis 1:2: "And the earth was without form, and void; and darkness was upon the face of the deep. And the Spirit of God moved upon the waters." see 214, 86.

צורי my rock. Psalm 18:2: "The Lord is my rock, and my fortress, and my deliverer; my God, my strength, in whom I will trust; my buckler, and the horn of my salvation, and my high tower." [אלי, my God, accompanies this. see 347]

עיר יהוה city of IHVH. Isaiah 60:14: "The sons also of them that afflicted thee shall come bending unto thee; and all they that despised thee shall bow themselves down at the soles of they feet, and they shall call thee, the city of the Lord, the Zion of the Holy one of Israel."

צפעוני poisonous snake, viper, basilisk; a small hissing serpent, asp. Isaiah 11:8, 59:5: "And the sucking child shall play on the hole of the asp, and the weaned child shall put his hand on the cockatrice' den."; "They hatch cockatrice' eggs, and weave the spider's web: he that eats of their eggs dies, and that which is crushed breaks out into a viper."

אב הרחמים Father of mercies. Suggest Chesed, sphere of Jupiter and of cosmic memory; manifestation on the Cube of Space.

ביעור ugliness, sin. Attributed to Peh, the letter of Mars as one of its pairs of opposites (grace and sin); the direction north on the Cube of Space. *Sepher Yetzirah* 4:1: "Seven Doubles in speech and in transposition. The transpose of wisdom is Folly [Daleth]. The transpose of Wealth is Poverty [Kaph]. The Transpose of Seed [fruitfulness] is Desolation [Resh]. The transpose of Life is Death [Beth]. The transpose of dominance is Subjugation [Tav]. The transpose of Peace is War [Gimel]. The transpose of Grace is Ugliness [Peh]." [Kaplan, 1997, p. 162]

מטרונא matrona. *domina*; matron, lady, mistress. An epithet or name of Briah, the creative world, "or the throne, which keeps the garden [of manifestation]; when, moreover Malkuth is called the lady [*domina*], then Briah is her maid-servant." See K.D.L.C.K. (p.528).

ניצוצין sparks, sparkling lights; squirting, a drop of water. These sparks are said to be caused from the breaking up of the vessels of the braitic level, which are then raised into the fragments of light, which are connected with divine sparks and human individualities. see 288, רפח and K.D.L.C.K. (p.571).

רההעאל 39th Shem ha-Mephorash. "God who receives sinners." For the healing of the sick. Governs health and longevity. Influences paternal and filial affection. Negative influence: dead or condemned land. The cruelest known: infanticide and patricide.

I. Associated with the 2nd decanate and 3rd quinance of Aquarius; angel by day of 6 of Swords (Tiphareth of Yetzirah). 191-195. PTÉCHOUT, Saturn. April 27, July 8, September 18, November 29, February 9. 12:40-1:00 P.M. [Psalm 30:10] "Hear O Lord, and have mercy upon me: Lord, be thou my helper." To cure maladies and for obtaining the mercy of God. see 965 & Appendix 10.

II. "An angel of the Order of Powers. he rules over health and longevity, and inspire respect for one's parents... his corresponding angel is Ptechout." [Davidson, 1971, p. 243.]

פורך Goetia demon #50 by night of the 2nd decanate of Leo. In the Tarot minor arcana this decanate is attributed to the 6 of Wands, or the

operation of egoic principle in the archetypal world. see 786 & Appendix 11.

I. "Forcas... a fallen angel; in Hell he is renowned president or duke; and here he devotes his time to teaching rhetoric, logic and mathematics. He can render people invisible; he also knows how to restore lost property." Has 29 legions of demons to do his bidding, according to De Planky, *Dictionnaire Infernal*." [Davidson, 1971, p. 113.]

II. *Goetia*: "He is a knight, and appears in the from of a cruel old man with a long beard and a hoary head, riding upon a pale-colored horse, with a sharp weapon in his hand. His office is to teach the arts of philosophy, astrology, rhetoric, logic, chiromancy, and pyromancy, in all their parts, and perfectly. He has under his power 20 Legions of Spirits." [Mathers, 1995, p. 54]

שאה to rage, to be noisy; to rush, roar (of water). Isaiah 17:12: "Woe to the armies of many people, which make a noise like a roaring of the seas! and to the rushing of nations, that rush like the rushing of mighty waters." Also the 28th Shem ha-Mephorash, short form. see 321 & Appendix 10.

רימון malo-granatum [Sephir Sephiroth]. Rosenroth in K.D.L.C.K. (p.689) says Netzach and Hod are called two pomegranates in the Zoharic text.

307 (prime)

רבקה Rebekah. Fettering (thy beauty), The Great White One; i.e. the Moon, the celestial virgin, the embodiment of lovingness, Rebecca (Inman). Rebecca, the wife of Isaac [Genesis 24:15]. See 576.

Rosenroth in K.D.L.C.K. (p.681-682) gives *Ribqah* and says this name is called "Malkuth with the most vehement connotation of judgement and when she is united with her husband [i.e. Tiphareth], with Geburah."

אב רוחמן Merciful father. Suggest Chesed, sphere of Jupiter and of cosmic memory.

ודיאץ Goetia demon #59 by night of the 2nd decanate of Virgo. see 1117 & Appendix 11.

Goetia: "He is a great Marquis, and appears in the from of a lion, riding upon a horse mighty and strong, with a serpent's tail; and he holds in his right hand two great serpents hissing. His office is to teach the virtues of the stars, and to know the mansions of the planets, and how to understand their virtues. He also transforms men, and gives dignities, prelacies, and confirmation thereof; also favor with friends and with foes. He does govern 30 Legions of Spirits." [Mathers, 1995, p. 59]

שבה to carry off, to lead captive, to make prisoner. 1 Kings 8:46: "When they sin against you (for there is no man that does not sin), and you be angry with them and deliver them to the enemy so that they carry them away captives to the land of their enemies, far and near." (Hear their prayer and maintain their cause). see 352, 358.

שוא nothingness, vanity. In Psalm 41:6: "When they come to see me, they speak falsely (vanity) and their hearts devise evil; they go out into the street and gossip about me." Translated "vain" in Psalm 60:12: "Give us help from trouble: for vain is the help of man. "Deceit" in Job 31:5: "If I have walked with vanity, or if my foot has hastened to deceit." "Affliction" in Job 7:3: "So am I made to possess months of affliction, and wearisome nights are appointed to me."

רעואל Moses's father-in-law. Exodus 2:18: "When the girls return to *Revel* their father, he asked them, 'why have you returned so early today?'"

מאלכונעפאט Malkunofat. The Sentinel of the 23rd Path (Tunnel) of Mem on the Inverse Tree of Life.

I. The 23rd *kala* is under the dominion of Malkunofat who lies in the depth of the watery abyss. His number is 307 which is that of וריאץ, a 'night demon' of the 2nd decanate of Scorpio, and having therefore an essentially sexual reference. It is also the number of לורע, meaning 'to sow', derived from the root זרע, 'semen'.

There is in this number an element of panic terror exemplified in the word שוא, which means 'to make a noise', 'crash', 'be terrible'. It derives

from the Egyptian word *shefi*, signifying 'terror, terrify', 'terrible' or 'demon-like'. It is the root of the name Shiva, the Hindu god of destruction.

These ideas are apparent in the sigil which is in the form of a portrait of Malkunofat, with the letters נוה descending in that order beside a downward-pointing arrow. The key to this glyph lies in the number 61, which is the number of נוה. 61 is *Ain*, meaning 'Not'. *Ain* is identical with *Ayin*, the yoni or eye of the void. According to Crowley, 61 is 'a number rather like 31'. 31 is לא, 'Not', and אל, 'God', thus identifying the Absolute with the Void. *Ani*, the ego, 61, is also void. 61 is the number of Kali, Goddess of Time and Dissolution. Her color is black, which equates her on the one hand with the void of space, and on the other with the symbolism of sexual magick typified by the blackness of gestation, the silence and darkness of the womb. Above all, 61 is the number of the 'Negative conceiving itself as a Positive'. This it does through the בטן (*Beten*, 61) or womb of Kali. *Beten* derives from the Egyptian *but*, the determinative of which is the vagina sign. The womb is the nave or נוה (61) which in metathesis becomes הון, meaning 'wealth.' It pertains to the Goddess of the lunar serpent that appears only when it wishes to drink. It then rests its tail on the ground and thrusts its mouth into the water. It is said that 'he who finds the excrement of this serpent is rich forever' The excrement to which allusion is made is not anal, but menstrual.

The formula of the sigil may be interpreted as the subjection of the womb or woman by Malkunofat for the purpose of acquiring wealth. The Atu corresponding to the Tunnel of Malkunofat is entitled 'The Hanged Man,' The Spirit of the Mighty Waters. This is indicated by the downward pointing arrow alongside the נוה, and it implies the light (or gold) in the Depths. Ibis symbolism accords with the magic *siddhi* attributed to Path 23, i.e. the power of skrying.

The tunnel of Malkunofat is the abode of the Deep Ones, of which the Arch devil Leviathan is the generic symbol. The *Sepher Yetzirah* refers to Leviathan as *Theli*, the Dragon. Its number is 440 which is the number of לבבות, 'placenta', or 'cakes', a reference to the excrement above mentioned. It is also the number of **הם**, meaning 'to come to an end', from the Egyptian *atem*, to annihilate. This is the dragon of darkness whose number is 5, being the formula of the female in her lunar and nocturnal form.

Mathers calls attention to the fact that 'this dragon is said by the author of the Royal Valley to be the king of all the 'shells or 'demons', and he suggests comparison with the beast in Revelation. According to *The Book of Concealed Mystery* 'the serpent (i.e. Leviathan) came upon the woman, and formed in her a nucleus of impurity, in order that he might make the habitation evil. The nucleus of impurity is the substance of which water is the symbol. Water (i.e. blood) is the element attributed to the 23rd Path.

It is this 'nucleus of impurity' which the Adept gathers about him for the work of the next (24th) *kala*. It should be understood that the term 'nucleus of impurity' is a legacy of the Old Aeon [The Aeon of Osiris of which the Judaistic cults, including Christianity, are the last remaining forms], when all that pertained to woman was considered unwholesome. In terms of physiology she was considered unclean, impure, and, in the moral sphere, 'evil'. The substance thus vilified was the water of life i.e. blood; and because its manifestation in the female determined the period of negation or non-openness to the male, it was execrated by an all-male regime as detestable, noisome, and wholly negative. In the New Aeon of Horus, however, this water is the menstruum of manifestation without which the phenomenal universe would be an impossibility. It is the means of incarnation as well as of magical reification, and as such it is the prime substance of all being, which is NOT (Nuit). This Mystery is of a mystical order and can be understood only when the nature of the Goddess is fathomed in its fullness. [Grant, 1994, pp. 216-218.]

308

שׂח seach. thought meditation. With different pointing *shach*: depressed.

קרוב Near, close by; relation, relative, kinsman. In 2 Samuel 19:42: "And all the men of Judah answered the men of Israel, because the king is near of kin to us: wherefore then be ye angry for this matter? Have we eaten at all of the king's cost? or hath he given us any gift? The "King" is **מלך** Melek (90) or Tiphareth, Judah is connected with Leo, the Sun and alchemical digestion (30), Israel means "he shall rule as God." With different pointing *qerub*: nearness, contact. see 1633.

בוקר daybreak. Suggest the golden dawn of illumination. With different pointing: herdsman.

זרקא One who flings, strews, throws, tosses, sprinkles (water of purification). With different pointing *zahrayqa*: Name of a disjunctive accent. K.D.L.C.K. (p.329) gives: *sparsor*.

קרח ice, frost; baldness. With different pointing: to make bald. Suggests uncovering the secret of reality. See Key 9, where the ice is found at the summit of the mountain.

שׁאג roaring, groaning. Isaiah 5:29: "Their roaring shall be like a lion, and like the young-lions that roar, and take hold on the prey and carry it off; and none shall deliver it." Also in Psalm 22:2: "O my God, I call thee in the daytime but you answer me not; and in the nighttime you do not abide with me." And in Job 3:24: "For my sighing comes before I eat, and my moaning are poured out like water." see 304, 306.

שׁבו A precious stone; according to the Septuagint, an agate. In Exodus 28:19: "And the third row [of the High Priest's breastplate or Ephod] a jacinth (zircon), an agate, and an amethyst."

שׁגה to wander, to go astray. Ezekiel 34:6: "My sheep wandered through all the mountains, and upon every high hill: yea, my flock was scattered upon all the face of the earth, and none did search or seek after them." Figuratively, to err in Job 6:24: "Teach me, and I will hold my tongue: and cause me to understand wherein I have erred." To deviate from, in Proverbs 19:27: "Cease, my son, to hear the instruction that causes to deviate from the words of knowledge." Also to stumble, to stagger (from drink) in Isaiah 28:7: "But they also have erred through wine, and through strong drink are out of the way; the priest and the prophet have stumbled through strong drink; they err in vision, they stumble in judgement." To be ravished with, in Proverbs 5:20: "And why will you, my son, be ravished with a strange woman, and embrace to bosom of a stranger?" see 306, 311.

שדד to be even, level, hence. With different pointing *sidded*: to level (a field), to harrow in Isaiah 28:24: "Does the ploughman plow all day to sow? Does he open and harrow his ground? And in Job 39:10: "Can you bind the yoke on the neck of the unicorn? or will he harrow in a rugged place?"

שוב to turn, to be turned. Deuteronomy 30:2: "And [you] shall return to the Lord your God, and shall obey his voice according to all that I command you this day, you and your children, with all your heart, and with all your soul." To return, to come back, in Isaiah 52:8: "Your watchmen shall lift up the voice; they shall sing together with the voice: for they shall see eye to eye, when the Lord shall return to Zion." To go again, to repeat, hence again in Ecclesiastes 10:11: "I returned, and saw again under the sun, that the race is not to the swift, nor the battle to the strong, neither yet bread to the wise nor yet riches to men of understanding, not yet favor to men of skill; but time and change happen to them all. "

309

שדה field; wife, mistress. In Ecclesiastes 2:8: "I also gathered for myself silver and gold and the treasure of kings and provinces. I got me men singers and women singers, and the delights of the sons of men, concubines very many."

שאגה roar, roaring; strepitus cordis (din of the hearts), mussitatio (mumbling, muttering), sussuratio (whispering), rugitus (roaring). The instruction of the father is a still, small voice in the heart.

"Shut thine ears to the confusing of the world which surroudeth thee. Open thine inner hearing... it shall ring suddenly in thine inner ear." [Book of Tokens, Vav]

K.D.L.C.K. (p.694) says these are in Chesed when it inclines to justice (Geburah).

זרבעל Zerbal. (A.A.S.R.) [or Ancient Accepted Scottish Rite, see Massey] The reference that is associated with *Zerbal* has to do with the quadarature of the circle. This is directly relate to קטר, diameter. (Note that the circle with a diameter drawn across is, a symbol of alchemical salt, or the physical plane. Quadrature suggest the 4 elements of Malkuth (Fire, Water, Air, Earth].

מוסגר a leper. In Exodus 4:6: "His hand was leprous as snow", should be understood under the mystery of the leper, which is a sign that it is a world enclosed by choice. See K.D.L.C.K. (p.495).

שהדי witness. Job 16:19: "And now, behold, my witness is in heaven, and my acquaintance are on high."

שט set. transgression; one who turns aside, hence: revolter. Hosea 5:2: "The rebels [שטים] are deep in slaughter, I will discipline all of them."

I. The prototype of Shaitan or Satan, God of the South whose star is Sothis. Set, or Sut (Soot), means 'black', which is the chief color of Set. Black indicates the dark mysteries of this god which were originally enacted in the underworld, or 'other' world, of *Amenta* . Set, as Lord of Amenta, or the hidden land (i.e. hell), is the epitome of subconsciousness, and therefore of the True Will or Hidden Sun, the son behind the sun symbolized by the Star of Set. [Grant, 1994, p. 278.]

ασηρ. asehr (Gr). Straight, level; prosperous, happy, blessed. Son of Jacob connected with Libra and with alchemical sublimation. Septuagint translation of אשר (501) in Genesis 49:20: "Asher's food will be rich; he will provide delicacies for a king."

310

אור הכוכבים Light of the stars, astral light; The Great Magical Agent. Otherwise know as the alchemical first matter. see 49, 74, 103, 207, 870.

חבש to bind, to bridle, to rule, to govern.

יש is, are, essence, being. Lo in that day shall the light that is bind fast every hideous shape of darkness." [Book of Tokens]

כפיר a young lion. As a young lion, the initiate conquers all the phantoms of delusion.

דוש to trample on, to conquer. "As a young lion trampled upon his prey." [Book of Tokens]

סמך מים כף Samekh (spelt in full). Refers to "the fullness of that blessed vision [Book of Tokens]. see 536, 120.

מדורין habitations. "And all thy habitations shall be blessed by the white brilliance which descendeth from the crown." [Book of Tokens, Samekh] see 960.

רעם Thunder. Refers to the fiery nature of Shin. see 360.

יקר precious, costly, dear; rare; scarce; heavy; weighty; glorious; splendid. see 710.

י:ר:ק I:R:Q. the initials of (ha) Idra Rabba Qadisha האדרא רבא קדישא The Qabalistic treatise called "the Greater Holy Assembly". Note that each letter is half the value of the letter of כתר Kether.

ירק yereq. greenness; green things; vegetables; green herbs; herbage, grass.

עמר to sprout. Root of עמרה, Gomorrah. With different pointing: omer. the [dry] measure of manna [מן, 90] for each of the Israelites in the wilderness Exodus 16:32: "And Moses said, this is the thing which the Lord commands, fill an omer of it to be kept for your generations; that they may see the bread where with I have fed you in the wilderness, when I brought you forth from the land of Egypt. With different pointing: sheaf; awmahr: to heap up. see 315, 50, 106, 700; 78.

ייצר formed. From יצר, form, pottery, imagination.

שאט to despise; contempt.

שבח to praise, to laud. Daniel 4:34: "At the end that time, I Nebuchadnezzar, raised my eyes towards heaven, and my sanity was restored. Then I praised the most high; I honored and glorified him who lives forever. his dominions is an eternal dominion; his kingdom endures from generation to generation."

שי gift, present. Isaiah 18:7: "At that time the present shall be brought to the Lord of Hosts form a people dishonored and trodden under foot, whose land the rivers have spoiled, to the place of he name of the Lord of hosts, the Mount Zion." Plural in Psalm 68:29: "Out of your temple at Jerusalem shall kings bring presents to you."

רצהיה Ritziah, "Jah is a friend"; a Phoenician name, similar to Ratziel. see 331, 15.

granum pectoria Jesus Insitum (Lt). The seed planted in the breast of Jesus. A short phrase preceding the Latin *Elogium* or *Epitaph*, at the end of Book T in the Rosicrucian Allegory. see 95, 50, 66, 99 Latin, 74, 740.

311 (prime)

רפאל Raphael. "God the Healer", the Archangel of Hod, Air, East, and of Mercury. The name designates the Life-power as the active principle of intellect, whereby things are brought to fulfillment and perfection. Also the Angel of Chokmah in Briah, the world of creation.

שבט rod, stick, branch, staff or scepter, a clan or tribe. These meanings associate with the wand of the Magician and with the magic of self-conscious intellect. The month of Shebet in Hebrew corresponds to Aquarius and Man, the water bearer. Note also that the number of Raphael is the same as that of Tzaphquiel, the archangel of Binah manifesting Itself as the Divine Soul, Neshamah. see 1217.

The divine rod that was delivered into his hand, as we read: 'With the rod of God in my [Moses] hand' [Exodus 17:9]. This is the same rod which was created in the twilight on the eve of the Sabbath and on which there was engraved the divine name in sacred letters. Rod in Psalm 23:4: "Yea, though I walk through the valley of the shadow of death, I will fear no evil; for thou are with me; thy rod and thy staff they comfort me." Other meanings: lance, spear; reed, pen. see Moses (345), 1308, 1311, 1000.

צפקיאל Tzaphqiel. "Contemplation of God." The archangel associated with Binah (3 of Cups). It refers to the Divine Vision, which is the Life-power's perception of the logical consequences of what It knows Itself to be. This Contemplation look upwards to Yekhidah, The One Self, and is the "Beholder of God," as well as the One who looks down through the abyss and is "God's Sentry." The One Power manifesting itself as the divine soul, Neshamah. see 101, 97, 280, 246.

האשה ha-aisha. the women (Eve before named). Genesis 3:1: "And he (the serpent) said unto the woman, yea, has God said, you shall not eat of every tree of the garden?" Note that man is spelled **איש**, with a Yod, but these is no Yod in the name for women.

איש man (a particular individual, as distinguished from the generic man Adam). Tiphareth as husband or spouse to Malkuth, the bride. Intimates that personal man can partake of the Divine Vision when he succeeds in attuning himself to guidance from Neshamah. see 45, 52, 80, 1081, 478, 536, 548, 640, 301, 727.

I. "**איש**, *intellectual man...* Here is a new denomination given to man. It appears for the first time, when the Being of beings, having declared that it was not good for universal man, Adam, to live alone in the solitude of his universality, has effected his individuality, in giving him an auxiliary force, a companion, created in his light and destined to him to reflect his image.

I beg the reader to remark first of all, that Moses giving a name to this companion, does not derive it from that of Adam; for Adam considered as universal man, could not know a companion. The Hebraic word **אדם** has no feminine. The word **ארמה** which appears to be it, does not signify *universal woman*, as one might think; but, the elementary principle of Adam. **אדם**, *universal man*, posses the two sexes. Moses has taken care to repeat it several times so that one shall not be deceived. What therefore is this companion, this auxiliary force, as the word **עזר** expresses it? It is the volitive faculty developed by the Being of beings: it is the intellectual woman of universal man; it is the will proper which individualizes him, and in which he is

reflected and which, rendering him independent, becomes the creative force by means of which he realizes his conceptions, and makes them pass from power into action. For, this truth must come out from the darkness of the sanctuaries: the will was creator with universal man. Whatever this man willed was when and how it willed it. The power and the act were indivisible in his will.

Such is the difference between **אדם** and **איש**. The one characterizes man universalized by his homogeneous essence. The other designates man individualized the his efficient will.

This name springs from two contracted roots **אי-אש** ...**אי** develops every idea of desire, of inclination, of appetite, of election: **אש** is the power of movement, the elementary principle, fire, considered in the absence of these two roots only differs from the word **אוש**, which indicates natural, substantialized fire, by the median sign. In the former it is that of manifestation and duration: in the latter it is the bond between nothingness and being, which I name convertible. The one is a movement, intelligent, volitive, durable; the other, a movement, appetent, blind, fugacious.

Here is the hieroglyphic meaning of the word **איש** *intellectual man*. It is a new development of *universal man*, a development, which, without destroying his universality and his homogeneity, gives him, nevertheless, an independent individuality, and leaves him free to manifest himself in other and particular conceptions, by means of a companion, an auxiliary force, intended to reflect his image.

It is therefore with profound reason that Moses having especially in mind, in this companion, the volitive faculty which constitutes universal man, *intelligent-being*, that is to say, the faculty which renders him capable of will and of choosing, draws its name from the same name of intellectual man, **איש**. In this derivation, he as caused the sign of manifestation **י**, to disappear, and has replaced it with the final sign of life, in order to make it understood that it is not the volitive principle with resides in **אשה** [woman], but the principant will, existing, no longer in power, but in action." [d'Olivet, 1976, pp. 91-93.]

347

II. F.J. Mayers: Now let us study, somewhat in detail, this word Aish. The simple root **אי** denotes merely any 'desire', 'inclination', and way in which a being or individual seeks some 'self' expression or reveals itself. The root 'Ash' denotes 'potential activity', 'power', 'force', 'directed energy'. Aish denotes all activity in which ones individuality is expressed. It is he manifestation of one's 'intelligent being'. This 'intelligent being', it is that gives man any real 'self' to express, and makes him capable of conceiving ideas of his own; but to bring about the realization of the ideas one creates, something more than creative intelligence is required. That 'something' is the driving power of will, and will was what God 'built up' into a living, active force from its elemental germ, that had till then been lying dormant in the being of Adam. Now we can see the meaning of the name Aisha [see 306]. To the name Aish, one sign letter has been added, and one removed. The sign added is Heh the sign of 'Life', or movement towards some purpose or end. It has been referred to and explained may times... Aisha is that which gives life and realizing power to Aish, but that transliterated Aisha is spelt Aleph-Yod-Shin-Heh, and pronounced Aish, but that transliterated Aisha, Aleph-Shin-Heh without the Yod, although the Yod sound is retained in pronunciation. It was omitted from the written word for heiroglypic purposes. Had it been retained, the word Aisha, would not have been simply a feminine of Aish, and would have denoted that Aisha was a separate 'intelligent being' or 'female intelligence'; but the omission of the Yod showed that Aisha was not a separate being but a faculty of the being of Adam. [The Unknown god, pp.167-168]

בשדה in the field. Astrologically associated with Key 7, a field or fence. The "field" is the area of manifestation. **שדה** (Shiddah) means "a wife, as mistress of the house," also associated with Cheth and Cancer. see 418, 309, 524, 2054 (Greek).

I. Genesis 4:8: "Now Cain said to brother Abel, 'Let go out to the field.' And while they were in the field, Cain attacked his brother Abel and killed him."

II. I.R.Q. Para. 1046: "... 'In the field', which is known to be the supernal (field). 'in the field,' which is called the field of the apple-trees."

[Mathers, 1993, p. 241]

זהב אופיר Gold of Ophir. Job 22:24: "Then shall thou lay up gold as dust, and the Gold of Ophir as the stones of the brooks." *Aesch Mezareph* says this particular kind of gold refers to the path of Malkuth and Tiphareth [Westcott, 1997, p. 15]. Note the word *zahab* does not occur in this quotation but is inferred from the word **בצר** Bawtzer, in the preceding line meaning "precious ore, support"). see 14, 291, 418, 1244.

I. *The Aesch Mezareph*: "But Zahab Ophir, is referred to Malkuth Job c. 22, v.24, for it is the name of a land (or earth) as so called from ashes.

... And thence is referred that text in Job c. 22, v.24, and put it upon Opher, he would have said Opheret, Lead, Batsar, Silver, that is this white gold. For from hence you shall have silver. And to silver when it shall be in the state of a stone, and Nachlim, Rivers of Metallic Waters; from whence you shall have Ophir, that is Gold of Ophir, which was accounted the best." [ibid, p. 11] See also 1 Chronicles 29:4.

כסף נמאס reprobate silver (evil ones). Used in Jeremiah 6:30 as a symbol for wicked-those dominated by the unrestrained impulses of the animal nature. "Reprobate silver shall men call them, because Tetragrammaton hath rejected them." This makes them "grievous revolters, walking with slanderers." They are also compared to brass, lead-base metals. Here is a clue to the true meaning of the work of transmutation whereby the stone changes these base metals into gold. Silver is used as a symbol for these persons, because Yesod (moon, silver) is the seat of Nephesh, the animal soul. see 80, 160, 204, 270, 1031, 1454 (Greek).

יקרא the calling. See **קרא**, 301.

עריאל Ariel, Aurial. "God the Revealer". The 46th Shem ha-Mephorash. 226E-230E. TÉP SEUTH. 3:00-3:20 P.M. May 4, July 15, September 25, December 6, February 16. To have revelations. [Psalm 144:9] To thank God for the good he sends us. discovers hidden treasures; reveals the greatest secrets of nature, and enables one in dreams to the objects of one's desires. Person born: a spirit strong and subtle; has new ideas and sublime thoughts; is able to solve the most difficult problems; is discreet and acts with much circumspection. Associated with the 4th quinance of Pisces; angel by night of the 9 of Cups (Yesod of Briah). see Appendix 10.

312

מערב West. The direction west.

בקר morning.

חדש new moon, month, mating (of animals). With different pointing *khawdawsh*: new, fresh. As a verb: *kiddeysh*: to renew, restore, do afresh, to produce something new. Now is the only time when anything can be new. Only at the end of a cycle may a hitherto unheard of things exist. Also to promulgate a new law; establish a new reputation (describes the work undertaking by a Rosicrucian fraternity).

לך יום אף-לך לילה The day is thine, the night is also thine; "Day and night are both thine [Psalm 74:16]. This, too, is truth about Now. יום, day (56) = אור (light, 207) = טוב, good (17) and לילה, light (75) = חשך, darkness (328) = רע, evil (270). Evil is raw material of good; darkness = a higher vibration. This is the secret of the stone. Both are his, and לילה (night) precedes יום (day).

מרבע four-sided, a square, quadrilateral figure (Rabbinical Hebrew). Relates to 4, the number of the Sephirah Chesed, the sphere of צדק, from which the 21st Path (Kaph), also attributed to *Tedeq*, passes to Netzach.

עין יעקב ayin Jacob. the fountain (eye) of Jacob. Deuteronomy 33:28: "Israel then shall dwell in safety alone: the foundation of Jacob shall be upon a land of corn and wine; also his heavens shall drop down dew." These words occur in the blessing of Moses, a poem which constitutes the entire chapter cited above. They may also be translated, "The eye of Jacob." Jacob means: "to supplant". It is always the new that supplants the old. Thus in the Biblical story, Jacob, the younger brother, supplants Esau. And Jacob himself gives a blessing to the younger of Joseph's two sons, Ephraim. Jacob's name was changed to "Israel" or "He shall rule as God." Wherever Jacob is mentioned in the Old Testament or in the new, inner esoteric meaning has always to do with the idea of supplanting the

old by the new, the familiar by some novelty hitherto unheard of. "Behold, I make all things new" is the secret of those who have learned to rule as God. see 100, 194, 246, 636, 182.

שחד to give, to make a present. As a noun: a gift, bribe. This word ties in with the basic meanings of the 9 of Cups, and the Archangel of the West, as the card of wish fulfillment. The Elohim which are the active Divine Powers of creation described in the first chapter of Genesis are really powers of man. Man, when he attunes himself through the automatic consciousness to the Higher Creative Powers, is able to form the darkness by the WORD and bring forth the light, which is good. It is also related with the basic meaning of the 4th Path of Chesed (Intelligence of the Desirous Quest), as its source, and to Jupiter, as expressing its quality, has an obvious correspondence to the idea of divine providence, its spiritual and its temporal gifts, and the reconciliation brought about by man's intelligent use of these gifts. These gifts are redemptive, freeing from punishment. Hence, the 21st path is call the some, "The Conciliating Intelligence." Proverbs 17:8: "A gift is as a precious stone in the eyes of him that hath it: whithersoever it turns, it prospers."

שבי captivity; concretely, captives, prisoners. In Jeremiah 30:16: "Therefore, all who devour you shall be devoured; and al your enemies, every one of them, shall go into captivity; and those who trample over you shall be trampled over, and all those who plunder you I will give for prey." Also in Lamentations 1:5: "Her oppressors have become her rulers, and her adversaries have made an end of her [Zion]; for the Lord has afflicted her for the multitude of her sins; her children are gone into captivity before the oppressor." Captive in Isaiah 10:4: "So shall the king of Assyria lead away the Egyptian prisoners, and the Ethiopians captive, young and old, naked and barefoot, with there buttocks uncovered, to the shame of Egypt." And in Amos 4:10: "I have sent among you the pestilence after the manner of Egypt; I slew your young men with the sword, together with you captive horses..." see 317 (שביה).

שואה crashing, loud noise. Job 30:14: "They came upon me as a wide breaking of waters; amidst a loud noise they rolled themselves along." Hence storm, tempest in Proverbs 1:27:

"When you fear comes as desolation, and your destruction comes as a tempest (whirlwind); when distress and anguish come upon you." And desolation, wasting, destruction in Proverbs 3:25: "Do not be afraid of sudden fear, neither of the desolation of the wicked, when it comes." And in Psalm 63:9: "But those that seek my soul, to destroy it, shall go into the lower parts of the earth."

ושי Goetia demon #57 by night of the 3rd decanate of Libra. see Appendix 11.

Goetia: "He is a great president, and appears like a leopard at the first, but after a little time he puts on the shape of a man. His office is to make one cunning in the liberal sciences, and to give true answers of divine and secret things; also to change a man into any shape that the Exorcist pleases, so that he that is so changed will not think nay other things than that he is verity that creature or things he is changed into. He governs 30 Legions of Spirits." [Mathers, 1995, p. 58]

αγγελος.. aggelos (Gr). a messenger, an angel. Messenger from God. "A symbol of spiritual influences able to minister to the aspirations of the soul. They are messengers of the inner light to arouse the higher faculties. There are many intelligences who point the way to Truth, and are a means of aiding the soul's evolution." [Gaskell, 1981, p. 48.]

αβαρης. abarehs (Gr). not heavy or burdensome; not causing expense. see 2 Corinthians 11:9.
ακακος. akakos (Gr). Without evil, i.e. unsuspecting or simpleminded. see Romans 16:18.

βολις. bolis (Gr). a missle, i.e. javelin, arrow, dart, anything thrown about. Those of Apollo (Sun) and Artemis (moon) are used of sudden, easy death. Bel was a personification in Chaldea of the Sun Deity. May allude to Key 13. The Apocryphal Bel and the Dragon added to the Book of Daniel, as proof that the Idol was not a living God.

313 (prime)

בשגגה through error, inadvertently. Leviticus 4:2: "Speak to the children of Israel, saying if a person shall sin through error [i.e. ignorance] against any of the commandments of the Lord concerning things which ought not to be done,

and shall do any of them [he shall offer a sacrifice]. see 311, 306, 308.

החש 51st names of Shem ha-Mephorash, short form. see 328 & Appendix 10.

ומוראצם and the fear/dread of you. Genesis 9:2.

אשיב I will return. Genesis 24:5.
וקרבה and she draws near. Deuteronomy 25:11.

הושב has been restored, returned. Genesis 42:28.

314

הוא כהן לאל עליון He was priest of the most high God (said of Melchizedek) [Genesis 14:18]. The reference is to the mystical high priest, Melchizedek. see 294, 4824 (Greek).

הלל גמור perfect praise. Said of the Zohar to apply to Binah. K.D.L.C.K. (p.275): "... and that which is not perfect (praise) (is attributed) to Malkuth."

מטטרון Metatron. the Archangel of Kether and therefore related to the Ace of Cups. He is a personification of Yekhidah, the One Self. Metatron is also said to be angel of Tiphareth in the creative world. In this aspect he refers to the awakened Ego, conscious of its essential identity with Yekhidah. With different vowel points, is specially designated by the word na'ar, boy (נער). This is the boy in Key 20 who is the resurrected ego consciousness, turning inward and eastward to Kether. In our experience, Metatron is the Central Self, said to embrace the 6 directions of space from the point within. Charged with the word of restoration and with the task of glorifying the bodies of the just in their sepulcher's [Zohar]. see 101, 311, 246, 280, 97, 320.

רחוק far off, distant (as in time or place). Ezekiel 6:6: "In all your dwelling-places the cities shall be laid waste and the high places shall be desolate; that your altars may be laid waste and the high places shall be desolate." Refers to the remoteness of Yekhidah. With different pointing: distance, separation, loathsomeness, absurdity.

שדי shaddai. almightily. A name of God associated in Qabalah with Malkuth, and therefore with Shekhinah, the bride. It is the Life-power under the aspect of omnipotence. In Job 32:8 Neshamah is called the "Inspiration of the Almighty." "But here is a spirit in man: and the inspiration of the Almighty gives them understanding." see 345, 594.

שטה Acacia. The sacred wood of which the tabernacle and its furniture were made. Because this word is equivalent to שדי, Shaddi, Qabalists who wrote and edited the story of the tabernacle, used it to intimate that the actual substance of which the "House of God" is made, is actually the omnipotent power or energy of the Almighty. The "Most High God" the one reality seems to be far distant (רחוק), but it is really near at hand. Both the tabernacle and the temple of Solomon are symbols of Man. see 683, 36, 46, 252, 154, 224, 315, 731.

שגיא great, mighty. Job 36:26: "Behold, God is great, and we know him not, neither can the number of his years be searched out." Also in Daniel 2:6: "But if you show me the dream and its interpretation, you shall receive from me gifts and wealth and great honor…" Much, many in Daniel 7:5: "And behold another beast, a second, like to a bear, and is raised itself on one side, and it had three ribs in the mouth of it between the teeth of it: and they said to it thus: "Arise, devour much flesh.'" Very in Daniel 2:12: "Then the king was very furious and he angrily commanded that all the wise men of Babylon should be destroyed."

חיים לעולם Life for evermore. Psalm 133:3: "It is as if the dew of Hermon were falling on mount Zion-for there the Lord bestows his blessing, even life forevermore." Variant spelling see 293.

D.O.M.A. (Lt). Initials of the phrase *Deus Omnipotens Magister Artis*, God Almighty, Master of the Art (of Alchemy) [Secret Symbols, page 35]. The Life-power is the actual worker in the great art of alchemical transmutation. see 29, 45, 124, 84, 61.

μαγος. magos (Gr). a magician, sorcerer. One of the wise men or seers in Persia who interpreted dreams; any enchanter, wizard. in a bad sense, juggler or quack. see 676, 1060 (Greek).

γαμος. gamos (Gr). marriage; wedding-feast. John 2:1: "And on the third day there was a marriage feast in Cana of Galilee; and the mother of Jesus was there."

I. "*Gamos*, a wedding; union of the sexes; one of the arcane rites; the union of positive and negative forces, the blending of superior and lower natures. Here the marriage stands of the action of the dual magnetic force in wakening the 'third eye', in the attainment of seership; but at this stage of the allegory, it refers only to one of those rare visions that come long before the permanent state of illumination is reached." [Pryse, 1967, p. 89.] see 1014, 1785.

II. "A union of two, forming a Harmony. As a term in the Science of the Soul it means the union of the Higher and Lasting Principle (Spiritual Principle) which the Purified Soul (Human Principle): that is, the 'Mystic Marriage' into which every Soul enters at some advanced stage of its evolution, and form which the 'SON" (Spiritual Consciousness) is, in a Virgin Birth, eventually Born. The Purified Soul is the Bride: the Lasting Principle is the Husband. Souls thus 'Married' are becoming Perfect. Compare the Myth of Psyche and Eros." [Omikron, 1942, p. 251.]

315

גביש ice. In Job 28:18: crystal. [The English crystal, from the Greek κρυταλλος, meaning clear ice, ice, crystal, rock-crystal, preserves the ancient belief that crystal was a sort of ice.] In the magical language this ideas suggests that man is a reflecting medium, like a crystal. Case gives: hail, petrified. see Gomorrah below.

העולם הקטן the little world, the microcosm. An epithet of man. see I. Myer Qabbalah, p.147]

יצרה yetzirah. formation, formative power. The world of formation. In man, Yetzirah is the formative power operative in all 6 Sephiroth of the Lesser Countenance. The 7 of Swords refers particularly to the formative power of desire and to the influence of desire upon the Yetziratic plane of patterns and processes. The formative power, is the special power man, reflecting the creative power (Briah) of the Vast Countenance. Darkness and evil provide the raw material from which then God FORMS into light [Isaiah 45:1]. In man the formative power is imagination or phantasy. The characteristic power at work in the world or plane above that of Assiah, or action. Corresponding to Vav in IHVH, and the element Air.

אדם רע evil man. It refers to the consequences of human actions when the formative power of desire is exercised under the nightmare dream of separation. see 270, 469.

Paul Case: The prayer for deliverance may be understood as a prayer that the Psalmist himself may not enter into the consciousness, of evil and violence. Perhaps an even deeper meaning may be found. Since אדם רע = 315 = העולם הקטן, a Qabalistic term for the microcosm. It is also the number of יצירה, formation, and the personal Adam is the center of the world of formation, posted in Tiphareth. To be delivered from the evil man may well be to be freed from the apparent limitations of those whose consciousness does not extend beyond formation, or beyond the personalized ego. These are men of violence and their essential character is that described in Genesis 6:11 where we read 'The earth was filled with violence: איש המסים, the violent man (469) = היכל קדש holy temple, because in spite of his error, he is as truly the temple of God as is any other man. And this is always understood by those who know, so that they never make the mistake of setting, themselves in antagonism to the violent man. They pray to be delivered from his error, and they work, for his liberation from that error.' Father forgive them for they know not what they do' is the attitude taken by the truly awakened man against all who conspire against him, and all who seem to be his enemies, or the enemies of principles he holds dear. see Psalm 140

מראה הנוגה Vision of splendor, mirror of splendor. Marah מראה also means mirror and Nogah נוגה, is a title of Netzach. The astrological symbol of Venus is said to be a mirror which was one of the Goddess attributes. The idea of reflection links this to גביש (crystal) and יצרה (formation). The microcosmic man is the mirror of the macrocosm, and so far as the personal man is concerned, whatever is reflected from the macrocosm into his microcosmic consciousness is more or less colored by his desires and passions.

Given as as visio splendoris [whole view of splendor] in K.D.L.C.K. (p.553) and says it is Binah from the part of Chesed, for splendor always sees to the right side.

עמרה Gomorrah. Submersion. Name of city in the vale of Siddom, referred to in the Bible and known for its wickedness, especially in the perversions of desire. Has a special correspondence with אדם רע (Adam Roa).

Paul Case: Gomorrah means "Submersion or woodland" and is probably from the root עמר omar, to sprout. Compare נון, Nun, to sprout. Gomorrah represents Water and Sodom represents fire in alchemy. see 310, 106, 104, 354, 1000, 1813 (Greek).

ערמה subtlety, shrewdness, prudence, cunning, craft. From the same root as that which describes the serpent as more subtle [ערום, Genesis 3:1] than any other creature. This word is employed in both a good and bad sense. On the good side it signifies the prudence which comes from skill in managing the emotions. (also symbolized by the skill needed to construct the heptagon). On the bad side it consists of the same sort of skill but applied by someone to manage others through their desires and to their disadvantage. see 683, 36, 46, 252, 154, 224, 314, 29.

ושט gullet, esophagus, narrow canal.

רב הבונים Master of the Builders. A term used in the 3rd degree of Freemasonry, the Master Mason. This is accomplished by the subtlety which brings the "evil man" into the "vision of splendor". see 108.

מערה Arrangement, order; battle-line, rank, pile (of wood on altar); disposition of the stars, fate; proportion, act in a drama. Metathesis of ערמה here the reversal of separateness penetrates the veils of ignorance (Ayin + Mem) causing regeneration and order (Heh and Resh).

כורגסיטז Kurgasiax. The Sentinel of the 21st Path (Tunnel) of Kaph on the Inverse Tree of Life.

I. The 21st Kala is dominated by Jupiter and is

refracted into a Tunnel sentinelled by Kurgasiax whose number is 315 which is that of ישׁה, 'to stand', 'stand out', 'stand up'. It is derived from the Egyptian *As*, which indicates the 'secreting part of the body'; also *ash*, 'emission', and *asut*, 'the testicles'.

The sigil of Kurgasiax shows a horned (or crescented) sphere containing an equal armed cross mounted on a pole terminating in three caudiform appendages. The cross within the circle is the Mark of Set which denotes the place of the crossing indicated by the northern pole or axis, i.e. Daath, the Gateway of the Abyss. The triple tail suggests three modes of entry *via* the backward or caudal tunnels that connect Daath hindwardly with the power-zones of Pluto, Jupiter, and Venus. These modes are glossed by the number 315 which is also that of עמרה, 'Gomorrah', a secret formula of Pluto; ישׁה, 'the phallus'; and קרה, meaning 'her precious thing' (i.e. vulva), for Pluto, Jupiter, and Venus respectively. The horned circle containing the equal armed cross is the horned barb of Set (spermatozoon) generated by the formula 315.

This is born out by the title of the Tarot key of this Path 21, viz: The Lord of the Forces of Life, which, translated in terms of the Tunnel of Kurgasiax becomes The Lady of the Forces of Death; she who sends the incubus and the nightmare.

In the verse of 231 relevant to this *kala*, Jupiter appears as the Father whose reflection is the Mother:

> Now then the Father of an issued as a mighty Wheel; the Sphinx, and the dog-headed god, and Typhon, were bound on his circumference.

The Wheel is the sphere containing the Mark of the Beast which is a revolving chakra that activates the forces of the Sphinx [Male-female potencies], the dog-headed god [Pluto], and Typhon [The Mother], repeating the formula above described. In the Tarot, the wheel becomes the Wheel of the Goddess Fortuna who determines the fluctuation of earthly life.

The magical *siddhi* associated with this *kala* is Ascendancy, political or otherwise. Hence the ascription to this Ray of the Scepter as its typical magical weapon.

It is noteworthy that Crowley regarded the formula of Gomorrah, which is the key formula of the Tunnel of Kurgasiax, as the feminine version of the formula of Sodom that obtains on the other side of the Tree at this level. [Grant, 1994, p. 211-212.]

αγαμος. agamos (Gr). Unmarried. Directly connected with the Pythagorean notions of the number 7. May be considered also in connection with the Rosicrucian allegory, which is explicit in its declaration that the founders of the order were "vowed virgins," though some of the later members were not celibate. see 314 (Greek).

316

עָרוֹם subtle. In Genesis 3:1: "Now the serpent was more subtle than any beast of the field which the Lord God had made. And he said unto the woman, yea have God said, ye shall not eat of every tree of the Garden? see 315.

I. "Now Nahash (egoism, envy, covetousness, concupiscence) was an insidious passion (blind principle) in all elementary life which YAWHEW AElohim had made: and it said (this passion Nahash) unto Aisha (volitive faculty of Adam), Why, hath AElohim declared, ye shall not feed upon all the substance of the organic enclosure?" [d'Olivet, 1976, p. 317.]

He comments: עָרוֹם, *the-blind-and-general-passion*.... What proves that the Samartain translator has not understood the word, *orem*, is that he has completely missed the meaning of it. He renders it by... *keen, cunning, subtle*, and makes it agree thus, with the strange idea that he appears to have really had, that נחשׁ *signified a serpent*. The word עָרוֹם was nevertheless easy, very easy to explain; but how it could be said that a *serpent* is a passion, a vehemence, a blindness, and so to speak, an universal impulse in productive nature? That is, however, what is found in the root עָר or עוּר. This root is primitive אר which Moses causes to govern here by the sign of material sense עָ; a sign almost always taken in the bad sense. The final sign ם, which he adds to it, indicates that the idea is generalized and should be taken in the broadest sense.

All the derivatives of the root עוּר, present a certain calamitous idea; first, it is עָר, *a violent adversary*; עוּר, *a privation of sight*; then, it is עָרוֹם or עָרֹם עֵרֹם *a desert, a barrenness, a complete nakedness*, literally as well as figuratively; it is מְעָרָה *a devastated place*, an abyss, cavern; it is finally מְעֹרָן, *an absolute blindness, a total abandonment*. In the sequence of these words can be placed the name that the Persians gave to the infernal adversary *Hariman* which is nothing else than the word עָרֹם referred to this note, with the augmentative syllable וֹן." [ibid, 1976, pp. 97-98.]

II. The serpent more subtle than any beast of the field is: "a symbol of the desire-mind, which is more penetrative and captivating to the ego than any of the lower desires (beasts)." [Gaskell, 1981, p. 676.]

III. The Zohar [I:28B] Comments: "And the serpent was more subtle than any beast of the field which the Lord God had made; i.e. they are more subtle for evil than all the gentiles, and they are the offspring of the original serpent that beguiled Eve. The mixed multitude are the impurity which the serpent injected into Eve. From this impurity came forth Cain, who killed Abel... From Cain was descended Jethro, the father-in-law of Moses, as it is written, 'And the sons of the Kenite the father in law of Moses [Judges 1:16], and according to tradition he was called Kenite because he originated from Cain. Moses, in order to screen the reproach of this father-in-law, sought to convert the 'mixed multitude' (the descendants of Cain), although God warned him, saying, 'They are of an evil stock; beware of them'. Through them Moses was banished from his proper place and was not privileged to enter the land of Israel." [pp.108-109]

חבוש Given as *ligatus* [bound, tied, connected, united] in K.D.L.C.K. (p.331). He says it refers to Tiphareth, which is with Malkuth linked and connected with Binah, which binds part of itself to Malkuth, as in exile.

קוטרא (loathing, disgust) [Crowley, 1977, p. 36].

Of קן d'Olivet says: That which is indefinite, vague, indeterminate, unformed: it is matter suitable to be put in action, the mechanical movement which acts upon it, the obtuse, vague, blind irresistible force which leads it, necessity. Of the letters רא he writes: ...that kind of straight line which departing from the center converges at any point whatsoever of the circumference: it is, in a very restricted sense, *a streak*, in a broader sense, a way and metaphorically, *the visual ray*, visibility." [d'Olivet, 1976, pp. 439-440, 446.]

וְשָׁאנוּ Goetia demon by day of the 3rd decanate of Aries. [Mathers, 1995, p. 127]. see Appendix 11.

I. "This Spirit is of a Good Nature, and his office is to declare things Past and to Come, and to discover all things hid or Lost." [ibid, 1995, p. 28]

II. The influence of the demon suggest conscious imbalance, resulting in negative aspect of the qualities assigned to this decanate, which are generous, religion, idealistic. When adversely aspected, as here, the 4 of Wands can indicate loss of success through personal merit or the perfection of something built up after labor, determinant through travel, shipping and business with foreign countries; loss in consequence of unpreparedness of by hasty action. The remedy is to get beneath personal levels of recollection into the cosmic memory and learn to participate in the life-power perfect memory of the creative order symbolized by Key 10.

שׁחח to crouch, bow down; to be bowed down, be humbled, be dejected. Job 9:13: "If God will not withdraw his anger, the proud helpers do stop under him." False pride is but misuse of the Mars force. see Key 16.

שׁאיה crash, ruin; name of a demon. In K.D.L.C.K. (p.54) it is connected with the Qlippothic cortices, which are deserted places, and referred to by the wise under this name.

ירֹק greenish; yellow; green herb, green thing. Job 39:8: "The range of the mountains is his pasture, and he searches after every green thing." Green is the color of Venus; the mountains suggest the higher brain centers.

עמר a bundle, handful; sheaf, row of fallen grain Deuteronomy 24:19: "When thou cuts down thine harvest in thy field, and has forgot a sheaf in the field, thou shall not go again to fetch it: it shall be for the stranger for the fatherless, and for the widow: that the Lord thy God may bless thee in all the work of thine hands.[spelled עמר in text].

ישו Yeshu. Jesus [Latin *Jesu*], a variant of Joshua.

Paul Case: The meaning of this "name of names" is "The nature of reality is to liberate", or "reality set us free". "Jesus himself made explicit declaration of the power of his name. "Whoever may receive one such little child in my name, receives me. Where or three are assembled in my name, I am there in the midst of them. Whatsoever you shall ask in my name, that will I do, that the father may be glorified in the son. If you shall ask anything in my name, I will do it. In my name they will expel demons; they will speak with new tongues; they shall take up serpents; and if they should drink any deadly poison, it will not hurt them they shall lay hands upon the sick, and they shall recover.' St. John says: 'As many as received him, to them gave he power to become the sons of God, even to them that believe on his name. [The Name of Names, p.4] see 888 (Greek) & 326.

317 (prime)

השחד the gift.

פרזל iron (Chaldee); to shoe a house. Iron is the metal of Mars, which is the raw material, or metal, from which "gold" is created, or transmuted.

שיבה sojourning, dwelling; return, restoration. Restoration of gold to its purity is the return to ones true dwelling-place in the heart. With different pointing *shibaw*: grey hair, hoary head; old age. Suggests wisdom or Chokmah. To return to the heart is to be united to the father. This is Ehben אבן, the stone. see 53.

ואלפר Goetia demon #6 by day of the 3rd decanate of Taurus. This decanate is ruled by the 7 of Pentacles (Netzach of Assiah), or the desire nature in the material world.

Goetia: "He is a mighty duke, and appears in the shape of a loin with an ass's head, bellowing. He is a good familiar, but tempts them he is a familiar of to steal (sic). He governs 10 Legions of Spirits." [Mathers, 1995, p. 30]

שביה captivity. Nehemiah 4:4: "Hear, O our God, for we have become ridiculed; and turn their reproach upon their own head, and give them for a prey in the land of their captivity." Captives in Deuteronomy 32:42: "I will make the arrows drunk with blood, and My sword shall devour flesh with the blood of the slain and the captives, from the long-haired heads of the foe."

שבא זהב gold of sheba. Sheba שבע (372) is connected with the number seven, and thus relates to the alchemical peacock's color, i.e. the seven metals. Forty is the number of Mem, or alchemical water, which is said to be the seed of the metals. Sheba is also connected with Venus, which is the 7th Sephirah.

יבשה dry land, parched land. One of the 7 earths [Qlippotic Mansions] corresponding to Netzach. K.D.L.C.K. (p.375) gives: *arida*, and says that it is Malkuth when because of its sins, none of the supernal influences is able to flow down the paths. see Genesis 1:10, 7:22 & 8:14.

318

אליעזר God of help. [Genesis 15:2]. Name of Abram's steward. *Eliezer* came from Damascus, which means "Work" (444). Furthermore, he is steward of Abram's "House" (בית), and in Genesis 14:14, the number of servants in Abram's House is 318. The Hebrew noun which is translated in the authorized version as trained servants really means "Initiates," and Christian tradition, preserved in the apocryphal Epistle of Barnabas (chapter 8) asserts that ceremony of initiation included circumcision. see 88, 505, 4860.

אמרי בינה imeray binah. words of understanding. Binah is the seat of intuition. The words of understanding are perceived through the function of inner hearing שיח (Siyakh): to ponder, to converse with oneself, to meditate. It is also a reference to the inner school as the retainers of Wisdom in words or forms of understanding. Includes symbols that can be passed on to future generation. Refers also to the servants of light who are receptive to Neshamah in Binah as the hear her "words of understanding."

יסוד החכמה הקדבמה Foundation of Primordial Wisdom. A name of Binah. Its meaning rests on the fact that the root-idea connected with Binah is depth. It is regarded as being the foundation of basis for the Height (Chokmah). see 67, 42, 52, 61, 199, 395, 450, 713.

שיח siyakh. to ponder, meditate, to converse with oneself, pray. With different pointing: 1. contemplation, communication, complaint, meditation, prayer, talk; 2. a shoot (as if uttered or put forth), bush, plant, shrub. [Strong's Dictionary] In Psalm 102:1: "Hear my prayer O Lord, and let my cry [i.e. complaint) come to you." see 1 Kings 18:27 and Job 9:27: "If I say, will forget my complaint, I will leave of my heaviness, and comfort myself."

פרזלא Iron (Chaldean). Metal of Mars. alternate spelling. see 317, 80, 239, 12.

כיור וכנו Given by Rosenroth in K.D.L.C.K. (p.473) as: *labrum lavacri et basis ejus*, i.e. The elegant lip and his pedestal or basis. He says these denote Netzach and Hod, the lip being Netzach, and the base Hod.

ηλιος.. helios (Gr). sun.

319

סרטן Sartain. the Crab, the sign Cancer. Associated with Cheth, the enclosed field and with Prakriti, the mysterious power of the finitizing principle. As the crab protects and isolates himself by growing a shell, so may the adept protect and isolate himself from the illusions of his environment by learning the technique of magical speech. By this means he may even build for himself an indestructible body, which will resist every hostile external influence. Only one who is wholly unselfish may exercise powers of a Master of the Temple.

ידמ to stretch out, to extend. An intimation that the powers associated with Cheth, Cancer and the Page of Cups are those of expansion or extension. The fundamental idea is that Water is the subtle substance which forms itself into all manner of objects and is the principle of increase and growth. In physics, extension is defined as "that property of a body whereby it occupies a portion of space". The Briatic plane is the extension of the dynamic Life-force in Chokmah. Hints at the tremendous extension of powers which is the outcome of the adept's command, through occult speech, of the substance phase of the Life-power. see 85, 331, 311.

שׂחה speech. The faculty attributed to Cancer.

שׁיט An oar. Suggest that by which one drives and steers a boat through water. Has to do with artistic adaptation and control of the Water element associated with the 18th path through the sign Cancer. The adept learns the secret of adapting the astral fluid by specific employment of sound-vibrations related to mental images, as will tend to materialize these images as physical conditions.

מכון באמצע standing in the midst [Book of Formation 4:4]. Refers to the holy temple, or palace, standing in the interior center. This palace is connected with the letter Tav and Key 21. see 969, 799.

דרך המלך The Kings Highway; The Way of the King. The driver of the chariot is Key 7 is a King. Note the stream behind the chariot. This is the Highway. see 224, 74.

שגיאה error, transgression. Plural form in Psalm 19:13: "Keep back your servant also from presumptuous sins; let them not have dominion over me: then shall I be upright, and I shall be innocent from the great transgression." see 311, 306, 308.

זרע יעבדנו a seed shall serve him. Psalm 22:30: "A seed shall serve him; it shall be accounted to the Lord for a generation." Nun is the "seed". Literally "posterity he-will-serve-them" in the *Interlinear NIV Bible*. see 50, 106, 700, 277.

λιθος. lithos (Gr). stone. One of the 2 New Testament spellings used throughout the Greek text of the New Testament. see 53. It is what is symbolized by the cubical stone chariot in Key 7.

Rosa hierichuntis spiritualis (Lt). Spiritual rose of Jericho [Secret Symbols, pate 13]. At the place cited, the spiritual rose of Jericho is associated with animal blood. There is a deep esoteric connection between blood and the "House of Influence," and one of the meanings of the river in Key 7 has to do with this. A clue to the meaning of the gematria of this number. see 47, 139.

320

נער child, infant, boy. Refers to the boy shown in Key 20, Judgement, who represents the awakened Ego-consciousness turning inward and eastward to Yekhidah in Kether. Refers also to Metatron and Enoch. see 314, 37, 620.

In Exodus 2:6: "And when she had opened it [i.e. the ark], she saw the child, and behold, the babe was weeping. And she had compassion on him, and said, this is one of the Hebrew's children." Also boy in 1 Samuel 1:24: "And when she had weaned him, she took him up with her, with a tree your old bullock and an Ephah of flour and a skin of wine, and brought him to the house of the lord in Shiloh; and the boy was very young."

ישי Jesse. wealth. The grandson of Boaz; almost always mentioned in connection with his youngest son David. In 1 Samuel 16:1, 3:. "...Fill your horn with oil, and go, I will send thee to Jesse the Bethlehemite... and I will call Jesse to the sacrifice, and I will show thee what thou shall do. And thou shall anoint unto me-him whom I name unto three. see 386, 326, 24 (note), 321 (variant spelling).

Thomas Troward refers to the wonderful child in Isaiah 11:1 described as Immanuel and linked later as a prophecy of the Christ: "His grandfather's name is Jesse."

I. "A further description of him occurs in Isaiah 11:1, where we again find the same three stages-first Jesse, next the stem proceeding out of Jesse, and lastly the Rod or Branch growing out of the stem. No Jesse is the father of David, and therefore, 'the Branch' is the same person regarding whom Isaiah and Jesus propounded their conundrums. Placing these four remarkable

passage together, we get the following description of the Wonderful Child:

His name is Immanuel. His father's name is David. His grandfather's name is Jesse. And He is His own grandfather and Lord over His father.

What is it that answers to this description? Again we find the solution of the enigma in the names. 'Jesse' means 'to be,' or 'he that is,' which at once brings us back to all we have learned concerning the Universal I AM-the ONE Eternal Spirit which is 'the Everlasting Father.'" [Troward, 1942, p. 171.]

II. Paul Case: ישי = "The Living One" = 320 = שהיה "which hath been" [Ecclesiastes 1:9]. 320 is also the number of: יהוא כהן לאל נליון [Genesis 14:15] describing Melchizedek: "And he was a priest of the most high God" Here not that עמנואל = אל עליון (#197), Immanuel, so that Melchizedek is priest of Immanuel" (see 294). "And he is his own grandfather and Lord over this father." Case: i.e. ישי = ימנואל and he is אדני "my Lord" in Psalm 100:1: ("Make a joyful noise unto the Lord, all ye lands"), the master of David, because he is actually עליון אל, the most high God. That is, when אל עליון is manifest as עלנו אל. He is אדני "my Lord," the central directive principle in the breast, for דוד = Man." see דוד David (24).

אדמה נכר ademah. nekawr. strange land. Psalm 137:4: "How can we sing the songs of the Lord while in a strange land?" variant spelling. see 815, 270, 50.

רעים friends, associates; brothers, brethren. Refers to the 4 who founded the Rosicrucian order. see 100, 220, 240, 340.

שך abode, an enclosed dwelling; booth, pavilion. The indwelling presence. The first 2 letters of sakel, intelligence. With different pointing *sake*: thorn, pick. see 350, 294, 800.

סריטיאל Saritiel. Lesser assistant angel of Sagittarius. See 60, 120 & Key 14.

עירם Oiram. A duke of Edom [Crowley, 1977, p. 36]. Edom suggest unbalanced force.

metathesis of רעים. Eram is associated with Malkuth. Translated "naked" in Genesis 3:10: "And he said, 'Who told you that you were naked? Have you eaten from the tree that I commanded you not to eat from?'" see 880 & 777 (p. 22).

והוא כהן לאן לאל עליון "And he [was] a priest by the most high God." And in Genesis 14:18: :And Melchizedek King of Salem brought forth bread and wine: and we was the priest of the most high God." see 294.

מיער out of the wood. Psalm 80:18: "The boar out of the wood does waste it, and the wild beast of the field does devour it." Refers to the vine plucked out of Egypt and planted Psalm 80:8. The "vine" is the Christos; "Egypt" is the astral realm.

חביש bound, imprisoned; a bandage wound; to bind.

סינר apron. The symbolic apron of freemasonry binds the reproductive energy for higher use.

אפרודיטי Aphrodite. Goddess of love and desire; literal spelling transposed from the Greek. It is desire which binds. The relationship between Mars & Venus.

321

אישי Jesse. wealth." alternate spelling. see 320.

פראם Piram. "the wild one". Amorite king of Jarmuth ("haughtiest, pride") in Joshua 10:3. Represents the unrestrained license, which is the opposite of true liberty. see 56, 321, 170, 216.

שאהוה "God who cures maladies". 28th Shem ha-Mephorash. 136-140. SITHACER. April 16, June 27, September 7, November 18, January 29. 9:00-9:20 AM. Psalm 71:12: "O God, be not far from me: O my God, make haste for my help." Against infirmities and lighting. Protects against incendiaries, the destruction of battlements, falls, maladies, etc. Rules health and longevity. Person born: have much judgement; never moves but with prudence and circumspection. see 965, 360 & Appendix 10.

Angel of the 4th quinance (16E-20E) of Sagittarius, and the angel by night of the 9 of Wands [Yesod of Atziluth]. This is the operation of Yesod, the automatic pattern-world of subconsciousness or sphere of the Moon, in the archetypal world of ideas, or Atziluth.

אלינכיר Alinakir. Angel of 3rd decanate of Cancer. This decanate is ruled by Neptune and Jupiter and suggest qualities of sympathy, courtesy, and ceremony.

לסלרא Lasalra. Lesser angel governing triplicity by day of Virgo. This implies service, industry and discrimination, self-consciously applied.

אדימירון Adimiron. Qlippoth of Taurus. "the bloody ones." Misuse of the qualities of determination, practicality, duty. Variant spelling, see 517.

I. The serpent is a glyph of menstruation and 59, as נדה, means precisely this. It derives from the Egyptian word Neti, meaning 'being', 'existence', 'negative', 'forth'. 'the sign of bleeding', 'female source'. This number therefore explains why the Adimiron (the bloody) are the Qlippoth attributed to the tunnel of Uriens (i.e. Taurus)... at the termination of... [an] abominable repast of Adimron.. Swarm across the desolate places of the void leaving the 'rich brown juice' [the color attributed to this path] of annihilation in their wake. [Grant, 1994, p. 187, 189.]

דברי הימים Events of the days; Hebrew title of Chronicles. [Esther 6:1: "On that night could not the king sleep, and he commanded to bring the book of records of the chronicles; and they were read before the king." see 881, 100, 216.

322

עברים Hebrews. With the prefix Heh in Exodus 7:16: "And thou shall say unto him, the Lord God of the Hebrews hath sent me unto thee, saying, let my people go, that they may serve me in the wilderness: and behold, hitherto thou would not hear." see 882

כבש to subdue, dominate; a ram (just old enough to butt). With different pointing: 1. to tread down, hence, to disregard; to conqer, subjagate, violate, bring into bondage; 2. a footstool (as trodden upon). [Strong's Dictionary]

בן-נכר strange son, i.e. stranger, foreigner. Genesis 17:27: "And all the men of his [Abraham's] household, both born in the house and bought with money. He also circumcised some of the strangers with him." see 270, 301.

כשב lamb. see Genesis 30:32 (give in its plural form).

שבב to lie down; to rest, lodge. In Ezekiel 4:4, Numbers 24:8 and Proverbs 3:24. To lie with (have sexual intercourse) in Genesis 19:32, 33 and 39:10.

שבך net, lattice-work. "None may grasp me; and to those who seek to capture me in the net of thought, I am the eternal fugitive. Yet though I elude pursuit, I am the source and support, even of the pursuers." [Book of Tokens, Heh]

קו האמצעי K.D.L.C.K. (p.673) gives *lina media* [middle line] and says that Tiphareth thus called, because it is in the middle, ascending and descending from Atziluth to its own terminus. see 1081.

לברמים Lebarmem. Lesser assistant angel of Sagittarius; Lord of triplicity by night. Sagittarius is a mutable Fire sign, attributed to support and to the Holy Guardian Angel. the name may be analyzed as לב heart = 32 + ר face, head = 300 + מים water = 90 = Tzaddi meditation. see Key 14.

323

ארבעים forty (40). Number of Mem, the 'waters of consciousness.' in Exodus 16:35: And the children of Israel did eat manna [90] forty years, until they came to a land inhabited; they did eat manna, until they came unto the borders of the land of Canaan." see 883, 90, 541, 190.

אורנוס Uranus.

סמנדר Satnadar. Angel of the 3rd decanate of Aries. This decanate is ruled by Jupiter, and suggest the qualities of: generous, religious, idealistic. It is also assigned to the 4 of Wands,

or Chesed in Atziluth. This refers to the cosmic memory in the archetypal world. This is referred to the attributes of kindness, good will and compassion, as well as eager, earnest desire, and adore or real toward anything, and the principle behind these qualities. The qualities of Chesed suggest we must continually exercise memory by recalling the truth that the Life-power is present everywhere and in all beings. This helps to develop our beneficence and compassion toward all things and creatures. Benevolent thought and speech have actual weight and set up movement of actual substance and corresponds to the 'powder of projection' of the alchemist. This is the secret of beneficence and wealth associated with Chesed and Jupiter.

יש אחד There is one that is alone. Ecclesiastes 4:8: "There is one that is alone, and he has not a second; yes, he has neither son nor brother; yet is there no end of all his labor, neither is his eye satisfied with riches: 'For whom then do I labor, and bereave my soul of pleasure? This also is vanity, yes, it is a grievous business.'" The Zohar [II:187A, pp.214-215]: "'There is one that is alone' [Ecclesiastes 4:8] is an allusion to the man who is improperly alone, without a wife; 'and he hath not a second', no one to uphold him, no son to establish his name in Israel, or to bring him to his due need; 'yet there is no end of all his labor', as he is always laboring, day and night; 'neither is his eye satisfied with riches' [IBID] and he has not the sense to reflect: 'For whom, then, do I labor and bereave my soul of pleasure? You may say that he has pleasure in that he eats and drinks and feasts every day; but it is not so, inasmuch as his soul (nefesh) does not share in his pleasure, so that assuredly he bereaves his soul of pleasure, of the blissful illumination of the world to come; for it is left stunted without attaining its full and proper growth. For God cares for his works, and so desires that a man should be set right and not perish from the world to come.' see 13.

בהימירון Bahimiron. "The bestial ones"; Qlippoth of Aquarius. Related to Behemoth, animality. Aquarius is related to meditation and revelation. see 453, 259, 973.

324

I. (4 x 9 x 9) or 2^2 x 9^2

פוכלור Goetia demon #41 by night of the 2nd decanate of Taurus. see Appendix 11.

Goetia: "He is a mighty duke and strong. He appears in the form of a man with gryphon's wings. His office is to slay men, and to drown them in the waters, and to overthrow ships of war, for he has power over both winds and seas; but he will not hurt any man or thing if he be commanded to the contrary by the Exorcist. He also has hopes to return to the seventh throne after 1,000 years. He governs 30 Legions of Spirits." [Mathers, 1995, p. 49]

בנאים הדביר Builders of the Adytum. see 103, 221.

מיטטרון Metatron. Angle of God's presence.

השיגו attained, the are equal. see Genesis 47:9.

בקרבך in the midst of you, among you. see Exodus 33:3.

325

I. (5 x 5 x 13) or 5^2 x 13

II. Σ25 = 325. The magic line of Mars.

ברצבאל Bartzbel. Spirit of Mars.
גראפיאל Graphiel. Intelligence of Mars.

נינדהר Nundahar. Angel of 2nd decanate of Scorpio.

הנער the lad. Genesis 18:7. With different pointing: the damsel. Genesis 34:3.

ויקטר and he burnt, made it smoke. see Exodus 40:27.

הרעים the evil, the horrible ones. see Deuteronomy 7:15.

הסירים the thorns. see Ecclesiastes 7:6.

הפרם he nullifed them see Numbers 30:13.

ויגשו and they moved. Genesis 19:9.

וישגו and they overtook. 2 King 25:5

ושיזב and he saved (rescued) [from a fire]. Daniel 3:28.

יקירה difficult. Daniel 2:11.

ישגיב He (God, אל) is exalted. see Job 36.22.

לטרוף to tear prey. Psalms 17:12.

לצרה for adversity. Proverbs 17:17

ελπις. (Gr). elpis. hope.

326

יהשוה Yeheshuah. Jesus. Mystical spelling of Jesus. The divine name IHVH has the "Holy Letter" Shin inserted, and thus the son is united to the father. The meaning is "The nature of reality is to liberate (or set free)." Jesus is also Joshua, and Hoshua was the son of Nun (נון). Also "Yah liberates." Yah is a divine name for Chokmah. Thus the name of Jesus really signifies "Wisdom is the principle of liberation." The essential nature of the creative order is the eternal tendency toward liberation. The central ego is begotten son, in perfect union with the father. see 426, 386, 26.

"St. Martin has a curious remark respecting the foundation of the two testaments. He asserts it to consist in the true pronunciation of the two great names (Theo. corr., p.244)*; This involves more than his words convey to common sense; as showing what really and originally the Old and New Testament is a development and fulfillment of the promise of the old, and with that fulfillment gives another promise." [Atwood, 1918, p. 576]

* Paul Case: יהוה and יהשוה or ישוע, for יהוה is the revealer of the law, and יהשוה by the addition of Shin = 300 = רוח אלהים, is the fulfillment thereof."

שאיה Vision. The Vision of the mystical Christ is what transforms Home Sapiens, natural man, into Homo Spiritualis, spiritual man. see 139, 45.

כוש Cush. In Exodus 2:13: "The name of the

second river is the Gihon; it winds through the entire land of Cush." This land is connected with Ethiopia or Abyssinia. In Isaiah 18:1: "Woe to the land Shadowing with wings, which is beyond the rivers of Ethiopia (Cush). A son of Ham in Genesis 10:6. Cush means "black or dark-colored" [Ancient Faiths VI, p.417] Ham is connected with Kehm or Egypt (subconsciousness). Gihon is "a stream" Eden is "time", the garden of delight. The influence from Kether, which fashions the son of God is seen by the materialist as the mechanical force (Kaph) behind manifestation, but (Vav) intuition guides the seeker to direct knowledge of the secret fire of regeneration (Shin). The son is conceived in the "darkness of Egypt" and brought through the stream of consciousness from time, into the "Garden of Delight". see 77, 124, 702.

I. כוש Chush... The elemental root אש, which signifies in general, the *igneous principle*, being verbalized by the signs ו or י has reduced the word אוש or איש; that is to say, *fire*, physical or moral: and this word contracted by the assimilative sign כ, has given rise to the one of which we are speaking. This name which is found in the sacred books of the Brahmans, and whose origin is consequently, very ancient, has been rendered by that of the *Aethi-ops*, which is to say, the sympathetic fire of the globe. All allegorical names of which Moses makes use come evidently from the Egyptian sanctuaries." [d'Olivet, 1976, pp. 80-81.] see 77; 858 (Greek).

II. Monitory of Freemasonry (p.33): "A Mason in the Master Mason ritual asks an old man whether he has seen any travelers passing by: "Yes; as I was down near the coast of Joppa (96) this morning, I saw three, and from their dress and appearances I supposed them to be men of Tyre (צור, 296), and workmen from the temple. They sought a passage to Ethiopia [Cush], but could not obtain one, in consequence of an embargo recently laid on the shipping."

שכו A place where Samuel stopped near Raman in 1 Samuel 19:22.

and suggest subconscious imbalance, resulting in negative aspects of qualities: profound, aloof, taciturn. This expresses in suspicious of the motives of others, conniving and ruthless determination for materialistic goals. The second decanate of Capricorn corresponds to the 4 of Pentacles, of Chesed, sphere of Jupiter in Assiah, the material world. This is particularly related to alchemical earth as the source of all manifestation. [Here recall that Capricorn is a cardinal earth sing, ruled by Saturn and with Mars, the "fire of the Lord" exalted]. In this context it denotes absence of grasp of the principles of manifestation in the immediate present, and is related to the symbol of Mercury on the devil's belly in Key 15. The self of man is seen to be dominated by the elements composing his physical environment.

שבכה net, snare. Job 18:8: "For he has stretched out his feet into the net, and he walks upon a snare." Also lattice-work or reticulated ornament, in regard to Solomon's pillars, in 1 Kings 7:17: "And he [Hiram] made carved ornaments of network and wreaths of chain work for the capitals which were upon the top of the pillars seven for one capital and seven for the other." see 322 (masculine form).

בוטיש Goetia demon #17 by day of the 2nd decanate of Virgo. see Appendix 11.

I. *Goetia*: "… a great president, and an Earl. He appears at the first show in the from of an ugly viper, then at the command of the Magician he putts on a human shape with great teeth, and two horns, carrying a bright and sharp sword in his hand. He tells all things past, and to come, and reconciles friends and foes. He rules over 60 Legions of Sprits."

הערבים dusk. Exodus 12:6.
הכבש the lamb. see Exodus 29:39.

השחטה the slaughtered, the one being killed. see Leviticus 14:6.

327

כיצאור Kitzaur. Night demon of 3rd decanate of Capricorn. This decanate is ruled by Mercury

328

חשך darkness, adversity. This suggests that no matter how much we investigate it, the material world remains ever a great field of the Unknown.

The adversity which is the "dark night" of the soul. Also the ninth of the ten plagues against Egypt, mentioned in Exodus 10:22: "So Moses stretched out his hand toward the sky, and total darkness covered Egypt for three days." see 70, 444, 116.

"It designates the immeasurable reservoir of undifferentiated energy (8) [ח]in relationship with the cosmic metabolism (300) [ש]and the cosmic life (500)[ם,ך]. This "darkness" is swarming with all that *could* be, and its living power transcends all human thought. From it, the action of *Yavdel Veyn* [יודל בין, 110], in time, order and measure, gives birth to all that *can* become and be." [Suraes, 1992, p. 88.]

בצל כנפיך יהוה *sub umbra alararum tuarum, IHVH.* under the shadow of thy wings, Jehovah. בצל = in the shadow; צלב = to hang, crucify, impale; cross.

Psalms 36:7: "How priceless is your unfailing love! Both high and low among men find refuge in the shadow of your wings." Psalm 57:1: "Have mercy on me, O God, have mercy on me, for in you my soul takes refuge. I will take refuge in the shadow of your wings until the disaster has passed." Psalm 61:4: "I long to dwell in your tent forever and taken refuge in the shelter of your wings." Psalm 91:4: "He will cover you with his feathers, and under his wings you will find refuge." All of the above without IHVH. see 303, 3926 (Greek).

החשיה God concealed. 51st Shem ha-Mephorash. 251E-255E. SESMÉ. Psalm 104:31: "The glory of the Lord shall endure forever: the Lord shall rejoice in his works." To raise the soul to the contemplation of things divine, and for discovering the mysterious of wisdom, rules chemistry and physics; reveals the greatest secretes of nature, notably the philosopher's stone and the universal medicine. Person born: loves abstract sciences; applied himself particularly to learning the properties and virtues attributed to animals, vegetables, and minerals; distinguishes himself in medicine by his marvelous cures, and makes many discoveries useful to society. Angel of the 3rd quinance (11E-15E) of Aries; angel by day of the 3 of Wands (Binah of Atziluth). see 965, 313 & Appendix 10.

329

מרסני Tarasni. Angel of 1st decanate of Libra [Crowley, 1977, p. 37].

בשכבה when she lay down. In Genesis 19:33: That night they got their father to drink wine, and the older daughter went in and lay with him. he was not aware of it *when she laid down* or when she got up.

והשיבו and they shall return, and they returned. see Genesis 29:3.

ושחטב and there shall slaughter. see Exodus 12:6.

והשיגה and he grows in wealth, and he prospers. see Leviticus 25:26.

330

של error, fault, transgression. With different pointing: *shel.* of, belonging to. Carelessness belongs to the ignorant man, to whom desires appear to originate from the personality level. True source of desire belongs to the life-power. see 331,

מצר Boundary; 60th name of Shem ha-Mephorash; short form. see 361 & Appendix 10.

פרים oxen, bulls. see Exodus 24:5.

לכפר to atone. see Exodus 30:15.

יפרם he shall rend, he must tear. see Leviticus 21:10.

הנערה the damsel. Deuteronomy 22:19.

331 (prime)

רציאל Ratziel. "Secret of God". Archangel of Supreme mysteries. The Archangel of Chokmah in Assiah, the material world; and is the aspect of creative force active in the Chokmah of Briah. Ratziel is the angel who is Chief of the Supreme Mysteries which ties him in with the idea of Wisdom. The hierophant is one personification of the great teacher. Symbolized by this archangel by his hands was sent down the secret and supreme book, source of all wisdom and knowledge. see 248 for Godwin's spelling.

Ratziel brought to Adam in Eden, a book containing supernal inscriptions of the secret wisdom, and 72 branches of wisdom, expounding so as to show the formation of 670 inscriptions of higher mysteries. In the middle of the book was a secret writing explaining the 1500 keys which were not revealed even to the Holy Angels, and all of which were locked up in this book until it came into the hands of Adam.[Zohar 1, page 176].

אפרים Ephraim. double fruit. The Tribe of Israel corresponding to Vav (Taurus), The Hierophant. The Hierophant is one personification of the Great Teacher, also symbolized by the Archangel Ratziel. Associated with alchemical Congelation, the 2ⁿᵈ stage of the Great Work. The standard of this tribe was an ox. Ephraim was the second son of Joseph ('Multiplier"), Menasseh being the first-born in Deuteronomy 29:7, Mennaseh is referred to as a "half-tribe." see 95, 30, 570, 501, 54, 7 Genesis 41:52 and Deuteronomy 34:17.

אשל Tamarisk tree, a "grove". One of the several cryptic words in the magical language, of which אבן is the most important. Its first two letters spell אש, aysh, fire. The letters Shin and Lamed spell של, Shal, "of, belonging to." Thus the mystical significance has to do with the fire of illumination which consumes error.

Rosenroth in K.D.L.C.K. (p.165) gives *arbor magna* (great tree), and cites Genesis 21:33: "Abraham planted a Tamarisk tree in Beersheba, and there he called upon the name of the Lord, the eternal God."

Paul Case: It is the great tree Abraham planted at Beer-sheba ("well of the covenant", or of seven = בור + שבעה = 585 = אלהים צבאות , the divine name of Hod'.) "Note אשל conceals אש: fire; foundation = ground, and של: erring, trespass, offence." see 301, 330, 585.

מימרא די יהוה Memra di Tetragrammaton. The Word of God. Memra is the Aramaic for word (of God). see 72, 670, 1500, 248.

שאל to ask, demand, to inquire, to request. to desire earnestly, to wish, to seek, to discuss; to lecture. Note that the mental attitude expressed by this verb is that which makes possible our communication with the inner teacher. see 12, 158, 506.

שבטך thy rod Psalm 23:4:. "Thy rod and thy staff they comfort me." The magic of self-conscious intellect. see 311, 1217.

רפאים shades; extinct giants; ghost In Job 26:5 used with Heh prefixed: "The shades tremble beneath the waters and the inhabitants thereof." Also used in Isaiah 26"19: "(For thy dew is as the dew of light) and the earth shall being to life the shades." From רפא to heal, cure. Venus (creative imagination) which is exalted in Taurus (the "earth") cures the maladies of false images and desires (the "shades").

שאל to beg (alms).

סיסרא Sisera. Judges 5:20"... the star in their courses fought against Sisera." In Judges 4:2, a captain of the army of King Jabin of Canaan, who dwelt in Hardsheth of the gentiles. Hardsheth means: "the enchanters." From HVSh, to engrave, cut, plough, to shine, to grow, to whisper or mutter (compare with Isaiah 8:18, Wizards that peep and mutter), to be soft or viscous, like clay, loam, a forest, deaf, a worker in brass, a cutting tool. All these meanings relate to Venus and to Taurus. Sisera is typical of inharmonious desires.

שאול Sheol. Underworld Grave. In Proverbs 7:27, Nether-world. Variant spelling see 337.

332

אפראים Ephraim. a double fruit, a Tribe of Israel associated with Taurus [Godwin's spelling]. see 331, 892.

מקום פנוי an empty place. Note that מקום (186) means: place, locality, spot; existence, substance. "Having emptied yourself, remain where you are" -This is essential for receptivity. The Hebrew dictionary gives: המקום, the existence, God. God is the all-existence, whose substance is in all things. פנוי means: empty, vacant; free, without work; unmarried man. This last implies control and direction of the life-force, which works freely, without forcing, to enlighten the receptive mind. see K.D.L.C.K. (p.551).

אנדרומאל Andaromael. Goetia demon #72 by night of 3rd the decanate of Pisces. This decanate corresponds to the 10 of Cups, or the power of Malkuth, the physical plane in Briah, the creative world. see Appendix 11.

Goetia: "He is an Earl, great and mighty, appearing in the from of a man holding a great serpent in his hand. His office is to bring back both a thief, and the goods which be stolen; and to discover all wickedness, and underhand dealing; and to punish all thieves and other wicked people; and also to discover treasures that be hid. He rules over 36 Legions of Spirits." [Mathers, 1995, p. 65]

מבצר Mabatzar. A duke of Edom [Crowley, 1977, p. 37]. Associated with Magdiel and Yesod . Edom (literally, red) signifies unbalanced force. It is spelled with the same letters as אדם Adam, or generic humanity. In Genesis 36:42,43: "Kenaz, Teman, Mibzar, Magdiel and Iram. These were the chiefs of Edom, according to their sentiments in the land they occupied." see 45, 51 & *777* (p. 22).

שאלא Demand. Daniel 4:17: "This decree is by the command of the angel at the demand of the Holy One to the intent that the living may know that the most high God rules in the kingdom of men and gives it to whomsoever he will, and appoints it over the lowest of men." see 331.

שבל to move, to wave, to flow, whence, with different pointing, *sebel*: the train of a robe (so-called from its waving). Translated skirts in Isaiah 47:2: "Take the millstone and grind flour; remove your veil, lift up your skirts, bare your legs, and wade through the streams."

מאראץ Goetia demon #21 by day of the 3rd decanate of Libra. Also known as Forfax. "A great earl and president of the underworld, in command of 36 legions of spirits; he gives skill in astronomy and liberal arts. He is also called Foraii (by Weirus). Manifest in the form of a heifer." [Dictionary of Angels, pp. 113-114] see 1142 & Appendix 11.

Goetia: ".He is a great earl and president. He appears like a great bull with a man's face. His office is to make men very knowing in astronomy, and other liberal sciences; also he can give good familiars, and wise, knowing the virtues of herbs and stones which be precious. He governs 30 Legions of Spirits. [Mathers, 1995, p. 37]

אור היקוד *Lux* [light] *Ardoris* [burning, heat, of the feelings of passion, eagerness] [Crowley, 1977, p. 37]. In K.D.LC.K. (p. 64) Rosenroth says that Netzach is called by this name, since its sphere refers to Venus, who introduces love, tightening the ties of amorous desires.

יומם בעמוד ענן "by day in a pillar of cloud." Exodus 13:21. Note that his expression is equivalent to "firmament" and "thick cloud".

333

יהוה עזוז וגבור The Lord, strong and mighty [Psalm 24:8]. see 127.

עזרנו our help (is in the name IHVH) [Psalm 124:8]. Which is said to be "in the name IHVH, who made heaven and earth."

ויהי בקר and it was morning (one day) [Genesis 1:5].

וכבשה כבש (and fill the earth) "and subdue it" [Genesis 1:28]. Kabbash כבש means: to tread down, to subdue, bring into bondage, to press, force, violate, to preserve, pickle, to store, hide, to detain, suppress; to pave a road. With different pointing: Lamb. see 322.

החשך the darkness. Genesis 1:4: "And God saw the light, that it was good, and God divided the light from the darkness." In Isaiah 45:7: "I form the light and create darkness..." this darkness is connected with הרע, "the evil"-the implications of Genesis 1:4, first clause. see 328, 270.

איק בכר Aiq Bekar. Qabalah of the 9 chambers.

גלש to lie down. to glide down, to seethe, run over; to stretch oneself. With different pointing *gelesh*: seething water.

שָׁגַל to ravish, violate; to lie with, to be sexually excited. Deuteronomy 28:30: "Thou shall betroth a wife, and another man shall lie with her..." (curse for disobedience).

שֵׁגַל royal paramour, consort, King's wife in Psalm 45:9:. "Daughters of kings are among your honored women; at your right hand is the royal bride in gold of Ophir." In Daniel 5:3: "Then they brought the golden vessels that were taken out to the temple of the house of God which was at Jerusalem; and the King, and his princes, his wives [שֵׁגְלָתֵהּ, wives-of-them, Interlinar Bible] and his concubines, drank in them. And Daniel 5:23: "But instead you have set up yourself up against the Lord of heaven. You had the goblets from his temple brought to you, and you and your nobles, your wives [שֵׁגְלָתָךְ, wives-of-you, Interlinar Bible], and your concubines drank wine from them..."

שֶׁלֶג snow. A symbol of purity, and of Kether, the crown.

ακρασια. akrasia (Gr). incontinence. The character of powerless-not having power or command over a thing; in a moral sense: without power or command over oneself, incontinent. Also, sensuality, want of self-restrain, excess. Note well that akrasia is want of control.

η ελπις. heh elpis (Gr). the hope, to anticipate, usually with pleasure; confidence, faith, hope [Strong's Dictionary]. Later usage: expectation of either good or evil, hope or fear (Latin *spes*). Acts 27:20: "And neither sun nor stars appearing for several days, and no small tempest pressing on us, all remaining hope of our being saved was taken away". Romans 4:5: "And this hope is not put to shame, because the love of God has been diffused in our hearts, through the holy spirit which has been given to us." A title of Christ in Colossians 1:27: "To whom God wished to make known, what is the glorious wealth of this secret among the nations, which is Christ in you, the hope and glory." In Timothy 1:1: "Paul, an apostle of Jesus Christ, according to an appointment of God our savior, and of Christ Jesus our hope." see 1183, 2368, 3330.

εκτη. hekteh (Gr). sixth. Septuagint translation of שֵׁשׁ (610) in Genesis 1:31: "Elohim saw all that they had made, and it was very good. And there was evening, and it was morning - the 6th

day." The Zohar says this word is the foundation or Yesod, which is the sixth sephirah of those constituting *Ben*, the son, in Microprosopus. It is also related to lust and desire. see 610.

οικοδομημα. oikodemehma (Gr). a dwelling, building, edifice. see 370, 111, 518 (Greek), Mark 13:2 and 1 Corinthians 3:9:

η ελπις. heh elpis (Gr). the hope.

334

הַבּוֹנִים הַדְּבִיר The builders of the Adytum. Those who are using the seed-power to build the organ of illumination. see 323.

וְחֹשֶׁךְ and darkness. In Genesis 1:2: "And the earth was without form, and void; and darkness was upon the face of the deep. And the spirit of God [Elohim] moved upon the face of the waters." The processes of transformation take place gradually and in relative "darkness" until the light dawns. Kaph = 500, see 334, 1389.

וְכִחֵשׁ and deal falsely, and he deceives. see Leviticus 5:21.

Εκατη Hecate. Greek Goddess of Magic.

335

הַר סִינַי Har Sinai. Mount Sinai. Recall that Sinai was the place where Moses (345) received the law. see 130, 376.

שָׁלָה to be quiet, tranquil, at ease, to draw out, extract; to draw out (from water). Ecclesiastics 47:13: "Solomon reigned in a peaceable time, and was honored, for God made all quiet round about him, that he might build a house; in his name, and prepare his sanctuary forever." With different pointing *shelaw*: request, petition. Note that Solomon is connected with the Sun, and that stilling of the waters of consciousness, draws out peace. see 370, 90, Key 12.

אֶבֶן הָעֵזֶר stone of help; Stone of strength.

כַּשְׂדָּיָא (The) Chaldeans" Daniel 4:7: "Then came in the magicians, the enchanters, the Chaldeans and the astrologers: and I told the dream before them; but they did not make known unto me the interpretation thereof." The Chaldeans were in possession of the flame alphabet. see 268, 392, 221.

ימי רעה evil days. "Days of trouble" in Ecclesiastes 12:1: "Remember your creator in the days of your youth, before the days of trouble come and the years approach when you will say, 'I find no pleasure in them'".

מלך מלכי המלכים The king above. The (Kether), above the kings Chokmah and Binah; the king [or] the seven interior [lower sephiroth], which involve the entire decade [of the tree]. "The Chaldeans and the kings thus represent the 32 paths of wisdom, ignorance brings the "evil days" but knowledge of the paths beings one into contact with the "companions", or Masters of Compassion.

336

נר אלהים lamp of the Elohim; Lamp of God. 1 Samuel 3:3: "And ere the lamp of God went out in the temple of the Lord, where the ark of God was, and Samuel was laid down to sleep." see 899.

פרוים A region where gold was mined. ." In 2 Chronicles 3:6: "And he [Solomon] garnished the house [temple] with precious stones for beauty: and the gold was of *Parvaim*."

I. *The Aesch Mezareph* says that *zahab parvajim* is "referred to Hod... From its likeness to the blood of young bullocks, for this kind is red at the left hand." [Westcott, 1997, p. 13] see 1 Kings 6:20.

II. Westcott adds: "Paravahim, appears to be the name of a place: but also לדם le-dam, the blood means for the blood of Heh the פרו bullock: left-hand means "of the sephirotic place

שבכיד Night demon of the 1st decanate of Gemini [Sephir Sephiroth]. Gemini is ruled by Mercury and suggest subconscious imbalance, resulting in negative qualities connected with versatility and acuteness. This can be lack of comprehension, ability to pay attention and quickly perceive differences, encouraging the sense of separateness. The 1st decanate of

Gemini corresponds to the 8 of Swords or Hod of Yetzirah. This is human intellect and the activities and results of human mentation informing patterns. Here it implies an inability to honestly evaluate motives. Progress is inhibited by becoming fixated on the delusive thought forms in the lower levels of the pattern world, or race consciousness. It can result in ill-directed action, wasted force, pettiness, gossip and great to do about nothing. These negative Gemini qualities show need for balancing quick mindedness and penchant for action with depth of feeling and emotional warmth corresponding to Netzach and Venus. see 331, 466.

שאלה sheelah asking, request, loan. Spelled השאלה "the loan" in 1 Samuel 2:20: "And Eli blessed Eilkanah and his wife, and said, 'the Lord gave you another offspring from the woman for the loan which he has lent to the Lord.' And they went to their own home." Translated request in Psalm 106:15: "And he [God] gave them their request; and he supplied them with abundance." see 331, 332.

337 (prime)

שאול Sheol. Underworld Grave. In Proverbs 7:27, Nether-world. Also hades, one of the 7 infernal mansions; pictured on the diagram of the 4 seas. see 57, 911, 99, 1026, 566, 108, 291, 331.

שאול Saul. "Asked of God." The first king of Israel; the apostle Paul. Also Hill of Supernals," A City of Edom; "The place of asking." the place of Saul. see 701.

As a proper name Saul meaning, "Asked of God", the first king of Israel. In 1 Samuel 9:2: "He had a son named Saul, an impressive young man without equal among the Israelites-a head taller than any of the others." Saul is also the name of the apostle Paul who before his conversion persecuted the Christians. see Acts 9:1, 901 (Greek).

זהב שחוט Fine and drawn gold. In 2 Chronicles 9:15 "beaten gold." שחוט means sharpened, slaughtered; hammered, beaten.

אליצור God of the Rock.

פוֹרלאַךְ Phorlakh, Phorlak. Ruler of Earth. Ruling angel of element Earth. Name of an angel inscribed on the 7th Pentacle of the Sun in the *The Key of Solomon the King*. [Mathers, 1972, p. 74] The angel's name suggest the power of Mars or activity (Peh) receptive to the instruction of intuition (Vav) in the use of solar regenerative force (Resh) and guided through balanced action (Lamed) into new adventures of experience (Aleph) in never-ending cycles of growth (Kaph).

338

שלח to send, to stretch out, extend; to dismiss, drive out; to throw off, undress, flay. In Ecclesiastics 48:18: "There was also Jeroboam, the son of Nebat, who caused Israel to sin, and showed Ephraim the way of sin: and their sins were multiplied exceedingly, that they were divine out of the land." Jeroboam (ירבעם, 322) means "the people increase." Nebat is reproduction (Nun) through concentration (Beth) of the serpent power (Teth). Ephraim is connected with Taurus and alchemical congelation (331). With different pointing "*shilach*: to send away, send off; to send out; to let go, let loose, set free; to stretch out, dismiss; to divorce. The same force that is driven out is used to set free from bondage. Note that this word is an metathesis of the two preceding and shows the spiritual fire (Shin) as a goad (Lamed) to receptivity of the one self (Cheth).

שלח dart, missile, weapon, sword; sprout, slip, shoot; extension, space (projective aspect of the life-power); With different pointing 1.*shiloah*: skin, hide; pressed olive; 2. *Shiloam*, foundation near Jerusalem; 3. *shalawkh*: worker in hides, tanner. see 784.

לבוש garment, covering, clothing, fig. marriage. Daniel 12:6,7: "And one said to the man clothed in linen, which was upon the waters of the river, how long shall it be to the end of the wonders? And I heard the man clothed in linen, which was upon the waters of the river, when he held up his right hand and his left hand unto heaven, and swore by him that lives forever, that is shall be for a time, times and a half; and when he shall have accomplished to scatter the power of an holy people, all these things shall be finished."

יכבוש He hath pardoned (or overcome); He will subdue. In Micah 7:19: "He will turn again, he will have compassion upon us; he will subdue our iniquities; and thou wilt cast all their sins into the depths of the sea." [כבוש means conquest, subjugation].

שחל Lion; (poetical use only). In Hosea 5:14: "For I will be unto Ephraim as a lion, and as a young lion to the house of Judah: I, even I, will tear and go away; I will take away, and none shall rescue him." And in Psalm 9:13: "Thou shall tread upon the lion and adder: the young lion and the dragon shall thou trample under feet." see 211, 310, 340, 43, 460, 1702.

חלש to cast down [Crowley, 1977, p. 37].

339

זבל + מעמקים to enclose, to dwell + depths, profundities. The one life dwells within the depths of the physical plane, and in the heart of its creation, mankind, אדם Adam. see 45, 300, 39.

מועד + טהרה cleansing, purification + appointed time. Illumination of the microcosm comes at the appointed time, after cleansing of the heart of all impurities and separative thoughts. see 120, 219. "And none knoweth the time, Save he who hath appointed it." [Book of Tokens, Ayin]

לטש forger, forging. see Genesis 4:22.

אפרחים young ones. Deuteronomy 22:6.

340

If the founder's of the Rosicrucian order be taken as C.R.C. and added to the number of the 3 co-founder's initials of the order, the total value is 340.

שם there, then. With different pointing *shem*: location, sign, token, memorial, monument, name, son of Noah. Often used in Qabalistic writing to designate the divine name IHVH. Refers to Tav and Mem at the center of the cube of space. see 26, 441, 476, 345.

Translated "name" in Genesis 11:4: "And they said 'come, let us build ourselves a city, and a tower whose top may reach to the heaven; and let us make a name for ourselves, lest we be scattered abroad upon the face of the whole earth." And in Genesis 12:8: "From there he [Abram] went on toward the hills east of Bethel and pitched his tent, with Bethel on the west and Ai on the east. There he built an altar to the Lord and called on the name of the Lord." Bethel means "house of God". East is the direction of illumination. see 366.

שם "Shem... The sign of relative duration and movement which is connected here, and the sign of exterior action used as final collective sign, composed a root which produces the idea of that which is distinguished exteriorly by its elevation, its splendor, its own dignity. It is, in its most restricted acceptation, the proper name of a thing, the particular designation of a remarkable place, or of a remote time; it is the mark, the sign by which they are recognized; it is the renown, the splendor, the glory which is attached to them. In its broadest acceptation, it is ethereal space, the empyrean, the heavens over God. That one finds designated by the singular word, in Hebrew as well as in Samaritan, in Chaldaic, or in Syraic.

Its extremely difficult to choose, among so many significations, that which is most consistent with the son of *Noah*. Nevertheless one can without erring translate it by the words, *the sublime, the splendid, the radiant*, etc." [d'Olivet, 1976, p.170.]

נצר to watch, guard, keep; to keep from danger; preserve; observe, to keep secret. "He that keeps Israel shall neither slumber nor sleep." see 541.

נצר shoot, sprout (a Christian convert). Branch in Isaiah 60:20: "All you righteous people shall inherit the land forever; the branch of my planting, the work of my hands shall be glorified." Figuratively, a descendant, in Isaiah 11:1: "And there shall come forth a shoot out of the stem of Jesse, and a branch shall grow out of his roots." And In Daniel 11:7: "But an heir from his posterity shall rise over his land, and he shall come with an army and might against the king of the north, and he shall deal against them, and shall prevail."

ספר Sepher. Book. a reference to the mystical

book of 7 seals mentioned in Revelations 5:1. In the *Fama* the work of the first 4 brethren was making of the magical language (gematria) with a large dictionary, and the creation of Book M. . see 4, 16, 34, 64, 240, 220, 320.

מרק to polish, scour, be purged. As a verb to polish up; to finish, complete; to cleanse from sin by suffering. With different pointing: broth, soup. This implies purification of thinking by water, i.e. right memory, to be able to read the "name" in the "book" of life. see 42, 97 (Lt).

ליש Lion. see 211, 338, 310, 43, 460, 1702, Isaiah 30:6.

Inman: (Jud. 18:7), 'properly strength, lustiness,' hence 'a lion,' [Inman, 1942, Vol. 2., p. 201]

שלי rest, quite. Quietly in 2 Samuel 3:37: "And when Abner had returned to Hebron, Joab took him aside in the gate to speak with him quietly, and hit him under the fifth rib, that he died, for the blood of Asahel his brother."

ישגדי ברודיאל Yasgedi Barodiel. Angel of the 3rd decanate of Sagittarius [Crowley, 1977, p. 37]. Godwin gives the 3rd decanate of Capricorn.

מנרופיא *uncus focarius*; fire shovel [Sepher Sephiroth].

341

ש + מ + א The sum of 3 mother letters. Emesh.

In the Cube of Space Aleph connects above to below. Aleph is associated with the Element Air and Key 0, The Fool. In the ancient sky Air is compared with river, suggesting height and depth. And since every day moves from east to west, so the stream of man's existence is compared to a river. In the Cube of Space Mem (Root of Water) connects east to west, or Venus (sea-born) to Jupiter (lord of rain. The north-south line of Shin links Mars and the Sun.

The Zohar refers to this in [II:231A, p.339]: "This world did not come into being until God took a certain stone, which is called the 'foundation stone', and cast it into the abyss so that it held fast there, and from it the world was planted. This is the central point of the universe and on this point stands the holy of holies. This is the stone referred to in the verse, 'who laid the corner-stone thereof' [Job 38:6], 'the stone of testing, the precious corner stone' [Isaiah 28:16: and 'the stone that the builders despise became the head of the corner.' [Psalm 118:22]. This stone is compounded of Fire, Water, and Air, and rest on the abyss." (that is) so Aleph, Mem and Shin, the three mothers. Note that the stone is set in the center.

חם בארץ "in the land of Ham". In Psalm 105:27: "They showed his signs among them, and wonders in the land of Ham." Ham (heat, warmth, 48) is connected with the concentration of energy, setting up whirling motion which generates heat at the beginning of a cycle of manifestation. see 936, 291.

אשם guilt, offense; guilt-offering. With different pointing *aswhahm*: to commit an offense, be guilty. Proverbs 14:9: "Fools make a mock at sin [guilt]: but among the righteous there is favor."

שמא the name. In the name of the Lord offenses are pardoned, and liberation comes.

פרה אדומה a red cow. [פרה means to bear, fruit, be fruitful]. This may also be read "fruitful ground". see 50.

פרסא *pharasa expanse*, diaphragm. Suggest the abdominal center, related to Jupiter and to Kaph. K.D.L.C.K. (p.648) gives: *expansun, septimentum, diaphragma*, and refers to the space between the first emanation, and the crown, i.e. Kether, which is Adam Qadmon, then Briah.

ספרא Siphra; book of Halakhic Midrash on Leviticus [Aramaic]. With different pointing: *safra*. scribe, copyist. The book of law is written on characters hidden in nature, or the manifested world. The meaning of Kaph is to grasp this law of cycles.

342

בשם dealer or maker of spices, perfumer, druggist; With different pointing: to be spiced, to be tipsy.

שלהבה a blaze, flame. With different pointing: to kindle, inflame. Formation is the operation of divine Fire or the Father (Chokmah) upon the divine Water or the "mother" (Binah); this produces the Air or "son" (Tiphareth), which is a "living soul".

מרבק stall, stable. The "place" where the Christ-child is born. It corresponds to the Virgo area in the microcosm. see 78, 490.

ארץ אדום land of Edom. In Isaiah 34:6: "The sword of the Lord is filled with blood, it is made fat with fatness, and with the blood of lambs and goats, with the fat of the kidneys of Rams: for the Lord hath a sacrifice in Bozrah, and a great slaughter of the land of Idumea (Edom)." Edom means "red" and is connected with blood as a vehicle of consciousness; lamb and ram are associated with Aries, goat with Capricorn, both influence by Mars; the sword is that of Justice, or equilibrium (kidneys = Lamed, connected with the path linking Geburah and Tiphareth); בצרה Bozrah (fortress, 297) was the capital of Edom, which also connotes unbalanced force. see 344, 51, 45.

פוכלור Paklur. Night demon of the 2nd decanate of Taurus. This decanate is ruled by Mercury, and suggest subconscious imbalance, resulting in concentration which is deliberative, destructive and reactionary. The 2nd decanate of Taurus is attributed to the 6 of Pentacles, corresponding to Tiphareth, sphere of the Sun, as it expresses in Assiah, the material world. As subconsciousness is freed with correct self-direction, both mental and physical alterations are accomplished. The goal of this stage of development is the level of adeptship associated with Tiphareth wherein one is liberated from the limitations of physical matter and circumstances. There is need to devote much time to attentive, concentrative observations of what is going on in one's environment.

כורסון Korson. Demon king of the west [Godwin, 1999, p. 168]. see 992 & Appendix 11.

יהוה מלך עולם ועד The Lord is king for ever and ever. Psalm 10:16: "The Lord is king for ever and ever: the heathen have perished from his land." The Zohar [I:34A, p.127] comments: "There are two worlds, an upper world and a lower world, the lower being on the pattern of the upper. There is a higher king and a lower king. It is written: "The Lord reigns, the Lord has reigned, the Lord will reign for evermore'. i.e. 'The Lord reigns' above, 'the Lord has reigned' in the middle, 'the Lord will reign' below. Rabbi Aha said: "The Lord refers to the supernal wisdom; beauty of Israel; 'The Lord will reign' signifies the ark of the covenant. At another time David reversed the order and said, 'The Lord is king forever and ever' [Psalm 10:16] i.e. 'The Lord is king', below 'forever', in the middle, 'and ever'. above for there is the reunion and the perfection of all. God is 'king' above, and 'will reign' below." see 26, 90, 146, 74.

שׁוֹיִל   path, way. Psalm 77:19: "Your path led through the sea, your way through the mighty waters, though your footprints were not seen."

343

I. (7 x 7 x 7) or 7^3

גשׁם   to rain violently. As a noun: a hard shower. Root of the Corporeal Intelligence (Qoph), see 739, 389.

ו-יאמר אלהים   and God said [Genesis 1:2]. Refers to the creative word or powers, which brought forth the universe from the unmanifest. see 414, 86.

טל חרמון   the dew of Hermon. In Psalm 133:3: "(Unity is) as the dew of Hermon, and as the dew that descended upon the mountains of Zion: for there the Lord commanded the blessing, even life forever-more." The dew is the watery essence which, according to the Zohar, flows from the brain of Macroprosopus (Kether) to the lower sephiroth. see 39, 304.

לב-אישׁ   hearts of men. This dew flows into Microprosopus (Tiphareth), which is the Ego seated in the hearts of men. see 32, 311.

שׁלחה   let loose. Genesis 49:21: "Naphtali is a hind let loose: he gives goodly words."

זפרון   a sweet smell; to be fragrant; a city in north Palestine. The "words" brought forth by Naphtali (Virgo) give the odor of sanctity.

ארון אלהים   The ark of the Elohim (God). 1 Samuel 3:3: "And ere the lamp of God went out in the temple of the Lord, where the ark of God was..." see 257, 86.

בהסירון   Bahisiron. Qlippoth of Aquarius. Implies wrongly directed meditation.

יאו + יהושׁה   I.A.O. + Yeheshua. I.A.O. = 17 = the swastika; Yeheshua = the pentagram. There total = 343, as 7^3 is the formation of the stone of the wise, from the seven-fold regimen and the fixation of the volatile (the wanderers of planets). Part of training of lesser adept 8 = 6. see 98, 48, 17, 326.

344

פרדס   A park; paradise. In Canticles 4:13:. "Thy plants are a park of pomegranates..." or "pleasure-garden." see 671 Greek.

לשׁוח   to meditate. see Genesis 24:63.

שׁלחו   send, send! see Genesis 42:16.

345

שׁילה   Tranquil, tranquility, inner peace. A mystical name referring to the process of liberation. "Shiloh shall come" [Genesis 49:10]. Refers to the Messiah. see 376.

Also a city in Ephraim (Taurus, congelation, 331, 656), north of Bethel, first capital of the Hebrews after the conquest of Palestine and seat of the tabernacle till Samuel. In Joshua 18:1: "And the whole congregation of the children of Israel assembled together at Shiloh, and set up the tabernacle of the congregation there. And the land was subdued before them."

אל שׁדי   El Shaddai. God Almighty. This name occurs 6 times in Genesis and 3 times in the rest of the Pentateuch. With different vowel points: to appall; to be horrified, to make desolate, devastate. see 340.

In Genesis 17:1: "And when Abram was 99 years old, the Lord appeared to Abram, the said to him, "I am the almighty God; walk before me, and be faultless.'" And in Exodus 6:3: "And I appeared to Abraham, unto Isaac and to Jacob, by the name of God Almighty, but by name IHVH I was not known to them."

השם Ha-Shem. The name; Tetragrammaton.

משה Moses. With different vowel points: 1. to draw out, to pull out; 2. debt, loan; 3. to massage.

שהם beryl crystal; onyx stone. In Genesis 2:12: a precious stone. Contains the pattern of the 6-pointed star. Concerning Onyx Webster dictionary says it is of Greek origin. "The nail," from the color of the gem resembling that of a nail. Any stone exhibiting layers or two or more colors contrasted, especially when it is marked and stratified with opaque and translucent lines. Onyx was valued highly by the ancients, and is much used for cameos, the figure being cut in one layer and the background consisting of the next layer. Webster Beryl: "A hard, colorless, yellowish, bluish or less brilliant green variety or emerald, the prevailing hue being green or various shades, but always pale... Some of the finer and transparent varieties of it are called aquamarine." In Song of Solomon 5:15 תרשיש is used to mean Beryl or Jasper, precious stone. see 44, 59, 64.

Beryls are found under the heavenly Taurus. Connected with the hexagonal crystal, Venus, the "eye-stone" and are a symbol of undying youth. They are also linked with Sardonyz, Leo, the Tribe of Judah of the Ephod (breastplate) of the high priest. The angel of Beryl is Anael, linked to Venus. see 409, 1210, 5, 403, 1207.

שבכה He was appeased. In Esther 7:10: "Then was the king's wrath pacified (i.e. appeased)" "Wrath pacified" or "Wrath appeased."

I. I.R.Q. para. 387: "*Shekaka* is the name which includes all names,* in consequence of which that holy blessed one makes his wrath to pass away. And caused Microprosopus to be at peace, and takes away all those extraneous (matters) from the midst." [Mathers, 1993, p. 155]

* It is not at first sight evident why this word should be the 'the name which includes all names." *Shekaka* [345] = Shemah = Ha Shem, The Name. This title Shemah is applied to the Tetragrammaton frequently as being the name of all names, and therefore *Shekaka* is taken as

concealing Tetragrammaton.

שולט dominator [i.e. both "the name" and Shiloh (king messiah)]. Dominator in K.D.L.C.K. (p.707) and says Tiphareth is thus called, when it is considered under the idea of Yesod; i.e. as ruler of the vital soul.

אש להט the flaming fire; the consuming fire. In Psalm 104.4: "Who makes his angels spirits; his ministers a flaming fire." (Lahat = Magical fire) see 44.

בטל-הרמון like the dew of Hermon [Psalm 133:3]. see 343.

שמה Thither, there [Genesis 29:3]. "Is there" in Ezekiel 48:35: "And the name of that city from that day shall be יהוה שמה, 'the Lord is there.'" It is the heavenly Jerusalem with 12 Gates, each gate a tribe of Israel. North: Gates of Reuiben, Judah, Levi; East: Joseph, Benjamen, Dan; South: Simeon, Issachar, Zebulun; West: Gad, Asher, Napthali. See 371.

אלהים אחרים The responsible creative powers; the creative guarantor or surety of God. Given as *dii alieni* in K.D.L.C.K. (p.106); for none other than God is exacted and elevated, eternally living, etc.

בשגם in that also; as also. In Genesis 6:3: "My spirit shall not always strive with man, for that he also is flesh: yet his days shall be an hundred and twenty years." Referred to Da'ath and to Moses [Zohar 1:38A]. see 474.

The Zohar [I:38A, p.140] comments: "And his days shall be a hundred and twenty years." This is an allusion to Moses, through whose agency the law was given, and who thus bestowed life on men from the Tree of Life. And in truth had Israel not sinned, they would have been proof against death, since the Tree of Life had been brought down to them. All this was through Moses, who is called בשגם beshagam*, and hence we have learnt: 'Moses did not die, but how haw gathered in from the world, and caused the moon to shine', being in this respect like the sun, which also after setting does not expire, but gives light to the moon.' According to another explanation we translate, 'for that it, to wit, the spirit, is also flesh', i.e. it is long converted into flesh, in the sense of following the body and seeking the pleasures of this world."

* בשגם = 345 = משה, Moses. בשגם = "as also", or according to others, "because of their erring."

לישה lioness. In K.D.L.C.K. (p. 501) kneading. "Lion; great and with abundant shaggy hair, also fierce. In the Zohar Noah refers her to the sphere of Geburah, and moreover in Job 4:11, "the old lion" indicates a total lack of influence.

שלהי end, tail (Aramaic). The lion's tail in Key 8 is a symbol of the serpent power.

משגב secure height; refuge, strength, safety Psalm 46:11 and 46:8:. "The God of Jacob is in our high tower."

שליה after-birth; secundine.* Deuteronomy 28:57: (The woman who lives a luxurious life, her eye shall be evil) "And toward the afterbirth that comes from between her feet, and toward her child whom she shall bear, when she eats them for want of all things in the siege and distress with which your enemy shall harass you in all your cities." Part of the covenant which the Lord gave to Moses.

*According to Webster, in botany the secundine is the second coat, or integument of an ovule (immature seed), within the primene (1st) coat, investing the nucleus or center.

מדיש 5th Shem ha-Mephorash, short form. see 360 & Appendix 10.

346

רצון will, good will, delight, favor, good pleasure, acceptance, favor, satisfaction graciousness, and good will. With different pointing: intent, purpose, determination, desire, wish, inclination; purpose. Name of the 20th path of Yod. It is good-will toward man and toward the rest of creation. The formative potency of the creative hand shapes things favorably for mankind. The star in the Hermit's Lantern or the hexagram is a synthesis of the alchemical symbols for the 4 elements, and the letters of רצון (ר: Fire; צ: Air; ו: Earth, נ: water) represent these same four elements as phases in the manifestation of Light. One of the 4 occult maxims. The magical will is the radiant power of the Sun (Resh). It is something perceptible throughout nature (Tzaddi). He who learns by practice the art of true meditation becomes a powerful center of that Natural Intelligence. He who knows the one will goes through Life guided by the inner voice (Vav). The magical will is a power of development and dissolving power as well. It takes form in mental imagery (Nun). see 474, 131, 70, 701, 107, 20.

Translated grace in Lesser Holy Assembly (p. 102, 108, 110, 111) "If this רצון grace, be revealed, all those judgements are enlightened and are diverted from their concealed rigor." "And when this head, which is concealed in the head of the ancient one, which is not known, extendeth a certain frontal formation, which is formed for brilliance, then flasheth forth the lighting of his brain." "And is produceth and designeth (a certain effect) in this light (otherwise in this opening), in this forehead, whereon is inscribed a certain light, which is called רצון, grace." "And this grace is extended backward into the head, even unto that place where it can remain in the beard, and it is called the supernal, חסד Chesed, Mercy."

Rawtzone, meaning grace and good will is numerically the same as maqor (see below), meaning, something dug, a spring, a well and tzanir, meaning, a water-pipe, a canal or channel. Thus we see that will has to do with the transmission of occult Water from a primary source through a channel. In this connection one would be lead to the conclusion that Geburah, the seat of Will is a watery sephiroth.

Note that the letters of rawtzone are composed of the 4 elements. Resh, Key 19, the Sun and the element Fire. Tzaddi, Key 17, The Star and the sign Aquarius, a fixed air sign; Vav, Key 5, the Hierophant and the sign Taurus, a fixed earth sign, and Nun, Key 13, the sign Scorpion, a fixed water sign. Note that three of these letters are related to fixed signs, and the Sun, Resh, rules the fixed fire sign of Leo. This is represented by the animals shown in the corners of Tarot Keys 10 and 21.

This intimates that Will is a synthesis of the elemental powers which are also represented by the word יהוה, because each of the letters also stands for one of the 4 elements (see 26).

The true magical will is to identify or align the personal will with the cosmic Will. The keynote of this practice found in the meaning of *rawtzone*, delight and acceptance. Through obedience to the cosmic will the Magician becomes a channel for its expression. And without exception the Primal Will-to-Good bestowes its gifts and favor.

צנור A water pipe, channel. From a root meaning to be hollow. Personality is but a channel for the out-flowing of the divine will into the outer world of name and form.

מקור A well, a spring, fountain, source; flow. This power which flows out into manifestation through personality is life water-the "Living water" of Chesed. With different pointing: the interior of the womb. see 504.

347 (prime)

אלי צורי my God, my rock. In Psalm 18:3: "The Lord is my rock, and my fortress, and my deliverer; my God, my rock (strength); in whom I will trust; my buckler, and the horn of my salvation, and my high tower." [in the first line "the Lord (IHVH) is my rock, סלעי is used]. Note that in Key 7 the Charioteer stands in a rock or cubic stone with a canopy overhead. see 306, 41.

ליבשה the dry land. In Genesis 1:10: "and God called the dry land earth; and the gathering together of the waters called he seas..." In Genesis 1:9 this word also occurs but preceded by Heh the definite article, instead of Lamed}. The 'earth' or dry land is here connected with 2 "metals" - Sun = gold = frankincense, Saturn = lead = myrrh, thus implying that the work of Elohim, the creative power, in building the "rock" or stone of the wise, is to transmute the force of Saturn into the Sun center, with the goad (Lamed) of equilibrated action.

בצהרים as noon, at the midday. see Deuteronomy 28:29.

להקדיב to present, bring near, to bring. see Leviticus 7:38.

משאו his burden, his load. Exodus 23:5.

הבשם the spice. Exodus 35:28.

348

משח oil (for anointing); to anoint; consecrate, to smear, measure. Root of Messiah. see 358, 868.

רוח-מים-דם spirit, water, blood. Symbolic of the 3 principles: spirit, soul, body.

שמח to shine, to be bright, to rejoice; to glitter, sparkle [Leviticus 23:40, Deuteronomy 12:7]. Joyful, glad, merry in Psalm 45:15.

חמש one-fifth, fifth part of something; belly; one of the books of the Pentateuch; to be strong, to equip, to arm for war; lion, abdomen. Relates to Geburah, the 5th Sephirah. The lions are the seat of strength; to gird the lions, or to arm generally. With different pointing *chawmesh*: Five; number of the pentagram. Note that the reduction of 348 is 15, which is the secret number, or extension of 5.

Of the root חם, Fabre writes: "The sign of elementary existence, symbol of every effort and every labor, united to the sign of exterior activity, and employed as collective and generalizing sign, forms an important root whose purpose it to signify, in a broad sense, a general envelopment and warmth which results, considered as an effect of contractile movement. Idea of that which *is obtuse; curved, hot, obscure; enveloping, striking; a curvature; dejection; a compressive force: natural heat, solar fire, torrefaction* and the *burnish amorous passion, wrath*, etc." [d'Olivet, 1976, p. 351.]

Of the root מש, he writes: "From the union of the sign of exterior activity with that of relative movement, or by contraction with elementary root אש sprigs a root whose purpose is to express that which is stirred by contractile movement. The Arabic signifies properly *to feel, touch, softly, brush lightly*. מש everything *palpable, compact, gathered*: every *pile*, as *a crop, a harvest*. That which is *drawn, extracted, shrunken*, as *silk*, etc." [d'Olivet, 1976, p.394.]

לעולם עקב to the end of the age (world). In

Psalm 114:112: "I have inclined my heart to perform thy statues always, even unto the end." Hebrew translation is: forever at every step. see the many meanings of עקב, 172, 2678 (Greek).

בבל-הארץ in all the world. The world is the physical plane. see 291.

חשם *Husham* a king of Edom, associated with Geburah. Edom signifies unbalanced force; Geburah is the sphere of Mars. In Genesis 36:34: "When Jobab died, Husham from the land of the Temanites succeeded him as king." see 348 for correct numeration. see 51, 216.

349 (Prime)

Ισραηλ. Israel (Gr). "He shall rule as God", Greek spelling. see 703.

350

שכל intelligence, consciousness, insight, awareness, understanding. Use to describe the Paths of Wisdom. Both awareness and ability to make practical use of insight. Applies to each of the 32 Paths of Wisdom combines שך (Soke) abode, with כל (Kole) all, the whole, every. True insight always perceives that whatever the form degree or category may be under consideration, each is really an abode for the whole being of the Life-power. Shin (Shin) symbolizes the creative Life-breath. Kaph (Kaph) represents conscious grasp, or comprehension of the universal order. Lamed (Lamed) symbolizes action to establish poise and equilibrium in man's conscious expression of spiritual powers. see 300, 868.

עפר dust. Out of the dust of the ground was the essence of man (Adam) created by Jehovah-Elohim. One spelling of Ophir. With different pointing: dry and loose earth soil, powder; ashes; also: young mule, youth. roe. see 297, 45, 50, 451, 795, 1881, 422.

"(*Aafar:* 70.80.200 translated "dust", of *Adama)* sets into indeterminate motion (70) the lowest strata of energy (80) in the cosmos (200).

This so-called 'dust' (symbolic of crumbled rocklike rigidity) leads us by means of its letter-numbers to the realization that *Eretz* is not only the Earth. This schema stands for all cosmic bodies and for every aspect of their components, from their simplest chemical elements up to their highest biological aggregates." [Suraes, 1992, p. 104.]

ספיר sapphire, the dark, delicate colored semi-precious stone. It also means beam or ray of light from the sun. Part of the breastplate of the High Priest in Exodus 28:18: "And the second row shall be an emerald, a sapphire, and a diamond." Note that 350 is 3 and 50, the numeration of the stone (53).

I. This stone is attributed by Kowminsky to the 11th gem of the breastplate of the high priest, and to the zodiacal sign Aquarius. He refers to is as lapis lazuli; the Septuagint of Exodus 28:20: "And the forth row a serpentine, a lapis lazuli, and a crystal; they shall be set in gold in their enclosings." see 839 (Greek). For the other stones of the breastplate see 45, 98, 702, 150, 345, 395, 370, 308, 84, 85.

II. Isdore Kosminsky writes: For reasons state the sapir is placed in the eleventh division of the breastplate instead of the shoham, and we thus have complete harmony between the eleventh sign of the zodiac Aquarius, the eleventh division of the breastplate and the sapir stone which is translated as sapphire in the Hebrew Bible, the authorized version, the vulgate; as lapis lazuli or sapphire by Mr. Wodiska, and as lapis lazuli by Dr. Hirsch, Rev. J.R. Dummelow, and others. The Targums indicate a stone of blue color, and that this is the lapis lazuli there is no reason to doubt. In ancient times the lapis lazuli was termed sapphirus [Greek, σαπψειρος , 1166]; Puny describes it accurately as 'opaque, sprinkled with specks of gold.' The lapis lazuli was a very highly esteemed stone amongst the old world peoples, who called it 'the stone of heaven', the gem of the stars', and the Zemech stone connected with all things heavenly. Traditionally it is the stone on which was engraved the law of Moses... The connector of a blue stone with the blue heaven is consistent with ancient philosophy, and authorities agree in connecting this color with the sign of the mighty heavens... Aquarius... the Lapis lazuli then, is the stone of the eleventh division of the breastplate and on it was engraved the name Joseph. [The Magic and Science of Jewels and Stones, pp. 50-

III. With different pointing: chickpea; kidney bean. The feminine form of the word: ספירה means counting, numbering; writing, recording, degree, quantitative category; sephirah, divine emanation, sphere]. see 403, 408; 186, 536, 604, 674; 1166 (Greek).

קרן horn; head; figuratively a sign of strength, might, power; glory, pride. A sign of strength and power in Daniel 7:8: "I considered the horns, and behold, there came up among them another little horn, before whom there were three of the first horns plucked up by the roots: and, behold, in this horn were eyes like the eyes of man, and a mouth speaking great things." Psalm 148:14:. "He also exacted the horn of his people, the praise of all his saints, even of the children of Israel, a people near unto him. Praise ye the Lord." With different pointing: grandeur; corner point, peak, ray; principal, capital; damage done by an animal's horns. see 752, 326 (Greek), 1000.

ריקם emptiness, vacuum. "Having emptied yourself, remain where you are." [Lao Tze] The influx of spirit when personality is put aside. Also: empty, void, vain, without cause, without effort. see 910.

K.D.L.C.K. (p.689) givens *vacuum*, and says it refers to the cortices (i.e. Qlippoth), where there is no water but serpents and scorpions. He cites Genesis 37:24 in regard to Joseph and his brothers: "And they took him and threw him into the cistern. Now the cistern was empty; there was no water in it." [Note that in this passage empty is spelled רק, Interlinar Bible]

According to Young's Concordance this word means: empthy, vain. In the Interlinar Old Testament Bible it is translated empty handed in Genesis 31:42; Exodus 3:21.

וירא אלהים כי טוב "And good saw that it was good." In Genesis 1:10: "God called the dry ground 'land', and gathered waters [המים] he called 'seas [ימים].' And God saw that it was good."

אלינוש Goetia demon #15 by day of the 3rd decanate of Leo. see Appendix 11.

I. *Goetia*: "...a great duke, and appears in the from of a goodly Knight carrying a Lance, and ensign, and a serpent. He discovers hidden things, and knows things to come; and of wars, and how the soldiers will or shall meet. He causes the love of lords and great persons. He governs 60 Legions of Spirits." [Mathers, 199, p. 35]

שן shan. prong, point, edge, tooth. Variant spelling of Shin (שין). see 360.

שן two. "שן [350], שני [360], or שנים [400] two. The root שן, composed of the sign of relative duration Shin, and that of produced being or growth Nun, contains all ideas of mutation, of transition, of passing from one state to another, of redundancy. Thus the name of this number in bringing diversity, change and variation, is the opposite in everything form the preceding number [one], which, as we have seen, arrests division and tends to immutability. The feminine is שת, שתי and שתים." [d'Olivet, 1976, p. 152.]

יהוה בקרבך IHVH be-qirebbek. Tetragrammaton is with you.. In Zephaniah 3:15: "The Lord has taken away your punishment, he has turned back your enemy. The Lord, the King of Israel, is with you; never again will you fear any harm. see 830.

351

I. Σ26 = 351

הרצון the Will, the good pleasure. The 20th Path of Yod. "The 20th path is called the intelligence of Will. It forms all patterns, and to know this intelligence is to know all the reality of the primordial wisdom. Rawtzone [רצון], "Will," by its four letters represent radiant energy or fire (ר); air (צ); earth (ו); and water (נ). The occult significance of the word relates to the idea of a synthesis of the 4 elements, which synthesis is none other than the One Reality, the Ancient of Days represented by the Hermit, and customarily designated by the Divine Name Jehovah. What men feel in their very bodies as the power called "will" is the surge of the light-force through blood stream and nerve and tissue. see 346, 701, 1001.

אנש man (Chaldean). A title of Tiphareth. This relates once again to the personality complex of man-- the six subdivisions of Ruach--as the instrument of dominion over the formative Yetziratic forces. see 357.

נשא Exalted; elevated, lofty. Suggest the forces of Malkuth as the bride who sits on the throne of Binah. Consider also as an Epithet of *Jah* (15). K.D.L.C.K. (p.599) gives: *elevatus*, and says it is regarded by some as Tiphareth, by others as Kether; the Zohar refers it to Binah which is above Geburah.

נשא to lend, be a creditor, to forget. In the sense of "to forget," as מנשה, Manasseh. With different pointing *nasa*: to lift up, to raise, to exact. Implies that the extension of the powers represented by the name IHVH has a tendency to raise man above the level of mere homo sapiens, or man as the result of the evolutionary process, to the higher level of adeptship or sainthood.

שמיא heaven, heavens (Chaldee) Daniel 4:20: "The tree that thou saw, which grew, and was strong, whose height reached unto the heaven, and the sign thereof to all the earth." Shemia always represents the level of life activity called super-consciousness. Root-meaning is lifted up. see 1035.

אשים The fiery ones, flames. The choir of angles associated with Malkuth in Yetzirah (10 of Swords). The masculine plural of אש, fire. "Burnt or incense offering" [Crowley, 1977, p. 38]. see 80, 301, 911.

אדני המלך נאצו The faithful King

ארץ נוד "The land of Nod", where Cain found his wife. In Genesis 4:16: "And Cain went out from the presence of the Lord, and dwelt in the land of Nod, on the east of Eden. see 570, 443, 20, 60, 1161.

פרי בטן children, offspring. literally "fruit of the womb".

נקרא to call oneself; to be called, be summoned; to be called, be named; to happen to be, to meet by chance; to be read aloud, be recited. From קרא, "to call".

שומה determination; determined, intention. 2 Samuel 13:32: "But Jonadab son of Shimeah, David's brother, said, 'My Lord should not think that they killed all the princes; only Ammnon is dead. This has been Absalom's expressed intention ever since the day Amnon raped his sister Tamar.'"

אשכל cluster of grapes, bunch; fig. great scholar; cyclopedia. see 439.

מושה Moses, the initiator. variant spelling. see 345.

352

ברקים lighting. see 912.

בשן soft, rich soil [Psalm 68:16]. The name of a country east of Jordan, famous for its Oak forest and meadows. see 581.

לא-החזיק לעד אפו He retains not His anger forever. Micah 7:18: "Who is a God like unto thee, that pardons iniquity, and passes by the transgression of the remnant of his heritage? He retains not his anger forever, because he delights in mercy." Refers to the fifth conformation of the beard of Macroprosopus in I.R.Q. or The Greater Holy Assembly [Mathers, 1993, para. 382, p. 154]. see 848, 291, 126, 201, 713, 406, 400, 581.

צורנו our rock [Deuteronomy 32:31]. see 336, 296, 301, 352.

קרון offering, sacrifice; form of a vow.

רצונו His favor [Proverbs 16:15]. May also be read, His will, His grace, His desire. see 476.

אור מעלה "The exalted light." A title of Kether. Aur (אור) means fire and Aor (אור) means light.

צורון necklace; collar. Form of a word (chain) used in Song of Solomon 4:9: "Thou has ravished my heart, my sister, my spouse; thou has ravished my heart with one of your eyes, with one chain of thy neck." see 416, 220.

אֶרֶךְ אַפִּים long of nose; i.e. merciful. אֶרֶךְ refers to Kether. see 221; 912, 1392.

לְהַבְדִּיל בֵּין הַיּוֹם וּבֵין הַלַּיְלָה "to divide between the day and between the night." Genesis 1:14: "And God [Elohim] said, let there be lights in the firmament of the heaven to divide the day from the night; and let them be for signs, and for seasons, and for days and for years." see 666, 777.

שֹׁבִים captor. In Isaiah 14:2: "And the Gentiles shall take them and bring them to their place; and the house of Israel shall posses them in the land of the Lord for men-servants and women-servants; and they shall take them captive, whose captors they were; and they shall rule over their oppressors." see 307, 358.

η οδος. he-odos (Gr). the way. John 14:6.

Μαριας. Marias (Gr). Mary, the mother of Jesus, as spelled in Matthew 1:18. "Now the birth of Jesus was thus: Mary his mother had been pledged to Joseph; but before they were united, she was discovered to be pregnant with the Holy Spirit." The name means "seas", and is attributed in Qabalah to the "Great Sea", Binah. see 146, 152.

πλασμα. plasma (Gr). Thing formed Romans 9:20: "O Man, who are thou, replying against God? Shall the thing formed say to its maker, 'why didst thou make me thus?'" Also means: anything molded or modeled in clay or wax, an image, That which is imitated, a forgery.

353 (prime)

חֲמִשָׁה five, the fifth. Suggest the quintessence, or fifth essence, which is akasha, spirit and the stone of the wise.

נָגַשׁ to draw near, approach; to stand back, recede; to lie with. The approach to unity is identification with the source of all. With different pointing nawgas: to press, drive, impel; to exact (debt); to rule oppressively.

גֹּשֶׁן A district of Egypt in which Jacob and his family were placed. In Genesis 47:6: "The land of Egypt is before thee; in the best of the land make thy father and brethren to dwell; in the land

of Goshen let them dwell..." Goshen was in the eastern portion of Egypt, North of the southern point of the delta. Egypt is a symbol of the astral plane; the east is the source of light. Goshen is the memory of the source uniting all things and creatures (Gimel), the perpetual resurrection out of darkness (Egypt) (Shin) and the seed of change which turns Jacob ("Supplanter", 182) into Israel ("He shall rule as God", 541) (Nun).

זָהָב וּלְבֹנָה וָמֹר Gold and Frankincense and Myrrh. Gifts of the three magi to the infant Christ-child. see 240, 246, 347.

חֲמִשָּׁה the fifty. see Genesis 18:28.

הִבְשִׁילוּ ripened. see Genesis 40:10.

כַּשֶּׁלֶג like snow, like the snow. see Exodus 4:6.

הַמּוּשָׁב the restitution. see Numbers 5:8.

354

שִׂדִּים Siddim. Plain. Vale in which Sodom and Gomorrah with 3 other cities, were located. It is the present site of the Dead Sea. "*Shedim*; demons." [Godwin, 1999, p. 550] See 345, 50, 152, 287, 104, 315.

דֶּשֶׁן fatness, fat land. Sacrificing fat or excess is part of transmutation of personality. see 826, 1004.

שְׁמִטָּה remission of debt, release. In Deuteronomy 15:1: "At the end of every seven years you shall make release [the-cancel-of-debt, Interlinar Bible]." With different pointing: sabbatical year; failure, bankruptcy.

K.D.L.C.K. (p.720) gives: *heptaeteris intermissoria* and says it is Malkuth, and relates to the 7 years and seven Sephiroth.

עֶזְרָא כַהֲנָא Ezra the priest. Ezra means: "aid, help". Help is in the "ark" of the Lord. see 278, 76 & Ezra 7:11.

שְׁלִיטָה power, control. Control over the power that flows through the personality, brings the priesthood of Ezra.

חֶצְרוֹן Hetzron. Hezron. "A courtyard". Son of

פרץ Perets (Perez = "a breach") in Numbers 20:21. Herzon is a son of Reuben (259, multiplication) in Genesis 46:9. The "courtyard" is the field (Cheth) into which the life-power flows, through the breach made by the higher self. This is a direct consequence of alchemical multiplication. see 1004.

שבבים fragments. From שבב to break, split. In Hosea 8:6: "For from Israel was it also: the workman made it; therefore it [the idol] is not God: but the calf of Samaria shall be broken in fragments."

355

נשה thigh-nerve; to forget, to lend, to exact payment.

ספירה a sphere, divine emanation; number, counting, writing, recording, quantitative category. A technical term employed to designate one of the 10 distinct intelligible aspects of the Life-power.

שנה year; to do again, repeat, to change, alter, to be different; to study; to teach. Suggest the spiraling cycles of emanation and the paths linking the spheres of the Tree of Life. With different pointing: *shenah*. sleep, slumber. The pralaya or resting period between cycles of manifestation. it is said that "life is a dream"; the universe is thought into manifestation periodically, by the meditation of God.

In Genesis 5:3: "And Adam lived a hundred and thirty years [שנה], and begat a son in his own likeness, after his image; and called his name Seth." This verse is rendered by d'Olivet: "And Adam existed three tens and one hundred cycles (of temporal ontological mutation); and he produced according to his assimilating action, in his reflected shadow, and emanated being, and he called his name Sheth (basis and foundation of all things)." [d'Olivet, 1976, p. 325.]

He comments: שנה, revolving change... The Hellenists, and Saint Jerome following these unreliable masters, have rendered it by ετος, "annus", *a year*. But they have restricted what was taken in a broad sense, and applied to a particular revolution, that which was applicable to an universal, ontological revolution. Its root is

שן to be that of number *two* and containing every idea of mutation, of variation, of passing from one state to another. Thus the word שנה, expresses a temporal mutation, relative to the being which is this object. The Hebraic tongue has several terms for expressing the idea of temporal duration. עד characterizes the same state continued, an actual duration; as relation, we translate it be *still*; חדש, carries the idea of a beginning of existence, either in the order of things, or in the order to time: in its most restricted sense, it means a monthly duration: שנה is applied to the transition of this same existence, to a mutation of the being: that is to say, that the being which is its object, is not found at the end of the period which it expresses, at the same point or the same state that it was at its beginning: in the more restricted sense, it is the space of a year: finally, the last of these terms it שנב, which should mean every revolution which replaces the being in its original state. These divers periods, always relative to the being to which they are applied, can mean the most limited duration as well as that whose limits escape human understanding. The numbers *one*, *two* and *seven* take their roots from this." [d'Olivet, 1976, p.155-156.]

ליסבהר Lisna-har. Angel ruling the 1st decanate of Leo. This decanate is ruled by the Sun, and suggest the qualities of sincerity; amiableness and dignity. The sun is the center of the local universe.

אשמדי Asmodi. Asmodeus "Creature of Judgement", King of the Demons. A Persian rather than a Jewish devil (Aeshma deva), he is regarded in Jewish lore as a evil spirit. An opponent of Solomon and ruler of the south. It was Ashmodai who made Noah (rest, cessation, 58) drunk, slew the 7 bridegrooms of the young Sarah (princess, 510), and who, overcome by the anger Raphael (God the Healer, 311), was finally 'banished to upper Egypt', [Dictionary of Angels p.57]. Egypt is a symbol of the astral plane; "Princess" suggest Malkuth, the physical plane. Alternate spelling, see 122, 355.

מענה אלהי קדם The eternal God is thy refuge (dwelling place). Deuteronomy 33:27: "The eternal God is thy refuge, and underneath are the everlasting arms: and he shall thrust out his enemy from before thee; and shall say, destroy them. see 915.

356

עורף Ophrah, mother of Goliath. Goliath (443) means "captivity, bondage" and is related to the dark body (Key 15) which fills the alchemical vase of art. see 1076, 443.

רוחין רחין spirits of the living. Suggest immortality. Luke 24:5: "Why do you seek the living among the dead?" see 214, 18, 1656.

בתל היש. Self-annulment, negation of false ego. "The destruction of the glamorous bondage which the Ruach [the ego] elects over us, thus permuting the light of the Neshamah and the higher principles to shine through to illumine our minds and our daily lives, is one of the all-important task of mysticism. In fact, the abnegation of the false ego (bitol hoyesh) is the essential accomplishment of all spiritual development." [Regardie: Garden of Pomegranates, p.102] see 310, 41.

פעור to open; uncovered oneself, behaving obscenely. "Also, uncovering the pudenda, to give oneself up to fornication.. Peor.. signifies 'a pitor hole', or rather, 'an opening, properly the opening of the maiden's hymen.' It was also the name of a [male] Moadite deity [Belphegor] in whose honor virgins sacrificed themselves" [Ancient Faiths, VII, p. 471] Numbers 23:28: "And Malak Brought Balaam unto the top of peor, that looks toward Jeshimon (barren desert)".

עופר a young mule, hart, stag. Canticles 4:5: "Thy two breasts are like two young roes that are twins, which feed among the lilies." (plural form spelled עפרים here). "Oofer... one of its meanings [is] the raw material into which Aleph (אלף) introduces the organic motion of Lamed. The fawn is a very young life, mobile as dust" [Suarez: The Song of Songs, p.95] Lilies suggest Mercury.

357

אנוש Man, mankind. The separate man, who is in error. The personality. As a proper name Enosh, son of Seth and father of Kenan. The state of the sons of God when they suppose themselves to be merely the sons of Adam, and the return to the original angelic condition. see 107, 45, 311, 1200, 148 and Genesis 4:26.

"And unto Sheth likewise, was generated a son: and he called his name Aenosh (mutable being, corporeal man): then hope was caused (to support his sorrow), by calling upon (invocation of) the name of YAHEH." [d'Olivet, 1976, p. 324.]

He comments: אנוש, *corporeal man...* This is the third name which Moses has employed to designate man. By the first, Adam [אדם], he designated universal man, divine similitude; by the second, איש, he characterized intellectual man, considered relative to the volitive faculty, free and efficient, which individualizes him and makes him a particular being; he now considers man in relation to his physical faculties and he call him אנוש, *corporeal man.*

Two roots are found here contracted אוּן-נוֹשׁ. The first אוּן develops the contradictory ideas of being and nothingness, of strength and weakness, of virtue and vice. The second, נוֹשׁ, expresses the instability of temporal things, their caducity, their infirmity.

Thus constituted, the word אנוֹשׁ produces its feminine נשה: but here the hieroglyphic meaning is discovered. Moses or his instructors, wishing to draw form the intellectual principle איש, the volitive facility אשה, makes the sign of manifestation disappear. Now, in order to deduce the physical faculties of the corporeal being אנוֹשׁ they suppress the initial sign of power א, and that of light וֹ, and put the word נש thus restricted, in the masculine plural נשים, a number which, as we have learned by the Grammar is confounded with the dual feminine. Here already are three different names to man, considered as universal, intellectual or corporeal, of which the translators have made no distinction. Further on we shall find a fourth. I urge the reader to reflect upon the gradation that Moses has kept in the employment of these terms. At first, it is the Divinity who creates אדם *Adam*, universal man, and who gives him companion אשה, efficient volitive facility. This facility, becomes הוה, *Hewah*, elementary life, creates in its turn אִישׁ, intellectual being, man individualized by his will. Afterward, it is the intellectual being, who, under the name of *Sheth*, son of *Adam*, brings forth corporeal man אֱנוֹשׁ, *AEnosh*, but already the physical faculties נשים *Noshim*, had been named as wives of *Lamech*, descendant of *Adam*, by *Kain* in the sixth generation.

Compare carefully *Kain* and *Sheth*, and the posterity of the one, with the posterity of the other. If he recalls that *Kain* produced *Henoch* and if he examines now the one which produces *Sheth*, he will find that the name of *AEnosh*, here referred to, differs only from the former by a certain softening in the characters of which both are composed. The vowel ה, which begins the name of *Henoch*, indicates a painful effort: the constant כ, which terminates it, a sharp compression: on the contrary, the vowel א, which begins that of *AEnosh*, announces a tranquil power, and the consonant, שׁ, which terminates it, a gentile movement relative to a transient duration. *Henoch* arrest, fixes, centralizes: *AEnosh* lets go, relaxes, carries to the circumference." [bid., p. 148-149]

אֱנוֹשׁ severe, incurable.

נשא to lead astray, to delude, to beguile, to exact usury. With different pointing *nosay*: subject (grammatical); thesis, theme, topic. see 666.

וגבהם מלאים עינים And their backs full of eyes. Ezekiel 10:12: "And their whole body [Cherubim], and their backs and their hands, and their wings, and their wheels, were full of eyes round about, even the wheels that they four had." I.R.Q. says that this passage and Daniel 10:6 and 9:21. All refer to the analogy of the man. see 1661, 568.

Daniel 10:6: "His body also was like the beryl, and his face as the appearance of lighting, and his eyes as lamps of fire, and his arms and his feet like in color to polished brass, and the voice of his words like the voice of a multitude."

Daniel 9:21: "Yea, while I was speaking in prayer, even the man Gabriel, whom I had seen in the vision at the beginning, being caused to fly swiftly, touched me at about the time of the evening oblation."

אש אכלה a consuming fire. Deuteronomy 4:24: "For the Lord thy God is a consuming fire, even a jealous God." הוא connects "consuming fire" with a "a jealous God." see 12, 182, 301; 1333 (Greek).

כגד יבש 42-fold name of Geburah in Yetzirah (5 of Swords). Has to do with divine volition, as it relates to the formative plane or Air activity. What is consumed is the appearance of separation.

שאון noise, tumults, roar. "The sons of tumult". i.e. noisy warriors, in Jeremiah. In Hosea 10:14 "battle roar." see 565.

358

The divine proportion of Pluto (Sheen:300), Scorpio (Nun:50) and Mars (Peh:80), 3:5:8, the relationship between Nature, Humanity and God.

מחודש Renewing, renovating. The 26th path of Ayin connection Hod and Tiphareth. The root of this adjective is akin to the verb in Psalm 51:10: "Create in me a clean heart, O God; and *renew* a right spirit within me." The same verb appears in Psalm 104:30: "Thou sends forth thy spirit, they are created: and thou *renews* the face of the earth." Of similar import is the passage in Revelation 21:5: "Behold, I make all things new." The renewal of the mind begins in "walking in all things contrary to the world," seeing that the One-life is the performer of all action (Mem). When personality has become as the hanged man, then is it transformed into the chariot of the divine self. All that makes up the personality becomes a vehicle for the One (Cheth). Then the voice of that life speaks in the silence which follows and the revelation of the mysteries begins (Vav). Love, sprung from understanding, the perfect love which cast out our fear, the unfailing love whose sphere is victory continues the renewal (Daleth) into the purifying fire of the superconscious Life-breath the devil is cast, become one with it (Shin). see 708.

בן-אשה Son of a woman [1 Kings 7:14]; son of fire. The person so designated is Hiram Abiff, the hero of masonry. Thus it is also a hint connecting with all three citations in the list under 780.

1 King 7:14: "Whose mother was a widow from the tribe of Naphtali, and whose father was a man of Tyre, a worker of brass, and he was filled with wisdom and understanding, and cunning to work all works in brass. And he came to King Solomon, and wrought all his works."?

The person so designated is Haram Abiff, the hero of Masonry. Also means "son of fire", and thus relates to the archetypal man of the Tree of Life (Adom Qadom), the architect of the Universe. Note that אשה is the feminine plural of fire. It suggest that fire is the womb of manifestation from which all things are brought forth. The Tree of life is a diagram of the progressive stages in man's mastery of fire; it represent the "son of a woman", who is also the "son of fire"; whose secret powers are connected with the serpent and the anointed... represented by the master-builder in Masonry and in Gnostic Christianity by the Logos or Word. see 200, 1008, 484.

דביר: היכל: אולם adytum-temple-vestibule.
Words designating the Holy of Holies, the temple, and its vestibule, respectively. see 216, 65, 77.

חשן Breastplate of the High Priest. The breastplate was set with 12 stones, corresponding to the Tribes of Israel, the 12 zodiacal signs. It was considered an oracle of great power and the 12 stones had the mysterious power of lighting up with divine glory. According to the Rosicrucian's these gems symbolized 12 great qualities and virtues: illumination, love, wisdom, truth, justice, peace, equilibrium, humility, faith, strength, joy and victory. Please note that the breastplate were worn over the heart or sun center. see 1008.

"...The word חשן, khoshen, the name of the high priest's breastplate, brings in another mathematical element. For the breast plate was a perfect square, subdivided into 12 parts, so that each of its division was a rectangle of 3x4 units. In this arrangement is concealed a geometrical formula having to do with the series of numbers 0,1,2,5,8,13,34,55. The number 358 is composed of the 4th, 5th, and 6th terms of this series. In what manner this is connected with the

breastplate is too intricate for explanation here." [Case, 1985, p. 215.]

חשן Choshen, Chassan. Angel of Air; listed by Mathers in *The Key of Solomon the King*; his name is inscribed on the 7th Pentacle of the Sun. [Mathers, 1974, p. 74]

נחש Nachash. serpent, tempter. Kundalini. The serpent of temptation. Also disease of the eye (masculine noun), brass or copper; divination, magic, an omen. The sign Leo and tribe of Judah. The letter Teth (Key 8). The metal of Venus (copper), the planet represented by the letter Daleth and the Empress. The desire nature seems to be the tempter, but liberation and redemption are found by rightly directing its force. The serpent of temptation in the allegory of the fall. Hence there is a direct connection, with Key 15. Its feminine plural form, נחשת means: copper brass, filthiness, harlotry; vessel made of brass or copper. With different pointing: pungent poisonous fluid, polished smooth, side of skin (hide). see 130, 601, 708, 854, 130, 780, 830, 1702.

358 is the number of *genshenah*, shame, *yaba Shiloh*, Shiloh shall come, and *messiah*. Thus the serpent who tempted Eve and brought 'shame' into her consciousness is occultly related to the promised messiah (Christ). Note that in the wilderness Moses raised a serpent of brass on a Tau cross. Brass or Copper is related to Venus and the serpent power that enchanted Eve. Compare this to the story of C.R. whose brother PAL (אלף, Aleph, 111),died at Cyprus (Kupros, Κμπος), meaning copper, or magician. In 1 Samuel 11:1,2 and 12:12 it was It is the name of an Ammonite who demanded of the men of Jabesh-Gilead ('dry-rocky region') that they should allow him to put out their right eyes. see 870 (Greek).

I. In Genesis 3:1: Now the serpent was more subtle than all the wild beast that the Lord God had made. And the serpent said to the woman, 'truly has God said that you shall not eat of any tree of the Garden.'

II. d'Olivet translates: "Now Nahash (egoism, envy, covetousness, concupiscence) was an insidious passion (blind principle) in all elementary life which YAHWEH Aelohim had made: and it said (this passion Nahash) unto

Aishah (volitive faculty of Adam), Why, hath Aelohim declared, ye shall not feed upon all the substance of the organic enclosure?"

He comments: והנחש *Now-eager-Covetousness...* it is well know that the Hellenists and Saint Jerome, have seen here, only a snake, a serpent, properly speaking: indeed according to the former a very wise serpent, οφις φρονιμωτατος and according to the latter, a serpent very skillful and very cunning, *serpens callidor*. This wretched interpretation appears to go back to the epoch of the captivity of Babylon and to coincide with the total loss of the Hebraic tongue: at least, it is there that the Chaldaic paraphrase has followed it. He says חויא הכים *a most insidious serpent*.

The word נחש, as it is employed in this case, cannot mean *a serpent*. It is an eager covetousness, self-conceited, envious, egoistic, which indeed winds about in the heat of man and envelops it in its coils, but which has nothing to do with a serpent, other than a name sometimes given metaphorically. It is only by restricting this figurative expression that ignorant people have been able to bring it to a point of signifying only a serpent. The Hellenists have followed this crude idea. If, through delicacy of sentiment or respect for Moses, they had wished to rid the veil in this passage, what would have become of the garden, the tree, the rib, etc. etc.? I have already said, in the part they had taken, they had to sacrifice all to the fear of exposing the mysteries.

The root חש which, as I have said in explaining the word חשך, *darkness*, indicates always an inner covetousness, a centralized fire, which acts with a violent movement and which seeks to distend itself. The Chaldaic, derives a great many expressions from it, all of which are related to anxiety, agony, sorrow and painful passions. It is literally, a *torrefaction*; figuratively, *an eager covetousness*, in Arabic, it is *suffering, a grievous passion*. It is finally, a *turbulent agitation*. In the Ethiopic this root verbalized in the Hebraic חוש, depicts the action of being precipitated, of being carried with violence toward a thing. The analogous verbs have the same meaning in Arabic, Ethopic and Syriac. There is nothing in these which restricts us to the idea of a serpent.

The hieroglyphic analysis can perhaps give us the key to this mystery. The reader will remember that I set down two different roots, אר and אש, to designate equally, the first principle, the elementary principle and the unknown principle of things. I shall now state the important differences that the Egyptian priest conceived between these two roots, and in what manner they expressed this difference.

They attached to both, the idea of movement; but they considered אר as the symbol of movement proper, rectilinear; and אש at that of relative movement circular. The hieroglyphic character which corresponds to these two movements was likewise *a serpent*: but a serpent sometimes straight and passing through the center of a sphere, to represent the principle אר; sometimes coiled upon itself and enveloping the circumference of this sphere, to represent the principle אש. When these same priests wished to indicate the union of the two movements or the two principles, they depicted a serpent upright, uncoiling itself in a spiral line, or two serpents interlacing their mobile rings. It is form this last symbol that the famous caduceus of the Greeks has come.

The priest were silent as to the inner nature of both these principles; they used indifferently the radicals אר or אש to characterize the ethereal, igneous, aerial, aqueous, terreous or mineral principle; as it they had wished to make it understood that they did not believe these simple and homogenous things, but the composite ones. Nevertheless, among all these several significations, that which appeared the most frequently was that of fire. In this case, they considered the igneous principle under its different relations, sentient or intelligible, good or evil, and modified the radical word which represented it, by means of the signs. Thus, for example, the primitive אר became אור to designate *elementary fire*, אור, *light*, איר *intelligible brightness*, etc. If the initial vowels is hardened, it takes a character more and more vehement. הר represented *an exaltation*, literally as well as figuratively: הר, *a burning center*, ע, *a passionate, disordered, blind ardor*. The primate אש was nearly the same.

The movement alone still distinguished the two

382

principles, whether, they were exalted or whether they were debased. The rectilinear movement inherent in the primitive אֵר, prevented the confusing of its derivatives with those of the primitive אֵשׁ, in which the gyratory movement dominated. The two radicals דֵּר and חֵשׁ represented alike *a central fire*; but in the first דֵּר, it was a central fire form which the igneous principle radiated with violence; whereas in the second חֵשׁ, it was, on the contrary, a central fire, from which the same principle being moved in a circular movement, was concentrated more and more and destroyed itself.

Such was the hieroglyphic meaning of this root which I have already examined under its idiomatic relations. This coincidence ought not to leave any doubt in the mind of the reader. Now the sign which governs it in the word נֵחֵשׁ, is that of passive action, individual and corporeal; so that the devouring ardor expressed by the root חֵשׁ, becomes by means of this sign, a passive ardor, cold in its vehemence, contained, astringent and compressive. Literally, it is every hard and refractory body; everything acrid, cutting and corroding; as *copper*, for example, which this word signifies in a very restricted sense, figuratively, it is every sentiment, painful, intense or savage, as *envy, egoism, cupidity*, it is, in a word vice.

This is the real signification of the word נֵחֵשׁ. I have been obligate to extend my proofs more than usual; but its importance demands it. It can be clearly seen that it does not signify simply a serpent. Moses, who has spoken so much of the reptilian life, in the beginning of the Beraeshith, was carefully not to employ it. The word שֶׁרֶץ which he uses, is that which, in his idiom, indicates veritable *a serpent*. One can easily recognize here the source of the French and Latin word, and that of the Celtic *sertz*, which is preserved without alteration in the modern Oscan." [d'Olivet, 1976, p. 94-97]

III. Swendenborg: "By the 'serpent' is here meant the sensuous part of man in which he trusts... The sensuous things in man they (the most ancient people) called 'serpents', because as serpents live close to the earth, so sensuous things are those next the body. Hence also reasoning concerning the mysteries of faith, founded on the evidence of the senses, were

called by them the 'poison of a serpent', and the reasoners themselves 'serpent'; and because such persons reason much from sensuous, that is, from visible things (such as are things terrestrial, corporeal, mundane and natural), its is said that 'the serpent was more subtle than any wild animal of the field... Among the most ancient people, who were celestial men, by the 'serpent' was signified circumspection, and also the sensuous part through which they exercised circumspection so as to be secure from injury." [Arcana Coelestia, pp.83-84, 86]

IV. Inman: This word gives us an insight into the association of ideas which prevailed in ancient times. It signifies 'a serpent.' Yet there is nothing very particular about serpents in general; but some, the cobra in India, and the asp in Egypt, for example, have the peculiarity of being able to raise and distend themselves, thus becoming erect. Hence, either or both of these creatures were emblematic of male activity, and covertly represented the phallus. The same word signifies 'a serpent,' and 'to be hard or firm;' and this again is associated with *nahash*, 'to be unclean, or adulterous.' Moreover, the serpent, being an emblem of diving power, neither roars, bleats, nor sings; it simply *hisses*. ...that serpents were supposed to utter oracles, those who taught the credulous to believe so utter words of their own therefore, in a hissing manner; hence the same nahash expressed 'to whisper,' 'to give an oracle,' and 'an omen.' It also signified 'brass, or copper.' ...the reader of Scripture is struck by the fact that the same Moses, who, amidst the thunders of Sinai, was forbidden to make any graven image... (Exodus 20:4), should be told by the same authority to make a serpent of brass, which was not only the emblem of life, but was to become itself a life-giver, and remain for may succeeding centuries an object of veneration to the faithful (2 Kings 18:4).

מָשִׁיחַ messiah. "the anointed" (one), king, high priest, which is translated Christos in Greek, and Christ in English. Assigned to Tiphareth on the Tree of Life along with Adam (humanity) and Melekh (king). The connection between the serpent and the messiah is one of the profoundest esoteric doctrines. The secret powers connected the serpent and the anointed are of fire, the element corresponding to the sign Leo. All practical occultism has to do with the right use of these fiery powers. Hence, it is written, "salvation is of the Jews" because the liberation men seek is a direct result of what is pictured in Key 8, where a woman tames a lion. The Tree of Life is a diagram of the progressive stages in man's mastery of the serpent fire and of his attainment of the kingship of messiah. Messiah is also the "redeemer" and the deliverer of the lower personality from its bondage to the elements, for it is the one Ego or higher self. see 45, 90, 656 (Greek), 859.

Recall the brazen serpent (Nachash) of Moses that whas lifted up on a T-cross. This was understood by the early Christians to be a foreshadowing of the crucifixion of Jesus. Think of the crucifixion in terms of a renewal in relation to the word *makhodash*, and its connection with the 26th path of Ayin connecting Hod and Tiphareth.

Nachash means copper, the metal of Venus, and the door of the vault of Brother C.R. is attributed to Venus. *The Perfect Way* says about Satan is the keeper of the Keys of the Sanctuary ["Satan is the doorkeeper of the temple of the king: he stands in Solomon's Porch; he holds the Keys of the sanctuary; that no man may enter therein save the **anointed**, having the arcanum of Hermes..."]

אנושא Of men. In Daniel 4:17 it is a reference is to the Kingdom of men. Only man has the capacity to create mentally. That capacity is both the source of sin and salvation.

יבא שילה Shiloh shall come, peace shall come. A mystical expression in Genesis 49:10 referring to the coming of the Redeemer, or Messiah. We begin in bondage (Key 15) which has Time (Saturn, Key 21) for its primary condition. Please note that for 4 fixed signs of the zodiac shown in the corners of the Key 21 symbolize time. As we perform the Great Work we reach a point of peace. Key 21 is a symbol of the completion of the Great Work and the mastery of the forces and govern the Universe. see 345. 713.

גושנה shame. It is past sins in earlier lives that cause shame in relation to the Mars force and its bodily activities. "Shame has more to do with the renewal of consciousness than may appear at first. It is with some understanding of this that evangelical churches put so much stress on 'conviction of sin.' When one is thoroughly disgusted with one's own state, or with one's

circumstances, it seems to be easier to make the required effort to begin afresh." [Case, 1985, p. 215.]

בר-יושף Son of Joseph, i.e. Jesus. see 744.

אור מעלה The exalted light.

בשומי when I made [the clouds]. see Job 38:9.

שבוים shebuim. captives. Isaiah 61:1: "The spirit of the Lord is upon me, because the Lord has anointed me and sent me to preach good tidings to the meek; to bind the broken hearted, to proclaim liberty to captives and release to prisoners. see 307, 352.

359 (prime)

שטן Satan. Adversary, accuser; archdemon of Kether.

I. "In other Old Testament Books [Job, 1 Chronicles, Psalm, Zechariah], the term likewise designates an office; and the angel investing that office is not apostate or fallen. He becomes such starting in early new Testament times and writings, when he emerges as Satan (Capital S), the prince of evil and enemy of God, and is characterized by such titles as 'Prince of this world' (John 16:11) and 'Prince of the Power of the Air' [Ephesians 2:2]. When Peter was rebuked by Jesus, he was called Satan in Luke 4:8. Reading back into Genesis, medieval writer like Peter Lombard... saw Satan in the guise of the serpent tempting eve, although other writers, like the 9th century bishop Agobard, held that Satan tempted Eve *through* the serpent. As Langton say in *Satan, A Portrait*: 'In the later Jewish literature, Satan and the serpent are either identified, or one is made the vehicle of the other.' Originally, Satan (as *ha-Satan*) was a great Angel, chief of the Seraphim, head of the order of virtues. While Seraphim were usually pictured as 6-winged, Satan was shown as 12-winged. Gregory, the great in his *Moralia*, after listing the nine hierarchic order, pays this tribute to Satan: 'He wore all of them [all the angels] as a garment, transcending all in glory and knowledge.'" [Dictionary of Angels, p. 261]

II. Inman: (1 Chronicles 21:1). 'The lier in wait,' 'the adversary.' Furst remarks, 'The view of an intermediate angle of evil between God and men arose at the time when the Zoroastrian doctrine became known amongst the Hebrews. In later judaism, Satan appears as the prince of evil spirits (Ephesians 2:2) the opponet fo the kngdom of God. In Revelations (12:10), Satan is spoken of as 'the accuser,' ο χατηγωρ. WE notice the fact that Satan does not appear in any writings which we believe to have been comosed before the period when the Jews became familiar with the Persian faith. For example, we are told that the Lord, not Satan, hardened Pharaoh's heart against Israel (Ecodus 7:13).

When we examine diligently into the use of the word שטן, in the Old Testament, we alight upon some remarkable facts. Satan is translated 'adversary' in Numbers 22:22, 32; 1 Samuel 29:4; 2 Samuel 19:22, (23); 1 Kings 5:4 (18), 11:14, 23, 25. Consulting these texts we find, literally, 'an angle of the Lord' is Satan; that David might become Satan if he went to fight; That Abishai and Joab were Satanic… whilst, if we turn successively to 2 Samuel 24:1, and 1 Chronicles 21:1, we recognize that astounding fact that Satan and Jehovah are identical! Peter, the rock upon which the Christian church is said to have been built was designated 'Satan' by the his master (Matthew 26:23). Jesus teaches his disciples to pray to their Almighty father (Matthew 6:13), 'lead us not into temptation;' whilst James 1:13 declares that God tempts no man. These apparent discrepancies may be reconciled by comparing Jehovah and Satan to the Hindu Siva, who is both creator and destroyer. [Inman, 1942, Vol. 2., pp. 697-698]

סטריף Satariph. Angel of the 3rd decanate of Pisces. This decanate is ruled by Mars and suggest the qualities of: vigilant, cordial, suave. This brings keen alertness to the actualities of personal environment, unusual ability to sense the reactions and wants of other people, with a cordial, tactful manner. The 3rd decanate of Pisces is attributed to the 10 of Cups, or the power of Malkuth, which is physical existence, in Briah, the creative thoughts and images. The influence form Briah in Malkuth, when misunderstood, results in the misinterpretations that binds us, and too much reliance on physical sense reports. When we understand this plane, the dark antagonist is seen to be the perfect order of the kingdom. It is here that we must become aware of our dwelling place in Briah, where all

aspiration are actualities. Then there is permanent and last success through inspiration from higher levels of consciousness. see 1079.

שטים acacia trees. This wood is a symbol of immorality and initiation-the Greek work means "innocence, without guile, harmlessness". Wood is a substance which absorbs personal emanations of the astral light. With different pointing: *Sittim*, a place east of the Jordan. "The sacred wind." [Crowley, 1977, p. 39] see 53 (Greek).

360

Number of degrees in a circle. 1/7 of a week of times (2520 years).

השנה ha-shawnaw. The year (as a revolution of time, 360 degrees) [Psalm 135:13]. As a verb: to do again, to repeat, to change, alter, to be different, to study, to teach. With different pointing: sleep. K.D.L.C.K. (p.235): "A year of 365 days, and in humanity (man) which is microcomus, 365 nerves."

שין Letter name Shin. flame, tooth, fang. see 300, 814.

The Golden Treatise of Hermes, IV says: "The whole matter I know to be only one thing. But who is he that understands the true investigation and inquires rationally in this matter? There is not from man anything but what is like him; not from the ox or bullock; and if any creature conjoins with one of another species, that which is brought forth in like neither." Paul Case: "The 'ox or bullock' is Aleph = Air = רוח אלהים = 300 = Shin = Fire. Verb. sap. Now Shin in its plentitude is שין = 360 = 9 and 'man' = אדם = 45 = 9. furthermore שין as 360 is the circle, and this is a mode of the ellipse, or egg, symbol of the first matter."

אשו הגדולה his great fire. Deuteronomy 4:36: "And upon the earth he showed thee his great fire." see 53.

הנשה (That) which shrank [Genesis 32:32]. Nawsheh written נשה, nahshah, means: "to forget, to lend, become a creditor; demand, exact payment. Pronounced *nishshaw*: to be forgotten, to cause to forget.

יהוה בקרבך Tetragrammaton (is) in the midst of thee [Zephaniah 3:15]. קרב: midst, interior, inward part, bowels. see 302, 98.

יהוה גבור מלחמה The Lord Mighty in battle [Psalm 24:8]. According to the text, this is the "King of Glory".

ישים The Flames, Fiery Ones. Angles of Yesod, also spelled אשים. Yesod is associated with the reproductive organs of the grand man. Shin is the center of that fire which builds all patterns in the vital soul; this is the "Almighty Living God." see 80, 570, 220, 127, 314, 31, 18.

ישן to be weary, to wither, to sleep, old, inactive. The misuse or loss of the power of Shin.

כובי בקר the Morning Stars. Job 38:7: (Who laid the corner-stone of) "when the morning stars sang together, and all the sons of God shouted for Joy?"

נשהי loan, debt; forgetfulness; the world.

צור ילבך Rock that begat thee [Deuteronomy 32:18]. Shin is associated with The Morning Stars, the Lord Mighty in Battle and this entry because of its connection with fire and spirit. A clear indication of the power associated with *tzoor*. see 300, 127, 333, 301, 464.

רעמים Thunders [Psalm 81:7]. The power of the letter Shin, is the power of the "Mighty Thunders of the swift flash, which divideth the one into the two.."[Book of Tokens]. Singular רעם (310).

Rosenroth cites *Jonitrua* in K.D.L.C.K.(p.690) and says they refer to Geburah, as in Job 26:14: "And these are but the outer fringe of his works; how faint the whisper we hear of him? Who then can understand the thunder [רעם, then-thunder-of] of his power?"

שכם shoulder-blades, the shoulder, back; portion of land; to load. The heart-center is between the shoulders-see Jesus "my burden is light", i.e. the Fire of Shin which renews and

transforms.

With different pointing: *shawkam*. to bend, to incline oneself; to lead up for a journey (early in the morning); to rise or get up early; to go early to a place; to do early, readily, earnestly, urgently, as in Jeremiah 7:13: "And now, because you have done all these works, says the Lord, and I warned you in advance and spoke to you (urgently), but you did not listen; and I called out, but you did not answer." Shoulder in Genesis 49:15: (Issachar) "And he saw that his dwelling place was good, and his land fertile; and he bowed his shoulder to servitude, and became a servant to tribute." see 365, 373.

שכם Sekem. The name of the Old Testament city, represented by the standard of the tribe of Simeon (Gemini). See Key 6 and compare with Key 20.

שלל booty, gain, plunder, spoil, profit, to pull out. As a verb: "to pull out, draw out; to plunder, pillage, to hang on, chain, negate. The profit of Shin is the higher octave of Mars.

שמך Thy Name (Tetragrammaton). Psalm 135:13: "Thy name, O Lord, endures forever; and thy memorial, O Lord, throughout all generations." See Psalm 8:1.

שני scarlet, crimson. With different pointing: the second.

עפיר ophir. "earth." [Godwin, 1999, p. 551] see 350 for alternate spelling.

המשיה Ha-Messiah. The Anointed One. Variant spelling of the word ordinarily rendered Messiah. see 303, 355, 358.

מהשיה 5th Shem ha-Mephorash. "God the Savior." To live in peace with everyone. Governs: high science, occult philosophy, theology, the liberal arts. Positive influence: learns easily, keen for honest pleasures. Negative: ignorance, licentiousness, bad qualities of body and mind.

Angel of the 3rd decanate and 5th quinance of Leo, attributed to the 7 of Wands. see Appendix 10.

אש הגדולה His Great Fire. in Deuteronomy

4:36: "And upon the earth he showed thee His Great Fire."

d'Olivet writes of עם: "This root, considered as a compound of the sign of material sense, limited to that of interior activity, has only the idea of obscurity and of darkness; but its greatest usage is onomatopoetic to depict movements which are easy, agile, light, swift. That which *rises, expands, opens out* into the air; that which *soars, flies*, etc." [d'Olivet, 1976, p. 420.] Of יר he adds: "Every idea of respect, of fear, of reverence, of veneration. The Arabic signifies a thing which is polished, smooth, without roughness, but firm, as crystal." [ibid., p. 367.]

αρθρικον. Arthrikon (Gr). The uttered (articulated) Word. A Greek mystery term.

η νικη αληθειας. He nikeh aletheias (Gr). The true victory.

προβολη. proboleh (Gr). a putting forward (as a weapon), spacial projection. The basic power of movement away from a center whereby the Limitless Light concentrated at a center produces a cosmos. The Greek dictionary defines this word: A putting forward, especially of a weapon for defense; of a boxer, a lunging out with fists. Anything held out before one, a guard, defense.

οσιοι. hosioi (Gr). the saints. Septuagint translation of חסידים (132) in Psalm 149:5: "Let the saints rejoice in this honor and sing for joy on their beds." These are the masters of compassion-those who have attained the consciousness of Chesed, who express the quality of Jupiterian benevolence, and are exempt, as adepts, from reacting in any way other than with true compassion for their fellow men. see 132, note.

361

I. (19x19) or 19^2

אדני הארץ Adonai Ha-Eretz. Lord of Earth (Malkuth). Divine name associated with Malkuth, Earth and the North. see 7, 496.

באר מים חיים A well of living waters. Song of Songs 4:15: "A fountain of gardens, a well of living waters, and streams from Lebanon."

Lebanon is the 'white mountain'. see 138, 53, 130.

כשיאל Cassiel. Angel ruler of Saturn. "The angel of solitudes and tears who 'shews forth the unity of the eternal kingdom'. Cassiel is one of the rulers of the planet Saturn, also a ruling prince of the 7th Heaven and of the sarim (princes) the order of powers. Sometimes he appears as the angel of temperance [Key 14 in the Tarot]. [Davidson, 1971, p. 82.] Liberator of the kundalini force-the "fire of illumination." see 400, 406.

מצראל Justus; "God who comforts the oppressed." 60th Shem ha-Mephorash, GENA. 296E-300E. For the cure of mental illness and deliverance form those who persecute us. Psalm 145:17: "The Lord is righteous in all his ways, and holy in all his works." Persons born are virtuous and have longevity. Associated with the 6th quinance (26E-30E) of Taurus; angle by night of the 7 of Pentacles. Corresponds to the operation of Netzach, sphere of Venus, in Assiah, the material of manifested results.

"One of the archangels in cabalistic lore. Mitzrael induces obedience on the part of inferiors toward superiors. His corresponding angel is Homath." [Davidson, 1971, p. 197.] see 330, 965 & Appendix 10.

יה שמו "his name Yah" Psalm 68:4: "Sing unto God, sing praises to his name: extol him who rides upon the heavens by his name Jah, and rejoice before him." see 363.

αμνος.. amnos (Gr). Lamb; an epithet of Christ, who is "the lamb of God", sacrificed for the remission of sins. Acts 8:32: "Now the portion of the scripture which he was reading was this: 'As to a sheep he was led to the slaughter, and like a lamb before the shearer is dumb, so he opens not his mouth." see 431, 915, 1665, 1685, 1785.

διαθηκη αλος.. diathekeh halos (Gr). "A covenant of salt". Septuagint translation of ברי תמלח (690) in 2 Chronicles 13:5: "Do you know that the Lord God of Israel has given the kingdom of Israel to David and his descendants forever, by a covenant of salt?" Note that salt is the third alchemical principle, denoting embodiment. It is attributed to Binah, sphere of Saturn. see 690; 60 (Greek).

Ανδρεας. Andrew (Gr). "The nature of the *aner* [159]: that is, the possession of an inner power: a condition of having been tried and approved. *Andreia* is a strength of soul, but *rhome* is a strength of body. *Andria* is greater than the nature of the *polites*, being begotten from the enthusiasm of the Soul. Compare the Cross of Saint Andrew. X." [Omikron, 1942, p. 249.]

362

אריך אפים   Long of Face; a title of Microprosupus, or Tiphareth [an other source cites Kether]. K.D.L.C.K. (p.155) says that some Qabalists assign this name as a prefix to Chesed, sphere of memory. see 922, 1422, 620, 1402, 422.

שבילך   thy path. Psalm 77:19: "Thy way is in the sea, and thy path is in the great waters, but thy footsteps are not seen." see 498.

שנואה   hated, being unloved. Genesis 29:31.

בשמך   in your name. Exodus 5:23.

363

שדי אל חי   Shaddai El Chai. Almighty God of Life, The Almighty Living God, Lord of the Universe. The Divine Name attributed to Yesod and to the Nine of Wands. The Almighty ever-living one which centers itself in all animate forms and finds its highest expression in the life of man. see 80, 11, 18, 23, 207, 570, 220, 127, 314, 31.

Throughout eternity, with no cessation does the utterance of the Ruach Elohim the might of El Shaddai the source of Life; and the Living Soul Nephesh is the vehicle of that utterance. Note that in the letters of Nephesh (נפש), Perpetuity [Nun], Utterance [Peh], and Ruach Elohim [Shin] the Fiery Breath of the Eternal Spirit of Life. Shaddai El Chai refers to Nephesh, or the Vital Soul and is that same Almighty Ever living One. It is the center in all animate forms, as well as in the and life of man. Through countless generations that Life perpetuates Its utterance by means of successive generations of human bodies. It is because of this that Yesod is the field of renewal through procreation. Shaddai El

Chai is Lord of the Universe, and Holy is His Name, Blessed be He.

Shaddai El Chai is the source of life, as in the command "be fruitful and multiply." This commandment can also be fulfilled be the generation of children as well as the generation of something more subtle. The clue is in the word Yesod (יסוד) because it can be read as Yod-Sod, or the secret of Yod. Yod is the Creative Power of the Hand, as well as the channel for the transmission of Life. Life is Chaiah, seated in Chokmah, to which Yod especially pertains. Chaiah is light (Aur, אור). Aur is 207, or 9 x 23. Twenty-three is the number of חיה, Chaiah, and 9 is Yesod. Furthermore Chaiah is in Chokmah and is the power of *Ab* the Father. Thus Life and Light are one; that Light is always pure and always Holy, and that the extension of Light is its multiplication through forms. But forms are manifest in varying degrees, and when it is your office to bring forth subtle forms, you fail if you miss your opportunity through the false belief that in the bringing forth of forms less subtle there is any essential failure. Failure is the missing of one's highest possibility. But what may be failure for you, may be supreme attainment for you Brother. Wherever Life is multiplied the giver of increase is Shaddai El Chai, and nothing that He effects has in it any loss or evil. Evil are man's judgments, but Life Itself remains forever good.

The name שדי (314) אל (31) חי (18) adds to 363, and this is 11 x 11 x 3. Eleven is אוד (Od), and 3 is Gimel. אוד is the magic power and Gimel is the beginning of Guph, the body. Aleph is the Breath, Vav is the Link, Daleth is the Door of Life and is Nogah also, which gives the Victory. In Gimel or 3 is Recollection and Union. Thus the letters of *Od* speak loud. In Yesod is all this centered and they who know the secret of Yod, become the extenders of the paternal Life and Light. Thus is Yesod called the Sphere of the Moon. Note also that Key 2, The Moon, pertains to the letter Gimel, the letter of Union.

Do not seak the spiritual at the expense of the body. Do not repudiate that which pertains to Yesod due to misunderstand of its significance. The mystery of the 9th Sephirah is a secret of

Yod. The letter Yod is the letter of אב, the Father in Chokmah, and dilates upon Chiah. The secret of Yod has to do with the radiance of the stars, that is with Light, which is one with Life. See **27**.

זרע אלהים a godly seed, seed of God, offspring of God. Malachi 2:15: "And did not he make one [covenant]? Yet had he the residue of the spirit. And wherefore one? That he might seek a godly seed. Therefore take heed to your spirit, and let none deal treacherously against the wife of his youth." Literally, seed of God, or offspring of God. This connects with the attribution of Yesod to the reproductive organs of the Grand Man. Brother C.R. is described in the *Fama Fraternitatis* as "A seed planted in the breast of Jesus." Note that the New Testament says the "seed" is the 'word". see 220, 430, 923, 277, 86; 878 (Greek).

המשיח ha-Messiach. The Messiah. The Messiah is the Christ consciousness seated in Tiphareth. Yesod is the reflection of the Ego in Tiphareth and is thus of the same essential nature. Note that the New Testament says the "seed" is the "word". The serpent is the savior in disguise. see 220, 358, 430.

ביה שמו By (or in) His name, Yah [Psalm 68:4]. The American translation gives: whose name is Yah. Applied to the rider of the heavens, described in verse 5 by the word (ב)ערבות, which, in addition to meaning sky or heaven, also means desert-plain, wilderness, literally the vast expanse of the sky. But in verse 33 of the same Psalm he is called the rider in the heavens again: לרכב בשמי שמי-קדם , "Who rides upon the heavens, the heavens of ancient days," (i.e. primordial heavens). קדם is the word for ancient days, or the primordial heavens. It also means: east, front (as the opposite of back).

בן-איש Son of Man. The scripture says Adam was formed from the 'dust of the ground", and careless superficial reading of the letter of this text and others like it, has led to an erroneous conception that man is a creature essentially different from his creator. To correct this, Qabalists add אדם and איש the noun בן, Ben, son, in order to bring out the idea that the essential man is 'begotten, not made'. Humanity is of the same essence as divinity. 'Man" and

'God' are members of the same genus. As an old Rosicrucian aphorism puts it: 'Man is the son of God, and there is no God but man." [TL 26:3] see 97.

גן בעדן מקדם A Garden of Eden Eastward. In Genesis 2:8: "And the Lord God planted a garden eastward in Eden; and there he put the man whom he had formed." see 144, 53, 124.

הנחש the serpent. Genesis 3:1: "Now the serpent was more subtle than any beast which the Lord God made. And he said unto the woman, 'yea, hath God said, you shall not eat of every tree of the garden?" see 585, 358.

364

אור מופלא Hidden Light. A name of Kether or alchemical Mercury, the first matter; sattva, "the illumination material." see 620, 207, 157, 397, 727.

שטנה resistance. "The hidden light, veiled in those forms of manifestation to which man does not understand, seems to offer resistance to man. But in itself it is the hidden light, a way and forever." [The Flaming Cube]

שטנה accusation. With different pointing: opposition, resistance, hatred, enmity. In Genesis 26:21: "Then they dug another well, but they quarreled over that one also; so he named it Sitnah [opposition] see Ezra 4:6.

אבני אש Precious stone. Literally fiery stones, or stones of fire. [Secret Fire pages 444, 453]. see 63, 301, 53.

השטן ha-Shatan. Satan; adversary; accuser. The "Father of Lies". What takes man out of bondage (the bondage of Egypt) to renewal is mirth-cosmic joy of the One. see 69 (Lt) and Key 15.

משיחו His anointed. Note that "His Anointed" is numerical equal to "The Satan," as is Messiah (358) and Serpent. see 358, 890, 526.

נחש magic divination. With different pointing: nachush: brazen, of bronze, of copper. This is the root of נחושה (Nechushah), copper. see Key 3, creative imagination, Venus and desire.

ארץ החיים Land of the Living. In Psalm 142:5: "I cry to you, O Lord; I say, 'You are my refuge, my portion in the land of the living [**בארץ החיים**, in-land-of living-ones] .'" In this quotation it is "in" (Beth) the land of the living. Relates to Hidden Light and "his anointed"-in this, says Case, is the whole secret.

The Zohar [I:66A, pp.216-217] adds: "The esoteric doctrine is that in the same way as the soul has to be clothed in a bodily garment in order to exist in this world, so is she given an ethereal supernal garment where with to exist in the other world, and to be enabled to gaze at the effulgence of life radiating from that 'land of the living'. Hence it is that Moses was not able to draw near to the place of God and to fix his gaze on what was to be seen there until he was first enveloped in another garment, as we read: 'And Moses entered into the midst of the cloud, and went up unto the mount' [Exodus 24:18], that is, he enveloped himself in the cloud, as in a garment, and then he 'drew near into the thick darkness where God was' [Exodus 20:18], and 'was in the mount forty days and forty nights' [Exodus 24:18], and was able to see what he did see. In similar fashion the souls of the righteous in the other world clothe themselves in garments belonging to that world, so that they can endure to gaze on the light which is diffused in that 'land of the living'. This is what Hezekiah meant when he said 'God, God in the land of the living' in Isaiah 38:11. He was afraid that he would be found unworthy to gaze on that light because he had allowed the life-giving stream to cease with him, through not begetting children.
Isaiah 38:11: "I said, I shall not see the Lord, even the Lord, in the land of the living: I shall behold man no more with the inhabitants of the world."

שדין demons, devils. From **שד**, the singular feminine of **שדרה**.

ולחשך and the darkness. Genesis 1:5: "...the darkness he called night..."

חשון Cheshvan. The 2nd Hebrew month, October-November, corresponding roughly to the period when the sun is in Scorpio. see 1014.

365

I. The number of years Enoch lived in Genesis 5:23.

II. The hypotenuse of the 13th Pythagorean triangle having altitude of 27 and base of 364.

נשיה Forgetfulness, Oblivion; Pasture land. One of the 7 Earths corresponding to Tiphareth. Psalm 88:12: "Shall thy wonders by known in the Dark? Or thy faithfulness in Oblivion." see 656, 23, 291, 50, 14, 105, 302, 432, 337.

מה-שהיה The thing that hath been [Ecclesiastes 1:9, 3:14]. In the Hebrew translation: "That which hath been." **מה** also meaning: "what", it may be "What has been." ["That which has been is that which shall be." **הוא** is translated "That," as a demonstrative pronoun.] see 707.

פריעה uncovering, removing mourner's wrap; removing the membrane of the corona at circumcision; paying of debt; letting hair grown neglect; destruction; ruination.

רוח אלהים אדני Ruach Elohim Adonai. The Spirit (or life) of the Creative Powers of the Lord. A divine name of God. see 300, 65, 216, 86.

אמרו חכמים "The wise men have spoken it." [Vaughan: Magica Adamica, page 87].

יהוה יגמר בעדי "The Lord will fulfill [his purpose] for me." In Psalm 138:8: "The Lord will full [his purpose] for me; your love, O Lord, endures forever-do not abandon the works of your hands." **יגמר** means (Hebrew Lexicon): to end, finish, complete, accomplish, to conclude, decide, resolve. **בעד** means: through, about, for, in behalf of, for the sake of. Literally: Tetragammaton will perfect what is around me, viz. perfection of environmental conditions.

בעד means: through, about, for, in behalf of, for the sake of. "If we do not oppose (Verse 8) God's working he can perfect it in us. It is the self-manifestation of the of the divine in us, as us and through us, and is therefore the supreme evolution; and we therefor we must never fear its failure to work forwards, to perpetual advance, if we recognize and follow its principles"

(Philippians 1:6 " Being confident of this very thing, that he which hath begun a good work in you will perform it until the day of Jesus Christ.") [Torward on Psalms, p.184] see 86, 253, 26.

Paul Case: Tetragrammaton will perfect that which concerns me, יהוה יגמר בעדי literally. 'Tetragrammaton will perfect what is around me' viz. perfection of environmental conditions. The number itself is suggestive, for there is no doubt the Qabalist knew the approximate number of days in the year. The idea is that Tetragrammaton is a power which completes and brings to perfection the environment of man. Not that 'what is around me' is בעדי = 86 = עברי = servants = הטבע nature = אלהים, Gods. 'in him we live and move and have our being'. The surrounding of man (בעדי) are what he calls 'nature' (הטבע), but nature is simply the complex of forces which are the servants of Tetragrammaton (עברי) cf.

השׁין the tooth. A reference to the letter Shin connected with spiritual fire and transfiguration or resurrection. A transposition of letters or metathesis of שׁינה (sleep). see 360, 300.

שׁינה Sleep. The function assigned to Qoph, Key 18 and the Corporeal Intelligence. In The Book of Formation [13] sleep is assigned to Samekh and is written שׁנה; laughing is assigned to Qoph: "He let the letter Samekh predominate in sleep, crowned it, combined one with the other, and formed by them: Sagittarius (the Archer) in the world, the month Kislev in the year, and the stomach of the human body, male and female. see 100, 186.

Nilus (Lt). The Nile, principal River of Egypt. Here may symbolize the subconscious flow of the mind-stuff. see Key 2.

Sardin, Sardis (Lt). One of the most ancient and famous cities of Asia Minor; identified with on of the 7 alchemical "churches," corresponding to Venus and the throat center, or laryngeal plexus, one of the Keys to inner hearing.

עֲרוּמִים naked. Genesis 2:25: "And they were both naked, the man and his wife, and were not ashamed before each other." In Key 6, The Lovers, the alchemical male (Adam) or self-consciousness, and female (Eve) or subconsciousness must be completely open to he influence of the angel (Super-consciousness). This word ends in מִם, water. The first two letters seem to be from עָרה, to be naked, be bare [from הֶעֱרה, to make naked, uncover, to pour out; to have sexual contact; to mix liquids. Water is certainly prominent in these meanings.] see 90.

שׁנוּי change, alteration. Cultivation of "fruit" goes through many changes of consciousness, in the process of maturation. see Key 13.

חשׁבון reckoning, account, calculation; arithmetic; bill, account, invoice. Attributed to *Hod* (15). Hod is the lower mind, or intellect, represented by the man in Key 6. Arithmetic is the basis of all practical occultism. A knowledge of the esoteric properties and uses of number is indispensable to every seeker for liberation.

"...all things are brought forth through number.
All works of power accomplished by the wise have number for their foundation.
For the circle of the tally is the coiled fiery power which comes from the sun
and to rule this, thou must learn to count." [Book of Tokens, Teth and note]. see 1016.

צוֹעֵר small, little; servant boy; shepherd boy. The birth of the higher self is likened to the boy in Key 19, Key 20-it is the servant of the personality, until the personality allows it to be its guide and shepherd.

אנדראלף Goetia demon #65 by night of the 2nd decanate of Capricorn. see Appendix 11.

Goetia: "He is a might Marquis, appearing at first in the form of a peacock, with great noises. But after a time he puts on human shape. He can teach geometry perfectly. He makes men very subtle therein; and in all things pertaining unto mensuration or astronomy. He can transform a man into the likeness of a bird. He governs 30 Legions of Infernal Spirits." [Mathers, 1995, p.

ανεμος, anemos (Gr). A wind, by implication the four quarters of the earth [Strong's Dictionary]. Refers to the Life-breath, or spirit. see 720 Greek, 214, 90 Latin.

367 (prime)

ז + ס + שׁ Shin + Samekh + Zain. tooth (spiritual fire) + prop, support + sword. Shin is the letter of truth, of communion with God, and connects the Mars and Sun faces on the Cube of Space. Samekh connects Tiphareth and *Yesod* (80) on the Tree of Life. *Yesod* represents the form-giving power of Binah which supports all forms of manifestation below it on the tree. The letter Zain is a combination of Yod (Yod or wisdom, *Yah* (15) and Vav (Vav or beauty, *Ben* [52]). Thus Ben-Yah or "son of God" (Zain) plus mother (Samekh) plus perpetuity (Shin). see 300, 60, 7.

פאיכורן Phaikuron. Day demon of 3ʳᵈ decanate of Gemini. This decanate is co-ruled by Saturn and Uranus and suggest conscious imbalance, resulting in negative qualities of secretiveness and adaptability to persons and surroundings, characterized by the co-rulers of Aquarius. The 3ʳᵈ decanate of Gemini is also attributed to the 10 of Swords or Malkuth, the kingdom of physical manifestation expressing the primal formative forces. The subtle astral forces in limited specific forms veil and conceal their true nature. Negative habit patterns and responses impressed in the formative Yetziratic substance have here been crystallized into automatic expression, resulting in failure, desolation, misery and destruction. The remedy is to use concentration to put an end to delusion, overthrow limiting conditions and break-up of physical, psychical and emotional restrictions by perceiving the core reality behind all things.

השׂנואה the hated, the being loved. see Deuteronomy 21:16.

ולארצם and unto their land. see Deuteronomy 31:4.

חמישׁי fifth.

שׁחין Boil, ulcer, eruption. Deuteronomy 28:35: "The Lord will afflict your knees and legs with painful boils that cannot be cured, spreading from the soles of your feet to top of your head." Note that the legs and knees correspond to Aquarius and Capricorn, and to alchemical fermentation (Capricorn, 830) and dissolution (Aquarius, 395). In the text the punishment was for disobedience to the Lord. In Job 2:7: "So went Satan froth from the presence of the Lord, and smote Job with sore boils from the sole of his foot unto his crown." Satan (359, 364) personifies the principle of limitation or Saturn, and Job ("the greatly afflicted one, 19) typifies the right knowledge which overcomes this limitation. With different pointing *saykayawn*: swimmer. One who navigates the "waters" of consciousness. Remember that the waters are also fiery; hence, the boil or eruption. see 1018. Boils is also the 5ᵗʰ of the ten plagues of Egypt. In Exodus 9:9: (8) "Then the Lord said to Moses and Aaron, 'Take handfuls of soot from a furnace and have Moses toss it into the air in the presence of Pharaoh. (9) It will become fine dust over the whole land of Egypt, and festering boils will break out on men and animals throughout the land."

כוכב בקר the Morning Star.

שׁלול snail (so called from its flowing away). Psalm 58:9: "As a snail that melts (into a slime), let every one of them pass away: like the untimely birth of a woman, that they may not see the sun." see 332, שׁבל.

369

I. Constant summation of a magic square of the Moon.

עולם הבריאה World of Creation. The world includes Chesed, Geburah, and Tiphareth. Briah is the world of created intelligence, and of the emanation of created forces. These are the Elohim (86), which are designated in the English Bible as "God" in Genesis 1:1. There association with the Spirit of the Moon hints that the creative forces are powers where by the Life-power reflects itself to itself, as the Moon reflects the Light of the Sun. see 217.

נחושה copper, (brass). In Job 28:2: "Brass is molten out of the stone." Copper is the metal of Venus and is therefore connected with ideas of fecundity, germination, growth and desire fulfillment (Key 3). The creative forces behind all growth are mental powers, because all cosmic activities are expressions of Life and Mind. There a the forces of imagery, giving from to the manifestations of the Life-power. It is highly probable that copper was chosen as the mental representing these forces because: 1) The mirrors of the ancients were made of burnished copper; 2) copper, being soft, is easily shaped. This connects it also with the 9 of Cups whose specific meaning is fulfillment of desire. The correspondence between נחושה, copper and עולם הבריאה is of special importance, see 9, 80, 628; 921 (Greek); 1458, 3321.

חשמודאי Kasmodai. Spirit of the Moon.

כלל פרט to liberate and complete, generally and specially. In this case it refers to the great work in the microcosm. see 80, 289.

שהדני Shahdani. Angel ruling the 2nd decanate of Gemini. This decanate is ruled by Venus, and suggest qualities of: kindness, cleverness and polished in speech and writing. Natives are more artistic and feeling, and have sympathy and an understanding and acceptance of various points of view These qualities are essential to the creation of the "new man".

שגיון enthusiastic song, hymn, dythyramb (according to some, a musical instrument). see 14, 326, 162 and Psalm 7:1.

והנחש and (now) the serpent. see Genesis 3:1.
אשיבנו I will bring back. see Genesis 42:37.

במשכבה her bed, on her bed. Leviticus 15:21.

ה-שוטמי the Shuhamite. see 2 Kings 4:8.

ירשנה may he accept (your offerings). Psalms 20:4.

חקרנוה we examined (her). Job 5:27.

שדיהן their breast. Ezekiel 23:3.

שטני my accusers. Psalms 71:13.
קטרין difficult problems. Daniel 5:12

ונשובה and we will come back. Genesis 22:5
ונחקרה and let us test. Lamentations 3:40

השמדך you be destroyed, to destroy you. Deuteronomy 28:24. Destruction is the Foundation of Existence (Book of Tokens). Peh = 80 = Yesod.

באישון at the middle of. Proverbs 7:9.

השודדים the ones destroying. Jeremiah 51:48.

נגשיו the ones driving him. Exodus 3:7.

שניון Shiggaion, title, probably a literary or musical term. Psalm 7:1

θεμελιος. themelios (Gr). foundation, the foundation-stone. Also elementary doctrine and instruction. The Hebrew word for foundation is יסוד Yesod. see 80, 439, 1254, 1850.

μαθηται. mathehtai (Gr). Learners (of mental discipline). Persons instructed in "Methesis," the special mental discipline of the secret schools. It means literally "the learners," and as a noun: "Mathematics". Thus it has to do with the knowledge of numbers and geometry. In the New Testament, the same noun, Mathetai, is used to designate the disciples.

370

שלם shalom. whole, complete, healthy; to complete, to be safe, peace, perfect. It has a great variety of shades of meaning, including peace, health, prosperity, completeness, wholeness, perfection, concord, friendship and good of every kind. The name is applied to the 8th Sephirah as a Path of Wisdom. As a proper noun, the same word is the place-name Salem, as when Genesis 14:18 mentions Melchizedek, King of Salem. This is one of the clues to the meaning of the Masonic legend concerning Hiram Abiff, please note here that the whole mystery of Masonry has to do with geometry (a science invented, say the ancient glyphs, by Hermes or Mercury), and with the application of geometry to the art of building. The temple "not made with hands, eternal in the heavens," is the house of the Divine Spirit. It is the perfected, completed personality of man. It combines the values of Ayin (Renewal) which carries the powers of Tiphareth down to Hod, and Shin (Judgement, completion) which carries the power of Hod into physical embodiment in Malkuth. Note that both letters are aspects of the Mars force. see 2327 (Greek), 15, 20, 428, 764, 930.

To be whole, safe, uninjured, in Job 9:4: "He is wise in heart, and might in strength who has hardened himself against him, and haw escaped uninjured?" To be full, ended, completed, in 1 Kings 7:51: "So was ended all the work that Solomon made for the house of the Lord. And Solomon brought in the things which David his father had dedicated; even the silver, the gold and the vessels, did he put among the treasures of the house of the Lord." To be at rest, at peace in Psalm 7:4: "If I have rewarded evil to him that was at peace with me; (yea, I have delivered him that without cause is my enemy)." To restore, to pay, to repay, to reward, recompense in Job 8:6: "If you were put and upright, surely now he would awake for you, and restore your righteous habitation. To make peace in 1 Chronicles 19:19: "And when the servants of Havarezer saw that they were put to the worse before Israel, they made peace with David, and became his servants..."

With different pointing *shawlem*: whole, entire, perfect, in 2 Kings 20:3: "I beseech you, O Lord, remember now how I have walked before you in truth and with a perfect heart, and have done good in your sight..." Health, full of strength, in Nahum 1:12: "Thus says the Lord; though they be in full strength, and likewise manly, yet thus shall they be cut down, when he shall pass through. Though I have afflicted you, I will afflict you no more."

The recompense [as a result of forgiveness] is *shalom*, 370, or יחידה (Yekhidah ,37), multiplied by 10. This is the perfect manifestation of the Indivisible ONE through the ten aspects on the Tree of Life. Perfect fulfillment is the perfect expression of the Will to Good (Kether, the seat of Yekhidah). Love condemns nothing, and because it never seeks it own, inflicts no lasting

penalties for the failures of ignorance. See **16**, 190; 477 (Greek).

לשם a precious stone [Hebrew Lexicon]. Metathesis of שלם.

דרך עולם the way everlasting. Psalm 139:24: "And see if there be any wicked way in me, and lead me in the way everlasting." The Psalmist's figure of speech for the divine order. עולם is the Hebrew for what the Latin expresses by seclorum and דרך corresponds to ordo in Latin. see 1746 (Greek).

עקר stem, root, essence, reality, main object, dogma, principle, God (Aramaic). Case: foundation, basis. With different pointing: *aqar*, *awaqqar*. to pluck up, to root out; to be sterile; to castrate; to make barren; to eradicate, undo, abolish; to move, remove; a stump, the trunk of a tree.

In Daniel 4:15: "Nevertheless leave the stump of his roots in the earth, even with a band of iron and brass, in the tender grass of the field; and let it be wet with the dew of heaven, and let his portion be with the beast in the grass of the earth." Suggesting the futile, worthless activity of intellect when it has nothing to work on except the reports of the physical senses. Without illumination from above (the dew of heaven), intellect is lifeless.

In I Chronicles 2:27: "The sons of Ram the first born of Jerahmeel: ma'az, and jamin, and Eker [ועקר, and-Eker]." Inman: A shoot, stock or trunk. A euphemism for the testes; 'he is a son of Ram' or 'the high one', עקר alker, is however probable a lesser euphuism for אכר achar, or ichar, 'to plow or dig'. [Ancient Faiths, VI, pp. 472-473]

צרף to refine, to smelt, to melt together, solder; to connect, to combine. With different pointing: to try, to examine; to cleanse, purify, to tighten, harden. All these meanings are connected with the deeper alchemical significance of the 8th path of Hod. see 1090.

קרע to rend, to tear. Related to the analytical power of intellect, the power which can tear things apart. The same power is represented by

Zain, the sword. Misused, it leads to evil results. As a verb *qarah* meaning: "to slander, to revile." For the false judgments of intellect are separative. They slander man to himself, and make him project his own bad estimate, his own inaccurate self-measurement, on all his fellows. see 15, 585, 720.

עַרְבֵי-נַחַל willows of a brook, populars. Leviticus 23:40: [וְעַרְבֵי-נַחַל, and-popuars-of stream] "And on the first day you are to take choice fruit from the trees, and palm fronds, leafy branches and poplars, and rejoice before the Lord your God for seven days." Seven is attributed to Venus (victory) on the Tree.

פֶּרֶץ "a bringing forth". Son of Tamer, "Date Palm". The fruit of the symbol of masculinity, pictured in Key 2, the High Priestess.

צִפֹּר K.D.L.C.K.(p.668): "The bird", which is called the shekinah, which is the bird wandering from his nest, from whence it departs its nest of union. The passage goes on to say that "bird" also refers to Malkuth and to Metatron, which makes its nest in Tiphareth. see 376 for alternate spelling (**צוֹפֵר**).

שָׁכַן to settle down (of a cloud); to lie down (of an animal). Deuteronomy 33:20: "And of Gad he said, 'blessed be he who enlarges Gad's domain! Gad lives there like a lion, tearing at arm or head." With different pointing: to be at rest, to rest in Psalm 55:6: "And I said, "Oh that I had wings like a dove! For then I would fly away, and be at rest." To abide, to dwell in Psalm 120:6: "My soul has long dwelled with him who hates peace." see 444.

קַסְטְרָא White lead, tin. see 380.

רַעֲנָן green. [Crowley, 1977, p. 40]. Figuratively flourishing. Job 15:32: "Before his time he will be paid in full, and his branches will not flourish [**רַעֲנָנָה לֹא**, she-will-flourish not]."

לֶשֶׁם ligure, jacinth, or opal.

עָשׁ a constellation, the Great Bear, moth, creation [Case].

οικος. oikos (Gr). House (1 Peter 2:5). Greek equivalent for Beth, the name of the letter corresponding to Mercury, whose influence is at work in the 8th Sephirah. A symbol of the New Order on the Great Seal of the U.S. is pictured as a piece of Egyptian masonry, an unfinished pyramid, of 13 courses. In Rosicrucian symbolism, this house is the vault of the adepts or burial-place of the founder of the order Brother C.R.C. see 126.

Annuit Coeptis Novus Ordo Seclorum (Lt). He hath prospered our undertakings, A new order of the ages (or, a new order of the aeons). These are the two Latin mottoes on the reverse of the Great Seal of the United States of America. It is an order which brings about perpetual renewal, hence Novus. And because it never comes to an end, there is a sense in which it never is finished, although it is perfect in the sense that all its parts are framed together.

εμνησθης. emnehsthen (Gr). "I call to remembrance". Septuagint translation of **חָשַׁבְתִּי** (720) in Psalm 77:6: "I call to remembrance my song in the night; I commune with my own heart and my spirit made diligent search.

ειπε ινα οι λιθοι. epie hina hoi lithoi (Gr). "Command that these stones". Part of the temptation of Jesus by the Devil, in Matthew 4:2: "Then the tempter approaching him, said: "If you be a son of God, command that these stones become loaves [i.e. bread]." see 1964, 710, 1059 (Greek).

371

שְׂמֹאל left-hand or left side; north. On the Cube of Space the northern face is attributed to Peh or Mars; the left-hand pillar of the Tree of Life is the of Geburah, or severity, and represents the future. The intimation is that out of the darkness of the unmanifest, the life-power, Mars, is there. See Genesis 13:19.

Left hand in Genesis 48:14: "And Israel stretched out his right hand, and laid it upon Ephraim's head, who was the younger, and his left-hand upon Manasseh's head, guiding his hands wittingly; for Manasseh was the first-born."

שַׂלְמָא clothing; Salma: an individual (or family) of Calebites who are represented as having founded Bethlehem . In 1 Chronicles 2:51, 54] " These were the descendants of

Caleb: ...Salma the father of Bethlehem..." and from who David was descended. Caleb (dog, 52) is כל kole, the all and לב laib, the heart, and is also connected with Beth and Mercury. Bethlehem (house of bread, 490) is the birthplace of Jesus (reality liberates) David (beloved, 14) is connected with the sun and Tiphareth, the dwelling place of the Christ. This dwelling place is also the city, where the Lord is.

372

עקרב Scorpion, Scorpio, a fixed water sign.

כבשים young lambs. A direct reference to the fiery quality hidden in alchemical water. The male lamb symbolizes the alchemical fire of Aries, the Ram. Both Aries and Scorpio are ruled by Mars.

עשב green herbs, tender plants, green fodder. Human life is also represented by the word *esayb*, as in the phrase: "They of the city shall flourish like grass (esayb) of the earth" (Psalm 72:16). In Key 13, alchemical water-the sperm of the world is the substance man seems to multiply in the reproduction of his species. Used in Psalm 102 as a figure of speech for the transitory, ephemeral life of the human personality. "My days are like a shadow that declines; and I am withered like grass". Compare with St. German's mention of a green branch, under אססידבא. see 2625.

In Genesis 3:18 this word is translated "herbs": "Thorns also and thistles shall it bring forth to you; and you shall eat the herb of the field."

1. d'Olivet renders this verse: "And harsh and rough (imperfect and disordered) productions shall germinate abundantly for thee; and thou shall feed upon bitter and withered fruits of elementary nature."

He comments: עשב, *upon the most sharp and wasted fruits of nature... we know that the* primitive root אש is applied, in general, to the elementary principle of things, and in particular, to *fire*. We also know that by reinforcing the initial vowel א, it suffices to increase progressively its force. Now, if the word which is the subject of this note, is composed of the contracted roots עש-אש, of which will signify

not simply Χορτος, *dried grass, herb of the field*, following the interpretation of the Hellenist, weakened by Saint Jerome; but indeed, *a sharp and wasted fructification*. For this is the true meaning of the word עשב." [d'Olivet, 1976, p. 115.]

2. F.J. Mayers: "All that on a casual reading sounds like punitive measures, proves, on closer examination to be remedial and helpful, intended to lead man to happiness and to strengthen him with hope. The disturbance and disordering of the Adamah results in human development becoming a matter of anxiety and labor. But the first thing God says is that in spite of thorns and thistles (of the mind and soul), "Adam" shall eat of the green herb-the grass of the field. That was exactly the food provided by nature for the higher animals (taking the words quite in a literal sense); and in their limited, animal existence it suffices for their needs; they flourish on it happily enough... just as he gives the cattle on a thousand hill their 'meat in due season', so God promises to provide for the simple material needs of man. But it means more than that. Adam's trouble was 'human' trouble, trouble of the mind and spirit. Ignorance of the way to use his higher faculties aright... God promises to continue to him, while his human elements are developing, the 'instinctive' guidance by which the lives of animals are ordered." [The Unknown God, pp.204-205]

אססידבא Water of Mercury, or mercurial water, astral water, spherical water. A term applying to alchemical Mercury and "spherical water" (*aqua spherica,* 109 Latin*)* symbolized in St. Germaine's Trinosophia, by a picture of the bird of Hermes.) This water is the fiery solar fluid which as it flows through the human nervous system, is the actual substance which is given shape and form. see 153 (miha-koaim).

The Aesch Mezareph: "This argent vive [living silver], in the *gemara tract gittin*, chapter 7, vol. 69, is called *espherica*, i.e. spherical water, because it flows from the mundane sphere." [Westcott, 1997, p. 39]

שבע to be full, filled, satisfied; sated, have in excess. This substance contains all we can desire for the satisfaction of every need. In Proverbs 27:7: "The full soul loathes a honeycomb; but to the human soul every bitter thing is sweet." And in Deuteronomy 33:23: "And of Naphitali [570] he [Moses] said, "O Naphtali, satisfied with favor, and fill with the blessing of the Lord: possess the west and the south."

שבע plenty, abundance, fill, satiety, copiousness. It is available in abundance-a direct result of reproduction. Ecclesiastes 5:10: "He that loves silver shall not be satisfied with silver; nor he that loves abundance with increase: this is also vanity." And in Genesis 41:29: "Behold, there come seven years of great plenty throughout all the land of Egypt." With different pointing: *sabah.* satiety, fullness. In Exodus 16:3: "The children of Israel said to them, 'Would to God we had died by the hand of the Lord in the Land of Egypt, when we sat by the fleshpots, and when we ate bread to fullness; for you have brought us out into this wilderness, to kill this whole assembly with hunger." And in Psalm 16:11: "You will show me the path of life: in your presence is fullness of joy; at your right hand there are pleasures forevermore."

שבע to swear, to bind with an oath, take an oath. Our use of the this power (Scorpio) entail certain definite obligations. In Genesis 21:31: "Therefore he [Abraham] called that place Beersheba; because there they swore [an oath], both of them" And in Genesis 22:16: "And [the angel of the Lord] said. 'by myself have I sworn', says the Lord, 'for because you have done this thing, and have not withheld your son, your only son."

With different pointing: *shehba.* The numeral 7, seven times, sevenfold [1 Kings 10:1]. The queen of Sheba is read as the Queen of Seven. The 7th Sephirah is the sphere of Venus. The Queen of Sheba is another aspect of what is called Hadassah (Myrtle) in the story of Esther (Ishtar). The seven are the occult planets, alchemical metals or interior stars (chakras). Also alchemical water is said to be the seed of the metals, which are 7 in number. see 74, 106, 756, 54, 50, 377, 764 and Isaiah 4:1.

"*seven.* ...ideas of complement, of accomplishment, and of the consummation of things and of times." [d'Olivet, 1976, p. 153.] see also 390 (seventh)

ישבו בנב "Resident of Nob". One of the sons of the giant [2 Samuel 21:16]. A priestly city, Nob, was on al hill immediately to the North of Jerusalem.

שביס net-work, hence, hair-net, headband. In Isaiah 3:18: "In that day the Lord will snatch away their finery: the bangles and headbands and crescent necklaces." (Because the daughters of Zion have become haughty).

יהוה שמו IHVH is his name. see 26, 340.

373 (prime)

אלהי העברים God of the Hebrews.
געש quaking.

שגע to wander about, hence to rave, be mad, frenzied. Deuteronomy 28:34: "So that you shall be mad for the sight which your eyes shall see." And Hosea 9:7: "The days of visitation are come, the days of recompense are come; Israel shall know it: the prophet is a fool, the spiritual man is mad, for the multitude of your iniquity, and the great hatred." see 429.

שכם אחד With one shoulder, i.e. of one mind. With one consent in Zephaniah 3:9: "For then I will restore to the people a pure speech, that they may call upon the name of the Lord to serve him with one consent." see 360, 365.

Λογος. Logos (Gr). The Word. The divine word or consciousness which called all manifestation into being, and which is the substance of all things. see 13, 150, 67, 785, 284, 358, 1008, 206, John 1:1.

374

כשדים Chaldees (reference to Astrology). see Genesis 11:28.

וישבנו and we will dwell, and we will settle. see Genesis 34:16.

אופנים + זקף the "wheels" + to raise up, lifted up. The wheels are attributed to Chokmah and are the circlings or circuits of celestial forces in the human body. When the vibratory rate is accelerated or lifted up, thin illumination occurs. see 187.

αγρος.. agros (Gr). "field". see Matthew 6:28, 30.

see 444.

375

I. (3 x 5 x 5 x 5) or 3 x 5^3

עשה   Assiah; the 4th Qabalistic world corresponding to the physical plane. The material world or world of action or manifestation.

עשה   to be made, formed. With different pointing *issawh*: to press, squeeze; to force, enforce. see 385, 425.

עשה   yielding (Genesis 1:11, 12).

שלמה   Solomon, meaning "peaceful". Wise King of Israel. Connected with the Sun and Tiphareth. see 1081, 470, 596, 640.

שעה   to be closed, dim, blind; for a moment, a while, an hour. Metathesis of עשה. With different pointing: to gaze at, to regard; to look about, behold; to look away from (followed by Mem). When one regards the handiwork of the eternal, one is amazed. "Except the Lord build the house, they labor in vain that build it."

גיר פחם וטיט   chalk, charcoal, and clay. Three elements of the lower man, used to "raise" him to a master builder, in a Freemasonry ritual. see 935; 213, 128, 28.

Mackey, in his Encyclopedia of Freemasonry (p.156) writes: "By these three substances are beautifully symbolized the three qualification for the servitude of an entered apprentice-freedom, fervency, and zeal. Chalk is the freest of all substances, because the slightest touch leaves a trace behind. Charcoal, the most fervent, because to it, when ignited, the most obdurate metals yield; and clay, the most zealous, because it's constancy employed in man's service, and is as constantly reminding us that from it we all came, and to it we all must return. In the earlier lectures of the last century, the symbols, with the same interpretation, were given as 'chalk, charcoal, and earthen pan'... Pan once signified hard earth, a meaning which is now obsolete." (p.237).

שמלה   A king of Edom, associated with Netzach. "A City of Edom." [Crowley, 1977, p. 40] Edom suggest unbalance force. see 51, 148, *777*, Table Table IV, Column CIX & Genesis 36:36.

השלם   the wholeness. Note it is equivalent to Solomon. Suggest balanced force. see 370.

צפרה   Zipporah, "bird", wife of Moses. Exodus 2:21: "Moses agreed to stay with the man [in Midian], who gave his daughter *Zipporah* to Moses in marriage."

כלל ופרט   generally and specially [Crowley, 1977, p. 40].

שעה   respect, he had favor. see Genesis 4:5.

עקרה   barren. see Genesis 11:30.

שלמה   perfect, accurate. see Deuteronomy 25:15.

376

שולם   Shalom. peace, health, prosperity, friend. Variant spelling. See 370.

Welfare, well-being, safety, health, in Exodus 18:7: "And Moses went out to meet his father-in-law, and did obeisance, and kissed him; and they asked each other of their welfare; and they came into the tent" [Spelled לשלום, "about-welfare", in the *Interlinear NIV Bible*]. Peace in Leviticus 26:6: "And I will give peace in the land, and you shall lie down, and none shall make you afraid; and I will rid evil bests out of the land, neither shall the sword go through you land."

צפור   bird, fowl; sparrow. According to Westcott, this is one of the three names for 'bird' in alchemy, which generally means sublimations. *The Aesch Mezareph*: "A beast with four wings like a bird was given power over the lion and bear that he may extract their gluten or blood. [Westcott, 1997, p. 25] see 156, 480 and Key 3 (the Empress' shield).

מדבר סיני   the wilderness of Sinai. Exodus 19:1: "In the third month, when the children of Israel were gone forth out of the land of Egypt, the same day came they into the wilderness of Sinai." Note מדבר means wilderness and also mouth, speech. see 246, 130; 1662 (Greek).

שוע   cry for help. Psalm 5:2: "Listen to the voice of my cry, my king and my God; for unto you will I pray."

שוע riches, wealth. In Job 36:19: "Will he esteem your riches? No, not gold, nor all the forces of strength." With different pointing *shoah*: liberal, bountiful, respected. In Isaiah 32:5: "No longer will the fool be called noble, nor the scoundrel be highly respected." see 381.

עשו "Hairy". Old Testament name in Genesis 25:25: "And the first came out red, all over like an hairy garment; and they called his name *Esau*." When Ayin is put before Shin it presents a false appearance on the origin of will, making personal intuition the fallible source of guidance (Vav), represented by Edom. [Inman says that Edom is connected with Adam (red), that Esau was hairy and frequented Mt. Seir, or creative power, produced by digging]. see 605, 620.

I. Another name for Edom. Esau means 'red'. According to Kuhn 'Tradition shows Esau imaged by the solar hawk, which symbolizes blood'. The Kings of Edom therefore were Kings of the Red Land, or place of blood, hence their association with the idea of 'unbalanced force' typical of the Qliphoth. [Grant, 1994, p. 263.]

Rosae (Lt). of the rose. see 371.

377

I. $(11^2 + 16^2)$ or $(4^2 + 19^2)$

גיד הנשה the sinew that shrank [Genesis 32:32]. Cited in K.D.L.C.K. (p.235), who connects גיד with Shekhinah. see 360.

הרפו ודעו be still and know (Psalm 46:10).

מבנה-עיר The frame of a city. Ezekiel 40:2: "In the visions of God he brought me into the land of Israel, and set me upon a very high mountain, like the frame of a city on the south."

שבעה seven (7). Alternate spelling. see 372.

שבעה fullness, plenty; With different pointing sawbeyawh: satiety. In Isaiah 56:11: "Yes, they are greedy dogs that can never have satiety (enough), they are so wicked that they cannot understand; they all have turned aside to their own way, everyone for his own gain and to his

own advantage."

שמואל Samuel. "God hath heard." Old Testament name. The prophet or seer of Israel, linked to hearing (Key 5). Inman suggest that the name *Samuel* means "elis high" or "shines afar". In 1 Samuel 1:20: "Wherefore it came to pass, when the time was come about that Hannah had conceived that she bare a son, and called his name Samuel, saying, because I have asked him of the Lord." See Number 34:20.

Inman: Now שמה, *shamah*, signifies 'to be high, to project, to be elevated to shine afar;' and if we adopt this etymon, *Shamael* signifies 'El is high,' or 'Shines afar.' Again שמא, *shama*, means 'to shine, to be bright, to glitter,' which equally tends to the same conclusion as the preceding; and שם, *shem*, signifies 'renown, fame,' etc.; Shami, in the Babylonian or Assyrian, = heat. [Ancient Faiths, Vol. 2, p. 689-690]

378

I. Σ27 = 378

חשמל amber, shining metal. Metallic alloy, composed of Gold and copper, which was used for mirrors. Derived from the noun נחש (358). Refers to the 14th Path of Daleth, and suggests the idea of reflection which is basic in creative imagination and is "the instructor of secret foundations of holiness and perfection." The copper shield held by the Empress in Key 3 bears the symbol of the Holy Spirit, a white dove. What begins as temptation (Neshash, the serpent), when we learn how to manage it, may be transformed into the shield of protection. In Ezekiel it is translated as "amber".

אשבעה I shall be satisfied. Psalm 17:15: "As for me, I will behold thy face in righteousness: I shall be satisfied, when I awake, with thy likeness." The light of satisfaction is the manifestation of the One Reality. 378 as the extension of 27 represents the <u>complete</u> manifestation of the One Reality, "I shall be satisfied". see 916, 207, 376, 370.

בשלום in peace; safety, safe, sound. see 938, 376, 370 and Genesis 26:29.

שבוע seven days, week; seven years, heptad of

the feast of weeks; Pentecost [חג השבועות].
K.D.L.C.K. (p.695) gives: *juramentum*, "oath"
and links this "oath" to other septenaries. Seven
days, one week in Daniel 9:27 and Deuteronomy
16:9. A week of years, seven years, in Daniel
9:24. see 383.

שבנוך Goetia demon by night of the first
decanate of Gemini. This decanate is ruled by
Mercury and has the qualities of: literary,
versitle, and acute. It corresponds, in the Tarot
minor arcana, with the 8 of Swords, which is the
operation of Hod, the lower mind, in Yetzirah,
the formative world. The negative influence of
the demon can bring mental confusion, resulting
in ill-directed action, wasted force, pettiness,
gossip, and great 'to do' about nothing. Control
of the emotions is lost. There is malice and too
much concern with personalities, portending the
need to balance the quick-mindedness and
penchant for action with depth of feeling and
emotional warmth corresponding to Netzach and
Venus. The demon's name suggest the use of the
spiritual fire (Shin) to break down attention and
concentration (Beth) to negative use of the Mars
force, such as anger and hate (Nun), to linkage
with the false 'voices' (Vav), resulting in
expansive 'spinning of wheels" and wasted
energy (Kaph).see 858.

כ-נחש of the serpent.

כמשיח of the Messiah.

כבו-אשה Of the son of fire.

מחודש Renewing.

εποιησε. epoiehse (Gr). made. Septuagint
translation of עשות (776) in Genesis 2:4: "These
are the generations of the heavens and of the
earth when they were created, in the say that the
Lord God [IHVH Elohim] made the earth and
the heavens. see 776.

379 (prime)

בשמאלו in his left hand. see Genesis 48:13.

בשבעה with an oath. see Leviticus 5:4.

בהקריבכם with you bring, sacrifice. see
Numbers 28:26.

Sum of the defining dimensions of Noah's ark
(Genesis 16:15)-Length 300 cubits, breath 50
cubits, height 30 cubits.

The summation of the letters of IHVH multiplied
severally by those of Adonai; [(י×ה) + (ה×ד) +
(נ×ו) + (י×ה)]. [Crowley, 1977, p. 41].

מספר number. The secret number of Egypt and
of occult science is "hid in number" [Book of
Tokens, Teth] which veils the power of the
Elohim. see 828.

ערפה darkness. The "pure darkness" in which
the creative force is made to rise is the obscurity
of the subconscious plane of life-activity
represented by the ninth path of Yesod. Initiates
perceive the radiant darkness (Ayin) as veiling
the liberating regenerative power (Resh). It tears
down the prison of false separation (Peh) and is
the source of power of adjustment (Lamed)
which preserves the balance of forces in action
throughout the universe. The power of Heh
constitutes this creative force (see Path name
commentary on Heh). see 219, 80, 423, 514.

מצרים Name given to Egypt by the Jews. The
Uraeus, or Royal serpent is the characteristic
symbol of Egypt. Paul Case: difficulty,
straitness, narrowness. The singular male noun is
מצר, meaning distress, straits; boundary, narrow
pass; strait, channel of the sea, isthmus, neck of
the land. The land of Egypt is connected with the
physical plane and with subconsciousness. see
30, 142, 358, 409, 671, 1702, 667.

עיש Ursa Major; constellation of the Great Bear.

רקיע firmament, expanse, sky. In Genesis 1:6:
"And God said, let there be a firmament in the
midst of the waters." (from Latin *firmamentum*.
"a strengthening support".) It has for its
meanings: 1. The region of the Air; the sky or
heavens; 2. established foundation; 3. the orb of
fixed stars in early astronomy; 4. Paul Case: The
2nd Heaven, corresponding to Hod. Psalm 150:1:
"Praise God in his sanctuary; praise him in the
firmament of his power."

"*Raquiy,* and is an energy which, not being fixed
in extent, has the intrinsic quality of expansion.
Energy in expansion: that is the definition of

space according to Qabala. It is in expansion because, as its own container, energy cannot cope with itself. It cannot but be perpetually its own overflowing.

We are very far indeed from the 'firmament' which is supposed to translate *Raquiy,* and further still from its other name "heaven" of the canonical text." [Suraes, 1992, pp. 91-92.]

שמם to be desolate, be ruined; to be amazed, be appalled.

עצב עצבון pain, affliction, trouble, misery. From the root meaning, labor, pain; idol, image. The process of dissolving cells which reflect the illusion of separation.

קסטירא white lead, tin. see 370.

לשן to slander. Paul Case: tongue, language. In Daniel 7:14 it is used in the plural for language. see Key 15, the Devil or "slanderer".

נשל to slip, drop off; to draw off (shoe); to drive out, eject. With different pointing to stumble, fall in Exodus 3:5 and Joshua 5:15; To cast out, eject in Deuteronomy 7:1. The same "darkness" where the power of Nun works to drive out illusion, through the agency of the spiritual fire (Shin) to balance cause and effect in all action (Lamed), also causes the ignorant to stumble and fall, but at the last it brings perfect justice and true faith.

פי-צדק יהגה חכמה "the mouth of the righteous speaks wisdom." Psalm 37:30: ("and his tongue talks of judgement").

פרק to remove, take off; to release, unload; to take apart, to solve a problem; to discharge (electricity). With different pointing: pahraq. to untie, loosen; to rescue, deliver. It is the power of the Mars-force (Peh working through the agency of regeneration (Resh) to bring about a perfected body (Qoph).

פש folly; haughtiness, arrogance. Job 35:15: "And further, that his anger never punishes and he does not take the least notice of great arrogance."

משלי Proverbs; title of Biblical text. [Godwin, 1999, p. 554]

ערפל thick darkness. see Job 22:13.

381

אשף astrologer, enchanter, magician.

שועה a cry for help. Jeremiah 8:19: "Behold the voice of the cry of the daughter of my people because of them that dwell in a far country..." Lamentations 3:56: "Thou has heard my voice: hide not thine ear at by breathing, at my cry."

שאף to draw breath, to breathe, to pant. Psalm 119:131: "I opened my mouth, and panted, for I longed for your commandments." To swallow up greedily in Psalm 56:1: "Be merciful to me, O God: for man would swallow me up; he oppresses me fighting daily. To long for, desire. Job 7:2: "As a servant earnestly desires the shadow, and as a hireling looks for the reward of his works." To strive for, to hasten to, in Ecclesiastes 1:5: "The sun also rises, and the sun goes down, and hastens to his place where he goes." To crush, bruise, in Amos 2:7: "Who crush in the dust of the earth the heads of the poor, and turn aside the way of the meek: and a man and his father will go in to the same maid, to profane my holy name."

משאם their burden. see Numbers 4:27.

οργης. orgehs (Gr). anger, wrath. Septuagint translation of זעף (887) in Isaiah 30:30: "And the Lord shall cause his glorious voice to be heard, and shall show the lighting down of his arm, with the indignation of his anger, and with the flame of a devouring fire, with cloudbursts and tempest and hailstones." see 877, 157.

382

שבניך Goetia demon #43 by night of the 1st decanate of Gemini. see Appendix 11.

Goetia: "He is a Marquis, mighty, great and strong, appearing in the from of an armed soldier with a lion's head, riding on a pale-colored horse. His office is to build high towers, castles, and cities, and to furnish them with armor, etc. also he can afflict men for many days with wounds and with sores rotten and full of worms.

He gives good Familiars at the request of the Exorcist. He commands 50 Legions of Spirits." [Mathers, 1995, p. 50]

ב-רקיע in the firmament; literally, "in-expanse-of." See *Interlinear NIV Bible* & Genesis 1:14.

Eliphas Levi: "The physical expression of the duad is the firmament which separate the waters from the waters; it is the point of fixation which rules the movements of matters. It was represented at the gate of Solomon's temple by the pillars of Jakin and Boaz. "The duad is unity reproducing itself to create, and this is why the sacred allegories picture Eve issuing from the very beast of Adam. Paul Case: Levi calls the duad the number of the firmament. It is also, according to him, the number of woman, i.e. of Eve = חוה = 19, and רקיע = 20 x 19. see 380, 2.

ב-מספר in number, by number. Deuteronomy 25:2. see 380.

Per spiritum sanctum reviviscimus (Lt). "Through the Holy Spirit we become alive again." This phrase is part of an inscription found in the vault of C.R. in the Allegory. see 683, 35, 113, 81, 153 Latin.

383 (prime)

ע-י-ב-א + רוח אלהים Rauch Elohim + Aleph-Beth-Yod-Ayin. The Life breath of the (7) creative powers plus the Hebrew initials of the names of the 4 Qabalistic worlds, corresponding to the "name" IHVH. see 300, 83; 214.

בא + יסוד + יצר to mold, create + foundation or basis + coming, future, or "to go out and in". The creation of man came from the foundation into manifestation and shall go out again in the cycle of evolution. see 300, 80, 3.

אב + ערפל darkness + the father. The darkness in which the latent creative force of the "father", i.e. Chokmah is made to rise, is the obscurity of the subconscious plane represented by Yesod. see 380, 3.

פעולה + בטן הסוס work, deed, action + horse's womb. The place of 'work' for the life-

power is the serpent fire working in darkness; the belly is physical embodiment. see 191, 192.

למשחה to be anointed, attain great office. see Exodus 29:29.

כנחשה as brass, like bronze. see Leviticus 26:19.

384

הפצי-בה + זלעפה my delight is in her; + raging heat, zeal. Understanding is the delight of the divine mother; zealousness is characteristic of unbalanced strength - in itself, it is raging heat. see 192.

שדף to scorch, to blast. Genesis 41:6: "And behold, seven thin ears and blasted with the east wind sprung up after them." see 389, 440.

ושבעו and be satisfied. Deuteronomy 14:29.

Γομορρα. Gomorhra (Gr). "Gomorrah"; the city in the Bible infamous for wickedness, and especially for perversions of desire. Septuagint translation of עמרה (315) in Genesis 19:24: "Then the Lord (IHVH) rained down burning sulphur on Sodom and Gomorrah - from the Lord out of the heavens." see 315.

385

I. Sum of the first 10 square numbers. $1^2+2^2+3^2+4^2+5^2+6^2+7^2+8^2+9^2+10^2 = 385$.

עשיה Assiah. World of Action or Manifestation.

שבינה Shekinah. Divine Presence. Attributed to Binah, the divine mother. A spark of which, carried into manifestation is part of Adam (humanity) and will lead him into redemption and mastery. A title of Malkuth, the "Cohabiting Glory," the actual presence of divinity in creation. Also called "Mirror of Tetragrammaton," Elohim (86), Adonai (65). In Qabalah she is exactly what Hindu philosophy terms maya-shakti, the feminine productive power. see 395, 422, 426.

I. "The qabalistic version of *Shakti* (q.v.). The female embodiment of power." [Grant, 1994, p. 279.]

II. The Zohar [II: 199A, p.256]: "'After God created the moon [i.e. the shekinah] he had her constantly before his eyes' [Deuteronomy 11:12] In regard to this it is also written: "Then did he see it, and declare it (vayesaphah); he established it, yea, and searched it out." [Job 28:27]. 'He saw it' means that through his providence the sun is reflected in it. The term vayesaphah we may translate, 'he made it like sapphire'. He established it 'so that it should fall properly into twelve division [or tribes], and be further distributed among seventy kingdoms [of the world-Genesis 10], supported by seven celestial pillars, that it might be perfectly illuminated. 'An searched it out': to guard it with an eternal and never ending vigilance. And then he gave a warning to man, as we read further: 'and unto man he said: behold the fear of the Lord, that is wisdom: and to depart from evil is understanding' [The Zohar, 28:28], since wisdom is the means to attain to the fear of the holy one, and understanding is the power by which to separate and keep away the refuse, and thus attain to a knowledge of and an insight into the glory of the most high king."

III. The Zohar [Prologue, 13A, p.55]: "The eighth percept is to love the proselyte who comes to be circumcised and to be brought under the wings of the 'divine presence' (Shekinah), which takes under its wings those who separate themselves from the impure 'unholy region', and come near unto her, as it is written: "Let the earth bring forth a living soul according to its kind."

שממה Devastation, desolation, sterility. One of the pair of opposites (sterility) assigned to the letter Resh. Identical except in outer aspect with fertility. With different pointing: waste; horror, amazement. The disintegrative expression of Resh, the תמורת or זרע (seed or fruitfulness). It is not, as Kalisch translates it, childishness, but the sterility of desert country, directly attributed to the sun. Resh is sterile when not jointed to the bride, shekinah. see 277, 822.

פדהצור "a rock has ransomed". Personal name in Numbers 1:10: ("the rock redeemed"). From פדה to ransom, redeem, deliver. The redemption of the stone from the physical plane by shekinah.

שפה lip, language, speech; border, shore; edge,

margin, rim. Zephaniah 3:9: "For then will I turn to the people a pure language, that they may all call upon the name of the Lord, to serve him with due consent." Case: This is the "language" of vibratory attunement through the intonation of divine names, a form of mantra yoga. With different pointing: 1 curds, cheese; 2. to plane, trim; 3. to incline, make a slanting; to be quite, be at ease. The divine presence is met in silence. The organ which takes up, the mouth, the lip.

ηραδοδ. heh rabdos (Gr). the rod (of the stem of Jesse). see 377, 1210 (Greek).

ιερος. hieros (Gr). sacred. "A derivative of this word is hiereus, priest [ιερευς, #370] who strength his 'sheep': 'to bear wool' seems to suggest maturity of power. The root meaning appears to be either purity or maturity: probably both these ideas are included. So that the compound word hiearche would signify the benevolent rule of those who were both pure and highly developed [as spiritual hierarchy] compare hierophant, hieroglyphics." [Omikron, 1942, pp. 255-256.] see 720 (Greek).

386

ישוע Jesus. Aramaic spelling of the name of a great Master. see 300, 86, 326, 67 Latin.

I. "The short form of "Joshua"...shows Shin, the letter of Fire, combined with Yod, Vav and Ayin, the three letters that are assigned in the Sepher Yetzirah to the earth signs, Virgo, Taurus, and Capricorn, respectively. The name Jesus is the number 358, or 300 and 86. 300 is Shin (Fire), 86 is אהיה אדני, a name of God, asserting the identity of Kether and Malkuth; אלהים; and כוס, to preserve, to conceal; cup, goblet, hence, and pelican, a bird used in Rosicrucian symbology, so called on account of its throat resembling a cup or bag.

II. Paul Case: The name אהיה אדני, which asserts the identity of Kether and Malkuth is the secret of the saying 'I and the Father are one.' In this connection remember that the Holy Ghost came as fire, and that כוס, in all its meanings suggests the concealment, virgin birth, and preservation of the fire through the feminine principle.

He continues in his notebook, From Day to Day, March 12, 1916: "Jesus is יֵשׁוּעַ Jehovah is יהוה. Thus Jesus and Jehovah, in Hebrew are identical in respect to the first and third letters, but different in respect to the 2nd and 4th. A Shin takes the place of the first Heh, and a Ayin of the second Heh. Now Shin corresponds to the Perpetual Intelligence, knowledge of perpetuity, changeless consciousness of the real nature of the Ego, and it is the liberating consciousness of personal immorality, that this recognition is the dominant characteristic of Jesus teaching and personal consciousness. In the Tarot Shin corresponds to Judgement, a picture of resurrection with which the name of Jesus is inseparably identified. Thus the substitution of Shin for Heh in Jesus name is the substitution of Liberation for rulership. Jehovah is the ruler (For Heh is the Emperor) and his self-consciousness is that of the Constituting Intelligence. Jesus is the liberator, and his self-consciousness centers upon the idea of releasing men from bondage and death. The final letter of Jesus name is Ayin. In the Kabalah this is Renovating Intelligence, the knowledge that preserves and renews the personal existence. This letters is associated with the Devil, because the first step towards liberation is to recognize what evil really is, so that we can attribute to it absolutely no power to determine the course of our lives. The story of Jesus temptation is a clue to this Jesus did not teach because he had to overcome the Devil. And his way of doing so was the command: 'Get thee behind me Satan! Thou shall not tempt the Lord thy God.' When we realize that God is the principle of our lives, all evil is recognized as subordinate and without power. To fear the devil is to worship him. Therefore the Lord's prayer asks God not to lead us into temptation instead of pensioning him to allow us to be tempted by Satan. Jesus, according to Cabalistic attributions of the letters, is consciousness of the Divine Will (Intelligence of Will) reflected in the realization that human personality is essentially immortal (Perpetual Intelligence, "My word shall not pass away."), and these two modes of consciousness are combined in the knowledge or Wisdom destined to Triumph over all error and failure (Vav, Triumphant and Eternal Intelligence) which is the true catholic church, having for its foundation Jesus' personal triumph over the Devil, and of the subordination of matter to thought, which is destined to make all things new (Renovating Intelligence, Ayin). If we know the will of God (Yod) if we, by daily meditation, become habitually conscious of personal immorality (Shin); if we rely upon the ever-victorious and eternal wisdom within for guidance (Vav), if we fear no evil, and see no evil, and are conscious of our power to make all things new (Ayin), we have in us the mind which was in Christ Jesus.

The sum of the letters in Jesus name is 386. Articulated this is 300, 80, 6, or Shin, Peh, Vav. Consciousness if immorality (Shin) overthrows the structure of false science and common-sense (Peh), and makes us rely wholly on the guidance of the indwelling spirit (Vav). By reduction 386 is 17. Articulated this is 10, 7 or Yod and Zain. Consciousness of divine will and of our relation to it (Yod) is expressed in the harmonious relationship of the objective and subjective minds to each other, and to the supreme spirit, and this is a consciousness that enables us to make a right deposition of all our talents, powers and possession (Disposing Intelligence, Zain). By reduction 17 is 8, the same number that represent the final reduction of the letter values of IHVH. Thus the name Jehovah and the name Jesus are represented by the same root-idea. Thus the I AM, Jesus is the recognition of the identity of the personal self with the universal I AM. Both names imply knowledge of the dwelling place of the supreme spirit (Intelligence of House of Influence). Jehovah is the I AM saying: 'My temple is man, and my knowledge is the hearts of men.' Jesus is man saying 'I am the temple of God; God and I are essentially One, He rules in my heart.' The same truth is revealed in both names from opposites points of view.

The sum of the two names is 412. Articulated, this is 400, 10, 2 or Tav, Yod, Beth; Administrative Intelligence, Intelligence of Will, Intelligence of Transparency; the World, the Hermit, the Magician. By analogy 412 is the number of the Holy Ghost; since it proceeds from 26 (the Father) and the Son (386). Now the Hebrew word for Spirit is Rauch, spelled רוח, so that its numerical value is the sum of 200, 6 and 8. or 214. Note that 214 is 412 reversed. The same figures, then that enter into the number produced by the addition of the names of the father and son, which by analogy as the product of the numerical equivalent of the names of father and son, should be a number corresponding to spirit, are found in the number of the word, Rauch. The reduction is 7, the number of Zain, and the Holy Ghost is therefore seen to be the Disposing Intelligence, represented in Tarot by the Lovers. Now the sum of the reductions of three names is 8+8+7 or 23. Articulated, this is 20, 3 or Kaph and Gimel (Intelligence of Conciliation and Uniting Intelligence): Wheel and High Priestess. The Trinity, then is that which expresses itself in the Wisdom that reconciles all opposites, and the wisdom that unites man and God. The reduction of 23 is 5 or Heh: Constituting Intelligence or the Emperor. The Emperor, then is the symbol of trinity, regarding as the supreme wisdom constituting all the conditions of existence.

386 - 26 = 360. This significant number is that which added to the number of Jehovah, produces Jesus. It is the number of the circumference, and the son is the circumference having the father for its center. Articulated 360 is 300, 60 or Shin and Samekh. Perpetual Intelligence and Intelligence of Probation or Trial. Jesus is the I AM, consciousness of immorality, and demonstrates that immorality by actual test or trial. Reduced to 360 is 9 or Teth. Intelligence of the Secret. Jesus is the I AM or God's knowledge that he dwells in the temple of man, expressed as consciousness of the Great Arcanum, that all the forces of nature are subject to the subjective mind of man when that reflects the I AM. This, as we see is the central doctrine of Jesus teachings."

חרב ליהוה מלאה דם The sword of Tetragrammaton is filled with blood. In Isaiah 34:6: "The sword of Tetragrammaton is filled with blood, it is made fat with fatness, and with the blood of the lambs and goats, with the fat of the kidneys of rams: for the lord has a sacrifice in Bozrah, and a great slaughter in the land of Idumea." see 946.

επτα. hepta (Gr). Seven. A mystical number of Great Importance. see 2112 Greek, 7.

387

רקיע-דג firmament, expanse, sky, established foundation + fish. The fixed stars or heavens are the foundation of the infinite potentiality of Atziluth, the archetypal world, represented by the "fish". The abundance multiplication is by "lighting". see 380, 7.

הוא אל-קנא + זין יוד נון "He is a jealous God"

+ the letter name for Zain, the sword. It is discrimination (Zain) of the divine will (Yod) which multiplies its potentialities (Nun). The word for jealous, קנה also means to set a measure to. The more one complies with the laws of nature, the more one get full measure in return. see 193, 194.

In Joshua 24:19: "Joshu said to the people, 'You are not able to serve the Lord. He is a holy god; He is a jealous God [הוא אל-קנא]. He will not forgive our rebellion and your sins. Note that jealous in this passage is spelled קנוא.

שזף shawzaph. to burn, scorch. In Canticles 1:6: "Do not look at me because I have dark skin, because the sun has tanned me (i.e. burnt me); my mother's sons contended with me; they made me the keeper of the vineyards; but my own vineyard I have not kept."

שביל החלב Shevil ha-Chalav. Milky Way.

Διαβολος.. Diabolos (Gr). Slanderer, devil.

388

חלמיש flint, Silex; the hardest rock. Psalm 114:8: "Who turned the rock into a pool of water, the flint into a fountain of water." The reference is to the God of Jacob (supplanter). see 182.

צור חסיו בו The rock in which they took refuge. In Deuteronomy 32:37: "And he [the Lord] shall say, where are their gods, the rock in whom they trusted?" Only inner peace is the true rock in which to seek refuge. see 296.

יהוה צורי וגואלי IHVH my rock (strength) and my redeemer. In Psalm 19:14: "Let the words of my mouth, and the meditation of my heart, be acceptable in thy sight, O Lord, my strength and my redeemer."

חפש to search, search out; to investigate. With different pointing hiphes: to search through; search for; to inquire, investigate.

חפש freedom, liberty. Proverbs 21:27: "The spirit of man is the candle of the Lord, searching all the inward parts of the belly." The belly is the womb of manifestation in the macrocosm, and the Virgo area in the microcosm.

שלחן table, board, bread; money-changer's table. Psalm 23:5: "Thou prepares a table before me in the presence of mine enemies: thou anoints my head with oil; my cup runs over."

389 (prime)

I. $(10^2 + 17^2)$

מוגשם Corporeal, incarnating, realized, materialized. The 29th Path of Qoph. The adjective *mogashem* is derived from a verb גשם, *gawsham*, which means "to rain violently," or from a noun spelled the same signifying, "a hard shower." Note Key 18 has for part of its symbolism a shower of 18 Yods, the total they represent is 10 x 18, or 180. This is the number of degrees in a semicircle, and, because the sun follows the apparent path of a semicircle from east to west during the course of a day, the number 180 is a symbol of the "day," or incarnation period, of a personality.

אילה שלחה a hind let loose, a free-running dear [Genesis 49:21]. Said of the Tribe of Naphtali, corresponding to Virgo. Virgo is the Tarot is pictured by the Hermit, and the Hermit is standing at the summit to which leads the path in Key 18. He is free to range, because he is altogether liberated. The path in Key 18 is what must be followed to attain liberation. It is the path of progress, made possible by incarnation.

דכר ונוקבא male and female (Aramaic). "Come and behold. When the most Holy and Ancient One, the concealed with all concealment (Key 9), desired to be formed froth, he conformed all things under the form of male and female" [Lesser Holy Assembly, Ch 8 Sec 218]. The process by means of which bodies are incarnated and forms marked out. Physical existence is the starting point for higher levels of awareness. In order to attain to conscious participation in higher realms of existence, the physical body must be purified and transmuted so that it may serve as an instrument for the expression of spiritual powers and as a receiving station for impressions from levels of existence above and beyond the limits of the physical plane. The practices of true occultism help us to overthrow the errors in our conscious thinking, which in turn affect our subconscious mentation which is in charge of bodily function. This is partly the work of Mars. As related to the 10 of Cups, it is the Scorpio aspect of Mars. When rightly utilized in meditation, the Scorpio force rises through the spinal cord and gives the organ of inner vision, the pineal gland, the strength to open. see 390.

שפמ is fat. In Psalm 119:70: There heart is fat as grease. The Jewish translation from the Hassoretic text is: "Their hearts is gross like fat." With different pointing: to be gross, be dull, stupid, foolish.

מגרשם magician, sorcerer. connected with the negative magic which some associate with the Corporeal Intelligence.

שלטן Power of office, Rulership, dominion, sultan [Daniel 4:3]. see 57, 259, 186, 100, 394.

שפמ judge, judgement; to judge. This is the root of the name Jeehoshphat, the Valley [Joel 3:2, 12]. It also means the name of the father of the prophet Elisha [1 Kings 9:16]. It evidently means Lily. This word has a solar significance. Shin (Fire), Peh (Mars) and Teth (Leo). Lilies are white, a solar color. see 985 (Lt).

שם הבדלח There (is) the Bdellium [Genesis 2:12]. One of the ingredients of the Land of Havilah "where there is Gold", variously taken to be a gum, precious stone or pearl. This could be the "pearl of Great price," otherwise known as the stone.

שמף overflowing, flood. Job 38:25: "Who has divided a watercourse for the overflowing of waters, or a way for the lightning of thunder." In Psalm 32:6: "For this let every one that is chosen pray to you at an appointed time; surely even the flood of great waters shall not come near him."

ο λιθος. ho lithos (Gr). the stone. The "Everlasting Dominion" designated by שלטן is symbolized in Daniel 2:34 and 44 as a stone. One of the results of making the Philosopher's Stone is the adept's ability to utilize the power of the 29th Path (Qoph) so as to form for himself a physical body adjusted to any physical environment. With this ability go certain other power's and all of them have to do with determining the rates of vibration which constitute the forms of physical objects. see 949, 53.

390

שמן oil, fatness. the oil is identical with the power of the heavens. With different pointing: stout, robust, fertile, rich (soil). see 434, 696,

Fatness in Psalm 109:24: "My knees are weak through fasting; and my flesh fail of fatness." [Spelled משמן, from-fat, *Interlinear NIV Bible*] Fertile [שמנים] in Isaiah 28:1; oil in Genesis 28:18. see 807.

שמים heavens, firmament, sky, height. Literally, "what is heaved up." It is the superior term of the first great pair of opposites: that which is above. Genesis 1:1: "In the beginning the Elohim cut part the heavens and the earth." שם means name word, sign; therefore *shamaim* means names and signifies the creative name or the Word. This is the element Fire (ש) with the element Water (מים) and symbolizes the hexagram, or the two interlace triangles. The oil expresses the forces of the heavens. see 430, 291, 451.

I. Paul Case: This masculine noun שם by taking the feminine plural or הת instead of ים makes a distinction between the creative name and all lesser names derived form it. The name שמים is written in the plural known to scholars as the "plural of majesty." By such device the priestly writers who invented written Hebrew as a secret code were able to conceal the mysteries from all but initiates. Solomon built his temple to this Name. In St. John's gospel Jesus says: "I have declared unto them thy name." This is the doctrine that he power "which is above" is the power of the creative Word. see 800, 895, 1499, 1356, 1775, 1856.

II. "The so-called 'heaven' in the first verse, the name of which *is Shamaim*, contains a *Yod* between two *Mem*. This sequence indicates the cosmic movement of *Sheen* acting against Mayim, the so-called waters: the two *Mem* (40) between which *Yod* is playing against its partner *Aleph* in the game of existence versus life. *Yod is* all we know and all that exists, and all that we can think about. Its mass, its space, its time are the mass, the space, the time, and the dwelling of all that exists. And it plays against its very destruction. And that which plays against it is the so-called Spirit of God, which is the tremendous vital energy of *Sheen* originated by *Aleph*. (The word God is the inadequate translation of Elohim, previously defined as a summing-up of *Aleph* in action and having nothing to do with the general idea of God, which is beyond thought.)" [Suraes, 1992, p. 81.]

זכר ונקבה male and female (he created them) [Genesis 1:27]. The oil is manifested on every plane as male and female. see 389 for Aramaic spelling.

"זכר ונקבה *male and female*... the root of the first of these words is כר, which expresses that which is apparent, eminent that which serves as monument or as character, to preserve the memory of things. It is the elementary root אך united to the assimilative sign כ, and ruled by the demonstrative sign ר." [d'Olivet, 1976, p. 59.]

ספרים letters, numbers, numberings. These forces are represented by the 22 letters or the Hebrew alphabet. Each letter having a numerical value explains the *Sepher Yetzirah*'s declaration that by these 22 letters God created the universe. They imply a mathematical and geometrical creative order. Indeed knowing how to "count" with these tools is an essential ingredient in personal evolution.

צלע rib. Written הצלע in Genesis 2:22: "And the rib, which the Lord God had taken from man, made he a woman, and brought her unto the man."

d'Olivet translates: And YAHWEH AElohim restored this involution (exterior envelope) which He had broken from (the substance of) Adam, for (shaping the form of) Aishah (volitive faculty, intellectual companion) and He brought her unto Adam.

He comments: "מצלעתיו *of-the-involutions-of-him*... One cannot, in a word wherein are formed so many different images choose an idea more petty and more material, than that which the Hellenist have rendered by the word πλευρα, a rib. Saint Jerome who has said in bad Latin 'unam de cotis', could not do otherwise, because the course of error was irresistibly marked out. The word צלע can only be composed of one root and of one sign, or of the two contracted roots. If it is the first, it is צל-ע, for לע, is not an Hebraic root; if it is the second, it is צל-ע‍, in neither case, the meaning is the same, for the root עה or עוה is only an extension of the sign ע.

According to this data, let us examine the ideas contained in the root צל. They are those of shadow, of an object extending above, and making shadow as a canopy, a curtain, a screen, hangings, roof, etc.

Now what is the meaning of the root עה? Is it that which is attributed to all curving, all circumferential form, to all exterior superficies of things.

Therefore the word צלע signifies exactly an envelope, an exterior covering, a protecting shelter. This is what the facultative צולע proves, *to be enclosing, covering, enveloping*: This word which is derived form the root על, characterizes a thing raised to serve as covering, canopy, etc. The Chaldaic makes use of the word עלע, analogous to the Samaritan and having the same signification." [d'Olivet, 1976, pp. 88-89.]

שץ   Goetia demon #44 by night of the 2nd decanate of Gemini. see Apendix 11.

Goetia: "He is a great Marquis and appears in the form of a stock-dove, speaking with a voice hoarse, but subtle. His office is to take away the sight, hearing, or understanding of any man or women at the command of the Exorcist; and to steal money out of the houses of Kings, and to carry it again in 1,200 years. If commanded he will fetch horses at the request of the Exorcist, or any other tings. But he must first be commanded into a triangle, or else he will deceive him, and tell him may lies. He can discover all things that are hidden, and not kept by wicked spirits. He gives good Familiars, sometimes. He governs 30 Legions of Spirits." [Mathers, 1995, p. 51]

פרנס   Rosenroth in K.D.L.C.K. (p.648) uses these words and says Binah is thus called with respect to supernal works constituted beneath her

and Malkuth with respect to the inferior copy [i.e. the Qlippoth] existing beneath it.

391

יהושע   Joshua, Jesus [Godwin's spelling] see 386 and Exodus 17:9.

רום מעלה   the inscrutable height, a title of Kether, the crown. [רום = height; on high. מעלה = height, heaven; ascent, stair, step, rise, degree]. see 630, 246.

נשמא   soul (variant spelling). The soul, when liberated form the bondage of materialism sees God face to face and ascend to the crown. see 395.

אשמים   guilty, punished ones. see Genesis 42:21.

והערפל   and the thick darkness. see Job 22:13.

392

כפר + סוכו   pavilion, "his tabernacle" + atonement, to pacify. The dwelling-place of the Lord is said to be in the peace, which is the result of unity. see 300, 92.

מציון + יהוה סלעי   "The Lord is my rock" + stone, as well as the heart. see 196.

שבילים   Paths; suggest the 32 Paths of Wisdom. A different word is used in Psalm 23:3: "He leads me in the paths [במעלי] of righteousness for his name's sake." In Jerimiah 18:15 it is spelled שמילי. see 952, 362.

שביעי   the seventh. Genesis 2:2: "And on the seventh day Elohim finished his works which he had made; and he rested on the seventh day from all his works which he and made." see 372 (seven).

D'Olivet: He translates this verse: "And Elohim accomplished in the seven day (phenomenal manifestation), the sovereign work which he and made, and he returned to his ineffable self, in the seventh day (phenomenal manifestation), from

all the sovereign work which he had made."
[p.313]

השביעי, *the seventh...* This is the number of complete restitution, of cyclic fullness. It is true that שבע signifies seven, and that שביעי can be taken for *seventh* or *septenary*; but the name of this number draws with it in the Hebraic tongue, the idea of the consummation of things, and of the fullness of times. One of the roots of which it is composed שוב expresses the idea of return to the place form which one had departed, and the one which is joined to it by contraction עו, indicated every kind of curve, of inversion, of cycle.

The Hebrews make use of the verb שבוע, to express the oath by virtue of which they affirm that a thing promised will be fulfilled."
[d'Olivet, 1976, p. 66.]

393

רוח אלהים + לבונה "The "spirit of God" which moved upon the waters + Frankincense, a symbol of aspiration, attributed to the sun or heart center (Tiphareth). see 300, 93.

עמנואל + ימסוף "God with us", one of the epithets of Jesus Christ + the boundless sea, a name of Malkuth, when the paternal light of Chokmah illuminates it. It denotes what is "below". see 196, 197.

שפחה handmaid, maidservant. see Genesis 16:1.
חפשה freedom, free. see Leviticus 19:20.

החלמיש the flint, the hard [rock, מצור]. see Deuteronomy 8:15.

גרגופיאץ Gargophias. Sentenial of the 13th Path of Gimel on the inverse Tree of Life.

I. The 13th path is charged with the lunar kala. The name of its shadow guardian is Gargophias and her number is 393, a number of supreme importance in the Draconian Cult in its Thelemic phase. Furthermore, 3 + 9 + 3 = 15 = Atu XV, The Devil; and 393 is thrice 131, the number of Pan and of Samael whose wife is the elder Lilith, the Lady of Night, or Not, the Great Negative.

393 is also the number of שפחה, the typical concubine or whore who later became Sefekh, the consort of Thoth. Sefekh means the number seven; she is therefore an image of Typhon.

According to Gerald Massey, Sefekh is a survival of Khefekh or Khepsh of the Seven Stars, once worshipped at Ombos as the 'Living Word'. By the later solar cults she was abhorred as the Great Harlot. The word *khepsh* means, literally, the hinder thigh, a symbol of the vagina which is itself an image of the Primeval Typhon, the Mother of Set. She typified the first parent known at a time when the role of the male in procreation was unsuspected. Because she had no consort she was considered to be a goddess without a god, and her son - Set - being fatherless was also godless and was therefore the first 'devil',' the prototype of the Satan of later legends.

One of the totems of Typhon was the Dove. This was continued by the solar cults where it typified the male bearer of the *ruach* or creative spirit, attributed to the element air. The dove depicted on the Great Seal of the *Ordo Templi Orientis* (O.T.O.) is the Typhonian bird of blood, and it can be shown by gematria that the emblems contained in that seal are qabalistically equivalent to the number 393.

Astro-symbolically, 393 is Saturn-Luna-Saturn, the Moon warded on either side by the God Set. A remarkable property of the number 393 is that it reduces to Unity, viz: 3 into 9 is 3; 3 into 3 is 1, which is אחד, 13, 'Unity'.

The sigil of Gargophias shows an upright sword, with an eye each side of the blade, set over an egg and crescent. The sword is typical of the Woman as the first cutter in two. The haunch or thigh constellation of sickle shape was the celestial symbol of Typhon which, in terrestrial terms is the vagina of the woman that divides and becomes two; the slit or bifurcating One. The two eyes represent the dual lunation, celestially, and the two phases of the feminine cycle with emphasis on the periodic eclipse. The egg is three-quarters full, which indicates the nine months of gestation, the dry phase immediately preceding the deluge characterized by the outgush of the amniotic fluid. This aspect of the formula is latent in the egg and does not manifest until the 15th Path, the Path of the Mother. The animal sacred to this *kala* is the stork (traditionally associated with childbirth), the dog, companion of the virgin huntress [Artemis in her lunar phase], and the camel. The camel is the chief totem of this path for it traverses the desert of the Abyss; it is the traditional ark or ship of the desert. Its humps contain the vital liquid of life that sustains the Adept during his crossing. The 13th path is thus the path of the Virgin who contains within herself the unawakened potential of the wife who is ascribed to the next path. The position of these two paths - 13 and 14 - constitutes the Sign of the Cross. The Abyss is the place of crossing over from the world of appearance (phenomenon) represented by the obverse of the Tree, to that of dis-appearance (noumenon) represented by the hind side.

The magical powers of the kala of the moon include clairvoyance and divination. Not the kind of divination associated with the eleventh *kala* (q-v.) which issues ventriloquilly *via* the open womb, but divination by dreams emanating from the 'sealed womb at night, i.e. when the lunar light is eclipsed.

The 13th, 14th and 15th kalas, resuming as they do the full formula of the female, form the Primal Cross or place of crossing over from the material world into the world of ghosts or spirits. The virgin menstruates and is sealed, dark, unillumined, unawakened; the wife or whore is open, awakened, her formula is love; the mother again is sealed, but after a different fashion for she brings forth what is shut in her womb.

The fluid plasma of the astral light that permeates the tunnels is alive with potential that becomes manifest only when it comes to the surface of the Tree, splits into myriad forms, and swarms through the black hole in space represented by Daath, the Gateway to the Abyss. The manifestation of the non-manifest is effected, magically speaking, via the lunar current which characterizes the High Priestess of this kala in her virginal, unawakened, or 'dreaming' phase. The verse in the grimoire applicable to this kala reads: Now hath Nuit veiled herself, that she may open the gate of her sister.

Not two women, but one only is implied by this statement. Nuit veils herself in sleep, i.e. she becomes virginal, menstruous, in order to open the gate of her sister - the gate of dreams. In a naturalistic sense the veil is the clothing assumed by primitive woman at the onset of puberty. In a physiological sense it is the unruptured hymen. When Nuit opens the gate she veils herself and is therefore able to divine by dreams seen in the mirror of magical sleep or trance. This is the sense in which virginity, or the state of 'sleeping', is here intended. In yet another sense, the opening of the gate refers to the gate of the mother of Path 15 wherein the unmanifest is made manifest as the birth of the child through the gateway of matter. But this is a later formula and belongs properly below the Abyss, whereas the Gate here intended is the Gate of the Abyss itself.

The disease typical of this path is not surprisingly subsumed under the general label 'menstrual disorders', but it should be understood that whereas this disease is applicable to the path, the corresponding disorders obtaining in the tunnel beneath the path comport disorders of the lunar current itself, and the consequent spawning of lemurian horrors. This is substantiated by the magical weapon of the path, the Bow and Arrow. In the Tarot Trump attributed to this *kala*, the High Priestess is shown with the bow and arrow across her thighs. The bow is also a glyph of the rainbow which has a direct mystical connection with the lunar formula.

The symbolism of the bow, as the emblem of Sothis, the Star of Set, and of the rainbow. In ancient Hebrew the name of the rainbow - *qesheth* or *qashed* is a qabalistic synonym of *qadosh*, a method- of sexual magick involving the use of the lunar current.

The specific magical formula of *kala* 13 is אלים [signifying the 'Elemental Gods'], the number of which - 81 - is the number of witchcraft presided over by Hecate, or Hekt, the frog-headed goddess. It is necessary to guard against interpreting the term witchcraft in its usually accepted sense, which does not pertain to these higher levels of the Tree. The real meaning of witchcraft is to be sought in the image of the frog which has a secret significance for initiates that is far closer to the concept of Lovecraft's batrachian fantasies than is the puerile assessment of the subject by mediaeval churchmen and witch-hunters. [Grant, 1994, pp. 166-175.]

394

שולחן table. In Psalm 69:22: "Let their table become a snare to them: and that which should have been for their welfare, let it become a trap." Note that this word for table also means "bread". It is לחם the bread which gives birth to the Christ-child. see 87, 388.

כשדים Chaldees; proficient in Astrology. Abraham came from Ur אור or "light" of the Chaldees. see 934.

השפט the judge, the one judging. see Genesis 18:25.

395

נשמה Neshamah. Breath, the Divine Soul seated in Binah, whose essential power is intuition. Neshamah has for its basic meaning "breathing" and is so used in Genesis 7:22 and in 1 Kings 17:17. It is that aspect of the Life Breath, of the element of air which manifests itself as intuition. In Yetzirah this intuition or Causal Intelligence expresses itself as the understanding we have spoken of which is gained through experience and pain. We must not forget that it is through feeling the pain of our misinterpretations of the true nature of the One Life that we are finally lead to liberation. Its spiritual truth and guidance is represented by Key 5, the Hierophant. It is the superconscious reason above all material limitations. It is the soul, which according to Qabalists, cannot sin; and its purity is never touched by the defilement of lower personality. see 67, 385, 405.

In Genesis 7:22: "Everything on dry land that had the breath of [נשמת, breath-of] life in its nostrils died." In 1 Kings 17:17: "Some time later the son of the woman who owned the house became ill. He grew worse and worse, and finally stopped breathing [נשמה] ." In Proverbs 20:27: "The lamp of the Lord searches the spirit [נשמה] of a man [or The spirit of man is the Lord's lamp] , it searches out his inmost being [בטן, inmost-being, see 61]."

השמים the heavens [Genesis 1:1 and Psalm 19:1]. The archetypal plane of causes (Atziluth), the causal Intelligence of Kether (430). The power of the abstract mind is the power of the divine soul, Neshamah. The "order of nature" is the only kingdom of heaven. The fire that overthrows our houses of delusions and separateness is, the flash of inspiration coming down into our personal lives from the divine soul (786). The lighting flash of inspiration may be compared to the paths of the letters Cheth and Mem descending from the "heavens" of Binah. Through the path of Cheth the holy influence is reflected in the sphere of Mars and then, through the path of Mem it energizes the sphere of Mercury. Intuition is the operation, at the personal level, of the Causal Intelligence which established the cosmic order. see Keys 7, 12 #390, 859, 955, 796, 1356, 1499.

השמן the oil, the ointment [Psalm 133:2]. The esoteric meaning of oil relates to the influence of the illuminating. It is akin to the Sattva Guna of the Yogis and the "Illumination material" of the alchemists. Thus the influence from Neshamah is an actual substance. Ha-Shahmen have the same letters as Neshamah and in the Jewish translation of Psalm 133:2, it is rendered "like a precious oil," כשמן הטוב. The esoteric meaning of this "oil" relates it to the influence of Mezla (78), which descends through the 32 paths. As oil it is illuminating material. see 390, 1045, 78, 660 (Greek).

עולם הבריאה Olahm Ha Briah. The World of Creation, associated with the 9 of Cups and the creative powers of the Moon intimates that the creative forces are powers whereby the Life-power reflects Itself to Itself as the moon reflects the light of the sun.

מנשה Tribe of Manasseh. "causing to forget." Aquarius. He who causes forgetfulness of native country. Name of the half-tribe of Israel attributed to Aquarius. The forgotten "native country" is the state of ignorance into which we are born. Connected with alchemical dissolution or solution, the 11th stage of the Great Work. Also attributed to Tzaddi. Alchemical solution is the cause of congelation-it is the process which reduces all solid bodies in man's experience into their elemental "water," through meditation. The alchemist perceives the true fludic substance of forms reported by his physical sense. He uses the knowledge that the substance may be molded by mental imagery to alter his own body. Success in meditation established a current of subtle energy between the Mercury center in the upper brain, and the Sun center near the heart. Alchemical dissolution lifts up energy stored in subconscious reservoirs into the field of conscious awareness. It affects physical and subtle changes-in the metaphysical sensorium-to make the personality a better vehicle of expression for the Life-power. see 7, 95, 30, 162, 570, 500, 54, 331, 830, 127, 44.

אביר יעקב　Mighty one of Jacob. Genesis 49:24: "But his bow remained steady, his strong arms stayed, limber, because of the hand of the Mighty One Jacob, because of the hand Shepherd, the Rock of Israel." Isaiah 60:16: "And thou shall know that I the Lord an thy savior and thy redeemer, the mighty one of Jacob." K.D.L.C.K. (p.13) gives: *robustus*. Jacob and says it is connected with עד, time [74] and cites Job 39:29.

ישעיה　Isaiah. Salvation of Yah. This means qabalistically, the salvation of wisdom. the Zohar says: "Isaiah's very name is the cause of future redemption and the return of the supernal light to its place, and the restoration of the temple and all the splendor and glory thereof." The temple which is restored is the temple of human personality.

משנה　Twice, second in line; second in rank; second quarter, copy duplicate, repetition (masculine noun). As a feminine noun: oral study, traditional law, a paragraph of the Mishnah. Also teacher, tutor. The one teacher grows the twice-born through oral study. see 866.

פשוט　plain or literal sense; flat, level, simple, undressed, divested of clothes, simple. see 602, 554, 737, 159, 559.

שופט　judge. The judge of the law is Manasseh, bring the heavenly breath into the "oil" through "Isaiah".

שמנה　eight (8). Connects with ha-shamaim, the heavens (all the stars in Key 17, Aquarius have 8 rays); through the notion of beginning, connects with esoteric doctrine of the octave. The divine influence which flows down to the conscious mind is effected by a vibratory correlation related to the octave of music. see Mezla (78).

"שמנה *eight*. This word springs from the double root שום and מן. By the first שום, is understood the action of placing, of putting one thing upon another; by the second מן that of specifying, of distinguishing by forms. It is therefore, the accumulation of forms that should be understood by this number. This signification is made obvious by that of the verb שמון, which means literally, *to fatten, to make larger*." [d'Olivet, 1976, pp. 153-154.] For other numerals see 13, 400, 636, 273, 348, 600, 372, 770, 570, 441. see 90 for his commentary on מן.

עריהנס　Uriens. The Sentinel of the 16th Path (tunnel) of Vav on the inverse Tree of Life.

I. The 16th Path Transmits the influence of the Hierophant, and its tunnel is sentinelled by the demon Uriens, whose number is 395, and his sigil shows a seven-armed figure; the upper four arms terminate in *yods*; the lower three, in crosses. The seven-armed figure is a glyph of the Tree of Life [The upper three *sephiroth* are not always included in diagrams of the Tree]. It has relevance to the worlds below the abyss. The seven also refers to the original Light in Heaven represented by the stars of Ursa Major. Note that 395 - the number of Uriens -- is also that of השמים, the 'heavens'. The seven arms, the four *yods*, the three crosses, make a total of 59 in all (7 + 40 + 12) and this number furnishes a wealth of clues relevant to the meaning of the sigil.

According to the *Kabbalah Denudata*, 59 is אחים, meaning 'brethren'; it refers particularly to Samael who is stationed in the midst of the Zodiacal Qliphoth accompanied by his *shakti*, the Elder Lilith. She guards the South East Corner and her companions are the Serpent and the Man. The serpent is a glyph of menstruation and 59, as נדה, means precisely this. It derives from the Egyptian word *neti*, meaning 'being', 'existence', 'negative', 'froth', 'the sign of bleeding', 'female source'. This number therefore explains why the *Adimiron* (The Bloody) are the qliphoth attributed to the Tunnel of Uriens. In the list of Primes, Crowley describes 59 as 'The Yoni calling for the Lingam, as ovum, menstruum, or alkali'. Furthermore, and to endorse the interpretation, the word זנב (59) signifies 'tail' or 'extremities'.

The name Uriens suggests Oriens who, as Atlas, supported the universe on his shoulders. The idea of support or *bearing* is borne out by the general symbolism associated with this *kala* which endows the Adept with the magical siddhi of physical strength.

The magical instrument ascribed to the 16th Path is the Seat, Throne, or Altar, which are curiously feminine symbols for a *kala* associated with *the Hierophant* until it is remembered that, in the New Aeon, the 'Lord initiating' (i.e. the hierophant) is the god Set, who is identical with his Mother, Typhon, and therefore the continuation of her *kala*, 15. She is in fact the *Goddess 15*, a name given to the Woman Fulfilled whose symbol, the full moon, occurred on the 15th day. The 16th *kala* was therefore her child, i.e. Set, and Set-Typhon under a single image was typified by the Dog Star, Sothis. According to Wilkinson. Set-Typhon was known as 'The Giant' and this symbolism equates it with the pre-eval *Nephilim*.

The name of the seat in Egyptian is *Hes*, or Isis. The throne bears the God, as the woman bears the child, as the altar bears the priest. The part of the body associated with the 16th *kala* is the shoulder, an euphemism for that which bears or supports the world, i.e. the Mother. Hence the association with Atlas (Oriens) who bears the world on his shoulders.

Uriens or Oriens, as the name implies, is also attributable to the Orient, the place of the rising sun or solar-phallic power. This phenomenon, both in its cosmic (celestial) and in its microcosmic (biological) aspect lies behind the name of the *Ordo Templi Orientis*, O.T.0, which being interpreted means the Order of the Temple of the Exalted or Risen Phallus. The verse of 231 relating to this Path declares: Also is the Star of Flame (i.e. the Phallus) exalted, bringing benediction to the Universe.

A glance at the columns of *Liber 777* shows that Uriens is attributed to the eleventh *kala* which is ruled by air and whose tunnel is presided over by Satan, Prince of the Powers of the Air.

The number corresponding to the astral dimension of this *kala* is 45, the number of אדם

(Man). He is one of the entities accompanying Lilith in the spaces between the south and east cardinal points of the zodiacal *qliphoth* at the center of which is the 'evil' angel Samael. Within the inverted dimensions of these spaces stands the Throne of Samael. Before this stands the altar on which is stretched the nocturnal Lilith, Mother of Abortions [a reference to the *Nephilim*]. The concept is explicit in the number of Uriens, for 395 is משבלה *Abortiens*. Furthermore, the reflection of the Hierophant is refracted into the depths of the Abyss in the form of Set or Pan (Samael), the devil [or Satan, meaning opposer] or double being the 'opposite' image. Likewise, this concept is explicit in the number of Uriens, for 395 is משנה, meaning 'twofold', 'duplex'. It derives from the Egyptian *shen*, two', 'twofold circle', and 'the other', the alter ego. Thus are the Heavens (השמים, 395) reflected into the hells, and the Hierophant or Magus of the Eternal becomes the judge [שופט, 395] of the 'dead', whose symbol is the jackal, the howler in the haunts of the dead, and 'the eater of dung in the day of Be With Us'. At the termination of this abominable repast the *Adimiron* (The Bloody) swarm across the desolate places of the void leaving the 'rich brown juice' of annihilation in their wake.

Other denizens of the cell of Uriens are the gorgons and minotaurs which are linked with the sun-son symbolic of Taurus and the Hierophant, and with the magical force that turns to stone [The name Set means 'a standing stone'; and Isis means literally 'the Seat of Stone'.].

Another animal associated with this path is the hippopotamus, a primordial image of Typhon. In the African cultus the goddess Ife typifies the 16th *kala* and she is represented by the gaping vulva of Iyemoja, the source of the manifested universe borne upon the shoulders of Atlas (Orien/Uriens). The hippopotamus, or water-cow, is the great bearer in the waters, the equivalent of Taurus, the Bull of Earth, on dry land, hence the connection with the goddess (Venus rules Taurus) and the waters of the abyss. Iyemoja means literally 'Mother of Fish', which shows the specifically sexual nature of her function. [Grant, 1994, pp. 186-189.]

מושבל Intellectual (Aramaic). Muskal - idea, concept (modern Hebrew).

יפרש Goetia demon #22 by day of the 1st decanate of Scorpio. Th is decanate is connected with the 5 of Cups or Geburah, sphere of Mars in Briah, the creative world. In Briah, the Geburah force expresses in its aspect of dissolution, destruction and change. see Appendix 11.

I. *Goetia*: "He is an Earl, and a mighty prince, and appears in the from of an angel with a lion's heard, and a goose's feet, and hare's tail. He knows all things past, present, and to come. He makes men witty and bold. He governs 36 Legions of Spirits." [Mathers, 1995, p. 38]

ושמים and heaven, and heavens. see Genesis 2:4.

ושמן and oil. olive, [זית]. see Exodus 30:24.

לשניאה that was hated, and the being unloved. see Deuteronomy 21:15.

397 (prime)

I. $(6^2 + 19^2)$ or $(12^3 - 11^3)$

אור פנימי Inner Light. A title of Kether and the number one. At the first principle, mercury, of the first matter (white light or brilliance). Sattva, the "illumination materia." From פנימי, inner, interior, inside; hidden, concealed. see 736, 207, 198, 364, 602, 620.

ויהושע and Joshua, with Joshua. see Exodus 24:13.

יהושע Joshua. Jah sets free. see Deuteronomy 3:21.

ואשימם and I will appoint them, and I will set them. see Deuteronomy 1:13.

ויעשהו and he made it. see Exodus 32:4.

חמשים fifty (50). see Genesis 6:15.

סמרעטן Satarotan. Lesser angel governing the triplicity by day of Capricorn. Note that Capricorn is depicted in Key 15 and contains the positive suggestion of renewal through mirth. Bondage is overcome by seeing through the illusions of the appearances of materiality. The energy of the serpent and of the lion, which brings death to the ignorant, is the savior of those who seek illumination. Note also that Mars is exalted in Capricorn.

שחיף thin board, plank. Ezekiel 41:1: "And [he measured] the door post and the narrow windows and the arches round about on their three stories, over against the three gates that were ceiled with wood [planks] round above, from the ground up to the windows." This is Ezekiel's vision of the temple, in part.

חפשי free. Exodus see 21:5.

שלחני send me, he sent me. see Numbers 16:29.

ישנלנה shall lie with her, he will ravish her. see Deuteronomy 28:30.

אמונה אמון + עצם **basis or faith + body,** substance, essence or life. The responsiveness of subconsciousness to suggestion is the psychological truth behind this designation, which is a title of Binah. The cosmic mother is the ground in which the suggestive power of true perception sows the seed of faith. The substance is the universal radiant energy; *etzem* is closely related to the word for tree and intimates that the human body is the Tree of Life, whose essence is that life. see 199, 200.

גן בעדן + ורדי **A garden in Eden + of a rose;** rosy. The garden is = 53 = אבן = the Stone, or union of father (אב) and son (בן); Eden means "time", the place where the garden of subconsciousness is cultivated, to build the stone. The rose is a symbol of spiritual aspiration; the red rose represents desire of Venus; the white rose, purified desire, or attainment. see 220, 179, 53, 124.

שגופי Given without explanation in *Sepher Sephiroth* [Crowley, 1977, p. 42]. This word does not appear in scripture.

d'Olivet comments on the root שג: "The sign of relative movement united to the organic sign, indicates a movement of the organ deprived of intelligence, a covetous movement; the same sign joined by contraction to the root אב, symbol of organic development, characterizes every kind of increase. Thence, *blind desire, thoughtless, inclination*; figuratively, *error, degeneration*; action of growing, augmenting in number, volume, duration." [d'Olivet, 1976, p. 457.]

If the middle letter Vav, is read as "and", we may take פי in its root sense as follows: פיה *a beak; the orifice* of anything; the prominent part, *an angle; a discourse*, and particularly *a message.*" [ibid., p. 426.] This is suggestive of error in communication.

השמידם **destroyed them, they destroyed them.** see Deuteronomy 2:23.

CPSIA information can be obtained
at www.ICGtesting.com
Printed in the USA
BVOW09s2030201116
468018BV00021B/18/P